Social Work
and the Law

Social Work and the Law

Second Edition

Donald Brieland

Dean, Jane Addams College of Social Work
University of Illinois at Chicago

John Allen Lemmon

Professor of Social Work at
San Francisco State University

WEST PUBLISHING COMPANY

St. Paul   New York   Los Angeles   San Francisco

Sample contract on pages 250 and 251 is from Lenore J. Weitzman, *The Marriage Contract: Spouses, Lovers, and the Law*. New York: Free Press, 1981. Reprinted by permission.

Photograph on page 1 © Jim Anderson, reproduced by permission of Woodfin Camp.

Photograph on page 73 © Sylvia Johnson, reproduced by permission of Woodfin Camp.

Photograph on page 219 © Erika Stone, reproduced by permission.

Photograph on page 379 © Sam Falk, reproduced by permission of Monkmeyer Press Photo Service.

Photograph on page 565 © Freda Leinwand, reproduced by permission.

Editorial services: Cobb/Dunlop Publisher Services, Inc.

Composition: Harper Graphics, Inc.

Copy editor: Peggy Hoover

Library of Congress Cataloging in Publication Data

Brieland, Donald, 1924–
    Social Work and the law.

    Bibliography: p.
    Includes index.
    1. Legal assistance to the poor—United States—Cases.
I. Lemmon, John. II. Title.
KF390.5.P6B7 1985   340'.024362   84-21001
ISBN 0-314-77848-9

Contents

PART II   THE COURTS AND THE USE OF EVIDENCE

Chapter 5   Criminal Procedure and Criminal Justice   75

Chapter 23   Health   493

Chapter 24   Mental Health and Institutionalized Persons   513

Table of Cases

Preface

Since the publication of the first edition of *Social Work and the Law*, nearly every graduate school of social work has come to offer at least one course on legal topics. Many of them adopted the first edition of this reference-text.

Like the first edition, this book provides cases in family law, poverty law, consumer law, and civil rights. After teaching the course for over ten years, we are convinced that the use of actual court decisions provides an appreciation of legal reasoning that mere summaries cannot. The book introduces the reader to the legislative process and social action and deals with the legal authority of social agencies including their powers to make rules. The text provides suggestions on how to testify and on rules of evidence employed by the courts. A new chapter is included on health. The final topics are legal assistance and the regulation of social work activity, including malpractice.

Meanwhile, there have been changes in society—in legislation and in court procedures. Criminal justice has moved significantly from discretion and rehabilitation to fixed sentences. The juvenile status offender has been given over to social service workers in many jurisdictions. The juvenile felon is more likely to be processed as an adult.

In family law, marriage provisions have changed little, but divorce is characterized by no-fault suits. In the past two years the divorce rates have decreased. The courts are more likely to examine child custody and approve or modify plans and to seek social work consultation in doing so. In the care of children who live in unstable families, the goal has become permanence, whether in the biological family or through adoption.

The Supreme Court has been less responsive to civil rights over the past decade. It has sanctioned corporal punishment in the school without due process, parental use of commitment to a mental hospital for children without attention to rights of the patient, and authorized searches of high school students by school officials. Since civil rights is a theme of principal interest to social workers, some of the major civil rights related cases from the 1970s have been retained as examples in this edition.

Poverty is on the increase, and homelessness is now an acute problem. Federal grants-in-aid have been combined into block grants with a net loss to the states and cities. Minorities participate widely in elections, but are not better off economically.

The practice of social work comes under closer scrutiny with the responsibility to predict dangerousness of our clients who make threats during the treatment process. Social work also seems more preoccupied with private practice and with third-party payments and less with the plight of the poor or the emotionally disturbed.

All of these developments are reflected in the second edition of *Social Work and the Law*.

We thank over a thousand students who have been in our classes for their reactions and comments. We acknowledge the assistance of many colleagues teaching social work and the law who have contributed materials and ideas for this edition.

The senior author, who had responsibility for the final manuscript, acknowledges the significant contributions of Wynne S. Korr; she made many suggestions on various drafts and shared her experience in the field of mental health. Josefina Gonzales gave invaluable help in word processing, and Kathleen McKenzie proofread every word. We are especially grateful to them.

March, 1985   D.B.
                                                                   J.A.L.

Social Work
and the Law

PART
I

Introduction to Legal and Legislative Processes

CHAPTER

1

Social Work and the Law: An Overview

Both social workers and lawyers are necessary to deal with major human problems. An understanding of basic values and similarities and differences between the two professions is essential for cooperation to be effective. Poor people have a special need for legal services and often come to social workers with their legal problems. Sometimes they are in trouble with the law; sometimes they have personal problems that require a lawyer. This chapter treats the question of contrasting values and philosophies and introduces major topics that will receive detailed consideration later in the volume.

Social workers and lawyers generally show a high regard for the dignity and worth of people and for the rights of individuals. The professions of law and social work both exist to help people. Their practice recognizes that every case differs in some respects from every other case. They share the concept of individualization and base their efforts on the unique characteristics of the case.

THE BASIC VALUES OF SOCIAL WORK

The following concepts are basic to social work practice:

■ The individual is the primary concern of this society.

■ Individuals in this society are interdependent.

■ Individuals in this society have social responsibility for one another.

■ Each person shows some common human needs, yet each person is essentially unique and different from the others.

■ In a democratic society each individual should be able to realize his or her full potential and assume his or her social responsibility through active participation in society.

■ Society has a responsibility to provide ways in which obstacles to this self-realization (i.e., disequilibrium between the individual and the environment) can be overcome or prevented.*

Social workers generally believe that they can best help those reach their full potential who seek help voluntarily and who have considerable freedom to make their own decisions. Yet social workers often must help people who are in trouble

---

*For more on the basic values of social work, see *Working Definition of Social Work Practice* (1958) and *Working Statement on the Purpose of Social Work* (1981).

3

with the law, including those whose freedom may be restricted. Commitment of mental patients; work with delinquents, criminals, and child abusers; termination of parental rights; and protection of consumers are a few examples of the application of authority that enters into social service.

Maximum client participation in solving a problem is also an important goal of social work. In court, however, a client may be overawed by the situation and unable to give spontaneous reactions, thereby inhibiting participation. A witness cannot recount facts freely, but must do so in response to questions raised by opposing counsel.

Confidentiality is a basic value of social work that conflicts with the use of information in adult hearings held in open court, where names must be given and a record of testimony is kept. This issue is of particular importance when the accused is found not guilty but there is a possibility of character damage.

How does the law accord with these emphases of social work?

THE ROLE OF THE LAW

Law is "a formal means of social control that involves the use of rules that are interpreted and are enforceable by the courts of a political community" (Davis, 1962: 41). The law provides standards and means of social control that have become necessary because people live together in groups. Society requires order, and human relations must be subject to certain social controls. Current and past manners, habits, fashions, and morals influence the standards found in laws. The law also provides for negative sanctions when there is a failure to conform to group norms and to expectations based on the values of society. These sanctions are imposed through a decision-making process governed by rules set forth in advance. Many of the values of society affect the family—one of the main concerns of social work.

Many people are frustrated because they feel the law does not keep up with social changes. The court's traditional view of marriage when many people just want to live together is one example. Both the social control function of the law and the slowness of the system to accept change may make the laws seem out of date. In some cases, however, change has been rapid, as in the acceptance of the concept of "no-fault" divorce.

It is helpful to differentiate three kinds of laws: common law, natural law, substantive law. **Common law** is the basis for the English legal system and was derived from church law and local customs and standards that led to the establishment of substantive rules. Decisions became precedents for further decisions. **Natural law** includes those immutable laws that are assumed, such as rights to "life, liberty, and the pursuit of happiness." These laws apply to all persons irrespective of gender, race, or handicapping condition and have resulted in a tremendous body of cases. **Substantive law** refers to common rules that have been applied to many situations, for example, marriage, the acquisition and transfer of property, obligations for child care that impinge on the family and the state, and the safeguarding of society by keeping the peace.

Crimes, torts, and contracts are three other terms that require attention.

Crimes are actions against the state that may involve the penalty of loss of liberty. Because of the threat to society, the state acts as the prosecution. **Torts** involve alleged harm to another person which results in suits brought by persons or organizations for monetary damages or an injunction to stop harmful behavior. A **contract** is a legal agreement to carry out certain actions or to avoid carrying them out. Leases, employment agreements, and bills of sale are all contracts involving the exchange of money. In a lease, one's property is used in return for money; in employment, work is exchanged for wages or salary; in bills of sale, property is conveyed from one owner to another. An employment contract may include the agreement that on termination of employment a person will not accept employment from a directly competing firm for a specified time. To execute a contract, one must be of legal age and not of "unsound mind." Breach of contract may result in litigation and assessment of damages. In social work, by contrast the term *contract* is used to designate an understanding between social worker and client without any clear consequences for penalty. For example, a client who pledges to see a social worker for eight sessions is not absolutely required to come eight times.

NEED FOR KNOWLEDGE OF THE LAW

What do social workers need to know about the law? Recent developments, both in society and in the social work profession, demand an understanding of the law. This chapter identifies the reasons for increased attention to legal processes, summarizes the roles of social workers in court, and suggests some of the attitudes that impede effective cooperation between social workers and lawyers. The discussion continues with an introduction to the substantive areas of greatest relevance, especially family law. It concludes with the impact of law on social work practice and the skills related to law that social workers need. This chapter poses basic questions that will be discussed later.

Administrative Hearings

The courts would be inundated if the complaints of most people against a public social service agency resulted in litigation. To meet the need to handle grievances, administrative "fair" hearings are held under the agencies' auspices using a judicial procedure. Unfortunately, many of the clients are poor, but counsel is not provided for people who cannot pay for it. Social workers need skills to assist clients in this process and to provide facts related to their claims. They may need to help a client who gets an adverse decision decide whether or not to file suit.

Goldberg (1960: 197) stresses that social workers must have a good understanding of adjudication and of fair hearings:

> In our system of government, courts exist primarily to protect rights and to enforce legal responsibilities. Our adjudication process is a precious heritage, the result of valiant struggles for human liberties. This heritage is a cluster of rights such as the right not to be called to court without notice of the matter to be litigated; the right to be notified with time to prepare when one's interests are to be litigated; and the right to a fair hearing. These are rights that attorneys protect.
>
> Briefly, a fair hearing means (1) the right to be represented by a lawyer, (2) an opportunity to be heard, (3) freedom from secret proceedings, (4) the right to know what data are used by the judge as a basis for his findings concerning the allegations of the petition or complaint, and (5) orderly proceedings. Another essential to justice is a judicial record for review purposes.
>
> Our adjudication process has been tested and refined throughout centuries of juridical experience. In adjudication, the right of due process with its requisite ingredients of notice and a fair hearing becomes a reality. If either of these essential ingredients is missing, the adjudication is a travesty upon justice.

LEGAL REASONING VS. SOCIAL DIAGNOSIS

The process in legal reasoning is different from that of social diagnosis. Since law is concerned mainly with cases that are interpreted in light of the Constitution, statutes, and previous case decisions, the reasoning and research processes may seem elaborate and confusing.

Social workers often see the law as a set of rules which judges are called upon to apply. They may fail to recognize how much discretion judges exercise in their interpretation and application of the law. Some judges rely on precedents more than others. In dealing with offenders, the judge's discretion is particularly important. How much should the personality or social class of convicted persons serve to mitigate the penalty? Recent court decisions have led judges to emphasize equal treatment and to avoid biases based on social class or personal appearance.

Levi (1963) emphasizes that the law must be flexible enough to respond to new societal situations. Changes in people's wants are particularly pertinent to the social work view of the law. He stresses that legal reasoning is reasoning by example from case to case. A proposition descriptive of the first case becomes a rule of law and is then applied to similar situations. Similarity is observed between cases; the rule of law inherent in the first case is announced; the rule of law becomes applicable to the second case.

> The problem for the law is: When will it be just to treat different cases as though they were the same? A working legal system must therefore be willing to pick out key similarities and to reason from them to the justice of applying a common classification. (Levi, 1963: 3)

> In the legal process, the classification changes as the classification is made. The rules change as the rules are applied. More important, the rules arise out of a process which, while comparing fact situations, creates the rules and then applies them. But this kind of reasoning is open to the charge that it is classifying things as equal when they are somewhat different, justifying the classification by rules made up as the reasoning or classification proceeds. In a sense all reasoning is of this type, but there is an additional requirement which compels the legal process to be this way. Not only do new situations arise, but in addition peoples' wants change. The categories used in the legal process must be left ambiguous in order to permit the infusion of new ideas. And this is true even where legislation or a constitution is involved. The words used by the legislature or the constitutional convention must come to have new meanings. Furthermore, agreement on any other basis would be impossible. In this manner the laws come to express the ideas of the community and even when written in general terms, in statute or constitution, are molded for the specific case. (Levi, 1963: 4)

This book includes case examples that illustrate legal reasoning and provide a basis for understanding the approaches of lawyers and judges. Such understanding is more effectively achieved by means of specific examples from cases than by broad generalizations.

GREATER RELIANCE ON LAW A larger population and increasing urbanism have led to less reliance on informal methods of social control and greater reliance on law. Because over the last century more people have continued to choose to live in metropolitan areas, urbanism increases the need for law to govern. Recourse to legislation and enforcement becomes necessary to protect the public.

Greater reliance on law has also been the result of increased affluence, which tends to reduce cohesiveness and lessen the effectiveness of informal social controls. As people improve their standard of living, they move to other neighborhoods, breaking racial and ethnic ties that traditionally promoted cohesiveness and interdependence.

Along with the demographic trends, an increased number of individuals are asserting their legal rights more aggressively and using the courts to obtain them. Civil rights of minorities has been a dominant theme since the school desegregation controversy of the 1950s. In the past three decades the rights of the accused have also been defined and protected. Public service employees have gradually obtained the rights to bargain collectively and to strike. Every year, U.S. Supreme Court decisions deal with fundamental questions that are of concern to social work. This book will identify Supreme Court decisions that have affected social welfare programs and their clients.

Class action suits, in which a person sues not only on behalf of himself or herself but on behalf of all persons similarly injured, have become important in social welfare cases. Townsend v. Swank, 404 U.S. 282, decided by the Supreme Court in 1971, is a typical example. The action was brought successfully by parents of several college students on behalf of all the recipients of Aid to Families with Dependent Children who were discriminated against by being removed from the rolls because they chose to go to college rather than trade school.

Class action suits have become more difficult to win. As a result of the Supreme Court decision in Eisen v. Carlile and Jacquelin, 417 U.S. 156 (1974), all parties included in the class must now be notified before a class action suit is filed, and plaintiffs must bear the cost of notification.

Clients are becoming less passive and are beginning to regard services more as a matter of right than of privilege. When they feel wronged, they are likely to challenge the actions of public and voluntary agencies. If they are poor, they are now able to receive free legal assistance to do so. The increased development of free legal aid services as a result of the Economic Opportunity Act helped to further suits on behalf of the poor. *Townsend v. Swank* is one welfare case that illustrates the interest of legal aid lawyers in statutory reform.

THE COURT SYSTEM

A **court** is a public tribunal for the administration of justice to deal with offenses against the state and controversies among individuals. The staff consists of at least one judge, a clerk, and a marshall to preserve order.

States have **trial courts** that exercise original jurisdiction, and courts of appeals. A trial court can be called a **court of original jurisdiction** or a **court of record**, since it is the only court in which original testimony is taken and recorded. The **U.S. Supreme Court** has final appellate power. However, in the term beginning October, 1983, the Court was involved with 5,099 cases but decided only 194 of them (Supreme Court Library).

Ninety-three **federal district courts** hear cases involving the U.S. Constitution, federal laws, or parties who are citizens of different states. Appeals go to one of the eleven **circuit courts of appeals** and then may proceed to the U.S. Supreme Court. Federal courts may decline to hear cases that involve questions for which they think the state courts should be responsible. Some actions may be brought either in a federal court or a state court.

City or municipal courts, or justices' courts whose jurisdiction is limited to the city, are trial courts that hear criminal cases involving only misdemeanors and civil cases for limited money damages; litigants may handle their own cases. **Small-claims courts** dispense justice on an assembly-line basis, but they are highly satisfactory.

Other trial courts have unlimited jurisdiction over cases involving unlimited amounts of money, probate equity, divorce, and felony cases rather than merely misdemeanors. They are called circuit courts (e.g., Illinois, Indiana, Michigan); superior courts (e.g., California, Massachusetts); supreme courts (e.g., New York); district courts (e.g., Iowa, Minnesota, Oklahoma, Wyoming); and courts of common pleas (e.g., Ohio, Pennsylvania).

In the appeal process, the court reviews the record of the trial court and the briefs from both sides that identify possible errors made by the trial judge. Each side will present oral arguments. The appeals court may grant relief, remand (send back) the case for retrial, or affirm the action of the trial court.

SOCIAL WORKERS AND THE COURTS

The growth of social agencies and the development of advocacy roles have brought more social workers into court. Public agencies have increased in number, and new private agencies have also been established to promote specialized programs. Associations for parents of the mentally retarded are examples of the use of advocacy.

With the growth of agencies and with increased litigation has come increased autonomy of staff members within social agencies. No longer is testifying automatically the prerogative of a senior social work supervisor or of the agency's executive director. The direct service worker is likely to deal with legal problems and appear in court. Lawyers and judges often will not accept hearsay; they seek primary testimony from the worker rather than secondhand information from an agency administrator.

Social Workers' Roles in Court

In court, the social worker usually serves one of five roles:

Petitioner. The social worker who alleges child neglect or abuse, for example, and files a petition to place the child in foster care represents society's interest by seeking protection of the child through court action.

Defendant. The social worker may be called on to answer the charge for an agency that is being sued and also may occasionally be named personally as a co-

FIGURE 1.1
THE COURT SYSTEM

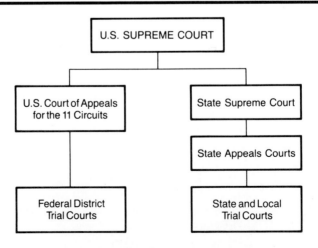

defendant. A suit by foster parents asking the court to restrain the agency and its worker from removing a child is one example.

Client Advocate.   A social worker may appear on behalf of clients to explain their problems, to justify their behavior, or to plead for services needed.

Expert Witness.   Because of their expertise, social workers may be asked to testify on a situation of which they have no direct knowledge but in which their experience is valuable. For example, one social worker was asked to provide data on the annual cost of rearing a child as a means of assessing damages in a wrongful death case.

Colleague.   In the social services department of a court, social workers function as colleagues of the court staff to aid in fact-finding and supervision. They are often responsible for the court report on which a disposition is based.

NATIONAL CONFERENCE OF SOCIAL WORKERS AND LAWYERS

The National Conference of Social Workers and Lawyers was created in 1962 by the American Bar Association and the National Association of Social Workers. Its purpose was to:

1.   Draft statements of principles defining the legitimate activities of social workers and lawyers
2.   Prevent the unauthorized practice of law by defining those areas in family law that are within the competence only of lawyers
3.   Serve as a clearinghouse for the interests of social welfare agencies and/or legal groups in the development of legislation
4.   Gather and disseminate information concerning research projects
5.   Promote a better understanding between lawyers and social workers

(National Conference of Lawyers and Social Workers, 1973)

Answerable to the Standing Committee on the Unauthorized Practice of Law and the Section of Family Law of the American Bar Association, the conference was active for over a decade and produced a series of position papers (National Conference of Lawyers and Social Workers, 1973). Sol Morton Isaac, who served as chairman of the conference, observed:

> [A] lack of cordiality between lawyers and social workers grew out of a lack of understanding and appreciation of the nature of the service that each was trained and competent to perform. When lawyers attempt to practice social work and social workers attempt to practice law, it is largely because neither fully appreciates the dimensions of the other's profession. Whenever lawyers and social workers are required, the results are immeasurably enhanced if they work together with conviction and are seriously retarded if they fail to do so. It has been demonstrated time and again, both nationally and locally, that there is no basic incompatibility between these two groups and that they can readily reach accord once they sit down together to counsel with each other. (National Conference of Lawyers and Social Workers, 1973: 53–54)

There is still a great need for joint deliberations by lawyers and social workers, not only on the national level but also in local communities.

ATTITUDES OF SOCIAL WORKERS AND LAWYERS

Stereotypes suggest that lawyers demand the facts while social workers value feelings, that the former tend to stress evidence and the latter rely on intentions and motives. Along these lines, it might also be said that lawyers emphasize sanctions and authority, and social workers stress self-determination and voluntary relationships.

Schottland (1968: 724) identified the lawyer's perception of the social worker as:

> associated with church-sponsored charity, work with homeless children, public assistance with its problems of dependency and family breakdown, activities carried on by persons who have not been accorded professional status by law and whose professional relationship to the client is colored (in his mind) by the fact that the social worker is employed by an agency and not by a client.

Sloane (1967) summarized the differences between lawyers and social workers based on interviews of a sample of lawyers and social workers in New England. He presented the responses of social workers first:

1. *The lawyer-client relationship.* The social workers interviewed clearly saw this relationship as confidential and client-focused but also as essentially different from the social worker-client relationship. In the social worker's view, the lawyer as a representative of his client carries out his bidding. In this he becomes a partisan and thus his relationship with his client is that of a "hired gun." The group of social workers interviewed felt that this was determined by the adversary system. For the most part, they overlooked other ways of settling disputes such as mediation, conciliation, and arbitration.

The social workers wanted to restrict the lawyer's counseling function to legal advice or associated business advice. They thought lawyers often went beyond this restricted role and offered marital and other counseling. The social workers saw them as ill prepared for the role of marital counselor.

2. *A specialized body of knowledge.* The social worker sees the law as a specialized body of knowledge and therefore he has no question about the need for expertise acquired by intellectual effort. He sees it as technical, rigid, logical and precise—the compulsive's delight!

The social workers interviewed found it hard to accept technical rules of evidence, particularly the hearsay rules, and thought the laws pertaining to divorce completely inappropriate. For them, hearsay rules seemed to typify the technical and hairsplitting aspects of the law. Divorce laws, based as they are on concepts of fault and subject to adversary action on specified grounds, were viewed as irrelevant and unhelpful. To the social worker, a marital problem is a psychosocial event, the causes and resolution of which should be approached by clinical process and conference, not as a dispute to be resolved by adversary action and cross-examination.

3. *Sanctions regulating practice.* Social workers know that the lawyer's activities are regulated not only by the law itself but by a canon of ethics, that his admission to practice is subject to licensing, and that he may be disbarred for improper conduct. Generally associated with improper conduct of the lawyer is outright criminal behavior or such clearly unethical activity as "ambulance-chasing."

The social workers had not considered the complexity and stresses of the ethical problems faced by the lawyer in independent practice, for instance, the problems of defending clients who are known to be guilty, drawing the line between preparing and coaching a friendly witness, advising a couple who agree on divorce when no valid grounds for such exist within the state of jurisdiction.

On the other hand, the social worker sees law as a masculine, aggressive profession and the lawyer as rigid, technical, and pettifogging. He is seen primarily as an advocate who rightly or wrongly identifies himself in a partisan way with his client and will use any legal loophole to win. He pays no attention to feelings and will see any complex human situation only in legalistic and financial terms. The lawyer patronizes the social worker, is hostile to clinical points of view and is skeptical about innovations suggested by the human relations professions. His profession has great power and authority and he is jealous of surrendering any vestige of them. (Sloane, 1967: 88–91)

The views of the lawyers were quite different:

For his part the lawyer associates social work with religion, charity, and humanitarianism. These views tend to be diffused and are not organized into a developed point of view about the nature and role of social work in the social structure. The lawyers interviewed also tended to identify public welfare agencies with controversial issues such as fostering immorality, dependency, or welfare-statism and private agencies with noncontroversial issues or more approved attitudes such as voluntarism and helping people to help themselves.

1. *The social worker–client relationship.* To judge from these interviews, the lawyer is not convinced that the social worker's relationship with his client is a professional one. He is aware that the law has not accorded a privileged status to these communications and his tendency is to limit this privilege.

Of more significance is that the lawyer is not aware of the therapeutic nature of the relationship or that it is central to the helping process. When a social agency offers a specific service, the lawyer sees the social worker as a kind of supplier of, let us say, a shelter to an unfortunate unmarried mother. Or, when counseling services are furnished, the lawyer thinks of the process in terms of his own activities of advice-giving, conciliation, mediation, or arbitration. Indeed, marital counseling services attached to courts are characteristically called "conciliation" services and marital partners may be asked to sign contractual agreements in settlement of differences.

2. *A specialized body of knowledge.* The lawyer sees the social worker as an agency representative, not a practicing professional using a specialized expertise within an agency structure. In carrying out the policies of the agency, he offers tactful and kind services calculated not to hurt or anger clients. True, administering these services requires intellectual knowledge, for example, of child development, but this is considered to be a smattering of knowledge borrowed from other disciplines rather than a distinctive body of applied knowledge. The lawyer thus fails to identify any area of true expertise for the caseworker.

This view was not shared by the two judges and the two law educators who were interviewed. They saw the social worker as an expert witness in specialized areas of practice, such as child welfare or adoption. Indeed, one of the judges interviewed stated a preference for the testimony of the trained social worker to the psychiatrist on family matters since the social worker is "family focused" while the psychiatrist as a physician is "patient focused."

3. *Sanctions regulating practice.* As one might expect from knowing that the lawyer views the social worker as an agency representative or employee, he then sees the work and activity of the social worker as being controlled by agency policy in the usual employer-employee relationship, not as self-regulatory. The lawyers thought of the social worker as an ineffectual, giving, nursing female who wants to and does do much good, but at the same time is impractical, utopian, overidentified with and overprotective of her client, "all heart and no head," subjective and not objective, concerned only with feelings and not logic. Even so, she knows less than she thinks she knows even about human relations. She is too defensive about what she does know. . . .

She will often complain about the law and how it hampers the effective resolution of a social situation but does not know how to be effective in altering the law. Her understanding of legal processes is scanty. She wants to be exempt from cross-examination, to confine her court reports to the judge's attention alone without scrutiny by the attorney, to obtain privilege for her communications to her clients. But she does not see that there are other public interests such as "due process" competing with hers that must be considered by the law. She has gone overboard on "psychology" and sees juvenile delinquents and criminals either as victims of faulty environment or as mentally ill—in both cases personal responsibility of the client is thus disclaimed. (Sloane, 1967: 89–91)

Obviously, these comments do not provide adequate evidence to generalize about the two professions. Sloane summarizes the differences:

Certainly the adversary system is a red flag to social workers and a complex of grievances arises from this basic legal apparatus. Upon reflection it seems clear that the difference in this respect does not involve basic values. It is not clear to social workers that the adversary system, with its right to confrontation and cross-examination of witnesses, is essential to the concept of a fair hearing and thus to due process of law. To them, freedom itself is the basic value. Without a doubt basic civil liberties are part of social work's value system.

What is in conflict, however, is the *methods* of the two professions. The social worker tries to resolve differences by case conference and consensus, not the clash of adversaries. The legal approaches of conciliation and mediation at least are comprehensible to the social worker, but the adversary system is entirely beyond his conception of the usual means of conflict resolution. Perhaps the social worker is not at home with aggression and conflict! (Sloane, 1967: 91–92)

Tamilia (1971: 579) presents a lawyer's view of the social worker in the adversary situation:

In presenting proof, the degree to which hearsay evidence should be admitted or considered is always an issue. Caseworkers are prone to incorporate in their reports and consideration material from numerous sources which are unavailable to the court or from persons unwilling to be involved. They are also impatient with legal requirements of proof and are inclined to make their case for agency or judicial intervention in a narrative summarization of their knowledge of the situation. When tested by lawyers in an adversary proceeding, the reaction is one of affront and personal injury and they tend to become polarized in the belief that they are protectors of the child against legal charlatanism.

ROLE CONFLICT   Brennan and Khinduka (1971) reported on role conflict between lawyers and social workers in juvenile courts. Lawyers felt that social workers usurped some legal tasks. Both lawyers and social workers considered informing juveniles of rights of custody, conducting factual investigations, and explaining reasons for adjudication to be elements of their role.

Overlapping functions between the two professions were also reported by Audrey Smith (1970). Social workers felt that they could conduct initial interviews, secure information for legal cases, complete the necessary forms for filing a divorce, interpret laws dealing with social functions, and arrange debt payment plans. These are all traditional responsibilities of the lawyer.

About one-quarter of the lawyers in the Smith study concluded that they could perform social work functions as well as the social workers. They saw the social worker's role as one of listening to the problems of others—something that "anyone" can do.

A conflict between judges and social workers has emerged in the latter's role as petitioner or advocate. Judges are often seen by social workers as advocates of parental rights, and social workers are seen as advocates of the child's rights and of **parens patriae**, the responsibility of the state to assume a parental interest in the well-being of the child. Another conflict occurs in that judges often take on administrative as well as judicial functions and make independent decisions about custody and foster care or the fitness of a couple to adopt a child. They may see the social worker as merely implementing the court's decision, but the social worker feels that child placement and custody are the domain of social work. This kind of professional territorial conflict is common.

From the literature and from training sessions with social workers and lawyers, several differences can be summarized:

Relative Status. Lawyers often regard social workers as lacking in status. They see them as technicians. It is no surprise that lawyers may be considered arrogant. Income differentials are cited as a measure of relative prestige. The traditional male personnel in law and female personnel in social work lead to conflict if differences are magnified by sexism. Male judges tend to be more sexist than attorneys or social workers.

Family Law. The lawyer in general practice rarely becomes involved in family law cases, with the possible exception of divorce. The lawyer may have little or no experience with issues involving juvenile delinquency, child custody, or mental health. The social worker often considers his or her knowledge to be superior and feels resentful because the lawyer is accorded deference as an expert.

Client Advocacy. Employment by an agency is seen as compromising the social worker's effectiveness as an advocate for the client. The agency is a force for social control. The social worker has divided loyalties: to society, the agency, and the client. Only the social worker in private practice is hired directly by the client. Even lawyers paid a salary in legal assistance programs see themselves as the client's representative just as if the client had hired them.

Guilt or Innocence. Lawyers, in emphasizing proof, defend people whom they may know are guilty. Social workers see this as an ethical conflict.

Adversary Methods Rather Than Conciliation. The lawyer seeks to prove a case. The social worker is a mediator and a conciliator. Except for plea-bargaining or some other compromise out of court, the lawyer seeks to win.

Evidence. The lawyer demands direct testimony—what was done, seen, or heard. The social worker is more likely to deal in summary judgments—what an incident meant or what its implications were. Even social work records may lack specific facts. Lawyers have little respect for diagnostic formulations. They do not consider the social worker serving a client to be an expert witness.

Professional Practice. The lawyer does not want social workers giving legal advice; in fact, it is illegal. But lawyers frequently provide clients with advice on marriage, child-rearing, or mental health—areas of social work competence. Lawyers may practice social work, but social workers may not practice law.

Confidentiality.   Names and events are needed in testimony. Highly personal information is revealed in open court. The social worker seeks to preserve privacy for the client and keep personal information confidential. Confidentiality is more likely to be protected in juvenile matters than in matters involving adults.

Too Much Intervention or Too Little.   In cases involving the authority of the court, the social worker is perceived as a child snatcher who makes a shambles of parents' rights, or by contrast as a sentimental, permissive client-centered person who cannot assess danger to children, thereby leaving them prey to child abuse and neglect. Lawyers can easily be critical because they do not have to provide continuing direct service to those parents who tend to be emotional and inconsistent at best.

Few recent articles have been published to highlight conflicts between social workers and lawyers. This may be a sign that relations between the two professions are improving.

In a recent study, Weil (1982) reported encouraging results. Her respondents—lawyers and social workers—all associated the responsibility of the disposition phase of juvenile court process with social workers. They recommended transferring to lawyers some preadjudication functions commonly carried by social workers. The organizational climate in Weil's Los Angeles sample differed markedly from that found by Brennan and Khinduka.

Weil reported other interesting findings, among them that social workers working with child dependency perceived lawyers positively, while adoption workers perceived them negatively; that adoption attorneys viewed their own role as more satisfying than did dependency court attorneys; that dependency court lawyers had a more favorable view of social workers than did adoption lawyers; and that both social workers involved with dependency cases and their lawyer counterparts considered the other profession more effective than their own profession. Two-thirds of the respondents in the study had participated in a two-week course on social work in the courts; that might explain the optimistic findings on social workers handling dependency cases.

INCREASING SOCIAL WORK'S KNOWLEDGE OF THE LAW

Weil (1982) also reported a successful project to increase social work students' understanding of problems of professional collaboration with lawyers. The project also sought to increase their knowledge of the family court. Scores on a knowledge test doubled. Attitudes toward interprofessional collaboration improved. But, first-year students in the project showed more negative attitudes toward lawyers at the end of the year, while attitudes of a comparison group of students did not change. Weil summarizes the outcome:

> At the completion of the planned learning experiences, the practicum group differed markedly in a number of respects from the comparison groups. They demonstrated a more heightened understanding of the complexities of interprofessional work than did the two comparison groups. They showed greatly increased knowledge of law content and processes in comparison with the other groups, where the knowledge gains were considerably less. They demonstrated greater ability than the other groups to define, describe, and differentiate the roles and responsibilities of social workers and lawyers operating in social welfare and the family-court system. In addition, they demonstrated increased sophistication in ability to identify interprofessional work problems such as

status differentiation, issues of confidentiality, conflicts in allegiance, protection of clients' rights, and value conflicts. They evaluated the learning experiences as very useful in aiding them in understanding the legal-social system and professional roles. (Weil, 1982: 402–403)

Increased professional knowledge and skill for both lawyers and social workers can result in less conflict between the two professions. Both professions now provide better clinical training for students, the value of which has been demonstrated by Weil. As the volume of work has increased, courts have turned over more administrative matters to social workers both on the court staff and in other agencies. Clearly, however, effectiveness of professional cooperation depends on the social worker's understanding of rules of evidence. In detention and in the disposition of cases, social workers find that their recommendations will be taken seriously only when a factual review logically leads to the recommended course of action. We will return to this topic in a later chapter.

One way to get the required knowledge base is to obtain academic degrees in both social work and law. Washington University in St. Louis pioneered a joint program in 1970, and similar opportunities have been developed at a dozen other universities. While we can expect dual social work and law degree programs to become more popular, most students do not have the time or the financial resources to pursue a joint program. Too little time is saved by a degree program to make it widely attractive. It is usually not practical for the social worker also to be a lawyer, but an improved knowledge of the law is necessary.

Social work students desire a single course that will give them the essentials of law. Courses with legal content are offered in over 85 percent of the graduate schools of social work. Practitioners want a handbook that will meet all their practical needs for information. With the wide range of possible content, a single course or a handbook can provide only a foundation for developing specialized knowledge. Books like this one can help social workers learn where to find legal documents and precedents and acquaint them with illustrative cases and major court decisions. They will need to become familiar with statutes and practices in their own state. No single text can accomplish this goal.

KNOWLEDGE OF GOVERNMENTAL STRUCTURE

Social workers need a basic knowledge of governmental structure. They are aware that our system involves three branches of government: the legislative branch, which passes the laws; the executive branch, which approves the laws and develops programs to carry them out; and the judicial branch, which interprets the laws.

Social workers soon realize that the relationships among the three branches are both complex and subtle. We went from a weak executive branch when the Constitution was adopted, to a strong executive beginning in the 1930s. Since then, Congress has exerted its right to veto on the executive branch in many types of legislation, including the War Powers Act. This traditional power will apparently be curtailed by a 1983 decision, Immigration & Naturalization Service v. Chadha, 103 S.Ct. 2764 (1983), which prohibited legislative vetoes and cast doubt on at least two hundred acts of Congress. It may take several years to see how Congress responds.

Meanwhile the importance of the Supreme Court has increased as it deals with many fundamental issues including not only separation of powers but also due process and rule-making authority, which affect social programs.

AREAS OF LEGAL KNOWLEDGE

For social workers, four areas of legal knowledge are especially important: **family law**, for example, marriage and divorce, child-bearing, child-rearing, and child custody; **delinquency and crime**, behavior that violates the law and involves resultant processing of offenders; **the legal rights of special groups that seek social services**—for example, the poor, women, adolescents, racial and ethnic minorities, consumers, tenants, mental patients, and the aged; and **issues related to social work practice**—legal authority for social welfare programs, clients' needs for legal assistance, the legal rights and responsibilities of social workers, and protection of the public and professional staff members.

Family Law

Social workers deal primarily with the area of family law. With over fifty systems of family law (one for each state, plus the District of Columbia, Puerto Rico, Guam, and American Samoa), courts must generally give **full faith and credit** to laws and actions of other jurisdictions by recognizing their validity and cooperating in enforcing them. If they did not do so, marriages could be annulled, divorces overthrown, and children taken from their homes simply because someone moves across a state line.

The Sanctity of Marriage.   The courts used to function as advocates of the sanctity of marriage by making annulment and divorce difficult; most states also outlawed common law marriages. However, more couples are now choosing to live together without marriage—not just the poor, but people with superior education and economic potential. The law has not accommodated itself to these changes.

Most courts no longer strongly defend the sanctity of marriage. They have found that compulsory counseling and mandatory waiting periods have not saved marriages. For many reasons, divorce has become much easier to obtain once a financial settlement has been worked out. What are the implications for social work? To what extent have the changes in attitude been accompanied by changes in the statutes? Has getting a divorce without any allegation of fault and without detailed testimony of the damage to the spouses really changed the divorce process? Is there really much difference between no-fault and adversary grounds such as mental cruelty or incompatibility? How is no-fault divorce important to the practice of social work? These questions will be considered in Chapter 14.

Child-bearing.   Social workers used to help the unmarried pregnant woman decide what to do with her baby, but there are now many options available to her. If she chooses not to terminate the pregnancy, she has usually decided to keep the child by the time she comes to the agency; she may seek service solely to implement that decision. What does the law have to say about contraception, abortion, illegitimacy, and meeting the financial needs of single parents? What new decisions affect the rights of the woman, her husband, and her parents? What controversial questions remain unanswered? This topic is discussed in Chapter 12.

Child-rearing.   When family dependency, neglect, or abuse develop, child-rearing is likely to involve the law. Sometimes problem behaviors of the child must be dealt with by the police. Older children beyond the control of their parents or of other adults may be declared by the courts to be "persons, children, or minors in need of supervision." Such labels have been considered preferable to "incorrigible" or "delinquent" because they are more benign. Negative labels are thought to reinforce negative behaviors. Labeling a juvenile with adult criminal terms may make subsequent delinquent behavior more likely. Some of the problems of labeling theory will be considered in several of the following chapters.

Child Custody and Placement. Custody is a major legal topic arising from the need to place children in adoption and foster care and to assure adequate parental responsibility in the case of divorce. Substitute care for children is one of the social service programs most costly to society and requires exceptional professional skill. Substitute care arrangements are intended to be temporary. The courts are reluctant to terminate parental rights permanently if the family can possibly resume parental responsibility, but this often puts children in an ambiguous situation. The basic laws to protect children from abuse and neglect also cover a wide range of circumstances in which the social worker becomes involved. When to take criminal action against abusing parents is a major controversial question.

Delinquency and Crime

Social services are available to alleged delinquents and to adult offenders. The juvenile court was largely a creation of social workers who felt that adult criminal proceedings were inappropriate for children and youths. Recent litigation has formalized and systematized the procedures to make processing more like that of adult criminal courts.

Many juvenile offenses are a function of the age-status of the offender rather than of the violation of statutes that apply to adults. Such status offenses include truancy, running away, curfew violations, use of tobacco and intoxicants, and disobeying adults, primarily parents or teachers.

In adult corrections, social workers are likely to work with lower-income prisoners charged with crimes against persons or property. Except for major felons, the intent of criminal justice programs has been to divert offenders from correctional institutions primarily through the use of probation, or to return them to society by means of parole. Social work roles in probation and parole have expanded, especially in the federal justice system. Social workers need to have an understanding of the correctional process: the complaint, apprehension by the police, processing at the station, detention, adjudication, disposition, and diversion. If the person is sent to a correctional institution, rehabilitative services may be offered. Supervision after parole should include provision for social services.

Rights of Special Groups

The Poor. Without attempting to define poverty precisely, both social work and law have had a particular concern with the poor. Personal income is negatively correlated with most major life problems. Following the English system, our laws have required the poor to prove their need for financial help, and for centuries financial aid has been tied to work requirements. Financial assistance benefits constituted a lien, a financial claim against property and other assets, present or future. Persons receiving assistance have often been denied privacy, especially women who head families.

Poverty has other consequences. While a disproportionate number of defendants are poor, the poor are also underrepresented on juries. Because of an inadequate bail system, poor people have had to stay in jail while awaiting trial and have faced greater risk of mistreatment as part of official interrogation. The poor have also been denied access to divorce and other legal services that cost money. They have been victimized by tradespeople because they have inadequate knowledge, limited buying power, and no effective way to lodge consumer complaints.

Racial and Ethnic Minorities.   For some years the National Association of Social Workers chose racism and poverty as two major priorities. Racial and ethnic minorities have been the subject of great concern. Desegregation was the legal goal of the 1950s and voting rights the goal of the 1960s; busing gained special attention in the 1970s. To provide jobs for minorities, affirmative action in employment is a goal of minorities. Now there is also concern about reverse discrimination, not only in hiring but in layoffs and terminations.

Women.   Laws protecting the rights of women have expanded broadly from the pioneering efforts that once prevented them from working in hazardous occupations. Rights to equal opportunity for employment, pay, and advancement have become important. Occupations that used to be closed to one sex have opened up; we have female telephone "linemen" and male "cabin attendants" on airplanes. Rights of women to own property and to make contracts have undergone change. Yet more than one-third of the states refused to ratify the Equal Rights Amendment to the Constitution. And some recent cases have included examples of sex-based discrimination against men, too.

Other Special Groups.   Social work has increasingly recognized fields of practice as a way to organize professional education. Current social work education places greater emphasis on specialized functions and clienteles—for example, health, mental health, child welfare, education, the poor, the handicapped, and the aged.

Adolescents have been of special concern in both casework and group work. Critical legal questions are the age of majority and the rights of the child who has not reached that age but who is emancipated by his or her own choice or by actions of the parents.

Consumers and tenants have organized, and federal and state legislation has reflected increasing awareness of their needs. Most state attorneys general are involved in preventing consumer fraud. Rent withholding to improve the quality of housing has been sanctioned by law in some states. Social workers have played the roles of organizers, enablers, and advocates.

Institutionalized persons include those of all ages. Mental patients have received particular attention with regard to their right to treatment and their right to release, both subjects of Supreme Court action.

Finally, the aged are becoming an increasingly important client group. They vote more regularly than most younger adults, and they are currently concerned about the right to work and the injustice of mandatory retirement. They need a wide variety of legal services but often have limited ability to obtain them. When the aged become senile, the courts can restrict their right to make decisions for themselves by appointing a guardian.

Social Work Practice

State Regulation of Social Work Practice.   Licensing of social workers has been a major goal, mainly to protect the public. Licensing conveys authority to carry on a specific activity. In the face of violations, licenses can be revoked, so that a person may no longer engage in his or her profession. Licensing also usually specifies certain levels of education and experience needed to practice a profession. One major problem in legal regulation is the broad and unspecific use by society of the term *social worker*. Other general terms for helping persons, such as counselor and adviser, are also ambiguous and sometimes misunderstood by the public.

Malpractice.   Malpractice raises several questions that require detailed discussion. To what extent is the social worker subject to malpractice suits? While charges against a social worker are less likely than against a surgeon, malpractice suits are possible. Are suggestions given by a therapist that turn out to be inappropriate for the patient basis for a malpractice suit? If the worker advises a client to file for a divorce, can the other marital partner file suit against the worker for alienation of affection? In some states, the answer is yes. Is sexual intercourse with the therapist or a surrogate as part of treatment grounds for a malpractice suit?

Privileged Communication.   The privilege not to testify, which provides a legal base for confidentiality, has traditionally been extended to husband and wife, priest and penitent, lawyer and client. In some instances professional social workers have the same privilege. In others they must testify and may be questioned in detail about what occurred in a therapeutic relationship. Most social workers value privileged communication highly and consider it essential to the most effective treatment efforts.

The Social Worker as Employee.   What protections does the social worker enjoy as an employee? Is employment protected by an adequate contractual arrangement? Does a staff member have tenure? Can he or she join a union? Does the union have the right to bargain, to strike, and to have a closed shop? If an employee works for a public agency, what protections are accorded by civil service? Can geographic transfer be used punitively? What are the effects of agency reorganization on employee rights? What are the risks of being sued? Exhibit 1.1 shows how liability insurance provides some protection against malpractice suits.

EXHIBIT 1.1
AN ADVERTISEMENT FOR LIABILITY INSURANCE

COULD ONE OF THESE SOCIAL WORKERS BE YOU?

A couple comes to you for counseling. After several months, one partner files for divorce. The other partner sues you for $350,000, claiming alienation of the spouse's affections.

Your agency places a child in an adoptive home. Several months later, you determine that the adoptive parents are unsuitable and remove the child. The parents sue your agency and name you as co-defendant.

These are actual cases, typical of many everyday situations that can leave a professional social worker open to accusations of malpractice. Social work demands involvement—yours with a client, your agency's with the community. This involvement makes you and your agency vulnerable to legal action.

Any client who believes there has been negligence or error in his or her treatment can bring suit. Court judgments in such cases are becoming increasingly large. More important, *any* claim (even if it is totally groundless) must be defended, and the cost of legal defense can be extremely high.

That is why the National Association of Social Workers has developed a comprehensive program of professional liability insurance specially designed for social workers and social service agencies and underwritten by the American Home Assurance Company. This program includes two flexible plans, which can be tailored to fit your unique situation:

Individual Liability Plan—Protection for yourself that may be extended to include partners and employees.

Agency Liability Plan—Vital coverage for social service agencies. Qualified individual professionals may be included under the agency policy.

SOCIAL WORK SKILLS

This book is concerned with development of basic skills to: (1) present evidence competently in court; (2) protect the legal rights of clients and obtain the legal services they need; (3) understand the major provisions of the family laws of one's own state; (4) find and interpret the relevant laws of other states when clients require such information; (5) keep up with major changes as the result of new legislation and court decisions; (6) affect legislation through testimony or lobbying; (7) seek legal protection for professional social work practice; and (8) make effective use of legal services on the social worker's behalf.

Questions for Review

1. Define *law*.

2. Explain the legal reasoning process from case to case.

3. How do population and urbanization trends increase the need for law?

4. What is the purpose of filing class action suits?

5. What was the "class" in *Townsend v. Swank?*

6. What areas of law are of special importance to social workers?

7. Identify basic areas of conflict between social workers and lawyers.

8. Why is the social worker's employment by an agency considered a problem by lawyers?

9. Illustrate the need to know how to find provisions of family laws in other states.

10. What is "full faith and credit?"

11. How would you generalize about the courts' concern for the sanctity of marriage?

12. Why is labeling important in serving youthful offenders?

13. How may licensing of social workers protect the public?

14. If a social worker suggests that a client file for divorce, what legal action against the social worker might result?

15. What are the major topics in family law about which the social worker should be knowledgeable?

Questions for Debate and Discussion

1. How important is a common value system for social workers and lawyers? Does differential emphasis on self-realization and social control result in basic conflict between them?

2. What issues are likely to be regarded differently by social workers and judges?

3. How can social workers and lawyers achieve better understanding?

4. Discuss the viewpoint that there are too many legal restrictions on human conduct.

5. Do you think that social workers have the same potential for damage to clients through malpractice as physicians do?

6.   What aspects of law discussed in this chapter seem most important to the type of social work practice in which you hope to engage?

7.   What needs do social workers have for legal knowledge to solve their own personal problems?

Selected Readings   Barrett, Edward Jr. *Constitutional Law: Cases and Materials.* Mineola, N.Y.: Foundation Press, 1977.

Edwards, Clark (ed.). *Government's Role in Solving Societal Problems.* Washington, D.C.: Graduate School Press, 1982.

Harnett, Bertram N. *Law, Lawyers, and Laymen: Making Sense Out of the American Legal System.* New York: Harcourt Brace Jovanovich, 1984.

Howard, Woodford J., Jr. *Courts of Appeals in the Federal Judicial System.* Princeton: Princeton University Press, 1981.

McDonald, Forrest. *A Constitutional History of the United States.* New York: Franklin Watts, 1982.

"National Conference on Social Work and the Law." *Children's Legal Rights Journal* 4 (1982): 33–41.

Schroeder, Leila Obler. *The Legal Environment of Social Work.* Englewood Cliffs, N.J.: Prentice-Hall, 1982.

Siffin, William J. *The Legislative Council in the American States.* Westport, Conn.: Greenwood Press, 1982.

Sloan, Irving J. *Law of Family Relations.* Dobbs Ferry, N.Y.: Oceana Publications, 1984.

Starr, Isidore. *Justice: Due Process of Law.* St. Paul, Minn.: West Publishing Co., 1981.

Stern, Robert L. *Appellate Practice in the United States.* Washington, D.C.: Bureau of National Affairs, 1981.

Weyrauch, Walter O., and Sanford N. Katz. *American Family Law in Transition.* Washington, D.C.: Bureau of National Affairs, 1982.

Williams, Robert F. "State Constitutional Law Processes." *William and Mary Law Review* 24 (1983): 169–228.

Woody, Robert H. *Law and the Practice of Human Services.* San Francisco: Jossey Bass, 1984.

CHAPTER

2

The Use of Legal References and Materials

Social workers who read legal literature for the first time may find themselves in a confusing world. The form of legal materials, the vocabulary, and the citation system are all unique. This chapter introduces the use of such materials. It serves the reader who is interested in understanding this book, but it is also detailed enough to be of use for elementary legal research.

For writing papers, consulting original materials, or analyzing a series of related decisions, a summary of the legal sources and research tools is helpful. The reader who needs more information may consult the several books on legal research which are available.

Laws are compiled and coded by subject. Decisions on given topics are collected in **casebooks**. "**Hornbooks**" are textbooks that summarize legal principles and precedents, according to West Publishing Company's terminology. West also publishes general paperback summaries of legal topics, "**nutshells**."

The legal documents referred to in this chapter are available in specialized libraries. Many larger public libraries are federal depositories. Smaller libraries at least have the federal and state constitutions and current state statutes. Social agencies often collect legal documents related to their particular field.

The key single rule in legal citations of cases is that the volume number always precedes the name of the publication and the page number follows it. For example: Townsend v. Swank, *404* U.S. 282 (1971), is found on page 282 of volume 404 of the U.S. Supreme Court Reports; Santosky v. Kramer, *455* U.S. *745* (1982), is found on page 745 of volume 455 of the same publication. References to other material may be designated *supra* or *infra*. *Supra* means earlier in this book and *infra* means later.

THE LEGAL STRUCTURE IN THE UNITED STATES

Many of the problems in dealing with legal materials arise from our governmental structure, which includes one federal legal system and fifty state systems. Any given transaction may be governed solely by federal law or solely by state law or by a combination of both. It is generally necessary to be familiar with both federal laws and state laws on a specific topic. Some cases of interest to social workers involve federal jurisdiction, others involve state jurisdiction. As we have seen,

23

conflicts between state laws are a particular problem because of the high mobility of the population.

The government of the United States is derived from the Constitution, the acts of Congress, and the interpretations of both by the U.S. Supreme Court and lower federal courts. State governments derive authority from the state constitutions, the enactments of the state legislatures, and, in some cases, laws enacted directly by the electorate. The states, except for Louisiana (which followed the French model), also created statutes by which they adopted provisions of English common law—law derived by judges rather than by legislative bodies.

REPORTING COURT DECISIONS

The law undergoes constant change. Justice Oliver W. Holmes observed that over a generation a given jurisdiction takes up the whole body of law and restates it in current terms. Thus earlier decisions perform a historical function but do not preclude change; today's dissent may become tomorrow's majority opinion.

Because court decisions are based on judicial precedents, reports of court decisions are important to the development of our laws. Some 3 million judicial opinions and the publication of 30,000 cases each year create problems of information retrieval and high costs. Computers are becoming increasingly helpful in providing the necessary information base for legal researchers. The Lexis system provides computerized references. Cases are indexed by key words to facilitate retrieval.

As indicated in Chapter 1, systems of court organization differ somewhat from state to state. In all jurisdictions, however, the initial judicial decision takes place in the *trial court,* where the parties appear, witnesses are heard, and evidence is offered. Determination of questions of fact and application of the rules of law are the functions of the trial courts.

The appellate stage, which may follow, requires action by the losing party, who appeals the original decision based on an alleged error in the trial court. No new testimony is taken, and a written opinion must be given. Decisions are made on the basis of the trial court record.

In the appellate court, both parties submit written briefs, which contain a summary of the facts and arguments on the points of law. The court may hear oral arguments by the respective attorneys. The court then writes an opinion stating the reasons for its decision. *Opinion* and *decision* are synonyms.

Written decisions routinely provide certain information:

1. The names of the parties to a lawsuit for use in indexing

■ *Townsend v. Swank* — The form used in an adversary action that does not involve criminal charges.

■ *Illinois v. Smith* — The form used for criminal actions. The state or the federal government is the plaintiff.

■ *In re Gault* — The form used if the action is not adversary. In the *Gault* case there was no plaintiff or defendant. In a table of cases it will appear *Gault, In re.* This form is often used in juvenile court matters.

■ *State on the relation of Watts v. Watts* — The form for a custody proceeding. It appears in a table of cases as *State ex rel. Watts v. Watts.*

2. Docket number
The docket number identifies the case while it is in progress. The numbers for *Townsend v. Swank* were 70-5021 and 70-5032 because two similar

cases were joined in this decision. The first number indicates the year, and the second number identifies the specific case as numbered by the court.

3. Date of decision The date of decision generally appears after the docket number. Sometimes the date of argument is also given.

4. Prefatory statement The prefatory statement explains the nature of the case, its disposition in the lower court, the judge, and the disposition by the appellate court—affirmed, reversed, or remanded (sent back to the lower court with specific instructions for further action).

5. Headnotes or syllabi Headnotes are summaries of the legal rules and significant facts in a case drafted by the editors of a report. Syllabi are the points of law covered by a case and written by the judge. Only the opinion affects the law, headnotes and syllabi do not.

6. Counsel The names of counsel for both parties may precede the opinion of the court.

7. Statement of facts A statement of the facts in the case usually follows.

8. Opinion of the court The opinion of the court explains the decision. After the majority has agreed on the decision, one of its members writes the opinion. If one judge agrees with the results but disagrees with the reasoning, a concurring opinion is included. The views of the minority are presented in one or more dissenting opinions. A *per curiam* opinion is an opinion of the whole court.

9. Decision and judgment The actual disposition of the case by the court.

FEDERAL COURT DECISIONS

As we saw in Chapter 1, the federal court system has three main divisions: (1) the Supreme Court of the United States (the highest court), (2) the courts of appeals (intermediate appellate courts), and (3) the district courts (courts of original jurisdiction). All written opinions of the U.S. Supreme Court are published in official and unofficial reports. Official reports are directed by statute, unofficial reports are produced by private sources. Both originate with the courts. There is no difference in accuracy. All written decisions of the courts of appeals and special courts are unofficially published, but only selected opinions of the district courts are reported.

U.S. Supreme Court Reports

Decisions of the U.S. Supreme Court are printed first on loose sheets called *slips* and sometimes revised before the final printing. They are available from five sources that include different supplementary materials. Any one of the five is suitable for study by social work students.

United States Reports (Official Edition). The *United States Reports* have been published by official reporters since 1817. (See Exhibit 2.1.)

United States Supreme Court Reports (Lawyer's Edition). This reprint edition of the U.S. Supreme Court opinions also contains all decisions. Tables included in the lawyer's edition cross-reference the pages from the official edition. The text of the decisions is given in full. Case summaries precede the headnotes, which are prepared by the editors. Briefs of counsel are summarized. Annotations in the form of essays on significant legal issues appear after the decision. (See Exhibit 2.2.)

Supreme Court Reporter.   This publication is part of the *National Reporter System* published by West Publishing Company. It begins with the 1882 volume of the official set. The full text of the decisions and edited headnotes are included in the *Supreme Court Reporter*. Summaries of the arguments of counsel are not included. The advance sheets of the *Supreme Court Reporter* also contain cumulative lists of cases. (See Exhibit 2.3.)

The United States Law Week.   This publication is available in loose-leaf form and consists of a Supreme Court section and a General Law section. *Law Week* reproduces the full texts of new Supreme Court opinions within twenty-four hours. The general law sections include the current federal statutes, analysis of federal legal trends, federal agency rulings, and new court decisions not yet reported in general or regional law reports. (See Exhibit 2.4.)

The Commerce Clearing House, United States Supreme Court Bulletin.   The *Clearing House Bulletin* includes the docket of the Supreme Court cases and the texts reproduced from the official "slip" opinions. Like *Law Week*, this bulletin reports Supreme Court opinions soon after they are rendered.

The first two pages of these five reports are reproduced for the same case, *Santosky v. Kramer*, to show the differences in presentation. (See Exhibit 2.5.)

Lower Federal Court Decisions   Lower federal court decisions are printed in the *Federal Reporter*, the *Federal Supplement*, and the *Federal Rules Decisions* as part of the *National Reporter System*. The first series of the *Federal Reporter* ended with volume 300. The second series started numbering from volume 1 to avoid long, unmanageable numbers. In 1932, the *Federal Supplement* was introduced. It contains the opinions of the U.S. district courts, the District Court of the U.S. for the District of Columbia, and (since volume 135) the U.S. Customs Court. Beginning with volume 276, 2d, the court of claims cases are included in the *Federal Reporter*.

The reports contain only those federal cases designated for publication by the courts. All written appellate opinions are published. Some federal district court opinions remain unreported but can be obtained from the clerks of the respective courts.

THE NATIONAL REPORTER SYSTEM   The *National Reporter System* includes opinions of the state appellate and trial courts and opinions of the federal courts. This system was initiated in 1879 with the *North Western Reporter*. Seven regional reporters are now published, arranged roughly by geographical divisions. The four federal units cover the various federal courts. Two state reports are also a part of the National Reporter System: *New York Supplement* and *California Reporter*. The coverage of each set is summarized in Table 2.1 on page 36.

"SHEPARDIZING" A DECISION   A decision must be checked to see whether it has been reviewed by a higher court or overruled by a subsequent decision of the same court.

The **Shepard Citation System** accumulates subsequent decisions that relate to a given decision. To use the system, you must learn to interpret the legal

EXHIBIT 2.1
EXAMPLE OF A UNITED STATES SUPREME COURT REPORT

SANTOSKY et al. v. *KRAMER, COMMISSIONER, ULSTER COUNTY DEPARTMENT OF SOCIAL SERVICES, et al.*

Certiorari to the Appellate Division, Supreme Court of New York, Third Judicial Department

No. 80–5889. Argued November 10, 1981—Decided March 24, 1982

Under New York law, the State may terminate, over parental objection, the rights of parents in their natural child upon a finding that the child is "permanently neglected." The New York Family Court Act (§ 622) requires that only a "fair preponderance of the evidence" support that finding. Neglect proceedings were brought in Family Court to terminate petitioners' rights as natural parents in their three children. Rejecting petitioners' challenge to the constitutionality of § 622's "fair preponderance of the evidence" standard, the Family Court weighed the evidence under that standard and found permanent neglect. After a subsequent dispositional hearing, the Family Court ruled that the best interests of the children required permanent termination of petitioners' custody. The Appellate Division of the New York Supreme Court affirmed, and the New York Court of Appeals dismissed petitioners' appeal to that court.

Held:

1. Process is constitutionally due a natural parent at a state-initiated parental rights termination proceeding. Pp. 752–757.

(a) The fundamental liberty interest of natural parents in the care, custody, and management of their child is protected by the Fourteenth Amendment, and does not evaporate simply because they have not been model parents or have lost temporary custody of their child to the State. A parental rights termination proceeding interferes with that fundamental liberty interest. When the State moves to destroy weakened familial bonds, it must provide the parents with fundamentally fair procedures. Pp. 752–754.

(b) The nature of the process due in parental rights termination proceedings turns on a balancing of three factors: the private interests affected by the proceedings; the risk of error created by the State's chosen procedure; and the countervailing governmental interest supporting use of the challenged procedure. *Mathews* v. *Eldridge*, 424 U.S. 319, 335. In any given proceeding, the minimum standard of proof tolerated by the due process requirement reflects not only the weight of the public and private interests affected, but also a societal judgment about how the risk of error should be distributed between the litigants. The minimum standard is a question of federal law which this Court may resolve. Retrospective case-by-case review cannot preserve fundamental fairness when a class of proceedings is governed by a constitutionally defective evidentiary standard. Pp. 754–757.

2. The "fair preponderance of the evidence" standard prescribed by § 622 violates the Due Process Clause of the Fourteenth Amendment. Pp. 758–768.

(a) The balance of private interests affected weighs heavily against use of such a standard in parental rights termination proceedings, since the private interest affected is commanding and the threatened loss is permanent. Once affirmed on appeal, a New York decision terminating parental rights is *final* and irrevocable. pp. 758–761.

(b) A preponderance standard does not fairly allocate the risk of an erroneous factfinding between the State and the natural parents. In parental rights termination proceedings, which bear many of the indicia of a criminal trial, numerous factors combine to magnify the risk of erroneous factfinding. Coupled with the preponderance standard, these factors create a significant prospect of erroneous termination of parental rights. A standard of proof that allocates the risk of error nearly equally between an erroneous failure to terminate, which leaves the child in an uneasy status quo, and an erroneous termination, which unnecessarily destroys the natural family, does not reflect properly the relative severity of these two outcomes. Pp. 761–766.

(c) A standard of proof more strict than preponderance of the evidence is consistent with the two state interests at stake in parental rights termination proceedings—a *parens patriae* interest in preserving and promoting the child's welfare and a fiscal and administrative interest in reducing the cost and burden of such proceedings. Pp. 766–768.

3. Before a State may sever completely and irrevocably the rights of parents in their natural child, due process requires that the State support its allegations by at least clear and convincing evidence. A "clear and convincing evidence" standard adequately conveys to the factfinder the level of subjective certainty about his factual conclusions necessary to satisfy due process. Determination of the precise burden equal to or greater than that standard is a matter of state law properly left to state legislatures and state courts. Pp. 768–770.

75 App. Div.2d 910, 427 N.Y.S.2d 319, vacated and remanded.

EXHIBIT 2.2
EXAMPLE OF UNITED STATES SUPREME COURT REPORT (LAWYERS' EDITION)

JOHN SANTOSKY II and ANNIE SANTOSKY, Petitioners,
v.
BERNHARDT S. KRAMER, Commissioner, Ulster County Department of
Social Services, et al.

455 US 745, 71 L Ed 2d 599, 102 S Ct 1388
[No. 80–5889]
Argued November 10, 1981. Decided March 24, 1982.

Decision: Application of at least "clear and convincing evidence" standard of proof to state's parental rights termination proceeding, held required by Fourteenth Amendment due process clause.

Summary

In an action brought in the Ulster County, New York, Family Court to terminate the rights of certain natural parents in their three children, the parents challenged the constitutionality of a provision of a New York statute under which the state may terminate the rights of parents in their natural child upon a finding that the child is "permanently neglected," when such a finding is supported by a fair preponderance of the evidence. The Family Court rejected the challenge, weighed the evidence under the "fair preponderance of the evidence" standard, found permanent neglect, and ultimately ruled that the best interests of the children required permanent termination of the parents' custody. The Appellate Division of the New York Supreme Court affirmed, holding application of the preponderance of the evidence standard proper and constitutional (75 App Div 2d 910, 427 NYS2d 319), and the New York Court of Appeals dismissed the parents' appeal to that court.

On certiorari, the United States Supreme Court vacated and remanded. In an opinion by Blackmun, J., joined by Brennan, Marshall, Powell and Stevens, JJ., it was held that (1) process is constitutionally due a natural parent at a state's parental rights termination proceedings, and (2) the "fair preponderance of the evidence" standard prescribed by the state statute violated the due process clause of the Fourteenth Amendment, due process requiring proof by clear and convincing evidence in such a proceeding.

Briefs of Counsel, p 981, infra.

U.S. SUPREME COURT REPORTS

Rehnquist, J., joined by Burger, Ch. J., and White and O'Connor, JJ., dissenting, expressed the view that the "fair preponderance of the evidence" standard prescribed by the New York statute must be considered in the context of New York's overall scheme of procedures relating to the termination of parental rights on the basis of permanent neglect, that such standard, when considered in that context, did not violate the due process clause of the Fourteenth Amendment, and that the majority decision, by holding the statutory standard unconstitutional without evaluation of the overall effect of New York's scheme of procedures for terminating parental rights, invited further federal court intrusion into every facet of state family law.

Headnotes
Classified to U.S. Supreme Court Digest, Lawyers' Edition
Constitutional Law § 830.7—due process—severance of parental rights—requirement of clear and convincing evidence
1a–1c. Before a state may sever completely and irrevocably the rights of parents in their natural child, due process requires that the state support its allegations by at least clear and convincing evidence; therefore a state statute violates the due process clause of the Fourteenth Amendment insofar as it authorizes termination, over parental objection, of the rights of parents in their natural child upon a finding that the child is "permanently neglected," when that finding is supported by a "fair preponderance of the evidence." (Rehnquist, J., Burger, Ch. J., White, J., and O'Connor, J., dissented from this holding.) . . .

EXHIBIT 2.2 (cont'd)

TOTAL CLIENT-SERVICE LIBRARY®
REFERENCES

16A Am Jur 2d, Constitutional Law § 568; 59 Am Jur 2d, Parent and Child § 5
USCS, Constitution, 14th Amendment
US L Ed Digest, Constitutional Law § 830.7
L Ed Index to Annos, Burden of Proof; Children and Minors; Due Process of Law
ALR Quick Index, Parent and Child; Presumptions and Burden of Proof
Federal Quick Index, Burden of Proof; Child Abuse and Neglect; Children and Minors;
  Custody of Children

ANNOTATION REFERENCE

Supreme Court's views as to concept of "liberty" under due process clauses of Fifth and Fourteenth Amendments. 47 L Ed 2d 975.

EXHIBIT 2.3
EXAMPLE OF U.S. SUPREME COURT REPORT (*NATIONAL REPORTER SYSTEM*)

102 SUPREME COURT REPORTER

Accordingly, the judgment of the Court of Appeals is
Affirmed.

John *SANTOSKY II and Annie*
Santosky, Petitioners
v.
Bernhardt S. KRAMER, Commissioner,
Ulster County Department of Social
Services, et al.
No. 80–5889.
Argued Nov. 10, 1981
Decided March 24, 1982

Parents appealed from judgment of the Family Court, Ulster County, Elwyn, J., which adjudged their children to be permanently neglected. The New York Supreme Court, Appellate Division, affirmed, 75 A.D.2d 910, 427 N.Y.S.2d 319. The New York Court of Appeals dismissed the parents' appeal. Certiorari was granted. The Supreme Court, Justice Blackmun, held that before a state may sever completely and irrevocably the rights of parents in their natural child, due process required that the state support its allegations by at least clear and convincing evidence, and, therefore, the "fair preponderance of the evidence" standard prescribed by the New York Family Court Act for the termination of parental rights denied the parents due process.

Judgment vacated and remanded.

Justice Rehnquist, filed a dissenting opinion in which Chief Justice Burger, Justice White and Justice O'Connor, joined.

1. Parent and Child ← 2(3.3, 3.7)
    Fundamental liberty interest of natural parents in care, custody and management of their child does not evaporate simply because they have not been model parents or have lost temporary custody of their child to State. U.S.C.A.Const.Amends. 5, 14.

2. Infants ← 191
    Even when blood relationships are strained, parents retain vital interest in preventing irretrievable destruction of their family life; if anything, persons faced with forced dissolution of their parental rights have more critical need for procedural protections than do those resisting state intervention into ongoing family affairs. U.S.C.A.Const.Amends. 5, 14.

EXHIBIT 2.3 (cont'd)

3. Infants ← 194

When state moves to destroy weakened familial bonds, it must provide parents with fundamentally fair procedures. U.S.C.A. Const.Amends. 5, 14,

4. Constitutional Law ← 274(5)

Nature of process due in parental rights termination proceedings turns on balancing of private interests affected by proceedings; risk of error created by state's chosen procedure; and countervailing governmental interest supporting use of challenged procedure. U.S.C.A.Const.Amends. 5,14.

5. Constitutional Law ← 311

In any given proceeding, minimum standard of proof tolerated by due process requirement reflects not only weight of private and public interests affected, but also societal judgment about how risk of error should be distributed between litigants. U.S.C.A.Const.Amends. 5, 14.

6. Federal Courts ← 416

Minimum standard of proof mandated by due process is question of federal law which Supreme Court may resolve. U.S.C.A.Const.Amends. 5, 14.

SANTOSKY v. KRAMER
Cite as 102 S.Ct. 1388 (1982)

7. Constitutional Law ← 251.5

Retrospective case-by-case review cannot preserve fundamental fairness when class of proceedings is governed by constitutionally defective evidentiary standard. U.S.C.A.Const.Amends. 5, 14.

8. Constitutional Law ← 251.5

Whether loss threatened by particular type of proceeding is sufficiently grave to warrant more than average certainty on part of fact finder turns on both nature of private interest threatened and permanency of threatened loss. U.S.C.A.Const.Amends. 5, 14.

9. Infants ← 179

In parental rights termination proceedings, private interest affected weighs heavily against use of preponderance of the evidence standard at state-initiated permanent neglect proceeding. U.S.C.A.Const.Amends. 5, 14.

10. Constitutional Law ← 274(5)

Until state proves parental unfitness under New York law, child and his parents share vital interest in preventing erroneous termination of the natural relationship, and, therefore, preponderance of the evidence standard provided under New York law does not satisfy due process clause. N.Y.McKinney's Social Service Law § 384-b, subds. 4(d), 7(a); N.Y.McKinney's Family Court Act § 622; U.S.C.A.Const.Amends. 5, 14.

11. Constitutional Law ← 274(5)

Preponderance of the evidence standard provided for in New York statutes governing termination of parental rights upon finding that child is "permanently neglected" does not properly allocate risk of error between parent and child, since, for child, likely consequence of erroneous failure to terminate is preservation of uneasy status quo, but for natural parents, consequence of erroneous termination is unnecessary destruction of natrual family, and, therefore, due process mandates standard of proof greater than fair preponderance of the evidence. N.Y.McKinney's Social Service Law § 384-b, subds. 4(d), 7(a); N.Y.McKinney's Family Court Act § 622; U.S.C.A.Const.Amends. 5, 14.

12. Infants ← 178

Standard of proof more strict than fair preponderance of the evidence is consistent with two state interests at stake in parental rights termination proceedings, *parens patriae* interest in preserving and promoting child's welfare and fiscal and administrative interest in reducing costs and burden of such proceedings. N.Y.McKinney's Social Service Law § 384-b, subds. 1(a)(i, ii, iv), 3(g), 4(e); N.Y.McKinney's Family Court Act § 622; U.S.C.A.Const.Amends. 5, 14.

13. Constitutional Law ← 274(5)

Before state may sever completely and irrevocably rights of parents in their natural child, due process requires that state support its allegations by at least clear and convincing evidence. N.Y.McKinney's Social Service Law § 384-b, subds. 4(d), 7(a); N.Y.McKinney's Family Court Act § 622; U.S.C.A.Const.Amends. 5, 14.

EXHIBIT 2.3 (cont'd)

14. Constitutional Law ← 274(5)

Clear and convincing evidence standard adequately conveys to fact finder level of subjective certainty about his factual conclusions necessary to satisfy due process in proceedings in which state seeks to completely and irrevocably sever rights of parents in their natural child. N.Y.McKinney's Social Service Law § 384-b, subds. 4(d), 7(a); N.Y.McKinney's Family Court Act § 622; U.S.C.A.Const.Amends. 5, 14.

15. Federal Courts ← 416

Determination of precise burden of proof equal to or greater than clear and convincing evidence standard, for purpose of proceedings in which parental rights are terminated, is matter of state law properly left to the state legislatures and state courts. N.Y.McKinney's Social Service Law § 384-b, subds. 4(d), 7(a); N.Y.McKinney's Family Court Act § 622; U.S.C.A.Const.Amends. 5, 14.

EXHIBIT 2.4
EXAMPLE OF U.S. SUPREME COURT REPORT (THE UNITED STATES LAW WEEK)

No. 80–5889

JOHN SANTOSKY II and ANNIE SANTOSKY, PETITIONERS v. BERNHARDT S. KRAMER, COMMISSIONER, ULSTER COUNTY DEPARTMENT OF SOCIAL SERVICES, et al.

ON WRIT OF CERTIORARI TO THE APPELLATE DIVISION, SUPREME COURT OF NEW YORK, THIRD JUD. DEPT.

Syllabus

No. 80–5889. Argued November 10, 1981—Decided March 24, 1982

Under New York law, the State may terminate, over parental objection, the rights of parents in their natural child upon a finding that the child is "permanently neglected." The New York Family Court Act (§ 622) requires that only a "fair preponderance of the evidence" support that finding. Neglect proceedings were brought in Family Court to terminate petitioners' rights as natural parents in their three children. Rejecting petitioners' challenge to the constitutionality of § 622's "fair preponderance of the evidence" standard, the Family Court weighed the evidence under that standard and found permanent neglect. After a subsequent dispositional hearing, the Family Court ruled that the best interests of the children required permanent termination of petitioners' custody. The Appellate Division of the New York Supreme Court affirmed, and the New York Court of Appeals dismissed petitioners' appeal to that court.

Held:

1. Process is constitutionally due a natural parent at a state-initiated parental rights termination proceeding.

(a) The fundamental liberty interest of natural parents in the care, custody, and management of their child is protected by the Fourteenth Amendment, and does not evaporate simply because they have not been model parents or have lost temporary custody of their child to the State. A parental rights termination proceeding interferes with that fundamental liberty interest. When the State moves to destroy weakened familial bonds, it must provide the parents with fundamentally fair procedures.

(b) The nature of the process due in parental rights termination proceedings turns on a balancing of three factors: the private interest affected by the proceedings; the risk of error created by the State's chosen procedure; and the countervailing governmental interest supporting use of the challenged procedure. *Matthews v. Eldridge*, 424 U.S. 319, 235. In any given proceeding, the minimum standard of proof tolerated by the due process requirement reflects not only the weight of the public and private interests affected, but also a societal judgment about how the risk of error should be distributed between the litigants. The minimum standard is a question of federal law which this Court may resolve. Retrospective case-by-case review cannot preserve fundamental fairness when a class of proceedings is governed by a constitutionally defective evidentiary standard.

2. The "fair preponderance of the evidence" standard prescribed by § 622 violates the Due Process Clause of the Fourteenth Amendment.

EXHIBIT 2.4 (cont'd)

(a) The balance of private interests affected weighs heavily against use of such a standard in parental rights termination proceedings, since the private interest affected is commanding and the threatened loss is permanent. Once affirmed on appeal, a New York decision terminating parental rights is *final* and irrevocable.

(b) A preponderance standard does not fairly allocate the risk of an erroneous fact-finding between the State and the natural parents. In parental rights termination proceedings, which bear many of the indicia of a criminal trial, numerous factors combine to magnify the risk of erroneous factfinding. Coupled with the preponderance standard, these factors create a significant prospect of erroneous termination of parental rights. A standard of proof that allocates the risk of error nearly equally between an erroneous failure to terminate, which leaves the child in an uneasy status quo, and an erroneous termination, which unnecessarily destroys the natural family, does not reflect properly the relative severity of these two outcomes.

(c) A standard of proof more strict than preponderance of the evidence is consistent with the two state interests at stake in parental rights termination proceedings—a *parens patriae* interest in preserving and promoting the child's welfare and a fiscal and administrative interest in reducing the cost and burden of such proceedings.

3. Before a State may sever completely and irrevocably the rights of parents in their natural child, due process requires that the State support its allegations by at least clear and convincing evidence. A "clear and convincing evidence" standard adequately conveys to the factfinder the level of subjective certainty about his factual conclusions necessary to satisfy due process. Determination of the precise burden equal to or greater than that standard is a matter of state law properly left to state legislatures and state courts.

75 App. Div. 2d 910, 427 N.Y.S.2d 319, vacated and remanded.

BLACKMUN, J., delivered the opinion of the Court, in which BRENNAN, MARSHALL, POWELL, and STEVENS, JJ., joined. REHNQUIST, J., filed a dissenting opinion, in which BURGER, C.J., and WHITE and O'CONNOR, JJ., *joined*.

JUSTICE BLACKMUN delivered the opinion of the Court.

Under New York law, the State may terminate, over parental objection, the rights of parents in their natural child upon a finding that the child is "permanently neglected." N.Y. Soc. Serv. Law §§ 384-b.4.(d), 384-b.7.(a) (McKinney Supp. 1981–1982) (Soc. Serv. Law). The New York Family Court Act § 622 (McKinney 1975 & Supp. 1981–1982) (Fam. Ct. At) requires that only a "fair preponderance of the evidence" support that finding. Thus, in New York, the factual certainty required to extinguish the parent-child relationship is no greater than that necessary to award money damages in an ordinary civil action.

Today we hold that the Due Process Clause of the Fourteenth Amendment demands more than this. Before a State may sever completely and irrevocably the rights of parents in their natural child, due process requires that the State support its allegations by at least clear and convincing evidence.

I

A

New York authorizes its officials to remove a child temporarily from his or her home if the child appears "neglected," within the meaning of Art. 10 of the Family Court Act. See §§ 1012(f), 1021–1029. Once removed, a child under the age of 18 customarily is placed "in the care of an authorized agency," Soc. Serv. Law § 384-b.7(a), usually a state institution or a foster home. At that point, "the state's first obligation is to help the family with services to . . . reunite it. . . ." § 384-b.1.(a)(iii). But if convinced that "positive, nurturing parent-child relationships no longer exist," § 384-b.1.(b), the State may initiate "permanent neglect" proceedings to free the child for adoption.

The State bifurcates its permanent neglect proceeding into "fact-finding" and "dispositional" hearings. Fam. Ct. Act §§ 622, 623. At the factfinding stage, the State must prove that the child has been "permanently neglected," as defined by Fam. Ct. Act §§ 614.1.(a)–(d) and Soc. Serv. Law § 384-b.7.(a). See Fam. Ct. Act § 622. The Family Court judge then determines at a subsequent dispositional hearing what placement would serve the child's best interests. §§ 623, 631.

At the factfinding hearing, the State must establish, among other things, that for more than a year after the child entered state custody, the agency "made diligent efforts to encourage and strengthen the parental relationship." Fam. Ct. Act §§ 614.1.(c), 611. The State must further prove that during that same period, the child's natural parents failed "substantially and continuously or repeatedly to maintain contact with or plan for the future of the child although physically and financially able to do so." § 614.1.(d). Should the State support its allegations by "a fair preponderance of the evidence," § 622, the child may be declared permanently

EXHIBIT 2.4 (cont'd)

neglected. § 611. That declaration empowers the Family Court judge to terminate permanently the natural parents' rights in the child. §§ 631(c), 634. Termination denies the natural parents physical custody, as well as the rights ever to visit, communicate with, or regain custody of the child.[1]

New York's permanent neglect statute provides natural parents with certain procedural protections.[2] But New York permits its officials to establish "permanent neglect" with less proof than most States require. Thirty-three States, the District of Columbia, and the Virgin Islands currently specify a higher standard of proof, in prenatal rights termination proceedings, than a "fair preponderance of the evidence."[3] The only analogous federal statute of which we are aware permits termination of parental rights solely upon "evidence beyond a reasonable doubt." Indian Child Welfare Act of 1978, Pub. L. 95–608, § 102(f), 92 Stat. 3072, 25 U. S. C. § 1912(f) (1976 ed., Supp. III). The question here is whether New York's "fair preponderance of the evidence" standard is constitutionally sufficient.

B

Petitioners John Santosky II and Annie Santosky are the natural parents of Tina and John III. In November 1973, after incidents reflecting parental neglect, respondent Kramer, Commissioner of the Ulster County Department of Social Services, initiated a neglect proceeding under Fam. Ct. Act § 1022 and removed Tina from her natural home. About 10 months later, he removed John III and placed him with foster parents. On the day John was taken, Annie Santosky gave birth to a third child, Jed. When Jed was only three days old, respondent transferred him to a foster home on the ground that immediate removal was necessary to avoid imminent danger to his life or health.

---

[1] At oral argument, counsel for petitioners asserted that, in New York, natural parents have no means of restoring terminated parental rights. Tr. of Oral Arg. 9. Counsel for respondent, citing Fam. Ct. Act § 1061, answered that parents may petition the Family Court to vacate or set aside an earlier order on narrow grounds, such as newly discoverd evidence or fraud. Tr. of Oral Arg. 26. Counsel for respondent conceded, however, that this statutory provision has never been invoked to set aside a permanent neglect finding. *Id.*, at 27.

[2] Most notably, natural parents have a statutory right to the assistance of counsel and of court-appointed counsel if they are indigent. Fam. Ct. Act § 262(a)(iii).

[3] Fourteen States, by statute, have required "clear and convincing evidence" or its equivalent. See Alaska Stat. Ann. § 47.10.080(c)(3) (1980); Cal. Civ. Code Ann. § 232(a)(7) (West Supp. 1982); Ga. Code §§ 24A–2201(c), 24A–3201 (1981); Iowa Code § 600A.8 (Supp. 1981) ("clear and convincing proof"); Me. Rev. Stat. Ann., Tit. 22, § 4055.1.B.(2) (Supp. 1981–1982); Mich. Comp. Laws § 722.25 (Supp. 1981–1982); Mo. Rev. Stat. § 211.447.2(2) (Supp. 1982) ("clear, cogent and convincing evidence"); N.M. Stat. Ann. § 40–7–4.J. (Supp. 1981); N.C. Gen. Stat. § 7A–289.30(e) (Supp. 1979) ("clear, cogent, and convincing evidence"); R.I. Gen. Laws § 15–7–7(d) (Supp. 1980); Tenn. Code Ann. § 37–246(d) (Supp. 1981); Va. Code § 16.1–283.B. (Supp. 1981); W. Va. Code § 49–6–2(c) (1980) ("clear and convincing proof"); Wis. Stat. § 48.31(1) (Supp. 1981–1982).

Sixteen States, the District of Columbia, and the Virgin Islands, by court decision, have required "clear and convincing evidence" or its equivalent. See *Dale County Dept. of Pensions & Security* v. *Robles*, 368 So. 2d 39, 42 (Ala. App. 1979); *Harper* v. *Caskin*, 265 Ark. 558, 560–561, 580 S.W.2d 176, 178 (1979); *In re J. S. R.*, 374 A. 2d 860, 864 (D.C. 1977); *Torres* v. *Van Eepoet*, 98 So. 2d 735, 737 (Fla. 1957); *Blakey* v. *Blakey*, 72 Ill. App.3d 946, 947, 391 N.E.2d 222, 223 (1979); *In re Kerns*, 225 Kan. 746, 753, 594 P. 2d 187, 193 (1979); *In re Rosenbloom*, 266 N.W.2d 888, 889 (Minn. 1978) ("clear and convincing proof"); *In re J. L. B.* Mont., 594 P.2d 1127, 1136 (1979); *In re Souza*, 204 Neb. 503, 510, 283 N.W.2d 48, 52 (1979); *J. and E.* v. *M. and F.*, 157 N.J. Super. 478, 489, 385 A.2d 240, 246 (App. Div. 1978); *In re J.A.*, 283 N.W.2d 83, 92(N.D. 1979); *In re Darren Todd H.*, 615 P. 2d 287, 289 (Okla. 1980); *In re William L.*, 477 Pa. 322, 332, 383 A.2d 1228, 1233, cert. denied *sub nom. Lehman* v. *Lycoming County Children's Services*, 439 U.S. 880 (1978); *In re G. M.*, 596 S.W.2d 846, 847 (Tex. 1980); *In re Pitts*, 535 P.2d 1244, 1248 (Utah 1975); *In re Maria*, 15 V.I. 368, 384 (1978); *In re Sego*, 82 Wash. 736, 739, 513 P.2d 831, 833 (1973) ("clear, cogent, and convincing evidence"); *In re X.*, 607 P.2d 911, 919 (Wyo. 1980) ("clear and unequivocal"). South Dakota's Supreme Court has required a "clear preponderance" of the evidence in a dependency proceeding. See *In re B.E.*, 287 N.W.2d 91, 96 (1979). Two states, New Hampshire and Louisiana, have barred parental rights terminations unless the key allegations have been proved beyond a reasonable doubt. See *State* v. *Robert H.*, 118 N.H. 713, 716, 393 A.2d 1387, 1389 (1978); La. Rev. Stat. Ann. § 13:1603.A (West Supp. 1982).

So far as we are aware, only two federal courts have addressed the issue. Each has held that allegations supporting parental rights termination must be proved by clear and convincing evidence. *Sims* v. *State Dept. of Public Welfare*, 438 F. Supp. 1179, 1194 (SD Tex. 1977), rev'd on other grounds *sub nom. Moore* v. *Sims*, 442 U.S. 415 (1979); *Alsager* v. *District Court of Polk Cty.*, 406 F. Supp. 10, 25 (SD Iowa 1975), aff'd on other grounds, 545 F.2d 1137 (CA8 1976).

EXHIBIT 2.4 (cont'd)

In October 1978, respondent petitioned the Ulster County Family Court to terminate petitioners' parental rights in the three children.[4] Petitioners challenged the constitutionality of the "fair preponderance of the evidence" standard specified in Fam. Ct. Act § 622. The Family Court judge rejected this constitutional challenge, App. 29–30, and weighed the evidence under the statutory standard. While acknowledging that the Santoskys had maintained contact with their children, the judge found those visits "at best superficial and devoid of any real emotional content." *Id.*, at 21. After deciding that the agency had made " 'diligent efforts' to encourage and strengthen the parental relationship," *id.*, at 30, he concluded that the Santoskys were incapable, even with public assistance, of planning for the future of their children. *Id.*, at 33–37. The judge later held a dispositional hearing and ruled that the best interests of the three children required permanent termination of the Santoskys' custody.[5] *Id.*, at 39.

Petitioners appealed, again contesting the constitutionality of § 622's standard of proof.[6]

---

[4]Respondent had made an earlier and unsuccessful termination effort in September 1976. After a factfinding hearing, the Family Court judge dismissed respondent's petition for failure to prove an essential element of Fam. Ct. Act § 614.1.(d). See *In re Santosky*, 89 Misc. 2d 730, 393 N.Y.S. 2d 486 (1977). The New York Supreme Court. Appellate Division, affirmed, finding that "the record as a whole" revealed that petitioners had "substantially planned for the future of the children." *In re John W.*, 63 App. Div. 2d 750, 751, 404 N.Y.S. 2d 717, 719 (1978).

[5]Since respondent took custody of Tina, John III, and Jed, the Santoskys have had two other children, James and Jeremy. The State has taken no action to remove these younger children. At oral argument counsel for respondent replied affirmatively when asked whether he was asserting that petitioners were "unfit to handle the three older ones but not unfit to handle the two younger ones." Tr. of Oral Arg. 24.

[6]Petitioners initially had sought review in the New York Court of Appeals.

EXHIBIT 2.5
EXAMPLE OF UNITED STATES SUPREME COURT REPORT
(COMMERCE CLEARINGHOUSE)

SUPREME COURT OF THE UNITED STATES

No. 80–5889

JOHN SANTOSKY II AND *ANNIE SANTOSKY,*
PETITIONERS v. *BERNHARDT S. KRAMER, COMMISSIONER,*
ULSTER COUNTY DEPARTMENT OF SOCIAL SERVICES, ET AL.

ON WRIT OF CERTIORARI TO THE APPELLATE DIVISION,
SUPREME COURT OF NEW YORK, THIRD JUD. DEPT.

[March 24, 1982]

JUSTICE BLACKMUN delivered the opinion of the Court.

Under New York law, the State may terminate, over parental objection, the rights of parents in their natural child upon a finding that the child is "permanently neglected." N.Y. Soc. Serv. Law §§384–b.4.(d), 384–b.7.(a) (McKinney Supp. 1981–1982) (Soc. Serv. Law). The New York Family Court Act §622 (McKinney 1975 & Supp. 1981–1982) (Fam. Ct. Act) requires that only a "fair preponderance of the evidence" support that finding. Thus, in New York, the factual certainty required to extinguish the parent-child relationship is no greater than that necessary to award money damages in an ordinary civil action.

Today we hold that the Due Process Clause of the Fourteenth Amendment demands more than this. Before a State may sever completely and irrevocably the rights of parents in their natural child, due process requires that the State support its allegations by at least clear and convincing evidence.

EXHIBIT 2.5 (cont'd)

I

A

New York authorizes its officials to remove a child temporarily from his or her home if the child appears "neglected," within the meaning of Art. 10 of the Family Court Act. See §§1012(f), 1021–1029. Once removed, a child under the age of 18 customarily is placed "in the care of an authorized agency," Soc. Serv. Law §382–b.7.(a), usually a state institution or a foster home. At that point, "the state's first obligation is to help the family with services to . . . reunite it. . . ." §384–b.1.(a)(iii). But if convinced that "positive, nurturing parent-child relationships no longer exist," §384–b.1.(b), the State may initiate "permanent neglect" proceedings to free the child for adoption.

The State bifurcates its permanent neglect proceeding into "fact-finding" and "dispositional" hearings. Fam. Ct. Act §§622, 623. At the factfinding stage, the State must prove that the child has been "permanently neglected," as defined by Fam. Ct. Act §§614.1.(a)–(d) and Soc. Serv. Law §384–b.7.(a). See Fam. Ct. Act §622. The Family Court judge then determines at a subsequent dispositional hearing what placement would serve the child's best interests. §§623, 631.

At the factfinding hearing, the State must establish, among other things, that for more than a year after the child entered state custody, the agency "made diligent efforts to encourage and strengthen the parental relationship." Fam. Ct. Act §§614.1.(c), 611. The State must further prove that during that same period, the child's natural parents failed "substantially and continuously or repeatedly to maintain contact with or plan for the future of the child although physically and financially able to do so." §614.1.(d). Should the State support its allegations by "a fair preponderance of the evidence," §622, the child may be declared permanently neglected. §611. That declaration empowers the Family Court judge to terminate permanently the natural parents' rights in the child. §§631(c), 634. Termination denies the natural parents physical custody, as well as the rights ever to visit, communicate with, or regain custody of the child.

---

citations for cases. Then you can find a listing of other decisions that involve the basic one. The citations in Shepard for *Townsend v. Swank* are found under volume 404 of its index for the Supreme Court of the United States. Find page 282, and you see how the decision has been applied in other cases.

Separate Shepard indexes of citations are available for regional reports, federal reports, and the *Federal Supplement*, and each of the fifty states.

THE FEDERAL CONSTITUTION

Three documents preceded the U.S. Constitution: the Declaration of Independence in 1776, the Articles of Confederation of 1777, and the Ordinance of 1787, providing for the government of the Northwest Territory. The Constitution of the United States was signed by a majority of the delegates to the constitutional convention on September 17, 1787. After ratification by the states, operation of the government under the new Constitution began on March 4, 1789. The text of the U.S. Constitution can be found in the various federal, state, and city codes, treatises, pamphlets, and most civics textbooks.

STATE CONSTITUTIONS

The state constitutions are published together with the state codes in pamphlets and in appropriate local treatises. The constitutions are generally available from the respective secretaries of states' offices on request. Analysis of one's own state constitution provides a valuable orientation for social workers to begin to understand relevant laws.

Popular names used to refer to provisions of individual state constitutions are indicated in *Shepard's Federal and State Acts and Cases by Popular Names*. A cumulative pamphlet supplement keeps the publication current.

TABLE 2.1
COVERAGE OF THE NATIONAL REPORTER SYSTEM

Reporter	Coverage
Regional:	
Atlantic Reporter	Connecticut, Delaware, Maine, Maryland, New Hampshire, New Jersey, Pennsylvania, Rhode Island, Vermont, and District of Columbia Municipal Court of Appeals
North Eastern Reporter	Illinois, Indiana, Massachusetts, New York, Ohio
North Western Reporter	Iowa, Michigan, Minnesota, Nebraska, North Dakota, South Dakota, Wisconsin
Pacific Reporter	Alaska, Arizona, California to 1960, California Supreme Court since 1960, Colorado, Hawaii, Idaho, Kansas, Montana, Nevada, New Mexico, Oklahoma, Oregon, Utah, Washington, Wyoming
South Eastern Reporter	Georgia, North Carolina, South Carolina, Virginia, West Virginia
South Western Reporter	Arkansas, Kentucky, Indian Territory, Missouri, Tennessee, Texas.
Southern Reporter	Alabama, Florida, Louisiana, Mississippi
Federal:	
Supreme Court Reporter	U.S. Supreme Court
Federal Reporter	From 1880 to 1932: Circuit courts of appeals and district courts of the U.S., U.S. Court of Customs and Patent Appeals, Court of Claims of the U.S., and Court of Appeals of the District of Columbia
	From 1932 to date: U.S. courts of appeals and U.S. Court of Customs and Patent Appeals
	From 1942 to 1961: U.S. Emergency Court of Appeals
	Since 1960: U.S. Court of Claims
Federal Supplement	U.S. District Courts, Court of Claims to 1960, U.S. Customs Court since vol. 135 (1949)
Federal Rules Decisions	District courts of the U.S.
State:	
New York Supplement	New York (all state courts). Since 1932, the New York Court of Appeals opinions are published here as well as in the North Eastern Reporter.
California Reporter	California Supreme Court, District Courts of Appeal and Appellate Department Superior Court
The states also publish their own decisions separately.	

CURRENT FEDERAL LAWS

After a law has been passed by Congress and signed by the president (or enacted over his veto), it is classified as either a **public law** of general applicability or a **private law** applying only to specifically designated persons. This book is concerned almost entirely with public laws.

The first law to be passed in a session of Congress is designated by the congressional session number and either as Public Law (P.L.) No. 1 or Private Law No. 1. Each succeeding law is then numbered in numerical sequence throughout the two-year life of a Congress.

Each law as passed is first issued by the U.S. Government Printing Office in **slip** or pamphlet form. Every law is published separately and may vary in length from less than one page to several hundred pages. Four sources provide current federal laws:

Slip Laws.   Available at all libraries that are depositories for the publications of the U.S. Government Printing Office and in certain law libraries.

U.S. Code Congressional and Administrative News Service.   Published by the West Publishing Company in connection with the *United States Code Annotated* (U.S.C.A.). During each session of Congress, the service is issued monthly in pamphlet form and includes the full text of all public laws. After each session of Congress, the pamphlets are reissued in bound volumes.

Current Public Laws and Administrative Service.   Published by the Lawyers Co-operative Publishing Company. It is similar to the *U.S. Code*, above.

U.S. Law Week.   A loose-leaf service that publishes the text of the more important laws passed during the previous week.

Codification of U.S. Statutes

At the end of each session of Congress all the slip laws are published together in numerical order in the *Statutes-at-Large*. All the laws enacted since 1789 are contained in this set. Chronological arrangement of congressional laws creates obvious problems in determining the statutory provisions on any given subject because they are found in many places. To be useful, laws are brought together topically as codes.

Codification of laws has three objectives: (1) to collate the original law and all subsequently passed amendments together with the deletion or addition of language changed by the amendments; (2) to bring all laws on the same subject or topic together; and (3) to eliminate all repealed, superseded, or expired laws.

The first codification of the *Statutes-at-Large* was authorized by the Congress in 1866 and resulted in publication of the *Revised Statutes of 1875*. All the laws on one topic were arranged in a separate chapter and then bound in one volume with a subject index.

Congress in 1925 authorized the preparation of the *United States Code*. A new edition of the *United States Code* (U.S.C.) is published every six years, and cumulative supplement volumes are issued during the intervening years. In the *United States Code Annotated* (U.S.C.A.), each of the fifty titles is published in a separate volume and kept up-to-date with annual cumulative pocket supplements and a quarterly pamphlet service. It follows the arrangement of the *United States Code* and contains the same text.

The *United States Code Service*, Lawyers Edition, provides another source for reference.

Popular Names of Federal Acts

Many laws are ascribed popular names. To find the law, it is necessary to reconcile the popular name with the official name. It is important for social workers to know how to do this because they are often familiar only with the popular name of an act. *Shepard's Federal and State Acts and Cases by Popular Names* and *United States Code Annotated*, which contains a table of acts cited by popular name are useful for this purpose. The popular names for federal acts are also listed in alphabetical order in the general indexes to the *United States Code Annotated* and the *United States Code Service*.

Table of Federal Statutes

The basic tables volume of the *United States Code* contains six tables to locate various materials in the code.

1. Revised titles (former sections of titles of the code)
2. Revised Statutes 1878
3. Statutes-at-Large (the Acts of Congress)
4. Executive Orders "that implement general and permanent law as contained in U.S.C."
5. Proclamations
6. Reorganization Plans

The tables in the U.S.C.A. cover the same materials listed for the U.S.C.

State Statutes

State statutes are published in codified form. Students must consult statutes of their own states. Most college libraries will have them, but if laws of other states are needed, students may have to consult a law library.

ADMINISTRATIVE PROCEDURES— REGULATIONS

The power to issue regulations and to hold hearings for people who have complaints against public agencies is delegated to those agencies by Congress or the state legislatures. As we shall see in Chapter 4, rule-making often provides these agencies with great power. Regulations to implement statutes may interpret the law narrowly or with great latitude. They are classified by subject in the *Code of Federal Regulations* (C.F.R.) under fifty titles.

To be legally effective, a regulation must be presented in the *Federal Register*, which has been published since 1936. The requirement applies to every document proscribing a penalty or a course of conduct, conferring a right, privilege, authority, or immunity, or imposing an obligation, relevant or applicable to the general public, the members of a class or the persons of a locality. The public often has a period of time to suggest revisions of regulations before they become final.

The following example presents a proposed federal regulation (42 C.F.R. 59 [2/22/82]) to require family-planning service projects receiving federal financial assistance to notify the parents of unemancipated minors that the minor has been provided with prescription drugs or prescription devices; unless such notification can be verified, the project shall not provide additional drugs or devices. The proposed regulation met with widespread opposition, and its implementation was barred by two federal district courts. It was struck down by the Washington, D.C., federal court in July 1983 because it violated privacy rights.

The *Federal Register* also includes a weekly compilation of presidential documents that includes proclamations, executive orders, and reorganization plans.

The *U.S. Government Manual* published by the General Services Administration provides general information about federal departments and agencies, including those no longer in existence. The major federal regulatory agencies also publish their own administrative decisions.

UNIFORM AND MODEL ACTS

Model acts are drafted by various groups on many subjects to try to promote law reform. The Commission on Uniform State Laws, sponsored by the American Bar

Association, establishes committees to develop drafts. **Uniform acts** have special status because of the prestige of their sponsorship, but states do not enact all of them. When they adopt a uniform law or a model act, states make modifications to reflect their court systems and other particular problems. If the states show little interest, a suggested act may be withdrawn or just forgotten. Federal agencies develop both suggested legislative guidelines and model acts.

EXHIBIT 2.6
EXAMPLE OF A PROPOSED REGULATION

DEPARTMENT OF HEALTH AND HUMAN SERVICES
Public Health Service
42 CFR Part 59
Requirements Applicable to Projects for Family Planning Services

Agency: Public Health Service (PHS), HHS.

Action: Proposed rule.

Summary: The Secretary of Health and Human Services proposes to amend the regulations governing the program for family planning services funded under Title X of the Public Health Service Act in order to implement a recent amendment of that Act. The statutory amendment requires family planning projects to encourage family participation in the provision of services by the projects, to the extent practical. The Secretary proposes to implement this amendment by requiring projects to notify the parents of unemancipated minors seeking family planning services when prescription drugs or devices are provided. In addition, where state law requires family planning providers to provide Title X services to unemancipated minors only with notification to or the consent of their parents, projects would be required to comply with that law.

Date: Comments on the proposed rules must be submitted in writing to the address below on or before April 23, 1982.

Address: Comments should be submitted to Marjory Mecklenburg, Acting Deputy Assistant Secretary for Population Affairs, Room 725H, 200 Independence Avenue, SW, Washington, D.C. 20201.

For further information contact: Marjory Mecklenburg (202) 472-9093.

Supplementary information: Title X of the Public Health Service Act (42 U.S.C. 300 et seq.) establishes a program of Federal financial assistance to public and private nonprofit entities for the provision of voluntary family planning services. Under section 1001(a) of that title, the Secretary of Health and Human Services may make grants to such entities for projects which will provide a "broad range of acceptable and effective family planning services," including "services to adolescents." The regulations implementing this section provide, among other things, that family planning services will be made available without regard to age or marital status. 42 CFR 59.5(a)(4).

On August 13, 1981, Congress amended section 1001(a). Section 931(b)(1) of Publ. L. 97–35 adds to section 1001(a) the following provision:

To the extent practical, entities which receive grants or contracts under this subsection shall encourage family (sic) participation in projects assisted under this subsection.

The Conference Report on Pub. L. 97–35 explains section 931(b)(1) as follows:

The conferees believe that, while family involvement is not mandated, it is important that families participate in the activities authorized by this title as much as possible. It is the intent of the Conferees that grantees will encourage participants in Title X programs to include their families in counseling and involve them in decisions about services. House Rep. No. 97–208, at 799.

The Secretary proposes to implement section 931(b)(1) by adding the following requirements to the Title X regulations. First, grantees would be required to notify the parents or guardian of unemancipated minors when prescription drugs or prescription devices are provided to such minors. Projects would also be required to inform the minor, prior to the provision of the service, about the notification requirement. Projects would be required to notify the parent or guardian within 10 working days following the initial provision of services by the project, except when the project director determines that notification would result in physical harm to the minor by a parent or guardian. Projects would be required to verify that the notifications were received. If the project was unable to verify that the notification was received, the project

EXHIBIT 2.6 (cont'd)

could not provide additional prescription drugs or prescription devices to the minor. Projects would be required to keep records on the notifications, verifications, and the number of cases in which a determination to forego parental notification has been made, along with the reasons for the determination. Second, grantees would be required to comply with any State law requiring that notification be provided to or consent obtained from the parents or guardian of unemancipated minors regarding the provision of family planning services to unemancipated minors. Third, the definition of "low income family" in the current regulations would be changed by eliminating the requirement that projects consider adolescents on the basis of their own resources for purposes of charging for services.

The proposed regulation limits application of section 931(b)(1) to "unemancipated minors." However, the definition of "unemancipated minor" varies under this regulation, depending on which requirement is involved. Since the first requirement applies to all grantees, we have proposed a Federal definition of the term for purposes of that requirement. This definition treats minors age 17 or under as unemancipated generally, but otherwise looks to State law to determine what specific acts, such as marriage or parenthood, constitute acts of emancipation. Thus, if State law would treat persons age 12 or older as emancipated for purposes of consent to medical care, Title X project would nonetheless have to treat them as unemancipated for purposes of complying with the first requirement, unless some other circumstance recognized as an act of emancipation under state law were present. With respect to the second regulatory requirement, by contrast, the term "unemancipated minor" is determined entirely by state law. We believe this is appropriate, since the intent of that requirement is to have Title X grantees comply with state laws requiring parental notification or consent. We do not expect that this variation in the applicable definition of emancipation will create difficulties for grantees, since the result is simply that, in addition to any state law requirement, the Federal notification requirement applies to otherwise unemancipated minors up to age 18. Nor do we expect that making a determination concerning emancipation will present any special problems for grantees, since they presently must decide who is emancipated in order to determine whether appropriate consent has been obtained in the course of providing medical services.

Under the proposed rules, projects would be required to notify the parents or guardian of an unemancipated minor where prescription drugs or prescription devices were provided. We believe that this requirement is consistent with the concern underlying section 931(b)(1). The Congressional policy of encouraging family participation in decision-making about family planning services is most clearly relevant where medical services are being provided to adolescents. In our view, implicit in section 931(b)(1) is an assumption that these individuals will generally benefit from the exercise of a parent's mature judgment on their behalf on matters that may affect their physical well-being. Particularly where prescription drugs or prescription devices are being considered, parents have a direct and legitimate concern in participating in a decision that may have long-term health consequences for the adolescent. It is our view that such involvement cannot occur unless the adolescent's parents or guardian are given the opportunity to participate, an opportunity which notification will provide. Thus, while we believe that grantees should encourage involvement of a minor's parents to the maximum extent possible in the provision of Title X services generally, the proposed rule ensures that Title X grantees will encourage parental involvement in those cases where it is most likely to be of the most significant value.

At the same time, the proposed rule provides that notification need not precede the provision of services, but rather that it must occur after services are provided. We believe this policy establishes a reasonable balance between competing concerns. On the one hand, it is the policy of the Act to make services available to adolescents, as evidenced by the statute's inclusion of "service to adolescents" as a mandatory project requirement. Requiring notification before services are provided could unduly delay or otherwise serve to restrict access to services, contrary to the statute's policy. On the other hand, as stated above, parents may reasonably be concerned about the potential medical consequences of prescription drugs and prescription devices, and should be afforded the opportunity to have input into a decision to use them. Notification of the minor's parents or guardian after service should minimize the access problem, while the 10 day rule will assure that parents can become involved promptly where there are serious concerns about the health of their child. To effectuate the notification requirement, projects must verify that the notification was received. If projects are unable to verify that the notification was received, projects may not provide additional prescription drugs and prescription devices to the minor. Also, projects must maintain records on the notifications and verifications.

In addition, the proposed rule provides that the minor must be informed about the notification requirement and permits an exception to the notification requirement where the project director finds that it would result in physical harm to the minor by a parent or guardian. The exception is meant to apply to cases where there is evidence of a history of child abuse, sexual

EXHIBIT 2.6 (cont'd)

abuse, or incest, or where there are other substantial grounds to determine that notification would result in physical harm to the minor by a parent or guardian. The exception does not apply to cases where notification would result in no more than disciplinary actions of an unsubstantial nature. This exception implements the statutory recognition of the fact that family involvement may not be advisable in all cases: under the statute such involvement is required only "to the extent practical." In our view, situations where notification of a minor's parents or guardian about the receipt of services would physically endanger the minor clearly come within the ambit of this statutory exception. The requirement that the minor be informed about notification will, among other things, provide an opportunity for the project to ascertain whether the exception applies. We recognize that any such exception contains the potential for abuse. Therefore, project directors will be required to keep a record of the number of exception determinations they have made, along with the reasons for each exception.

Finally, the proposed rule provides that the notification requirement shall not apply in cases where a project is providing prescription drugs for the treatment of venereal disease. This is consistent with the overriding public health necessity of ensuring prevention of infection of others.

The second requirement—for parental notification or consent where such a State requirement exists—is being proposed to resolve a dilemma presently facing some grantees. From time to time, States enact family laws that seek to require family planning providers to provide family planning services to unemancipated minors only with parental consent or notification. Now, where the State's underlying law of consent renders minors unable to give legally effective consent, Federal regulations do not require a project to provide services to the minor without the consent of a parent or guardian. However, where the minor can provide legally effective consent under State law, the project is required by 42 CFR 59.5(a)(4) to make services available to the minor to the extent it would to any otherwise similarly situated (for example, with respect to income) individual, even if the State has enacted a parental consent requirement intended to apply to Title X providers. Similarly, § 59.5(a)(4) presently precludes States from requiring grantees to condition services to minors upon parental notification.

The Secretary has concluded that the above policies are inconsistent with the statutory policy expressed by section 931(b)(1). Section 931(b)(1) expresses a Congressional judgment that, in an area as sensitive and difficult as family planning services, family involvement in the decisionmaking of minors should be encouraged. Traditionally, this has been an area which States, in their role as *parens patriae*, have regulated, for example, through statutes requiring parental notification or consent to certain types of medical services. In light of this traditional State role, and in order to remedy an often conflicting and confusing situation for grantees, the Secretary believes that it would be appropriate to implement section 931(b)(1) by deferring to legislative judgments made by the States, as expressed by State statutes. Accordingly, the Secretary proposes to amend the regulations to require grantees to adhere to any applicable State parental consent or notification statutes.

Finally, the proposed rules would amend the present definition of "low income family" to eliminate the requirement that projects consider minors who wish to receive services on a confidential basis on the basis of their own, and not their parents', resources. Since persons who are members of low income families receive services without charge, the present policy has the inappropriate effect of skewing the distribution of limited Federal grant funds away from the patients who are the most financially needy. In addition, the present policy indirectly discourages family involvement in the receipt of services by certain minors and thus is inconsistent with section 931(b)(1).

The Secretary solicits comments on the ramifications of the above proposals and suggestions as to how he might more effectively implement the intent of Congress. If there are particular operational problems with any of the proposals, the Secretary would appreciate being so informed. Statistical or other data supporting suggestions for change in the proposals would be particularly welcomed.

Impact Analysis

Executive Order 12291

E.O. 12291 requires that a regulatory impact analysis be prepared for major rules, which are defined in the order as any rule that has an annual effect on the national economy of $100 million or more, or certain other economic effects. The Secretary concludes that these regulations are not major rules within the meaning of the Executive Order, because they will not have an effect on the economy of $100 million or more or otherwise meet the threshold criteria. To the contrary, they effect a minor alteration in grantee operations that will cost little, if anything, to implement.

EXHIBIT 2.6 (cont'd)
Regulatory Flexibility Analysis

The Regulatory Flexibility Act (5 U.S.C. Ch.6) requires the Federal Government to anticipate and reduce the impact of rules and paperwork requirements on small businesses. For each proposed rule with a "significant economic impact on a substantial number of small entities" an initial analysis must be prepared describing the proposed rule's impact on small entities. The required change in grantee operations will be minimal in cost, as it will generally consist of a slight revision of present intake and counseling procedures applicable to only a small percentage of each grantee's total client population. Therefore, the Secretary hereby certifies that an initial regulatory flexibility analysis is not required.

For the reasons set forth above, the Assistant Secretary for Health, with the approval of the Secretary of Health and Human Services, therefore proposes to amend 42 CFR Part 59, Subpart A, as set forth below.

Dated: December 2, 1981.

Edward N. Brandt, Jr.,
Assistant Secretary for Health.

Approved: December 21, 1981.

Richard S. Schweiker,
Secretary.

Uniform laws are published in bound form by West Publishing Company as *Uniform Laws Annotated* (U.L.A.). They are also published separately by the Commission on Uniform State Laws. Model acts are published by the various organizations that sponsor them.

This book uses as illustrations several uniform and model acts because they usually represent a consensus of informed legal opinion and deal with current issues. They are also less provincial and more satisfactory as illustrations than a state statute influenced by local conditions.

OTHER USEFUL MATERIALS

Legislation, court decisions, and other developments are included in specialized reporting services: The *Poverty Law Reporter* and the *Family Law Reporter* are of special interest to social workers. Much legal scholarship is available from law reviews and journals. Articles often review major decisions and provide legal research on them. Articles are frequently quoted in court decisions. Several are included as references in this book. Law journals and reviews are summarized in the *Guide to Legal Periodicals*, which also includes a useful table of cases.

News magazines and other popular periodicals often present comments on cases and decisions. Most are indexed in the *Reader's Guide to Periodical Literature*. Book-length discussions of legal problems are also useful. Citations for books are generally similar to those for periodicals.

GENERAL INDEXES AND DICTIONARIES

For searches of the legal literature, two general indexes are particularly useful: the *Guide to Legal Periodicals* and *Law Books in Print*.

Every serious student using legal materials will need a law dictionary. Two standard works designed for lawyers are *Black's Law Dictionary* and *Ballantine's Law Dictionary*. The paperback *Oran's Dictionary of the Law* is an inexpensive resource.

ANALYZING A CASE: AN EXAMPLE

Students often find it desirable to analyze, or brief, a case. The following unpublished outline form developed by Professor Stuart Nagel is useful for that purpose. *Townsend v. Swank* was chosen as the subject matter for a sample analysis.

EXHIBIT 2.7
EXAMPLE OF CASE ANALYSIS

ANALYSIS OF TOWNSEND V. SWANK

I. Identification

Townsend v. Swank, 404 U.S. 282 (1971).

II. Preliminary facts

A. The plaintiffs were two college students and their mothers who had been receiving AFDC benefits until the children entered college.

B. Harold Swank was the director of the Illinois Department of Public Aid.

C. Restoration of two college students, Jerome Alexander and Omega Minor, to the AFDC rolls was sought though a request for injunctive and declaratory relief against the termination of AFDC benefits.

D. A class action was sought because SS 4-1.1 of the Illinois Public Aid Code implementing Illinois Public Aid Regulation 150 allegedly violates the equal protection clause of the Fourteen Amendment and SS 406(a)(2) of the Social Security Act and violates the supremacy clause of Article 6 of the U.S. Constitution.

  Needy dependent children 18–20 years of age attending high school or vocational school qualify for AFDC, but such children attending college or university do not qualify.

E. The plaintiffs lost their case in federal district court, 314 F. Supp. at 1088–1089. The U.S. Supreme Court reversed the decision on appeal.

III. Majority opinion

A. If under section 402(a)(10) state plans submitted under the AFDC program must provide such aid with reasonable promptness to *all eligible* individuals, then a state eligibility standard that excludes persons eligible for assistance under federal AFDC standards violates the Social Security Act and therefore is invalid under the supremacy clause.

B. Congress did not authorize the states to include only students attending vocational school.

C. AFDC payments up to age twenty-one were optional to a state. States that choose to make such payments have to conform their eligibility requirements to the new federal standards. The Illinois classification cannot withstand the equal protection clause.

IV. Concurring opinions

A. Chief Justice Burger held that rather than the supremacy clause, the appropriate inquiry involved whether the state had adhered to federal provisions and is accordingly entitled to utilize federal funds.

V. Dissenting opinions

A. None.

SOCIAL WORK AND LEGAL LITERATURE

What legal materials are of greatest value to the social worker?

The provisions of the U.S. Constitution are central because they establish the concept of individual rights and the concept of the general welfare as well as the supremacy of federal laws over state and local laws. Therefore they limit local and state discretion. The broad issues of due process and equal protection are of special interest to social work. An understanding of cases illustrating these issues is essential.

State constitutions deal with the structure of state government, civil rights, the system of taxation used to finance social services, and educational entitlements, all of which are important to the social worker.

Specific legislation is of major concern as well, for it authorizes human services programs and provides the basis for social action. Family law, welfare law (including poverty law), and juvenile and criminal law are key areas. The law of torts covers personal injury and is of relevance to workman's compensation; it also affects cases where a family member is responsible for injury to another family member.

Because of the dominant role of public agencies, a knowledge of administrative rules and regulations is important for they provide the framework both for the licensing of agencies and the licensing of the professionals employed therein. The social worker is also interested in product safety, the commercial code, and other aspects of consumer protection, both personally and for clients. Social workers need also to be aware of their own rights as employees and the legal implications of possible malpractice.

Familiarity with the legal literature and the means of enacting laws and testing them affords the social worker insights into the legal process, which can lead to more effective performance in court and serve as the basis for more effective co-operation between social work and law.

Table 2.2 summarizes the major sources of legal material.

TABLE 2.2
THE MAJOR SOURCES OF LEGAL MATERIAL

Documents	Sources
Constitutions	
United States	Any U.S. civics text
State	Secretary of state's office
Court Decisions	
U.S. Supreme Court	*Supreme Court Reports*
Federal courts of appeals	*Federal Reporter*
State courts of appeals	*National Reporter System* (see *supra* for specific states)
Congressional Debates	*Congressional Record*
Regulations	
Federal	*Federal Register*
State	From issuing agency
Federal Departments and Agencies	*U.S. Government Organization Manual*
Statutes	
Federal	*U.S. Code*
State codes	*Revised Statutes*
Textbooks	
Texts of major cases	Casebooks by topic
Legal principles	Hornbooks by topic
Brief summaries of topics	"Nutshells"
Periodicals	
Law reviews and journals	*Guide to Legal Periodicals*
Popular sources, e.g., news magazines	*Readers' Guide to Periodical Literature*

Questions for Review

1. What is the main rule for citation of legal cases?

2. What characteristic of modern society increases the importance of conflicting state laws?

3. What procedures in trial courts are eliminated in appellate courts?

4. In a legal decision, what is contained in headnotes?

5. Why are U.S. Supreme Court cases reported by several different publishers?

6. What two sources are most helpful to get the most recent U.S. Supreme Court decisions?

7. In the *National Reporter System*, where would you look for decisions from appellate courts in your home state?

8. In what publication does congressional debate appear?

9. Why is codification of laws necessary?

10. What is the purpose of U.S. **codes**?

11. From analyzing your own state constitution, who is given the power to operate the public social services at the state level?

Questions for Debate and Discussion

1. How would you respond to the criticism by social workers that the law is often too complicated?

2. What information traditionally in footnotes is omitted from the brief legal form? Are the omissions of great importance?

3. Why is it necessary to report court decisions in full? With full reporting, why are there still conflicts in law?

4. In analyzing the constitution of a state, social workers are often advised to pay particular attention to the revenue article. Why is this advice given?

5. Why do students of family law pay more attention to state constitutions than to the U.S. Constitution?

Selected Readings Dougherty, Douglas B. "How to Make High-Quality Requests for Computer-Assisted Research." *Clearinghouse Review* 16 (1982): 82–83.

Eres, Beth K. *Legal and Legislative Information Processing.* Westport, Conn.: Greenwood Press, 1980.

"The Federal Register: What It Is and How to Use It." Washington, D.C.: Office of the Federal Register, 1977.

Jacobstein, Myron, and Roy M. Mersky. *Fundamentals of Legal Research.* Mineola, N.Y.: Foundation Press, 1981.

Regal, Jill M. "Employing Research Concepts: Principles and Problems in the Case Method." *Legal Research Journal* 4 (1980): 6–11.

Statsky, William P. *Legal Research Writing and Analysis.* St. Paul, Minn.: West Publishing Co., 1982.

CHAPTER

3

The Legislative Process and Social Action

Governmental structure is often confusing. Departments, bureaus, and commissions seem to serve differing but overlapping purposes. Federal agencies under the president are often investigated by Congress, those under a governor are scrutinized and evaluated by the state legislature. Executives have found many ways to exert controls, including the withholding of funds.

The process of getting bills passed seems difficult. In some states, ethical questions are raised about the ways legislation is supported. The term *lobbyist* may suggest corruption, but lobbyists are absolutely necessary to lawmakers as sources of technical information.

Social work efforts at social action are needed, but they are frequently primitive and disorganized. This chapter considers all these problems and suggests some means for effective political intervention.

LEGISLATIVE AUTHORIZATION OF SOCIAL PROGRAMS

Legislation authorizes the major social service programs and provides the appropriations for them. Bills that directly affect economic policy and indirectly affect the need for social services are introduced. Other bills deal with social values, such as civil rights. The importance of legislative activities suggests the need for understanding how a bill is enacted into law and how its content and passage can be influenced. These are times in the life of a bill when the response of citizens can be particularly effective.

Simply authorizing a program by law does not mean that it will be put into operation. If the legislature fails to appropriate funds, the program is effectively curtailed; if appropriations are made later, the program can be restored. Appropriations must be enacted at each session, because one legislature cannot obligate the succeeding one. Does passage of an appropriation for a given purpose provide the authority to operate a program not already specified within the powers and duties of a governmental agency? Agencies will assume such authority, but the courts may rule that the unauthorized activity must be suspended.

METHODS OF EXECUTIVE CONTROL

How can the president or a governor modify the intentions of the legislative branch of government? An **executive agency** is under the control of the president or the governor, who appoints the cabinet officer who has direct charge of the agency. The chief executive may order the agency to impound funds.

Impoundment

An executive-level decision not to spend appropriated funds, **impoundment** became a frequent strategy in the 1970s, but such action was challenged in the courts. The time needed to bring such actions, however, resulted in delays that saved money. Since appropriation bills must be signed by the chief executive, ethical questions result when he or she approves a bill and then forbids executive agencies to spend funds for the designated purpose. The Supreme Court, in Train v. New York (420 U.S. 35 [1975]), generally rejected impoundment. The Congressional Budget and Impoundment Control Act of 1974 (P.L. 93-344) had been passed earlier to formalize the procedure for impounding and unimpounding.

Both political pressure and court action have been used successfully to "unimpound" funds. Interest groups may bring pressure, and Congress may delay other necessary legislation until funds are released. Impoundment is important, because the courts must determine the constitutional boundary between the executive and Congress regarding the power to spend. In *Train*, the Court avoided constitutional questions and considered only statutory questions. Litigation is useful to parties that have less political influence, while more powerful groups will find political pressure more effective.

Under the 1974 act, the president must notify Congress of each proposed deferral, and either house may pass an impoundment resolution requiring the president to make the funds available. Action may also be brought in the courts. Impoundment is likely to continue to be attempted, and both judicial and political methods will be employed to counter it. However, a strong commitment from Congress for budget reduction has reduced concern with impoundment in the 1980s. Ironically, President Ronald Reagan used the budget reconciliation device in the Anti-impoundment Act to bypass the congressional appropriation process to make significant cuts in social programs.

Freezes

To keep the budget in balance, **freezes** are common. In a freeze, executive agencies may be ordered to hire no new employees and replace none that leave, which reduces staff by attrition and thereby saves money. Agencies may also be required to curtail travel. Freezes for these purposes are generally considered acceptable. When direct client benefits are reduced by a freeze, the orders are more likely to be challenged than if only staff and travel are frozen. The alternative to a freeze is to ask the legislature for a **deficiency appropriation**. If such a request is refused, an agency that has overspent its budget will be in financial chaos. Recent fiscal crises have shown that state agencies may also demote, lay off, or terminate personnel in order to balance their budgets. Many state constitutions require a balanced budget, leading to drastic actions affecting personnel when funds fall short.

Line-item Veto

In several states, governors also have the power to reduce appropriations at the time they sign a bill. This is known as **line-item veto**. Such reductions are rarely overridden. In fact, lawmakers at the outset may take the credit for supporting appropriations and then later support the amended reductions.

LEGISLATIVE PROCESS

Understanding legislative power is a prerequisite to understanding both the legislative process and the strategies of lobbying. The social worker interested in legislation must identify the key persons in a given system. Often the success or failure of a bill may depend on who sponsors it or how a key person says he or she plans to vote.

Speakers and party leaders exercise special power and some legislators and congresspeople become specialists on certain types of bills. Colleagues who may be less well informed may follow the leads of the specialists.

Some committees are much more powerful than others. The classic example used to be the House Ways and Means Committee, and the chairperson of the Finance Committee exercised similar power in the Senate. Given the size of the two houses of Congress, the committee structure is especially important. Committees often rewrite bills, and the committee chairperson has considerable power to determine the fate of a bill—much more than is the case in most state legislatures. Changes over the last decade, however, seem to have diluted some of the centralization of power in committee chairpersons.

Although many similarities are found in the federal and state legislative processes, there are also major differences.

The Federal Enactment Process

The term **bill** is used until a proposal is fully approved. Then it becomes a **law**.

Step One.   A bill is introduced and assigned a number: A U.S. House of Representatives bill is designated "H.R. _____"; a U.S. Senate bill is identified "S. _____." Bills do not carry over from one Congress to another; they must be reintroduced in each new Congress (every two years). Every bill is separately printed in each of its several stages of progress through both houses.

Step Two.   The bill is assigned to the appropriate committee. If the bill is acted on favorably, it is "reported out of committee." Bills are generally accorded hearings by the committee to determine the views of the public on the subject and to obtain expert testimony. A committee report is printed. The reports are numbered consecutively for each Congress and are identified as "H.R.Rep.No. _____" or "S.Rep.No. _____." Hearings may or may not be printed.

Step Three.   The bill is "reported out" by the chairperson with the committee recommendation for passage.

Step Four.   The bill is debated. The debates appear in the *Congressional Record*. The House or Senate votes on the bill; when it passes, it is sent to the other body to go through the same four steps. If the second house passes the bill with amendments, it is returned to the first house. When the first house does not accept the amended bill, a **conference committee** consisting of members of both houses is appointed. If the conferees agree to compromise, the report of the conference committee is printed and both houses vote on the conference bill.

Step Five.   The bill is submitted to the president for signature and approval. If it is vetoed by the president, the bill must be passed again by a two-thirds vote in both houses in order to become law.

Authorization and Appropriations Bills.   Unlike the states, Congress generally first passes an **authorization bill** as a guide to appropriations over several years. The authorization bill is followed by an **appropriations bill**, which determines the actual amount of money available. Generally the appropriation will be less than the authorization. Authorizations are seen as planning tools, but they do not convey any actual funds.

Citizen Involvement on the Federal Level

Since most of the federal support for social welfare services stems from the authority in the Social Security Act (1935), amendments to that act are closely watched. Title XX of that act was an example of major legislation dealing with social services in which the National Association of Social Workers (NASW) and similar groups expressed strong support. Federal funding of social services, labor legislation, bills on education and rehabilitation, and revenue measures are of key interest to social workers because of their effect on people with special problems.

Individuals who are recognized as experts and legislative specialists from national organizations play an important role in federal legislation by drafting bills and testifying on their behalf. The NASW and many other social welfare organizations maintain offices in Washington, D.C., and encourage individual members to see or write their own representative or senator. Testimony before committees is most often given by the officers of such organizations and other leaders whose knowledge in a given area is well recognized. Time for testimony is strictly limited. Schedule changes may mean that a witness must stay in Washington for several days waiting to be heard. Cost, distance, and time constraints discourage many concerned citizens from testifying before congressional committees, so personal contacts, letters, and telegrams are important when a bill is being drafted, when it is heard before a committee, and when it comes up for passage. Such approaches may also be used to influence the president to sign or veto the bill.

The State Enactment Process: An Illinois Example

Social workers are more likely to be directly involved in state legislation. Comparisons of the fifty state legislatures with each other and with the U.S. Congress reveal wide differences. In general, state legislatures are less well organized and administered than their federal counterparts. Testimony before committees and floor debate is often not recorded. Committees also may have minimal staff resources. Legislators who are not in positions of leadership sometimes have no private office and may try to conduct office business on the floor of the legislature. The best place to see a legislator during a session may be in a neighborhood bar.

Citizens who visit a legislature for the first time are often amazed at the chaos. Although nonmembers do not have floor privileges while the body is in session, they learn how to avoid the sergeants-at-arms. If proceedings are not published, debate becomes only a means to impress the galleries. Nonetheless, the legislative system functions better than anyone might have a right to hope. In spite of primitive conditions, laws do get passed. Ultimate success is probably due to the specific rules and procedures that mandate deliberate action, plus the devoted service of many members and supporting staff who have a high sense of commitment.

The Idea of the Bill.   The interest in a bill does not usually originate with the legislator who sponsors it. More likely, it comes from the administration (if the legislator is a member of the party in power), from a constituent, or from some outside organization. Nevertheless, the sponsor who introduces the bill will have full control over it. He or she may schedule it for a committee hearing or may have no real interest in it and let it die.

Drafting the Language.   The first task in drafting a bill is to state its purpose and outline its provisions in simple terms. The office for the drafting of bills is usually called the **Legislative Reference Bureau**. Its staff takes the version supplied by the legislator and drafts the bill according to the prescribed format. The drafters are nonpartisan experts who are not interested in the details of the bill but only in giving it acceptable form. They serve all legislators and other major state officers.

To pass a bill, the following process used in Illinois is typical in other states as well:

Introduction of the Bill—"First Reading." To introduce the bill, the sponsor delivers it to the presiding officer. By the time of introduction, the sponsor will usually have added the names of other members willing to co-sponsor it. Multiple sponsorship implies a broader base of support for the bill. Sponsors of many social legislation measures will include members of the opposite party as well as members of one's own party.

The bill is numbered and will bear that number throughout the session. It is then read by title by the reading clerk and placed on "first reading," which simply means that the bill has been officially introduced. Theoretically, it could be advanced to "second reading" the following day by passing a motion to bypass reference to committee, but that rarely happens.

Assignment to one committee rather than another may be important, since certain committees are typically hostile or friendly to certain types of legislation. Therefore, the Speaker of the House and the Committee on the Assignment of Bills in the Illinois Senate, for example, wield considerable power.

The Committee Hearing. The sponsor of the bill lets the chairperson of the committee know when he or she wants to call the bill for a hearing. Any citizen may appear as a witness, but the public is allowed to testify only during the committee hearing. Thus the committee hearing is most important. The committee secretary knows what bills will be considered in a given session. People who are interested in testifying on a bill should be sure that the sponsor or a legislative staff member keeps them informed on when hearings will be held, otherwise the hearing may take place without the interested person being aware of it.

Before the bill is read, witnesses register as proponents or opponents. The sponsor begins by explaining the bill briefly and introducing witnesses favorable to the bill to present their testimony. The committee chairperson will then ask the opponents to testify. Committee members may question the witnesses. Before witnesses are heard, the sponsor will sometimes offer amendments to correct defects. Other amendments may be offered by the sponsor or any committee member. All amendments must all be voted on. Finally the chairperson asks for a motion on the bill.

Usually a committee member moves that "the bill be voted out DO PASS." If the vote fails or a DO NOT PASS motion carries, the bill is defeated. If the votes are not forthcoming, a committee member can ask to postpone consideration to a later time. The request is usually granted routinely.

If a bill carries an appropriation, it will not advance to "second reading" until it has also been heard by the appropriations committee. The procedure is similar to the one already described, except the focus is on the costs involved. Appropriations are also subject to amendment. The question "Is the cost of this program included in the governor's official budget?" is often raised. If not, chances for passage may be reduced, because the bill is more likely to be vetoed.

Second Reading—The Floor Amendment Stage.   When a bill passed out by committee is called for "second reading," it is subject to possible amendments from the floor. If it has already been amended in the committee hearing, the amendments will have been printed and the bill will be referred to as "House # _____ as amended." After the whole body has considered it, or if no amendments are offered from the floor, the bill is advanced to "third reading."

Third Reading—The Voting Stage.   The sponsor will ordinarily call the bill for vote when the members are present to make passage most likely. If a close vote is anticipated, the sponsor will not proceed if several supporters are absent. If votes are tallied mechanically, a tentative count is often shown before the machine is locked for the final count. Before the tally is final, members can switch their votes. This occurs, for example, when members are willing to vote for a bill but prefer not to do so unless their vote is needed. They may fear that that vote will offend some key constituents. If the votes are lacking, the sponsor may ask that the bill be postponed. Postponement is granted as a matter of courtesy and allows the bill to be brought up again.

Passage in the Other House.   Unless there is a one-house legislature, as in Nebraska, a bill passed in the first house is introduced in the other house. The principal sponsor asks a member of the second house to handle the bill, and the process is repeated. The original sponsor usually attends the committee hearing to explain the bill. The readings and committee process are similar to those already described. If the bill passes in the second house without alteration, it goes to the governor for possible signature. If amendments are passed in the second house, the first house will be asked to concur. If it does not do so, a conference committee will be appointed.

The Conference Committee.   Several members from each house are appointed to the conference committee to work out a compromise, which will be returned to the two houses for adoption. If both houses fail to adopt the report, a second conference committee may be appointed. If no agreement is reached, the bill will die.

The Bill Becomes Law.   If the chief executive signs the bill, it becomes an **act** and a new law has been created. In some states a bill that is not actually vetoed by the governor is considered to have received a "pocket veto." In other states, a bill may become law without signature after a given number of days. Some states allow the governor to make changes in substance or to reduce appropriations through an amendatory veto. The bill must then be returned to the legislature for approval of the changes. To restore the original provisions, the bill would have to be repassed by a two-thirds or three-fifths majority, depending on the provisions of the state constitution.

State Legislative Safeguards

The three readings assure that bills will not ordinarily be passed in less than six days. Usually the process will take much longer. Each step requires deliberate effort. The committee hearing is considered a major safeguard; subcommittees may also be used. Amendments may be offered by the committee or on second reading from the floor. After the final vote, the entire process is repeated in the other house. Finally, the chief executive signs the bill. If he or she does not do so, the legislature may be persuaded to pass it over the veto. Sustained efforts can be successful in influencing such a complex process, but letters or telephone calls may not be enough to have any effect.

CITIZEN ACTION ON BEHALF OF LEGISLATION

The critical stages for contacting a legislator include:

The Drafting Process. Being pro-active on behalf of a bill is desirable. The most appropriate time to influence a bill is while it is still tentative. After it has been introduced, amendments are more difficult to achieve.

The Committee Hearings. The committee hearings are the only occasions for public testimony. Amendments are easiest to pass at this time, particularly if they are proposed by the sponsor. Testimony at the appropriations hearing is important too.

The Third Reading. The final vote—the time to be sure that all members are contacted, that they understand the bill and the recommendations on it, and that they will be present for the vote.

The Signing of the Bill. It is necessary to influence the governor to sign or veto the bill.

Influencing the Legislator

Citizens have both the right and the responsibility to make their views known on major legislative matters. Such efforts are likely to be most effective if the citizen is known to the legislator and is a resident of the legislator's home district. The most influential people are those who enjoy the status of expert in a particular field or whose views are supported by a number of like-minded citizens who also make their position clear. Nevertheless, an individual who is persistent in communicating a specific viewpoint may influence legislation.

Collective social action is the goal of organizations interested in lobbying. Personal visits, letters or telegrams, petitions, and mass demonstrations are the most common social action methods. Few systematic studies have been made of the comparative value of these techniques. What is very effective with one person may not be as effective with another. The nature of the issue, the number of people responding, and the timing of the action are all important. A personal relationship assures access to the lawmaker. Personal contact is more likely to be effective in the earlier stages of a legislative session and in the earlier stages of consideration of a given bill. Perhaps the greatest advantage for the legislative advocate is to already be acquainted with the legislator and to have his or her respect.

Generally a visit to the legislator at office or home is recommended. It is difficult to try to transact business on the floor of the legislature. Establishing contact with a legislator in the home district clearly identifies the person as a constituent whose opinion matters.

A personal visit to a legislator conveys the idea that the advocate considers the issue to be really important. While a delegation is sometimes more effective, the legislator may feel pressured and be less willing to discuss the bill than if only one or two people were present. Instead of effective interchange, a delegation may receive only a polite hearing. Advocates sometimes expect a definite commitment as the result of a visit, but they may be disappointed. Most lawmakers keep their options open. A fair request is to ask for a response when the legislator has decided what his or her final position will be. That leaves the door open for the advocate to make another contact later. The visit may motivate the lawmaker to read the bill for the first time.

The personal visit should be followed by a letter setting forth the desired position clearly and recommending definite action: support, support with amendments, or opposition. Clear identification is particularly important. If the bill has been introduced, the letter should not only summarize its purpose but also give the bill number.

Telephone contacts to a legislator during a session are often unsatisfying. If the lawmaker must be called from the floor, a call may do more harm than good. When a vote is to be taken in committee or a bill reaches the final passage stage, telegrams serve as a reminder of a previous contact. Special low rates are available for messages to legislators. Whatever the method of communication, the advocate should be sure that the reasons for his or her recommendation are set forth clearly and concisely.

Petitions and duplicated letters and postcards requiring only a signature are less effective in influencing a lawmaker because they reflect minimal commitment on the part of the citizen. They merely convey that some kind of organized effort is being carried on. Large numbers of such communications can sometimes lead to impressive results, but many legislators say that they discount any communications that are not personalized.

The use of marches and other demonstrations or packing the galleries at the time of a vote alienates some lawmakers. In addition, a person who organizes a demonstration may have no assurance that members of his or her group will act responsibly.

ORGANIZATIONS AND SOCIAL ACTION

Most of the social action efforts by individuals are generated by their membership in organizations. The organization usually presents its position to the members and advises them to support that position by highlighting some aspect most important to each member individually. In that way, responses differ somewhat but serve a common purpose. Members may also be encouraged to add personal views not in the organization's position statement, although that discretion may be risky for an organization.

Pro-action

"Pro-action" involves formulation of one's position even before a piece of legislation is drafted. A major example has been the American Medical Association's (AMA) efforts on governmental involvement in medical care. Although the AMA's political power has diminished recently, anyone who proposes health legislation knows that the AMA or the state medical association must be considered. Social work groups have less power, and their positions may be less consistent, but pro-activity is also a major goal for their social action strategies. A continuing campaign of public information and interpretation will serve to clarify social work positions on major issues. Organizations also have a responsibility to keep members informed on the progress of a bill. Rapid action is often needed—especially when amendments change a bill's substance.

The National Association of Social Workers has developed ELAN (the Educational Legislative Action Network). Members from each congressional district provide a response system so that national lawmakers can be contacted quickly when major issues develop. State NASW chapters are also encouraged to use ELAN as a pattern for responding to issues facing the legislature. One of the key goals is to develop relationships with lawmakers so they will depend on the ELAN representative for advice on social welfare legislation.

NASW also formed a political action committee, PACE (Political Action for Candidate Election), in 1976. Social workers are encouraged to contribute to a fund used to support candidates favorable to NASW positions. Contributions are kept separate from other NASW funds since they are not tax exempt. Efforts in the Florida chapter to support candidates were reported in a volume on political action for social workers (Abrams and Goldstein, 1982).

Lobbying   Organizations with the most effective social action programs generally retain paid lobbyists who are registered with the legislature and work year-round on public information and legislative action. Registered lobbyists serve several major functions. They are advocates, they are watchdogs, but mainly they are sources of data. Legislators depend on lobbyists for information because they cannot possibly be informed about several thousand bills. While some small organizations may share the time of a lobbyist with others, this may result in conflicts of interest and make it difficult for the lobbyist to devote the time needed at critical points in the legislative process.

An important duty of many professional lobbyists is to organize the social action efforts of the organization's members. Support from a number of regular members is generally more effective than support from a paid lobbyist. The lobbyist must be sure that members are informed. Members may need help on committee testimony and, most important, must be in the right places at the right times. With the scheduling of legislative activities, especially toward the end of a session, last-minute changes often require a responsible person on the scene.

The value of a lobbyist's knowledge and contacts grows from session to session. Experienced lobbyists become experts in their field and are well regarded by legislators. The lobbyist may be a useful consultant as legislation is being developed.

Historically, social work lobbying efforts have been sporadic and underfinanced, especially at the state level. When social workers do not enjoy high prestige, the lobbyist must obtain testimony from influential citizens who are interested in social issues but not included in social agency payrolls. To gain strength, coalitions are also necessary.

Coalitions   Issues that interest social workers usually involve major social policy questions with widespread general impact. They also involve large appropriations. Organizations find that their social action programs are much more effective if they seek to develop coalitions on a broad, continuing basis, so they join with other health and welfare organizations. Such nonprofit groups as the League of Women Voters and the Parent–Teachers Association study questions of social policy and generally develop positions compatible with those of social work. Exploration will reveal many other organizations that are potential members of a coalition.

Broad and noncontroversial issues, such as prevention of child abuse, provide a basis for large coalitions. Financing of public welfare and other more controversial topics involve a wider spectrum of positions. Sometimes coalitions are formed to deal with one single issue and then they disappear. A lobbyist is often of great help in designing and implementing needed coalitions because of special knowledge of other organizations.

SPECIAL PROBLEMS OF SOCIAL WORK LEGISLATION

Bills dealing with the profession of social work often incur the opposition of other professions and related disciplines. Psychiatry and psychology, for example, may take exception to bills that accord licensing to social workers in clinical practice or that authorize payment for social work treatment from health insurance. At the same time, groups with a lesser level of education that perform social work functions may also oppose legislation for licensing of social workers.

All relevant professional groups must be consulted in order to present a unified position. Legislators tend to back off from bills on which professionals cannot agree. They are particularly confused when groups within social work strongly oppose one another's efforts. If caseworkers in agencies and those in private practice disagree on a bill, for example, the legislator tends to vote no.

ADVOCACY: A LONG-TERM VIEW

Advocates of a bill often feel betrayed when a legislator appears to fail them by voting contrary to their position. While a lawmaker may be asked to justify such a vote, successful social action requires perspective. One's efforts at influencing the legislator in the future may be enhanced by knowing how to lose gracefully and respecting the lawmaker's right to vote independently.

Advocacy by individuals, organizations, and lobbyists is the way to obtain legislation, and legislation is a means of obtaining social change.

This discussion has introduced the legislative process and identified specific stages in the passage of a bill when social action will be most effective. Suggestions have been made for continuing efforts to involve lobbyists and social workers in influencing legislation on behalf of their profession and in concert with groups with similar interests. Since in each session one-third of the legislators are usually new, maintaining and broadening of the support base require constant effort. Although each new session will always be different from the last, gains will gradually be made as long as social action is sustained, responsive, and informed.

Questions for Review

1. What is meant by an executive agency?

2. Explain what is meant by a freeze on funds or personnel. How does a freeze differ from impoundment?

3. How does an authorization differ from an appropriation?

4. What is a line-item veto?

5. Given limitations of space and distance, how can an individual influence federal legislation?

6. Summarize the steps in the passage of a bill in each house of a state legislature.

7. Who is allowed to participate in floor debate in the legislature?

8. When is the first opportunity to amend a bill?

9. What is the purpose of the "first reading"?

10. Explain the purpose of a conference committee.

11. Identify the most appropriate stages for citizen input on a bill.

12. Compare the value of a personal visit and a letter to a legislator on behalf of a bill.

13. Explain the statement "Most social action efforts by individuals are generated by their membership in organizations."

14. Explain "pro-active" techniques.

15. Why do social work lobbying efforts tend to be ineffective?

Questions for Debate and Discussion

1. Why is this chapter concerned mainly with the state level, rather than with the federal level?

2. Why would there be considerable opposition to speeding up the legislative process?

3. What would be the advantages and disadvantages of a unicameral (one-house) legislature, such as that in Nebraska?

4. In preparing a talk to an NASW chapter on lobbying, what main points would you stress?

5. Choose a topic for proposed legislation concerning social services. Develop a plan for a coalition on that topic.

Selected Readings Culyer, A. J. *The Political Economy of Social Policy*. New York: St. Martin's Press, 1980.

Davidson, Roger, and Walter Oleszek. *Congress and Its Members*. Washington, D.C.: Congressional Quarterly, 1981.

Edwards, Clark (ed.). *Government's Role in Solving Societal Problems*. Washington, D.C.: Graduate School Press, 1982.

Eres, Beth K. *Legal and Legislative Information Processing*. Westport, Conn.: Greenwood Press, 1980.

Olson, David M. *The Legislative Process: A Comparative Approach*. New York: Harper & Row, 1980.

Williams, Robert F. "State Constitutional Law Processes." *William and Mary Law Review* 24 (1983): 169–228.

CHAPTER

4

Legal Authority for Social Welfare Programs

People who have had little experience with welfare services find them confusing. The sponsorship, financing, and eligibility policies of the various programs make it impossible to develop normative organizational patterns. This chapter looks at the structure of social welfare agencies and provides some clarification. A useful way to test out understanding of a state or local system is to reduce it to a series of organizational charts. The discussion that follows will help you make such a study. The scope of the social welfare endeavor, the relative responsibilities and roles of the federal, state, and private sectors, and the legal authority of each are discussed in this chapter.

THE SCOPE OF SOCIAL WELFARE

In the past decade, social welfare expenditures have rivalled the budget for national defense. In 1982, social welfare expenditures totaled nearly $600 billion—19.3 percent of the gross national product. This figure includes the cost of health, education, public assistance, and social service programs. The federal government supplies about 60 percent and state and local governments about 40 percent of the funding. Social welfare expenditures include all programs operating under public law that are of direct benefit to individuals and families. Figure 4.1 shows the growth since 1950. Figure 4.2 shows the changes in proportionate expenditures since 1950. The vast growth of social insurance involved 9.8 percent of the gross national product in 1983, up from 14.7 percent in 1970.* Public expenditures play a dominant role in the large total expense of social welfare, and although state and local governments operate most welfare programs, federal support of social welfare in the public sector is of critical importance.

EARLY EFFORTS AT PROMOTING THE GENERAL WELFARE

The federal government has the power to "promote the general welfare." This is the only phrase in the U.S. Constitution which authorizes governmental participation in welfare programs. With a few exceptions, until the last half-century the federal government left such programs to the states and to local charities. This section will identify several early federal efforts, and then we will consider the Social Security Act occasioned by the Depression of the 1930s.

---

* For statistical data, see the latest *Social Security Bulletin*, Annual Statistical Supplement.

FIGURE 4.1

SOCIAL WELFARE EXPENDITURES UNDER PUBLIC PROGRAMS
AS A PERCENT OF THE GROSS NATIONAL PRODUCT (GNP)

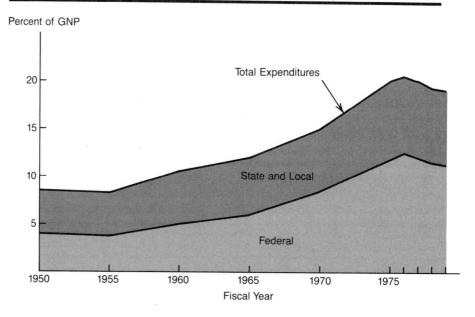

Source: *Social Security Bulletin* 44 (November 1981): 99.

Federal Land Grants

In 1848 Dorothea Dix, a leader in mental health reform, proposed the distribution of federal lands to the states. Proceeds from the sale of land were to be applied toward support of the indigent insane. Six years later, a bill was passed which reserved 10 million acres for this purpose. However, President Franklin Pierce vetoed it, stating:

> I cannot find any authority in the Constitution for making the Federal Government the great almoner of public charity throughout the United States. If the several States . . . shall be led to suppose . . . that congress is to make provision for such objects, the fountains of charity will be dried up at home and the several states instead of bestowing their own means on social wants of their own people may themselves through the strong temptation which appeals to States as to individuals become humble suppliants for the bounty of the Federal Government, reversing their true relation to this Union.

The Pierce veto formed the basis for Justice James C. McReynolds' dissent in the suit that held the Social Security Act to be constitutional.

The Morrill Acts of 1862 for the support of higher education were patterned on Dorothea Dix's original proposal. The acts provided each state with land to establish colleges of agriculture and engineering, and 30,000 acres were awarded for each senatorial and representative district.

WAR VETERANS

War veterans were the only group of disabled persons for whom the federal government assumed direct responsibility. Veterans' benefits have included transfer payments from the federal government to the states since before 1800. By 1790,

FIGURE 4.2
PERCENTAGE DISTRIBUTION OF SOCIAL WELFARE EXPENDITURES,
BY PROGRAM, SELECTED FISCAL YEARS 1950–80

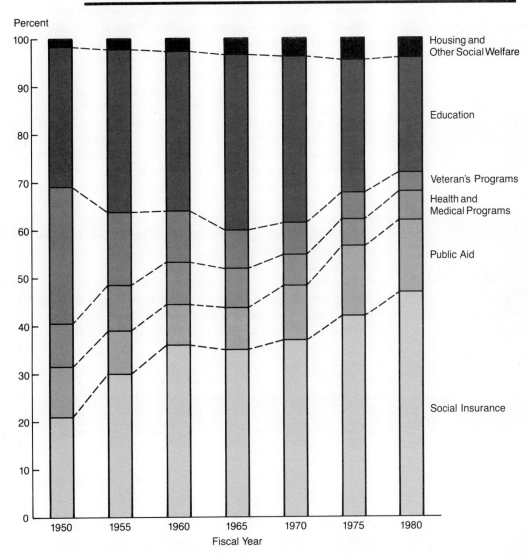

Source: *Social Security Bulletin* 39 (January 1976): 14; 45

the federal government had assumed responsibility for financial support of disabled veterans, veterans' widows, and orphans of veterans. Pensions were established for participants in the revolutionary war and in subsequent wars. President Abraham Lincoln signed a bill in 1865 to incorporate a national military and naval asylum for the relief of totally disabled officers and men of the U.S. armed forces. In 1873, national homes for veterans were authorized. Residence in the homes was considered to be earned by the veteran through his military service. The homes were specifically not to be almshouses.

The Pension Act of 1890 eliminated the need to be disabled in order to receive a pension. Financial need became the basic criterion. By the turn of the century, the social welfare of veterans included state and federal benefits—cash payments, medical services, and domiciliary care—but benefits were not extended to Confederate veterans.

Following World War I, a Veterans Bureau (now the Veterans Administration) was created to bring together most benefits—medical care, insurance payments, and vocational rehabilitation services. In 1924, hospital services were made available to honorably discharged veterans who did not have service-connected disabilities. During the Great Depression, veterans marched on Washington seeking bonus payments. Their efforts returned $3.5 billion to the economy in 1937.

Post–World War II benefits were provided under the Servicemen's Readjustment Act of 1944, the GI Bill of Rights. The philosophical basis of this legislation was that "the country owes an obligation to the veteran to restore him to civilian status and opportunities he would have enjoyed had there not been a war." Education and training, loans to purchase a home or business, unemployment payments, and employment services were provided. As Figure 4.2 illustrates, in 1950 veterans' services and benefits reached a peak of 23 percent of federal expenditures, involving a cost of over $9 billion.

Social workers should be aware of special benefits for veterans. The following were available at the end of 1984:

Social Security Credits.   Veterans are entitled to $160 per month earnings credits for each month spent in the armed forces from September 15, 1940, through December 1956. Deductions for Social Security have been taken out since 1957. Provision was made later for $100 per month of credits to be added to the earnings record of anyone who served after 1956.

Home Loans.   Veterans Administration guarantees are available for up to 60 percent of the loan, with a maximum guarantee of $27,500.

Disability Compensation.   Benefits are paid for service-connected disability ranging from $66 to $1,295 per month. In severe cases, payments can go to over $4,005 per month. Non-service-connected disabilities make one eligible for pension benefits if income is under $6,273 for a person without dependents and $8,435 with dependents.

Survivor's Benefits.   Widows receive pensions. Minor children get additional amounts; their eligibility continues to age twenty-three if dependents are in school when the veteran's death was service-connected. For non-service-connected cases, benefits are available if income levels do not exceed the limits outlined above under Disability Compensation.

Burial Expenses.   Benefits of $1,100 are available if the death is service-connected, and $300 if not. Headstones, gravemarkers, plot, and burial flag allowances, are available. Burial for the veteran and a spouse is available without charge in a national cemetery.

Medical Care.   Hospital care is available for veterans with service-connected disabilities on an inpatient or outpatient basis. Non-service-connected conditions are treated for veterans who cannot afford to pay.

Federal Employment The federal government has a policy of promoting maximum job opportunities for qualified disabled veterans and Vietnam era veterans. Additional points may be added to passing scores in job examinations, and certain physical requirements are subject to waiver.

Life Insurance. Insurance is available for group life coverage in the amount of $10,000, plus additional coverage if dividends are used to purchase it. Service-disabled and mortgage insurance are also available to veterans under certain conditions.

Educational Benefits. GI education benefits are available on a contributing basis to people who entered the military in or after 1977. They may have $25 to $100 deducted each month, up to $2,700. On discharge, this will be matched to cover educational expenses, with $2 for each $1 withheld.

Veteran's benefits are also offered by each state. The local Veterans Administration office has details on state benefits.

Legal Precedents for Federal Grants-in-aid

Federal grants-in-aid providing support for state and local programs began before the Social Security Act was passed. A Maternity Act (42 Stat. 224) was passed in 1921, providing appropriations for reducing maternal and infant mortality. Monies were to be appropriated to the several states that accepted and complied with its provisions. Periodic reports were required on operations and expenditures much as they are on grants-in-aid today.

The constitutionality of the act was challenged by a state in *Massachusetts v. Mellon* and by a taxpayer in *Frothingham v. Mellon*. The two suits were considered together (262 U.S. 447 [1923]). The decision established federal authority to make the grants. To bar the action, the plaintiff "must be able to show not only that the statute is invalid but that he has sustained or is immediately in danger of sustaining some direct injury as a result of its enforcement and not merely that he suffers in some indefinite way in common with people generally" (262 U.S. at 488). To declare the act unconstitutional "would be to assume a position of authority over the governmental acts of another and co-equal department [Congress]—authority which we plainly do not possess." This precedent was to be important in the test of the Social Security Act a decade later.

The U.S. Supreme Court later specifically provided that Congress may tax in order to raise money to promote broad national public welfare (United States v. Butler, 297 U.S. 1 [1936]). It also extended financial backing to the general welfare clause of the Constitution.

THE SOCIAL SECURITY ACT

The Social Security Act, passed in August 1935, marked the beginning of large-scale federal involvement in social welfare. It launched the unemployment compensation program, old-age benefits to be financed by taxes on employees and employers, and an elaborate system of credits and subsidies to obtain the cooperation of the states. Federal aid was also authorized for dependent children, maternal and child welfare, and public health. Grants-in-aid were authorized originally for development of health and welfare services in rural areas, but they came to be used for special urban problems as well. The act contained no provisions for health insurance because it was considered politically hazardous. Aid programs for the blind and disabled were added later.

The Social Security Act augmented local responsibility with federal aid for social welfare activities to the states on a permanent basis. Poverty was recognized as a fundamental social and economic issue that required a response from society as a whole. People were entitled to public benefits—justice replaced charity.

The simple structure of the original Social Security Act and its vast expansion make it of special interest to social work students. The present amended act is over thirty times as long as the original legislation.

Challenges to the
Social
Security Act

The constitutionality of the Social Security Act was unsuccessfully challenged in Steward Machine Co. v. Davis, 301 U.S. 548 (1937), and Helvering v. Davis, 301 U.S. 619 (1937). The former dealt with taxes on employers, and the decision held that the exceptions provided did not render the act "obnoxious to" (in conflict with) the Fifth Amendment.

Helvering v. Davis affirmed that federal old-age benefits in Title II did not violate the Tenth Amendment, which entrusts to the states those powers not specifically delegated to the federal government. The decision related to federal powers and the rationale for them:

> Congress may spend money in aid of the general welfare . . . It is now settled by decision—United States v. Butler. . . . The line must still be drawn between one welfare and another. . . . The discretion belongs to Congress. . . . Nor is the concept of general welfare static. Needs that were narrow and parochial a century ago may be interwoven in our day with the well-being of the Nation. What is critical or urgent changes with the times. (301 U.S. at 640)

> Spreading from State to State, unemployment is an ill not particular but general, which may be checked, if Congress so determines by the resources of the Nation. . . . But the ill is all one, or at least not greatly different, whether men are thrown out of work because there is no longer work to do or because the disabilities of age make them incapable of doing it. Rescue becomes necessary irrespective of the cause. The hope behind this statute is to save men and women from the rigors of the poorhouse as well as from the haunting fear that such a lot awaits them when journey's end is near. (301 U.S. at 641)

> The problem is plainly national in area and dimensions. Moreover, laws of the separate states cannot deal with it effectively. Congress, at least, had a basis for that belief. States and local governments are often lacking in the resources that are necessary to finance an adequate program of security for the aged. This is brought out with a wealth of illustration in recent studies of the problem. Apart from the failure of resources, states and local governments are at times reluctant to increase so heavily the burden of taxation to be borne by their residents for fear of placing themselves in a position of economic disadvantage as compared with neighbors or competitors. We have seen this in our study of the problem of unemployment compensation. Steward Machine Co. v. Davis, supra. A system of old age pensions has special dangers of its own, if put in force in one state and rejected in another. The existence of such a system is a bait to the needy and dependent elsewhere, encouraging them to migrate and seek a haven of repose. Only a power that is national can serve the interests of all. (301 U.S. at 644)

Social insurance provisions of the Social Security Act are directly administered by the federal government, and clients are served by Social Security field offices. The growth of federal participation in social insurance and in welfare programs since 1935 has been phenomenal and has become the subject of increasing controversy.

THE OPERATION OF GRANTS-IN-AID

Federal grants-in-aid to state and local government are of special interest to social workers because they support public assistance, child welfare, services to crippled children, and maternal and child health programs. Special grants have been intended to encourage state initiative. Monies are allocated by a formula that takes into account population, income, and other factors related to need.

Grants-in-aid have been made in many other areas—rehabilitation services, hospital construction, mental health planning and construction, education, environmental protection projects, and highways, to name but a few. The states theoretically have the option of applying or not applying for such grants. Obviously, states apply because they need the funds, but then they must conform with many specific requirements. For social welfare programs, the state must file a plan for spending the funds, make periodic reports on how the plan was carried out, and be subject to federal audit concerning disbursement of funds.

States may not pass laws or frame regulations that are inconsistent with federal statutes as provided by the supremacy clause of the U.S. Constitution (Article 6, Section 2): the laws of the United States "shall be the supreme law of the land; and the judges in every state shall be bound thereby, anything in the Constitution or laws of any state to the contrary notwithstanding."

Grants-in-aid must generally add to the programs and not replace state monies. In P.L. 93-247, the Child Abuse Prevention and Treatment Act, the accompanying regulations require an affirmative answer to the question "Does the state provide that the aggregate of support for programs or projects related to child abuse and neglect *assisted* by State funds has not been reduced below the level the state has been providing?" This **maintenance of present effort** means that federal dollars cannot be used to replace state dollars.

Requirements for receiving federal funds are specific. Although some state child abuse laws covered children up to age twelve, while others covered children up to age twenty-one, federal regulations now specify that the program must include children up to age eighteen. Some states object, but the money offered is usually attractive enough for them to accept federal regulations, albeit in some cases reluctantly.

Traditionally, the states were expected to bear a large part of the financial responsibility for public social services, but the federal share has increased—most notably by the federalization of the Supplementary Security Income Program. Court decisions have helped to increase the demands from the states for federalization. Shapiro v. Thompson, 394 U.S. 618 (1969), outlawed residence requirements for public assistance and affirmed the fundamental right of interstate movement. This major decision held that discrimination against recent arrivals deprived those otherwise eligible of equal protection. This led to demands for total federal financing of assistance programs, especially from the states that provided higher benefits. State officials unsuccessfully applied pressure to federalize Aid to Families with Dependent Children (AFDC) or to substitute a negative income tax. The Reagan administration promoted plans for the federal government to take full responsibility for Medicaid while the states would pick up the costs for other welfare programs, including AFDC. The states opposed these plans because of added cost to them.

Grants-in-aid vs. Revenue-sharing

Many citizens resented both the taxing power of the federal government and arbitrary regulations and guidelines. They wanted to see revenue-sharing replace grants-in-aid, to give states and localities more flexibility. However, social welfare generally has not fared well from revenue-sharing. It is difficult for social services to compete with priorities for new fire trucks or a new police station. Federal control is often resisted, but federal requirements may be more successful in meeting the concerns of social work than increased state or local discretion. Such standards have tended to help maintain quality and reduce discrimination.

President Reagan has combined a number of federal programs into block grants that give state and local governments broader discretion but significantly fewer federal dollars. Congress has successfully resisted the proposed curtailment of some social programs which was to result from the block grants.

FEDERAL GRANTS

For the most part, grant programs are located in the U.S. Department of Health and Human Services, HHS, which has been reorganized several times in recent years. Social workers from other agencies are most likely to deal with federal programs in HHS which provide public assistance, child welfare and child care, health and mental health, and services for older people. Correctional programs are supported through the U.S. Department of Justice. The U.S. Department of Labor is responsible for dealing with unemployment. The U.S. Department of Education was separated from Health and Welfare in the Carter administration, and President Reagan proposed its abolition.

Direct Operation of Services

The federal government both operates programs directly and gives grants. It operates the Old Age and Survivors Insurance Program (usually called Social Security); Medicare, for the aged, is also a federal program. The Veterans Administration, the Public Health Service, and the federal correctional system are important users of specialized social work personnel. Military outposts throughout the world use human services workers.

Freedom of Information

The legal right of access to public records is of long standing, but agencies have not always been cooperative. The Freedom of Information Act of 1966 (80 Stat. 250) sets forth the information to which the public is entitled and the machinery for compelling disclosure. Social workers who are investigating the operation of agencies may be particularly interested in this act. Thurman (1973:v) offers an explanation for freedom of information:

> The common law had always recognized a legal right of access to public records prior to any statute authorizing such disclosure. Both in England and in the United States, the courts would enforce the citizen's right of access against any public official who denied that right unlawfully. However, under the common law, the person seeking access to records had to establish an "interest" and a "legitimate purpose." This act requires no such showing. Its intention is to afford broad access to public records to all citizens, whether or not they are able to demonstrate any personal or particular interest in the material which they seek to examine.
>
> Essentially, the "Freedom of Information Act" provides for (1) publication in the daily Federal Register of data concerning an agency's organization, functions, and rules of procedure; (2) making available for public inspection all orders, decisions, transcripts of testimony, manuals, etc.—with certain specified exceptions—primarily for the protection of privacy and providing an index to these documents; (3) an appeal procedure in the event an agency bureaucrat declines to furnish information guaranteed under the Act.

Federal law requires some fifty federal agencies to conduct their business regularly in public session. Meetings can be closed only for one of the following reasons: (1) national defense or foreign policy considerations; (2) agency personnel rules and practices; (3) information required by other laws to be kept confidential; (4) trade secrets or commercial information received under a pledge of confidentiality; (5) accusation of a crime; (6) disclosing information that would constitute an unwarranted invasion of privacy; (7) certain law enforcement investigatory records; (8) bank examination records and financial audits; (9) information that would lead to financial speculation; and (10) involvement in federal or state civil actions. Informal contacts between agency officials and outsiders to discuss pending business are banned. Transcripts of closed meetings are required.

STATE SOCIAL SERVICES

The primary responsibility for administration and operation of social welfare programs lies with states and to a lesser extent with the counties and cities. Both are the costs of specialized programs and dependence on larger governmental units have increased. Control has shifted to those who provide the money. Federal officials prefer state-level rather than local administration of social services, because there are fewer people to deal with and programs are more uniform.

Legal Authority

Although state programs differ, in each case their authority comes from the statutes. The organizational units are named in state statutes and their powers and duties are defined there. The simplest system involves directors appointed by the governor for the several departments of state government. A director is generally confirmed by the senate, but serves at the pleasure of the governor and is directly responsible to him. The director is able to appoint some people to policy positions, but most employees are career civil servants. If there are many smaller departments, the pattern is decentralized. The existence of only a few large departments suggests increased power for the large units.

Organization

The departments of the state of Illinois illustrate a decentralized system (Chapter 127 Ill. Rev. Stat.): In 1985 they included Departments of Agriculture, Labor, Mines and Minerals, Transportation, Mental Health and Developmental Disabilities, Public Health, Registration and Education, Rehabilitation Services, Conservation, Insurance, Law Enforcement, Corrections, Revenue, Financial Institutions, Public Aid, Children and Family Services, Commerce and Community Affairs, Central Management Services, Aging, Veterans Affairs, Nuclear Safety, Human Rights, Energy and Natural Resources, and Alcoholism and Substance Abuse.

A centralized structure would perhaps involve combining the programs for mental health, public aid, corrections, and children and family services into a Department of Human Services or a Department of Social Welfare. Public health and education would be likely to remain separate from such a department, but the vocational rehabilitation program and the program serving crippled children might well be included. Powers and duties are illustrated by the Illinois Department of Children and Family Services (Ill. Rev. Stat. 23-5005): "To provide direct child welfare services when not available through other public or private child care or program facilities." The definitions and ramifications of this mandate are spelled out in three columns of explanation.

Other forms of organization for state services are less popular than executive departments. Sometimes a commission of prominent citizens is used to reduce political influence. The commission hires the executive and may be able to assure better continuity of leadership. If the agency has to be included in the governor's budget, however, politics may be necessary to obtain fiscal resources.

Education departments sometimes have an elected superintendent. More often, a state board of education appoints the chief school officer. A state's powers in education are usually limited, but with increasing state financial aid, regulatory powers have increased.

State agencies may be organized to offer services through a number of decentralized field offices. Attempts are made to involve the various communities in decision-making through advisory boards and other mechanisms. In addition, decentralization encourages regional or field offices to develop their own priorities and to plan and defend their own budget requests.

Funding The state operates its programs from tax funds, federal grants, and payments from users. The state may also be the recipient of foundation grants for research or other special purposes. While foundations used to give funds only to private agencies, grants to public bodies for innovative purposes are now common.

One of the major responsibilities of state agencies is to obtain and account for federal funds. The state agency is in the same position with federal officials as voluntary agencies are with state agencies. They all have to comply with certain standards for program and fiscal auditing. Just as the state is concerned about the various federal requirements, the voluntary agencies question state procedures.

Many state departments have the power to buy care and service from individuals or private organizations. A state child welfare program may pay a private agency to provide foster or institutional care for a child. The agency then bills the state for the care, and the state reimburses the cost. Citizens object less to purchase of care and services by public agencies than to block grants or subsidies that do not specify clearly how the money is to be used.

Program authority in the statutes is meaningless if there is no provision for fiscal support. The fiscal flexibility of a public agency is often determined by the form of its budget. Specific line items provide less flexibility than more general categories. A line item for purchase of child care makes it impossible for an agency to use those monies for its own child care services. A category like "child care and counseling" would permit more options.

CIVIL SERVICE Selection of public employees by merit rather than political patronage has been provided by the federal government and by the states. The civil service system involves competitive examinations. Usually employees must be selected from the three names at the top of the list on examination performance. Policy-making positions are exempt from the civil service system. Civil service often has disadvantages in that employees need not be very creative to retain their jobs and salary provisions attached to the system often make it impossible to recognize meritorious performance adequately. Nonetheless, the system is probably superior to a system in which jobs are given out to members of a victorious political party, the patronage system.

The U.S. Supreme Court ruled on use of patronage in Elrod v. Burns, 427 U.S. 347 (1976). Republican employees of the Cook County, Illinois, sheriff's office brought a class action suit alleging they were discharged solely because they were not members of the Democratic party. The Supreme Court upheld the appeals court decision:

> In summary, patronage dismissals severely restrict political belief and association. Though there is a vital need for government efficiency and effectiveness, such dismissals are on balance not the least restrictive means for fostering that end. There is also a need to insure that policies which the electorate has sanctioned are effectively implemented. That interest can be fully satisfied by limiting patronage dismissals to policymaking positions. Finally, patronage dismissals cannot be justified by their contribution to the proper functioning of our democratic process through their assistance to partisan politics since political parties are nurtured by other, less intrusive and equally effective methods. More fundamentally, however, any contribution of patronage dismissals to the democratic process does not suffice to override their severe encroachment on First Amendment freedoms. We hold, therefore, that the practice of patronage dismissals is unconstitutional under the First and Fourteenth Amendments, and the respondents thus stated a valid claim for relief. (427 U.S. at 372)

VOLUNTARY SERVICES

The legal authority for voluntary services is quite different from that for public agencies, and the situation is confusing because the name of the agency does not indicate its auspices. For example, "Smith County Mental Health Clinic" could be either public or voluntary.

A voluntary or private agency is generally organized as a not-for-profit corporation chartered by the secretary of state. The office of the state attorney general may have an interest in its fund-raising activities because it is concerned with consumer fraud. The application for a charter typically requests a statement of purpose and the names of the officers and directors of the proposed corporation.

Many social agencies are included under the licensing laws of the state. When this is the case, the state agency holding the licensing authority investigates the application for incorporation and makes a recommendation to the secretary of state. Agencies handling adoptions or providing child care are generally licensed by the child welfare authority and those providing mental health services are licensed by the Department of Mental Health. Regulation of hospitals and nursing homes is provided by the Department of Public Health. Licenses may be withheld or suspended for cause. Without a license, the agency may not operate. On an appeal to restore a license, an administrative hearing is held first. If the finding is negative, recourse comes through the courts.

Licensing statutes usually establish basic policies. Regulations made by the licensing authority fill in the details. For example, for a day-care center, the square footage of floor space required per child, the number of toilets, and the fire protection provisions are specified in the regulations rather than in the licensing law. The operator of a facility generally regards the licensing standards as reasonable minimum standards for care. Licensing staff members like to work with more ideal standards and use their roles for program consultation in order to upgrade services that already meet accepted minimums. The program improvement function is recognized in the licensing law in some states.

Two types of private agencies subject to licensing are most frequently operated for profit: day-care centers and nursing homes.

How Private Are Private Agencies?

Many people have thought of private agencies as the embodiment of private charity because such agencies have considerable freedom to develop programs as they see fit. It is no longer that simple. Agencies that are members of the United Way are restricted by that body in both raising and spending funds. Also, receipt of large amounts of public money for purchase of care and service have made voluntary agencies semiprivate. Private agencies may obtain local governmental money from revenue-sharing or from tax income for mental health or other purposes. Often the agencies must be politically sensitive to the wishes of the county board or other governmental bodies to receive such funds.

New Attitudes of Citizen Givers

Inflation has made it difficult to expand existing programs with private contributions; programs have been lucky even to maintain their current volume of service. In addition, the citizen giver who is paying higher taxes feels that the public agencies will have to assume responsibility for the dependent members of society. Therefore the private contributor may support those causes in which his or her family can participate and let taxes support the poor. These attitudes are in direct contrast to President Reagan's emphasis on returning to private resources to support welfare endeavors.

RULE-MAKING AND PROCESSING GRIEVANCES

The rule-making powers of public agencies have implications for voluntary agencies and for clients. Rule-making is a major invention of modern government. As we saw in Chapter 2, federal regulations are published in the *Federal Register*.

The rules spell out the means to carry out the intent of a statute and provide a framework for program operation. Tentative rules are drafted and published in order to provide for public response before they become final. Once the rules have been adopted, an agency must live within them.

Increasingly, both state and federal agencies sponsor public hearings when major changes in rules are proposed. Agencies that are subject to license have a strong concern with licensing standards. Their suggestions in public hearings often serve to modify the rules to be adopted by the licensee.

Questions for Review

1.   What proportion of total welfare spending comes from federal sources?

2.   Identify the reason for the large increase in public assistance expenditures since the mid-1970s.

3.   Why did President Pierce veto the proposal by Dorothea Dix to benefit the "indigent insane"?

4.   Why is the constitutionality of grants-in-aid of major importance to social services?

5.   On what basis were grants-in-aid affirmed in *Massachusetts v. Mellon?*

6.   What major authority concerning the general welfare is clarified by *United States v. Butler* ?

7.   According to *Helvering v. Davis,* why should a system of old-age pensions be national in scope?

8.   What two major provisions were omitted in the original Social Security Act?

9.   What responsibilities do the states assume when they apply for federal grants-in-aid?

10. Explain the philosophy of the Reagan administration concerning federal block grants.

11. Explain requirements for "maintenance of present effort."

12. Why did *Shapiro v. Thompson* increase the demand to federalize welfare programs?

13. Where does the authority for operating state public agencies originate?

14. What conveys legal authority to voluntary agencies?

15. What two types of agencies are most typically operated for profit?

16. Explain how and why some voluntary agencies are licensed.

17. What constraints restrict the independence of voluntary agencies?

Questions for Debate and Discussion

1. Summarize the arguments for and against grants-in-aid versus revenue-sharing or block grants.

2. What are the advantages and disadvantages of a centralized state structure over having more separate governmental departments?

3. Explain and evaluate a commission pattern of organization for state agencies.

4. Why are many voluntary agencies having difficulty maintaining their present scope and impact? What are some solutions to their problems?

Selected Readings   Buntz, Gregory C., and Beryl Radin. "Managing Intergovernmental Conflicts: The Case of Human Services." *Public Administration Review* 43 (1983): 403–410.

Gossen, Hermann H. *The Law of Human Relations and the Rules of Human Actions Derived Therefrom.* Cambridge, Mass: MIT Publications, 1983.

Hagebak, Beaumont R. "The Forgiveness Factor: Taking the Risk Out of Efforts to Integrate Human Services." *Public Order Review* 42 (1982):72–76.

Lorenz, Patsy H. "The Politics of Fund Raising through Grantsmanship in the Human Services." *Public Administration Review* 42 (1982): 244–251.

Prottas, Jeffrey Manditch. "The Cost of Free Services: Organizational Impediments to Public Services." *Public Administration Review* 41 (1981): 526–534.

The Courts and the Use of Evidence

CHAPTER

5

Criminal Procedure and Criminal Justice

Serving clients who are charged with criminal acts, members of the family of the accused, and victims of crimes requires that the social worker understand the criminal justice system. Social workers also serve on court staffs and carry out investigations for pre-sentencing, probation, or parole. They may be involved as well with processing alleged criminals, improving prison conditions, and developing programs for education and rehabilitation.

The decision-making process in criminal justice is different from that in most other areas of social work practice. The law is concerned with alleged transgressions, not with conforming behavior or good intentions. Theoretically, a person can avoid contact with the law by knowing in advance what acts are unlawful and the penalties for them. Another difference is that the convicted criminal is an involuntary client; like the other officials in corrections, the social worker is perceived as an authority figure within the system.

A new federal Comprehensive Crime Control Act (P.L.98-473) became law in the fall of 1984. Several of its major provisions are included in this chapter.

CIVIL AND CRIMINAL LAW

Civil law concerns settling disputes between individuals or organizations. The alleged injuries are called **torts**. The typical remedy is provided by damages paid to the party who can demonstrate the basis for his or her injury to the court. Even highly motivated disputants tend to accept the ultimate findings of the courts and rarely visit revenge on an adversary once the courts have acted.

In addition to disputes between individuals, major conflicts with the law include breaches of the peace and illegal conduct. Maintaining law and order is a major task of law enforcement personnel. A major role is responding to family disputes that affect the peace. The presence of the police is also supposed to prevent illegal conduct.

The police apprehend violators and testify about their behavior in court. Correctional programs are used to protect society, to carry out sanctions against law violators, and to attempt to rehabilitate offenders.*

---

* For a view stressing training and opposing rehabilitation, see Bean, 1976.

Criminal law deals with actions that threaten the well-being of the state. A **crime** is an injury against the state that may be punished by fine or imprisonment or both. The fine goes to the state treasury. One act may be both a crime and a tort because it jeopardizes the community and at the same time inflicts private personal injury. Kerper (1972: 31) provides an example:

> If A attacks B without provocation and puts out B's eye, the state will punish A in a criminal action and fine him, imprison him, or both. The victim B, in a civil action, can recover money damages from A for the personal injury he suffered in losing an eye. A's unprovoked attack was an offense against the state, hence a crime. At the same time, it inflicted injury on the individual B, and was a tort against B. In the criminal action against A, the state (not B) would be the plaintiff, and the form of the action would be (for example) State of Wyoming v. A. The remedy sought in this action would be the fine or imprisonment of A. In the civil action against A, B (not the state) would be the plaintiff, and the form of the action would be B v. A. The remedy sought in the civil action would be money damages to be paid by A to B. We can distinguish the criminal action from the civil action in two ways: (1) by the remedy sought, and (2) by the character of the plaintiff, i.e., the state or an individual.

For example, although John Hinckley was acquitted of the attempted assassination of President Reagan because of an insanity plea, civil suits were filed against him by those persons who were wounded in the attempt.

Laws frequently elicit a sharp conflict in values. For instance, regulation of marijuana or abortion generates different procedures and sanctions from state to state. A vast legal mechanism has been developed by government agencies as well. General agency authority comes from statutes but is often spelled out in the form of complex administrative regulations.

The law cannot exist independently from other socializing elements in society— the family, the church, and the school. Values inherent in these institutions simplify the task of law enforcement. While the social worker may be assigned by the police department, a court, or a correctional program to work with the lawbreaker, forcing the offender to comply with rehabilitation efforts will achieve only limited success. The relationship may begin authoritatively, but it must develop trust to ensure cooperation.

CLASSIFICATION OF CRIMES

A **crime** involves a law prohibiting the act, the criminal action, the intent of the actor, an injury, a causal relationship between the action and the injury and finally a penalty. If no punishment is prescribed by law, there can be no crime.

Crimes are usually classified by their seriousness. **Felonies** are offenses punishable by death or imprisonment in the penitentiary (not in a jail). Lesser offenses are **misdemeanors.** Some states classify all offenses involving imprisonment of a year or longer as felonies. Either the place of punishment or its length may be the basis for classification.

Crimes may be directed against persons, property, morality, decency, public peace or tranquility, or the functioning of government. Other classifications include violent crimes, such as murder or armed robbery; nonviolent crimes, such as forgery; and victimless crimes like prostitution. Persons interested in a more detailed classification of crimes will find the Model Penal Code (1962) of interest.

A crime committed by a juvenile is termed a **delinquent act.** As we will see in the following chapter, the term *juvenile* is not synonymous with *infant* or *minor.*

The Uniform Crime Reporting Program provides the classification system used by most law enforcement agencies (Federal Bureau of Investigation, 1980). Offenses in Uniform Crime Reporting are divided into two groupings, designated Part I offenses and Part II offenses. Crime rates are generally based on Part I offenses. Offense and arrest information are reported for Part I offenses on a monthly basis, whereas only arrest information is reported for Part II offenses.

Part I offenses include seven different categories: criminal homicide; forcible rape; robbery; aggravated assault; burglary, or breaking and entering; larceny theft; motor vehicle theft; and arson. **Part II offenses** include simple nonaggravated assaults; forgery and counterfeiting; fraud; embezzlement; buying, receiving, or possessing stolen property; vandalism; carrying or possessing weapons; prostitution and commercialized vice; sex offenses (except forcible rape, prostitution, and commercialized vice); drug abuse violations; gambling; offenses against the family and children; driving under the influence; violation of liquor laws; drunkenness; disorderly conduct; vagrancy; and all other offenses. Suspicion arrests where persons are released are classified separately. Running away, curfew violations, and loitering are described as **Part II juvenile offenses.**

MAJOR CRIMES AGAINST PERSONS

The social worker is more likely to be involved with offenders accused of crimes against persons, as opposed to crimes against property. Murder and assault are important not only in conflicts between adults but also in child abuse. Rape and incest are associated with frustrations and anger. Robbery is often identified with unemployment and poverty, while extortion and embezzlement are less commonly acts of the poor and the emotionally disturbed.

Homicide

Homicide may be a crime or a justifiable act. **Criminal homicide** involves the death of a human being by the act of another without justification or excuse. **Murder** is the deliberate premeditated killing of another person. This offense is often classified as murder in the **first degree**. Murder in the heat of passion is a less serious offense and is classified in the **second degree**. Although the intent is not to commit murder, a burglar who grabs a gun in the house he is robbing and kills someone will be tried for murder in the first degree. (Under the felony murder rule, one felony transfers to another.) If robbery is intended, the murder could not be considered a crime of passion.

The term **manslaughter** is used for acts involving recklessness or negligence, but not malice or disregard for human life. Some states distinguish degrees, including voluntary or involuntary manslaughter. Death resulting from a fight would be voluntary manslaughter; killing someone while playing with a gun could be considered involuntary. Manslaughter involving driving a motor vehicle may be a separate category.

Assault

Assault is similar to homicide, except that death does not result. **Assault** involves threat of bodily harm or fear of bodily harm created by a person who is able and intends to commit the offense. Assault may lead to **battery**, or touching a person with an injurious purpose. **Aggravated assault** involves threat of serious bodily injury as with a weapon. **Simple assault** involves threat of lesser injuries. The former is a felony, the latter is generally a misdemeanor. In general usage, *assault* is often used to encompass both the threat and the injury. The Model Penal Code

(Section 211) classifies "recklessly endangering another person" and "terroristic threats" with assault.

Rape

Rape has traditionally involved sexual intercourse by a man with a woman not his wife against her will, compelled by force or threat. **Statutory rape**—sexual intercourse with a female below a given age—need not involve threat; in the Model Penal Code (Section 213.13) the female must be sixteen or under and the male four years or more older than the female for statutory rape to be charged. **Criminal sexual assault** is replacing the term *rape* in some state statutes, because it applies to both men and women.

The statutes also include other sexual offenses. In many states, **deviate sexual behavior** includes oral or anal intercourse between husband and wife. The conduct described in modern marriage manuals such as *The Joy of Sex* is often illegal. The U.S. Supreme Court refused to review a lower court decision upholding the constitutionality of a Virginia law against sodomy (Doe v. Commonwealth's Attorney for City of Richmond, 425 U.S. 901 [1976]). Statutes in a number of other states legalize such practices by consenting adults in private.

Spousal rape has become an actionable offense in several states, and this trend can be expected to continue.

Robbery

Robbery is both a crime against the person and a crime against property. The elements include personal threat and unlawful taking of personal property to be used for the robber's benefit. Robbery is often accompanied by both larceny and assault. According to this definition, snatching a purse without warning is theft because it lacks threat. Robbery often takes place with a deadly weapon. Armed robbery, as we have indicated, can involve the death penalty. The value of the property taken may also influence penalties for robbery.

CRIMINAL RESPONSIBILITY

Criminal responsibility requires awareness of purpose and an act to be committed knowingly, recklessly, or negligently. The punishment for acting knowingly and with purpose is greater than that for acting negligently or recklessly. **Negligence** involves violating the standards of the "reasonable person." **Recklessness** involves similar violations of the standards of the "law-abiding person." Such subtle distinctions between criteria lead to disagreements among judges and juries alike.

CRIMINAL PENALTIES

Crimes that involve the greatest damage to the victim tend to bring the most severe punishment. Treason, murder, and kidnapping have often carried the death penalty. In some states, armed robbery and rape have also been punishable by death.

The same types of crimes may carry different penalties because of varying standards of society. Drug use and gambling, for example, are both victimless crimes, but possession of drugs carries a higher penalty than gambling.

The Death Penalty

Most social workers are opposed to the death penalty because they consider it to be a "cruel and unusual punishment" and do not find that it deters crime. Thirty-eight states have laws authorizing capital punishment. Social workers often may be involved in helping the families of those sentenced to death, but there is also a strong philosophical interest in the death penalty—generally in opposition to it. Until an execution in Utah in 1977, the death penalty had not been carried out in the United States for ten years. Between 1977 and the end of 1983 there were twelve executions. There were 21 in 1984 and 5 in January 1985. In a typical year there are about 1,300 people on death row. Capital punishment with its drawn-out legal process can still be considered both indecisive and cruel.

In 1972, in Furman v. Georgia, 408 U.S. 238, the U.S. Supreme Court struck down the death penalty as unconstitutional because it was "cruel and unusual punishment" and therefore violated the Eighth Amendment of the Constitution. In 1976, the Court declared constitutional laws providing for the death penalty in Georgia, Florida, and Texas and voided laws of Louisiana and North Carolina. In Gregg v. Georgia, 428 U.S. 153 (1976), Justice Potter Stewart's prevailing opinion held in part:

> The basic concern of Furman centered on those defendants who were being condemned to death capriciously and arbitrarily. Under the procedures before the Court in that case, sentencing authorities were not directed to give attention to the nature or circumstances of the crime committed or to the character or record of the defendant. Left unguided, juries imposed the death sentence in a way that could only be called freakish. The new Georgia sentencing procedures, by contrast, focus the jury's attention on the particularized nature of the crime and the particularized characteristics of the individual defendant. While the jury is permitted to consider any aggravating or mitigating circumstances, it must find and identify at least one statutory aggravating factor before it may impose a penalty of death. In this way the jury's discretion is channeled. No longer can a jury wantonly and freakishly impose the death sentence; it is always circumscribed by the legislative guidelines. In addition, the review function of the Supreme Court of Georgia affords additional assurance that the concerns that prompted our decision in Furman are not present to any significant degree in the Georgia procedure applied here. (428 U.S. at 206)

In Woodson v. North Carolina, 428 U.S. 280 (1976), the North Carolina statute was found to violate the Eighth and Fourteenth Amendments because it departed markedly from the contemporary standards respecting the imposition of the punishment of death, gave unbridled jury discretion in the imposition of capital sentences, and failed to allow consideration of relevant aspects of the character and record of each convicted defendant.

State legislatures favoring the death penalty have made their laws conform to those acceptable to the U.S. Supreme Court. Decisions in the early 1980s had little effect on capital punishment. In many states where it has been authorized, there is still a great reluctance to use it.

A person sentenced to life imprisonment was later retried because women had been automatically excused from jury service. At the second trial, the death penalty was prescribed, but the U.S. Supreme Court held that this constituted double jeopardy and violated Fifth Amendment rights (Bullington v. Missouri, 451 U.S. 430 [1981]).

In Eddings v. Oklahoma, 455 U.S. 104 (1982), the Supreme Court held that a death sentence imposed on a defendant who was sixteen years old at the time of his crime be vacated because the trial court refused to consider his family history as a mitigating factor in the death penalty. The Court did not rule on whether execution of a person this age or younger would have constituted cruel or unusual punishment.

The Court has also ruled that a nontriggerman in a felony murder who had not intended that a killing occur or that lethal force be used in the commission of the felony may not be sentenced to death (Enmund v. Florida, 458 U.S. 782 [1982]).

As a result of the decision in Barefoot v. Estelle, 463 U.S. 880 (1983), last-minute habeas corpus appeals to the U.S. Supreme Court may be reduced, but this will not necessarily lead to increased executions because of opposition to carrying out the death penalty.

LEGAL DEFENSES

Defenses for a crime may be used to establish legal innocence or to reduce the penalty. Defenses include:

Age.   Below a certain specified age (often thirteen or fourteen) a child cannot be expected to know enough about distinguishing right from wrong to commit a criminal offense.

Insanity.   Unsoundness of mind is determined legally rather than medically. Section 4.01 of the Model Penal Code illustrates how general the standard is and how difficult it is to interpret the definition in a specific case:

> A person is not responsible for criminal conduct if at the time of such conduct as a result of mental disease or defect he lacks substantial capacity either to appreciate the wrongfulness of his conduct or to conform his conduct to the requirements of the law.

Four different rules are applied in the insanity plea: (1) the M'Naghten rule, developed in England; the "right and wrong" test, from Durham v. United States, 214 F.2d 862 (D.C.Cir.1954); the "irresistible impulse" test; and the American Law Institute rule, which is now most widely applied. The last rule has been included in the excerpt from the Model Penal Code above.

In the insanity defense, both expert testimony and the social history of the accused are relied on. Insanity at the time an act is committed does not mean that the accused will be incompetent at the time of the trial. Recovery from temporary insanity is often claimed.

The Comprehensive Crime Control Act of 1984 alters the use of the insanity plea in federal cases by shifting the burden of proof of insanity to the defendant. It will be interesting to see whether this provision will be enacted into state law.

Impairment of the capacity of a defendant as described above may also be used as an argument for imprisonment rather than capital punishment.

Intoxication.   Extreme drunkenness may be considered equivalent to insanity.

Duress or Coercion or Threat of Force.   These become possible defenses if the accused was unable to resist.

Military orders, consent of the victim, entrapment by a public law enforcement official, or **ignorance** are other defenses. **Self-defense** is also commonly used in cases of homicide. Use of force to carry out one's public duty and to protect others is frequently used as a defense by police officers. In such instances, the issue is the appropriate use of deadly force.

Criminal responsibility is often restricted if a criminal action is not begun within a specified time. In the Model Penal Code, a felony of the first degree must be prosecuted within three years, but a petty misdemeanor must be prosecuted within six months. In addition, criminal responsibility has been eliminated if the person is found to be insane, mentally retarded, or otherwise incapable of criminal intent. Deaf people or those who speak some obscure foreign language may not come to trial unless they can understand the proceedings or assist with their own defense.

CONSTITU-TIONAL PROTECTIONS

To bring suit in a criminal action requires an actual controversy. Arrest cannot be based on mere suspicion but must be based on information that is "reasonably trustworthy" and sufficient to support the belief that an offense has been or is being committed. Both criminal convictions and adjudications of delinquency require proof beyond a reasonable doubt. A preponderance of evidence is not adequate.

After all circumstances have been considered and all witnesses heard, the state must prove that its evidence sustains the allegations concerning the defendant's guilt. The accused in the criminal process is protected by the Bill of Rights of the U.S. Constitution:

The *Fourth Amendment* deals with searches and seizures:

The right of the people to be secure in their persons, houses, papers, and effects, against unreasonable searches and seizures, shall not be violated, and no warrants shall issue, but upon probable cause, supported by oath or affirmation, and particularly describing the place to be searched, and the persons or things to be seized.

The *Fifth Amendment* establishes the grand jury as the mechanism for indictment for an "infamous" crime and also guarantees due process:

No person shall be held to answer for a capital, or otherwise infamous crime, unless on a presentment or indictment of a Grand Jury, except in cases arising in the land or naval forces, or in the militia, when in actual service in time of war or public danger; nor shall any person be subject for the same offense to be twice put in jeopardy of life or limb; nor shall be compelled in any criminal case to be a witness against himself, nor be deprived of life, liberty, or property, without due process of law; nor shall private property be taken for public use, without just compensation.

In the *Sixth Amendment* is the right to a speedy and public trial by a jury:

In all criminal prosecutions, the accused shall enjoy the right to a speedy and public trial, by an impartial jury of the State and district wherein the crime shall have been committed, which district shall have been previously ascertained by law, and to be informed of the nature and cause of the accusation; to be confronted with the witness against him; to have compulsory process for obtaining witnesses in his favor, and to have the assistance of counsel for his defense.

The Speedy Trial Act was passed by Congress in 1975 to limit the period between arrest and indictment to thirty-five days and to mandate a trial within one year unless delays are requested by the defendant.

The *Seventh Amendment* reserves the decision on facts to the jury:

> In suits at common law, where the value in controversy shall exceed twenty dollars, the right of trial by jury shall be preserved, and no fact tried by a jury, shall be otherwise reexamined in any court of the United States, than according to the rules of the common law.

The *Eighth Amendment* forbids excessive bail and cruel and unusual punishment:

> Excessive bail shall not be required, nor excessive fines imposed, nor cruel and unusual punishments inflicted.

Article 4 of the U.S. Constitution provides for full faith and credit of public acts in each state by every other state: an offender who flees to another state shall "be delivered up, to be removed to the state having jurisdiction of the scene." Extradition is covered in the Uniform General Extradition Act in force in forty-seven states.

The *Fourteenth Amendment*, covering due process and equal protection, has been used as justification for applying the provisions of the Bill of Rights to the states.

Rights in a Criminal Proceeding

In a criminal proceeding, the accused has the following rights: to be protected from unreasonable searches and seizures, to be informed of his or her constitutional rights, to remain silent, to avoid self-incrimination, and to have counsel at every stage of the proceeding. In addition, the accused must receive reasonable notice of the charges, be able to appear in court and confront witnesses, and have a fair, speedy, and public trial by jury. Finally, no one may be tried twice for the same offense.

The accused may use a writ of habeas corpus to obtain freedom at any time if the court determines there is no legal reason to hold him or her.

In the American adversary system, all accused are considered innocent until proven guilty, and all have the services of a lawyer to represent them. The jury evaluates the facts on behalf of the community.

Jurisdiction. The right of a court to hear a case is limited by geographic boundaries and the nature of the case. A juvenile court, for example, can hear only juvenile matters and does not deal with other topics. Determination of jurisdiction is especially important when the parties live in different states or counties. Federal and state jurisdiction are complex issues. Federal courts hear criminal matters when the offense is covered by federal statutes. The U.S. Supreme Court reviews criminal cases when a federal question has been successfully raised. The due process right guaranteed by the U.S. Constitution is frequently at issue in criminal cases reviewed by the Supreme Court.

Venue. The place of the trial is subject to specific rules. While criminal actions should be heard where the offense occurred, venue may be changed for cause. The potential effect of press coverage on a murder trial illustrates the possible need for change of venue.

DIVERSION

If everyone accused of a serious crime were actually incarcerated, the criminal justice system could not possibly cope with all the prisoners. The police in effect decide who actually goes into the system. Only about 20 percent of those involved with the police are arrested. The police divert many people through **station adjustments**—one-shot counseling and advice, followed by some assurance that the person will not repeat the act. A station adjustment culminates in release. A station adjustment may also include referral to a social agency. The diversion process is illustrated in Figure 5.1. A decision not to prosecute may be based on a judgment of the best strategy for rehabilitation or simply on the fact that the evidence is inadequate.

The criminal justice system can be thought of as a leaky funnel. It continues to function by means of perforations along the sides through which it can divert at least 50 percent of the cases before trial, thus relieving the pressure. Each of the major decision-makers listed in Figure 5.1 can use various mechanisms for diverting offenders, such as those listed on the right-hand side of the figure. When an offender has been diverted, he or she has been removed from the criminal justice system, at least for the present. Diversion is much more frequently used with juveniles than with adult offenders, but many adults are diverted too. The system is not efficient when persons charged with a serious crime may have to wait six months to a year before trial.

Pretrial diversion involves the decision not to prosecute on the condition that the accused does something in return. Enrolling in some type of rehabilitation program is a typical example. Social workers generally approve of such an alternative, but Nancy Goldberg (1973:490) of the National Legal Aid and Defenders Association indicated possible problems:

1. Diversion can be coercive in that the prosecutor might otherwise seek a maximum penalty.

2. Heavy reliance is placed on the correctional philosophy of the intake officer and his knowledge of services.

3. Failure in the rehabilitation program may affect subsequent sentencing.

4. Investigations related to diversion may violate the standard related to arrest that pre-sentence reports should not be initiated until an adjudication of guilt.

5. An innocent defendant may accept the offer of diversion rather than contest the charge.

6. As a safeguard the defense counsel should be made an integral part of the diversion proceedings.

INVESTIGATION AND ARREST

Sheriffs, police, and federal agents all engage in investigations of possible criminal behavior. In an arrest at the scene of a crime, **interrogation** is usually the first step. The police official must have probable cause to believe a crime has been committed. The investigator may stop and question persons who may have information about a suspected crime. **Stop and frisk**, a limited search of the outer clothing to detect weapons, is often used. A police officer may confiscate a weapon, but ultimately must either return it or arrest the person. See Terry v. State of Ohio, 392 U.S. 1 (1968).

When a complaint has been filed, **arrest** requires a warrant that sets forth the charge. **Warrants** must be based on probable cause, reasonable evidence that the

FIGURE 5.1
THE DIVERSION PROCESS

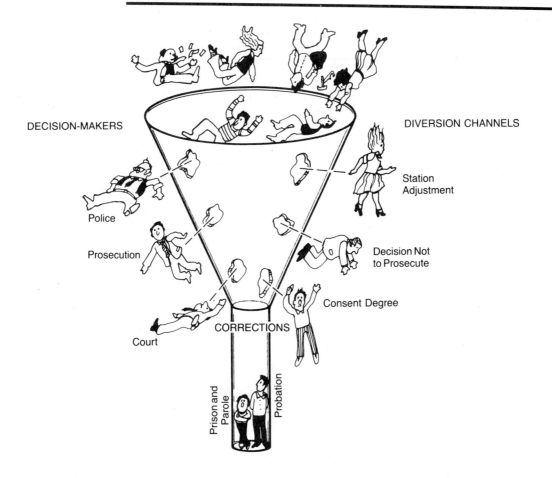

DECISION-MAKERS

DIVERSION CHANNELS

Station
Adjustment

Police

Prosecution

Decision Not
to Prosecute

Consent Degree

CORRECTIONS

Court

Prison and
Parole

Probation

accused committed the crime. A suspect is taken to the police station or sheriff's office. The intent to arrest must be understood.

Without the required warrant, searches to gather needed evidence are questionable (Mapp v. Ohio, 367 U.S. 643 [1961]). A warrant describing the place to be searched and the property to be seized, issued by a magistrate on the basis of probable cause, provides the best legal protection for a search. It must be supported by a sworn affidavit. Modifications and classifications of search and seizure rules will be discussed under that topic heading below.

The Suspect's Rights   Escobedo v. Illinois, 378 U.S. 478 (1964), and Miranda v. Arizona, 384 U.S. 436 (1966), determined that the suspect must be informed of his or her rights: that any statements the suspect makes may be used against him or her and that the suspect is entitled to counsel and may remain silent. If the suspect is not thus informed of the above rights, any statements the suspect makes are not admissible as evidence. A Uniform Arrest Act has been specifically proposed to assure the recommended procedures (Warner, 1942). Compliance with *Miranda* requirements can be verified if the confession is videotaped, an increasingly common procedure.

The right to counsel for capital crimes was established in Powell v. Alabama, 287 U.S. 45 (1932) and for other crimes in Gideon v. Wainwright, 372 U.S. 335 (1963). Misdemeanors involving loss of liberty were covered ten years later by Argersinger v. Hamlin, 407 U.S. 25 (1973).

In 1976 a Supreme Court ruling in Doyle v. Ohio, 426 U.S. 610 (1976), extended the *Miranda* principle: After being advised of the right to remain silent, a defendant's silence cannot be used against him or her in a trial. Prosecutors may not cross-examine defendants about why they did not tell their story when first arrested.

Brewer v. Williams, 430 U.S. 387 (1977), evoked strong disagreement in the Court over *Miranda* rights. The respondent who acted on an appeal by a police officer to locate the body of a victim to make possible "a Christian burial" was held to have been deprived of the right to assistance of counsel. Chief Justice Warren E. Burger's dissent illustrates the objections of the minority:

> Williams is guilty of the savage murder of a small child; no Member of the Court contends he is not. While in custody, and after no fewer than five warnings of his rights to silence and to counsel, he led police to the concealed body of his victim. The court concedes Williams was not threatened or coerced and that he spoke and acted voluntarily and with full awareness of his constitutional rights. In the face of all this, the Court now holds that because Williams was prompted by the detective's statement—not interrogation but a statement—the jury must not be told how the police found the body.

Search and Seizure

Since Mapp v. Ohio, 367 U.S. 643 (1961), the U.S. Supreme Court has considered many specific issues regarding the exclusion of evidence obtained from "unreasonable searches and seizures" under provisions of the Fourth Amendment. Decisions in 1983 included five that served to limit the exclusion of evidence and thereby reduce the need for a search warrant:

1. An electronic beeper could be used to monitor the movements of a car carrying material to produce illegal drugs (United States v. Knotts, 460 U.S. 276 [1983]).

2. The warrantless seizure of a balloon containing heroin in a routine police stop of a car was permissible (Texas v. Brown, 460 U.S. 730 [1983]).

3. Customs officials do not need search warrants to board seagoing vessels for routine document checks (United States v. Villamonte-Marquez, 462 U.S. 579 [1983]).

4. Police may detain a traveler's luggage briefly for a sniff test by a dog trained to detect narcotics (Singleton v. United States, certiorari denied, 459 U.S. 828 [1982]).

5. Police do not need a warrant to search the bags, purses, and personal effects of persons under arrest at the police station (Illinois v. Lafayette, 462 U.S. 640 [1983]).

Detaining Suspects

The U.S. Supreme Court held that police could stop or seize a person when they suspected he or she was about to commit a crime (Terry, v. Ohio, 392 U.S. 1 [1968]) or when the person was committing a crime at the moment of the stop (Adams v. Williams, 407 U.S. 143 [1972]).

In 1985, the court extended this power in a unanimous opinion. When police have a reasonable suspicion that a person they encounter is wanted in connection with a completed felony, they may stop the person to investigate that suspicion. The case involved stopping a suspect and checking "a wanted flyer" issued by a local police department (United States v. Hensley, 53 U.S.L.W. 4053).

BOOKING AND LEGAL APPEARANCES

Booking provides a record of the arrest and all the essential circumstances. It may include searches and the taking of photographs and fingerprints. Witnesses may be shown several possible people in a lineup, from which they are expected to identify the suspect. Since 1967, the attorney for the accused must be present at the preliminary lineup (United States v. Wade, 388 U.S. 218).

The accused is then taken before the court to be identified, to hear the nature of the charge, and to enter a plea of guilty. Bail is set so that the accused can be released from custody.

The Eighth Amendment prohibits excessive bail. Usually bail is obtained from persons called sureties (bond makers) who sign the bail bond, guaranteeing payment if the accused fails to appear in accordance with his or her agreement. While the sureties generally charge the accused only 10 percent of the face amount of the bail, they are obliged to pay the court the full amount in the event the accused fails to show up. However, the Comprehensive Crime Control Act of 1984 provides in federal cases that a defendant may be held without bail pending his or her trial if it is shown that the defendant is a "danger to the community."

Many poor people are unable to obtain bail and cannot be freed before trial. Recent practice has shown that most offenders will not skip out on a court appearance if they are released on recognizance—without any financial security such as bail or case bond. The accused merely signs his or her own bond. Release on recognizance reduces the time in jail and is considered a more humane procedure than bail. Very few people commit offenses while awaiting trial.

Generally, the next step is for the prosecution and the accused to appear at a preliminary hearing, during which a judge determines whether there was probable cause to arrest and sufficient proof to pursue prosecution. A *prima facie* case—one that will suffice until contradicted—must be established. The preliminary hearing gives defendants an early look at the state's case against them.

Indictment for felonies comes from the grand jury, which reviews the evidence to determine whether there is presumption of probable cause. The grand jury does not determine guilt or innocence. If probable cause is established, an indictment is returned, stipulating that the defendant be tried.

Although grand jury indictments are required by the U.S. Constitution in federal courts, many states use an information instead. An information is an accusation from a prosecuting attorney naming the defendant and setting forth the offense "against the peace and dignity of the state." The information is filed in the court where the defendant will be tried and replaces a grand jury indictiment.

After hearing the indictment or information, the defendant is asked, "How do you plead?" A plea of guilty is an admission to every allegation in the indictment or information. A plea of not guilty requires the state to prove all the material elements of its case. The time of the trial is set, and a new bond may be executed or the former one continued.

A study published by the U.S. Department of Justice Bureau of Justice Statistics (1984) indicated wide variety in the use of guilty pleas in fourteen jurisdictions studied. The median number of guilty pleas for each person who went to trial on a felony charge was 11, the lowest 4, and the highest 37. Clearly the vast majority of persons charged with felonies choose to plead guilty.

Plea-bargaining

Plea-bargaining is common. In plea-bargaining, negotiations between the prosecution and the defense result in a plea of guilty in return for an agreed-upon sentence. The accused is assured that the prosecutor will recommend a particular sentence, to which the accused agrees. Often the bargain includes a guilty plea to a lesser charge. Plea-bargaining saves the time and expense of a trial. The judge will generally follow the recommendation of the prosecutor, but need not do so; in that case, the plea of guilty can be withdrawn and the trial may proceed.

Before pleading guilty, it is essential that the accused understand the highest possible penalty that can be exacted. The accused must understand the nature of the charge and that a guilty plea waives the right to trial by jury. A plea of not guilty gives one the constitutional right to a speedy trial. Nevertheless, long delays may still result, making it especially difficult for the prisoner who is held without bail.

Under rule 11e of the Amended Federal Rules of Criminal Procedure, judges can approve or disapprove of plea bargains but shall not participate in any discussions or agreements regarding guilty pleas. Plea-bargaining involving a judge was prohibited in United States v. Werker, 535 F.2d 198 (2d Cir. 1976). The federal prosecutor had been asked to recommend a sentence of no more than ten years, rather than the maximum twenty-five years provided by law. The judge had been involved in the plea-bargaining discussion. The court held that "Participation in the plea bargaining process depreciates the image of the trial judge that is necessary to public confidence in the impartial and objective administration of criminal justice."

THE JURY TRIAL

While jury trials are guaranteed by the Sixth Amendment of the U.S. Constitution, they are rare. Some 90 percent of persons charged with felonies or misdemeanors plead guilty. Others waive the right to a jury trial. In a **bench trial**, the judge serves the role of the jury. If there is a jury, it decides questions of fact. Questions of law are always decided by the judge. Some states do not permit waiver of jury trial for offenses that can involve the death penalty.

The jury is selected by lot from a panel of qualified persons assembled by the court from voter lists and other recommendations. No person may be excluded from jury duty solely by race or color, but until recently, panels have included a smaller proportion of minority members and women than is found in the population. This situation leads the accused minority person to question whether the jury members are truly peers. The membership of women on juries is considered in Chapter 18. Since the 1960s, nearly all states have considered men and women equally for jury service. Juries must be drawn from lists representative of the community.

Two suits were brought by accused persons claiming that restrictions on jury selection deprived them of a fair trial. In Louisiana, women had to volunteer for jury service (Taylor v. Louisiana, 419 U.S. 522 [1975]). In Missouri, women had been allowed to claim automatic exemption from jury service (Duren v. Missouri, 439 U.S. 357 [1979]). Both practices were barred by the U.S. Supreme Court.

Recently the trend has been for a majority of jury members to be women, because men are more often excused from jury service.

Prospective jury candidates are usually questioned as a group by the court as to their qualifications. Then one name is selected. That person takes his or her place in the jury box, and the prosecutor and the defense attorney examine the candidate. A prospective juror may be excused for cause. Perhaps he or she has already formed an opinion on the case, is related to the defendant, or has a physical infirmity, such as deafness. Each side may also exercise peremptory challenges in order to reject a jury candidate without cause. For capital cases, twenty challenges are often allowed to each side. Fewer are permitted for lesser offenses. Finally, twelve members must be accepted by both sides.

After the evidence has been presented and witnesses examined, arguments to the jury are summarized by both sides. The judge charges the jury and explains the possible verdicts. In some states, both the verdict and the degree of the offense is determined by the jury.

The jury remains isolated until they either reach a verdict or find that they cannot agree unanimously. Members remain in the custody of the bailiff and may not be permitted to leave the jury room. They may request any necessary transcripts and may also seek additional instructions from the judge. Deliberations often begin by taking a vote. Discussions then go back and forth, with votes being retaken until unanimous agreement is achieved.

When the jury returns to the courtroom the verdict is read. Sometimes individual jurors are polled to attest to the accuracy of the verdict. If the verdict is "not guilty," the defendant will be released immediately; if "guilty," the time for sentencing may be set. Appeals may be filed or errors charged that can result in motions for a new trial.

<table>
<tr><td>

THE PRE-SENTENCE REPORT

</td><td>

The pre-sentence report, prepared by a probation officer, summarizes the background factors to be taken into account in sentencing an individual. The report includes such data as education and employment, family history, and the record of previous offenses. This evidence is used in determining the appropriate sentence. Exhibit 5.1 is a brief fictional version of a pre-sentence investigation report.*

</td></tr>
<tr><td>

SENTENCING

</td><td>

The maximum sentence is determined by the legislature. Under the laws of some states, habitual criminals (those with two or more felonies) may receive special sentences, such as life imprisonment. While the judge usually imposes sentences, in some states the jury passes sentence, especially in the case of the death penalty.

Sentences may be for a definite period of time or indeterminate; the judge may set a high minimum period to discourage early parole. When several crimes are involved, sentences may run concurrently or consecutively. The latter results in much longer sentences and is rarely followed. Concurrent sentences are adopted in the Model Penal Code. There are still many discrepancies in sentencing. Racial, age, and sex bias have been alleged.

</td></tr>
</table>

---

* From a forthcoming publication by the U.S. Probation Service.

EXHIBIT 5.1
EXAMPLE OF A PRE-SENTENCE REPORT

UNITED STATES DISTRICT COURT
Presentence report

Name:	Hesse, Herman	*Date:*	October 26, 1983
Address:	Hampden County House of Correction Hampden, MA	*Offense:*	Distribution of Heroin, 21:U.S.C.,841(a)(1) (one count)
Legal Residence:	71 Lee Avenue 28 Holyoke, MA	*Penalty:*	At 21:U.S.C.(b)(1)(A), 15 yrs. and/or $25,000 and SPT of at least 3 yrs.
Age:	28	*Plea:*	Guilty to D-MA indictment 9/29/83; will plead under Rule 20 to WD-TX indictment.
Date of Birth:	9/16/55		
Sex:	Male	*Verdict:*	
Citizenship:	U.S.	*Custody:*	In custody in lieu of $100,000 surety bond
Education:	10th grade	*Other Defendants:*	Nancy Rooney in federal custody in Texas pending trial
Marital Status:	Divorced		
Dependents:	One, in custody of wife	*Asst. U.S. Atty:*	David Crawford
Social Security No.:	987-65-4321	*Defense Counsel:*	Philip Pratt, Esq. (Retained)
FBI No.:	124 568 B9	*Sentencing Judge:*	Hon. Dwight Lester Reid

Charges Pending: Rule 20 WD-TX, Docket No. 82-00135-01, violation of 21:U.S.C., 952(a) and 960(a)(1) and 841(a)(1), two counts, same penalty 4

Offense

Prosecution Version. Herman Hesse is the subject of two separate indictments, one in the District of Massachusetts returned an indictment against Hesse and Nancy Rooney, charging that on June 23, 1983, they distributed a quantity of heroin. On August 26, 1983, a grand jury in El Paso, Texas, returned an indictment against Hesse and Rooney charging that they imported 101.7 grams of heroin into the United States on or about July 30, 1983, and that they distributed that heroin on the same date in El Paso, Texas. Hesse appeared on September 29, 1983, and pled guilty on the Massachusetts indictment. He has indicated his intention to plead guilty to both counts of the Texas indictment under Rule 20.

The Drug Enforcement agent's report indicated that this investigation began in May 1983 when the Drug Enforcement Administration received information that Hesse was looking for a buyer for a large quantity of heroin. On May 28, 1983, an undercover agent was introduced to Hesse at a bar in Springfield and Hesse acknowledged that he was looking for a buyer for a kilo of heroin. He was initially reluctant to deal with a stranger, but after four meetings, he offered to make the agent a partner if the agent agreed to purchase the heroin as soon as it

EXHIBIT 5.1 (cont'd)

came across the border into Texas. The agent accepted the offer but insisted on first receiving a sample of the heroin.

On June 23, 1983, the agent and Hesse met in Springfield and drove to a shopping mall where they met Hesse's girlfriend, Nancy Rooney. After receiving instructions from Hesse, Rooney went to her car and returned with a sample of 2.70 grams of heroin, which she gave to the agent. The latter paid Hesse $300. The substance was tested and found to contain 31.7 percent heroin or .86 grams of pure heroin (total net weight).

On July 21, 1983, the agent informed Hesse that the sample was of acceptable quality. On July 24, Hesse instructed the agent to meet him in El Paso, Texas, on July 29. The agent flew to El Paso where he met with Hesse and Nancy Rooney at the Yellow Rose Motel.

On July 30, Hesse and Rooney crossed the border into Juarez. They returned 2 hours later and Hesse told the agent that he was able to obtain only a quarter kilogram of heroin. The agent expressed his disappointment, but Hesse said that the heroin was of very high quality and could be cut many times. Hesse then sold the agent the first installment of 101.7 grams for $6,000. Tests determined that this substance contained 44.6 percent heroin or 45.36 grams of pure heroin (total net weight). Hesse explained that Rooney and he would return to Mexico that afternoon to obtain the balance.

Hesse and Rooney crossed from Juarez into the United States and were arrested by U.S. Customs later in the day. Nancy Rooney had 147.3 grams of heroin in her possession (44.6 percent heroin or 65.7 grams of pure heroin (total net weight). No heroin was found on Hesse, who was released that day. Rooney was held for trial. Hesse returned to Massachusetts where he was arrested on August 15, 1983. (Total net weight = 111.92 grams of pure heroin from the three sales.)

Defendant's Version. "I was going to Mexico on a vacation and Nancy decided to come with me. This guy she met in Springfield was pestering her to get him some heroin. I had seen him a couple of times in June. All of a sudden he shows up in El Paso and demands to know where the stuff is. She finally agreed to get him some, and she asked me to come in case anything happened. I was there so I guess I'm guilty. All of a sudden I was arrested by customs but they let me go because they didn't have anything on me. Then, all of a sudden I'm arrested up here. My lawyer says entrapment is hard to prove so I guess I'm guilty. But I didn't say all those things the narc claims. I don't deserve to go to jail."

Prior record

Juvenile Adjudications

Age 14	10/6/69: Using motor vehicle without authority	Springfield, Mass. Juvenile Court	11/5/69 1 year probation Probation expired 11/4/70

Mr. Hesse was represented by counsel. He and two other juveniles stole a car and went on a "joy ride." Mr. Hesse made a good adjustment on probation during the initial months, but became increasingly uncooperative thereafter.

Age 15	10/28/70 Breaking & entering	Holyoke, Mass. District Court	11/17/70 Committed, Youth Service Board (paroled on 6/1/71; parole expired 6/1/72)

Mr. Hesse was represented by counsel. He and one other juvenile broke into a home in Holyoke. The Youth Service Board sent him to the Industrial School at Shirley, Massachusetts, where he remained until June 1971 when he was paroled. His institutional performance was routine. He participated in a woodworking course and was placed on report on one occasion for fighting in the dining hall.

Adult Record

Age 20	12/23/75 Shoplifting	Springfield, Mass. Police Dept.	12/24/75 Dismissed, lack of prosecution

Hesse was arrested after he allegedly attempted to steal several jewelry items from a department store. The store manager declined to press charges.

EXHIBIT 5.1 (cont'd)

| Age 20 | 4/11/76: Receiving stolen property | Holyoke, Mass. District Court | 5/11/76 4 months county jail; ss; Probation 1 year; Expired 5/10/77 |

Mr. Hesse was represented by counsel. He was arrested after he sold a stolen television set to a pawnshop. The probation officer reports that he had little success with Mr. Hesse, who was constantly on the borderline of violation.

| Age 21 | 9/16/76 Burglary & entering in the nighttime | Northampton, Mass. District Court | 11/15/76: 6 months Hampshire County Jail; released on 5/14/77 |

Mr. Hesse was represented by counsel. He was apprehended at 2:15 a.m. inside a drug-store. He had activated a silent alarm when he entered the building. Jail officials recall that Mr. Hesse tended to be reclusive while incarcerated. He voluntarily spent several months in segregation because of his fear of attack by other inmates. Holyoke District Court declined to revoke probation.

| Age 24 | 4/13/80 Larceny over $100 and forgery | Hampden Cty., Mass. Superior Court | 6/27/80: 2 years prison ss; 12 months probation with restitution; Probation expired 6/26/81 |

Mr. Hesse was represented by counsel. He withdrew $500 from a bank account using a stolen passbook and forged withdrawal slips. He was identified through bank photographs. Mr. Hesse paid $310 in restitution and the balance was remitted. He performed well under probation supervision.

Personal and family data

Defendant. Herman Hesse was born on September 16, 1955, in Boston, Massachusetts. His parents, natives of Austria, came to the United States as displaced persons after World War II. The family has lived for the last 15 years at their residence in Holyoke. The defendant's early years were turbulent because of many violent arguments between his parents. These were caused by Mrs. Hesse's belief that her husband was an excessive drinker. She summoned police assistance on several occasions, although no arrests were made. In 1966, Mrs. Hesse contracted tuberculosis. She was hospitalized for almost one year and the father was unable to keep the family together. Hesse was placed in St. Vincent's Home for Children, but the family was reunited when Mrs. Hesse recovered. The defendant remained with his family until he married at the age of 20. He returned to the family home after his divorce 3 years later.

Mr. and Mrs. Hesse picture their son as a well-intentioned individual whose difficulties with the law were caused by his unwise selection of associates. They are bitter towards co-defendant Nancy Rooney, who they believe was responsible for this offense. They view his previous juvenile and adult transgressions as minor matters which were treated with undue harshness by police and the courts. His parents describe the defendant as an intelligent and ambitious individual, who values financial success above all else. They are proud of the fact that, in recent years, the defendant has acquired such material possessions as an expensive automobile and a boat. They also note that he has been especially generous with his younger brother and sister.

Parents and Siblings. The father, Henry Hesse, age 59, resides with his family and for the last 17 years has been employed as a machine operator earning a moderate salary. The home atmosphere improved considerably when Mr. Hesse stopped drinking approximately 5 years ago. The mother, Geraldine Ericksen Hesse, age 58, resides with her husband and is a housewife. Her health is poor due to respiratory ailments.

There are two siblings. Stanley Hesse, age 24, resides with his parents and is unemployed. Stanley believes that his brother is the victim of harassment by law enforcement authorities. Audrey Hess, age 19, resides with her parents and is a community college student.

EXHIBIT 5.1 (cont'd)

Marital. Herman Hesse married Barbara Raymond in a civil ceremony in Hartford, Connecticut, on November 22, 1975. Both parties were 20 years old at the time and she was pregnant. The couple had one child, Herman, Jr., who was born on April 29, 1976. Mrs. Hesse reports that the marriage was troubled from the start by financial problems since the defendant was unemployed. He turned to illegal means of supporting the family and his subsequent arrests caused even more strain on the couple's relationship. There were several brief separations during 1976 and a longer one when the defendant was sentenced to serve 6 months in September 1976. When he was released, Mrs. Hesse found him a "different man" and it was impossible to reconcile their relationship. The Hampden County Probate Court granted a divorce on December 28, 1978, on grounds of incompatibility and awarded her custody of the child. The defendant was required to pay $20 a week child support. Mrs. Hesse is employed as a telephone operator. She reports that her ex-husband's support payments have been sporadic. He often goes for months without visiting the child or making any payments, but he will then arrive with lavish gifts for his son and lump-sum support payments. Mrs. Hesse says that her relationship with the defendant is now amicable, but they see each other infrequently.

Mr. Hesse asserts that he has no plans to marry again. He stated that Nancy Rooney was merely a friend.

Education. Mr. Hesse was educated in local public schools. He left junior high school in October 1970 when he was committed to the Youth Service Board. He returned to Baran High School in Holyoke, in the fall of 1971, and dropped out of the 11th grade in November 1982.

School officials describe Mr. Hesse as an intelligent individual who never worked up to his capabilities. His grades were generally C's and D's. Mr. Hesse left school because he was older than most of his classmates, and wanted to get a job.

Employment. Between November 1982 and the time of his arrest, Mr. Hesse was unemployed and collected unemployment compensation of $72 a week. From August 1980 to November 1982 he was a forklift operator at the Smith Chemical Company in Northampton. He earned $4.10 an hour, but he was subject to frequent layoffs. Company officials described him as an uncooperative employee with a high degree of tardiness. He would not be considered for reemployment.

Between March 1978 and December 1979, Mr. Hesse worked in the warehouse of the United Rug Company in Easthampton, Massachusetts. He earned $2.75 an hour and he quit after a disagreement over hours. Between 1974 and 1977, Mr. Hesse was sporadically employed in the roofing business. This work paid well but he seldom was able to get more than 3 or 4 months work in any year.

After he left high school, Mr. Hesse worked on a delivery truck for Central Bakery, Inc., of Holyoke. He held this job between April 1972 and October 1974 and earned the minimum wage. He lost his job when the company went out of business. Mr. Hesse said that he would like some day to open his own business.

Health

Physical. Mr. Hesse is in good physical condition. He denies having used drugs of any kind and he specifically disclaims the use of heroin. Discussion with family members, as well as with law enforcement sources, and urinalysis test performed at the jail were negative for heroin use.

Mental and Emotional. On two occasions, Mr. Hesse was tested in public schools and received I.Q. scores of 102 and 103.

Mr. Hesse has been examined by mental health professionals on two occasions. The first occurred shortly after Mr. Hesse was committed to the Youth Service Board in 1970. A psychologist diagnosed him as "a person whose anxiety is stimulated by a frustrated need for affection. Herman has developed no healthy conscience. His response to social demands is not based on any close committment to moral principles."

Mr. Hesse was examined once again as a result of this court's pretrial order. Dr. Robert Land administered a battery of psychological tests, the results of which suggested, "that he seems to be unusually fearful of the power and influence of others. It is obvious that he has been unable to resolve childhood problems and continues to feel quite rejected. He tends to view threatening environmental forces as coming outside his control."

Financial condition

Assets. Mr. Hesse lists two main assets: one is a 1983 Cadillac purchased in January 1983, for $16,640. This automobile was confiscated by the Drug Enforcement Administration.

EXHIBIT 5.1 (cont'd)

The other asset is a 19-foot fiberglass speedboat with a 115 horsepower Mercury outboard engine worth approximately $5,500.

Mr. Hesse's parents displayed to the probation officer a savings account passbook with a present balance of $7,146.23. The account was listed to Mr. Hesse and his mother, but the parents made it clear that the defendant made the deposits. When questioned about this, Mr. Hesse asserted that the account, in fact, belonged to his mother and that his name was on it only as a matter of convenience. His mother subsequently contacted the probation officer and retracted her earlier statement. She said that she made a mistake and that the money in the account belonged to her.

Liabilities. The only debt Mr. Hesse lists is a loan from GMAC to finance the purchase of his 1983 Cadillac. The loan balance is presently $6,200 and Mr. Hesse plans to make no further payments until such time as his car is returned to him by the government.

Evaluation

Probation Officer's Assessment. Although he attempts to shift responsibility to his co-defendant, Mr. Hesse was the principal figure in the importation and sale of over 100 grams (net weight) of pure heroin. Were it not for the intervention of the U.S. authorities, he would have completed the sale of an additional quarter kilogram to an undercover agent. Mr. Hesse is not a user of the drug. He apparently values financial success to the point that he made a calculated decision that heroin trafficking was profitable. His lack of concern about the moral aspects of his decision confirms the observation of mental health professionals that his personality lacks some of the restraints under which most people operate. For Mr. Hesse, participation in this offense, as well as in earlier offenses, was a logical means of satisfying his economic motives.

The members of Mr. Hesse's family are intensely loyal to him and they have an unrealistic view of his participation in criminal activities. They do not question the sources of his assets, which are surprisingly large for a person with his employment history. The family cannot be counted upon to exert the pressure that might convince Mr. Hesse to conform to law-abiding behavior. Mr. Hesse, himself, is unrealistic in his personal goals. Without much education or skill, he expects a high degree of financial compensation, but he has not thus far shown a willingness to work towards that goal. It is unlikely that Mr. Hesse will attempt conventional paths to economic success until he is convinced that illegal means are too hazardous.

Parole Guideline Data. (Estimate) Offender Characteristics (SFS): 6; Offense Category: VI; Adult Guideline Range: 52–64 months.

Sentencing Data. The following information was obtained from the Statistical Analysis and Reports Division of the Administrative Office of the U.S. Courts for 1983. (The data could contain statistical errors and it is provided only to give a national or district pattern.)

Offense: Drugs

	National		District: D/MA	
	Number	Percent	Number	Percent
Total defendants sentenced:	2,438		35	
Imprisonment	1,856	76.1	28	80
1–12 months	150	6.2	4	11.4
13–35 months	250	10.3	7	20
36–59 months	355	14.6	4	11.4
60 months and over	618	25.3	2	5.7
Average number of months of				
imprisonment	62.7		28.1	
Split sentence	219	9	10	28.6
Indeterminate	187	7.7	0	0
YCA	77	3.2	1	2.9
Probation	570	2.3	7	20
Average number of months	40.3		36	
Fine only	2		0	

EXHIBIT 5.1 (cont'd)

Special Sentencing Provisions. Adult sentencing provisions apply in this case, along with a statutory requirement for a special parole term of at least 3 years, and a possible fine of $25,000.

Respectfully submitted,

Susan Deavers
U.S. Probation Officer

Recommendation

It is recommended that the defendant be committed to the custody of the Attorney General for 5 years and a special parole term of 3 years. This recommendation considers the quantity and quality of the heroin involved, the defendant's prior record, and Mr. Hesse's central involvement in a serious offense in which he fails to exhibit concern for his illegal behavior. This officer believes that punishment is the most appropriate sentencing objective in this case.

The court may wish to consider imposing sentence under 18 U.S.C. 4205(b)(2) to permit flexibility as to the release date. The court might also consider recommending commitment to a minimum security institution, where Mr. Hesse might feel less threatened.

Eventually, under most sentences imposed, Mr. Hesse will come under the supervision of a probation officer. For at least 6 months of supervision it would appear that Mr. Hesse will have to have, *at least*, semimonthly contact with a probation officer. It is also believed that Mr. Hesse would best respond to supervision in a highly structured environment which a halfway house could provide. Mr. Hesse would need to focus on his lack of job skills. The probation officer will need to engage him in a job skills program and scrutinize his finances.

Voluntary Surrender. If the court imposes a custody sentence, voluntary surrender would not appear wise. Mr. Hesse lacks maturity and ability to assume responsibility for his conduct.

Respectfully submitted,

Susan Deavers
U.S. Probation Officer

Approved: _____
   J. Grant Hogan
   Supervising U.S. Probation Officer

Information excluded from the pre-sentence report as potentially exempt from disclosure: Rule 32(c)(3)(A)

Marital. The defendant's ex-wife reported that when he was released from jail in early 1977, he showed no interest in resuming sexual relations with her. His behavior was also unusual in other respects, and he exhibited great tension and insomnia. Mrs. Hesse began to suspect that he had some experience in jail that had affected his sexual function. She questioned him about this on several occasions and he responded with bitter denials. Mrs. Hesse became convinced that it was impossible to save the marriage and she filed for divorce. Mrs. Hesse was adamant that her husband not learn that she provided this information.

Officials of the Hampshire County Jail confirmed that Mr. Hesse was the victim of a homosexual assault in the jail. He refused to identify his attackers but he asked to be moved to an isolated cell. This request was granted.

Officials of the Hampden County Jail, where Mr. Hesse is now lodged, report that he has displayed acute anxiety during his confinement. They are not aware of the reasons for this, but they note that Mr. Hesse has requested a transfer to the administrative segregation section. The jail has not complied with this request because of overcrowding.

Mental and Emotional. The latest psychological report suggest that Mr. Hesse will continue to experience acute anxiety whenever he is placed in a situation that threatens recurrence of the homosexual assault. The psychologist believes that Mr. Hesse is not overtly homosexual, but that his orientation is ambiguous. Since this attack, Mr. Hesse has reportedly experienced complete sexual dysfunction.

EXHIBIT 5.1 (cont'd)

Summary of withheld factual information

If the court is of the view that the above information is excludable under Rule 32(c)(3)(A) and if the court intends to rely on that information in determining sentence, a summary of the withheld factual information is provided for disclosure to the defendant or his counsel:

The court has received information about experiences of the defendant while previously incarcerated which caused him to have serious emotional problems. Subsequent psychological examination confirmed this existence.

The ultimate time served is affected by the prisoner's conduct. Specific formulas are used to calculate time off for good behavior, which is an incentive for prisoners to avoid disruptive behavior. This should not be confused with parole.

The American Bar Association has developed recommended "Standards Relating to Sentencing Alternatives and Procedures." The standards hold that sentences should be determined by the judge rather than by juries and that all crimes should be classified by a single system. Probation is recommended as the basic form of sentence. Jail time before the trial should count toward the sentence. Pre-sentence reports should be mandatory when the offender risks incarceration for more than a year, is under twenty-one, or a first offender. Guides for judges to develop comparable sentencing standards are included in the standards. Another suggestion is for routine review of lower court sentences by higher courts, in order to correct any unjust actions.

Indeterminate sentences were intended to take into account individual differences among offenders. However, the Twentieth Century Fund observed in a study report that the indeterminate sentence was a noble experiment that failed. The report recommends that the "presumptive sentence" for each crime be set by legislatures or by judicial bodies. In addition to specifying sentences for particular crimes on the first offense, these bodies would also suggest rapidly increasing sentences for repeated offenses.

In homicide cases, the report suggests ten years for a premeditated killing which could be increased by 50 percent if "**aggravating factors**" are present or decreased if there are "**mitigating factors**." It does not recommend capital punishment for murder under any conditions.

Aggravating Factors

1. The defendant was the leader of the criminal enterprise.

2. The crime involved several perpetrators.

3. The crime involved several victims.

4. The victim or victims were particularly vulnerable.

5. The victim or victims were treated with particular cruelty during the perpetration of the crime.

6. The degree of physical harm inflicted on the victim or victims was particularly great.

7. The amounts of money or property taken were considerable.

8. The defendant, though able to make restitution, has refused to do so.

9. The defendant had no pressing need for the money taken; he was motivated by thrills or by the desire for luxuries.

10. The defendant has threatened witness or has a history of violence against witnesses.

Mitigating Factors

1.   The defendant played a minor role in the crime.

2.   The defendant committed the crime under some degree of duress, coercion, threat, or compulsion insufficient to constitute a complete defense but which significantly affected his conduct.

3.   The defendant exercised extreme caution in carrying out the crime.

4.   The victim or victims provoked the crime to a significant degree by their conduct.

5.   The defendant believed he had a claim or a right to the property.

6.   The defendant was motivated by a desire to provide necessities for his family or himself.

7.   The defendant was suffering from a mental or physical condition that significantly reduced his culpability for the offense.

8.   The defendant, because of his youth or old age, lacked substantial judgement in committing the crime.

9.   The amounts of money or property taken were deliberately very small and no harm was done or gratuitously threatened against the victim or victims.

10.   The defendant, though technically guilty of the crime, committed the offense under such unusual circumstances that it is unlikely that a sustained intent to violate the law motivated his conduct. (Twentieth Century Fund, 1976:44–45)

The major flaw in our system, according to the Twentieth Century Fund report, may be the capricious and arbitrary nature of criminal sentencing. By failing to administer either equitable or sure punishment, the sentencing system—if anything permitting such wide latitude for the individual discretion of various authorities can be so signified—undermines the entire criminal justice structure. Proposed presumptive sentences for first offenders should be set considerably lower than the prison sentences authorized today.

The report also contends that a larger number of criminals who have committed offenses should serve time in confinement and adds that the discretion of sentencing judges and parole boards should be narrowed considerably. It recommends that sentences should be predictable before the offense is committed.

States that adopted mandatory sentences for major felonies have not experienced a salutary effect on crime rates. The major consequence has been increased overcrowding in the prisons. If early release is necessary, it defeats the purpose of fixed sentences.

The Comprehensive Crime Control Act of 1984 creates a special commission to set ranges of minimum and maximum sentences on all federal crimes, thus leading to more uniform sentences. A judge who imposes a sentence outside the range must give reasons in writing. Either the defendant or the government may appeal if sentences are on the high or the low side. In five years, parole boards will be eliminated and inmates will not be released before the end of their sentences.

APPEALS The Comprehensive Crime Control Act provides that to stay out of prison, a convicted defendant must convince the trial judge that he has a liklihood of winning the appeal.

PROBATION Probation provides an alternative to incarceration and can be considered a posttrial diversion from loss of liberty. Sometimes a jury has the power to mandate probation, but usually the decision is made by the judge. Probation is often desirable because it maintains the support of the offender's family, allows the offender to be self-supporting, and avoids the stigma of incarceration. Probation is equivalent to serving a sentence within the community and is important in diverting people from the correctional system.

Granted and regulated by the court, probation has the effect of suspending a sentence while the convicted defendant attempts to fulfill the conditions of probation. The offender remains in the custody of the trial court under the supervision of a probation officer. In some states, persons convicted of violent crimes or prior felonies are ineligible for probation. Although conditions of probation vary, they usually require active employment or continuance in school and avoidance of contact with criminals or other persons who may lead the offender into further crime. Restrictions are sometimes placed on driving a car, drinking liquor, and the use of credit. Occasionally, restitution to the victim of a crime is also specified. Violations of probation conditions may lead to revocation of probation.

Probation is also often revoked for failure to report to the probation officer. Such failure is frequently attributable to the commission of a new crime. The probation violator is generally offered a chance for a hearing, at which time he or she is entitled to counsel. Due process in probation was specified in Gagnon v. Scarpelli, 411 U.S. 778 (1973). Upon revocation, a sentence of imprisonment may be imposed. Some states allow credit for the previous probation time, while others do not.

Due process in probation was further explicated in Bearden v. Georgia, 461 U.S. 660 (1983), in which a defendant was given probation on condition that he pay a $500 fine and make restitution for $250. The offender held that he could not make payment because he could not get a job. Probation was revoked. The Supreme Court held:

> A sentencing court must inquire into the reasons for failure to pay. . . . If the petitioner could not pay despite sufficient bona fide efforts to do so, the court must consider alternate means of punishment other than imprisonment. (103 S.Ct. 2702)

INCARCERATION

When an offender is to be incarcerated, commitment is usually made by the court to the director of adult corrections. Once delivery of a prisoner has taken place, the court has no further control over the offender. Assignment may be made to a diagnostic center and then to the most appropriate facility. In some states, the offender may be sentenced to a specific institution, thus reducing the control of the Department of Corrections.

PAROLE

With increased support for determinate sentences, parole has been eliminated in some states. Parole is intended to provide a transition from prison to freedom. As with probation, everyone is entitled to consideration for parole unless specifically prohibited by law. The inmate usually appears personally before the parole board, but often may not be permitted to bring an attorney to the hearing. The balance of the sentence yet to be served usually constitutes the length of parole.

Parole officers assist the parolee in adjusting to society and help prevent violations of the conditions of parole. Conditions imposed are similar to those of probation. Parole may be revoked for cause. In general, fewer rights accompany parole than probation. All states have signed an Interstate Compact for the Supervision of Parolees and Prisoners, making it possible for parolees to go where relatives are located or obtain jobs in other states. If parole is violated, parolees may be returned to the state of origin without extradition. Due process requirements for alleged parole violators were established in Morrissey v. Brewer, 408 U.S. 471 (1972).

One of the variables of parole is the time allowance given for good behavior. Sometimes "time off" also makes it possible to apply for early parole. Behavior modification systems where various rewards are provided for good behavior, have been inaugurated in many prison programs. Performance in these programs can be called to the attention of a parole board.

LOSS OF CIVIL RIGHTS

Incarceration usually involves loss of the right to vote, to hold public office, and to serve on a jury after release. Convicted felons and major juvenile offenders are not accepted into the armed forces. States with provisions for declaring life-term prisoners "civilly dead" may dissolve their marriages and terminate their parental rights as well. Various types of licensing and the right to practice in certain professions are denied to ex-convicts. Some types of business, such as the operation of a liquor store, are especially restricted.

One of the most important aspects of criminal justice concerns maintaining contact with family members, a major social work role. Divorce is a common problem, especially for prisoners who face long sentences. A social worker may also assist the prisoner to maintain parental rights. With the "tender years" doctrine, the problem of parental rights was limited to female prisoners, but now male prisoners often have responsibilities as single custodial parents.

For a number of years, Wisconsin has fully restored a prisoner's rights on completion of sentence. In some states the only way for a prisoner to regain his civil rights is through a pardon—an act of executive clemency—usually from the governor.

The prisoner is deprived of physical freedom, the right to carry on a business, the right to heterosexual activity (although conjugal visits are allowed in a few states), and the right to sue or be sued. The Eighth Amendment protects the prisoner against cruel and unusual punishment. In making appeals or seeking parole, inmates are entitled to legal assistance from professional attorneys or "jailhouse lawyers"—inmates who have become experts on certain types of offenses. Prisoners are also entitled to the use of law books on their own behalf.

"Detainers" used to be common, that is, another jurisdiction would request that an inmate be held in order to answer for an offense committed in that jurisdiction. Recent decisions facilitate speedy trials by permitting a prisoner to stand trial on charges in another jurisdiction while he or she is simultaneously serving a previous sentence. In this way, long delays are avoided and the prisoner is not deprived of the right to a speedy trial.

COMMUNITY-BASED CORRECTIONS

Social workers have had a particular interest in community-based corrections, including probation and parole, furloughs that maintain a relationship with the family, and work-release as a means to maintain economic stability. Halfway houses and shelter programs for released prisoners are useful innovations.

AIDING VICTIMS OF CRIMES So far, the emphasis in this chapter has been on the accused, but social workers also work with victims of crimes, especially rape and domestic violence, in prosecution of the offender. They assist the victim and the prosecuting attorney and are often instrumental in convincing the victim to decide to file charges. The social worker also enlists the cooperation of the police when they are not particularly sympathetic to the victims of rape or domestic violence.

CITIZEN SUPPORT FOR CORRECTIONS Citizens support correctional programs less than they do such services as mental health and child welfare. As a result of inadequate correctional programs, prisoners frequently find themselves in need of many services after their release. Services offered during a prison term help the inmate adequately prepare to return to society. Major goals include public support of efforts to help offenders and of research that will develop and test new approaches.

Questions for Review

1. What issues related to criminal justice are most likely to concern the social worker as a private citizen?

2. What are victimless crimes, and why are they so described?

3. What generally differentiates murder in the first degree from murder in the second degree?

4. Explain the felony murder rule.

5. Does assault have to involve bodily harm? Explain.

6. What are some of the paradoxes in sexual conduct codes?

7. How is robbery considered a combination of two types of crime?

8. How does an adversary procedure help protect the rights of the accused?

9. Explain and illustrate jurisdiction.

10. Explain each step in criminal legal procedure, beginning with investigation.

11. What is meant by diversion? What is the most common means of diversion for serious offenses?

12. Explain plea-bargaining. Indicate its advantages and its dangers.

13. Differentiate between probation and parole.

14. How do social workers assist victims of crimes?

15. Why do correctional programs receive inadequate financial support from citizens?

16. Identify and evaluate techniques used in community-based corrections. Discuss problems of citizen acceptance of such programs.

Questions for Debate and Discussion

1. Select an issue like adoption or legal control of marijuana. What are some of the major value conflicts that affect legal controls?

2. Are felonies uniformly defined by the fifty states? Is uniformity a good idea?

3.   Do you feel that determinate sentences discourage criminal behavior? Why?

4.   Why is release on recognizance now widely accepted?

5.   Debate the following statement: All sentences for criminals should be precisely specified, thereby eliminating parole.

Selected Readings   Alpert, Geoffrey P. (ed.). *Legal Rights of Prisoners.* Beverly Hills, Calif.: Sage, 1980.

Culbertson, Robert G., and Mark R. Tezak. *Order Under Law: Readings in Criminal Justice.* Prospect Height, Ill.: Waveland Press, 1981.

Foote, Caleb, and Robert J. Levy. *Criminal Law: Cases and Materials.* Boston: Little, Brown, 1981.

Gottfieldson, Michael R., Marilyn H. Chandler, and Lawrence E. Cohen. "Legal Aim, Discretion, and Social Control: A Case Study of the Federal Corrections Act." *Criminology* 21 (1983): 95–118.

Kadish, Shulhoffer. *Criminal Law and Its Processes.* Boston: Little, Brown, 1982.

CHAPTER
6

The Juvenile Court: Delinquency and Incorrigibility

Social workers have had a special interest in the juvenile court because it was created largely out of their efforts. It has had a unique focus and has permitted judges to use wide discretion in determining the child's needs and selecting from a range of possible alternatives to meet them. Traditionally, the court was supposed to create the same atmosphere of trust that a social worker would establish in dealing with a voluntary client.

The juvenile court is considered a civil court rather than a criminal court. It usually has original jurisdiction over (1) juvenile delinquents, (2) children in need of supervision, (3) neglected and dependent children, and (4) the victims of child abuse.

This chapter will focus on juvenile delinquency and children in need of supervision. Child dependency, neglect, and abuse will be considered in Chapter 7, and child placement and guardianship in Chapter 8.

HISTORY AND RATIONALE OF JUVENILE COURT

The first juvenile court was established in Chicago in 1899. Much earlier, in 1861, the mayor of Chicago was authorized to appoint a commissioner to place boys from ages six to seventeen under probationary supervision or in reform schools. By 1867, placements were being made by regular judges. In 1877, New York prohibited contact between juvenile and adult offenders in courts and institutions, and by 1892 separate trials and records were mandatory.

The movement to establish juvenile courts spread rapidly until all states had them. The Illinois law became the model. Juvenile courts have existed for over fifty years in all but two states—Maine and Wyoming. Wyoming was the last state to act; its juvenile court was not created until 1945. The juvenile court is often established as a division of another court. In California and Illinois, for example, it operates within the Superior and Circuit Courts, respectively.

A Uniform Juvenile Court Act was drafted in 1968 by the Commission on Uniform State Laws (§1–64, 9A U.L.A. [1968]). Subsequently, a Model Act for Family Courts and State–Local Children's Programs was prepared by W. H. Sheridan and H. W. Beaser (1975) for the Office of Youth Development of the Department of Health, Education, and Welfare. The Model Act for Family Courts will be cited hereafter as MAFC (1975).

The MAFC recommends that the court "should be a division of the highest court of general trial jurisdiction since an integrated court system is preferred rather than a proliferation of specialized courts. The establishment of the court at this level is also desirable since it is more likely to attract individuals of high judicial caliber and command the respect of the bar and the community."

Early advocates of the juvenile court held that although crimes are committed out of "free will," children are not fully responsible for their misbehavior. Consequently, an age standard is required to determine criminal responsibility. According to common law, a child began to be held responsible for his or her own actions at the age of seven. However, neither the MAFC (1975) nor most state laws specify a minimum age for juvenile court jurisdiction. Because the juvenile court deals with civil matters, the question of criminal responsibility is relevant for juveniles only when waiver to a criminal court is contemplated.

All states stipulate a maximum age for jurisdiction. In more than two-thirds of them, it is eighteen years. For the child who reaches the maximum age after committing an offense but before appearing in court, the date of the offense determines jurisdiction in some states, while the date of court appearance is used in others.

Criminal processing gave inadequate attention to the child's history and to the influence of the environment on his or her behavior. The juvenile court, however, was designed to operate as a clinic in which medicine, psychology, and other services could be brought to bear on behalf of children in trouble. Legal terminology reflected this change in focus. Children were not to be "arrested," but "held in custody." Instead of "charges," "petitions" were to be filed on their behalf. Rather than a "trial," the minor was entitled to a "hearing" involving a final "disposition" instead of a "verdict" or "sentence." The press and the public were denied access to records, and labels were minimized.

The specific goal of the juvenile court was to discover reasons for antisocial behavior and develop means by which to change it. Thus the services provided need not necessarily reflect the seriousness of the offense. The court system was to be entirely separate from the one used to process adults. Children's needs were to be met through informal procedures. Judges were supposed to be socially minded and to have wide discretion to act on behalf of the child. The juvenile court concept required that probation officers, physicians, psychologists, and psychiatrists be available to gather data for a just decision and to provide direct service and appropriate referrals to other community programs.

Prosecution was alien and undesirable. Public trial, traditional rules of evidence, and the right to avoid self-incrimination were held to be out of place in juvenile court. The concept of *parens patriae* (the state as parent) was considered adequate to safeguard children's rights, to empower the court to remove a child from parental control when necessary to protect his or her best interest, and to provide for appropriate placement outside the family. Delinquency was perceived not so much as an outcome of defects within the individual but as a product of societal influences to be dealt with primarily by social and economic intervention, improvements in schools, housing, employment, occupational training, and a range of supportive resources.

Not everyone has regarded the juvenile court movement as liberal or liberating. In *The Child Savers*, Platt (1969) held that the juvenile courts actually diminished the civil liberties of youths. Early proponents of the juvenile court suggested removal of children from their homes and recommended increased imprisonment as an alternative to protect delinquents from corrupting influences. The juvenile court imposed sanctions on premature independence and behavior unbecoming to youths. Correctional programs inculcated middle-class values and lower-class skills, according to Platt. Most important, the juvenile court abandoned the due process element in justice.

Two inconsistent developments resulted from the operation of the juvenile court. Through a series of U.S. Supreme Court decisions in the 1965–75 decade, the rights of juveniles in delinquency actions came to approximate those of adult offenders, reducing the informality of proceedings. The decisions will be discussed in detail later in this chapter. At the same time, a need for more services at the neighborhood level was recognized. Youth service bureaus were developed and required to accept all referrals and to provide or obtain group and individual counseling, foster placements, and work programs, as well as education for special needs.

Few major developments in juvenile justice have come in the late 1970s and the 1980s. Recent years have been characterized principally by frustration with a juvenile crime rate increase that is double the adult rate and with how to deal with youths who commit violent crimes.

The Purposes of Juvenile Court

A juvenile court act should emphasize diversion of children from the juvenile justice system to community-based programs, guarantee constitutional safeguards of due process, and separate a child from parents only when absolutely necessary. The Model Act for Family Courts (1975) reads in part:

> This (act) shall be interpreted and construed so as to effectuate the following purposes:
> (1) To divert from the juvenile justice system, to the extent possible, consistent with the protection of the public safety, those children who can be cared for or treated through community-based alternative programs;
> (2) To provide non-criminal judicial procedures through which the provisions of this (act) are executed and enforced and in which the parties are assured a fair hearing and their constitutional and other rights are recognized and enforced; and
> (3) To separate a child from such child's parents only when necessary for the child's welfare or in the interests of public safety.

The model act also includes the following definition: " 'Delinquent child' means a child who has committed a delinquent act and is in need of care or rehabilitation."

Jurisdiction over Children and Adults

The following sections of the MAFC (1975) deal with the juvenile court's jurisdiction over children.

Section 7. Jurisdiction—Children

(a) The court shall have exclusive original jurisdiction of the following proceedings, which shall be governed by the provisions of this act: (1) proceedings in which a child is alleged to be delinquent or neglected.

(b) The court shall also have exclusive original jurisdiction of the following proceedings, which shall be governed by the laws relating thereto without regard to the other provisions of this [act]: (1) the termination of parental rights; (2) proceedings for the adoption of an individual of any age; (3) proceedings under the Interstate Compact on Juveniles; (4) proceedings under the Interstate Compact on the Placement of Children; (5) proceedings to determine the custody or to appoint a legal custodian or a guardian of the person of a child; and (6) proceedings for the commitment of a mentally retarded or mentally ill child.

Section 9. Retention of Jurisdiction

(a) For the purposes of this [act], jurisdiction obtained by the court in the case of a child shall be retained by it until the child becomes 19 years of age, unless terminated prior thereto. This section does not affect the jurisdiction of other courts over offenses committed by the child after such child reaches the age of 18 years.

(b) If a defendant already under jurisdiction of the court is convicted in a criminal court of a crime committed after the age of 18, the conviction shall terminate the jurisdiction of the family court.

[Section 10 of the MAFC (1975) establishes a family court rather than a juvenile court. Functions *c*, *d*, and *e* below are typical of family courts but not juvenile courts.]

Section 10. Jurisdiction—Adults

The court shall have exclusive original jurisdiction:

(a) To try any offense committed against a child by the child's parent, guardian, or any other adult having the legal or physical custody of such child.

(b) To try any adult charged with (1) deserting, abandoning, or failing to provide support for any person in violation of law; (2) an offense committed by one spouse against the other.

In any case within this section, the court in its discretion may transfer the proceedings to a court which has criminal jurisdiction of the offense charged.

(c) In proceedings for support, alimony, divorce, separation and annulment, and to establish paternity of a child born out of wedlock.

(d) In proceedings under the Uniform Reciprocal Enforcement of Support Act.

(e) In proceedings to commit an adult found to be mentally retarded or mentally ill.

DEALING WITH DELINQUENCY AND INCORRIGIBILITY

Before considering the steps in processing juveniles, it may be well to look at juvenile misbehavior and typical youth-police interaction, especially in problem neighborhoods. Seldom is conflict occasioned by clear law violations, and seldom will the juveniles ultimately be prosecuted.

Youth-Police Interaction

Those who are unfamiliar with juvenile behavior problems are likely to visualize one individual youth committing a criminal act. Problems are much more often the result of group activity and are more disruptive than criminal activity, involving an acting out of value conflicts between youths and the police. Bittner (1976:82) comments:

> In matters ranging from riotous and destructive conduct, to noisy and boisterous behavior, to groups of youngsters hanging around some street corner, patrolmen must deal with aggregations of young people in which individual culpability cannot be easily determined. Where alleged deeds cannot be associated with doers and the business at hand cannot be readily defined by what has happened, patrolmen's attention tends to focus on what is taking place during the intervention. The decision of what has to be done takes shape in relationship to how the young people act toward the intervening patrolmen. Within a considerable range, police judgment of substantive misconduct

will be mitigated by expressions of diffidence on the part of young people and aggravated by their arrogance.

The police are likely to be predisposed toward pro-active intervention—preventive surveillance. Bittner (1976:85) observes further:

> To forestall lurking danger, to gain advantage over what might happen, patrolmen engage in what is euphemistically called proactive intervention. They consider it especially necessary to engage in this practice in blighted areas of the city simply because the young people there are very often found in places where they are not supposed to be—other places being in short supply. Moreover, they act in this way because there has grown up a stabilized relationship of conflict, or at least contest, between the police and kids who feel that they have nothing to lose in giving the police a hard time because they would not be left alone under any circumstances. . . . Some of the efforts of young people to bedevil police attempts at preventative surveillance are undertaken in the spirit of fun and adventure. But often the resentment at being hassled is bitter enough to produce the more serious reactions associated with overly strict controls of all kinds. . . . Thus the proactive approach, far from preventing troubles, is a source of them. Aside from occasionally leading to ugly flareups, the patrolmen's gratuitous poking around in their affairs causes many young people to grow up accepting hostility between cops and kids as a natural fact of life. . . . Believing that cops always accuse and insult people for no good reason, they search anything a policeman says for the accusation or insult supposedly contained in it. The result comes to be a pervasive atmosphere of distrust on both sides, and a free-wheeling search for opportunities to get at each other.

In trying to prevent juvenile nuisance behavior, the police often encourage it. In these contacts, patrol officers rather than specialized youth officers experience continuing difficulties with teenagers. Notwithstanding a high level of frustration, the police rarely follow through to the arrest of juveniles in such conflictual situations. Although they sometimes single out for action the apparent leaders of a group, police are generally convinced that arrest should be a last resort and used only when absolutely necessary. Police frequently contend that the permissiveness of the courts undermines their attempts to keep juveniles under control.

Labeling Juvenile Misbehavior   The juvenile court may impose penalties on delinquents which restrict their liberty. Many juvenile courts are empowered to transfer the minor's case to the adult court. Therefore the most careful safeguards of children's rights have concerned delinquency. Traditionally **delinquency** involves offenses that would be crimes if committed by adults, but delinquency also originally included truancy, running away, and curfew violations—behavior problems related to the age status of the offender. These **status offenses**—offenses that would not be considered crimes if they were committed by adults—are usually not considered very seriously. Many people feel that they should not be under the juvenile court's jurisdiction.

Juvenile offenses have resulted in major attention to labeling. We have already considered the use of benign terminology such as "held in custody" rather than "arrested." To advocates of juvenile justice, the delinquency label was the source of stigma just as was the criminal label prior to creation of the juvenile court. To them, the child who was disobedient or unruly did not deserve to be considered delinquent. Also the person who committed a delinquent act might be less easily rehabilitated after the label had been applied. Other delinquent acts would likely result, and labeling would have contributed to a self-fulfilling prophecy.

Research indicates that avoidance of labeling does not necessarily serve to eliminate deviant behavior. Thorsell and Klemke (1972:401–402) specify several conditions under which labeling theory is most likely to be useful:

1.   If the labeled person is a primary rather than a secondary deviant

2.   If the labeling is carried out in a confidential setting with the understanding that future deviance will result in public exposure

3.   If the labeling has been carried out by an in-group member or significant other

4.   The more easily the label is removable when the deviant behavior has ceased

5.   The more the labeling results in efforts to reintegrate the deviant into the community

6.   If the label is favorable rather than derogatory

Some states still include a less serious category—PINS, CHINS, OR MINS (persons, children, or minors in need of supervision)—for children considered unruly or incorrigible. States that use these categories tend to conclude that the children should be served by the child welfare system rather than the correctional system.

The MAFC (1975) eliminates the "person in need of supervision" category. The rationale is:

> In common usage, these types of cases have come to be known as **juvenile status offenders**—children who are brought within the jurisdiction of the court for having committed actions which are illegal only for juveniles.
>
> It is obvious that such actions on the part of the child, while they may be indicative of the imperative need of the child to receive some type of care or treatment, do not necessarily pose a threat to society. They, therefore, will represent the bulk of the cases which can safely be diverted from the juvenile justice system, i.e., referred, prior to the filing of a petition, for service or care to a community agency which is not part of the juvenile justice system.
>
> Even in such situations, there will be cases in which an agreement for care and service cannot be achieved, thus necessitating referral to court. In this section, the traditional definition of neglect has been somewhat broadened by adding a child "whose parents, guardian, or other custodian are unable to discharge their responsibilities to and for the child." This provision alleges a condition or status but does not require a finding of fault on the part of any individual or social institution. (Section II, p. 14)

If this suggestion is followed, curfew violations, truancy, drinking, and running away will be accommodated under the neglect category.

If other public or private agencies are to serve status offenders, we must be sure that they develop the needed programs. The minor who is beyond the control of adult supervision generally has not been well accepted for service either by child welfare or by mental health agencies.

Court Discretion   The same type of incident that brings the person to court can result in several different findings based on the total situation. A youth picked up driving a car that he has taken may be found delinquent, but he may also be considered in need of supervision. Lack of parental supervision may lead to a finding of neglect, or economic deprivation may lead to a finding of dependency. While the precipitating incident is the same, both the finding and the prognosis may be different.

The courts tend to deal more benignly with the offender who has no previous history of delinquency, who has a cooperative family, and who is polite and submissive. The circumstances that lead to wide differences in disposition also lead many people to consider juvenile courts inconsistent, if not too soft on "bad" behavior. Nevertheless, such discretion has been considered essential to successful outcomes based on the juvenile's best interests. The history and the total context of the child's environment contribute to the nature of the finding.

STEPS IN PROCESSING JUVENILES

Although organization and administration of juvenile courts vary from state to state, five basic steps in processing alleged juvenile delinquents and minors in need of supervision have evolved: (1) arrest and detention, (2) filing a petition, (3) the detention hearing, (4) the adjudicatory hearing, and (5) the dispositional hearing. The steps in processing a person in need of supervision are similar to those in delinquency because the individual's liberty can be restricted.

Arrest and detention bring the minor into contact with the court. The petition requests a certain action of the court, such as a finding of delinquency. The detention hearing asks, "Is there a basis to retain jurisdiction over the juvenile?" The adjudicatory hearing asks, "Is the juvenile a person described under the Juvenile Court Act, i.e., guilty of behavior covered by the act?" The disposition hearing asks, "What should be done in the best interests of the juvenile?"

The majority of children do not proceed through all three hearings, but are diverted from the juvenile justice system. Diversion may occur on the street at the time of initial questioning of the youngster by police, at the police station during the pre-judicial process, or subsequent to detention.

Arrest and Detention

The initial step in the juvenile court process brings the alleged delinquent or minor in need of supervision to the attention of the court. The police are generally first to discover that an offense has been committed. Rather than actually detain juveniles, the police usually prefer to issue a warning. They may take a child to the police station and bring the matter to the attention of the parents. Detention is more likely to result when the child is already known to the police and has had several warnings.

Parents frequently make a complaint against their own child. A minor who is considered incorrigible or unruly is often referred to the police by the parents as "beyond their control."

Morris and Hawkins (1970:71) provided statistics to show the influence of police on how many youths are arrested in Chicago:

> We found that of every hundred youth arrested, only forty reach the court intake process. Of those forty, only twenty actually reach the court. Those figures are accurate. . . . We believe, and the police in the areas share this view, that the hundred they arrest represent five hundred "probable cause" arrest situations.

The MAFC (1975) indicates the conditions under which the juvenile may be taken into custody:

Section 18. Taking into Custody

A child may be taken into custody:

(1) Pursuant to the order of the court under Sections 15 and 19;

(2) For a delinquent act pursuant to the laws of arrest;

(3) By a law enforcement officer having reasonable grounds to believe that the child has run away from a correctional facility;

(4) By a law enforcement officer who has reasonable grounds to believe that the child is suffering from illness or injury or in immediate danger from the child's surroundings and that the child's immediate removal from such surroundings is necessary for the protection of the health and safety of such child;

(5) By a law enforcement officer who has reasonable grounds to believe that the child has run away from a residential, non-correctional, child-caring facility in which he had been lawfully placed;

(6) By a law enforcement officer who has reasonable grounds to believe that the child has no parent, guardian, custodian or other suitable person willing and able to provide supervision and care for such child; or

(7) By a probation officer or social service worker, pursuant to Section 6(b) of this [act].

The drafters comment:

> In the past, statutes have provided that taking into custody shall not be considered an arrest. However, for all practical purposes, this has been a legal fiction since the child is being held in involuntary custody. It is particularly important that this be recognized in the light of recent decisions and also in order to facilitate the development of appropriate guidelines for law enforcement practices. Therefore, under this section, the taking into custody of a child for a delinquent act is to be considered an arrest for the purpose of determining the validity of taking him into custody or the validity of any actions or procedures related to the arrest. It should be noted that a child who has run away from home may be taken into custody under subsections (3), (4), (5) and (6), depending upon the circumstances of the situation.

Most minors can be detained without a warrant for behaviors specified in the Juvenile Court Act. In general, they may be taken into custody on the same grounds as an adult. The Fourth Amendment to the U.S. Constitution provides protection against unreasonable search and seizure and a requirement that warrants be based on probable cause, that is, evidence that an offense has been or is in the process of being committed. The first step in detention may be a limited search without a warrant, as long as it is incident to a valid arrest (Chambers v. Maroney, 399 U.S. 42 [1970]). "Stop and frisk," involving patting down the outer clothing, is permitted without a warrant.

Several reasons for detention are recognized in addition to the nature of the offense: the minor is likely to flee if released, is dangerous to self or others, or is subject to home conditions that make release impossible.

The juvenile does not have a constitutional right to bail. Police are usually required to notify parents promptly when a child has been apprehended. However, parents are not entitled to waive their child's constitutional rights. The juvenile's ability to waive his own rights has been affirmed in West v. United States, 399 F.2d 467 (5th Cir. 1968). In that case, the defendant, who had been charged with transporting a stolen auto in interstate commerce, was only sixteen years old, but he was deemed capable of waiving his rights to counsel and to remain silent.

WEST v. UNITED STATES

United States Court of Appeals, Fifth Circuit, 399 F.2d 467 (1968).

CLAYTON, Circuit Judge:

Appellant, Louis West, was tried to the court on a charge of violating the Federal Juvenile Delinquency Act by reason of knowingly transporting a stolen motor vehicle in interstate commerce knowing it to have been stolen. He was found guilty and was committed to the custody of the Attorney General for the period of his minority. He appeals here, and we affirm.

The sufficiency of the evidence to warrant the conviction is not in question. In fact, it was more than enough to warrant the finding of guilt, and no good purpose would be served by a discussion of it.

Complaint is made here of the introduction into evidence of a statement given by Louis West to a special agent of the Federal Bureau of Investigation. The main thrust of the argument on this point is that a 16-year-old boy is per se incapable of waiving his rights to counsel and to remain silent even where, as here, the record demonstrates that he was given full *Miranda* warnings and that he signed a written waiver of his rights before making the statement. The written form used by the officer which includes a written waiver form as signed by Louis West is shown in the margin.

Appellant urges us to extend a landmark decision of the Supreme Court, in re Gault, 387 U.S. 1 (1967), in two major respects: first, by implication he says that the pre-interrogation warnings commanded in all criminal cases by *Miranda* also apply to pre-judicial stages of federal juvenile delinquency proceedings, and second, he suggests that any prejudicial statement made by a juvenile outside the presence of his parents is automatically tainted and can never be elevated to the status of competent evidence even where, as here, the juvenile has received a full-fledged *Miranda* warning and has knowingly waived his right to remain silent and his right to be represented by counsel. As has been said, all the warnings required by *Miranda* were given to Louis West before he made the statement about which complaint is made here. The entire interview consumed less than one hour. No claim was made at trial, nor is there any evidentiary basis for finding on appeal, that appellant did not understand the warnings given and the waiver of rights signed by him. Nor was this statement ever repudiated later. *Gault*, inter alia [among others], stands for the proposition that the concepts of due process and fundamental fairness serve as guides in determining whether a juvenile has waived his privilege against self-incrimination, a purely factual question. Factors considered by the courts in resolving this question include: (1) age of the accused; (2) education of the accused; (3) knowledge of the accused as to both the substance of the charge, if any has been filed, and the nature of his rights to consult with an attorney and remain silent; (4) whether the accused is held incommunicado or allowed to consult with relatives, friends or an attorney; (5) whether the accused was interrogated before or after formal charges had been filed; (6) methods used in interrogation; (7) length of interrogations; (8) whether vel non [or not] accused refused to voluntarily give statements on prior occasions; and (9) whether the accused has repudiated an extra judicial statement at a later date. . . . Although the age of the accused is one factor that is taken into account, no court, so far as we have been able to learn, has utilized age alone as the controlling factor and ignored the totality of circumstances in determining whether or not a juvenile has intelligently waived his rights against self-incrimination and to counsel.

Viewing the evidence in the light most favorable to the United States, Glasser v. United States, 315 U.S. 60 (1942), the facts sub judice [before the court] demonstrate that Louis West voluntarily and intelligently waived his privilege against self-incrimination prior to being interviewed by the officer. The totality of circumstances shows, inter alia, that appellant: (1) was fully informed of his rights to remain silent and to have the assistance of counsel; (2) was interviewed by the special agent of the Federal Bureau of Investigation at 11:55 a.m. in a county juvenile facility; (3) voluntarily and understandingly waived his rights; (4) was 16 years old at the time of the interview; (5) had completed a tenth-grade education; (6) had worked and lived as an adult with adults, hundreds of miles away from his parents; (7) was not held incommunicado; (8) and, had been permitted visits by his parents (who had been informed previously by the local police that the automobile in appellant's possession was a stolen vehicle). Moreover, no deceit, persuasion or coercion was present in the very brief interrogation procedures. There is no doubt that where a statement of this nature is sought to be introduced the prosecution bears a heavy burden in establishing that the statement is a product of the free will of the defendant. In this instance, this burden has been met. The appellant admits that this is so in his statement on the sole basis that he was 16 when the statement was given. But this just will not do, especially where the defendant takes the stand as a witness and reiterates the facts delineated in the statement.

The point made by the United States in brief and on oral argument with respect to the inadequacy of the objections made to the use of this statement by the prosecution need not be dealt with in light of what we have said heretofore. Even if the objections had been complete in every respect, the statement would have been available for use by the prosecution and admissible. . . . This case should be, and is,

Affirmed.

In *West v. United States* the waiver form that the juvenile was presented with and expected to sign raises a number of questions: Is there any assurance that the juvenile has read the waiver carefully? Does the juvenile understand its full implications? Does the juvenile ever have the right to change his or her mind and repudiate the waiver? Perfunctory use of the form may tend to short-circuit juvenile rights. The MAFC (1975) provides that in delinquency cases the juvenile may not waive counsel. It goes beyond the *Miranda* decision in that the child's statements may not be used against him or her later.

Intake Screening.   The intake process provides other means of diverting the juvenile from the court system. Paulsen and Whitebread (1974:125) describe the purposes of intake:

> Intake (screening procedures) after arrest are designed (a) to eliminate matters over which the court has no jurisdiction, (b) to eliminate cases in respect to which the petition would be insufficiently supported by evidence, (c) to eliminate from the process

cases not serious enough to require juvenile court adjudication and (d) more contro-versially, to arrange an "informal adjustment" which may involve a degree of supervision and treatment without the stigma of court adjudication.

The decision to send a case to the court for adjudication is made in different ways. In some places the petitioner may insist that the case go to court. In others the consent of an intake officer, a public prosecutor or the judge must be obtained before a petition will be entertained.

Some cases of alleged misbehavior will come to the attention of court personnel which are not appropriate for adjudication. To take an example, a youngster may have been technically a trespasser, but the true cause for filing a delinquency petition is that the child has been annoying to a neighbor because of his dress or general style of behavior. He may have been disrespectful and arrogant, yet such behavior is not a ground for court adjudication. The youth, his parents, and the court should not be troubled with such a trivial matter.

Often the sound judgment of a probation officer attached to a court intake service can determine that the law has not been violated. If so, the matter can be ended and the child sent home. Similarly, the person serving the intake function may judge that the evidence against the child is insufficient and eliminate the case for that reason. Unhappily, the court intake service's probation officers (speaking generally) do not have access to legal advice which, in many cases, would greatly assist them in making judgments.

A publication from the Offices of Human and Youth Development (Olson and Shepard, 1975:21) provided detailed screening guides for intake and a variety of screening practices:

> The nature and extent of processing varies extensively among juvenile court intake units particularly in the area of decision-making. Intake practices range from little or no screening to extensive screening and referral. Overall, the screening is generally inadequate. Large numbers of youth are still being funneled into the court for minor crimes or status offenses. . . .
>
> Many youth are brought to the attention of the police and the juvenile court because no community resources are available to address the special needs of acting-out children and youth, or because such resources—when available—are not utilized. This creates more problems than it solves. When intake personnel accept these referrals of further service in the overburdened justice system they create an illusion of services, thereby allowing the community to feel comfortable that someone has taken care of the situation.

Decisions are influenced by the age of the offender, the seriousness of the offense, the person's previous record, and the standards of the community. In Colorado, for example, a preliminary investigation determines "whether the in-terests of the public or of the child require that further action be taken."

Two types of intake disposition are "letter dismissal" and "informal handling." **Letter dismissals** are made for minor offenses when recurrence is unlikely. The letter informs the parents of the offense and indicates that further action is not contemplated. It also explains their responsibility to correct and guide their child's behavior, indicating that the court will act if repetition occurs. After the letter is sent, the case is officially closed unless the parents request help.

Informal handling describes casework given to children and their parents when the behavior is symptomatic, that is, when the child's action reveals problems deeper than the severity of the offense would indicate. This leads to an exploratory interview to determine what casework service the family needs. The child and parents are then counseled on the recommended treatment. A contact with a community or private agency may be a condition of dismissal.

The individual worker handling the matter has the responsibility to prepare the case for disposition. A letter is sent to the parents, requesting them to bring the child to the court at an appointed date and time. Should the parents fail to respond, a registered letter is sent stating when the hearing has been rescheduled and that a second failure to appear will cause a formal petition to be filed. If the parents do not cooperate, the case will be returned for rescreening.

An intake department lacks power to compel compliance, but the threat of a formal petition is usually sufficient. After interviewing both the child and the parent(s), the worker may either dismiss the action or recommend a rescreening for a formal hearing. This choice depends on the amount of available evidence, the admission or denial in the child's version of the incident, both the parents' and child's attitudes toward the behavior, any information gathered during the interview, and most important, the worker's evaluation of the situation. Dismissal may also be conditioned on some further requirements appropriate to the individual circumstances.

Filing a Petition

The petition (sometimes called the complaint) requests a particular finding from the court at the adjudicatory hearing. Petition forms may cover possible neglect and dependency as well as delinquency and need for supervision. The petitioner crosses out material that does not apply to the request. Forms vary from court to court. It will be useful to compare the sample petition form included as Exhibit 6.1 with those of other local courts.

The petition summarizes the charges in general terms. If termination of parental rights is not sought, the petition for the adjudicatory hearing should eliminate any references to unfitness and make no mention of consent to adoption.

The petition is usually completed by the state's attorney, but may be filed by an agency or a private individual. Social workers should know how to draft such petitions and be prepared to act as the petitioner.

The Detention Hearing

The minor who has been detained is entitled to a detention hearing within the time specified by law, generally thirty-six to forty-eight hours, excluding Sundays and holidays. Rules of evidence are not strictly applied, because the purpose is to determine whether there is sufficient legal basis for the court to hold the child. Also, the adjudicatory hearing must either be held within ten days or the juvenile released.

Usually no basis for detention is found. The child will usually be released to the parents. Then the adjudicatory hearing must be held within thirty days.

The decision to detain a juvenile involves holding him or her for later court action because release is considered unsafe for the juvenile or for society. Juveniles who have committed no crime but are runaways or beyond control are actually more likely to be detained than juvenile lawbreakers.

One of the main reasons for detention is concern that the juvenile will flee. Patricia Wald (1976) has suggested that requiring a juvenile to post his or her own money to obtain release may be an effective alternative to detention. Wald was especially critical of the services available during detention. In closed settings, schools and other supportive programs tend to be poor. Juveniles are also much too likely to be detained in jails. Only nine states categorically prohibit use of jails for juvenile detention.

EXHIBIT 6.1
EXAMPLE OF A PETITION

IN THE CIRCUIT COURT FOR THE
_____JUDICIAL CIRCUIT OF ILLINOIS,
COUNTY OF _____, STATE OF ILLINOIS

IN THE INTEREST OF

_____,

a minor.

NO. _____

PETITION—DELINQUENT MINOR*
    MINOR OTHERWISE IN NEED OF SUPERVISION
    NEGLECTED CHILD
    DEPENDENT CHILD
    NEGLECTED AND DEPENDENT CHILD

I, _____, _____, am an adult and on information and belief state the following:
    (name)   (title)

1. That the name, age, and address of the minor herein is as follows:

Name   **Date of Birth**   **Residence Address**   **City and State**

2. The names and residence addresses of the minor's parents, legal guardian, custodian, and nearest known relative are as follows:†

Father:
Mother:
Legal Guardian:
Nearest Known Relative:

The minor and the persons named in this paragraph are designated as respondents, and those names and addresses that are unknown are designated as respondents under the style "All Whom It May Concern."

3. The minor _____ _____ detained in custody.
              (is)   (is not)

4. A detention hearing _____ _____ the _____
               (was held) (has been set for)
day of _____, 19_, at _M.

5a. Said minor is a delinquent minor, pursuant to Section 2-2 of the Juvenile Court Act of the State of Illinois, in one or more of the following respects.‡

    (1) Said minor is below seventeen years of age and has violated or attempted to violate, regardless of where the act occurred, any Federal or State law or municipal ordinance, in that:

    (Here state facts forming a basis for the allegations.)

    _____

    _____

    _____

    (2) Said minor has violated a lawful order made under the Juvenile Court Act of the State of Illinois.

    (3) Said minor is an addict as defined in the "Drug Addiction Act."

    (4) Any minor who violates a lawful court order made under the Juvenile Court Act of the State of Illinois.

EXHIBIT 6.1 (cont'd)

5b.   That the aforesaid minor is in need of supervision, pursuant to Section 2-3 of the Juvenile Court Act of the State of Illinois, in one or more of the following respects:

(1) Said minor is under eighteen years of age and is beyond the control of h⎯ parents, guardian or other custodians, in that:

(Here state facts forming a basis for the allegations.)

_____

_____

_____

(2) Said minor is subject to compulsory school attendance and is habitually truant from school, in that:

(Here state facts forming a basis for the allegations.)

_____

_____

_____

5c.   That the aforesaid minor is neglected pursuant to Section 2-4 of the Juvenile Court of the State of Illinois, in one or more of the following respects:

(1) Failure to receive proper or necessary support, education as required by law, or medical or other remedial care recognized under State law or other care necessary for h⎯ well-being in that:

(Here state facts forming a basis for the allegations.)

_____

_____

_____

(2) Said minor has been abandoned by h⎯ parents, guardian or custodian in that:

(Here state facts forming a basis for the allegations.)

_____

_____

_____

(3) The environment is injurious to h⎯ welfare or h⎯ behavior is injurious to h⎯ own welfare or that of others in that:

(Here state facts forming a basis for the allegations.)

_____

_____

_____

5d.   That the aforesaid minor is dependent pursuant to Section 2-5 of the Juvenile Court Act of the State of Illinois, in the following respects:

(1) Said minor is without a parent, guardian or legal custodian in that:

(Here state facts forming a basis for the allegations.)

_____

_____

_____

(2) Said minor is without proper care because of the physical or mental disability of h⎯ parent, guardian or custodian, in that:

EXHIBIT 6.1 (cont'd)

(Here state facts forming a basis for the allegations.)

_____

_____

_____

(3) H___ parent, guardian or legal custodian, with good cause, wishes to be relieved of all residual parental rights and responsibilities, guardianship or custody, and desires the appointment of a guardian of the person with the power to consent to the adoption of the minor under Section 5-9.

6. That _____, as the natural _____,
                                                    (father) (mother) (father and mother)
_____ consented, or indicated a willingness to consent, to the entrance of
(has) (have)
an Order in this proceeding which would authorize a guardian of the person to be appointed to consent to the later adoption of the minor child.**

Alternate Paragraph 6:

6. In accordance with Section 5-9 of the Juvenile Court Act incorporating the Adoption Act, that _____
is an unfit parent in one or more of the following respects.

(a) abandonment of the aforesaid minor child, in that:

_____

_____

(b) failure to maintain a reasonable degree of interest, concern or responsibility as to the child's welfare in that:

_____

_____

(c) desertion of the child for more than three (3) months next preceding the commencement of this proceeding, in that:

_____

_____

(d) substantial neglect of the child of a continuous, or repeated nature, in that:

_____

_____

(e) extreme or repeated cruelty to the child, in that:

_____

_____

(f) failure to protect the child from conditions within h___ environment injurious to the child's welfare, in that:

_____

_____

(g) other neglect of or misconduct toward the child, in that:

_____

_____

(h) depravity, in that:

_____

_____

(i) open and notorious adultery or fornication, in that:

_____

_____

EXHIBIT 6.1 (cont'd)

(j) habitual drunkenness for the space of one (1) year prior to the commencement of the adoption proceeding, in that:

_____

_____

(k) Failure to demonstrate a reasonable degree of interest, concern or responsibility as to the welfare of a newborn child during the first 30 days after its birth.

(l) Failure to make reasonable efforts to correct the conditions which were the basis for the removal of the child from his parents or to make reasonable progress toward the return of the child to his parents within twenty-four months after an adjudication of neglect under Section 2-4 of the Juvenile Court Act.

7. That an order of Protection under Section 5-5 of the Juvenile Court Act is sought against _____, who resides at _____,
                                                        (street address)
_____, _____ and that said person is hereby named as a Respondent
   (city)   (state)
for this purpose.††

8. That it is in the best interest of the minor and of the public that _he be adjudged a ward of the Court and that a Guardian of the person be appointed and authorized to consent to the adoption of the minor.

9. That _____, as Guardianship Administrator for the Illinois Department of Children and Family Services, or his successor in office, consents to being appointed Guardian for the person of said minor.

WHEREFORE, YOUR PETITIONER PRAYS AS FOLLOWS:

1. That a Guardian ad Litem be appointed to represent the rights of said minor.

2. That an adjudicatory hearing be set within the time limits prescribed by the Juvenile Court Act of the State of Illinois.

3. That the said minor be adjudicated a ward of the Court.

4. That said parents be adjudicated unfit parents, and that all parental rights be terminated, and that _____, Guardianship Administrator for the Department of Children and Family Services, State of Illinois, or his successor or successors in office, be appointed guardian of the person of said minor with the power to consent to h__ adoption.

5. For such other relief as is available under the terms of the Juvenile Court Act.

_____
Petitioner

STATE OF ILLINOIS
COUNTY OF _____   } SS:

I, the undersigned, on oath state that I have read the foregoing Petition and that the matters alleged therein are true and correct to the best of my information and belief.

_____
Petitioner

Subscribed and sworn to before me this _____day of _____, 19__.

_____
Notary Public

EXHIBIT 6.1 (cont'd)

My Commission Expires: _____
ATTORNEY FOR PETITIONER:
State's Attorney _____
Address _____
City _____
Telephone _____

    * Select the title which applies to the allegations contained in the petition.
    † The petition shall state the names and residences of the minor's parents *or* the name and residence of the legal guardian *or* the person or persons having custody or control of the minor, *or* the nearest known relative, if no parent or guardian can be found.
    ‡ In Paragraph 5 and the subparagraphs thereof, the draftsman should select those allegations which apply and delete all others.
    ** All parental consents should be taken in open court, where possible, and otherwise must be in writing and signed in the form and manner provided for in the Adoption Act.
    †† Delete this paragraph if inapplicable.

Criteria for detaining "dangerous" juveniles so they will not commit crimes are notoriously vague. Paradoxically, most juveniles held will be PINS, and PINS are detained the longest. Wald recommends prohibiting the use of secure detention homes and jails for status offenders. She recommends that the detention hearing be held within 24 hours and that reasons for detention be stated in writing. If the juvenile were still detained, another hearing would be held within seven days. Detention would be limited to fifteen days, and a similar period would be allowed between adjudication and disposition.

Wald's solution to detention problems is a crisis intervention system in which the activities currently initiated on the child's behalf after adjudication would begin after arrest. Interventions and therapists would be available at the time of arrest. Most juveniles can be worked with better at home or in the community than in a locked facility. Counselors would determine when the remand (hold order) would expire permitting the child's release. PINS cases would be the major beneficiaries of this system. With advice of counsel, the juvenile could, of course, choose the traditional process and stay in a detention facility until adjudication. This proposal presents the same dangers identified by Goldberg (1973) in her discussion of diversion for adults in that there is always the risk that help will become tyranny. The conflict is one of welfare vs. due process.

Wald (1976:135) concludes: "We do seem to need a theory and function for the post-arrest period that more nearly accommodates the reality that the vast majority of juveniles will never go to trial, as well as one that fits better into a community-based corrections program."

Figure 6.1 shows the decision tree involved up to the adjudicatory hearing.

The Adjudicatory Hearing

Adjudication determines whether the child has actually committed the offense for which he or she is accused. If delinquency is alleged, the required standard of evidence is proof beyond reasonable doubt—identical to that needed to sustain a criminal charge in an adult court. There should be no uncertainty about the guilt of the accused. When the juvenile appears to be "in need of supervision," proof in most states is established by a preponderance of evidence. Hearsay, a statement which is made other than by a witness and offered at a hearing to prove the truth

FIGURE 6.1
JUVENILE COURT INTAKE DECISIONS AND DISPOSITIONS

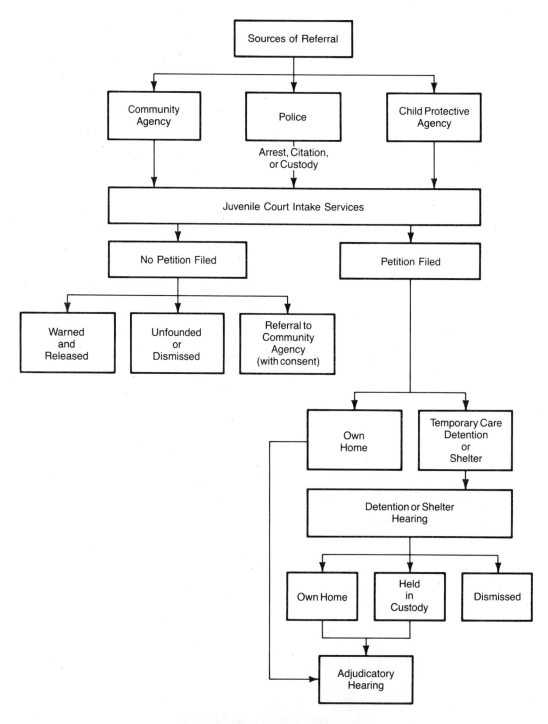

Source: Olson and Shepard (1975:18).

of the matter, is inadmissible at the adjudication hearing. Inadequacy of evidence is a frequent basis for appeal. The juvenile has the right to confront and cross-examine witnesses and is entitled to the due process safeguards of adequate, timely written notice of the allegations and sufficient time to formulate a response. The right to refuse to testify is also under the Fifth Amendment. The juvenile is entitled to counsel as a protection of his or her legal rights.

If a search has involved an invasion of a juvenile's right of privacy, evidence obtained may be inadmissible. A search of students' lockers by public school officials has become especially important in alleged drug violations. Constitutional restrictions do not generally apply to such searches because the law recognizes that the school representative acts *in loco parentis* (in the parents' place) and has a special duty to maintain discipline and safety in the school. On this basis, searches of lockers are justified.

To be valid, confessions must be voluntary, corroborated by someone other than an accomplice, and preceded by the *Miranda* warning. The Miranda requirement does not apply to social workers or other nonpolice personnel. Generally, the same warning should be given to the juvenile's parents, so they may be of greater help in protecting their child's Fifth Amendment rights.

A minor's arrest or juvenile court records may be inadmissible as evidence in subsequent juvenile proceedings in order to reduce the stigma of such a record. Photographing and fingerprinting of juveniles are generally more restricted than for adults.

The age of witnesses is one of the special problems in juvenile hearings. If young children are the victims or accomplices of alleged delinquents, their testimony may become critical. To be considered competent, a witness must be able to recall the event and report what happened. Regardless of whether or not a witness is sworn in by oath, he or she must recognize the importance of telling the truth. The problem of the age of witnesses is more common in cases of neglect and dependency than in delinquency, however, because children can offer firsthand evidence concerning parental practices and home conditions.

The Dispositional Hearing

Finally, when the child is found to be an offender, "What should be done next?" Hearsay evidence and opinion are admissible in planning for the child's future. The dispositional hearing often involves the social worker's expertise in presenting a service plan for the child.

Increasingly, juvenile courts are seeking the advice of social workers for recommendations in the dispositional hearing. This may work in the interests of the young offender by emphasizing supportive services more than punishment.

YOUTH SERVICE BUREAUS

To obtain community services, juveniles are referred to a variety of agencies. The youth service bureau has been created especially to deal with the problems of youths.

Youth service bureaus are designed for delinquents and nondelinquents. Referrals come from the police, the juvenile courts, parents, and schools, as well as from other sources. They are frequently located in neighborhood service centers. The service bureaus have a special target population, give priority to police and court referrals, and seek to coordinate neighborhood prevention activities. Services include psychological counseling, placement in group and foster homes, work and recreational programs, employment counseling, remedial education, and vocational training. This type of program is consistent with the goals of the generalist social worker. Acceptance of services is intended to be voluntary, but like the juvenile court, informal proceedings may give little or no attention to due process rights.

The bureaus stress that court action includes stigmatization. By handling problem behaviors, they free the courts to deal with serious delinquencies. Youth service bureaus have achieved dramatic decreases in court processing of less serious delinquencies and a reduction in the number of probation actions. in some communities, police referrals to youth service bureaus have been few because of differing philosophies. Police have commented that the bureaus use extralegal approaches and are too permissive in dealing with their clients.

JUVENILE PROBATION

Because fewer juveniles than adults receive sentences to correctional facilities, probation is more likely for juvenile offenders. Siegel and Senna (1981:422) summarize the role of the juvenile probation officer:

1. Providing direct counseling and casework services
2. Interviewing and collecting social service data
3. Making diagnostic recommendations
4. Maintaining working relationships with law enforcement agencies
5. Using community resources and services
6. Using volunteer case aides and probation officers
7. Writing predisposition reports
8. Working with families of children under supervision
9. Providing specialized services such as group work, behavior modification counseling, or reality therapy counseling
10. Supervising specialized caseloads involving children on drugs or with special psychological or emotional problems
11. Making decisions about the revocation of probation and its termination

While the American Bar Association has considered probation ineffective, a summary of recent studies is not as pessimistic. However, the optimistic accounts do not necessarily mean that the favorable results can be attributed to probation, since some youthful offenders are "self-correcting."

JUVENILE COURT RECORDS

One of the special interests of social workers is minimizing the stigma of juvenile offenses that will otherwise have a negative effect later in life. Use of juvenile records after a person becomes an adult is an especially important issue.

Charles Jordan filed suit in 1976 because his juvenile record was allegedly used by Los Angeles County as a basis to deny him employment. He had stolen a car at age fifteen and was charged with grand theft. He applied for a job with the county ten years later. The suit was filed as a class action by the Center for Law in the Public Interest on the basis that use of the record discriminates against black job applicants and is a violation of the 1964 Civil Rights Act. Unfortunately, the civil rights question of confidentiality of records was not decided, because Jordan accepted $500 in settlement of any claims against the county. The facts are presented in full in a subsequent appeal dealing with class action aspects of the suit (Jordan v. County of Los Angeles, 669 F.2d 1311 [9th Cir. 1982]).

The National Council of Juvenile Court Judges sponsored a model statute on juvenile and family court records (Larson, 1981) that provides for the sealing and destruction of such records under specified conditions after the juvenile reaches majority. It would be especially useful if Congress would pass legislation prohibiting inquiry into the juvenile court record, as suggested in the footnote of the excerpt from Section 105 of the following Model Statute.

Section 105. Disposition of Records—Delinquency and Noncriminal Offense Matters

(1) In all cases where the referral is not accepted by the court, or when the case is dismissed without adjudication, all identifying information collected by the court must be automatically destroyed at the end of six months, or sooner upon motion of the court or juvenile record subject, except when a subsequent referral is received within said period.

(2) At any time after the court's jurisdiction has been terminated, the juvenile record subject may apply to the court for destruction or sealing of the subject's records.

(3) Any court record not destroyed or sealed on application of the juvenile shall be destroyed or sealed by the court in accordance with the following procedures and conditions.

(a) Sixty days notice of the proposed action shall be given to the following: parties to the proceedings, involved law enforcement agencies, the prosecutor, defense attorney of record, and to any institution or agency if custody of the child had been transferred to said institution or agency.

(b) If any person or agency listed in Sec. 105(3)(a) objects to the proposed disposition of the records, the court shall grant the objecting party a hearing to determine the merits of the action. If there is no objection to the proposed action within the sixty day period, all identifying information shall be automatically removed from all indices.

(c) Unless waived by the court for good cause, the following conditions precedent must be met prior to the disposition of the records:

(i) the child has attained the upper age of the original jurisdiction of the court; (ii) two years have elapsed from the date of final discharge from the supervision of a court without a felony referral or a misdemeanor referral involving assaultive conduct against a person; (iii) one year has elapsed from the date of entry of a final dispositional court order; (iv) there are no proceedings pending regarding a delinquency and/or noncriminal offense matter; (v) there are no proceedings pending seeking conviction of a felony or of a crime involving injury to a person; and (vi) there have been no felony convictions or convictions for crimes involving injury to a person.

(4) Upon the entry of an order of destruction or sealing:

(a) The proceedings shall be deemed never to have occurred and the record subject may properly reply without swearing falsely upon any inquiry in the matter that he has never been arrested, taken into custody, placed under the supervision of the court, committed to a state agency or institution, or adjudged delinquent.*

(b) Index reference shall be destroyed.

(c) All inquiries concerning court records must be submitted in writing to the juvenile or family court judge;

---

*In lieu of this section, the drafting committee would prefer federal legislation prohibiting inquiry into the subject's juvenile court record, rather than having the subject deny the existence of a record which was previously destroyed or sealed.

(d)   A court order shall be sent to all offices or agencies in possession of the subject's records directing that all offices or agencies forward to the court all records and copies thereof, including the court order, within 60 days, unless sooner ordered by the court, and, further, certifying compliance;

(c)   All legal and social records shall be sent to the court's repository and shall be sealed. The record subject may petition the court to permit the inspection of the sealed records by the persons named in the petition; otherwise such records shall not be opened for inspection;

(f)   All sealed records may be physically destroyed ten years after the sealing order. (Larson, 1981:12–13)

MAJOR COURT DECISIONS AFFECTING JUVENILES

Requirements for the three hearings and clearer rules of evidence evolved in opposition to the fatherly judge image and atmosphere of informality in the juvenile court. While admirable in principle, informality ultimately failed to protect the rights of juveniles facing a delinquency finding. Incongruent as it may seem, juvenile courts had often punished trivial offenses by long-term commitment to training schools or other correctional facilities. Community standards for disposition of juvenile cases varied considerably. Some courts developed a reputation for being soft, while others were just the opposite. Many alleged delinquents learned from their peers who had been to juvenile court that they would receive less severe penalties by misrepresenting their age and being processed in adult courts.

Against this backdrop, several cases decided by the U.S. Supreme Court profoundly influenced the functioning of the juvenile court relative to alleged delinquents, but did not have comparable impact on need for supervision or neglect and dependency actions.

Unreasonable Search and Seizure—Mapp v. Ohio (1961).   According to Paulsen and Whitebread (1974:10), Mapp v. Ohio, 367 U.S. 643 (1961), affected the juvenile court significantly by requiring state courts to abide by Fourth Amendment protections against unreasonable search and seizure. Mapp challenged the right of police to seize evidence from her home without the proper warrant. The state of Ohio cited Wolf v. Colorado, 338 U.S. 25 (1949) as the authority for using such evidence. The Supreme Court ruled:

> Today we once again examine Wolf's constitutional documentation of the right to privacy free from unreasonable state intrusion, and, after its dozen years on our books, are led by it to close the only courtroom door remaining open to evidence secured by official lawlessness in flagrant abuse of that basic right, reserved to all persons as a specific guarantee against that very same unlawful conduct. We hold that all evidence obtained by searches and seizures in violation of the Constitution is, by that same authority, inadmissible in a state court. (Mapp v. Ohio 367 U.S. at 654-655)

This decision clearly extends to juveniles as well as adults. Juvenile rights have frequently been violated in searches and seizures.

Due Process in Waiver of Jurisdiction—Kent v. United States (1966)   Kent v. United States, 383 U.S. 541 (1966) was the first Supreme Court case to deal specifically with the juvenile court since its establishment. Morris Kent committed alleged offenses in the District of Columbia. After an earlier appearance in juvenile court when he was fourteen, Kent was charged at age sixteen with new allegations of housebreaking, robbery, and forcible rape. The juvenile court of the District waived its jurisdiction over him, and he was tried in a criminal court. In reaching the decision, the juvenile court judge did not hold a hearing, specify any findings, or avail Kent's lawyer of reports from the court staff. Neither did he give any reason for his action. The defendant was found guilty on six counts of housebreaking.

The U.S. Supreme Court reversed the convictions because the waiver procedure did not involve due process:

> The net, therefore, is that petitioner—then a boy of 16—was by statute entitled to certain procedures and benefits as a consequence of his statutory right to the "exclusive" jurisdiction of the Juvenile Court. In these circumstances, considering particularly that decision as to waiver of jurisdiction and transfer of the matter to the District Court was potentially as important to petitioner as the difference between five years' confinement and a death sentence, we conclude that, as a condition to a valid waiver order, petitioner was entitled to a hearing, including access by his counsel to the social records and probation or similar reports which presumably are considered by the court, and to a statement of reasons for the Juvenile Court's decision. We believe that this result is required by the statute read in the context of constitutional principles relating to due process and the assistance of counsel. (383 U.S. at 587)

Waiver hearings "must measure up to the essentials of due process and fair treatment" (383 U.S. at 562). Application of Gault, 387 U.S. 1 (1967) expressly approved the language of *Kent*, leaving no doubt about its constitutional authority.

The possibility of waiver to the criminal court is most likely for felonies or other serious offenses. Arizona, Louisiana, Nebraska, New York, and Vermont avoid the need for a waiver provision by either maintaining a low maximum age for jurisdiction or by instituting statutes that exclude serious offenses from the juvenile court's jurisdiction. Other states permit waiver over a certain age, regardless of the nature of the offense. In Illinois, for example, that age is thirteen. Kent specifically stipulates conditions for waiver:

1. Entitlement of a juvenile to a hearing

2. Representation by counsel

3. Access to social records on request of the juvenile's attorney

4. Statement of reasons if jurisdiction is waived (383 U.S. at 561–563)

Students may be surprised that *Kent* was not a naive youth who was ripped off by the justice system. He had apparently committed violent offenses. The basic question in the decision did not involve his guilt or innocence, but abrogation of rights. In order to protect the rights of everyone, the Constitution must also protect people who commit violent crimes, including Miranda and Kent.

Section 31 of the MAFC (1975) provides for transfer to criminal court.

Section 31. Transfer to Criminal Court

(a)   The prosecutor may, within 5 days of the date a delinquency petition has been filed and before a hearing on the petition on its merits, and following consultation with probation services, file a motion requesting the court to transfer the child for criminal prosecution, if: (1) the child was 16 or more years of age at the time of the conduct charged, and is alleged to have committed an act which would constitute a felony if committed by an adult; or (2) the child is 16 or more years of age and is already under commitment to an agency or institution as a delinquent; or (3) a person 18 years of age or older is alleged to have committed the delinquent act prior to having become 18 years of age.

(b)   Following the filing of the motion of the prosecutor, summonses shall be issued and served in conformity with the provision of Sections 15 and 16. A copy of the motion and a copy of the delinquency petition, if not already served, shall be attached to each summons.

(c)   The court shall conduct a hearing on all such motions for the purpose of determining whether there are reasonable prospects of rehabilitating the child prior to his 19th birthday. If the court finds that there are not reasonable prospects for rehabilitating the child prior to his 19th birthday and there are no reasonable grounds to believe he is committable to an institution or agency for the mentally retarded or mentally ill, it shall order the case transferred for criminal prosecution.

(d)   When there are grounds to believe that the child is committable to an institution or agency for the mentally retarded or mentally ill, the court shall proceed as provided in Section 40.

(e)   Evidence of the following factors shall be considered in determining whether there are reasonable prospects for rehabilitating a child prior to his 19th birthday: (1) the nature of the present alleged offenses and the extent and nature of the child's prior delinquency record; (2) the nature of past treatment efforts and the nature of the child's response to past treatment efforts; and (3) the techniques, facilities and personnel available to the court for rehabilitation.

(f)   Prior to a hearing on the motion by the prosecutor, a study and report to the court, in writing, relevant to the factors in subsection (e)(1), (2), and (3) shall be made by probation services.

(g)   When a person is transferred for criminal prosecution, the court shall set forth in writing its reasons for finding that there are no reasonable prospects for rehabilitating the person prior to his 19th birthday.

(h)   Transfer of a person 16 years of age or older for criminal prosecution terminates the jurisdiction of the family court over the child with respect to any subsequent delinquent acts.

(i)   A judge who conducts a hearing pursuant to this section shall not, over the objection of the child whose prospects for rehabilitation were at issue, participate in any subsequent proceedings relating to the offense.

The criterion for waiver is the assurance of no reasonable prospects of rehabilitation before the alleged offender's nineteenth birthday. The provisions conform to the requirements of *Kent*.

One case was remanded because the trial court did not make an explicit finding that the youth could not benefit from treatment before sentencing him as an adult on a manslaughter charge (United States v. Hopkins, 531 F.2d 576 [D.C. Cir. 1976]).

Relevant criteria for waiver are the seriousness of the offense, the juvenile's past history, the degree of aggressiveness, violence or premeditation involved in the offense, the juvenile's level of sophistication and maturity, and proximity to the maximum age of juvenile court jurisdiction. Unfortunately, judges often merely restate the general language of the statue, for example, that the juvenile "is not amenable to treatment or rehabilitation." The respective juvenile court acts should mandate that specific reasons for such a decision be explicated.

Due Process in Adjudicatory Hearings—Application of Gault (1967).   The landmark due process case, Application of Gault, 387 U.S. 1 (1967) concerned a fifteen-year-old juvenile who was brought before an Arizona juvenile court for allegedly making an obscene telephone call to a neighbor. Neither the accused nor his parent was given advanced notice of the charge against him. He was not informed of his legal rights and could have been held until he reached majority. The penalty for an adult making an obscene phone call was no more than sixty days in jail or a fine.

The procedure used with Gerald Gault was not without reason. Many juvenile judges felt that advance notice stigmatizes a child and also violates confidentiality, since many people have access to official records. However, a legitimate desire to be helpful to an alleged juvenile is insufficient reason to disregard procedural safeguards.

The U.S. Supreme Court held that due process requires adequate, timely, written notice of the allegations against a juvenile, allowing sufficient time for preparation of a response. In all cases involving the danger of loss of liberty, the juvenile must be accorded the right to counsel, privilege against self-incrimination, and the right to confront and cross-examine opposing witnesses under oath. The Court was careful to limit Gault to the adjudication hearing in a delinquency action. Gault's affirmation of *Kent* is especially interesting:

> In Kent v. United States, supra, we stated that the Juvenile Court Judge's exercise of the power of the state as *parens patriae* was not unlimited. We said that "the admonition to function in a 'parental' relationship is not an invitation to procedural arbitrariness." With respect to the waiver by the Juvenile Court to the adult court of jurisdiction over an offense committed by a youth, we said that "there is no place in our system of law for reaching a result of such tremendous consequences without ceremony— without hearing, without effective assistance of counsel, without a statement of reasons." We announced with respect to such waiver proceedings that while "We do not mean . . . to indicate that the hearing to be held must conform with all of the requirements of a criminal trial or even of the usual administrative hearing; but we do hold that the hearing must measure up to the essentials of due process and fair treatment." We reiterate this view, here in connection with a juvenile court adjudication of "delinquency," as a requirement which is part of the Due Process Clause of the Fourteenth Amendment of our Constitution (387 U. S. at 45).

The MAFC (1975) provides for hearings in Section 32, but no set number of hearings. Every attempt is made to avoid the adjudicatory phase. Section 33 provides for continuance under supervision to achieve this goal.

Section 32. Hearings—Findings—Dismissal

(a)   The parties shall be advised of their rights under law in their first appearance at intake and before the court. They shall be informed of the specific allegations in the petition and given an opportunity to admit or deny such allegations.

(b)   If the allegations are denied, the court shall proceed to hear evidence on the petition. The court shall record its findings on whether or not the child is a neglected child or, if the petition alleges delinquency, as to whether or not the acts ascribed to the child were committed by him. If the court finds that the allegations in the petition have not been established, it shall dismiss the petition and order the child discharged from any detention or temporary care theretofore ordered in the proceeding.

(c)   If the court finds on the basis of a valid admission or a finding on proof beyond a reasonable doubt, based upon competent, material, and relevant evidence, that a child committed the acts by reason of which he is alleged to be delinquent, it may, in the absence of objection, proceed immediately to hear evidence as to whether the child is in need of care or rehabilitation and to file its findings thereon. In the absence of evidence to the contrary, evidence of the commission of an act which constitutes a felony is sufficient to sustain a finding that the child is in need of care or rehabilitation. If the court finds that the child is not in need of care or rehabilitation, it shall dismiss the proceedings and discharge the child from any detention or other temporary care theretofore ordered.

(d)   If the court finds from clear and convincing evidence, competent, material, and relevant in nature, that the child is neglected and in need of care or supervision, or from clear and convincing evidence, relevant and material in nature, that the child is in need of care or rehabilitation as a delinquent child, the court may proceed immediately or at a postponed hearing to make proper disposition of the case.

(e)   In disposition hearings all relevant and material evidence helpful in determining the questions presented, including oral and written reports, may be received by the court and may be relied upon to the extent of its probative value, even though not competent in a hearing on the petition. The parties or their counsel shall be afforded an opportunity to examine and controvert written reports so received and to cross-examine individuals making reports when reasonably available, but sources of confidential information need not be disclosed.

(f)   On its own motion or that of a party, the court may continue the hearings under this section for a reasonable period to receive reports and other evidence bearing on the disposition or need for care or rehabilitation. In this event, the court shall make an appropriate order for detention or temporary care of the child or his release from detention or temporary care during the period of the continuance subject to such conditions as the court may impose pursuant to Section 23 of this [act].

Section 33. Continuance Under Supervision Without Adjudication—Consent Decree

(a)   At any time after the filing of a delinquency petition and before the entry of an adjudication order, the court may, on motion of the prosecutor or that of counsel for the child, suspend the proceedings, and continue the child under supervision in his own home, under terms and conditions negotiated with probation services and agreed to by all parties affected. The court's order continuing the child under supervision shall be known as a consent decree.

(b)   Where the child objects to a consent decree, the court shall proceed to findings, adjudication and disposition. Where the child does not object, but an objection is made by the prosecutor after consultation with probation services, the court shall, after considering the objections and reason therefore, proceed to determine whether it is appropriate to enter a consent decree.

(c)   A consent decree shall remain in force for 6 months unless the child is discharged sooner by probation services. Upon application of probation services or other agency supervising the child, made before expiration of the 6-month period, a consent decree may be extended by the court for an additional 6 months.

(d)   If prior to discharge by the probation services or expiration of the consent decree, a new delinquency petition is filed against the child, or the child otherwise fails to fulfill express terms and conditions for the decree, the petition under which the child was continued under supervision may, in the discretion of the prosecutor following consultation with probation services, be reinstated and the child held accountable just as if the consent decree had never been entered.

(e)   A child who is discharged by the probation services, or who completes a period of continuance under supervision without reinstatement of the original delinquency petition, shall not again be proceeded against in any court for the same offense alleged in the petition or an offense based upon the same conduct.

(f)   A judge who, pursuant to this section, elicits or examines information or material about a child which would be inadmissible in a hearing on the allegations in the petition shall not, over the objection of the child, participate in any subsequent proceedings on the delinquency petition if (1) a consent decree is denied and the allegations in the petition remain to be decided in a hearing where the child denies his guilt; or (2) a consent decree is granted but the delinquency petition is subsequently reinstated under subsection (d).

The traditional arguments that confession may be good for a child and that sworn testimony is unnecessary in juvenile proceedings were refuted by *Gault*. Furthermore, the state of Arizona provided the alleged delinquent no right to appeal or constitutional right to a transcript, and the court of original jurisdiction failed to set forth reasons for the conclusion. *Gault* observed "It would indeed be surprising if the privilege against self-incrimination were available to criminals but not to children" (387 U.S. at 47).

Kent and *Gault* suggest that traditional rehabilitative procedures have fallen short of their goal and highlight the gulf between the states' treatment of the adult and of the child. *Gault* held:

> Under the Constitution, the condition of being a boy does not justify a kangaroo court. The traditional ideas of Juvenile Court procedure, indeed, contemplated that time would be available and care would be used to establish precisely what the juvenile did and why he did it—was it a prank of adolescence or brutal act threatening serious consequences to himself or society unless corrected? Under traditional notions, one would assume that in a case like that of Gerald Gault, where the juvenile appears to have a home, a working mother and father, and an older brother, the Juvenile Judge would have made a careful inquiry and judgement as to the possibility that the boy could be disciplined and dealt with at home, despite his previous transgressions. Indeed, so far as appears in the record before us, except for some conversation with Gerald about his school work and his "wanting to go . . . [to the] Grand Canyon with his father," the points to which the judge directed his attention were little different from those that would be involved in determining any charge of violation of a penal statute. The essential difference between Gerald's case and a normal criminal case is that safeguards available to adults were discarded in Gerald's case. The summary procedure as well as the long commitment was possible because Gerald was 15 years of age instead of over 18. . . .
>
> So wide a gulf between the State's treatment of the adult and of the child requires a bridge sturdier than mere verbiage, and reasons more persuasive that cliché can provide. As Wheeler and Cottreil have put it, "The rhetoric of the juvenile court movement has developed without any necessarily close correspondence to the realities of court and institutional routines" (387 U.S. at 20–30).

The historical emphasis on preventing stigma had not been accomplished successfully by the juvenile court, since records on delinquency were readily available to the government, the armed forces, and sometimes to private employers.

Standard of Proof—In re Winship (1970).   In re Winship, 397 U.S. 358 (1970), established the principle of proof beyond reasonable doubt as a requirement in the adjudicatory stage of a delinquency proceeding. This standard is specifically inapplicable to the dispositional hearing and need not be extended to cases involving children in need of supervision.

Proof beyond reasonable doubt requires evidence that the allegations are true. Mere preponderance of evidence does not justify designation as a delinquent.

Since *Gault*, courts have uniformly held that fundamental fairness bars successive hearings on the same count of delinquency in different juvenile courts. Whether adjudication of delinquency in juvenile court precludes subsequent criminal prosecution will be considered later.

No Mandatory Trial by Jury—McKeiver v. Pennsylvania (1971).   McKeiver v. Pennsylvania, 403 U.S. 528 (1971), provided a major limitation to legal rights by holding that a juvenile is not constitutionally entitled to the right of trial by jury. Fairness is the applicable due process standard for juvenile proceedings. A jury was considered an unnecessary component of accurate fact-finding. In addition, a jury trial could lead to a full adversary process and eliminate the idealistic prospect of an "intimate, informal protective proceeding." Confidentiality would also be threatened. A further danger was that the jury trial might eventually cause the extinction of separate courts for children.

McKeiver does not prevent states from according juveniles the right to trial by jury. Colorado, Michigan, Montana, Oklahoma, South Dakota, Texas, West Virginia, Wisconsin and Wyoming do so under certain circumstances.

No Double Jeopardy—Breed v. Jones (1975).   Conflicting findings had existed as to whether a person processed through the adjudicatory hearing in the juvenile court could then be transferred for trial as an adult. This did occur in the California Superior Court after a youthful defendant, Jones, had already been put in jeopardy in the adjudicatory hearing. In Breed v. Jones, the U.S. Supreme Court vacated the judgment of the lower court:

> Respondent was subjected to the burden of two trials for the same offense: he was twice put to the task of marshalling his resources against those of the State, twice subjected to the "heavy personal strain" which such an experience represents (421 U.S. at 533).
>
>   Turning to the question whether there had been a constitutional violation in this case, the Court of Appeals pointed to the power of the Juvenile Court to "impose severe restrictions upon the juvenile's liberty" [citation omitted] in support of its conclusion that jeopardy attached in respondent's adjudicatory hearing. It rejected petitioner's contention that no new jeopardy attached when respondent was referred to Superior Court and subsequently tried and convicted, finding "continuing jeopardy" principles advanced by petitioner inapplicable. Finally, the Court of Appeals observed that acceptance of petitioner's position would "allow the prosecution to review in advance the accused's defense and, as here, hear him testify about the crime charged," a procedure it found offensive to "our concepts of basic, even-handed fairness." The court therefore held that once jeopardy attached at the adjudicatory hearing, a minor could not be retried as an adult or a juvenile "absent some exception to the double jeopardy prohibition," and that there "was none here" [citation omitted] (421 U.S. at 526–527).
>
>   What concerns us here is the dilemma that the possibility of transfer after an adjudicatory hearing present for a juvenile, a dilemma to which the Court of Appeals alluded. See supra, at 1784. Because of that possibility, a juvenile, thought to be the beneficiary of special consideration, may in fact suffer substantial disadvantages. If he appears uncooperative, he runs the risk of an adverse adjudication, as well as of an unfavorable dispositional recommendation. If, on the other hand, he is cooperative, he runs the risk of prejudicing his chances in adult court if transfer is ordered. We regard a procedure that results in such a dilemma as at odds with the goal that, to the extent fundamental fairness permits, adjudicatory hearings be informal and non-adversary. [Citation omitted.] Knowledge of the risk of transfer after an adjudicatory hearing can only undermine the potential for informality and cooperation which was intended to be the hallmark of the juvenile court system. Rather than concerning themselves with the matter at hand, establishing innocence or seeking a disposition best suited to individual correctional needs, the juvenile and his attorney are pressed

into a posture of adversary wariness that is conducive to neither [Citation omitted]. (421 U.S. at 540–541)

Since Jones was no longer subject to Juvenile Court jurisdiction, the decision gave him his freedom.

ROLES OF SOCIAL WORKERS AND LAWYERS IN JUVENILE CORRECTIONS

The traditional social work roles in juvenile corrections are clear. As public agency staff, social workers may be especially involved in filing the petition and in the dispositional hearing, since most juveniles who are adjudicated are served by correctional or "treatment" agencies.

The federal courts have tended to employ professional social workers as probation officers and supervisors more commonly than the local courts. More social workers are going into probation work—especially those with the professional bachelor's degree. Some states encourage the upgrading of probation staffs by providing subsidies to courts that comply with professional standards for probation personnel. Social workers interested in early intervention find increasing opportunities for employment with police departments.

Both increasing interest in juvenile corrections from social workers and increasing job openings have afforded social work a larger role. Social workers also have program responsibilities in training schools and other correctional facilities. In short, juvenile corrections is one of the more promising career areas for social workers.

Casework services in the court are provided for in the MAFC (1975). Section 5 establishes the services and section 6 defines the duties.

Section 5. Probation and Other Casework Services

Probation and other casework, clinical and related and supporting services shall be provided to the court by the department pursuant to the provisions of ( ) the cost thereof to be paid out of the general funds of the State as appropriated to the department pursuant to the provisions ( ) for such purposes.

[Sheridan and Beaser's (1975) rationale is:]

It is strongly recommended that probation services be established on a statewide basis, administered by an agency which is part of the executive branch of government. Continuity of responsibility and treatment is attained when service and care for delinquent children are in a single agency. Such a system also will provide continuity of administration and will promote a more equitable distribution of services in terms of both quality and quantity, as well as uniformity of procedure. These characteristics are currently lacking in most States because the localities have responsibility for the services and they are often not in a position to provide them adequately.

Administration of probation services by the executive branch of government will help to clarify the role of the probation officer as a professional without prosecutorial functions or subject to judicial control. Also, for legal as well as ethical reasons, the duties of the judge should not involve the administration of the probation services, the detention home, other foster care facilities or other casework or clinical services necessary for study or treatment.

Section 6. Powers and Duties of Probation Officers and Social Services Personnel

(a) For the purpose of carrying out the objectives and provisions of this (act), and subject to the limitations of this (act), probation and social services personnel shall have the power and duty to: (1) receive and examine complaints and allegations that a child is neglected or delinquent for the purpose of considering the commencement of proceedings under this (act); (2)   make appropriate referrals of cases to other private or public agencies of the community where their assistance appears to be needed or desirable; (3)   make predisposition studies and submit reports and recommendations to the court as required by this (act); (4)   supervise and assist a child placed on probation or under supervision by order of the court; and (5)   perform such other functions as are designated by this (act) or by rules of court pursuant thereto.

(b)   For the purposes of this (act), a probation officer or social service worker, with the approval of the court, shall have the power to take into custody and place in shelter or detention care a child who is under his supervision as a delinquent or neglected child when the probation officer or social service worker has reasonable cause to believe that the child has violated the conditions of his probation, or terms of protective supervision, or that he may flee from the jurisdiction of the court. A probation officer does not have the powers of a law enforcement officer nor may he sign a petition under this (act) with respect to a person who is not on probation or otherwise under his supervision.

In the position statement on Lawyer–Social Worker Relationships in the Family Court, the National Conference of Lawyers and Social Workers delineates the roles of social workers and lawyers (1973:32–33).

ROLES OF THE SOCIAL WORKER AND LAWYER IN FAMILY COURT
The social worker
The primary roles of the social worker in the various types of judicial hearings include acting as a witness to give substantial factual testimony; acting as an expert; performing the professional task of gathering, evaluating, and interpreting social and behavioral data for use by the court; and making recommendations as to predisposition detention or release and as to the final disposition best calculated to solve the presenting problems within the limits established by the statutes. In carrying out these roles, the social worker should:
1.   Explore with the defense counsel the resources of the family for coping with the problems at issue to the end that recommendations regarding predisposition detention and the final disposition may be mutually understood if not agreed upon.
2.   Work for the resolution of differences of opinion between himself and the lawyer prior to the hearing in court and avoid displays of antagonism or resentment when the differences are opened up in the hearing.
3.   Insofar as possible, and in concert with the defense counsel, keep the individual and family informed as to the nature of the upcoming hearing and share with them the recommendations that he plans to make, if any, and the reasons therefor.
4.   Obtain the advice and help of legal counsel concerning the validity and pertinence of the factual evidence that he is competent to give and the manner in which this testimony should be given.
5.   Present his oral and written information in a well-organized, clear, and concise fashion.
6.   Maintain his impartial, professional status in avoiding the role of an advocate.
7.   Abstain from furnishing advice or expressing opinions on questions of law.
8.   Encourage the individual or family concerned to seek legal counsel.
The lawyer
The lawyer representing litigants in family court should:
1.   Provide legal advice to his client and represent him at all stages of the proceedings.
2.   Participate with the social worker in evaluating circumstances and resources as they may affect detention and final disposition.
3.   To the extent permissible under local practice, minimize the adversary nature of the proceedings if, in his judgment, this is appropriate to the effective representation of his client's interests.
4.   Share with the social worker the recommendations he believes should be made concerning predisposition detention and the final disposition, in an effort to resolve as many differences as possible before the hearing.
5.   Demonstrate appreciation of the role and contribution of the social worker. Reinforce

the position of the social worker in carrying out responsibilities that he may have to assume after the hearing on behalf of the lawyer's client.

6. Encourage the social worker to participate in interpreting to the client and family the nature of the proceedings, the functioning of the court, and the reason for the findings of the court.

7. Establish with the client and the social worker the manner and extent to which he will provide postdispositional legal service, if any.

8. Advise the court when, in his estimation, additional counsel is needed for a separate member of the family to avoid a conflict-of-interest situation. (Pp.32-33)

Katz (1983) provides detailed suggestions for the social history on the basis that the social milieu is the predominant shaper of youth's activities.

TRENDS IN THE JUVENILE COURT

The *Kent, Gault, Winship,* and *McKeiver* decisions have shaped the contemporary juvenile court. Yet in spite of wide publicity, the safeguards provided by these cases are too often ignored. There is still a wide range of discretion in the thoroughness with which procedural safeguards are employed.

Paulsen and Whitebread (1974: 151-152) describe a hearing that may be all too representative of what still occurs in juvenile courts.

> A Rhode Island opinion, Gonsalves v. Devine (294 A.2d 206 [1972]) tells of a hearing held in March 1970. A 16-year-old respondent appeared in Family Court to answer a petition charging him (surely insufficiently under the *Gault* requirement of timely, written notice in sufficient detail so that the youth may make a response) with "a physical assault on [a] teacher at Central Junior High School." His mother was told she was entitled to counsel to defend the boy but was not told that if she had no funds to pay a lawyer, one would be provided. The judge said nothing to the respondent about the availability of counsel. Nor did he advise parent or child about the right to remain silent. The hearing consisted of listening to a school principal and a representative of the school tell of the incident which gave rise to the alleged assault. The representative had no first-hand information; the principal's recital was based partly on his own observations and partly on what he had been told. At no point during the fact-finding inquiry did the trail justice offer the juvenile an opportunity to question the school department's representative or the principal, to present testimony in his own defense, to address the court in his behalf, or to exercise what at common law was known as the right of allocution.* Instead, the record shows only that the trail justice, at the conclusion of the principal's statement and after observing that "any striking of a teacher just cannot be tolerated in our system," ordered the respondent detained at the state training school until further order of the court.

Some sources believe that Supreme Court decisions have gone too far toward formality, yet when one considers that juveniles often received stricter penalties than would have been accorded an adult under comparable circumstances, action had to be taken to protect their rights.

Several other areas need further clarification.

The right to counsel has been well established since *Gault,* but the courts might advise the juvenile of this right in such a way as to encourage a waiver. If

---

*Allocution refers to a statement from a defendant on behalf of mitigation of punishment.

used in a perfunctory manner, the waiver form applied in the *West* case will constitute poor legal practice.

Pretrial *discovery* is an important element in juvenile justice because it provides the child's attorney with the basis of the plaintiff's case. Besharov (1974:274) lists the evidence that may be important: (1) Witnesses, including their names, addresses, statements, and previous records, whether or not they will testify at trial; (2) Oral or written statements of the accused; (3) Physical evidence, including anything seized from the accused; (4) A line-up at which witnesses identified the accused; (5) The accused's or any potential witness' previous record; (6) Medical, psychiatric, or social work records or reports concerning the accused or any potential witness; (7) Medical or autopsy reports concerning the victim; and (8) Relevant photographs, diagrams, or demonstrative evidence. Only Ohio lists specific items that are considered discoverable.

Major problems for the juvenile court include an increase in violent crimes. In a single year in New York City, seventy-three youths were charged with fifty-one murders. Twenty-one were sent to institutions and five received probation. Thirty cases were withdrawn or dismissed. The records were unclear or missing on eleven. Six were still pending a year later.

One approach that will increase in popularity is stricter rules concerning juveniles who commit serious crimes of violence. The 1976 session of the New York Assembly mandated a minimum of two years of confinement and a maximum of five years for juveniles who commit such crimes. A thirteen-year-old charged with murder can be tried in an adult court and receive a life sentence. Sixteen-year-olds accused of violent crimes were already handled by the adult criminal justice system. Several other states have enacted similar legislation. In urban areas, juveniles in gangs that harass the community create more fear than alienated adults. Some people have advocated a reunification of adult and juvenile systems to give more options in the handling of dangerous youths.

Geoffrey Hazard (1976:18), in reviewing the state of the juvenile court, observes, "Most of the defiance that the law seeks to control is simply inaccessible from any external position." Both psychological factors and social environments are difficult to modify. Using legal compulsion to develop self-control is impossible. Hazard concludes, "It is possible for society to create government of sorts, but it has proved impossible for government to create society."

We tend to assign the juvenile justice system an impossible task, complicated by the lack of clear policies.

> Yet in doing so, the juvenile court has not gone very far in appropriating the concepts of reasonableness, notice, specification, reciprocity, and fiduciary duty that are the basic stuff of association law. If the school requires the child to attend, does it not have a duty to provide real tutelage? (Of all applications of the "right to treatment" concept, surely school attendance is potentially the most salient.) If young persons may not dally in tenement corridors, where can they dally? If they must obey their parents, what are they entitled to get in return? Again, on fairly elementary legal grounds, this branch of juvenile law is sustainable on the assumption that the persons subject to it can be regarded as having substantive legal responsibilities but no substantive legal rights. That, indeed, has been the assumption in the past, and even today the concept and content of substantive legal rights for children is barely in the formative stage.

> Although the juvenile law purports to have a "philosophy," there is no social philosophy on which is can draw, except perhaps for the question-begging precept that it serve the "best interests of the child." It often seems that the juvenile law is operating on an unarticulated wish that young people would behave as though they were members of an integrated and static society living in untroubled times. Such a wish, though understandable, is no substitute for policy. (Hazard, 1976:7-8)

Hazard also raises the troublesome issue of social class as it relates to diversion:

> The problems of substantive values and labeling are not serious in themselves, but they become serious in practice when the cases of middle-class juvenile offenders are resolved differently from those involving their lower-class counterparts. The difference is that middle-class children have access to means of mediation through private resources that are not available to lower-class children through public resources. These means include intervention by parents, teachers, clergy, lawyers, and others skilled in interpreting offenders' behavior in a way that elicits a more lenient response from legal authority and in formulating alternatives to the sanctions of juvenile law—dispositions such as psychological treatment, or special educational plans, for example. In essence, middle-class children can to a considerable extent escape the hand of the juvenile law because there are private hands in which to put them, whereas such resources are in short supply for the poor. The only way to avoid this discrimination would be to foreclose such diversions to the middle-class or to make equivalent resources available to the lower class. Neither alternative is a realistic possibility, and those administering the juvenile law cannot be held responsible for that fact. They can be held responsible, however, for recognizing that the law they administer is the official part of a two-part regime whose unofficial counterpart works more tenderly. (p. 10)

Gender discrimination also characterizes juveniles who are sent to correctional facilities. Huntington (1982:36) indicates that institutions for females are less likely to have doctors, nurses, or social workers or to use volunteers on a regular basis. She also found that such programs are more lenient with young women who had committed delinquent acts rather than sexual offenses. Sarri (1983) also deals with gender issues associated with the juvenile court.

Pabon (1983) considers detention as an informal correctional response to juvenile misdeeds—an alternative dispositional option to a lengthy stay at a training school.

The question of diversion is dealt with more comprehensively by Nejelski (1976), who indicates that the coercive power of the state is always present in diversion. The program that is agreed to by a youth, or one substantially more unpleasant, can be ordered by the judge. He quotes Coles' observations on children's perceptions of welfare workers:

> Welfare workers, in the pictures ghetto children draw, stand near the police like dogs, with huge piercing eyes, ears that seem twisted as they are oversize, and mouths noticeably absent or present as thick lines enclosing prominent and decidedly pointed and ragged teeth. To ghetto children, as to their parents, the welfare worker is the policemen's handmaiden, and together they come, as one child put it, "to keep us in line or send us away." (Coles, 1971:599–600)

There are neither adequate resources not adequate evaluations of diversion. Diversion programs under voluntary auspices may suffer a kinder fate than the juvenile court itself, only because the voluntary programs avoid public scrutiny.

Nejelski (1976:115) sounds the same warning on using diversion instead of giving attention to fundamental reform:

> In the adult system, society is coming to realize the impracticability of processing drunks or alcoholics as criminals. In contrast, where there is case by case diversion of minor cases, especially in the so-called status offenses, there is little pressure for radical change; sentiment for the repeal of the statutes which form the basis for state intervention does not develop. Instead, an administrator is deciding privately that some "juvenile offenders" are better treated in noncourt systems. Such a scheme currently calls for ad hoc decisions in individual cases by someone in the large system which deals with children in trouble. This discretion has low visibility and may be exercised in a discriminatory or arbitrary fashion.
>
> Discretionary screening of cases, which has the most serious impact on the poor and minorities, may have the unfortunate result of postponing more basic reform.

From developments in the 1980s thus far, it seems that the juvenile court has lost much of its distinctiveness and serious felonies by juveniles have deemphasized rehabilitation efforts. At the same time, handling status offenses through child welfare channels has decreased the need for counseling within the juvenile justice structure.

The current needs of juvenile courts are summarized in the recommendations from the National Association of Juvenile Court Judges published in 1984 in a special issue of the *Journal and Family Courts Journal*.

I Disposition Policies

1. Serious Juvenile Offenders Should Be Held Accountable by the Courts
2. Individualized Treatment Should Be Considered For Every Juvenile
3. Rehabilitation Should Be a Primary Goal of the Juvenile Court
4. Social Investigations Should Be Used for Individualized Treatment

II Causes and Prevention

5. Families and Schools Should Be Strengthened to Reduce Delinquency
6. Close Liaison Should Be Maintained between the Courts and the Schools
7. The Impact of School Problems on Delinquency Should Be Researched
8. Business and Labor Should Provide Jobs and Job Training for Juveniles
9. The Causes of Delinquency Should Be Studied in Depth

III Dispositional Guidelines

10. Guidelines Should Be Developed to Reduce Disparities
11. Provide Judicial Discretion for Individualized Treatment
12. A System-wide Commission Should Devise the Guidelines

IV Transfer to the Adult Criminal Court

13. Offenders Unamenable to Juvenile Treatment Should Be Transferred
14. The Juvenile Court Should Make the Transfer Decision
15. A New Transfer Decision Should Be Required for Subsequent Offenses

V Confidentiality

16. Open Hearings
17. Police Should Be Informed of Court Actions in Their Cases
18. Juvenile Records Should Be Provided to Adult Courts When Sentencing

Questions for Review

1. The juvenile court was created to achieve what specific goals?

2. What theory of causation of delinquency most influenced the efforts of the advocates of the juvenile courts?

3. How does juvenile-police interaction determine the volume of cases that actually come before the juvenile court?

4. Identify the major status offenses. Why are they given that name?

5. In the intake decision process, what three general courses of action are possible on behalf of the juvenile?

6. The sample petition form has been criticized as mechanical and legalistic. How would you revise the example given to overcome these criticisms?

7. Patricia Wald recommends that status offenders not be under the jurisdiction of the juvenile court. To what extent is this recommendation desirable? feasible?

8. Given the police attitudes toward juveniles as presented by Bittner, why would search and seizure violations by police be a particular problem?

9. What criteria permit waiver of a juvenile to an adult court?

10.   Why is *Gault* considered the most important single decision pertaining to the juvenile court?

11.   Explain the purpose of Section 33 of the model family court act dealing with continuance under supervision.

Questions for Debate and Discussion

1.   Evaluate Platt's criticisms of the juvenile court advocates in *The Child Savers*.

2.   Critics of labeling theory have held that labeling contributes little to future behavior—that the self-image is the by-product of many other more pervasive influences. Evaluate this statement.

3.   Evaluate Wald's analysis of the major problems in detention.

4.   *Gault* criticized the informality of juvenile court proceedings. *McKeiver* considered it essential. Can the two views be reconciled? How?

5.   From the comments of some police and judges, juvenile court disposition allegedly reduces adolescents' respect for law. Do you agree? If so, what should be done?

6.   How does Question 5 relate to use of diversion?

7.   What aspects of social work skills can be most effectively used to deal with problems in the juvenile court? Is the conflict between a welfare approach and a due process approach inevitable?

Selected Readings   Bailey, Ann Leslie. "Waiver of Miranda Rights by Juveniles: Is Parental Presence a Necessary Safeguard?" *Journal of Family Law* 21 (1983):725–743.

Barnett, Donald J., and Ola Barnett. "Enacting Legislation to identify and Treat Children with Conduct Disorders." *Pepperdine Law Review* 7 (1980): 827–864.

Coates, Robert. "Deinstitutionalization and the Serious Juvenile Offender: Some Policy Considerations." *Crime and Delinquency* 27 (1981):477–486.

Crow, Ruth, and Ginny McCarthy. "Teenage Women in the Juvenile Justice System." *Crime and Delinquency Review* (1980):103–105.

Davi, Donati. "Chance, Charge, and Challenge in Juvenile Corrections." *Juvenile and Family Courts Journal* 33 (May, 1982):45–50.

Fjeld, Stanton P., Lila Newsom, and Ruth M. Fjeld. "Delinquents and Status Offenders: The Similarity of Differences." *Juvenile and Family Courts Journal* 32 (May, 1981):3–10.

Fox, Sanford J. *Law of Juvenile Courts in a Nutshell.* St. Paul, Minn.: West Publishing Co., 1984.

Hahn, Paul H. (ed.). *The Juvenile Offender and the Law.* Cincinnati: Anderson Publishing Co., 1984.

King, Jane L. *A Comparative Analysis of Juvenile Codes.* Washington, D.C.: Government Printing Office, 1980.

Kogan, Lawrence. "A Family Systems Perspective on Status Offenders." *Juvenile and Family Courts Journal* 31 (1980):49–53.

McCarthy, Francis Barry, and James C. Carr. *Juvenile Law and Its Processes: Cases and Materials.* Indianapolis: Bobbs-Merrill, 1980.

Quinn, Luke, and Peter M. Hutchinson. "Status Offenders Should Be Removed from the Juvenile Court." *Pepperdine Law Review* 7 (1980):923–935.

Severy, Lawrence J., and J. Michael Whitaker. "Juvenile Diversion: An Experimental Analysis of Effectiveness." *Evaluation Review* 6 (1982):753–774.

Street Law: A Course in Practical Law. St. Paul, Minn.: West Publishing Co., 1981.

Turner, Kenneth A. "Treatment of Juvenile Delinquents." *Juvenile and Family Courts Journal* 32 (November, 1981):3–7.

CHAPTER

7

The Juvenile Court: Child Dependency, Neglect, and Abuse

In this chapter we consider how the juvenile court is involved with the parenting process. The focus shifts from a primary concern with delinquency and unruliness to home conditions that affect children's physical and emotional growth and development.

In the case of delinquency, criminal statutes have provided rather clear criteria for adjudication. In the case of neglect, dependency, or child abuse, however, vague statutory language and subjective values and standards predominate. In addition, the due process of law safeguards are also less clear for abused, neglected, and dependent children than they are for delinquent youths.

The social service agency plays a much larger role in making decisions about child neglect, dependency, or abuse than it does in cases of delinquency. Social workers may find themselves in the unenviable position of having to choose between an inadequate family home environment and an inadequate substitute home. Given this choice, the question often becomes "Is the continuity of the biological family preferable to the discontinuity of institutions or foster family homes?"

THE STATE AS PARENT

The state's parental function originates from the tradition of **parens patriae** by which the king authorized his chancellors to protect all infants in the realm. Their authority was limited to situations that threatened the children's present or future well-being and was justified by the ruler's desire to help subjects function effectively as citizens. The objective of *parens patriae* today is similar: to help children grow up to be responsible citizens and to prevent antisocial behavior.

Parens patriae has been defined as the responsibility to do "what is best in the interest of the child." In the judicial role, the judge has to assume the position of a wise, affectionate, and careful parent. Kadushin (1980:157) speaks from the perspective of a social worker and describes the obligation of the state in more explicit terms:

> The state is, ultimately, a parent to all children. When the natural parents neglect, abuse, or exploit the child, the state has the legal right and responsibility to intervene

137

to protect him. The state delegates this authority to the protective service agency, so that, in effect, the agency operates as an arm of the state and operates with legal sanctions. In such situations not only does the protective service agency have the right to intervene, they have the duty to intervene. All social agencies have an obligation to concern themselves with any situation of danger or potential danger to children, but the protective service agency has an explicitly delegated responsibility to intervene in such situations.

It follows, therefore, that protective services may be initiated on the basis of a request by someone other than a member of the family. In the case of services discussed earlier, client participation was voluntary. In the case of protective services, client involvement may be involuntary. Protective services deal with those instances of failure in parental role performance in which the parent is unaware of the need for service, or is unwilling and/or unable to avail himself of the services the community has provided.

Although *parens patriae* refers to the state's obligation and right to protect the young, the helpless, and the incompetent, its legal authority is lodged in the juvenile court charged with carrying out the state's authority on behalf of children in trouble. Yet Justice Abe Fortas noted in Application of Gault, 387 U.S. 1 (1967), that the meaning of *parens patriae* is "murky" and its historic credentials are of "dubious reference" to juvenile delinquency proceedings.

For the child who is in need of protection, but not delinquent, the standards of evidence and the emphasis on due process of law provided for the alleged delinquent in the *Winship*, *Gault*, and *Kent* cases have not been assured. Protective services are offered in a value-laden context. Each person involved uses different criteria to define "adequate" family life as well as to identify home conditions that require restriction of parental rights. Interpretation of evidence differs from one court to another and one judge to another, even in the same county. In some instances the state functions as a strict and demanding parent figure; in others it fulfills its parenting role cautiously or permissively.

Most of the decisions on child protection come from lower courts. Until *Kent* and *Gault*, the U.S. Supreme Court had not dealt with the rights of children. Since those rulings, the Court has shown great reluctance to rule on child-rearing and family life.

LABELING AND CLASSIFICATION

How does child protection involve labeling? Labels used to describe a child's behavior are based on (1) the child's actions; (2) supports that can be expected from the child's family; (3) the standards of the community in which the child lives; (4) the philosophy of the police, judges, and social agencies; and (5) the services one wishes to utilize.

The juvenile court handles two types of matters—those involving offenses of the child and those related to offenses or gross inadequacies on the part of parents. Labels used in juvenile courts reflect this dual focus and can be arranged in a descending order of seriousness:

Labels for the Problem Child

Criminal (committing offenses that bring the child under the jurisdiction of an adult court)

Delinquent (violating a law that may or may not apply to adults also)

In need of supervision (behaving in a way that indicates the child is beyond control of parents or other adults)

Labels for the Problem Parent

Abusing (inflicting injury)

Neglecting (failing to do that which is essential)

Dependent (providing inadequate care through no fault of the caretaker)

We have already noted that applying a label ultimately affects a person's self-image and encourages the very behavior it describes. Recognizing this fact, the juvenile court has generally attempted to apply benign labels. It is also important to note that categories are not mutually exclusive. Parental neglect can precipitate delinquent conduct, and the delinquent child may have been subjected to hostility and child abuse in the home. The neglected child may also be a delinquent who has not yet been caught.

Social class can affect labeling. A child from a "good family" who comes before the law is less likely to be adjudicated "delinquent" or given any formal label because the court trusts the parent to take responsibility for rehabilitation. Differential labeling may also arise in response to community standards or size. Many large urban courts require that there be repeated instances of lawbreaking to justify a finding of "delinquency," while smaller communities tend to apply the same designation for relatively minor infractions in order to teach the offender a lesson or to relay a warning to other youths in the community.

The types of services available can also affect the label chosen. In order to avail itself of a rehabilitative juvenile corrections program, for example, a court may be likely to find a youth "delinquent." If the same kinds of services were offered within the "child welfare" system, a finding of "neglect" might be entered principally to gain access to the service program.

Delinquency can be established by a single act, but **neglect** requires repeated acts on the part of parents or custodians. Neglect stems from violations of some parental standard—a failure to meet minimal parental behavior. Criteria for the neglect standard vary in accordance with the problem, the child's prognosis for change, and the disposition desired.

The MAFC (1975) defines *neglect* in Section 3:

(19) "Neglected child" means a child:

(a) who has been abandoned by his parents, guardian, or other custodian;

(b) who is physically abused by his parents, guardian, or other custodian or who is without proper parental care and control necessary for his well-being because of the faults or habits of his parents, guardian, or other custodian or their neglect or refusal, when able to do so, to provide them; or

(c) whose parents, guardian, or other custodian are unable to discharge their responsibilities to and for the child; or

(d) who has been placed for care or adoption in violation of law; and

(e) in any of the foregoing is in need of care or supervision.

Two definitions of neglect illustrate how two states can apply the label differently. The Minnesota statute specifies eight situations that can constitute neglect (M.S.A. §260.015, Subd. 10 [1982]). It is interesting to note that residence in an unlicensed foster home is included.

"Neglected child" means a child:

(a)   Who is abandoned by his parent, guardian, or other custodian; or

(b)   Who is without proper parental care because of the faults or habits of his parent, guardian, or other custodian; or

(c)   Who is without necessary subsistence, education, or other care necessary for his physical or mental health or morals because his parent, guardian, or other custodian neglects or refuses to provide it; or

(d)   Who is without the special care made necessary by his physical or mental condition because his parent, guardian, or other custodian neglects or refuses to provide it; or

(e)   Whose occupation, behavior, condition, environment, or associations are such as to be injurious or dangerous to himself or other; or

(f)   Who is living in a facility for foster care which is not licensed as required by law, unless the child is living in the facility under court order; or

(g)   Whose parent, guardian, or custodian has made arrangements for his placement in a manner detrimental to the welfare of the child or in violation of law; or

(h)   Who comes within the [juvenile delinquency] provisions of subdivision 5, but whose conduct results in whole or in part from parental neglect.

The New York statute on child neglect introduces the more abstract idea of impairment or imminent danger of impairment (N.Y. Family Ct. Act, 1012[f] [McKinney, 1973]):

"Neglected child" means a child less than eighteen years of age whose physical, mental or emotional condition has been impaired or is in imminent danger of becoming impaired as a result of the failure of his parent or other person legally responsible for his care to exercise a minimum degree or care

A.   in supplying the child with adequate food, clothing, shelter, or education, in accordance with the provisions of part one of article sixty-five of the education law, or medical, dental optometrical or surgical care, though financially able to do so or offered financial or other reasonable means to do so; or

B.   in providing the child with proper supervision or guardianship, by reasonably inflicting or allowing to be inflicted harm, or a substantial risk thereof including the infliction of excessive corporal punishment; or by using a drug or drugs; or by using alcoholic beverages to the extent that he loses self-control of his actions or by any other acts of similarly serious nature requiring the aid of the court; provided, however, that where the respondent is voluntarily and regularly participating in a rehabilitative program, evidence that the respondent has repeatedly misused a drug or drugs or alcoholic beverages to the extent that he loses self-control of his actions shall not establish that the child is a neglected child in the absence of evidence establishing that the child's physical, mental or emotional condition has been impaired or is in imminent danger of becoming impaired as set forth in paragraph (i) of this provision; or

C.   who has been abandoned, in accordance with the definition and the criteria set forth in subdivision five of section three hundred eighty-four b of the social services law, by his parents or other person legally responsible for his care.

Whatever definition is followed, social workers must be sure that allegations of neglect are based on evidence, not speculation. Bell and Mlyniec (1974:27) comment on In re Nyce, 268 N.E.2d 233 (Ill. App. 1971):

Two child welfare workers who had had limited contact with the young mother of an infant testified that they did not believe she would be a fit and proper parent. Since the young mother had not had actual custody of her child and since the petition did not claim she failed to insure proper care, the appellate court found that neglect as defined by the statute was not shown. The court held that the workers' testimony was speculative as to the future care of the child.

DEPENDENCY

Fault is often difficult to assess in determining parental failure. A **dependency** finding frequently results from poverty rather than parental fault. It allows the court to exercise necessary authority over the family without alleging parental neglect. In this sense, dependency is equivalent to no-fault neglect.

Poverty alone should not justify a finding of dependency leading to removal of a child from the home. The child from a family lacking material resources should not be subjected to judicial review; alternative means should be devised to meet the needs of the child and the family as well.

Mental retardation of parents is a cause of inadequate child care leading to a dependency action, as In re McDonald, 201 N.W.2d 447 (Iowa 1972). Note the key role of the social worker and the visiting nurse in this case.

IN RE McDONALD

Supreme Court of Iowa, 201 N.W.2d 447 (Iowa 1972).

This is an appeal from an order of the municipal court of the city of Davenport sitting as the juvenile court of Scott County terminating the relationship of parent and child existing between David McDonald, father, and Diane McDonald, mother, and their twin daughters, Joyce and Melissa McDonald. The parents challenge sufficiency of the evidence to support the order. . . .

The court, after summarizing the evidence produced at the hearing, noted in its findings of fact that the evidence compelled a finding "that Diane McDonald, primarily because of her very low IQ, is simply not able to give to these twins the proper care and attention, including but not limited to the stimulation which the twins need and to which they responded almost immediately when placed in the foster homes. Nor is there any reasonable probability that Diane McDonald would be able to substantially improve her past performance with the twins, should they continue for a further period even as long as a year, in foster care. The Court is reluctantly convinced that because of this mother's very low IQ she could never adequately take the proper care of these twins or at least provide them with the stimulation in her home that they must have to grow and develop into normal, healthy children. Unfortunately, although David McDonald is able to do considerably better, the best interests of the twins requires a termination as to him as well."

The court concluded: . . . That the relationship now existing between David McDonald, father, and Diane McDonald, mother, and Joyce McDonald and Melissa McDonald, children, should be terminated because the parents are unfit by reason of conduct found by the Court to be detrimental to the physical and mental health of said children.[Citations omitted.] . . .

. . . That the relationship now existing between David McDonald, father, and Diane McDonald, mother, and Joyce McDonald and Melissa McDonald, children, should be terminated because following an adjudication of dependency on March 3, 1969, reasonable efforts under the direction of the Court have failed to correct the conditions leading to such findings.[Citation omitted.] . . .

David McDonald, 20, and Diane Kroeger, 17, were married May 27, 1967. David testified that approximately two years before his marriage, a Davenport doctor had hospitalized him at the University Hospital in Iowa City for a nervous condition and general health. About nine months before his marriage he was again hospitalized, this time at Mercy Hospital in Davenport by his mother. After about two weeks David was transferred to Pine Knoll for observation and mental tests. During the time he was at Pine Knoll he was released during the daytime to work in Davenport. When discharged about two months before his marriage, David said he was "physically and mentally good." . . .

A visiting counselor with the Davenport public school system testified that David had been given the Wechsler Adult Intelligence Scale January 21, 1965, and recorded a full scale IQ of 74. David had quit school in the eleventh grade. Diane had been tested September 21, 1964 and her full scale score IQ was 47. We are not told about her background except that she came from "a very cruel and immoral home." . . .

Elaine Hughes, a registered nurse with 25 years' experience, presently serving as a nurse of Davenport Visiting Nurse Association, made one unannounced visit to McDonalds when the twins were four months old. When Miss Hughes arrived, David and Diane were upstairs in another apartment. They came down to show her the children. The nurse testified the babies were in a clean bed with "propped bottles," which she felt was dangerous as the babies might choke and that "a mother should hold their baby to feed it." She observed their diapers were both quite soiled and dirty. "They were pale, just unresponsive as far as—no stimulation, lack of stimulation is probably the way I would say." She noted in her office records following this visit "diaper rash and a possibility of a slight cold." . . .

[Miss Hughes] was asked why her office was seeking termination of the relationship. . . .

"Because children this age should not remain in foster care indefinitely. These children are now two and half years old. They should not remain in foster care for another two and a half years, for instance, and become of an age when adoption is more difficult. It would appear that it is only fair to the children, if the parents are not going to be in a position to have them back in their home, that there be a severance so they could have their own homes at this time. And the reason we filed the severance Petition was at the request of the Supervising agency."

Barbara Moore, a social worker employed by the Scott County Department of Social Services, first observed the McDonald twins October 7, 1968, during a visit to the Graves home. Miss Moore testified the children were listless, appeared to have colds and in general did not look very healthy. . . .

. . . After the twins were placed in foster homes Miss Moore visited with McDonalds 30 to 35 times; some of these visits were in the McDonald apartment, others at Miss Moore's office. . . .

The witness expressed doubts about Mrs. McDonald's ability to cope with the situation where Diane had to mother children, care for them, give them guidance and all the things a mother would have to do. She based this opinion upon Diane's responses when the witness attempted to talk with her. Mrs. McDonald never initiated any conversation, everything "had to be pulled out of her" and often times the witness didn't get too much response. Miss Moore expressed the opinion Mrs. McDonald had a general lack of concern about the twins during these visits. This was not true of David who was interested and concerned about his children. . . .

Respondents called Joyce Graves as a witness. She testified she knew David wanted to marry Diane but she was opposed to the marriage and signed necessary papers to place David in Mercy Hospital. From her experience of raising 11 children—six ranging in age from 2 to 19 still at home—it is evident Mrs. Graves had an appreciation of the care demanded of a mother. She said she foresaw difficulties arising from the marriage because of Diane's mental slowness. Although she felt her son could provide a home for the twins, she was concerned about Diane's capabilities to be a mother. This was the basic reason for opposing the marriage. . . .

Mrs. Graves could not honestly say that at the time of the hearing Diane could do the things necessary for the children although there were certain things she could do with training. She had improved in her housekeeping considerably. Mrs. Graves taught Diane to bathe the children, which she was afraid to do at first, and to make a formula. However, it took some coaxing and a lot of patience to accomplish this. Mrs. Graves expressed compassion for Diane because of her earlier home life, or lack thereof, and the indifference of her mother. . . .

The record discloses that McDonalds are presently experiencing physical problems with the third child. She has leakage of the heart, which will require surgery, and her arm was broken at birth.

Diane did not testify, on her doctor's advice.

Counsel for McDonalds point out that, "There is no evidence of their 'debauchery, intoxication, habitual use of narcotic drugs, repeated lewd and lascivious behavior, or other conduct—likely to be detrimental to the physical or mental health or morals of the children.' " . . . In the cited cases there was substantial evidence of infidelity, quarreling between parents, separations, illegitimate births and in one, attempts of suicide and in two, physical abuse inflicted upon the children involved.

It cannot be logically argued that there is substantial evidence in the record before us to support a finding of willingness on David's part to avoid responsibility of providing care and support for the twins. . . .

. . . The court reached the conclusion that the relationship should be terminated "because following an adjudication of dependency on March 3, 1969, reasonable efforts under the direction of the court have failed to correct the conditions leading to such findings." Section 232.41(2)(e).

"A dependent child includes one 'who is in need of special care and treatment required by his physical or mental condition which the parents, guardian, or other custodian is unable to provide.' Code section 232.2, subd. 14, par. b." . . .

There is substantial evidence that neither conditions leading to the twins being placed in foster homes November 8, 1968, nor those conditions leading to the court's finding of dependency following the March 3, 1969, hearing have been corrected by reasonable efforts under the court's direction.

Both procedures were made necessary by reason of Diane's inability to properly care for the children.

Although there has been considerable improvement in Diane's ability to keep house, there still remained at the time of the termination hearing held more than two years after the birth of the twins a serious doubt as to Diane's ability to cope with the situation requiring guidance and to perform those things a mother must do in raising children.

As noted in the quoted portion of its findings, the juvenile court was "reluctantly convinced that because of this mother's very low IQ she could never adequately take the proper care of these twins or at least provide them with the stimulation in her home that they must have to grow and develop into normal healthy children." There is substantial evidence to support this finding. Mrs. Graves, Miss Moore and Miss Hughes all expressed doubt as to Diane's ability to perform the functions of a mother because of her very low IQ.

Since there is no reasonable probability Diane would be able to substantially improve her past performance in caring for the children, the longer they remain in foster homes the more difficult adoption will become.

By the time this opinion is filed the twins will be four and half years old. They should have proper guidance and a healthy mental atmosphere from those who have their custody. . . .

When the twins were seen in May before the hearing they appeared to be normal children in all respects, mentally and physically.

. . . This court has repeatedly stated that in matters of this kind the primary consideration is the welfare and best interests of the child. While there is a presumption that the best interests of the child will be served by leaving it with its parents, this is not conclusive. The State, as *parens patriae*, has the duty to see that every child within its borders receives proper care and treatment. . . .

In equity matters, such as this, where our review is de novo, it is our responsibility to review the facts as well as the law and adjudicate rights anew on those propositions properly presented, provided issue has been raised and error, if any, preserved in the course of the trial court's proceedings. Therefore, we conclude, as did the juvenile court, that the best interests of the twins require termination of the relationship existing between David McDonald, father, and Diane McDonald, mother, and Joyce and Melissa McDonald, children.

CHILD NEGLECT   Statutory definitions of *neglect* frequently include abandonment, seriously inadequate or improper care, deprivation of education or health care, or subjection to an "unfit" environment. In most jurisdictions, courts handle child abuse under a neglect petition. If dependency is equivalent to no-fault neglect, child abuse may be considered "punitive" neglect. More recent additions to the statutes are *psychological neglect* or *mental injury*—terms that present particularly difficult problems of proof. The Children's Division of the American Humane Society (unpublished paper) identified conditions of child neglect:

IDENTIFYING CONDITIONS OF CHILD NEGLECT
Physical

1. Physically abused
2. Sexually abused
3. Exploited
    A. Excessive responsibilities placed on very young children to care for home and other younger children
    B. Overworked beyond physical endurance
    C. Forced to beg and steal
    D. Forced to sell commodities beyond child's ability to do so
4. Malnourished and emaciated
5. Failure to receive necessary immunizations
6. Suffers chronic illness and lacks essential medical care
7. Lack dental care
8. Failure to receive necessary prosthetics, including eyeglasses, hearing aids, etc.
9. Failure to receive proper hygiene
    A. Unwashed
    B. Unbathed
    C. Poor mouth and skin care
10. Failure to attend school regularly due to the faults of the parent
11. Without supervision
12. Left alone for hours and days
13. Abandoned

Emotional

1. Denied normal experiences that produce feelings of being loved, wanted, secure, and worthwhile
2. Rejected through indifference
3. Rejected overtly—left alone, shouted at, blamed for problems, etc.
4. Emotional neglect is intangible, but the child's behavior often reveals visible symptoms such as hyperactivity, withdrawal, overeating, fire-setting, nervous skin disorders, psychosomatic complaints, autism, suicide attempts, truancy, delinquencies, failure to thrive, aggressiveness, discipline problems, stuttering, enuresis, hypochondriasis, and overprotection.

Material

1. Insufficient clothing
    A. Fails to keep child warm and comfortable at home, at school, and at play
    B. Seriously fails to protect the child from the elements of the weather
2. Improper clothing
    A. Dirty, smelly, ragged, and generally in terrible disrepair
    B. Wearing of such clothing usually results in ridicule and harassment from the child's peers
3. Filthy living conditions
    A. Garbage and dirt strewn about the house and yard
    B. Floor and walls smeared with crusted feces
    C. Urine smell permeates throughout the house
    D. Vermin
    E. Soiled bedding and chairs
    F. Some conditions in total chaos—no evidence of routine housekeeping
4. Inadequate shelter
    A. Cold
    B. Overcrowded
    C. Makeshift sleeping arrangements
    D. Poor lighting
    E. Poor ventilation
    F. Fire hazards
    G. Poor sanitation as a result of inadequate or unrepaired plumbing
    H. Other hazardous conditions existing for children such as broken stairs, broken windows, broken porch and stair railings, etc.
5. Insufficient food
6. Haphazard meals
    A. Meals that consistently lack nutritional value
    B. Steady diet of potato chips, pop, candy, peanut butter, crackers, etc.

Demoralizing circumstances

1. Continuous friction in the home
2. Mentally ill parents
3. Marital discord
4. Immature parents
5. Excessive drinking
6. Addiction to drugs
7. Criminal environment
8. Illicit sex relations
9. Overly severe control and discipline
10. Encouraging delinquencies
11. Mental retardation of parents
12. Harsh and improper language
13. Nonsupport
14. Values in the home in conflict with society
15. Failures to inculcate value system in guidance and care of children (lack of moral training)
16. Broken home, divorce, and frequent remarriages
17. Failure to offer motivation and stimulation toward learning and receiving an education in keeping with child's ability and intelligence
18. Failure to provide healthy, wholesome recreation for family and children
19. Failure to individualize children and their needs
20. Failure to give constructive discipline for the child's proper development of good character, conduct, and habits
21. Failure to give good adult example
22. Promiscuity and prostitution

The conditions specified reflect a strong moral tone. Many children suffer from several of these conditions without being considered neglected. In some circumstances, a single condition will establish neglect. Some are more serious than others, and interpretations of seriousness differ.

Refusing Medical Treatment

Parental authority and religious freedom coexist as issues in cases concerning parental refusal of medical treatment or surgery. The best-known cases probably involve the ordering of blood transfusions for children of Jehovah's Witnesses who refuse transfusions on a religious basis. Courts usually refrain from ordering such medical procedures unless the need for intervention is to preserve life, but judges differ in their assessment. In re Green, 292 A.2d 387 (Pa. 1972), illustrates the case where the majority decided that the situation was not a life-or-death matter.

IN RE GREEN

Supreme Court of Pennsylvania, 292 A.2d 387 (Pa. 1972).

The Director of the State Hospital for Crippled Children at Elizabethtown, Pennsylvania, filed a "petition to initiate juvenile proceedings" under The Juvenile Court Law [citation omitted], which sought a judicial declaration that Ricky Ricardo Green (hereinafter "Ricky") was a "neglected child" within the meaning of the Act and the appointment of a guardian. After an evidentiary hearing, the Court of Common Pleas, Family Division, Juvenile Branch, of Philadelphia dismissed the petition. On appeal, the Superior Court unanimously reversed and remanded the matter for the appointment of a guardian. Green Case, 220 Pa. Super. Ct. 191, 286 A.2d 681 (1971). We granted allocatur [allowed the order].

Ricky was born on September 10, 1955, to Nathaniel and Ruth Green. He lives with his mother as his parents are separated and the father pays support pursuant to a court order. Ricky has had two attacks of poliomyelitis which have generated problems of obesity and, in addition, Ricky now suffers from paralytic scoliosis (94% curvature of the spine).

Due to this curvature of the spine, Ricky is presently a "sitter," unable to stand or ambulate due to the collapse of his spine; if nothing is done, Ricky could become a bed patient. Doctors have recommended a "spinal fusion" to relieve Ricky's bent position, which would involve moving bone from Ricky's pelvis to his spine. Although an orthopedic specialist testified, "there is no question that there is danger in this type of operation," the mother did consent conditionally to the surgery. The condition is that, since the mother is a Jehovah's Witness who believes that the Bible proscribes any blood transfusions which would be necessary for this surgery, she would not consent to any blood transfusions. Initially, we must recognize that, while the operation would be beneficial, there is no evidence that Ricky's life is in danger or that the operation must be performed immediately. Accordingly, we are faced with the situation of a parent who will not consent to a dangerous operation on her minor son requiring blood transfusions solely because of her religious beliefs.

By statute, a "neglected child"—"a child whose parent . . . neglects or refuses to provide proper or necessary . . . medical or surgical care"—may be committed "to the care, guidance and control of some respectable citizen of good moral character . . ." appointed by the court. . . .

Almost a century ago, the United States Supreme Court enunciated the twofold concept of the Free Exercise clause: "Laws are made for the government of actions, and while they cannot interfere with mere religious belief and opinions, they may with practices." . . .

Turning to the situation where an adult refuses to consent to blood transfusions necessary to save the life of his infant son or daughter, other jurisdictions have uniformly held that the state can order such blood transfusions over the parents' religious objections. . . .

In our view, the penultimate question presented by this appeal is whether the state may interfere with a parent's control over his or her child in order to enhance the child's physical well-being when the child's life is in no immediate danger and when the state's intrusion conflicts with the parent's religious beliefs. Stated differently, does the State have an interest of sufficient magnitude to warrant the abridgment of a parent's right to freely practice his or her religion when those beliefs preclude medical treatment of a son or daughter whose life is not in immediate danger? We are not confronted with a life or death situation. . . . Nor is there any question in the case at bar of a parent's omission or neglect for non-religious reasons. . . .

On facts virtually identical to this appeal, the Family Court of Ulster County ordered a blood transfusion in In re Sampson, 65 Misc.2d 658, 317 N.Y.S.2d 641 (1970). . . . That court further decided not to place this difficult decision on the boy and to order an immediate operation, thereby preventing psychological problems. On appeal, the Appellate Division, Third Department, unanimously affirmed the order in a memorandum decision. In re Sampson, 37 A.D.2d 668, 323 N.Y.S.2d 253 (1971). That court rejected the argument that "State intervention is permitted only where the life of the child is in danger by a failure to act . . . (as) a much too restricted approach."

(1) With all deference to the New York Court of Appeals, we disagree with the second observation in a non-fatal situation and express no view of the propriety of that statement in a life or death situation. If we were to

describe this surgery as "required," like the Court of Appeals, our decision would conflict with the mother's religious beliefs. Aside from religious considerations, one can also question the use of that adjective on medical grounds since an orthopedic specialist testified that the operation itself was dangerous. Indeed, one can question who, other than the Creator, has the right to term certain surgery as "required." This fatal/non-fatal distinction also steers the courts of this Commonwealth away from a medical and philosophical morass: if spinal surgery can be ordered, what about a hernia or gall bladder operation or a hysterectomy? The problems created by *Sampson* are endless. We are of the opinion that as between a parent and the state, the state does not have an interest of sufficient magnitude outweighing a parent's religious beliefs when the child's life is *not immediately imperiled* by his physical condition.

(2) Unlike *Yoder* and *Sampson*, our inquiry does not end at this point since we believe the wishes of this sixteen-year-old boy should be ascertained; the ultimate question, in our view, is whether a parent's religious beliefs are paramount to the possibly adverse decision of the child. . . .

It would be most anomalous to ignore Ricky in this situation when we consider the preference of an intelligent child of sufficient maturity in determining custody. Moreover, we have held that a child of the same age can waive constitutional rights and receive a life sentence. Indeed, minors can now bring a personal injury action in Pennsylvania against their parents. We need not extend this litany of the rights of children any further to support the proposition that Ricky should be heard. The record before us does not even note whether Ricky is a Jehovah's Witness or plans to become one. We shall, therefore, reserve any decision regarding a possible parent-child conflict and remand the matter for an evidentiary hearing similar to the one conducted in *Seiferth* in order to determine Ricky's wishes. . . .

EAGEN, Justice (dissenting). . . .

I also do not agree with the emphasis the majority places on the fact this is not a life or death situation. The statute with which we are dealing does not contain any such language, nor do I find support for this position in the case law. The statute in pertinent part states:

> "A child whose parent . . . neglects or refuses to provide *proper or necessary* subsistence, education, *medical or surgical care, or other care necessary for her health.* . . ." [Emphasis supplied.] 11 P.S. § 243(5)(c)

The statute only speaks in terms of "health," not life or death. If there is a substantial threat to health, then I believe the courts can and should intervene to protect Ricky. By the decision of this Court today, this boy may never enjoy any semblance of a normal life which the vast majority of our society has come to enjoy and cherish.

Lastly, I must take issue with the manner in which the majority finally disposes of the case. I do not believe that sending the case back to allow Ricky to be heard is an adequate solution. We are herein dealing with a young boy who has been crippled most of his life, consequently, he has been under the direct control and guidance of his parents for that time. To now presume that he could make an independent decision as to what is best for his welfare and health is not reasonable. Moreover, the mandate of the Court presents this youth with a most painful choice between the wishes of his parents and their religious convictions on the one hand, and his chance for a normal healthy life on the other hand. We should not confront him with this dilemma.

It is increasingly common and highly desirable for older children to be involved in reaching a decision on their own situations, but as the dissent indicates, the child is unlikely to be objective. An earlier case that did involve the question of life or death was People v. Labrenz, 104 N.E.2d 769 (Ill. 1952).

PEOPLE v. LABRENZ

Supreme Court of Illinois, 104 N.E.2d 769 (Ill. 1952).

After a hearing upon a petition filed in the circuit court of Cook County, an order was entered finding that Cheryl Linn Labrenz, an infant then eight days old, was a dependent child whose life was endangered by the refusal of her parents to consent to a necessary blood transfusion. The court appointed a guardian for the child and authorized the guardian to consent to a blood transfusion. The propriety of that action is challenged here upon a writ of error raising constitutional issues.

The petition was filed on April 17, 1951. It alleged that Cheryl Linn Labrenz was born on April 11, 1951, that she was then in a hospital in Chicago, and that her parents, Darrell and Rhoda Labrenz, were wholly unwilling to care for and protect her, so that she had become a dependent child. The petition prayed that the child be taken from its parents and placed under the guardianship of a suitable person to be appointed by the court.

At the hearing which was had on this petition on April 18, 1951, the evidence showed that the child suffered from erythrobastosis fetalis (commonly called the RH blood condition), a disease in which the red blood cells are destroyed by antibodies, or poisons. Hospital records and medical testimony established that the child's blood count had been dropping steadily since her birth; that the normal blood count of a child of her age was about 5,000,000, whereas her blood count was 1,950,000; that antibodies in the baby's bloodstream were gradually destroying all of the red blood cells; that her blood-supplying system was unable to furnish a supply of its own blood adequate to overcome the condition, and that a blood transfusion was necessary.

Three doctors testified. Two were certain that the child would die unless a transfusion was administered. The third doctor testified that the child had a slim chance to live without a transfusion, but that even if she did live, without a transfusion her brain would probably be so injured that she would be mentally impaired for life. The medical testimony also dealt with the degree of risk involved in a blood transfusion. One doctor testified that there would be no more hazard in a transfusion than in taking an aspirin. . . .

The parents of the child testified that their refusal to consent to a transfusion was based upon religious grounds. Darrell Labrenz, the child's father, testified: "it is my belief that the commandment given us in Genesis, Chapter 9, Verse 4, and subsequent commandment of Leviticus, Chapter 17, Verse 14, and also in the testimony after Christ's time and recorded in Acts, 15th Chapter, it is my opinion that any use of the blood is prohibited whether it be for food or whether it be for, as modern medical science puts it, for injections into the bloodstream and as such I object to it. The life is in the blood and the life belongs to our father, Jehovah, and it is only his to give or take; it isn't ours, and as such I object to the using of the blood in connection with this case."

Rhoda Labrenz, the mother, testified that "we believe it would be breaking God's commandment to take away blood which he told us to eat of the flesh but should not take of the blood into our systems. The life is in the blood and blood should not be drained out. We feel that we would be breaking God's commandment, also destroying the baby's life for the future, not only this life, in case the baby should die and breaks the commandment, not only destroys our chances but also the baby's chances for future life. We feel it is more important than this life."

. . . The court appointed its chief probation officer to be guardian of the person of Cheryl Linn Labrenz, directed him to consent to a blood transfusion, and retained jurisdiction for the purpose of making further orders for the welfare of the child. On May 4, 1951, the guardian reported to the court that a transfusion had been administered on April 18, 1951, and that the child's health had greatly improved. The court then ordered that the child be released from the hospital and returned to the custody of her parents but refused to discharge the guardian because it found that further periodic medical examinations would be necessary to determine the need for additional transfusions. On June 15, 1951, the court discharged the guardian, released the child to her parents, and ordered that the proceeding be dismissed.

Turning now to the merits of the case, plaintiffs in error first argue that the court below lacked jurisdiction because the child was not a "neglected" or "dependent" child within the meaning of the statute. The jurisdiction which was exercised in this case stems from the responsibility of government, in its character as *parens patriae*, to care for infants within its jurisdiction and to protect them from neglect, abuse and fraud. That ancient equitable jurisdiction was codified in our Juvenile Court Act, which expressly authorizes the court, if circumstances warrant, to remove the child from the custody of its parents and award its custody to an appointed guardian. [Citations omitted.]

So far as here pertinent, the statute defines a dependent or neglected child as one which "has not proper parental care." [Citations omitted.] The record contains no suggestion of any improper conduct on the part of the parents except in their refusal to consent to a blood transfusion. And it is argued that this refusal on the part of the parents does not show neglect, or a lack of parental care. Neglect, however, is the failure to exercise the care that the circumstances justly demand. It embraces wilful as well as unintentional disregard of duty. It is not a term of fixed and measured meaning. It takes its content always from specific circumstances, and its meaning varies as the context of surrounding circumstances changes. The question here is whether a child whose parents refuse to permit a blood transfusion, when lack of a transfusion means that the child will almost certainly die or at best will be mentally impaired for life, is a neglected child. In answering that question it is of no consequence that the parents have not failed in their duty in other respects. We entertain no doubt that this child, whose parents were deliberately depriving it of life or subjecting it to permanent mental impairment, was a neglected child within the meaning of the statute. The circuit court did not lack jurisdiction. . . .

It is next contended that if the Juvenile Court Act is held to be applicable, it deprives the parents of freedom of religion, and of their rights as parents, in violation of the Fourteenth Amendment to the Constitution of the United States and of section 3 of article II of the constitution of Illinois, S.H.A. This contention is based upon the parents' objection to the transfusion because of their belief that blood transfusions are forbidden by the Scriptures. Because the governing principles are well settled, this argument requires no extensive discussion. Concededly, freedom of religion and the right of parents to the care and training of their children are to be accorded the highest possible respect in our basic scheme.

Indeed, the early decision in the Reynolds case, upholding a Mormon's conviction for bigamy against the defense of interference with religious freedom as guaranteed in the First Amendment, leaves no doubt about the validity of the action here taken. The following language of that opinion is of particular interest, 98 U.S. at page 166: "Laws are made for the government of actions, and while they cannot interfere with mere religious belief and opinions, they may with practices. Suppose one believed that human sacrifices were a necessary part of religious worship, would it be seriously contended that the civil government under which he lived could not interfere to prevent a sacrifice? Or if a wife religiously believed it was her duty to burn herself upon the funeral pile of her dead husband, would it be beyond the power of the civil government to prevent her carrying her belief into practice?"

The recent Prince decision reinforces that conclusion. The court there held that a State, acting to safeguard the general interest in the well-being of its youth, could prohibit a Jehovah's Witness child from distributing religious pamphlets on the street even though the child was accompanied by her adult guardian. Obviously, the facts before us present a far stronger case for State intervention. Further, the court observed in reaching its conclusion in the Prince case, 321 U.S. at pages 166, 170, 64 S.Ct. at pages 442, 444: "The right to practice religion freely does not include liberty to expose the community or child to communicable disease or the latter to ill health or death. . . . Parents may be free to become martyrs themselves. But it does not follow they are free, in identical circumstances, to make martyrs of their children before they have reached the age of full and legal discretion when they can make that choice for themselves."

We hold, therefore, that neither the statute nor the action of the court pursuant to the statute violated the constitutional rights of plaintiffs in error.

Matters of life and death are considered to override religious practices and beliefs. The exclusive reliance on prayer for healing illustrates another controversial issue that is similarly considered.

CHILD NEGLECT AND DUE PROCESS OF LAW
The definition of neglect has been alleged to be so vague in its description of the parental acts proscribed as to deprive persons of due process of law. Parents consider their ability to raise a family without governmental interference a right and contend that the statutory definitions of neglect allow selective and discriminatory enforce-

ment by prosecuting officials and courts. These issues were the heart of the appeal in the People v. Schoos, 305 N.E.2d 560 (Ill. App. 1973).

PEOPLE v. SCHOOS

Illinois Appellant Court, 305 N.E.2d 560 (Ill. App. 1973).

The Circuit Court of Cook County entered findings of child neglect against the respondent, Delores Schoos, on September 7, 1972, pursuant to Section 2-4 of the Juvenile Court Act (Ill.Rev.Stat., 1971, Ch. 37, § 702–4). The issue presented for review is whether Section 2-4 is unconstitutionally vague and overly broad.

On May 9, 1972, the respondent was informed by police that her 14-year-old daughter by a previous marriage, Geraldine Rubo, had been taken into custody as a runaway child. Geraldine told the officers she had been sexually assaulted on two occasions by Leroy Gadson, the man who had been cohabiting with her mother. The police informed representatives of the Illinois Department of Children and Family Services, and the Department took five of the respondent's six children from her and placed them in foster homes. The respondent had legal custody of her children since her divorce seven years before.

On May 19, 1972, the Department filed petitions in the Juvenile Court charging the respondent with child neglect. On June 9, 1972, counsel for the respondent filed a motion to dismiss or, in the alternative, a motion for declaratory judgment, in which it was alleged that the statute in question was unconstitutionally vague and overly broad. After briefs were filed and arguments heard, the court denied the motion.

On September 7, 1972, a trial was held and there was testimony that Mrs. Schoos had been cohabiting with Leroy Gadson and that she had permitted her two oldest daughters, aged 14 and 15, to smoke marijuana that Gadson had brought into the home. There was no testimony that Gadson had sexually assaulted Geraldine, but Ann Rubo, aged 15, testified Gadson had asked her to have his child.

In its dispositional order of October 26, 1972, the court followed the recommendation of the Illinois Department of Children and Family Services and placed three of the children with their natural father and permitted two of them to remain with the respondent.

The respondent contends Section 2-4 of the Juvenile Court Act deprives her of due process of law in that it is so vague and overly broad as to lack adequate notice of what parental acts it proscribes, and allows selective and discriminatory enforcement by prosecuting officials and courts, and includes within its coverage parental acts which are constitutionally protected.

Section 2-4 of the Juvenile Court Act (Ill.Rev.Stat., Ch. 37 § 702–4) provides in part:

(1) Those who are neglected include any minor under 18 years of age (a) who is neglected as to proper or necessary support, education as required by law, or as to medical or other remedial care, recognized under State law or other care necessary for his well-being, or who is abandoned by his parents, guardian or custodian; or (b) whose environment is injurious to his welfare or whose behavior is injurious to his own welfare or that of others.

Mrs. Schoos argues that raising her family without governmental interference is a fundamental right, and the State must show it has a "compelling interest" in restricting that fundamental right.

(1) Both the United States and Illinois Supreme Courts have held a statute need not be more specific than is possible under the circumstances. . . .

(2) Child neglect is by its very nature incapable of a precise and detailed definition and, contrary to the respondent's contention, the child neglect statute does not infringe on any of the basic liberties protected by the United States Constitution. The United States Supreme Court has never held a parent has the right to treat his child as he wishes, subject only to limited and strictly defined state intervention. The court held parents have some rights with respect to their children's education irrespective of a state statute based on religious beliefs, but the court also recognized the state's broad powers as *parens patriae*. Consequently, the statute need not meet a higher standard of specificity than is ordinarily applied.

The state does have a compelling interest to protect children from abuse and neglect, and to narrow the statute would have the effect of diminishing the rights of children who have no other means of protecting themselves. If a parent believes the court abused its discretion in a particular instance, he may seek review in this court. In this case the respondent does not allege such an abuse of discretion by the trial court.

(3) The child neglect laws of Illinois have been in existence for over seventy years, and while the passage of time is not conclusive as to the validity and the constitutionality of a statute, it creates a strong presumption against its invalidity. People ex rel. Drobnick v. City of Waukegan, 1 Ill.2d 456, 166 N.E.2d 365 (1954).

(4) We hold that although the language of the statute is general, due process does not require standards more specific than can reasonably be applied.

For these reasons the judgment of the Circuit Court of Cook County is affirmed.

In spite of imprecise language, then, *parens patriae* sanctions such child protection efforts as those undertaken in the *Schoos* case.

Another action concerning due process of law was decided in State v. McMaster, 486 P.2d 567 (Or. 1971), in response to an appeal by the McMasters that the state's statutory basis for termination of their parental rights in a previous proceeding was unconstitutionally broad, uncertain, and vague.

STATE v. McMASTER

Oregon Supreme Court, 486 P.2d 567 (Or. 1971).

This is a proceeding to terminate parental rights in a four-year-old child under ORS 419.523(2)(a), which provides for such termination if parents are found to be "unfit by reason of conduct or condition seriously detrimental to the child." . . .

Two questions are presented for decision:

(1) Whether the trial court erred in overruling a demurrer [allegation that the facts were inadequate to proceed] to the petition to terminate parental rights upon the ground that ORS 419.523(2)(a) is unconstitutional as a vi-

olation of due process of law under the Fifth and Fourteenth Amendments of the Constitution of the United States and Art. I, § 10, of the Oregon Constitution "in that said statute is unconstitutionally broad, uncertain and vague," and

(2) Whether the evidence was "sufficient to hold that defendants were 'unfit by reason of conduct or conditions seriously detrimental to the child' " . . .

The procedure here is not the state against the parents. Three parties are involved: the state, the parents, and the child. The welfare of the child is the primary consideration of the Juvenile Code of 1959 (ORS 419.474). That the welfare of the child is the primary purpose does not lead to the conclusion that the rights of the parents are without constitutional protections. This emphasis upon the welfare of the child does imply, however, that, unlike criminal statutes in which the interests of only one set of individuals is involved, the constitutional issue must be examined with the interests of both the child and the parents. What might be unconstitutional if only the parents' rights were involved is constitutional if the statute adopts legitimate and necessary means to protect the child's interests. In our opinion it does. . . .

The flexibility granted the juvenile court by the legislature is epitomized by the general charge made in ORS 419.474(2):

> "The provisions of ORS 419.472 to 419.587 shall be liberally construed to the end that the child coming within the jurisdiction of the court may receive such care, guidance and control, preferably in his own home, as will lead to the child's welfare and the best interests of the public, and that when a child is removed from the control of his parents the court may secure for him care that best meets the needs of the child."

We are not shocked by a grant of flexibility to administrative agencies dealing with our material affairs such as businesses and professions. . . .

The United States Supreme Court has held that in the states' juvenile procedures at the adjudicatory stage, the states cannot ignore some of the procedural due process requirements. That Court, however, has not held that all the substantive due process requirements of the criminal law were applicable to juvenile proceedings, particularly the dispositional process of juvenile proceedings. It has indicated to the contrary.

In our opinion, to accomplish its primary purpose of caring for the welfare of the child, the legislature would have extreme difficulty being more specific. The legislature could specify certain conduct upon the part of the parents which would cause them to be deprived of their parental rights; however, that is not the intent of the legislature or of this court in interpreting this statute. The legislature and this court do not desire to sever parental rights for any conduct by the parents unless such conduct seriously affects the child's welfare. For example, imprisonment was not held conduct "seriously detrimental to the child"; wilful fraud upon the court likewise was held not sufficient to sever parental rights.

The legislature could "spell out" what aspects of the child's well-being harmed by the parents' conduct were grounds for severing parental rights [Citation omitted.] This does not add anything, however. Because the Oregon statute does not specify, the inference is that it is conduct detrimental to any major aspect of the child. This is undoubtedly what the legislature intended.

That we are not concerned with the criminal statute also makes inapplicable one of the bases for *State v. Hodges* [citation omitted], that is, "the terms of a penal statute creating an offense must be sufficiently explicit to inform those who are subject to it what conduct on their part will render them liable to its penalties." We would hope that in the case of the McMasters, or any parents, there is no need for explicit statute to "spell out" how poorly they can treat their child before risking loss of their parental rights.

If some notice of conduct which will cause a result is required in a noncriminal statute, the parental rights statute gives adequate notice of the kind of conduct involved and the result which will occur. The conduct is of a kind detrimental to the child, not beneficial. It is not just any detrimental conduct but seriously detrimental conduct. We see no policy to be furthered by attempting to elaborate on what conduct is seriously detrimental and what is not. The ordinary parent should "get the message" from the statute as it is now worded.

The other basis for *State v. Hodges* [citation omitted] is labeled "adjudication"; a statute must be certain enough so that a court or jury does not have uncontrolled discretion to act or withhold action. The history of the parental rights statute reveals that the juvenile court does not have unbridled discretion under that law. As this court and the Court of Appeals have held, under that statute, the juvenile court does not have uncontrolled discretion to terminate or not terminate parental rights. Only when the parents' conduct is seriously detrimental to the child can parental rights be terminated. As stated, in State v. Grady, supra (231 Or. 65, 371 P.2d 68), we held that imprisonment on a felony charge and the mother's commitment of a felony and of later acts causing her probation to be revoked was not sufficient to support the trial courts' finding that such conduct and condition were seriously detrimental to the child. . . .

On the other hand, in *State v. Blum* [citation omitted] the Court of Appeals found the parent's condition was seriously detrimental to the child and affirmed the termination of parental rights. The uncontradicted evidence was that the mother had a recurring mental illness and that the prognosis was that she never would be able to care for her child and that the mother's mental condition and the incapability accompanying such mental condition made her condition seriously detrimental to the child.

For these reasons we are of the opinion that the statute is not constitutionally vague.

We are further of the opinion, however, that the evidence does not support the juvenile court's finding that the conduct of the parents has been seriously detrimental to the child within the meaning of ORS 419.523(2)(a).

The child was born in June 1965. About two months later the child was taken from her mother and placed in emergency custody. This was done under a warrant issued pursuant to an affidavit stating that the Women's Protective Division (WPD) received complaint that the child was not receiving proper care and other allegations. The child was subsequently placed with a foster couple and in April 1966 made a ward of the juvenile court. The foster parents, who have had the child since some time before April 1966, desire to adopt the child and Mrs. McMaster refuses to consent.

The essence of the case against the McMasters is stated in the following testimony by a representative of the Multnomah County Welfare Department:

> "The original removal (emergency custody) would have been based on conditions in the home and the neglect of the child; but subsequently to that the primary problems have been the mutual instability of the parents, probably paramount, and numerous separations and lack of concern and consistency that they might have for anyone else that might be living in the home, the family's management. At times there has been adequate money. At times there has been money, not from the assistance grant, of sufficient nature to manage and it has not been managed properly; and also frequent moving because they have lived in many places during the past four years."

This testimony was elaborated by evidence that the parents frequently quarreled, McMaster never held a job more than a month and seldom that long, they were usually on welfare, and McMaster frequently left home with the welfare check, leaving Mrs. McMaster destitute. They were unable, particularly Mr. McMaster, to handle their financial affairs. The caseworker testified that the foster parents were the complete antithesis—stable, consistent and mutually supportive.

There was testimony which was uncontradicted that if the child were now taken from the foster parents and placed with her natural parents it would have a serious detrimental effect upon the child. This same testimony developed, however, that this is primarily because the child has lived with foster parents for almost all of her now almost six years. The detrimental effect on the child is not necessarily because of the conduct of her natural parents, except that the child may resent being taken from the better all-around environment provided by her foster parents as compared to that which would be provided by her natural parents.

However, a decision in favor of the natural parents in this termination proceeding does not result in the child being transferred to the custody of her natural parents. We are only deciding that the McMasters parental rights cannot be terminated at this time. The juvenile court must determine whether custody should remain with the foster parents. If it does, we realize that the foster parents may be kept in a state of anxiety never knowing when the child might be taken from their custody. Nevertheless, we are of the opinion that the natural parents' rights cannot now be terminated.

We are of the opinion that the state of the McMaster family is duplicated in hundreds of thousands of American families—transiency and incapacity, poverty and instability. The witness was undoubtedly correct when he stated that living in the McMasters' household would not "allow this child to maximize her potential." However, we do not believe the legislature contemplated that parental rights could be terminated because the natural parents are unable to furnish surroundings which would enable the child to grow up as we would desire all children to do. When the legislature used the phrase "seriously detrimental to the child," we believe that they had in mind a more serious and uncommon detriment than that caused by the conduct of parents such as the McMasters. The best interests of the child are paramount; however, the courts cannot sever the McMasters' parental rights when many thousands of children are being raised under basically the same circumstances as this child. The legislature had in mind conduct substantially departing from the norm and unfortunately for our children the McMasters' conduct is not such a departure.

Notwithstanding the Oregon Supreme Court's reversal of the original decision to terminate parental rights in this case, the McMasters subsequently consented to their daughter's adoption by the foster parents who had reared her. The case created controversy among courts as to the constitutionality of the termination statute. Subsequently, Oregon laws were revised to specify more clearly the grounds for termination. The statutory amendment now allows termination of parental rights

> if the court finds that the parent or parents are unfit by reason of conduct or condition seriously detrimental to the child and integration of the child into the home of the parent or parents is improbable in the foreseeable future due to conduct or conditions not likely to change.

Such conduct or conditions were considered to include, among other things,

> Lack of effort of the parent to adjust his circumstances, conduct, or conditions to make the return of the child possible or failure of the parent to effect a lasting adjustment after reasonable efforts by available social agencies for such extended duration of time that it appears reasonable that no lasting adjustment can be effected.

The McMasters later lost parental rights to a second daughter in 1974 (State ex rel. Juvenile Department of Multnomah County v. McMaster, 523 P.2d 604 [Or. App. 1974]), partly on the basis of the specific language contained in the statutory amendment described above.

An Iowa case, Alsager v. Polk County, Iowa, 406 F.Supp. 10 (D.C. Iowa, 1975), is widely cited as an example of the need for more precise standards for child neglect. The Alsagers had six children. After nearly five years of contact with the family, juvenile authorities sought to terminate parental rights. On recommendation of the probation office of the Polk County Juvenile Court, rights were terminated for five of the children on the basis of neglect. The appellate decision determined that the state parental termination statutes were "unconstitutionally vague." The parents were deprived of procedural due process when the court gave inadequate notice of the termination proceeding and used a standard of proof that required only a preponderance of the evidence.

The federal district court concluded that the Iowa statute menaced "the fundamental right to family integrity" protected by the due process clause of the Fourteenth Amendment. The U.S. Supreme Court held: "We insist that laws give the person of ordinary intelligence a reasonable opportunity to know what is prohibited, so that he may act accordingly (Grayned v. City of Richford, 408 U.S. 104 [1972]). Vague statutes carry three dangers: the absence of fair warning, the impermissible delegation of discretion, and the undue inhibition of the legitimate exercise of a constitutional right." The following evidence was included:

> The Alsagers sometimes permitted their children to leave the house in cold weather without winter clothing on, "allowed them" to play in traffic, to annoy neighbors, to eat mush for supper, to live in a house containing dirty dishes and laundry, and to sometimes arrive late at school.
>
> At the time of the termination, Mr. Alsager was a working man who had never been on public welfare rolls. He and his wife lived together, and shared an interest in keeping their family unit intact. The Court cites this evidence not to contradict the findings of the juvenile court, but simply to describe the general nature of the Alsagers' family situation in 1969. The Court accepts the juvenile court's factual findings, but agrees with Dr. Robert Kugel and Dr. Kenneth Berry, plaintiffs' trial experts, who testified that even if all of the evidence harmful to the Alsagers is assumed to be true, their home situation did not justify permanent termination. The probative termination

standard to which the Alsagers were subjected in 1969 and 1970 was simply not high enough to ensure that their fundamental parental rights would not be violated. Stated differently, the Alsager family unit was severed on the basis of evidence which was insufficient to give the state a "child-protection interest" compelling enough to require termination. . . .

The 1969–1970 familial situation of the Alsagers was simply not deficient enough to justify its end. These parents were trying to do the right thing. Under the facts of the case, they should have been allowed to continue to do so. (406 F. Supp. 10 at 22)

The case also indicated that *In re McDonald* had been improperly applied because the material facts differed substantially:

McDonald involved a parent with a clinically tested I.Q. of 47. This fact was heavily relied on by the McDonald court in concluding that the parent was unable to care for her children. In contrast, the record here reveals no intelligence testing of the Alsagers. Nor is there any evidence which suggests the Alsagers lacked the mental capacity to perform parental functions. The Iowa court's conclusion claiming an identity of material fact between these two divergent cases is not justified by the record. (406 F.Supp. at 21)

The comparative lack of success of the county authorities in providing stable homes for the children is revealed in the decision. From 1969 to 1974, four of the Alsager children had experienced fifteen separate foster home placements and eight juvenile home placements. During the appeal process, the two "well-adjusted" boys had rejected their foster home placements and were being considered for probationary placements with their parents.

Pennsylvania has had a standard of **clear necessity** to justify removal of a child. County welfare authorities declared a child deprived who had never been in their custody because the child was without proper parental care or control. The superior court reversed the lower court on the basis of insufficient evidence to show clear necessity (In re DeSavage, 174, 360 A.2d 237 [Pa. Super. 1976]). A similar decision, In Interest of La Rue, 366 A.2d 1271 (Pa. Super. 1976), was reached because the court based its decision on the child's "doing well" in a foster home, rather than on proof that the child was deprived:

A child may be separated from the parents *only* when *both* of two conditions are satisfied: there is "clear and convincing" evidence that the child is "deprived"; and there is proof of "clear necessity" for separating the child from the parents. (366 A.2d at 1279)

A rehearing to answer the two questions was ordered, specifying that a different judge hear the case.

Wald (1976: 252) contends that we should give substantial deference to parental autonomy in deciding whether coercive intervention is appropriate. We do not know the characteristics desired in children or adults, or how parental behavior and home environment affect their development. Public welfare agencies have untrained or poorly trained staffs and high turnover and tend to apply middle-class standards to poor and minority parents. "By focusing on the child [rather than on parental misconduct] it is possible to draft more specific statutes. . . . There are relatively few harms to children with which we should be concerned." The harm should be serious, and in general the remedy of coercive intervention should do more harm than good.

While some people advocate increased state intervention on behalf of neglected children, others take the opposite position. Wald developed a statutory definition of neglect that does not authorize a court to intervene unless one or more specific factors are present:

(a) A child has suffered a physical injury, inflicted upon him/her nonaccidentally, causing disfigurement, impairment of body functioning, or severe bodily harm, or there is substantial likelihood that the child will imminently suffer such an injury.

(b) A child has suffered physical injury causing disfigurement, impairment of body functioning, or severe bodily harm as a result of conditions uncorrected by his/her parents or by the failure of his/her parents to adequately supervise or protect him/her; or when there is a substantial risk that the child will imminently suffer such harm as a result of conditions uncorrected by his/her parents or by the failure of his/her parents to adequately supervise or protect him/her.

(c) A child is suffering serious emotional damage, evidenced by severe anxiety, depression or withdrawal, or untoward aggressive behavior toward others, and his/her parents are unwilling to provide when financially able to do so, or permit necessary treatment for him/her.

(d) A child has been sexually abused by a member of his/her household.

(e) A child is in need of medical treatment to cure, alleviate, or prevent him/her from suffering serious physical harm which may cause death, disfigurement, or substantial impairment of bodily functioning, and his/her parents are unwilling to provide, when financially able to do so, or consent to the medical treatment.

(f) A child is committing delinquent acts as a result of parental encouragement, guidance, or approval. (p. 274)

The standards advocated are relatively specific and designed to minimize state intervention. Basically, intervention is permitted only in cases where a child evidences serious physical or emotional damage. The guidelines are not designed to insure that every child receives adequate housing, medical care, education, or supportive home environment. Many children need more than they now have, but their needs should not be met through neglect proceedings, which even in the best circumstances will be perceived as punitive, rather than helpful, by parents. Instead, the state should establish general programs to help all families provide adequately for their children and intervene coercively only if the statutory grounds proposed herein are met. . . .

The approach suggested may be seen by some readers as more solicitous of parents' rights than of children's rights. As such, it may be interpreted as a defense of the old system against the mounting call for emphasis on children's rights and greater state protection for children. To me, such charges are unwarranted. Existing policies have too often destroyed families rather than helped them become viable units. The result has not only harmed the parents, it has failed to benefit the children. A new approach is needed if we are really to protect children's rights. (p. 172, 173)

The view of neglect expressed by Wald reminds one of the intent of *Gault* for delinquency: more care, more specificity, more caution, and more attention to parental autonomy and therefore to parental rights. It also involves a reluctance to act.

CHILD ABUSE LAWS Child abuse, defined narrowly, refers to willfully inflicted physical injury and sexual abuse. The realization that parents intentionally injure their own children is repugnant to most people, including those who advocate physical punishment as a means of discipline. In the 1950s, pediatric and social work groups collected evidence of widespread abuse. **Reporting laws** that clearly convey legal immunity from prosecution for libel or slander for persons acting in good faith in reporting child abusers were considered the effective remedy. From only one such law in 1960, the legislation spread, until five years later every state had some type of reporting law.

The Need for Legislation

Legally, the child abuse reporting laws may be considered redundant. Inflicted injury of children was already covered under existing statutes. Most states had an agency designated to investigate such cases and to provide protective services. People reporting child abuse in good faith were probably already immune to prosecution.

However, the laws do focus attention on reporting, and a few states specify a penalty for *failure* to report, although the difficulty of enforcing such a penalty is evident because alleged abuse involves a judgment call.

Provisions and Problems of Legislation

The major components of child abuse reporting laws are: (1) the ages of children covered under the laws; (2) the definition of abuse; (3) specification of persons mandated to report; (4) the reporting procedure; (5) the legal immunity clause; (6) the responsibility of the agency mandated to investigate such reports; and (7) a statement of confidentiality and sometimes a penalty for violating it.

It is interesting to note that state child abuse laws emphasize reporting and investigative procedures. Most mandate reporting on the part of medical, educational, social service, and law enforcement professionals, but not laypersons. If the latter choose to report, they are accorded the same legal immunity as the professional person. The services provided come under enabling legislation for the department of social welfare that authorizes protective services, and juvenile court acts and the criminal code provide for prosecution of abusers.

Over half the child abuse reports cannot be verified, and less than 10 percent of abuse cases reported result in prosecution. In some, the evidence of abuse is inadequate. In most others, the judgment is that the abuse can be decriminalized because the parents will respond to services or supervision of a child protection agency. Prosecution breaks up the family.

In spite of possible philosophical differences between the roles of police and social workers, neither group can function effectively alone. Social services are necessary for helping alleged abusers, and police services are needed for initial discovery of abuse, gathering of evidence, and protection of the social work investigator when the parents are emotionally disturbed. In addition, the support of hospitals and schools is important because of the role they play in detection and service to abused children.

Federal Guidelines

A decade or more after the first child abuse laws were passed, guidelines were developed for states to qualify for federal assistance for such programs under the Child Abuse Prevention and Treatment Act of 1974 (P.L. 93-247). The federal requirements for state legislation include coverage of all children under the age of eighteen, coverage of mental injury and physical injury, the inclusion of neglect reports as well as abuse reports, confidentiality of records, legal immunity for reporters, and a guardian ad litem for children whose cases come to court. Most states revised their legislation in order to qualify for federal funds under this act.

From a legal viewpoint, two provisions of these guidelines were unfortunate. Physical abuse is well understood, but adding both mental injury and neglect to the statutes attenuated the clarity of anti-abuse programs. The mental injury concept raises serious evidentiary problems, and adding the neglect concept, with its much more vague standards and a high volume of cases, strained the ability of public protective agencies to respond rapidly. A well-defined, limited law results in more effective enforcement.

CHILD ABUSE SERVICES

So far there is neither the knowledge nor the resources to deal effectively with child abuse. The causes of child abuse are complex. Services for child abusers are limited, and their effectiveness is by no means clear. Cases that are closed are rarely monitored to determine whether abusive behavior recurs. Reporting is of small value without successful remediation.

The nature of the problem makes earlier intervention difficult. Self-help groups such as Parents Anonymous may be more effective in deterring abuse than traditional social services, but they require that the parent acknowledge the problem.

RECORDS ON CHILD ABUSE

Child abuse and neglect matters require consideration of the question of destruction of records, as with juvenile delinquency. A single abuse or neglect proceeding should not be a permanent part of a person's record. The Model Statute on Juvenile and Family Court Records (Larson, 1981: 13–14) provides:

SUGGESTED PROCEDURE FOR RECORDS ON CHILD ABUSE AND NEGLECT

In all cases where the referral is not accepted by the court, or where the case is dismissed without adjudication, all identifying information collected by the court must be automatically destroyed at the end of six months, or sooner upon motion of the court or juvenile record subject, except when a subsequent referral is received within said period.

At any time after the court's jurisdiction has been terminated, the juvenile record subject may apply to the court for destruction or sealing of the subject's records.

Any court record not destroyed or sealed on application of the juvenile shall be destroyed or sealed by the court in accordance with the following procedures and conditions:

(a) Sixty days' notice of the proposed action shall be given to the following: parties to the proceedings, involved law enforcement agencies, attorney of record, guardian ad litem, and to any institution, agency, or person involved with the child;

(b) If any person or agency listed in Sec. 105(7)(a) objects to the proposed disposition of the records, the court shall grant the objecting party a hearing to determine the merits of the actions. If there is no objection to the proposed action within the sixty day period, all identifying information shall be automatically removed from all indices and the records shall be sealed;

(c) Unless waived by the court for good cause, the following conditions precedent must be met prior to the disposition of the records: (1) The child and all siblings have attained the upper age of the original jurisdiction of the court; (2) there are no subsequent proceedings pending concerning the record subject regarding delinquency non-criminal offenses, child abuse, neglect or termination of parental rights;

(d) The court records of child abuse and neglect matters shall be reviewed five years after their initial entry. If there are no subsequent proceedings concerning the record subject or his siblings regarding delinquency, non-criminal offenses, abuse or neglect matters, the court may order the removal of all identifying information from all indices and order the records sealed.

ACTIONS IN RESPONSE TO DEPENDENCY, NEGLECT, AND ABUSE

On reaching a finding of dependency, neglect, or abuse, the court may choose from three courses of action: (1) It may enter a supervisory order, allowing the child in need of protection to remain in the parental home; (2) it may allow the child to be removed from home temporarily, in hopes that parental rehabilitation may be effected in the child's absence and lead to eventual reunion of the family; or (3) it may terminate parental rights and have the child placed in foster care or adoption.

Supervisory Orders. Court orders are necessary when parents are unlikely to follow a course of action that the court considers necessary. For example, the order may require the family to place the child in day care or to attend a family life education class. Removal of the child may be the alternative.

Temporary Removal. Temporary removal from the home is usually followed by remediation efforts with the parents. The outcome of the temporary order will depend on parental rehabilitation. Some parents are greatly relieved to have the child removed from their care and do not cooperate with attempts to improve the family situation.

Termination of Parental Rights. Some parents are willing to have parental rights terminated, while others fight the action strongly. One main area of controversy in involuntary termination of parental rights is how much contact between parent and child represents adequate parental interest in the child. Some state statutes specify that if there has been no contact with the parent in a year the child may be considered abandoned. On the other hand, a Christmas card may be considered enough contact to comply with the law. Thus many children remain in foster care with no plan for a permanent home.

Most courts regard termination of parental rights as a serious step and will not order it without earnest efforts at rehabilitation. Santosky v. Kramer (455 U.S. 745 [1983]) provided that clear and convincing evidence rather than a preponderance is required. While it is hoped that termination of parental rights will lead to the child's adoption, many children are too old or too emotionally disturbed to be adoptable. Such children are usually assigned to a series of foster homes. If the older child maintains any basic loyalty to his or her natural parents, placement may present a serious conflict. Child welfare agencies have generally been able to provide foster homes, but they are not always able to provide supportive services to help children remain in their own homes. In addition, foster parents are beginning to claim rights of their own. Agencies may be enjoined from removing a child from the care of foster parents without due cause.

A New York case, In re Frances, 267 N.Y.S.2d 566 (1966), illustrates the role of the juvenile court in a battered child situation.

IN RE FRANCES

Family Court, City of New York, New York County, 267 N.Y.S.2d 566 (1966).

The first neglect petition on her behalf was filed by the Society for the Prevention of Cruelty to Children on November 5, 1965, when she was nearly three years old.

Earlier in 1965, Sydenham Hospital had reported to the Protective Unit of the Department of Welfare suspicion that injuries they found on August 18, 1965, could not have resulted from a fall in a bathtub as reported by the stepfather, and that this was a "battered child." The medical testimony before the court presented hospital findings including marked redness of both legs, softening of soles of both feet, bluish areas on the buttocks and legs, and red areas on back and chest. There were also discolored areas on the back, chest, abdomen, legs, face, forehead and neck. The lesions were suggestive of belt or strap marks. The abrasions were suggestive of fingernail marks. The child was extremely docile, apprehensive, petrified, but became less fearful during the hospital stay. On August 24, 1965, on the decision of the Protective Unit, the child was discharged to the parents with a referral for clinic care. There was no record of subsequent clinic attendance. There was no referral for court action.

Two months later this small child was taken to a different hospital (Harlem) on October 16, 1965, by the mother. At that time the physician could not obtain a history of the injury from the mother. Physical finding, however, included a lesion on the buttocks that appeared to be a healing second degree burn and a second lesion on the right leg. Treatment was given in the hospital and the mother was directed to take the infant to the clinic for further care. Although the examining physician testified that in his opinion the injuries were at least six to twelve hours old, he testified that it was not his business to investigate.

The suspicion of the first hospital was promptly reported to the Protective Unit. The second injury was not reported. On the undertaking of the Protective Unit in August to supervise the child, the child was discharged to the parents. The supervision was delegated to a professionally untrained worker, who made one visit on September 21, 1965, and one on October 22, 1965. He did not secure the written report from Sydenham Hospital until October 8, 1965. When it was then decided to "double-check," the investigator went out on a visit two weeks later. The child had already received the second injuries. The child was not present, and he did not investigate although the parents mentioned that the child had received a minor bruise from being pushed against a radiator by a dog.

It was only through the fortunate incident of a family wedding later in October 1965 that the grandmother called to take the child and discovered burns, raw open sores all over the baby's rectum, and bruises on her forehead and arms. It was she who took the baby home and called the Society for the Prevention of Cruelty to Children. When their representative called and observed the infant's condition, he insisted on hospital examination, notified the Department of Welfare and filed a neglect petition in this court.

At the hearing on December 21, 1965, both the mother and stepfather gave a history of the child having fallen while being bathed by the stepfather to explain the first injuries in August. They sought to explain the second injuries as resulting from the baby being pushed against a radiator by a dog. The mother, aged 19, testified that the child was born out of wedlock and that she had married the stepfather, who was also 19, some five months earlier. Both the mother and father were defensive and evasive throughout their testimony as to how this infant had been injured. A finding of neglect was made and the child was paroled in the custody of the maternal grandmother. Psychiatric studies of the mother and stepfather were ordered. . . .

In 1963 the *Journal of the American Medical Association* wrote:

"It is likely that it (physical abuse of children) will be found to be a more frequent cause of death than such well recognized and thoroughly studied diseases as leukemia, cystic fibrosis and muscular dystrophy, and may well rank with automobile accidents and the toxic and infectious encephalitis as causes of acquired disturbances of the central nervous system."

While accurate histories are seldom obtainable, the development of the use of X-ray has given additional confidence to the experienced clinician who suspects deliberate injury to an infant or young child. Dr. Finberg, Chief of the Division of Pediatrics at Montefiore Hospital, reports that while the history given is usually that the baby either fell from a bed or chair or that an arm or leg became caught in the slat of a crib "when something was found on X-ray, such as fracture, the odds have been four out of five (80%) that the trauma was deliberate and not accidental."

With such objective tools and such clinical experience one must question whether it is sound to leave the determination of whether the infant or young child is to be released to the adults who had care of the child to non-medical personnel in the Department of Welfare without full investigation by a court. . . .

The serious nature of the charge of "battering" or physical abuse of a child by a parent or guardian requires a judicial determination, where a court can subpoena witnesses and provide a forum in which all evidence can be submitted. The continuation of supervision by a social agency, without such an adjudication, fails to provide adequate protection for the child or a determination to which the parents or guardian are entitled.

Finally, in New York City, where anonymity is so easily achieved, it would seem that some procedure should be developed so that where there has been suspicion of abuse, a central clearinghouse would register such cases, and such information would immediately be available to any hospital which subsequently examined a child. There is no doubt that in the instant case the infant would, with such information, not have been released by Harlem Hospital after emergency care only to be subjected to further abuse. A method of identification for follow-up purposes is now being used in one area in Pennsylvania on a voluntary basis.

The case of Marion [sic] is but one example of the inadequate protection now afforded under existing legislation. No report of the serious first injuries discovered by Sydenham Hospital was made to either the police or the court. The worker assigned by the Protective Services unit was untrained and could not through monthly visits protect this infant from further abuse. No real service was rendered to the parents. The second hospital to which the infant was taken in October had no knowledge of the previous history at Sydenham. The reports of both hospitals were not submitted in writing until long after the incidents. In short, neither "protection" for the infant nor services to the parents were provided in timely or meaningful fashion. The law, as written, and its implementation in New York City fail to assure either.

It is directed that this child shall be discharged to the maternal grandmother under the supervision of the court. Visitation by the mother shall be arranged in the home of the grandmother on the mother's request, but the mother is directed not to remove the child, or take the child out except in the presence of the grandmother. The mother and stepfather are referred for casework services to a family casework agency. Order of protection to maternal grandmother to include terms of visitation. Progress report to be submitted to this court on September 15, 1966.

SAFEGUARDING PARENTAL RIGHTS   Although safeguards of parental rights have been applied to delinquency actions by virtue of *Gault* and related cases, no such provisions have been mandated for child dependency, neglect, and abuse actions. At least one case involving persons faced with termination of custody on a dependency finding established the right of counsel, Danforth v. State Department of Health and Welfare, 303 A.2d 794 (Maine 1973):

> The fact that a parent is not fined or imprisoned as a result of a neglect proceeding does not make the prospect of the loss of custody of one's child anything less than punishment in the eyes of the parent.
>
> Because of the nature of the interest protected by the Constitution we must and do hold that procedural due process requires that counsel be appointed at State's expense in any proceeding under 22 M.R.S.A. 3792 upon a proper showing that the party or parties against whom the proceeding is commenced is indigent unless the right to counsel is knowingly waived.

In 1980 the right to counsel in termination of parental rights cases was upheld in the federal district court, fifth circuit (Davis v. Page, 618 F.2d 374 [5th Cir. 1980]). However, the U.S. Supreme Court ruled in Lassiter v. Department of Social Services of Durham County, N.C., 452 U.S. 18 (1981), that a mother was not denied due process in a termination of parental rights case because she was not allowed to have counsel. The petition to terminate rights contained no allegations of neglect and abuse on which criminal charges could be based. The mother had declined to appear in an earlier custody case, and she had failed to contest the present termination proceedings.

Sobelson (1982) is critical of the *Lassiter* decision from several viewpoints: The Supreme Court's limiting of provision of counsel to instances involving physical liberty; the lack of concern for due process of law, since parental termination proceedings often leave the parent incapable of addressing the issues raised; and because there cannot be an adequate adversarial hearing without counsel, the decision made by the trial court, regardless of its true merit, will have to be approved by an appellate court. On due process, we agree with Sobelson's comments:

> The combination of exceedingly malleable grounds, lax evidentiary and procedural standards, and relatively low standards of proof required, unnecessarily infringes upon the parent's rights to notice and fair play. This jeopardizes the child's best interests, as well as the interests of the parent. Appointment of counsel would enhance not only the fairness of the proceedings, but also the reliability of results. (P. 770)

We may expect that eventually all the due process safeguards accorded delinquency would apply to neglect, dependency, and child abuse. Both the rights of the child and the rights of the parents should receive adequate attention.

Questions for Review

1. Describe the current view of *parens patriae*.

2. What are the possible consequences of serious failure in parental role performance?

3. What is the most serious civil action a juvenile court may take against a neglecting parent?

4. Explain why labeling has received so much attention in recent years. Give an example of the application of labeling theory.

5. Why would most people consider it desirable that neglected children not be housed in facilities with delinquent children? Is this argument simplistic? Why?

6.   How do continuity and constancy relate to establishment of neglect?

7.   What issues are involved in the major cases involving alleged neglect stemming from refusal of medical treatment for religious reasons? What criterion has determined whether the court will order medical treatment?

8.   How is due process of law an issue in neglect cases?

9.   What is the major purpose of child abuse laws?

10.   Why is it desirable to decriminalize child abuse?

11.   What are the components of a community network of services to deal with child abuse?

12.   Explain the purpose of supervisory orders and illustrate a situation in which such an order would be appropriate.

13.   What was the finding concerning right to counsel in *Danforth*? How is it related to *Gault*?

Questions for Debate and Discussion

1.   Has the *Gault* decision had much effect on the juvenile court? Indicate evidence for your answer.

2.   Do you prefer the Minnesota or New York definition of neglect? Why?

3.   What was the finding in *In re McDonald*? Do you agree with it? Why or why not?

4.   Many children lack dental care. Should these children be considered neglected?

5.   Would a sole emphasis on inflicted injury be a better focus for child abuse legislation than including mental injury and neglect as emergencies requiring immediate investigation?

Selected Readings   Besharov, Douglas J. "The Civil Prosecution of Child Abuse and Neglect." *Vermont Law Review* 6 (1982): 217–239.

Burt, Robert A., and Michael Wald. *Standards Relating to Abuse and Neglect*. Cambridge, Mass.: Ballinger Publishers, 1982.

Collier, Susan A. "Reporting Child Abuse: When Moral Obligations Fail." *Pacific Law Journal* 15 (1983): 189–215.

Costin, Lela B., and Charles A. Rap. *Child Welfare, Policies, and Practices*, 3d ed. New York: McGraw-Hill, 1984.

Edwards, Clark (ed.). *Government's Role in Solving Societal Problems*. Washington, D.C.: Graduate School Press, 1982.

Edwards, Leonard P., and Inger Sagatun. "Dealing with Parent and Child in Serious Cases." *Juvenile and Family Courts Journal* 34 (1983): 9–14.

Johnson, Clara L. "Representation for Neglected and Abused Children: So What, Unless?" *Juvenile and Family Courts Journal* 33 (1982): 51–54.

Kadushin, Alfred, and Judith Martin. *Child Abuse: An Interactional Event*. New York: Columbia University Press, 1981.

Lydeen, Lottie Finch. *Child Abuse: Medical and Scientific Guide for Reference and Research*. Washington, D.C.: ABBE Publications Association, 1984.

Robinson, Gregory E. "The Utah Child Abuse Law of 1981: Penal Sanctions Directed at Child Abusers." *Journal of Contemporary Law* 8 (1982): 133–141.

Schwartz, Arthur, and Harold L. Hirsh. "Child Abuse and Neglect: A Survey of the Law." *Medical Trial Technique Quarterly* 28 (1982): 293–334.

Sloan, Irving J. (ed.). *Child Abuse: Governing Law and Legislation*. Dobbs Ferry, N.Y.: Oceana Publications, 1982.

CHAPTER
8

The Juvenile Court: Child Placement and Guardianship

The juvenile or family court may determine that a child must be placed outside the family home due to dependency, neglect, abuse, juvenile delinquency, incorrigibility, or the death of both parents or their divorce. Such a decision gives rise to a series of issues concerning the rights and responsibilities of a court-appointed custodian and guardian for the child. This chapter deals with the principal elements of child custody and guardianship. Custody issues in divorce will be presented here and should be considered in conjunction with Chapter 14.

CUSTODY AND GUARDIANSHIP DEFINED

Custody denotes the normal transactions of living together. One person assumes the responsibilities of daily care, supervision, socialization, and education over another. In a separated family, the person who performs most parental functions is considered to have custody of the child. Arrangements following separation or divorce may involve a sharing of child custody, although generally the primary responsibility for care is assigned to one parent. Joint custody requires a friendly basis for separation or divorce. In 1985, thirty-one states had joint custody statutes: Alaska, California, Colorado, Connecticut, Delaware, Florida, Hawaii, Idaho, Indiana, Illinois, Iowa, Kansas, Kentucky, Louisiana, Maine, Massachusetts, Michigan, Minnesota, Mississippi, Missouri, Montana, Nevada, New Hampshire, New Mexico, North Carolina, Ohio, Oklahoma, Oregon, Pennsylvania, Texas and Wisconsin.

Many arrangements develop whereby nonparents rear children. Child-rearing on an informal basis is most frequently assumed by relatives. Court-ordered custody implies a finality that informal arrangements do not, because terms and conditions of custody are defined.

Social agencies sometimes encourage parents to sign a voluntary agreement for placement of their children in another home or in an institution. Voluntary arrangements are thought to facilitate eventual reestablishment of the family. Since voluntary agreements can be terminated whenever the parent desires, they are most appropriate for planned, short-term custody needs.

Guardianship entails a larger responsibility, whereby one person, the guardian, is responsible for protecting the interests of another, the ward. Guardianship recognizes legal incompetency of the ward because of age, mental ability, or mental or physical health and conveys parental rights to the guardian. The guardian is responsible for making all ordinary decisions about the ward's well-being and for the management of his or her person.

When parents do not fulfill their roles, the child may become a **ward of the court**. This term may be misleading because guardianship is not retained by the court but is conveyed to an agency or individual.

The responsibilities of the court-appointed guardian remain in force until the child reaches the age of majority or termination is ordered by the court. In agency-sponsored foster-care arrangements, the foster parents have custody but the agency usually retains guardianship.

PARENTAL CARE: NATURAL GUARDIANSHIP

Natural guardianship refers to the legal relationships between parent and child; it is reserved solely to the parents. Parental rights extending to education, religion, and physical welfare emerge from natural guardianship. Major court decisions have often been involved with the issue of religious preference in conjunction with the child's right to education or physical care.

Parental rights involving education will be discussed in detail in Chapter 22. Wisconsin v. Yoder, 406 U.S. 205 (1972), is of special interest because it confirmed the rights of Amish parents to withhold their children from high school. The majority decision has been criticized because it did not consider the wishes of the children themselves.

The preceding chapter indicated that appellate courts have considered cases in which parents denied their children adequate physical care of medical treatment on the basis of religious beliefs. Parental religious preferences are defended by the courts as rights of natural guardianship. Courts try to respect the religious preference of natural parents in selecting adoptive or foster parents.

Generally, the most serious problems result when the natural guardians disagree between themselves about religious upbringing of the child. The courts have been cautious to intervene in such disputes and generally recognize the importance of family privacy. In People ex rel. Sisson v. Sisson, 2 N.E.2d 660 (N.Y. 1936) the trial court had rescinded the father's custody over his daughter because the teachings of a religious sect to which he belonged kept her "from home to an unreasonable extent" and "alienated [her] in some respects from her mother." The appeals court held:

> The parents of this child are obviously interested only in her welfare. When they realize that for the good of the child, it is necessary for them to repress to some extent the natural desire of each to have the child educated solely according to his or her point of view, the remaining sources of difficulty doubtless will disappear.
>
> The court cannot regulate by its processes the internal affairs of the home. Dispute between parents when it does not involve anything immoral or harmful to the welfare of the child is beyond the reach of the law. The vast majority of matters concerning the upbringing of children must be left to the conscience, patience and self restraint of father and mother. *No end of difficulties would arise should judges try to tell parents how to bring up their children. Only when moral, mental and physical conditions are so bad as seriously to affect the health or morals of children should the courts be called upon to act.* [Emphasis added]

Kilgrow v. Kilgrow, 107 So.2d 885 (Ala. 1958), involved a dispute between two parents over whether their child would attend a parochial school or a public school. The appellate court reversed the decision of the trial court that had granted an injunction to the father. The reasoning was similar to that in *Sisson*:

> It seems to us, if we should hold that equity has jurisdiction in this case such holding will open wide the gates for settlement in equity of all sorts and varieties of intimate

family disputes concerning the upbringing of children. The absence of cases dealing with the question indicates a reluctance of the courts to assume jurisdiction in disputes arising out of the intimate family circle. It does not take much imagination to envision the extent to which explosive differences of opinion between parents as to the proper upbringing of their children could be brought into court for attempted solution.

In none of our cases has the court intervened to settle a controversy between unseparated parents as to some matter incident to the well-being of the child, where there was no question presented as to which parent should have custody. In all of our cases the real question has been which parent should properly be awarded custody. Never has the court put itself in the place of the parents and interposed its judgment as to the course which otherwise amicable parents should pursue in discharging their parental duty. Here, the sole differences between the parties is which school the child should attend. And that difference seems not to have affected the conjugal attitude of the parents one to the other.

The inherent jurisdiction of courts of equity over infants is a matter of necessity, coming into exercise only where there has been a failure of that natural power and obligation which is the province of parenthood. It is a jurisdiction assumed by the courts only when it is forfeited by a natural custodian incident to a broken home or neglect, or as a result of a natural custodian's incapacity, unfitness or death. It is only for compelling reason that a parent is deprived of the custody of his or her child. The court only interferes as between parents to the extent of awarding custody to the one or the other, with the welfare of the child in mind. And it is in awarding custody that the court invokes the principle that the welfare of the child is the controlling consideration. *We do not think a court of equity should undertake to settle a dispute between parents as to what is best for their minor child when there is no question concerning the child's custody.* [Emphasis added]

It would be anomalous to hold that a court of equity may sit in constant supervision over a household and see that either parent's will and determination in the upbringing of a child is obeyed, even though the parents' dispute might involve what is best for the child. Every difference of opinion between parents concerning their child's upbringing necessarily involves the question of the child's best interest.

The relationships between the natural guardian and the child enjoy considerable privacy. The state does not interfere unless it appears that the child may be exposed to serious mental or physical harm. Even then, parents often retain custody of their child under state supervision. Two guiding principles are involved: notwithstanding all their faults and mistakes, parents will generally be more successful in caring for their children than strangers or agencies of the state, and the emotional ties between parent and child should be respected regardless of whether the child might enjoy both better care and more material advantages under the care of someone else.

Natural guardians are responsible for the support and education of their children. They are legally free to claim their children's earnings. Children, however, have status as their parents' heirs. Parents may move wherever they wish with their children. None of these privileges or responsibilities is shared by a court-appointed guardian.

Even when a guardian is named, the natural parents continue to retain the responsibility for financial support and have the right to visit, to determine the child's religious affiliation, and to request judicial review of the court order appointing the guardian. The parents also have the right to consent or refuse to consent to adoption. Parental consent to adoption or a specific order by the court for sufficient cause terminates all parental rights and responsibilities.

THE GUARDIAN OF THE PERSON

The **guardian of the person,** like the parent, assumes responsibility for the child's care and nurturance but may or may not have physical custody of the child. Duties include choice of a living arrangement and decisions governing medical care, surgery, and education. In medical emergencies, attempts are made to obtain permission for necessary treatment from the natural parents as well. A guardian of the person is likewise responsible for granting permission for the minor's marriage and entry into the armed forces. The guardian also represents the child in legal actions. If parental rights have been terminated, the guardian must consent to the child's adoption.

THE TESTAMENTARY GUARDIAN

The **testamentary guardian** is nominated in a parental will to be guardian over the person and/or estate of the child in the event of the parent's death. The parental choice is usually confirmed by approval of the court unless the nominee can be shown to have some defect. The parents' wishes tend to dominate even when the child has been living with other relatives, as in Comerford v. Cherry, 100 So. 2d 385 (Fla. 1958). The rationale was stated in the decision:

> The courts have always seen to it that the property of a testator was received by those whom the testator intended. The upbringing of minor children is a matter which concerns every thoughtful human being more vitally than the disposition of his worldly possessions when he has passed on. No person is in a position to know as well who should have the custody of children as the surviving parent. They are his flesh and blood. He has observed them throughout their lives. By daily contact he knows their temperaments and habits, and by observation he knows those who have evidenced the greatest interest in his children, and those whose moral and spiritual values are in his judgment conducive to the best interests of his children. *A judge treads on sacred ground when he overrides the directions of the deceased with reference to the custody of his children.* [Emphasis added]

The appointment of a testamentary guardian is now required only rarely, because one or both parents usually survive until the children reach the age of majority. Automobile accidents are the most common cause of death of both parents.

THE GUARDIAN OF THE ESTATE

As a trustee responsible for managing the ward's property under the supervision of the court, the **guardian of the estate,** sometimes called a conservator, does not acquire legal title to the property of the ward, but may take possession of and manage the property and invest its proceeds. Property may not be co-mingled with the guardian's own, nor may profit be gained from fulfillment of the guardian role.

The guardian of the person does not have the right to receive and manage property belonging to the ward without designation by the court as guardian of the estate. A division of guardianship will safeguard the ward's funds or property and avoid any possible conflict of interest.

The Uniform Gifts to Minors Act provides a simple and inexpensive procedure for designating a custodian for property received by the minor. A custodian can be named within the instrument of the gift and thus formal appointment of a guardian of the estate can be avoided.

THE GUARDIAN AD LITEM

The **guardian ad litem** is the person who represents the interests of the child in specific actions of the court. With increasing attention to children's rights, such protection has become much more common. Advocates for children's rights hold that the child should be represented by counsel in divorce. The guardian may be a lawyer, but a layperson may also serve as a guardian ad litem. The federal guidelines for abuse and neglect statutes provide for a guardian ad litem in each case that comes before the court. When the parents are indigent, the guardian ad litem may be appointed by the court at public expense.

CUSTODY AFTER SEPARATION OR DIVORCE

Custody problems arise mainly as the result of separation and divorce. The impact of divorce on American children is illustrated by recent statistics. In 1981, some 20 percent of all children under eighteen years old were living with only one parent. Divorce is the major cause of single parenthood.

In separation and divorce, custody issues are limited to children of the marriage. Where parents remain separated, visitation rights are also now accorded to other specified relatives, especially grandparents. Custody is generally necessary whether a divorce is obtained or not. In divorce, one parent usually is awarded custody and the other is allowed visitation rights. Custody may occasionally have to be awarded to someone other than the parents, in which case the custodians should also be named in the divorce action.

Custody should be awarded in accordance with the child's best interests. Children often become victims of parental stress in a pending divorce suit when they are used as a weapon by the feuding spouses. Children of divorce require special protection under such circumstances if their needs are to be fulfilled. Family court judge Robert Hansen provided couples coming before his court with the following Bill of Rights from opinions of the Wisconsin Supreme Court.

THE BILL OF RIGHTS OF CHILDREN IN DIVORCE ACTIONS
The family court of Milwaukee County

I.   The right to be treated as an interested and affected person and not as a pawn, possession or chattel of either or both parents.

II.   The right to grow to maturity in that home environment which will best guarantee an opportunity for the child to grow to mature and responsible citizenship.

III.   The right to the day by day love, care, discipline and protection of the parent having custody of the child.

IV.   The right to know the non-custodial parent and to have the benefit of such parent's love and guidance through adequate visitations.

V.   The right to a positive and constructive relationship with both parents, with neither parent to be permitted to degrade or downgrade the other in the mind of the child.

VI.   The right to have moral and ethical values developed by precept and practices and to have limits set for behavior so that the child early in life may develop self-discipline and self-control.

VII.   The right to the most adequate level of economic support that can be provided by the best efforts of both parents.

VIII.   The right to the same opportunities for education that the child would have had if the family unit had not been broken.

IX.   The right to periodic review of custodial arrangements and child support orders as the circumstances of the parents and the benefit of the child may require.

X.   The right to recognition that children involved in a divorce are always disadvantaged parties and that the law must take affirmative steps to protect their welfare, including, where indicated, a social investigation to determine, and the appointment of a guardian ad litem to protect, their interests.

Judge Hansen said the bill of rights was developed to encourage reconciliation of the parents, to influence custody and visitation provisions, and to substantiate the need for a guardian ad litem in divorce cases involving special concern for the welfare of children. A guardian ad litem in such circumstances is now a requirement of Wisconsin law.

Goldstein, Freud, and Solnit (1973:37–38) proposed that one person serve as the child's "psychological parent—the person who assumes responsibility for day-to-day care of the child and who is best equipped to meet the child's total physical and emotional needs. Such selection might be made by voluntary agreement, by court order, or in accordance with the child's own wishes. Children of divorced or separated parents must be assured the total commitment of one "psychological parent":

> Child placements in divorce and separation proceedings are never final and often are conditional. The lack of finality, which stems from the court's retention of jurisdiction over its custody decision, invites challenges by a disappointed party claiming changed circumstances. This absence of finality coupled with the concomitant increase in opportunities for appeal are in conflict with the child's need for continuity. As in adoption, a custody decree should be final, that is, not subject to modification . . .
>
> Certain conditions such as visitations may themselves be a source of discontinuity. Children have difficulty in relating positively to, profiting from, and maintaining the contact with two psychological parents who are not in positive contact with each other. Loyalty conflicts are common and normal under such conditions and may have devastating consequences by destroying the child's positive relationships to both parents. A "visiting" or "visited" parent has little chance to serve as a true object for love, trust, and identification, since this role is based on his being available on an uninterrupted day-to-day basis.
>
> Once it is determined who will be the custodial parent, it is that parent, not the court, who must decide under what conditions he or she wishes to raise the child. *Thus, the non-custodial parent should have no legally enforceable right to visit the child, and the custodial parent should have the right to decide whether it is desirable for the child to have such visits.* [Emphasis added.] What we have said is designed to protect the security of an ongoing relationship—that between the child and the custodial parent. At the same time the state neither makes nor breaks the psychological relationship between the child and the noncustodial parent, which the adults involved may have jeopardized. It leaves to them what only they can ultimately resolve.

The courts tend to guard their prerogative to approve parental visiting privileges and have not usually adopted the idea of the psychological parent, except in cases where familial conflict is extreme. Divorced fathers have often attempted to gain more parental rights and have formed national organizations in order to do so.

In many jurisdictions, custody was automatically awarded to the wife, especially if young children were involved. This has been called the **tender years presumption**. The custody issue, including "tender years," was popularized in the Academy Award-winning movie, *Kramer vs. Kramer*. The approach to custody awards is changing, however, as is evident in the Family Court of New York ruling on the issue of fathers' rights in State ex rel. Watts v. Watts, 350 N.Y.S. 2d 285 (1973). By 1983 at least thirty-seven states had rejected the tender years presumption. The *Watts* decision included the following analysis:

STATE EX REL. WATTS v. WATTS

New York Court of Appeals, 350 N.Y.S. 2d 285 (Fam. Ct. 1973).

Although in theory, a father has an equal right with the mother to the custody of his children, in well over ninety percent of the cases adjudicated, the mother is awarded custody. . . .

Yet sound application of the "best interests of the child" criteria requires that the court not place a greater burden on the father in proving suitability for custody than on the mother.

Application of a presumption favoring the mother violates the law of New York State. Both section 240 of the Domestic Relations Law, dealing with custody of children in matrimonial actions, and section 70 of the Domestic Relations Law, dealing with habeas corpus for a child detained by a parent, provides in relevant part:

"In all cases there shall be no prima facie right to the custody of the child in either parent, but the court shall determine solely what is for the best interest of the child, and what will best promote its welfare and happiness. . . ."

Until recently, however, there has been a pattern of at least cursory invocation by the courts in New York and elsewhere, of the presumption that children of tender years, all other things being equal, should be given into the custody of their mother. In fact, this approach to deciding custody cases, since the Domestic Relations Law was amended to forbid such preference, constitutes judicial error—error, moreover, which does not promote the best interests of the children involved. As Foster and Freed, authors of the comprehensive treatise Law and the Family, New York, Vol. 2 (1967) stated:

"The statutory mandate in practice is ignored and instead of equality as between the parents, the mother's claim to the child is paramount. In reality instead of "best interests of the child" serving as the test, the "unfitness" rule which was designed to serve in all custody contests between parents and non-parents is being applied. . . ."

The "tender years presumption" is actually a blanket judicial finding of fact, a statement by a court that, until proven otherwise by the weight of substantial evidence, mothers are always better suited to care for young children than fathers. This flies in the face of the legislative finding of fact underlying the explicit command of section 240 and section 70 of the Domestic Relations Law, that the best interests of the child are served by the court's approaching the facts of the particular case before it without sex preconceptions of any kind.

However, the trend in legislation, legal commentary, and judicial decisions is away from the "tender years presumption."

Recent amendments of the Domestic Relations Law of several other states have codified as explicitly as New York the view that the child's best interest requires that neither parent have preference. In Florida, for example, the relevent provision, effective July 1, 1971, states:

"The court shall award custody and visitation rights of minor children of the parties as a part of proceeding for dissolution of marriage in accordance with the best interests of the child. Upon considering all relevant factors, the father of the child shall be given the same consideration as the mother in determining custody." Fla. Stat. 61.13(2), F.S.A. (1971).

Wisconsin's law, also revised in 1971, provides in relevant part:

"In determining the parent with whom a child shall remain, the court shall consider all facts in the best interest of the child and shall not prefer one parent over the other solely on the basis of the sex of the parent." Wis. Stat. 247.24(3) (1971).

Colorado Rev. Stats. 46-1-5(7) provides:

"No party shall be presumed to be able to serve the best interests of the child better than any other party because of sex."

Legal scholars advocate this evenhanded approach with near virtual unanimity. Evidence that the courts are taking long strides toward abandoning the "tender years presumption" in favor of an unbiased consideration of the best interests of the children solely on the basis of the individual characteristics and relationships of the parents and children involved is found in the large number of recent custody cases in which the parents were treated equally and the father prevailed. . . . [Citation omitted.]

Apart from the question of legality, the "tender years presumption" should be discarded because it is based on outdated social stereotypes rather than on rational and up-to-date consideration of the welfare of the children involved. . . .

Eminent psychologists and anthropologists have also acknowledged and asserted that both female and male parents are equally able to provide care and perform child-rearing functions.

"At present, the specific biological situation of the continuing relationship of the child to the biological mother and its need for care by human beings are being hopelessly confused in the . . . insistence that the child and mother or mother surrogate must never be separated; that all separation even for a few days is ultimately damaging and that if long enough it does irreversible damage. This is a mere and subtle form of anti-feminism which men—under the guise of exalting the importance of maternity—are tying women more tightly to their children than has been thought necessary since the invention of bottle feeding and baby carriages." Margaret Mead, "Some Theoretical Considerations of the Problems of Mother-Child Separation," 24 *Amer. Jrl. of Orthopsychiatry* 24 (1954).

Studies of maternal deprivation have shown that the essential experience for the child is that of mothering—the warmth, consistency and continuity of the relationship rather than the sex of the individual who is performing the mothering function. [Citations omitted.]

Finally, application of the "tender years presumption" would deprive respondent of his right to equal protection of the law under the Fourteenth Amendment to the United States Constitution.

Although courts have properly held that the primary consideration in awarding custody of children is the welfare of the child, it is indisputable that each parent's interests, their relationships with, rearing and custody of their children are of substantial importance. Recent decisions of the Supreme Court of the United States make clear that differential treatment on the basis of sex of the kind created by the "tender years presumption" is "suspect" and therefore subject to the strictest judicial scrutiny. In Frontiero v. Richardson (411 U.S. 677 [1973]) the court made explicit the incurable flaw in rules of law which accord different treatment to men and women on the basis of rigid and outdated sexual stereotypes:

> "Since sex, like race and national origin, is an immutable characteristic determined solely by the accident of birth, the imposition of special disabilities upon the members of a particular sex because of their sex would seem to violate 'the basic concept of our system that legal burdens should bear some relationship to individual responsibility [citation omitted]. . . .' And what differentiates sex from such non-suspect statutes as intelligence or physical disability, and aligns it with the recognized suspect criteria, is that the sex characteristic frequently bears no relation to ability to perform or to contribute to society."

The message of Frontiero is clear: persons similarly situated, whether male or female, must be accorded evenhanded treatment by the law. Legislative classifications may legitimately take account of need or ability; they may not be premised on unalterable sex characteristics that bear no necessary relationship to the individual's need, ability or life situation.

Classifications subject to "strict scrutiny" under the Fourteenth Amendment pass constitutional muster only if a "compelling state interest" requires their existence. The "best interests" of the child might well qualify as such a compelling state interest if, in fact, it were served by the "tender years presumption." But since, as has been shown, the presumption does not in fact serve the child's interests, it does not constitute a compelling state interest justifying the different treatment of parents on the basis of sex. *Thus, the "tender years presumption," in addition to its other faults, works an unconstitutional discrimination against the respondent.* [Emphasis added.] . . . This court, in arriving at its decision, has applied one criteria only—the best interests of the children.

Having listened to all the testimony, having read all the medical reports and records and having observed the demeanor and responses of the parties on the witness stand, this court concludes that it is in the best interests of the children for them to be in their father's custody.

Even though awards to fathers are increasing, more than eight out of ten children are awarded to mothers. The parents' moral behavior and ability to care for the child are both factors in custody decisions. Some courts also refuse to make custody awards that will remove the child from the state.

The child's own wishes are receiving increased attention—especially if the child is old enough to make a thoughtful decision about the living arrangement. The wishes of the children were given particular weight in Hammett v. Hammett, 239 So.2d 778 (Ala. App. 1970).

HAMMETT v.
HAMMETT

WRIGHT, J. This is an appeal from a decree of divorce by which the parties were each granted a divorce on complaint and cross-complaint. The authority for such decree is Title 34, Section 22(1), Code of Alabama 1940.

Alabama Court of Civil
Appeals,
239 So.2d 778
(Ala. App. [1970]).

This is the statute which permits a final divorce after there has been a decree of separate maintenance in effect for more than two years. By its decree, the trial court granted custody of three minor children, ranging in age from eight to thirteen years, to the mother-appellee, with reasonable visitation rights to the father-appellant.

The only error assigned is that the court erred in granting custody of the children to the mother rather than to the father.

Appellant is retired from military service after some thirty years of service. His career in the service was that of cook and NCO in charge of general mess. Appellee during most of the marriage years, worked as a beautician and is presently so employed. Appellant has suffered several heart attacks and is also a diabetic. His physical condition appears to have stabilized, but he is not able to be regularly employed. His income consists of retirement benefits and social security. His children receive $27.50 a month each from social security. He has purchased and lives in a comfortable home in Prattville, Alabama. Appellee is regularly employed as a beautician in Montgomery.

Following the decree of separate maintenance in 1966, appellee worked from early morning until late afternoon. The children were either alone or in the care of a sitter or watched by a neighbor. Appellant often met them in the afternoon after school, and had them with him on weekends. Appellant fully complied with the terms of the separate maintenance decree, and supplemented it by purchasing clothes and other necessities for the children.

Shortly before the filing of the petition for divorce by appellant, the appellee and the children moved back into the home in Prattville. Appellee testified that the return was at the request of appellant and the children, and was for the purpose of reconciliation. Appellant testified that the return was on appellee's own initiative and not at his request. However, appellant accepted the return, prepared meals and cared for the children. They were entered in school in Prattville and were living there at the time of the decree.

There was no order in the decree requiring appellee to move after the divorce, and insofar as the record discloses they may all still be living in the same residence, including appellee. . . . At the time of the decree in June 1969, the children were fourteen, twelve and eleven years of age. The oldest and youngest are girls and the other a boy. Throughout this marriage appellant had done substantially all the cooking for the family and had continued to do so after they returned home in 1968. Appellant is not employed and stays at home. Appellee is employed and is gone from home all day, six days a week. When questioned by the court the children expressed a desire to live with their father rather than their mother. The mother had discipline problems with the children, particularly the boy. Appellant has an excellent home near the schools where the children are enrolled located in Prattville "the best place to live in the United States."

The testimony was without serious conflict as to appellant or appellee being a fit and proper person to have custody of the children.

We have very carefully read and considered the testimony in this case. We have also considered the colloquy between the trial judge and counsel which appears in the record. It is obvious that the decision of the court concerning the custody of the children was reached after serious consideration. It is only after equally serious study and consideration that we have concluded that the award of the custody of these children to appellee is plainly wrong and does not represent the best interest of the children—which is the paramount matter for consideration. Calhoun v. Calhoun, 278 Ala. 610, 179 So.2d 737. . . . To summarize the evidence which forces us to decision—*The children prefer to live with their father.* [Emphasis added.] The father has prepared their meals almost exclusively since their birth. He is free to be at home with them at all times. He is undisputedly fitted morally and financially to provide them with a good home. The mother, whether from necessity or inclination, has worked throughout the children's lives, all day and every day, except Sunday, leaving their care to someone else. She, admittedly, cannot cook for them as well as the father. The children are enrolled in schools near the home of appellant. The children are in need of parental discipline.

It really matters not whether our determination of error in the decree is stated to be based upon a wrong conclusion of facts, or a wrong application of governing principles of law. In any event, it is clear that to serve the best interest of the children the decree in respect to custody must be reversed.

In the event there is not involved a child of such tender years as to be peculiarly dependent upon the mother, there is no rule requiring that custody be granted to the mother rather than the father, when either is a fit and proper custodian. From the facts in the instant case, it rather appears that the children are peculiarly dependent upon the father. In making such statement and in rendering this decision, we do not intend to appear derogatory to the appellee as a mother. We are certain she has attempted to do her best for her children under difficult circumstances. We are further certain that the trial court will insure that she has every opportunity, consonant with the welfare of the children, to be with them and have them with her.

The trial court is hereby directed to amend its decree wherein it granted to appellee the permanent care, custody and control of the children, and grant such custody to the appellant, granting appellee such reasonable rights of visitation as is deemed proper in the premises. It follows, that the portion of the decree as to payment of support for the children to appellee by appellant, be amended to conform with this decision.

Reversed and remanded with directions.

Other family members are frequently involved in child care following divorce. Vanden Heuvel v. Vanden Heuvel, 121 N.W.2d 216 (Iowa 1963), demonstrates the difficult issues in some custody cases. Of particular interest are the sharp differences in the dissent, and the court's willingness to give up jurisdiction by placing the son with his mother in Michigan.

VANDEN HEUVEL
v.
VANDEN HEUVEL
Iowa Supreme Court,
1963.
254 Iowa 1391, 121
N.W.2d 216.

This habeas corpus action of Howard Gene Vanden Heuvel, by his mother and next friend, Sally Vanden Heuvel, plaintiff, against Jaren G. Vanden Heuvel, the father, and Henry Vanden Heuvel and Gertrude Vanden Heuvel, paternal grandparents of the minor child, defendants, alleges the child is illegally restrained of his liberty by defendants, and Sally's rightful custody of him is prevented.

On April 3, 1962, a writ was issued and served upon the defendants, who appeared and filed pleadings in the matter, including a counterclaim asking that they be granted the full care and custody of Howard, then about two and one half years of age, and alleging that it would not be for the child's best interest and welfare to give custody to the mother, Sally. The issue for the court's determination here, as in the usual case of this kind, is in whose custody will the best interest and general welfare of the child be served—a very simple question with no completely satisfactory answer.

The trial court, after a lengthy trial, found the equities were with the mother and granted to her the care, custody and control of the plaintiff, Howard Gene Vanden Heuvel. The defendants have appealed contending the trial court erred in finding the mother was a fit and proper person to have custody of the child, that the best interest of the child would be obtained by granting the custody to the mother, and in permitting the removal of the child to the mother's residence in the State of Michigan. We shall consider these contentions in that order.

The record discloses that Sally, now 22 years of age, and Jaren, now 26 years of age, were married at Grand Rapids, Michigan, on January 29, 1960, after an acquaintance of about one year while both were attending Calvin College. They set up housekeeping in an apartment at Kalamazoo, Michigan, where Jaren was then attending Western Michigan University. Some financial and emotional difficulties arose, making the marriage somewhat less than ideal. Howard was born July 30, 1960. The evidence adequately supports a finding that due to illness, a not unusual product of mental and emotional disturbances at such time, Sally did not keep house in an acceptable manner subsequent to the marriage and that, after the child's birth, she failed to give him proper care and attention or exhibit love and affection for him. Up until the seventh month of her pregnancy Sally was employed, and at one time was the sole source of the family income. Conditions did not improve in the next two and one half months after Howard's birth and Jaren urged Sally to take the baby to his or her parents for a while. She consented to visit his parents in Iowa and, although obviously quite ill, Jaren sent her and the child alone by train to Ottumwa, Iowa, where they were met by his parents. The mother and child were then taken to the farm home near New Sharon, Iowa. After spending approximately two weeks at the Henry Vanden Heuvel home, Sally left the baby with the grandparents and went to Chicago, where Jaren met her. They then went to Grand Rapids, Michigan. On October 21, 1960, Sally was persuaded to become a voluntary patient at the Pine Rest Christian Hospital, a psychopathic institution maintained largely by the Christian Reformed religious sect. The baby has remained with the paternal grandmother on the Iowa farm except for two brief visits to Michigan, once to see Sally at the hospital and once to see his father at Kalamazoo. It appears Sally had been assured she could have her child when she was well and able to adequately care for him.

At the Pine Rest Hospital Sally's mental illness was diagnosed as being "that of a schizophrenic reaction and what is called the schizoaffective type." She remained at the hospital for about 8 or 9 months and received appropriate care and treatment as a patient of Dr. Stuart Bergsma, M.D., Clinical Director at Pine Rest (a Fellow of the American College of Surgeons and a

Diplomate of the American Board of Psychiatry and Neurology), whose specialty is psychiatry.

Sally's alleged disillusionment and disappointment from a lack of sympathy, love and understanding of her husband, was not altered when Jaren instituted a divorce action against her in the Circuit Court of Kalamazoo County, Michigan, on April 25, 1961. This action culminated in a "Final Decree of Divorce" dated December 8, 1961, granted Sally on her "Cross-Bill of Complaint." On July 12, 1961, she was discharged from the hospital, but she had been permitted to work outside the institution after June 10, 1961.

The record discloses that Sally is a high school graduate, has attended Calvin College at Grand Rapids for a year, and is now taking five hours of study there, making a B grade in her courses. Since her discharge from Pine Rest, she has been steadily employed as a practical nurse and now works at the Maple Grove Medical Facility operated by Kent County, Michigan, at Grand Rapids. Her work record is excellent and she earns $46.00 per week take-home pay. Her superiors speak highly of her work and personality.

Sally has been residing with her childless sister and brother-in-law, Jeanette and Marvin Diepstra, who own a neat, well-kept, modern and comfortable Cape Cod bungalow in a very nice residential section of Grand Rapids. It has a large fenced backyard with a sandbox. There are two rooms upstairs available for Sally and Howard, and there are two bedrooms, bath, kitchen, and living room downstairs, and a full basement. There are children in the family next door. Sally pays a modest sum for these facilities and Howard will be more than welcome in that home. Work schedules have been arranged between Sally and her employed sister so that Howard will be provided with full-time and adequate care and supervision in this home.

The record also discloses that since leaving Pine Rest Sally has become quite active in church youth activities and has demonstrated to authorities and acquaintances, many of whom testified for her, a sincere fondness for children and the patience and ability to manage and get along well with them. Her baby-sitting record reflects credit upon her present capabilities, and there was no evidence to the contrary.

The trial court observed that during the long trial, which by the very nature of it was a most emotional experience for her, "Sally demonstrated a marked degree of sincerity, composure, self-control, poise and stability."

As to charges of sexual irregularities, three or four of which Sally admitted, the court found they were properly attributed to her then immaturity and her later mental illness. After careful consideration of that evidence, it observed that while those incidents were regrettable, there is "no reasonably likelihood that they will reoccur." Only the interested parties gave testimony on this unusual relationship.

It appears an ill-advised attempt to obtain the physical control of Howard by self-help occurred in October 1961. When Sally was refused the return of her son and was denied the right to visit him on weekends, she sought the aid of a private detective, who unfortunately directed the abortive attempt to take the child from a store in Oskaloosa, Iowa. That activity was wholly improper, as Sally now sorrowfully admits. The mistake was made, she says, because of her great desire to regain her son and by accepting and following such poor advice from another.

Dr. Bergsma, Sally's psychiatrist, and Dr. Edwin M. Williamson, M.D. (chief of Staff of Plainwell Sanitarium, Kalamazoo, Michigan), who at the request of one of the attorneys representing Jaren in the divorce proceedings, made careful and thorough psychiatric examinations and evaluations of Sally just before this trial and sometime subsequent to her discharge from the Pine Rest Hospital, each expressed the opinion that Sally had recovered from her mental illness and is, from a psychiatric standpoint, a fit and proper person to have the care and custody of her minor child Howard. While it is true these doctors use the term "remission" in describing Sally's condition, it was the trial court's understanding, as it is ours, that they intended to indicate thereby that Sally has, for all practical purposes, recovered from her mental illness and that the possibility of any recurrence is remote.

Many substantial residents and church authorities of the Grand Rapids area who have had various and close relationships with Sally since her release from Pine Rest, testified that in their opinions Sally is fully capable of properly caring for her son and will be a loving and devoted mother to him. Thus the trial court's finding that Sally is now a mature and well-oriented person possessed of a normal outlook upon life and of a normal motherly instinct, that she has the ability and desire to assume the care, custody and control of her child Howard, is fully supported by the evidence.

On the other hand, Jaren holds degrees from Calvin College and from Western Michigan University. Since receiving his Master's degree, he has been employed as Clinical Psychologist at the Annie Wittenmyer Home for children at Davenport, Iowa, where he is well liked and his work has been entirely satisfactory. He bears a good reputation, is devoted to his son, and spends many weekends with him at the Henry Vanden Heuvel home.

Mr. and Mrs. Vanden Heuvel each have excellent reputations and are well regarded as parents, having raised two sons in addition to Jaren. The younger son, now age 14, still is at home, a high school student. They are devoted to Howard and have provided him with good care. The farm home is modern and is located on their 230 acre farm. At the time of the trial Gertrude Vanden Heuvel was 46 years of age, and Henry, who did not testify, was 48 years of age. Both are in good health and can furnish Howard a satisfactory home.

I.   Although some definite rules have been laid down and recognized as applicable to cases of this nature, it is obvious each case must depend largely upon the facts disclosed by the evidence. . . . So once again we are faced with the task of deciding whether under the revealed circumstances the interest and welfare of this child Howard will best be served by his being placed with his mother or with his father and his paternal grandparents. No one can be sure on this point, for as we pointed out in Patzner v. Patzner, 250 Iowa 155, 159, 93 N.W.2d 55, 57 (1958), a determination that appears wisest today may by a turn of events be found tomorrow to have been unfortunate. Courts realize they are human agencies and, as we cannot be positive as to the future, we admit the possibility of a mistake and decide such matters on the conditions as they now appear, with full confidence courts will correct inequities later appearing. Our attempt is, therefore, to arrive at what seemingly is the best solution under the facts and circumstances as they presently appear.

The trial court apparently believed the physical facilities offered by both parties were more than adequate, that the parties were both fit and proper parties to have the child's custody, and felt the small child's best interest would be served by placing him with his mother. We agree.

II. This action, instituted by the plaintiff, is a statutory proceeding. Where the custody of children is involved, we have adopted the rule that the scope of the writ of habeas corpus is enlarged and invokes the broad equitable powers of the court. The ultimate consideration in such cases, is, of course, the best interests and welfare of the children before it. . . .

We are, of course, mindful of the presumption that a young child will be best advantaged by being placed in the custody of the mother. We are also aware that this presumption has been weakened somewhat in recent years, so while it may be said such a presumption is not strong and can readily be overcome by other evidence, there must be some such substantial evidence. Thus, as a general rule the court would be right, save in exceptional circumstances, in holding the mother best-fitted to care for her child of tender years. . . . Where the record does not bear out a finding that the mother of a small child is presently suffering from a mental disease, but does show she has been discharged from treatment of such a disease with symptoms under remission for a reasonable length of time, and shows no probability of a recurrence, the mother should not be deprived of the care and custody of her child for that reason. . . .

The case at bar is much stronger in support of a finding of complete recovery of the mother. It clearly appears she has had no treatments or medication for over a year after her discharge and shows no signs of a recurrence of her illness. All the experts' testimony was to the effect that she did not have the permanent type of mental illness of that nature, would probably never have a recurrence of her illness, and that they knew of no reason why she should not have the care and custody of her child. Many lay witnesses gave the same opinion.

We agree with the trial court that the evidence fully justified the conclusion that the mother has fully recovered, that she will not be likely to encounter the disturbing conditions or relationships which originally brought on her mental illness and unusual behavior. Therefore, on the fitness of the mother issue we are satisfied the trial court's judgment was correct.

As to the fitness of defendants Henry Vanden Heuvel and Gertrude Vanden Heuvel to have the care and custody of Howard, there can be no doubt. Both are in good mental and physical health and have excellent reputations in the community as citizens and as parents. It is true Gertrude had some mental illness when her last son was born and had also taken treatment at the Pine Rest Institution some years ago. She too has completely recovered.

As to the fitness of defendant Jaren, we are not so sure. His testimony as to Sally's shortcomings appears too eagerly given. It is clear he too has made some mistakes in the past. While he bears a good reputation and holds a very responsible position, his conduct toward and treatment of Sally, his wife, at the time of her greatest need does not tally with the standard of conduct we would like to find in a father and devoted husband. Significant was his lack of concern for the welfare of his ill wife and baby as he sent them both on a hard train trip alone to his parents' home rather than obtain help for her in their apartment or take them to Iowa himself. His premature effort to divorce his wife when she was ill in the hospital discloses little or no love or sympathy for his unfortunate wife. . . . Clearly, he could not care for the boy without the help of his parents, and we have not favored joint custody of children, especially where the parties do not live in the same household.

Therefore, we are inclined to believe it best for this child to place him in the custody of his mother where the responsibility for his well being and discipline will be in a single person who loves and cherishes him as only a mother can. Under the circumstances it seems better than to have his custody in the father who only spends weekends with him, while his actual care and training are left to his paternal grandparents. Should Jaren remarry and remove the boy to his new home, status quo, the most persuasive contention for denying this writ, would not be maintained.

The question as to whether the mother should be given the custody of this child in view of the fact that she intends to remove him from this state naturally gives us some concern. We have several times approved the statement that it is against the policy of the law to permit the removal of a child from our jurisdiction unless its welfare would be better served thereby. . . .

The trial court considered carefully this question and decided it would be for Howard's welfare to permit his permanent return to the state of his birth to be with his mother, and that this transfer would not be in the nature of an experiment. We are inclined to agree, for if it was to be considered an experiment it clearly should not be allowed. To sustain this writ and grant Sally the right to take the child back to Michigan means the Iowa courts will not have a chance to correct a mistake if that action turns out to be such. Appellants contend that to permit the immediate removal of Howard from the jurisdiction of the Iowa court will amount to an abandonment of its duty to protect the welfare of the child when its jurisdiction had been invoked by an action of habeas corpus. We do not concede that fact.

Being satisfied the child's interest and welfare will best be served by the transfer, we fail to see any failure of Iowa courts to properly perform their duty to protect the child's best interest. This was the extent of the trial court's judgment and we find no such abuse of its discretion in this matter as to call for a reversal. There is ample evidence to support its decision and we can only hope, as we always do in such custody disputes, that tomorrow its expectations will be fulfilled.

In passing, however, we will not concede the contention that this child's welfare and best interest will not be as well and carefully protected by the Michigan courts as by ourselves, and feel certain that if the child's best interest should again be questioned in a habeas corpus proceeding in Michigan, such interest would be fully and carefully protected. . . .

THOMPSON, Justice (dissenting):

I.   The majority opinion removes this small child from the only home he has known, where he has been happy and well cared for about two and one-half years, almost all of his short life, and sends him to the care of a mother who has suffered serious mental illness in the past and had admittedly been guilty of acts of sex deviation. It may be true that she has re-covered from her mental troubles and that her sexual aberrations will not be repeated. But the child will be far removed from Iowa and it will be a practical impossibility for the father and the paternal grandparents in whose custody he has thrived to date to know what is happening to him or what the mother's mental condition and conduct may be, or for the Iowa courts to do anything about it if serious danger to his welfare develops. The mother voluntarily left him in his present home and for some time paid little or no attention to him.

As the majority rightly says it is impossible to know the future, and the courts can at best make only an educated guess as to what will best serve the interests of the child. In this situation there is an old rule which expresses the common sense experience of men over the centuries. It is that when we cannot be certain we should leave well enough alone. We know the boy will be well cared for and reared where he is; we are gambling with his future when we send him to a new home and a new life in a distant state. I would follow the rule of common sense.

II.   The majority states and follows another rule which it must be ad-mitted has become fixed in our consideration of child custody cases. It is that the trial court has discretion and we will reverse only when an abuse appears. . . . Our present rule, I apprehend, gives the appellant only a limited review, which amounts in effect to a determination whether there are facts which support the trial court's findings. The present rule makes our review little more than a review at law, in which the fact findings of the trial court have the force and effect of a special verdict. We should make our own examination and decision as to the weight of the evidence.

Visitation of grandparents were clarified in an appellate decision several years ago granted by the New York Supreme Court In the Matter of Gabriel Vacula v. Carol James Blume, 384 N.Y.S.2d 208 (1976). The grandparents had not seen their granddaughter for over three years. The parents had divorced in 1971 and the father died a year later. The mother's animosity extended to the grandparents. The appeals court held:

"Animosity between the mother of the children and their grandparents is not a proper basis for the denial of visitation privileges to the grandparents, nor is it a proper yardstick by which to measure the best interests of the children."

Courts are generally willing to reopen and modify custody decrees if the best interests of the child so require. Remarriage of the custodial parent is a common reason for modification. Custody may be awarded to the other parent in order to avoid any impediment the child's presence might present to the success of a new marriage. Unfortunately, in some instances neither parent may want to exercise custody.

CUSTODY AWARDS TO HOMOSEXUALS   When child custody is petitioned by a homosexual parent, social workers in child welfare are concerned both with the best interests of the child and with the rights of the parent. Traditionally, the major question has stemmed from the "tender years" principle: Should a mother living in a lesbian relationship retain custody of a young child? The problem for the male homosexual parent is more likely to concern visitation rights. Although "tender years" is an important issue, perhaps the decision should be considered more critical for the older child.

Recent decisions have depended increasingly on two questions: Is the homosexual parent unfit? Does the relationship with a partner concretely harm the child? Decisions depend on a nexus* requirement stated, for example, in Bezio v. Patenaude, 410 N.E.2d 1207 (Mass. 1980).

> A finding that a parent is unfit to further the welfare of the child must be predicated upon parental behavior which adversely affects the child. The state may not deprive parents of custody of their children simply because their households fail to meet the ideals approved by the community. . . or simply because the parents embrace ideologies or pursue a life-style at odds with the average. In *Bezio* the court found no correlation between the mother's homosexuality and her fitness as a parent.

In considering a Virginia decision favorable to the birth mother (Doe v. Doe, 222 Va. 736, 284 S.E.2d 799 [1981] Cardwell (1982) identifies eleven cases that protected the custody and visitation rights of homosexual parents.† Evans (1982) considers an Oklahoma case, M.J.P. v. J.G.P., 640 P.2d 966 (1982), in which a young child was removed from a lesbian mother:

> The court overlooked the present needs of the child for continuity in the placement in which he was flourishing. Absent evidence of present harm to J., further inquiry into the sexual activities of the mother was not required and was a violation of her right to privacy.
>
> An analysis of this fact situation shows a 2½-year-old boy with a masculine identity, who has lived with his mother since birth, and for whom she has been the psychological parent for the last eighteen months. The court did not address the effects of separation from her. It did not concern itself with the ensuing fears, regression, and loss of trust a child experiences after separation. Yet this should be the main issue in this case, in the absence of a showing of present harm.
>
> There is empirical evidence of what the child's response will almost certainly be. The damage done by separating J. from his psychological parent may far outweigh any damage that might be done if he has to defend his mother's choice of life-style at some future date. Indeed, he may not be spared that experience even now.
>
> The trial court apparently did not consider the tender years doctrine in making its judgment, nor did the Supreme Court mention it in upholding that judgment, despite the doctrine's validity and constitutionality. The trial court did acknowledge the doctrine's importance in its initial decision, but presumably it was outweighed by the change of condition. [Citations omitted]

The court has wide discretion in such cases. The right to specify restrictions has never been successfully challenged, so the court may require that a male parent may have a child stay with him only when the partner is not present. A mother may get custody if she agrees the partner will not live with her. The decisions also

---

* **Nexus** refers to the connection between the evidence and the decision.

† Nadler v. Superior Court, 63 Cal. Rptr. 352 (1967) (custody involving a homosexual father); Gay v. Gay, 253 S.E.2d 846 (Ga. App. 1979) (custody involving a lesbian); D.H. v. J.H., 418 N.E.2d 286 (Ind. App. 1981) (custody involving a lesbian); Bezio v. Patenaude, 410 N.E.2d 1207 (Mass. 1980) (custody involving a lesbian); Hall v. Hall, 291 N.W.2d 143 (Mich. 1980) (Custody involving a lesbian); M.P. v. S.P., 404 A.2d 1256 (N.J. Super. 1979) (custody involving a lesbian); DiStefano v. DiStefano, 401 N.Y.S.2d 636 (1978) (custody involving a lesbian); A. v. A., 514 P.2d 358 (Or. App. 1973) (custody involving a homosexual father); In re Breisch, 434 A.2d 815 (Pa. Super. 1981) (custody involving a lesbian); Kallas v. Kallas, 614 P.2d 641 (Utah 1980) (visitation involving a lesbian). Also Peterson v. Peterson, No. 0-66634 (Colo. Dist. Ct. April 26, 1978); Whitehead v. Black, 2 Fam. L. Rep. (BNA) 2593 (Me. Super. Ct. July 13, 1976); Ungland v. Ungland, No. 62380 (Minn. Dist. Ct. June 12, 1978); Anonymous v. Anonymous, No. 19028 (Super. Ct. Wash. 1976).

rely heavily on expert testimony. In addition, the social worker may play a key role.

Of course, the issue does not usually arise as long as parents do not officially separate. Homosexuality is rarely advanced as an issue in child neglect in a two-parent household, although a number of married couples do develop homosexual relationships.

INTERSTATE CUSTODY PROBLEMS

The bitter feelings and strife evoked by child custody are often complicated by jurisdictional problems among the states. It is not unusual for a parent to kidnap a child from the parent holding legal custody and to petition for custody in another state. The privilege of interstate visitation is also occasionally violated when a child is not returned according to the provisions of the court order. A Uniform Child Custody Jurisdiction Act (§§1-28, 9 U.L.A. 116-170 [1968]) was passed, and a federal act on Prevention of Parental Kidnapping (28 U.S.C.A. §1738A [1980]), was enacted later. The Uniform Child Custody Jurisdiction Act includes provisions for jurisdiction and abduction of a child:

Section 3. Jurisdiction

(a) A court of this State which is competent to decide child custody matters has jurisdiction to make a child custody determination by initial or modification decree if:

(1) this State (i) is the home state of the child at the time of commencement of the proceeding, or (ii) had been the child's home state within 6 months before commencement of the proceeding and the child is absent from this State because of his removal or retention by a person claiming his custody or for other reasons, and a parent or person acting as parent continues to live in this State; or

(2) it is in the best interest of the child that a court of this State assume jurisdiction because (i) the child and his parents, or the child and at least one contestant, have a significant connection with this State, and (ii) there is available in this State substantial evidence concerning the child's present or future care, protection, training, and personal relationships; or

(3) the child is physically present in this State and (i) the child has been abandoned or (ii) it is necessary in an emergency to protect the child because he has been subjected to or threatened with mistreatment or abuse or is otherwise neglected (or dependent); or

(4) (i) it appears that no other state would have jurisdiction under prerequisites substantially in accordance with paragraphs (1), (2), or (3) or another state has declined to exercise jurisdiction on the ground that this State is the more appropriate forum to determine the custody of the child, and (ii) it is in the best interest of the child that this court assume jurisdiction.

(b) Except under paragraphs (3) and (4) of subsection (a), physical presence in this State of the child, or of the child and one of the contestants, is not alone sufficient to confer jurisdiction on a court of this State to make a child custody determination.

(c) Physical presence of the child, while desirable, is not a prerequisite for jurisdiction to determine his custody.

Section 8. Jurisdiction Declined by Reason of Conduct

(a) If the petitioner for an initial decree has wrongfully taken the child from another state or has engaged in similar reprehensible conduct the court may decline to exercise jurisdiction if this is just and proper under the circumstances.

(b) *Unless required in the interest of the child, the court shall not exercise its jurisdiction to modify a custody decree of another state if the petitioner, without consent of the person entitled to custody, has improperly removed the child from the physical custody of the person entitled to custody or has improperly retained the child after a visit or other temporary relinquishment of physical custody. If the petitioner has violated any other provision of a custody decree of another state the court may decline to exercise its jurisdiction if this is just and proper under the circumstances.* [Emphasis added.]

(c) In appropriate cases a court dismissing a petition under this section may charge the petitioner with necessary travel and other expenses, including attorneys' fees, incurred by other parties of their witnesses.

With the high mobility of families and children, a formal set of policies is necessary between the states. The Interstate Compact on the Placement of Children serves this purpose. By 1985, the compact had been adopted by forty-seven states and the Virgin Islands as the result of a special project sponsored by the American Public Welfare Association. Only Hawaii, New Jersey, and Nevada had failed to enact it.

INTERSTATE COMPACT ON THE PLACEMENT OF CHILDREN*
Article I: Purpose and policy

It is the purpose and policy of the party states to cooperate with each other in the interstate placement of children to the end that:

(a) Each child requiring placement shall receive the maximum opportunity to be placed in a suitable environment and with persons or institutions having appropriate qualifications and facilities to provide a necessary and desirable degree and type of care.

(b) The appropriate authorities in a state where a child is to be placed may have full opportunity to ascertain the circumstances of the proposed placement, thereby promoting full compliance with applicable requirements for the protection of the child.

(c) The proper authorities of the state from which the placement is made may obtain the most complete information on the basis on which to evaluate a projected placement before it is made.

(d) Appropriate jurisdictional arrangements for the care of children will be promoted.

Article II: Definitions

As used in this compact:

(a) "Child" means a person who, by reason of minority, is legally subject to parental, guardianship or similar control.

(b) "Sending agency" means a party state, officer or employee thereof; a subdivision of a party state, or officer or employee thereof; a court of a party state; a person, corporation, association, charitable agency or other entity which sends, brings, or causes to be sent or brought any child to another party state.

(c) "Receiving state" means the state to which a child is sent, brought, or caused to be sent or brought, whether by public authorities or private persons or agencies, and whether for placement with state or local public authorities or for placement with private agencies or persons.

(d) "Placement" means the arrangement for the care of a child in a family free or boarding home or in a child-caring agency or institution but does not include any institution caring for the mentally ill, mentally defective or epileptic or any institution primarily educational in character, and any hospital or other medical facility.

Article III: Conditions for placement

(a) No sending agency shall send, bring, or cause to be sent or brought into any other party state any child for placement in foster care or as a preliminary to a possible adoption unless the sending agency shall comply with each and every requirement set forth in this article and with the applicable laws of the receiving state governing the placement of children therein.

---

*Source: Council of State Governments, *Interstate Placement of Children: A Preliminary Report* (Lexington, Ky., 1974), pp. 49–51.

(b)   Prior to sending, bringing or causing any child to be sent or brought into a receiving state for placement in foster care or as a preliminary to a possible adoption, the sending agency shall furnish the appropriate public authorities in receiving state written notice of the intention to send, bring, or place the child in the receiving state. The notice shall contain: (1) the name, date and place of birth of the child; (2) the identity and address or addresses of the parents or legal guardian; (3) the name and address of the person, agency or institution to or with which the sending agency proposes to send, bring, or place the child; (4) a full statement of the reasons for such proposed action and evidence of the authority pursuant to which the placement is proposed to be made.

(c)   Any public officer or agency in a receiving state which is in receipt of a notice pursuant to paragraph (b) of this article may request of the sending agency, or any other appropriate officer or agency of or in the sending agency's state, and shall be entitled to receive therefrom, such supporting or additional information as it may deem necessary under the circumstances to carry out the purpose and policy of this compact.

(d)   The child shall not be sent, brought, or caused to be sent or brought into the receiving state until the appropriate public authorities in the receiving state shall notify the sending agency, in writing, to the effect that the proposed placement does not appear to be contrary to the interests of the child.

Article IV: Penalty for illegal placement

The sending, bringing, or causing to be sent or brought into any receiving state of a child in violation of the terms of this compact shall constitute a violation of the laws respecting the placement of children of both the state in which the sending agency is located or from which it sends or brings the child and of the receiving state. Such violation may be punished or subjected to penalty in either jurisdiction in accordance with its laws. In addition to liability for any such punishment or penalty, any such violation shall constitute full and sufficient grounds for the suspension or revocation of any license, permit, or other legal authorization held by the sending agency which empowers or allows it to place, or care for children.

Article V: Retention of jurisdiction

(a)   The sending agency shall retain jurisdiction over the child sufficient to determine all matters in relation to the custody, supervision, care, treatment and disposition of the child which it would have had if the child had remained in the sending agency's state, until the child is adopted, reaches majority, becomes self-supporting or is discharged with the concurrence of the appropriate authority in the receiving state. Such jurisdiction shall also include the power to effect or cause the return of the child or its transfer to another location and custody pursuant to law. The sending agency shall continue to have financial responsibility for support and maintenance of the child during the period of the placement. Nothing contained herein shall defeat a claim of jurisdiction by a receiving state sufficient to deal with an act of delinquency or crime committed therein.

(b)   When the sending agency is a public agency, it may enter into an agreement with an authorized public or private agency in the receiving state providing for the performance of one or more services in respect of such case by the latter as agent for the sending agency.

(c)   Nothing in this compact shall be construed to prevent a private charitable agency authorized to place children in the receiving state from performing services or acting as agent in that state for a private charitable agency of the sending state; nor to prevent the agency in the receiving state from discharging financial responsibility for the support and maintenance of a child who has been placed on behalf of the sending agency without relieving the responsibility set forth in paragraph (a) hereof.

Article VI: Institutional care of delinquent children

A child adjudicated delinquent may be placed in an institution in another party jurisdiction pursuant to this compact but no such placement shall be made unless the child is given a court hearing on notice to the parent or guardian with opportunity to be heard, prior to his being sent to such other party jurisdiction for institutional care and the court finds that (1)   equivalent facilities for the child are not available in the sending agency's jurisdiction; and (2)   institutional care in the other jurisdiction is in the best interest of the child and will not produce undue hardship.

Article VII: Compact administrator

The executive head of each jurisdiction party to this compact shall designate an officer who shall be general coordinator of activities under this compact in his jurisdiction and who, acting jointly with like officers of other party jurisdictions, shall have power to promulgate rules and regulations to carry out more effectively the terms and provisions of this compact.

Article VIII: Limitations

This compact shall not apply to:

(a)   The sending or bringing of a child into a receiving state by his parent, step-parent, grandparent, adult brother or sister, adult uncle or aunt, or his guardian and leaving the child with any such relative or non-agency in the receiving state.

(b)   Any placement, sending or bringing of a child into a receiving state pursuant to any other interstate compact to which both the state from which the child is sent or brought and the receiving state are party, or to any other agreement between said states which has the force of law.

Article IX: Enactment and withdrawal

This compact shall be open to joinder by any state, territory or possession of the United States, the District of Columbia, the Commonwealth of Puerto Rico, and, with the consent of Congress, the Government of Canada or any province thereof. It shall become effective with respect to any such jurisdiction when such jurisdiction has enacted the same into law. Withdrawal from this compact shall be by the enactment of a statute repealing the same, but shall not take effect until two years after the effective date of such statute and until written notice of the withdrawal has been given by the withdrawing state to the Governor of each other party jurisdiction. Withdrawal of a party state shall not affect the rights, duties and obligations under this compact of any sending agency therein with respect to a placement made prior to the effective date of withdrawal.

Article X: Construction and severability

The provisions of this compact shall be liberally construed to effectuate the purposes thereof. The provisions of this compact shall be severable and if any phrase, clause, sentence or provision of this compact is declared to be contrary to the constitution of any party state or of the United States or the applicability thereof to any government, agency, person or circumstance is held invalid, the validity of the remainder of this compact and the applicability thereof to any government, agency, person or circumstance shall not be affected thereby. If this compact shall be held contrary to the constitution of any state party thereto, the compact shall remain in full force and effect as to the remaining states and in full force and effect as to the state affected as to all severable matters.

Section 2.   Financial responsibility for any child placed pursuant to the provisions of the Interstate Compact on the Placement of Children shall be determined in accordance with the provisions of Article V thereof in the first instance. However, in the event of partial or complete default of performance thereunder, the provisions of the Revised Uniform Reciprocal Enforcement of Support Act, approved August 28, 1969, as amended, also may be invoked.

Section 3.   The "appropriate public authorities" as used in Article III of the Interstate Compact on the Placement of Children shall, with reference to this state, mean the Department of _____ , and the Department shall receive and act with reference to notices required by Article III.

Section 4.   As used in paragraph (a) of Article V of the Interstate Compact on the Placement of Children, the phrase "Appropriate authority in the receiving state" with reference to this state means the Department of _____ .

Section 5.   The officers and agencies of this state and its subdivisions having authority to place children are empowered to enter into agreements with appropriate officers or agencies of or in other party states pursuant to paragraph (b) of Article V of the Interstate Compact on the Placement of Children. Any such agreement which contains a financial commitment or imposes a financial obligation on this state or subdivision or agency thereof shall not be binding unless it has the approval in writing of the State Comptroller in the case of the state and of the chief local fiscal officer in the case of a subdivision of the state.

Section 6.   Any requirements for visitation, inspection or supervision of children, homes, institutions or other agencies in another party state which may apply under the Interstate Compact on Juveniles or any other Act or regulation shall be deemed to be met if performed pursuant to an agreement entered into by appropriate officers or agencies of this state or a subdivision thereof as contemplated by paragraph (b) of Article V of the Interstate Compact on the Placement of Children.

Section 7.   No Act or regulation restricting out of state placement shall apply to placements made pursuant to the Interstate Compact on the Placement of Children.

Section 8.   Any court having jurisdiction to place delinquent children may place such a child in an institution in another state pursuant to Article VI of the Interstate Compact on the Placement of Children and shall retain jurisdiction as provided in Article V thereof.

Section 9.   As used in Article VII of the Interstate Compact on the Placement of Children, the term "executive head" means the Governor. The Governor is authorized to appoint a compact administrator in accordance with the terms of said Article VII.

SITUATIONS REQUIRING NONPARENTAL CARE

Separation and divorce create a need for custody decisions between parents but may also lead to placement of the child under the care of someone else. In low-income families, the mother may be unable to support both herself and her children when no help is received from the husband. Another family member may assume the substitute parental role for some mothers. Parents who lack appropriate family resources may be forced to place their children under the care of an agency or the court.

Death of the parents traditionally created the most common need for child care, but with increased life expectancy of parents, full or half orphans are now rare. The agencies that used to serve orphans have transferred their attention to children with emotional problems. The emotional difficulties experienced by such children are frequently characterized by a surplus rather than a deficit of parental figures. For example, in families where each parent remarries, the child may be exposed to four parent figures. The child may also typically be assigned two foster parents and a social worker, making a total of seven parental figures at the same time.

Abandonment of children is a cause for substitute care. This often occurs when a parent leaves children with someone else temporarily and never returns. Legally, abandonment is clear-cut evidence of child neglect.

Illegitimacy used to be a common basis for surrender of children for adoption or foster care. Now, as Chapter 12 will also indicate, unmarried mothers are initially more likely to keep their babies. They seek placement only when they have difficulty rearing a child alone. In the last decade, agencies also report that more married parents are surrendering children because they have had a first child sooner than planned or feel they cannot care for another child.

Children are often placed temporarily in response to **physical or mental illness** of the parents. Arrangements intended to be short-term may become permanent, however.

Other reasons for nonparental child care are related to dependency, neglect, or abuse, which are treated in the previous chapter.

Parental visiting of children in foster care is a key to discharge from such care, according to data from a study by Fanshel (1975). Visitation has implications for children who are placed informally as well as for those placed by social agencies.

> It is my view that it ought to be mandatory for all agencies to keep a log on the visitation of parents to their children in foster care. This information should be readily available as part of the computerized management information systems currently being developed in this area of service. The requirement that this information be available should be formalized into state law, and agency practices in this regard should be carefully monitored by the state departments of social service as part of their licensing function. Like the frequent monitoring of body temperature information for assessing the health of patients in hospitals, the visitation of children should be carefully scrutinized as the best indicator we have concerning the long-term fate of children in care. Consider the fact that 66 percent of the children who received no visits during the first year of care were still in care five years later. . . . Failure of parents to visit their children cannot long be tolerated unless the parent is physically or mentally incapacitated. The question of termination of parental rights naturally arises when a parent drops out of a child's life. Agencies should be held accountable for efforts made to involve the parent in more responsible visitation. The finding that frequency of casework contact, independent of the valuation of the mother, is associated with greater frequency of visiting is a good omen (Fanshel, 1975:513).

Custody and
Guardianship by
Relatives

In child welfare practice, strong preference is generally given to child-care arrangements with relatives rather than strangers. However, one must not assume that the child's best interests will automatically be assured by placement within the extended family. Experience has shown that blood ties do not necessarily assure parental competence or impeccable motivations in assuming the responsibility for care and supervision of a child. Busy court staffs are unlikely to investigate proposed family arrangements with the same thoroughness as they do qualifications of non-relatives. The frequency of child abuse and neglect by relatives suggests that uniform standards of evaluation should be mandatory in selection of custodians and guardians, regardless of blood relationships. Some cases involve a conflict between a parent and the grandparents for custody. The best known case is Painter v. Bannister, 140 N.W.2d 152 (Iowa 1966). The Iowa Supreme Court decided that seven-year-old Mark Painter should remain with his natural grandparents rather than his father. The decision was influenced by the expert testimony of a child psychologist. A major issue was the life-style of Mark's father.

**PAINTER v.
BANNISTER**

Iowa Supreme Court,
140 N.W.2d 152
(Iowa 1966).

Our conclusion as to the type of home Mr. Painter would offer is based upon his Bohemian approach to finances and life in general. We feel there is much evidence which supports this conclusion. His main ambition is to be a free lance writer and photographer. He has had some articles and picture stories published, but the income from these efforts has been negligible. At the time of the accident, Jeanne was willingly working to support the family so Harold could devote more time to his writing and photography. In the 10 years since he left college, he has changed jobs seven times. He was asked to leave two of them; two he quit because he didn't like the work; two because he wanted to devote more time to writing and the rest for better pay. He was contemplating a move to Berkeley at the time of the trial.

The psychiatrist classifies him as "a romantic and somewhat of a dreamer." An apt example are the plans he related for himself and Mark in February 1963: "My thought now is to settle Mark and myself in Sausalito, near San Francisco; this is a retreat for wealthy artists, writers, and such aspiring artists and writers as can fork up the rent money. My plan is to do expensive portraits ($150 and up), sell prints ($15 and up) to the tourists who flock in from all over the world. . . ."

The house in which Mr. Painter and his present wife live, compared with the well kept Bannister home, exemplifies the contrasting ways of life. In his words "it is a very old and beat up and lovely home. . . ." They live in the rear part. The interior is inexpensively but tastefully decorated. The large yard on a hill in the business district of Walnut Creek, California, is of uncut weeds and wild oats. The house "is not painted on the outside because I do not want it painted. I am very fond of the wood on the outside of the house."

The present Mrs. Painter has her master's degree in cinema design and apparently likes and has had considerable contact with children. She is anxious to have Mark in her home. Everything indicates she would provide a leveling influence on Mr. Painter and could ably care for Mark.

Mr. Painter is either an agnostic or atheist and has no concern for formal religious training. He has read a lot of Zen Buddhism and "has been very much influenced by it." Mrs. Painter is Roman Catholic. They plan to send Mark to a Congregational Church near the Catholic Church, on an irregular schedule.

There were "two funerals" for his wife. One in the basement of his home in which he alone was present. He conducted the service and wrote her a long letter. The second at a church in Pullman was for the gratification of her friends. He attended in a sport shirt and sweater.

These matters are not related as a criticism of Mr. Painter's conduct, way of life or sense of values. An individual is free to choose his own values, within bounds, which are not exceeded here. They do serve however to support our conclusion as to the kind of life Mark would be exposed to in the Painter household. We believe it would be unstable, unconventional, arty, Bohemian, and probably intellectually stimulating.

Were the question simply which household would be the most suitable in which to raise a child, we would have unhesitatingly chosen the Bannister home. We believe security and stability in the home are more important than intellectual stimulation in the proper development of a child. There are, however, several factors which have made us pause.

First, there is the presumption of parental preference, which though weakened in the past several years, exists by statute. . . . We have a great deal of sympathy for a father, who in the difficult period of adjustment following his wife's death, turns to the maternal grandparents for their help and then finds them unwilling to return the child. There is no merit in the Bannister claim that Mr. Painter permanently relinquished custody. It was intended to be a temporary arrangement. A father should be encouraged to look for help with the children, from those who love them without the risk of thereby losing the custody of the children permanently. . . .

Second, Jeanne's will named her husband guardian of her children and if he failed to qualify or ceased to act, named her mother. The parent's wishes are entitled to consideration. . . .

Third, the Banisters are 60 years old. By the time Mark graduates from high school they will be over 70 years old. Care of young children is a strain on grandparents and Mrs. Bannister's letters indicate as much.

We have considered all of these factors and have concluded that Mark's best interest demands that his custody remain with the Bannisters. Mark was five when he came to their home. The evidence clearly shows he was not well adjusted at that time. He did not distinguish fact from fiction and was inclined to tell "tall tales" emphasizing the big "I." He was very aggressive toward smaller children, cruel to animals, not liked by his classmates and did not seem to know what was acceptable conduct. As stated by one witness: "Mark knew where his freedom was and he didn't know where his boundaries were." In two years he made a great deal of improvement. He now appears to be well disciplined, happy, relatively secure and popular with his classmates, although still subject to more than normal anxiety.

We place a great deal of reliance on the testimony of Dr. Glenn R. Hawks, a child psychologist. The trial court, in effect, disregarded Dr. Hawks' opinions stating: "The court has given full consideration to the good doctor's testimony, but cannot accept it at full face value because of exaggerated statements and the witness' attitude on the stand." We, of course, do not have the advantage of viewing the witness' conduct on the stand, but we have carefully reviewed his testimony and find nothing in the written record to justify such a summary dismissal of the opinions of this eminent child psychologist. [Dr. Hawk's professional qualifications are summarized.]

Between June 15th and the time of trial, he spent approximately 25 hours acquiring information about Mark and the Bannisters, including appropriate testing of and "depth interviews" with Mark. Dr. Hawks' testimony covers 70 pages of the record and it is difficult to pinpoint any bit of testimony which precisely summarizes his opinion. He places great emphasis on the "father figure" and discounts the importance of the "biological father." "The father figure is a figure that the child sees as an authority figure, as a helper, he is a nutrient figure, and one who typifies maleness and stands as maleness as far as the child is concerned."

His investigation revealed: ". . . the strength of the father figure before Mark came to the Bannisters is very unclear. Mark is confused about the father figure prior to his contact with Mr. Bannister." Now, "Mark used Mr. Bannister as his father figure. This is very evident. It shows up in the depth interview, and it shows up in the description of Mark's life given by Mark. He has a very warm feeling for Mr. Bannister."

Dr. Hawks concluded that it was not for Mark's best interest to be removed from the Bannister home. He is criticized for reaching this conclusion without investigating the Painter home or finding out more about Mr. Painter's character. He answered:

"I was most concerned about the welfare of the child, not the welfare of Mr. Painter, not about the welfare of the Bannisters. Inasmuch as Mark has already made an adjustment and sees the Bannisters as his parental figures in his psychological makeup, to me this is the most critical factor. Disruption at this point, I think, would be detrimental to the child even though Mr. Painter might well be a paragon of virtue. I think this would be a kind of thing which would not be in the best interest of the child. I think knowing something about where the child is at the present time is vital. I think something about where he might go, in my way of thinking is essentially untenable to me, and relatively unimportant. It isn't even helpful. The thing I was most concerned about was Mark's view of his own reality in which he presently lives. If this is destroyed I think it will have rather bad effects on Mark. I think then if one were to make a determination whether it would be to the parents' household, or the McNelly household, or X-household, then I think the further study would be appropriate."

Dr. Hawks stated: "I am appalled at the tremendous task Mr. Painter would have if Mark were to return to him because he has got to build the relationship from scratch. There is essentially nothing on which to build at the present time. Mark is aware Mr. Painter is his father, but he is not very clear about what this means. In his own mind the father figure is Mr. Bannister. I think it would take a very strong person with everything in his favor in order to build a relationship as Mr. Painter would have to build at this point with Mark.". . .

We know more of Mr. Painter's way of life than Dr. Hawks. We have concluded that it does not offer as great a stability or security as the Bannister home. Throughout his testimony he emphasized Mark's need at this critical time is stability. He has it in the Bannister home.

Other items of Dr. Hawks' testimony which have a bearing on our decision follow. He did not consider the Bannisters' age anyway disqualifying. He was of the opinion that Mark could adjust to a change more easily later on, if one became necessary, when he would have better control over his environment.

He believes the presence of other children in the home would have a detrimental effect upon Mark's adjustment whether this occurred in the Bannister home or the Painter home.

The trial court does not say which of Dr. Hawks' statements he felt were exaggerated. We were most surprised at the inconsequential position to which he relegated the "biological father." He concedes "child psychologists are less concerned about natural parents than probably other professional groups are." We are not inclined to so lightly value the role of the natural father, but find much reason for his evaluation of this particular case.

Mark has established a father-son relationship with Mr. Bannister, which [Mark] apparently had never had with his natural father. He is happy, well adjusted and progressing nicely in his development. We do not believe it is for Mark's best interest to take him out of this stable atmosphere in the face of warnings of dire consequences from an eminent child psychologist and send him to an uncertain future in his father's home. Regardless of our appreciation of the father's love for his child and his desire to have him with him, we do not believe we have the moral right to gamble with this child's future. He should be encouraged in every way possible to know his father. We are sure there are many ways in which Mr. Painter can enrich Mark's life.

For the reasons stated, we reverse the trial court and remand the case for judgment in accordance herewith.

In 1969, the father obtained custody in a California court while Mark was visiting him. The grandparents did not oppose this petition. The case shows the essential conservatism of both the trial court and the state supreme court. Students regard the case as an arbitrary abuse of the father's parental rights.

Custody and Guardianship by Social Agencies

Both public and voluntary social agencies are guardians for large numbers of children. In re East, 288 N.E.2d 343 (Ohio 1972), is a typical illustration of how a public agency acquires custody of a dependent child:

IN RE EAST

Court of Common Pleas of Ohio, 32 Ohio Misc. 65, 288 N.E.2d 343 (Ohio 1972).

This matter is before the court on the complaint of the executive secretary of Highland County Children Services alleging that the two day old baby of an unwed mother is a dependent child whose condition and environment under R.C. 2151.04(C) is such as to warrant the state, in the interests of the child in assuming his guardianship. The court has assumed the custody of the two day old infant and ordered him placed with children services pending final disposition of this cause.

The court's first consideration should be and always is to place the child with the natural parent if possible.

The court finds from the evidence presented that the 16-year-old unwed mother has been an incorrigible child who has been sexually promiscuous and has no visible means of supporting herself or her infant. The welfare department has refused to approve aid for the child in the mother's home. Because her mother could not control her, she was previously in a foster home where she was unruly and disobedient. She has indicated a desire to take the baby into the home of her parents where she is now living. Her father is an 80-year-old invalid and her mother has on previous occasions asked children services to take the baby since she and her husband could not help take care of it. The court finds that the grandparents, into whose home the mother proposes to rear the child, can give little or no assistance financially or emotionally to either the mother or the baby.

Counsel for the mother raises two principal issues: (1) that the mother must be found unfit before she can be deprived of custody of the child and (2) that the mother cannot be deprived of the custody of the child until she has had the opportunity to prove that she can properly take care of the child.

The court is of the opinion that these propositions address themselves to a charge of neglect rather than a charge of dependency.

A brief analysis of the neglect and dependency statutes appears necessary to place the instant case in proper perspective. By definition, R.C. 2151.03 requires the commission of culpable acts by the parents of the child to constitute the child neglected. Thus, the parents must abandon the child, through their faults or habits cause the child to be without proper parental care, neglect or refuse to provide the child with necessities or the special care made necessary by the child's mental condition or place or attempt to place the child in violation of the placement law. Under the neglected child statutes, the fault, unfitness or unsuitability of the parent is the crux of the cause and a necessary element in the determination that a child is neglected.

This is not so in an action to determine that a child is dependent. By definition, R.C. 2151.04 does not require the commission of culpable acts or fault by the parents to constitute the child dependent. Rather, it specifically states in subsections (A) and (B) that if a child is homeless or destitute or without proper care or support, through no fault of his parents or that he lacks proper support by reason of the mental or physical condition of his parents, he is a dependent child.

Note that the neglect statute refers to lack of "proper parental care." The dependent statute refers to a child "without proper care" or [who] "lacks proper care," expressly omitting reference to parental responsibility. . . .

In the case at bar, this court finds that not only are the conditions and environment of the child set forth in the record such as to warrant the state, in the interests of the child in assuming his guardianship, but also that the mother is unfit to rear the child. Her emotional instability, financial irresponsibility and lack of support, direction or control by her parents has resulted in her moral and social impoverishment. There is little to indicate the child's best interest or welfare would be served living with his mother in her parents' home.

This does not mean that the mother will always be denied any child born to her. A child born to this mother at another time under circumstances indicating a substantial maturing and change of conduct on the mother's part and conditions and environment not substantially detrimental to the best interests of such child would prevent a finding of dependency.

The second issue, to wit: that the mother cannot be deprived of the custody of her child until she has had the opportunity to prove that she can properly take care of him is likewise not well taken. In re Turner, 12 Ohio Misc. 171, 231 N.E.2d 502, a permanent order of custody of a three-day old infant was granted on the grounds of dependency, although the mother had not had physical custody of the child. The court reasoned that the mother's unfitness could be predicted from her past history.

This court agrees that a child should not have to endure the inevitable to its great detriment and harm in order to give the mother an opportunity to prove her suitability. To anticipate the future, however, is at most, a difficult basis for a judicial determination. The child's present condition and environment is the subject for decision not the expected or anticipated behavior of unsuitability or unfitness of the mother. The child has been born into a condition and environment that demands his removal from the custody of the mother now. The law does not require the court to experiment with the child's welfare to see if he will suffer great detriment or harm.

Succinctly stated, in a dependency action, where the child's condition or environment warrant it, the child may be removed from the custody of the mother and it is not necessary that she first be given the opportunity to prove that she can properly care for said child.

It is therefore the opinion of this court that the permanent custody of the infant herein should be granted to the children services board.

A state director of child welfare may be designated as the guardian of tens of thousands of children, because having one person serve in this capacity for all wards is more administratively efficient. In such cases the actual role performance involved in guardianship must be delegated to a caseworker or perhaps to a foster parent. Costin and Rapp (1984:48) consider simultaneous fulfillment by one person of the role of guardian and social worker a potential conflict of interest, but the roles may be successfully carried out if the differences are recognized:

> If social workers do act as children's guardians, and they may find it necessary to do so for some time to come, their function as guardian with its judicial responsibilities and controls must be separated from their function as professional helper with its administrative responsibilities and controls. A social worker deals with defined and limited areas of a child's life, those relevant to the child's condition as they may be perceived and diagnosed as problems, or at least as areas of needed help. Social workers have professional, not personal, goals; their skills include techniques of treatment, and use of themselves in a professional capacity. They are accountable, not judicially to a court, but administratively to the social agency which employs them.

Social service agencies have been sued on behalf of foster children. The U.S. Supreme Court concluded that foster parents were not entitled to an adversary hearing when an agency removes a child (Smith v. Organization of Foster Families for Equality and Reform, 431 U.S. 816 [1977]). The Court held that the procedures for removal of foster children from foster homes did not violate the due process and equal protection clauses of the Fourteenth Amendment. Procedures of New

York State and New York City were considered adequate to protect the interests that foster parents may have:

> Before a child is removed from a foster home for transfer to another foster home, the foster parents may request an "independent review." Such a procedure would appear to give a more elaborate trial-type hearing to foster families than this Court has found required in other contexts of administrative determinations.
>
> Outside New York City, foster parents are provided not only with the procedures of a preremoval conference and postremoval hearing provided by 18 N.Y.C.R.R. §450.10 (1976) and Soc. Serv. Law §400 (McKinney 1976), but also with the preremoval judicial hearing available on request to foster parents who have in their care children who have been in foster care for 18 months or more, Soc. Serv. Law §392. As observed, a foster parent in such case may obtain an order that the child remain in his care. . . .
>
> The §392 hearing is available to foster parents, both in and outside New York City, even where the removal sought is for the purpose of returning the child to his natural parents. Since this remedy provides a sufficient constitutional preremoval hearing to protect whatever liberty interest might exist in the continued existence of the foster family when the State seeks to transfer the child to another foster home, a fortiori [with more reason] the procedure is adequate to protect the lesser interest of the foster family in remaining together at the expense of the disruption of the natural family.

INNOVATIONS IN GUARDIANSHIP

Because a bureaucratic approach to guardianship by large social agencies may be impossible, three innovations in guardianship have been proposed:

The Citizen Guardian. Guardianship could be publicized as an appropriate volunteer role for citizens interested in the welfare of children who might serve as advocates and give considerable attention to the needs of the individual child. Agencies would no doubt respond negatively to such a system, because lay guardians would generate a sharp increase in the number of demands for service on behalf of wards. In addition, given the large number of children to be served, the supply of potential "citizen guardians" would be too small.

The Foster Parent as Guardian. In short-term placements, the foster parent should not fulfill the guardian role. When long-term placement is envisioned, however, a potentially successful alternative might be to accord the foster parents' guardianship, implying the fullest possible responsibility for the child, on the basis of their day-to-day responsibility and identification with the child's best interests. Agencies that view foster parents as co-workers rather than purveyors of physical care should find this arrangement compatible with that role concept. Recently, encouraging foster parents to become adoptive parents has achieved the same goal.

The Social Worker as Guardian. The social worker need not necessarily be disqualified from serving as guardian because of possible conflict of interest. If the line caseworker is inappropriate for the role, local agency administrative personnel might serve as guardians for reasonable numbers of children and provide a personal relationship without risking a serious conflict of interest. They can have a more meaningful relationship with each child than the guardian who has several thousand children.

The traditional bureaucratic guardianship role in the large agency provides reason for developing creative alternatives.

FEDERAL CHILD WELFARE PROVISIONS

The child welfare services program from 1935 to 1958 emphasized improving services in rural areas. The program was broadened in 1962 to cover the well-being of all children. By 1975, the goal was to provide child welfare services on a statewide basis. The highest expenditure for the program before 1980 was $56.5 million.

Expenditures for AFDC foster care were not authorized until 1961. By 1979, $270 million was expended for this purpose.

The Adoption Assistance and Child Welfare Act created programs under Title IV of the Social Security Act. The main goal of the legislation was to obtain permanent homes for children.

The law required preventive and reunification services from the states as a condition of federal funding.

The act also seated financial incentives to facilitate adoption of children with special needs. Children who received federally reimbursed subsidies automatically became eligible for Medicare. Statewide information systems were required to gain knowledge of the movements of clients within the child welfare system.

States were also required to devise a case review system including written case plans and a status review of the placement every six months and a dispositional court hearing within 18 months of placement. Parents are encouraged to participate in the reviews.

Other federal legislation relevant to child welfare includes social service program provisions of Title XX of the Social Security Act (1975), the Child Abuse Prevention and Treatment Act (1974), the Juvenile Justice and Delinquency Prevention Act (1974), the Developmentally Disabled Assistance and Bill of Rights Act (1975), the Education for All Handicapped Children Act (1975), the Adoption Opportunities Act (1978), and the Indian Child Welfare Act (1978).

Title XX was incorporated into a social services block grant in 1981.

Federal provisions for participation in current child welfare programs are found in the Adoption Assistance and Child Welfare Act of 1980 that expanded federal involvement in child welfare services, foster care, and adoption assistance.

Table 8.1

Federal Support (in millions of dollars) for Child Welfare Services Under P.L. 96-272—The Adoption Assistance and Child Welfare Act of 1980

Program	Title 4B Child Welfare Services	Title 4-E Foster Care	Adoption Assistance
1981	163.5	349	5
1982	156.3	334	2.1
1983	156.3	373	7.3
1984	165	483	21.0
1985 (projected)	200	460	12

Source: Child Welfare League Information Service

While the Reagan Administration sought cuts in federal support, the amounts in Table 8.1 indicate growth in federal support for child welfare services, especially for children in foster care.

Questions for Review

1. What specific powers distinguish a *guardian* from a person who has *custody* of a child?

2.   What is misleading about the term *ward of the courts?*

3.   Identify typical informal custody arrangements in which the court is unlikely to be involved.

4.   Given the action of the courts in *Sisson* and in *Kilgrow*, where could the parents go for help?

5.   What action by the natural parents or the courts terminates parental rights irrevocably?

6.   What practical significance has the argument in *State ex rel. Watts v. Watts*, especially in light of the women's movement?

7.   Review the family situation in *Hammett v. Hammett*. What peculiarity is evident?

8.   What three common conditions require nonparental child care?

9.   Why is the testamentary guardian of limited importance? Why are there now few full orphans?

10.   To be most effective, what should be the special training and experience of a children's law guardian?

11.   Evaluate the decision in *In re East*. Would you have reached the same conclusion? Why?

Questions for Debate and Discussion

1.   Do you favor the psychological parent concept as a basis for custody? Why or why not?

2.   Explain and criticize the "tender years presumption."

3.   State the decision you would have preferred in *Vanden Heuvel* and the evidence to support your choice.

4.   Evaluate the remedies provided in the Uniform Child Custody Jurisdiction Act to deal with parental abduction of children.

5.   What innovations would you recommend in public agency guardianship?

Selected Readings   Buser, Paul J. "A Typical Joint Custody Agreement." *Family Advocate* 5 (1982): 26–28.

Hardin, Mark. *Foster Children in the Courts.* Newton Upper Falls, Mass.: Butterworth Legal Publications, 1983.

————. "When a Parent Is Unfit." *Family Advocate* 3 (1981): 8–12, 43.

Hubbell, Ruth. *Foster Care and Families: Conflicting Values and Policies.* Family Impact Seminar Series. Philadelphia: Temple University Press, 1981.

Kram, Shirley W., and Neil A. Frank. *Law of Child Custody: Application and Procedural Aspects.* Lexington, Mass.: Lexington Books, 1984.

Leroux, Charles. "Making Joint Custody Work: A Father's View." *Family Advocate* 5 (1982): 20.

Levy, Adler, and Carole R. Chambers. "The Folly of Joint Custody." *Family Advocate* 3 (1981): 6–10.

Levy, Alan M. "Disorders of Visitation in Child Custody Cases." *Journal of Psychology and Law* 10 (1982): 471–489.

McDaniel, Deborah. *Foster Care in the 1980s.* Elmsford, N.Y.: Pergamon Press, 1981.

Sheehan, David. "Who Gets the Child?" *Family Advocate* 4 (1981): 2–6.

Wald, Michael S. "Child Custody Disputes: Are We Abandoning the Child's Best Interests?" *Stanford Law Review* 16 (1981): 16–19.

Witt, Linda. "Making Joint Custody Work: A Mother's View." *Family Advocate* 5 (1982): 21.

CHAPTER

9

How to Testify in Court

The previous four chapters have considered the operation of the criminal and juvenile courts. Against this background, we shall look at the participation of social workers in the judicial process.

The major role of the social worker in relation to the courts is to gather and organize evidence and to present direct testimony or occasionally to serve as an expert witness. The social worker is also frequently involved in helping clients who are expected to testify. In some states, social work therapists are accorded the privilege of not testifying about details of treatment. The purpose of such privileged communication is to encourage people to seek help without violating their privacy.

As we have seen, a higher level of proof is required in criminal actions than in civil actions. In both civil and criminal actions, American law presumes that a person is not guilty until guilt has been established. Evidence is introduced by the testimony of a witness given under oath.

EVIDENCE IN CRIMINAL PROCEEDINGS
A **criminal proceeding** is instituted and conducted to prevent commission of a crime or to fix the guilt for a crime already committed and to punish the offender. Rules of evidence specify proof **beyond a reasonable doubt**—that is, the facts presented must establish guilt.

In a child abuse case in criminal court, the state must prove that the accused person willfully inflicted the injury. When there is a clear possibility that injuries were accidental or inflicted by the other parent or a baby-sitter, an alleged abusing parent will be found innocent of a criminal assault charge.

Criminal proceedings do not allow hearsay, that is, secondhand evidence. However, official records, documents, and photographs authenticated as true may be admissible. Rules of evidence are especially important because of the possible effects of evidence on a jury's decision.

Statements made to a social worker by a child or parent are admissible as evidence when they are presented by the social worker in court. For example, the parental statement "I beat the child with a strap to make him stop crying" would be admissible, but a statement from a neighbor indicating that the mother told her she beat the child with a strap would not. The police must use the *Miranda* warning to inform the parent of the right to remain silent because any statements he or she makes may be used in court. However, the law does not require a social work investigator to give such a warning.

EVIDENCE IN CIVIL PROCEEDINGS

Civil actions are intended to settle disputes between individuals. Most civil proceedings involve a lesser burden of proof—only a *preponderance of evidence*. A common civil action involves wrongful death. A person may be killed in an auto accident or in an industrial mishap. Insurance or worker's compensation claims generally lead to civil suits.

Since many courts regard termination of parental rights as one of the most serious civil procedures, unfitness must be proved. The standard of evidence demanded in custody hearings is *convincing proof*. Convincing proof is nearer to beyond a reasonable doubt than to preponderance of evidence. It was established as the standard in child neglect cases where rights may be terminated in Santosky v. Kramer, 455 U.S. 745 (1982).

In cases involving termination of parental rights, social workers usually appear as witnesses for the prosecution. In proving unfitness, the agency may be expected to document both its attempts to provide assistance and the parents' response to those attempts. The case for termination will be much stronger if the parents have failed to cooperate with sustained attempts to provide social services.

Consent and Default

An adult about to lose parental rights does not always obtain counsel and present a defense against the action. The parent may voluntarily consent to the placement of the child, or at least not contest termination of parental rights in court. By being absent from the custody hearing, the parent may choose to have the matter decided by default.

In most states, child welfare agencies have the authority to enter into voluntary agreements with parents to release custody. In that event the parent need make no admissions and can usually petition to regain custody after ten days. In some cases, obtaining a voluntary agreement may be inadvisable because the parent is apt to change his or her mind capriciously. In such instances, whenever an application for a voluntary agreement is denied, the agency should always provide reasons in writing.

ADMINISTRATIVE HEARINGS BY AGENCIES

Social workers deal extensively with civil administrative hearings conducted by public agencies. In such hearings, rules of evidence are less clearly established and procedures are informal. Counsel is not provided, but clients may retain counsel at their own expense. Two examples will show the range of subject matter of such hearings:

The family may contend that a mental patient is being overcharged for care on the basis of payments set by a state reimbursement schedule administered by the Department of Mental Health. The department holds a hearing to determine the facts. The family presents evidence that their income and net worth have been overstated and that therefore they should pay less than determined by the department. If the facts they present are authenticated, the department will revise its payment demand. If it does not do so, the family may appeal the ruling to the civil court.

Another example would be the contention of an employee of a state public aid agency that he or she has been fired because of racial bias. After following the grievance procedure of the agency to no avail, the employee appeals to the Civil Service Commission. The Civil Service Commission grants an administrative hearing to seek the facts from both the agency and the employee. The commission then rules on the case. The employee also has the right to appeal the matter to a civil court.

Due Process Concerns The decision concerning due process in administrative hearings most familiar to social workers is Goldberg v. Kelley, 397 U.S. 254 (1970), which established the rights of recipients to a hearing before welfare benefits could be terminated. In that decision, the following conditions were set:

1. The recipient should receive timely and adequate notice stating the reasons for termination of benefits.

2. The recipient should be able to cross-examine adverse witnesses.

3. There should be oral presentation of arguments and evidence.

4. The recipient should be represented by counsel if desired.

5. The decision should be made by an impartial hearing officer based solely on rules of law and evidence determined at the hearing.

Senna (1976:321) concludes that social workers can learn several lessons from *Goldberg v. Kelley:*

> First, philosophically, it may be realistic today to regard welfare entitlements as more like a property right than a gratuity. Second, the adversary proceeding may be applied within an administrative context. This gives the client the opportunity to challenge the government. Third, in thinking about the challenge, the client must consider its effect on his relationship with his caseworker. An appeal against agency action is basically a challenge to the caseworker. These are among the eventualities to be considered when introducing due process into one area of the administration of public welfare.

Dickson (1976:276) considers both social workers and lawyers generally effective in hearings involving due process. He reiterates the position that clients' awareness of their rights, coupled with a willingness to bring challenge, are the important factors. The benefits of winning must outweigh the costs of trying and losing. Dickson comments:

> Given these conflicts in role, it is not surprising to find indication that social workers in advocacy or quasi-judicial roles have not been effective. Data from welfare hearings suggest that there have been relatively few challenges to termination or reduction of benefits; those that have been brought are neither well argued nor documented.
>
> At the same time, there is evidence that lawyers also have not been particularly effective in a variety of due process settings. There is evidence suggesting that the presence of an attorney in the early stages of the juvenile justice process—which are essentially rudimentary due process settings—often results in decisions unfavorable to the client. Handler found that in welfare hearings, clients with lawyers did no better than those without. Furthermore, a number of studies have questioned the effectiveness of lawyers in juvenile court hearings.

Dickson also considers the consequences of the due process emphasis for the social worker:

> The expansion of due process has direct consequences for the social welfare client, the human service organization, and the individual social worker. If procedures and protections are adequate, the opportunity to challenge decisions, present his own case, and have access to an impartial forum should result in more appropriately timed and less arbitrary social services for the client. Moreover, the client may find himself in a different role vis-à-vis the human service organization—he is no longer powerless but is directly involved in decisions pertaining to his case. If procedures and protections are inadequate, the client may be no worse off, although he will probably be more

disillusioned with the agency and the law. He could suffer, however, if procedures penalize him or allow retaliation against him.

For the human service organization, effective due process will subject decisions and actions to unprecedented scrutiny, publicity, and challenge. Organizations will be forced to establish rules and criteria for decisions, especially in the allocation of resources or services. Another consequence is that agencies will have to become increasingly conscious of clients' rights in this area and, in the case of partial and rudimentary due process, will have to allocate necessary manpower and fiscal resources.

The social worker is placed in a difficult and anomalous position. As a representative of the agency, he may be forced to defend decisions that he believes are correct but that are difficult to justify except in terms of ideology or experience. If placed in a quasi-judicial role, the social worker must make decisions independent of agency needs or dictates. If he is providing assistance in the preparation of a case, he must argue for his client—even if he disagrees with the position—and against the agency. Such a situation could jeopardize his career and social relationships. (p. 276)

The effectiveness of fair hearings for welfare recipients was most recently studied by Hagen (1983). Only 21 percent of the cases culminated in the petitioner's winning or partially winning. About half the petitioners had legal assistance, mainly from legal aid attorneys. The effectiveness of those who did not have counsel was relatively low. Hagen suggests an important role for social workers:

Many social workers now employed in both public and private agencies serve potential and actual welfare recipients. To operate effectively as advocates for their clients, social workers need to be informed about the appeals mechanism and its procedures. Such familiarity would enhance their ability to protect their clients' interest and to provide appropriate referrals for legal assistance. Establishing linkages with legal aid service as a resource for clients would be particularly beneficial. In addition, social workers would be able to help their clients better prepare to represent themselves in adversarial hearings or to actually function as the client's advocate during the proceedings. Although the intricacies of welfare regulations and welfare law are complex, a clear and thorough presentation of and argument for the client's case, as well as thoughtful questioning of the county or state's basis for action, would certainly enhance the chances of fair and accurate hearing outcomes. (p. 191)

PREPARING THE EVIDENCE

The importance of preparation for testifying is presented by Bernstein (1975: 525):

Although it is a somewhat onerous task to the helping professional, the social worker is occasionally and reluctantly called upon to be a witness, sometimes for and sometimes against his own client. All the material garnered in months or years of consultation must be made available to the court. The social worker who walks into court at the appointed hour without preparation is performing a disservice to himself and to his client. Preparation must include a basic knowledge of the rules of evidence, court procedure, and techniques of examination and cross-examination and a rehearsal of testimony to be given at trial. Armed with this knowledge, the social worker enters the courtroom with confidence. Lacking it, the social worker enters into unfamiliar territory, traversing treacherous ground with highly technical rules. The client is entitled to a competent, prepared witness. The stakes are too high to enter the lists unprepared.

Developing the evidence must take into account the disposition sought—the purpose of the petition, the pertinent facts, and the availability of witnesses. Three types of evidence may be involved:

1. **Direct evidence**: from firsthand knowledge

2. **Real evidence**: documents and photographs

3. **Hearsay evidence**: secondhand comments admissible in some civil and juvenile court actions but not in the criminal courts

Direct evidence often has circumstantial elements. In child abuse, for example, observable welts and bruises are direct evidence, while the identity of the abuser is likely to be circumstantial because the actual infliction of the injuries has not been observed by the social worker, the police, or the physician. Written reports may be inadmissible unless the person making them is available to testify and submit to cross-examination. Sometimes, when a witness cannot appear personally, written statements known as **depositions** are used. They are usually admissible only if both sides agree to accept them.

An important element in the development of evidence is **discovery**. In order to protect individual rights, attorneys for both sides are expected to share the facts in advance so that there will be no surprises. When the social worker prepares a case for prosecution, pertinent evidence that is not known to defense counsel should always be discussed with the state's attorney to determine whether it should be communicated to the defense to satisfy the provisions of discovery.

Problems in social workers' use of evidence are illustrated in In re Pima County Juvenile Action No. J-31853, 501 P.2d 395 (Ariz. App. 1972). The case concerns a petition for dependency on behalf of a nine-year-old girl whose mother was recovering from cancer surgery.

IN RE PIMA COUNTY JUVENILE ACTION NO. J-31853

Court of Appeals of Arizona.
501 P.2d 395
(Ariz. App. 1972).

HATHAWAY, Judge.

This appeal is taken by the mother of a minor adjudicated by the juvenile court to be a dependent child.

On May 5, 1972, a petition was filed invoking the jurisdiction of the juvenile court for purposes of declaring the subject minor a dependent child. The petition alleged:

"Said child's home is unfit for her by reason of abuse by the parent in that during the period September 1971 to the present, said parent caused the deterioration of the child in that the parent failed to maintain reasonable care and treatment of the child by failing to send her to school, subjected or exposed said child to emotional and mental abuse or damage, thus endangering said child's well-being."

The petition was based on an affidavit of the child's father which stated inter alia [among other things] that he and the mother were divorced on June 11, 1971, that the child had been in the sole and exclusive custody of the mother since the date of divorce, that they had been living in California until approximately March 1972 when they returned to Tucson and checked in at the Tidelands Motel, that the mother had been examined by her family physician and surgeon who made a diagnosis of cancer and that surgery had been performed in the latter part of March. It further stated that the mother was presently recuperating at the motel, that the child had not attended school since Christmas of 1971 and was not adequately fed, that the mother was not emotionally stable, that a psychiatrist had found the child to be "emotionally affected" and that the father was ready to make a home for his daughter and do all things necessary to provide her with a normal childhood.

A hearing was duly held on June 8, 1972. The child's mother and father testified, as did the mother's physician, a welfare worker assigned to the case, a clinical psychologist, and an employee of the Tidelands Motel. At the conclusion of the hearing, the court spoke to the 9-year-old child in chambers and the record reflects that the court's impression of the youngster was that she was very precocious and extremely intelligent. The court concluded that since the conditions where the child was living were such as to cause concern, particularly the fact that she was not going to school, and the fact that she appeared to be living in somewhat of an isolated existence, she came under the definition of a dependent child.

A.R.S. § 8-201, subsec. 10, par. b, as amended, defines a "dependent child" as one who is adjudicated to be:

"Destitute or who is not provided with the necessities of life, or who is not provided with a home or suitable place of abode, or whose home is unfit for him by reason of abuse, neglect, cruelty, or depravity by either of his parents. . . ."

The welfare of a child is the prime consideration of a juvenile code. . . . If the evidence presented to the juvenile court is sufficient to support a finding of dependency, we as a reviewing court do not interfere. [Citations omitted.] In the instant case, however, with all due respect to the juvenile court's opportunity to assess the credibility of the witnesses, we are of the opinion that appellate intervention is appropriate. True, the burden of proof in a dependency adjudication is merely a preponderance of the evidence. . . . [V]iew of the evidence leads us to conclude that this burden was not met.

Viewing the evidence most favorable to support the order of the juvenile court, we find the following. The mother withdrew the child from school in California midway through the school year with the consent of the school authorities, the idea being that a trip to Europe would serve an educational purpose. There is no question but that the youngster was very bright and had no difficulty keeping up in school. The mother appears to have been inordinately fearful of having cancer but her fears were not groundless since, after coming to Tucson to be examined by the former family physician it was discovered that she did have a uterine cancer requiring surgery. She arranged for the child to stay at the home of the physician while she was in the hospital and then returned to the Tidelands Motel with the child to recuperate.

According to the mother, she attempted to enroll the youngster in a private boarding school so that the child could have "all around care" but was unsuccessful. She explained that she had not enrolled the child in public school because it would create an additional burden. Furthermore, she assumed, from what the doctor had told her, that she would be able to travel within four weeks. Also, it was her understanding that she had permission to keep the child out of school for the remainder of the school year. Although she made no attempt to obtain a tutor for the child, she did get "learning books on math and science" which the child worked on and the mother graded. After the filing of the petition in juvenile court, the child was placed in a foster home and attended public school for about a month. She did very well in school notwithstanding her absence of several months. She was promoted and received an award. There was some testimony that the mother was "possessive" and wanted the child close to her. Also, during the stay at the motel the child had little opportunity for contact with her peers.

The welfare worker assigned to the case testified as to the mother's fitness:

"A. I feel there is a possibility that she is unfit without some outside influence and supervision.
Q. What do you base that on?
A. On what had happened during the past six months, from the testimony of Dr. G. [the family physician] and other people I have talked to.
Q. Isn't your main concern the fact that [the child] was not in school?
A. Yes.
Q. And the fact that she hasn't been with other children during this period?
A. Yes."

A report prepared by a staff psychiatric social worker for Southern Arizona Mental Health Clinic recommended that the child be made a temporary ward of the court, that a psychiatric evaluation of the mother be obtained and that she be given assistance to help her through "her current emotional crises." We are inclined to discount the evidentiary value of this report since it was based solely on a consultation with the child and her father.

The child was examined by the mother's psychologist and by a psychiatrist hired by her father. The report of the latter stated, in part:

"From my observations, it is my impression that this child has no major emotional disturbance. From the adjustment she appears to have made in the foster home, she is not overly dependent on her mother, even though their life together would seem to have promoted this. . . .

In summary, it is my impression that [the child] is a precocious, bright 9-year-old girl, who has been somewhat socially isolated from peers and relates more easily to adults, and adjusts easily to new situations. She is dependent, but not to a pathological degree, on her mother and sees her mother as offering the most security in her future. She is mildly anxious, which is appropriate to her situation at the moment. There is no evidence of serious emotional disturbance."

The mother's psychologist, as the result of two consultations with the mother and one with the child, testified that he found no reason to conclude that the mother was unfit or that the child's well-being had been endangered by the mother's conduct during the preceding few months. He expressed lack of concern over the fact that the child had not been in school in view of her obvious potential and her very adequate school progress and adjustment. Further, he discounted the child's lack of association with her peers.:

"Q.   Was there anything you could tell in your examination of [the child to show] that this lack of dealing with children of her own age might have adversely affected her?

A.   I'm aware this is one of the very favorite sacred cows with regard to children. I don't think it's really as significant or important as to the degree it's often emphasized. I think this partly depends on the individual; in other words, let's say this is something that a child is very much seeking and is having difficulty doing it so that it, then, becomes a frustration and a source of dissatisfaction, then it may well represent a problem to that child.

Now [the child] on the other hand, doesn't seem to have that much of a need for contact with other people. As I say, she's a very self-contained young lady, and is able to occupy her time with her own interests and activities and pursuits, and generally keeps pretty busy with them so that it's not a source of frustration to her. I think this is an important distinction."

When cross-examined as to the fact that the child and her mother had been living at a motel, the psychologist testified:

"Q.   Did this in any way disturb you that these two people, that a nine-year-old child had been living in a motel room, was there anything unusual about that?

A.   I don't see that it's too different from an apartment the way motels are these days.

Q.   Are you speaking of facilities for food?

A.   Just living arrangements, the availability of services, et cetera, it was probably much handier for them than an apartment would be.

Q.   Do you feel [the child] is normal in the social relationship be it one of the hangups we have?

A.   I think she is able to relate to other children as the circumstances may require."

It is apparent that the juvenile court based its adjudication of dependency on a conclusion that (1) residing at the Tidelands Motel constituted a failure to provide a suitable place of abode, and (2) the subject minor was neglected because she was not attending school and was disassociated from her peers. We find, under the circumstances presented here, that we are unable to concur with the adjudication of dependency.

The recommendation of the Pima County Department of Public Welfare was that the child be placed in its care, custody and control, with return to the mother at the discretion of the welfare department. The court ordered the child placed in the temporary care, custody and control of the welfare department. Physical custody of the child was restored to the mother with the proviso that such placement might be changed at the discretion of the welfare department "consistent with the well-being of said child." It further prohibited removal of the child from the State of Arizona until further order of the court and directed that there be an annual review.

The expression "neglect" is not a term of fixed meaning—its meaning varies as the context of circumstances changes. . . . One court has defined the term as the disregard of duty owing to indifference or willfulness. . . . The record here reflects quite the contrary—the mother was extremely devoted to the child. We cannot equate the mother's concern with her physical health, even if some individuals considered it exaggerated, with indifference to the child's needs. In fact, we conceive that it is only natural that a mother be concerned about her health lest she be unable to fulfill her responsibility of caring for her young daughter.

Living at the motel, a situation clearly engendered by the circumstances, was no more than a makeshift arrangement. There was no showing that the child's physical or mental health were in jeopardy. In fact, her "confusion" was more likely precipitated by the conduct of others who did not approve of the child's "life-style."

While we agree that the child's non-attendance in school was a factor to be considered, we believe that undue emphasis was given it in view of the mother's belief, misguided though it may have been, that she had the approval of the California school authorities to keep the child out of school even if the trip to Europe did not materialize. We are also of the opinion that undue emphasis was placed on the fact that the child was deprived of association with her peers. As the testimony of the psychologist indicates, the salutary effect of such association cannot be decided in a vacuum. Rather, it must be considered in the light of the individual child's needs and situation. Here the record reflects neither unhappiness nor frustration on the part of the youngster nor any inability to adjust to a peer group setting.

Our review of the record convinces us that the sum and substance of the evidence in support of the petition reflects nothing more than an opinion of what an ideal home atmosphere should consist of, rather than a showing that this child's well-being was being endangered. Nor do we find sufficient evidentiary support for a finding of neglect. [Emphasis added.] We believe the following statement of Chief Justice Rosellini, dissenting in Todd v. Superior Court, 68 Wash.2d 587, 414 P.2d 605 (1966) is apropos:

> "Again, there was no finding that the home was an unfit place for the child. There was no showing that the mother neglected her, or was cruel to her, or that she acted in a depraved manner. . . . I do not think that the legislature intended this section to authorize the court to deprive a parent of the custody of his child simply because the parent is suffering from a mental illness, unless that illness causes him to mistreat or neglect the child or renders the home an unfit place, not merely an imperfect place, for the child.
>
> The mental illness of a parent will, of course, affect the attitudes and emotional well-being of a child; so will a physical illness, or any number of anti-social attitudes which are not necessarily classified as mental illnesses. I do not think that the legislature meant to empower the court to take charge of a child whenever its parent was not providing it with a perfectly healthy home atmosphere, for the perfect parent is the exception and not the rule.
>
> It is, of course unfortunate that a child should be subjected to the influence of its parent's delusions or prejudices or hostilities; but this is one of the hazards of family membership. I do not find in the statute an expression of legislative intent that parents who are devoted to their children should be deprived of their custody because of defects in their own personalities unless those defects have a seriously adverse effect upon the child." [Citation omitted.]

For the foregoing reasons we believe the adjudication of dependency is not supported by a preponderance of the evidence. Therefore, the order is reversed and the cause is remanded with directions to dismiss the petition.

KRUCKER, C.J., and HOWARD, J., concur.

Pima County is a good example of differing values of the social worker and the appeals court. Also, the cross-examination reported in question-and-answer form reveals little support for a finding of dependency.

Bell and Mlyniec (1974: p. 28) provide suggestions for preparing neglect and abuse cases that are useful for other types of cases as well. They emphasize particularly the importance of the *case record*. They also indicate the use of the record in discovery:

> Social workers will find the limited but growing case law in neglect and abuse instructive in their ongoing efforts to maximize their effectiveness in court. A review of this body of material reveals that some social workers have difficulty distinguishing facts from personal opinion and speculation; in addition, there may be reliance on hearsay evidence; poor record-keeping; and inadequate presentation techniques. From the reported cases and from experience, it appears that social workers need to strengthen their work in three areas: (a) collection, preservation, and analysis of factual data for court testimony; (b) management of second-hand information and hearsay testimony; and (c) participation in pretrial conferences with the county attorney.
>
> Building a legally usable record of facts for possible litigation begins *at intake* in all cases of suspected child abuse or neglect. Regardless of how receptive to services and workable a parent or guardian may appear, every protective service case has a potential for court action. For it is through such action that the ultimate protection of an endangered child lies.
>
> While a social worker should follow the practice of exploring all nonjudicial resolutions of neglect, such exploration does not obviate the value of laying a foundation of fact in each family case file from which to build an effective case in court should judicial action become necessary. Indeed, the very records kept can be used to make a determination of whether or not to go to court. Accurate, complete summaries of parental functioning, over time, can show or fail to show child-care improvement. In the area of neglect the pattern of conduct is considered, rather than one action or omission.
>
> Once the social worker has made the decision to go to court, the protective service records will have various uses. In order for the judicial proceeding to be initiated, the county attorney must file a petition or pleading with the court setting forth the allegations, which, if proven true, will give the court jurisdiction over the child. Failure to prove the allegations will result in a finding that the child is not neglected. It is essential both for the protection of the child and to accord due process to the parent that the petition accurately reflects the facts which the government will seek to prove. Since the worker will most often be the supplier of the information, an accurate case record will insure a valid petition.
>
> Once the case has been formally initiated in court, the primary value of the protective service record is to refresh the worker's memory so that testimony can be prepared for court. Social work records are not generally admissible at trial. Since many cases have long histories before court action, and since case loads are usually high, it is unrealistic to assume that a worker can remember all that has transpired. Also, in cases where termination of parental rights is being sought long after the original neglect finding, prior workers may no longer be associated with the case. If their testimony is essential to a ruling of termination, accurate records will be indispensable for refreshing their memory.
>
> The worker must assume that these records will be discoverable by all the attorneys in the case. The worker who keeps unbiased, well-documented records has no reason to be apprehensive about discovery. However, if the records are inaccurate, or unverified, or contain unsupportable conclusions, the worker can expect a vigorous and damaging cross-examination by the parent's attorney.

Social work recording has traditionally been geared to meeting administrative, supervisory, teaching, and research requirements. But too often, records have not been consistent or full enough to allow retrospective observations about effectiveness or even to permit factual statements about what the social worker did. Recording has focused upon social history, worker-client feelings, and diagnosis without documentation of what the social worker and the client heard, saw, said, and did to support the resultant diagnosis and subsequent treatment plan. It has been further noted that the casework record has received little attention, except for its deficiencies, in the professional literature.

THE PRETRIAL CONFERENCE

A pretrial conference with the state's attorney is essential, but it is often postponed until just before the hearing, when it is too late to be very effective. While the task of the state's attorney is to prepare witnesses, the social worker is often asked to outline the facts and introduce the other witnesses to be called. Since the witness cannot have any direct control over the questioning, main points should be clarified in the pretrial conference and written out for the state's attorney.

THE SUBPOENA

The social worker may have no option about testifying. In litigation, any party may subpoena a witness. A *subpoena* is a summons to appear before a particular court at a particular time. It commands you to appear. Otherwise, the sheriff can be requested to bring you physically before the court. If you cannot explain your absence or refuse to testify, the court can hold you in contempt until you purge yourself of such contempt by serving a sentence, paying a fine, or testifying.

Exhibit 9.1 shows a typical subpoena. It may not only command your appearance before the court but may also specify that you bring certain books and records. In states where social workers have no privileged communication, you can be required to bring in the names and addresses of patients individually or in groups. Notes, tape recordings, videotapes, or any other written materials pertaining to the services rendered may be subpoenaed.

EXHIBIT 9.1
EXAMPLE OF A SUBPOENA

SUBPOENA TO A WITNESS

Civil Court of _____County

State of _____

John Smith   PLAINTIFF

v.

William Brown   DEFENDANT

To Bradwell Jones, of 8 Maple Avenue, Smithville, Smith County, _____

WHEREAS it has been made to appear that you are likely to be called to give material evidence in the above entitled action for the plaintiff:

THIS COMMANDS YOU to attend the Civil Court of Smith County on the first day of April, 19 _____, at ten a.m. at room 418 to hold yourself in readiness to give evidence in the above-entitled action.

DATED this _____day of _____, 19 _____at Smith County, _____

_____
Clerk of the Court

Bernstein (1977) provides an example involving a social worker who was conducting a six-person group. One couple in the group also pursued individual counseling. In the course of their relationship with the social worker, both parties and the social worker were open and honest. Both husband and wife confessed to certain improprieties, but the wife was far more open and active. She confessed to a series of indiscretions that might put her ability to rear children in question. The husband knew of these confessions and also knew that the wife would deny their existence at the time of the trial. Only one professional person could testify to the true facts.

Thus the attorney for the husband subpoenaed the social worker, the social worker's records, and obtained a list of the other people in their group. The lawyer then issued a subpoena compelling the social worker and all members of the group to appear for a deposition, and, had the case not been settled for other reasons, would have had the right to take the deposition of the social worker, the wife, and all members of the group. The **deposition**, a series of questions and answers taken before a court reporter, which may be read into the record, subject only to objections made at the time of the trial, would have been devastating. It would have made public all the confessions made during therapy. Future therapy would have been almost impossible. Just receiving the subpoena upset all the members of the group.

TESTIFYING IN COURT

Presentation of formulations and recommendations is a major issue in a social worker's testimony. Judges want terms simpler than some social workers use, and insist on the background and reasons for recommendations. One effective procedure is to present and analyze all possible alternatives for disposition, concluding with the one to be recommended in simple, clear language.

Another problem concerns using general adjectives in presenting evidence. To say that a room was filthy is less effective than to say that there were feces in three corners of the room. The statement "I found it to be the dirtiest house I ever saw" may lead to a series of questions designed to create embarrassment—"How many houses have you seen?" "What is your definition of a dirty house?" It is far better to use specific facts: "The dishes in the sink were caked with dry food. There were dirty diapers on the floor. The dog had urinated in the corner."

Direct testimony should be given calmly, without tension. While a witness is generally expected to testify from memory, notes are sometimes permitted as a source of detailed data. The judge or opposing counsel may ask to see any notes used. Particularly in protective services cases, social workers have no idea when a record may become important in a court hearing, so care in case recording is important.

Dates and times are often crucial to evidence. Events should be described accurately. Although questions should be answered directly, one should take full advantage of the range of the question. "What did you find when you visited the home?" provides a better lead than more specific questions such as "What were the parents doing when you entered the home? Was there any evidence of a family argument? Did there seem to be any food in the house?"

The stresses of testimony and how to respond under cross-examination are discussed by Bernstein (1975: 523–524).

The infrequent witness is often intimidated by what may be asked and what may appear to be trick questions. As a minimum, the social worker should understand that direct questioning and cross-examination are different, and he should know the nature of these differences.

Under direct examination, the attorney will ask questions, each designed to elicit a fact considered relevant to the case. These questions cannot be suggestive of an answer. Direct examination involves a lawyer and his own witness. Generally, it is a more gentle type of examination, because the attorney has had the opportunity to meet the witness and discuss potential questions and answers. Under direct examination of a witness, he never asks a question the answer to which could be unexpected. This fear of a surprising answer is the reason for the pretrial interview.

When being cross-examined, the social worker witness would not be treated as gently. The cross-examining attorney is not limited in any way to general questions and may ask leading questions, suggest answers, and often assume a belligerent or hostile posture. . . . .

The social worker should be aware of this procedure and also the method by which written evidence or documents are introduced. The introduction of documents is a technical procedure which follows a natural flow or sequence in the courtroom—from attorney to opposing attorney to judge—and only at the end may an objection be made to the introduction of a given document. While this time-honored practice is taking place, the social worker cannot allow his personal feelings about the system to be obvious. The social worker should know that information relevant to the social worker's practice is often inadmissible as evidence and that no useful purpose is served by anger, outbursts, or manifestations of frustration. Every lawyer has been in the courtroom at some time when a witness has blurted out, "If you really wanted the truth, you would read this letter and let the jury read it." Such a demonstration of feeling only serves to destroy the objective credibility of the social worker as a witness.

If a question seems inappropriate, a look at the state's attorney may get him or her to register an objection. If not, you may ask the judge, "Must I answer that question?"

Tierney (1971:104) presents a succinct set of rules for direct testimony:

The art of testimony cannot be reduced to a science; there are few universal rules and it is impossible to foresee every possibility on the witness stand. Nevertheless, there are certain general principles which can aid a witness in all circumstances:

1. Keep your temper.
2. Answer a question in the shortest possible way.
3. Always be willing to admit ignorance of the subject-matter of a question, or that your memory has failed you, or that you are not sure.
4. Never show partiality, or vindictiveness, to either party to the litigation.
5. Never show reluctance to concede a point in the opposition's favor.
6. Use short, simple language so that your point is immediately comprehensible.
7. Ask for a question to be repeated or rephrased if you do not understand it.

A witness who acts according to these suggestions will not necessarily have an easy task, but he can rest assured that he will have performed his duty as a witness in a way that serves justice and does him credit as a citizen.

Several other steps are important in testifying. Check the court docket for possible changes in scheduling. Arrive at the hearing in plenty of time to be briefed on any last-minute developments. A conference of the parties in the judge's chambers may result in agreement that eliminates the need for the hearing. The social worker should be available to participate in the conference if asked to do so.

The attorney must be sure to establish the qualifications of the social worker as a witness. This may be done by direct questioning or in an introductory statement. For example:

————has been a professional social worker for fifteen years—ten of them in this state—served as a member of the standards committee of the Child Welfare League of America concerned with foster care, published three articles on the subject, was named Social Worker of the Year in this state in 1982, and has worked with over 500 children and their families.

The Human Element

Tierney (1971: 14) emphasized the importance of observation for testimony and called attention to sources of error:

The law depends on human observation for nearly all of its factual data and for this reason witnesses have been described as "the eyes and ears of justice." But it is a great mistake to place too much faith in the accuracy of human observation; many of the clearest miscarriages of justice have been caused by erroneous, though honest, observations. These can arise from all sorts of causes—the perspective from which a witness saw the things he described, the conditions in which he saw them, and so on—but the fundamental difficulty arises because human beings are not as well equipped for observation as they might be and they are not as good at it as they believe.

A witness giving evidence in court is actually involved in a quite complex mental activity, in which there are many opportunities for error. Put succinctly, it may be said that a witness is describing his memory of an event which he observed at some time in the past. From this, we can see that error may arise from three major causes: (1) a witness's initial observation of the event in question may have been faulty; (2) his memory may be inaccurate; (3) his description of his memory may be inadequate and misleading. In view of the importance of testimony, each of these possible sources of error will now be considered in turn. One of the greatest human delusions is an absolute faith in memory and it is the one which can do the most harm if a witness does not appreciate how fallible memory is. . . .

Since a witness is called before a court to recount the facts in his possession, his powers of expression are heavily relied on when he testifies; his knowledge is of no use unless it can be communicated. A witness may be articulate, or he may be tongue-tied; he may be quick-witted or slow; capable of bringing to life what is in his memory or not—but what he says is all the court has to go on. It is not enough that a witness exercises his capacity to observe; to be a good witness he must be able to memorize and recall accurately, under the formal conditions of a court of law.

This is demanding a great deal from a witness. Even in perfect conditions for reminiscence, there are few people who can produce a memory concisely and impartially. On the witness stand, a witness may find himself facing a barrage of specific questions, the answers to which he finds it almost impossible to summon up. One of the defects of the question-and-answer method by which testimony is elicited from witnesses is that the questions condition the answers so that much of what is relevant from a witness' point of view is left out. Since most people remember episodes or complete stories rather than isolated facts, many witnesses leave the stand dissatisfied with their attempt to tell what is in their minds.

THE SOCIAL WORKER AS EXPERT WITNESS

In a particularly important or perplexing case, persons with a known reputation may be called to testify as expert witnesses, in which case they will be paid travel and a per diem fee. The expert witness will not have observed the situation firsthand but will be told of the case and be given hypothetical questions to answer.

Question: If you were trying to make a permanent plan for an eight-year-old boy of above average intelligence who had been the victim of twenty severe beatings administered by his father, what plan would you make for him?

Answer: An eight-year-old should be consulted about his own wishes in planning for his care. The plan would be dependent largely on his emotional state. If he had no special emotional problems, I would try to select a foster home that has the potential for becoming an adoptive home. If the agency cannot provide a subsidy, the family must be able to afford to undertake the financial obligation of adoption. From the description given in your question, parental rights should be terminated without giving the father any more opportunities for violence. The child may not trust adults enough for adoption, but if the foster placement is successful for the first few months, adoption should be possible.

Another example would be the real-life case following the accidental death of a father in which the railroad for which he worked was sued on behalf of his five children. The question was the level of damages needed to pay for child care until the children became eighteen. A social worker was asked to determine the costs and present them on behalf of the plaintiffs in federal district court. The following statement was prepared as expert testimony:

The Commission on Population Growth and the American Future conducted research on the cost of rearing a child from birth to majority. Ritchie H. Reed and Susan McIntosh determined that the total cost of a child in 1969 was $17,576 or $976 per annum (Commission on Population Growth, 1972). This figure took into account neither the mother's wages sacrificed by child-rearing nor the costs of college.

This figure was corrected by an inflation factor based on the actual increases in the consumer price index from over the past five years—a mean rate of 6.6 percent and an estimated inflation rate of 6 percent in subsequent years.

The cost of rearing the five children from the time of death to their majority was estimated at a total of $73,770. This figure is substantially higher under current estimates—at least $75,000 per child. The railroad had originally offered $15,000, but partly as a result of this statement an out-of-court settlement of $35,000 was agreed on.

Often several expert witnesses will be used. In Mills v. Board of Education of the District of Columbia, 348 F. Supp. 866 (D.C.Cir. 1972), a class action suit filed to compel the school board to provide appropriate education for all types of handicapped children, the experts included three professionals with doctoral degrees. The special educator had twenty years of experience in his field and numerous publications. The economist had published a book on cost–benefit issues for programs for the mentally retarded. The chemist, who had also written articles on retardation, had a reputation as an advocate for retarded citizens.

Another interesting use of expert testimony is found in Painter v. Bannister, 140 N.W.2d 152 (Iowa 1966), discussed in Chapter 8.

PREPARING THE CLIENT AND OTHER WITNESSES TO TESTIFY

Preparing the client for a court appearance is part of the casework process. The parent must understand both the consequences of a neglect or dependency finding and his or her right to deny the allegation and to be represented by an attorney. If a parent is unable to afford a lawyer, in many states the court will appoint one.

The social worker should explain the general court procedure to the client, indicating exactly what to expect. The time of the hearing, location of the courtroom, the name of the presiding judge, and where the client is to sit should all be included. Any witness must know what is being alleged, the basis for allegations, and how the court procedure operates on behalf of the child and family. The suggestions earlier in this chapter that apply to the preparation of the social worker apply also to preparing the client and other witnesses. Without coaching the witness or adding facts, the social worker may have to help identify and organize information that will form the basis for testimony.

For all participants, factual accuracy is essential. In testimony, names must be correctly spelled, often letter by letter. Dates used in evidence must be precise. If unfitness is alleged, documentation of contacts between the parent and child may be very important. In depicting the child, behavioral descriptions are better than such global terms as anxiety, neurosis, inferiority complex, or shyness. An effective statement would be: "Bobby told me that he had no friends and that he was afraid to approach other people. When he did so, he said he felt sick. He said, 'I like to play alone. Then I don't have to try to please anyone else.' "

CHILDREN AS WITNESSES

Special problems are encountered with child witnesses. Increased attention to child abuse and neglect outside the family in day-care centers and nursery schools, and alleged child pornography rings has focused attention on problems of validity of children's testimony. Interviews of the child witness by social workers and others before actual testimony has been alleged to provide leads that distort factual reality. The younger the child, the greater the difficulty in establishing the validity of the testimony. Goodman (1984) edited a special number of the *Journal of Social Issues* on the child witness, dealing with the reliability of children's memories and the testimony of the child victim of sexual abuse, among other topics.

THE PRIVILEGE NOT TO TESTIFY

Privileged communication may seem confusing. The priest-penitent, doctor-patient, and lawyer-client privileges not to testify about what is revealed to them are intended to encourage people to seek help when they need it.* This privilege may or may not extend to the social worker in a therapeutic relationship with a client. The privilege serves the interests of the client. It is not a means to save social workers' time by keeping them from having to go to court. A New York Court decision in Yaron v. Yaron, 372 N.Y.S.2d 518 (1975), upheld social worker privilege.

YARON v. YARON

372 N.Y.S.2d 518 (1975).

This question arose in this matrimonial proceeding in which the plaintiff seeks the dissolution of the marriage and both the plaintiff and defendant wish custody of the three infant issues of the marriage.

A number of years prior to the commencement of this proceeding the parties, who had been having marital problems, sought the help, advice and guidance of the Jewish Family Service. Both were interviewed by staff personnel of that agency, including social workers and at least one psychiatrist. It is clear that both parties were interviewed together on a number of occasions. . . .

---

* Spousal privilege has been subject to modification. The U.S. Supreme Court held in Trammel v. United States, 445 U.S. 40 (1980), that the spouse may be neither compelled to testify nor foreclosed from testifying in a criminal proceeding. This was felt to "further the public interest in marital harmony."

During the trial the attorney for the defendant served a subpoena duces tecum on the Jewish Family Services calling upon it to produce its records and reports covering the consultations, examination, interviews, etc., relating to the parties. He also made an offer of proof to the effect that he wished to produce as a witness the psychiatrist on the staff of that agency who had interviewed the parties.

The attorney for the plaintiff objected to the production and admission into evidence of the records and reports of the agency on the grounds that they were not business records as defined in section 4518 of the CPLR [Civil Practice Laws and Rules] and that in any event they were privileged under the relevant section of the CPLR and that the offer of proof to produce the psychiatrist should be denied on the grounds of privilege. The court reserved decision at that time.

The Jewish Family Services thereafter informally sought permission to appear as amicus curiae and was permitted to submit a memorandum of law opposing the production of its records and reports on the grounds of the privilege granted in section 4508 of the CPLR. . . . Section 4508 for certified social worker-client relationships; section 4507 for registered psychologist-client relationships; and section 4504 for physician psychiatrist-patient relationships; and all of the other staff personnel of that agency by virtue of their relationship to the protected communications. . . . Persons who voluntarily seek the aid of such an agency in connection with inter-personal problems, whether the family unit or other, must, if such aid is to be successful, deal with the staff of such agency with the utmost candor, revealing and laying bare all of their secret feelings, resentments, hostilities, fantasies, desires, etc. To embark on this most difficult task of stark self-revelation the parties must have absolute confidence that total privacy (read privilege) protects such baring of their souls.

Some judges have dealt with privilege in a manner not calculated to encourage this essential element of confidence in the total privacy (read privilege) of such disclosures.

They have placed great reliance on Wigmore's four fundamental conditions claimed to be necessary to establish the privilege against disclosure between persons standing in given relationships (8 Wigmore, Evidence, McNaughton rev. 1961, section 2285, page 527).

They read as follows:

"(1) The communications must originate in a confidence that they will not be disclosed.

(2) This element of confidentiality must be essential to the full and satisfactory maintenance of the relation between the parties.

(3) The relation must be one which in the opinion of the community ought to be sedulously fostered.

(4) The injury that would inure to the relation by the disclosure of the communications must be greater than the benefit thereby gained for the correct disposal of litigation."

These judges have interpreted the fourth condition in such a way as to negate the privilege of section 4508 CPLR. . . .

The Legislature, when it enacted section 4508, CPLR, into law, included in its membership a large number of attorneys, and thus would be aware of Wigmore and his four fundamental conditions. Yet, when it did so it saw fit to provide only four exceptions to this privilege. Nowhere do we find any reference to the four fundamental conditions. . . . (T)he Legislature deemed the relationship between social worker and client to be one where communications "originate in a confidence that they will not be disclosed." (First condition) The Legislature further by such act deemed that the "element of confidentiality must be essential to the full and satisfactory maintenance of the relation between the parties." (Second condition) And finally by such act answered the third condition "The relation must be one which in the opinion of the community ought to be sedulously fostered."

Now if the Legislature meant to give the fourth condition any statutory validity it could and would have done so. There is no mention in section 4508 (which sets forth four exceptions to the privilege attaching) of any discretion to the court which is contained in the fourth condition: "The injury that would inure to the relation by the disclosure of the communications must be greater than the benefit thereby gained for the correct disposal of litigation." . . .

When a court says it is balancing the privilege with some other interest, whether denominated a community interest or anything else, and then goes on to say that the danger to the relationship of the social worker to the client is outweighed by such other interest, it misses the real point. It is not the individual relationship between a client and a social worker that is injured. It is the general relationship between all clients and their social workers that is injured. It is the chilling effect on such a general relationship that is overlooked by the courts when they apply the balancing act test.

If parties who are in need of help face the danger that some court will at some later date balance the privilege, which the clients believe they have every right to rely on, with some other so-called interest, what happens to the necessary "baring of the souls," the necessary "self revelation," the necessary honesty required to provide the basis for such aid?

Who would wish to be subjected to such self-revelation faced with the possibility that at some later time a court will do a balancing act and declare that the privilege relied upon was a myth? . . .

Privilege granted by the Legislature was not meant to be a myth. It was meant to cure the evil which had resulted from social workers either voluntarily or by court direction being forced to disclose communications given to them of the most intimate nature by people desperately in need of help. People were, and are, told that in order to be helped they must reveal the innermost parts of their emotional being—their most dreadful fantasies, their fears, their angers and desires. How can such persons have faith in this process if they become aware that some courts can subsequently find that the confidence in which such feelings were revealed can be betrayed? This court takes the position that by communication which is privileged when made remains privileged forever unless the privilege is waived by the client.

In most roles discussed in this chapter, privilege is not a major issue. In child abuse cases, as in most other protective roles, the social work investigator is acting as a representative of the state, and therefore no basis exists for privilege for the parent. Such a basis may exist, however, for the child who is the primary client in abuse and custody matters.

The court places the social worker in a world of fact leading to proof. The more we know about the functioning of the courts, and the more we can present facts accurately and confidently, the more we may make use of the judicial system to serve the best interests of clients.

Questions for Review

1. Contrast the standards of proof in criminal and civil proceedings.

2. Why is it necessary to establish the qualifications of a social worker as witness?

3. A social worker considers a child to have autistic tendencies. How could he or she best describe the behavior in court?

4. What are the steps in preparing evidence?

5. If the parent does not wish to risk a finding of neglect or dependency, what type of action may the parent take to provide custodial care for a child?

6. Why would there be no question of social worker–client privilege in a typical child abuse case?

7. Under what conditions may children be taken into custody? Once taken into custody, what right do they have in a specified time period?

8. When is hearsay admissible as evidence?

Questions for Debate and Discussion

1. Describe a case from your agency or field setting. Indicate the questions you would suggest that the state's attorney ask and the answers you would give as the social worker.

2. Give an example of default in a neglect or dependency hearing.

Selected Readings   Bernstein, Barton E. "Out of the Mouths of Babes: When Children Take the Witness Stand." *Children's Legal Rights Journal* 4 (1982): 11–17.

Dingwall, Robert, and John Echelaar. "Care Proceedings: A Practical Guide for Social Workers." *Health Visitors and Others*. Towanda, N.J.: Biblio Distribution Center, 1982.

Garnett, Stanley L. "Children as Witnesses: Competency and Rules Favoring Their Testimony." *Colorado Law* 12 (1983): 1.

Horsley, Jack E., and John Carlova. *Testifying in Court*. Oradell, N.Y.: Medical Economics Books, 1983.

Melton, Gary B. "Children's Competency to Testify." *Law and Human Behavior* 5 (1981): 73–85.

PART
III

Family Development and Crises

CHAPTER
10

Marriage

Marriage has been affected by changes in attitudes of society as well as by changes in individual goals and expectations. Unlike those who wish to divorce, couples who intend to marry rarely seek the professional services of a social worker in advance of the ceremony.

If a person meets the legal age requirements, has no current valid marriage, and has complied with license and blood test requirements, getting married is not difficult. It is simpler to obtain a marriage license than a driver's license.

Every effort is made to support the validity of marriage. Typically, it is assumed that both parties had the capacity to marry, that they followed laws governing licensing formalities, and that they had a wedding ceremony. The latest of successive marriages is generally presumed to be valid. The strength of these presumptions increases with the passage of time and the birth of children.

Social workers need to have a knowledge of marriage laws in order to help clients who encounter difficulties in living together without marriage, who want to marry in the face of parental objections, who are unhappy with their mate, or who do not know where to find their spouse.

Over the past decade, cohabitation has received more attention because of the increased number of couples who choose it. Middle-class young people and retired people who want to remarry but do not want to have retirement benefits curtailed are the most likely to live together without marriage. The social worker needs to know the provisions pertaining to the rights of nonmarital partners in such an arrangement in their state of residence.

The largest demand for social work services comes in marriage counseling—either to improve marital relationships or to help terminate them. Marriage counseling is now more likely to be divorce counseling. The social worker may also be involved in trying to find a spouse in order to enforce a child support order or to seek a release for adoption.

These issues, and the role annulment plays in terminating invalid marriages, constitute the substance of this chapter.

PREMARITAL CONTROVERSIES

Breach of promise, gifts to engaged persons, and contracts that restrict (or occasionally promote) marriage or facilitate retention of property rights are issues that precede marriage or result because a marriage does not take place.

Breach of Promise

Suits have been brought for more than three hundred years, but breach of promise no longer qualifies as a major premarital controversy; it is omitted from many basic family law textbooks. Breach of promise is anachronistic to the current concepts of dating and courtship, which consider engagement to be a period of final decision-making based on increasing intimacy from which either person may freely withdraw. If reluctance to marry develops, most people prefer to learn before rather than after the ceremony that the reticent partner did not really want to marry. In addition, people whose engagement fails do not want to undergo the publicity necessary to bring suit. The right to bring breach of promise and alienation of affection suits led to abuses. Such actions have been prohibited as a result of changing social norms because they encouraged scandal and blackmail.

Gifts When a proposed marriage does not take place, issues sometimes arise around courtship and engagement gifts. The engagement ring is clearly assumed to be conditional to the marriage. In Friedman v. Geller, 368 N.Y.S. 2d 980 (1975), the decision included these comments on the gift of an engagement ring:

> Here, the donee fails to reflect upon the significance of a diamond engagement ring. A ring is given by a donor to his fiancée as a sacred designation of conjugality. It is a pledge of betrothal growing out of the love and affection, which is coincidental, as well as part and parcel, of a culminating matrimonial relationship. Would the plaintiff have made the gift had not he contemplated a consummated marriage in the offing?
>
> The donor clearly has the right to recover engagement gifts. But to recover without summary judgment would convert a judicial forum into a bitter duel conjuring up traumatic tales of grievous hearts. The courtroom scene would be transposed into a grotesque marketplace whose wares would be the exposure of heart-rending episodes of wounded pride, which should be best kept private rather than public.

Some courts hold major gifts to be conditional, except possibly those related to specific occasions—a birthday or Christmas. If a gift is conditional and both parties consent to termination of the engagement, the gift is recoverable. However, the person who gives a gift and subsequently breaks the engagement unilaterally may be unable to recover it. Gifts made to the engaged couple by third parties are also usually considered conditional.

Contracts Contracts to prevent marriage are uncommon but have been found to be valid under some circumstances. For example there may be a contract not to marry before a certain age or outside a certain religious faith. Female public school teachers used to be prohibited from marrying during the school term, but such provisions would not now be enforceable because they involve sex discrimination.

Prenuptial contracts are most necessary to a second marriage of older persons who have considerable property and wish to retain control of it. Such agreements may be sought to obtain support for the marriage from children who see themselves as primary heirs. Both spouses must have a clear idea of the financial status of the other partner so they know what is being sacrificed.

To eliminate any confusion, the prenuptial agreement should include a disclosure clause indicating familiarity with the assets of the spouse. Where both partners bring substantial assets to the marriage, two forms of the disclosure clause should be included, with the husband's name and masculine pronouns in one and the wife's name and feminine pronouns in the other.

EXHIBIT 10.1
EXAMPLE OF A DISCLOSURE FORM

DISCLOSURE FORM

[———] acknowledges that:
(a) She is fully acquainted with the business and resources of [———];
(b) She understands that he is a person of [very] substantial wealth;
(c) He has answered all the questions she has asked about his income and assets;
(d) She understands that by entering into this agreement she will receive, as his widow, substantially less than the amount she would otherwise be entitled to receive if he died intestate or if she elected to take legal action against his last will and testament pursuant to statute;
(e) She has at all times received the advice of counsel of her own choosing;
(f) She has carefully weighed all the facts and circumstances and desires to marry [———] regardless of any financial arrangements made for her benefit; and
(g) She is entering into this agreement freely, voluntarily and with full knowledge.

In Posner v. Posner, 233 So.2d 381 (Fla. 1970), a Florida state appeals court had considered a prenuptial agreement that specified alimony of $600 a month in the event of divorce. The three appellate judges took different views of the agreement:

> (1) the parties may validly agree upon alimony in an antenuptial agreement but . . . the trial court is not bound by their agreement; (2) such an agreement is void as against public policy; and (3) an antenuptial agreement respecting alimony is entitled to the same consideration and should be just as binding as an antenuptial agreement settling the property rights of the wife in her husband's estate upon his death.

The Florida Supreme Court held the prenuptial agreement concerning alimony to be valid:

> We have given careful consideration to the question of whether the change in public policy towards divorce requires a change in the rule respecting antenuptial agreements settling alimony and property rights of the parties upon divorce and have concluded that such agreements should no longer be held to be void *ab initio* from the outset as "contrary to public policy." If such an agreement is valid when tested by the stringent rules prescribed in Del Vecchio v. Del Vecchio, supra, 143 So.2d 17 (Fla. 1962), for ante- and post-nuptial agreements settling the property rights of the spouses in the estate of the other upon death, and if, in addition, it is made to appear that the divorce was prosecuted in good faith, on proper grounds, so that, under the rules applicable to post-nuptial alimony and property settlement agreements referred to above, it could not be said to facilitate or promote the procurement of a divorce, then it should be held valid as to conditions existing at the time the agreement was made.

However, a prenuptial agreement in which the wife accepts a stated sum as full settlement in the event the marriage ends in divorce is usually considered invalid, mainly because the economic conditions of both husband and wife may change substantially between the time of the agreement and separation or divorce. Such a contract may also be invalid because it is seen as tending to encourage divorce.

SOCIAL WORK CONCERNS ABOUT MARRIAGE

Several legal aspects of marriage are of special interest to social workers: age and other legal requirements, common law and proxy marriages, the implications of bigamy, laws derived from the incest taboo, and legal age requirements.

Common law marriage is not recognized in most states. Where it is recognized, important benefits can accrue to the surviving spouse and children. *Proxy marriages,* in which a third party represents the bride or groom, are rare but may be desirable when a man and a woman living apart expect to assume a full marital relationship in the future. Some clients are casual about marriage and divorce and fail to realize that *bigamy* is a serious offense. Caseworkers often help straighten out situations that are at least technically bigamous.

People are also often confused about "forbidden degrees" of blood relationships that bar marriage, as in the case of first cousins. How far does the *incest taboo* extend? Does it apply only to persons who have a blood relationship, or does it also affect adopted or stepchildren reared together? On bigamy and forbidden degrees, the Uniform Marriage and Divorce Act, § 207 9A U.L.A. 108 (1973), states:

> (a) The following marriages are prohibited: (1) a marriage entered into prior to the dissolution of an earlier marriage of one of the parties; (2) a marriage between an ancestor and a descendant, or between a brother and a sister, whether the relationship is by the half or the whole blood, or by adoption; (3) a marriage between an uncle and a niece or between an aunt and a nephew, whether the relationship is by the half or the whole blood, except as to marriages permitted by the established customs of aboriginal cultures.
>
> (b) Parties to a marriage prohibited under this section who cohabit after removal of the impediment are lawfully married as of the date of the removal of the impediment.
>
> (c) Children born of a prohibited marriage are legitimate.

GOVERNMENT REGULATION OF MARRIAGE

In the United States, unlike Europe, the regulation of marriage rests with the state rather than the church. Nevertheless, there is also a strong element of privacy and freedom from state intervention in the marital relationship, as emphasized in the U.S. Supreme Court decision in Griswold v. State of Connecticut 381 U.S. 479 (1965), which dealt with the right to use contraceptives. Regulation of marriage is related to police powers inasmuch as it helps maintain the public welfare and discourage immorality. Marriage is regulated through licensing.

Most state statutes require blood tests to detect venereal diseases before a marriage license is issued, and some provide for physical examinations to determine other abnormalities, including epilepsy, tuberculosis, drug addiction, or alcoholism. Colorado also requires blood grouping to detect an Rh problem, and tests for rubella immunity for women of child-bearing age.

Licensing requires that the principals prove their age and attest that they are not validly married to anyone else and that they do not violate the forbidden degrees of familial relationships applicable in their state. Hasty marriages are supposedly discouraged by an obligatory waiting period of three to five days from the issuance of the license to the time of the ceremony. This is generally too short a time to eliminate precipitous marriage plans.

Section 203 of the Uniform Marriage and Divorce Act, (9A U.L.A. 102–103 [1973]), covers licensing and age requirements:

> When a marriage application has been completed and signed by both parties to a prospective marriage and at least one party has appeared before the [marriage license] clerk and paid the marriage license fee of [$————] the [marriage license] clerk shall issue a license to marry and a marriage certificate form upon being furnished:
>
> (1) satisfactory proof that each party to the marriage will have attained the age of 18 years at the time the marriage license is effective, or will have attained the age

of 16 years and has either the consent to the marriage of both parents or his guardian, or judicial approval; [or, if under the age of 16 years, has both the consent of both parents or his guardian and judicial approval;] and

(2) satisfactory proof that the marriage is not prohibited; [and]

[(3) a certificate of the results of any medical examination required by the laws of this State.]

A ceremony rather than issuance of the license validates a marriage and constitutes notice to the public that the marriage occurred. A ceremony may be civil, religious, or both and serves to eliminate the ambiguity associated with informal marriages based only on the private exchange of promises.

The Uniform Marriage and Divorce Act (§ 206, 9A U.L.A. 107 [1973]), also covers solemnization of the marriage, including the status of the rite when it is performed by an unqualified person:

Section 206

(a) A marriage may be solemnized by a judge of a court of record, by a public official whose powers include solemnization of marriages, or in accordance with any mode of solemnization recognized by any religious denomination, Indian Nation or Tribe, or Native Group. Either the person solemnizing the marriage, or, if no individual acting alone solemnized the marriage, a party to the marriage, shall complete the marriage certificate form and forward it to the [marriage license] clerk. . . .

(d) The solemnization of the marriage is not invalidated by the fact that the person solemnizing the marriage was not legally qualified to solemnize it, if either party to the marriage believed him to be so qualified.

Even when a license is shown to be defective, the marriage will probably be considered valid by virtue of the wedding ceremony.

Only in Maryland is performance of marriage rites limited to the clergy. Elsewhere, judges and justices of the peace are allowed to perform marriage ceremonies. Generally, there is no form prescribed for the marriage ceremony. Couples may write or adapt their own marriage service. The only requirement is that the parties declare before an officiating person and witnesses that they take each other as husband and wife.

In some states, the marriage ceremony must be performed in the county where the license is issued and where one of the principals is domiciled. In most instances two witnesses are required. Ceremonial marriages are considered valid regardless of whether they are consummated, but common law marriages require consummation.

AGE AND PARENTAL PERMISSION

Age provisions of the statutes are important when parents oppose a marriage. Generally, the female could marry without parental permission earlier than the male, but this has been challenged. Two decisions are presented below, the first (Phelps v. Bing, 316 N.E.2d 775 [Ill. 1974]) based on equal protection in the Illinois constitution, and the second (Friedrich v. Katz, 318 N.E.2d 606 [19xx]) on the traditional support obligations of the male and the need to "provide safeguards affecting the marriage of male minors":

PHELPS v. BING

**Supreme Court of
Illinois, 316 N.E.2d
775 (Ill. 1974).**

UNDERWOOD, Chief Justice.

The plaintiffs, Larry Phelps, age 20, and Nikki Rexroad, age 19, sought a marriage license in Champaign County where both were residents. The defendant, Champaign County Clerk Dennis Bing, refused to issue the license because Phelps was not 21 years old and had no parent or legal guardian to give consent as required by the provisions of sections 3 and 6 of the Marriage Act (Ill.Rev.Stat.1973, ch. 89, pars. 3, 6). Plaintiffs then filed a petition for a writ of *mandamus* alleging that section 3(b) of the Marriage Act is unconstitutional in that it discriminates in age requirements between males and females, and asking that the defendant clerk be ordered to issue a marriage license to the parties.

The trial court found that section 6 of the Marriage Act violated section 18 of article I of the Constitution of 1970, S.H.A., and was therefore invalid. . . .

Section 3 of the Marriage Act provides in pertinent part:

"The following persons may contract and be joined in marriage.
(a) Male persons of 21 or more years and female persons of 18 or more years; or
(b) Male persons of 18 or more years and female persons of 16 or more years. However, the parent or guardian of such person must appear before the county clerk in the county where either such minor person resides, or before the county clerk to whom application for a license under Section 6 is made, and make affidavit that he or she is the parent or guardian of such minor and give consent to the marriage. . . ."

Section 3.1 provides:

"Male persons of 16 or more years and female persons of 15 or more years may contract and be joined in marriage provided such persons first present to the county clerk who is requested to issue to them a marriage license, a certified copy of a court order which has been obtained pursuant to Section 3.2 of this Act. No county clerk shall issue a marriage license under this Section unless such order has been so obtained as provided in Section 3.2."

Section 6 provides:

"If the male is over the age of 18 years and under the age of 21 years, or the female is over the age of 16 years and under the age of 18 years, no license may be issued by the County Clerk, unless the consent in writing of the parents of the person under age, or one of such parents, or of his or her guardian, is presented to him, duly verified by such parents, or parent, or guardian, and such consent must be filed by the Clerk, and he must state such facts in the license.

The effect of this statutory scheme is that while a male must be 21 to obtain a license to marry without parental consent, 18 to marry with consent, and 16 to marry by court order, a female may obtain a license at 18 without parental consent, at 16 with consent, and at 15 by court order.

Section 18 of the Bill of Rights of the Constitution of 1970 (Ill. Const. [1970], art. I, sec. 18) provides:

"The equal protection of the laws shall not be denied or abridged on account of sex by the State or its units of local government and school districts."

In People v. Ellis (1974), 57 Ill.2d 127, 132, 133, 311 N.E.2d 98, 101, we found this section "was intended to supplement and expand the guaranties of the equal protection provision of the [Federal] Bill of Rights" and that any classification based on sex is a "suspect classification" which must withstand "strict judicial scrutiny" in order to be upheld. The age classifications found in sections 3, 3.1 and 6 of the Marriage Act are obviously based on sex.

It is not argued that there exists, and we do not find, any compelling State interest which justifies treating males and females of the same age differently for the purpose of determining their rights to a marriage license. Accordingly we hold the higher age limitations for males in sections 3, 3.1, and 6 are invalid and that the lesser age limits therein shall apply to both males and females. . . .

Accordingly, the judgment of the circuit court of Champaign County is affirmed.

The opposite conclusion was reached in New York at about the same time.

FRIEDRICH v. KATZ

Supreme Court,
Special Term,
New York County,
Part I,
341 N.Y.S.2d 932
(1973), reversed 34
N.Y.2d 987,
360 N.Y.S.2d 415,
318 N.E.2d 606.

Margaret Mary J. MANGAN, Justice.

Petitioner, an eighteen year old male, brings this special proceeding for an order directing the respondent, the Clerk of the City of New York, to issue him a marriage license without petitioner first obtaining his parents' written consent. He alleges that Domestic Relations Law 15(2) unconstitutionally discriminates against him as a male because there is no comparable provision requiring an eighteen year old female to obtain parental consent to marry.

Domestic Relations Law, Sec. 15(2) provides that if "the man is under twenty-one years of age . . . or . . . the woman is under eighteen years of age . . . then the town or city clerk before he shall issue a (marriage) license shall require the written consent to the marriage from both parents of the minor or minors."

. . . There is no dispute that marriage "is a social relation subject to the State's police power." The immediate issue presented is whether there is an appropriate governmental interest in requiring the petitioner to obtain parental consent to marry while not fixing the same requirement for an eighteen year old female. . . .

Discriminatory classification regarding the marriage of minors existed at common law—"males (could marry) at the age of fourteen and females at twelve." The matter is now regulated by statute, which in most jurisdictions has materially increased the age requirements. Forty of the states and the District of Columbia fix different ages for males and females to marry with parental consent. Twenty-nine of the states have different age requirements for marriage without parental consent. Only nine states allow an eighteen year old to marry without parental consent. In New York the different age requirements for marriage became law in 1907 and have remained the same to date. This discrimination, then is an ancient rule, time-honored, and the public policy of this state and much of the nation.

Paralleling this discrimination both at common law and presently by statute is the primary obligation of a husband or father to support his wife and children. Presumably, interwoven in the latter obligation is the recognition that natural order, taught both by history and reason, designates the male as the provider in the usual marriage relation. That duty, different in recognizable degree than the other mutual duties of marriage, is sufficient reason to require males to be older and generally more suited to their duty before they may independently decide to marry.

The court is not unmindful of the stringent rules applied in some equal protection cases, yet, "the Supreme Court . . . has not yet added sex to the list of suspect classifications. . . . Nor is the court unaware of the current legal thought on the subject of marital age restrictions and the recent legislation granting to eighteen year olds rights formerly limited to those over twenty-one. It is significant, however, that both proposed and accomplished reforms have been by the legislative process expressive of public opinion and policy. Indeed, it may be that the classification here will not survive if the proposed constitutional amendment relative to equal rights for men and women is ratified. Yet, even that law, in its present form, does not appear to create absolute equality between the sexes. "Congress and the State legislatures can take differences between the sexes into account in enacting laws which reasonably promote the health and safety of the people." (U.S. Code, Congressional and Administrative News, April 20, 1972, House Report No. 92-539, p. 836.)

The right to marry is no less important than the state's interest in the stability of marriage and society generally. Marriage is an "institution in the maintenance of which the public is deeply concerned" (Law and the Family, Henry H. Foster, Jr. and Doris Jonas Freed, Vol. I, Revised, Sec. 1:3). Accordingly, in the presence of a legitimate state interest in the marriage relation and the reasonably conceivable fact that the male will be the provider in the marriage relation, there is a rational basis for the state to provide safeguards affecting the marriage of male minors.

The petitioner has not met the "heavy burden (of) overcoming the strong presumption of constitutionality" of Domestic Relations Law, Sec. 15(2). The petition is denied and it is dismissed.

Following Stanton v. Stanton, 421 U.S. 7 (1975), the decision in *Phelps* should prevail.

Exceptions to age and permission provisions are often made in the case of pregnancy. The court may also have wide discretion to waive such rules for other causes.

CHANGE OF NAME   State laws differ widely concerning change of name. Married women generally may retain their unmarried surname, substitute the husband's name, or combine the two. The names of the children may be an issue. Problems with name changes also arise in the case of divorce. MacDougall (1981) reviewed the voluminous literature on this subject.

COMMON LAW MARRIAGES

Common law marriage statutes are now recognized in only thirteen states and the District of Columbia. Common law marriage requires an agreement to be husband and wife. The basis for testing a common law marriage has generally been to determine whether a couple has lived together professedly (or "put themselves forward") as husband and wife. In the past, common law marriage was limited to the poor, who either saw little need for a ceremonial marriage or were unable to afford one. As we have seen, however, many couples with greater financial means now live together in relationships that may be construed as common law marriages. It remains to be seen whether social changes will modify attitudes about such relationships.

Common law marriage depends largely on the nature and duration of the relationship between the man and woman. Was the marriage consummated? Did the couple live together? Did others regard them as husband and wife? In states recognizing common law marriages, less evidence is required to substantiate a marital relationship when attempting to establish the legitimacy of children than in suing for alimony. Similarly, when the deceased party to a common law marriage has left no will, it is more likely that worker's compensation benefits from government funds will be paid than an award from a personal estate. Although Oregon has no provision for common law marriage, a man and woman who have lived together for one year are subsequently entitled to the same worker's compensation rights as if they were legally married.

Attitudes in most states toward common law relationships have tended to be punitive. In non–common law states, a woman typically will not receive worker's compensation benefits if her mate suffers injury at work. A man may escape financial responsibility for child support if his mate and children leave him, because their relationship is not considered a valid marriage. The woman in this case may have only the rights of any unmarried mother.

A non–common law state usually recognizes such a marriage if the relationship is established in a common law state. Also, if a couple begins a relationship in a non–common law state and then moves to one that recognizes such marriages, the marriage may become and remain valid when the couple moves to another non–common law state. In brief, if domicile is acquired in any state that recognizes common law marriages, the marriage will be considered valid in most other states. A contrary finding was made in Kentucky in Vaughn v. Hufnagel, 473 S.W.2d 124 (Ky. 1971), because the couple did not establish themselves adequately as members of the community in Ohio.

VAUGHN v. HUFNAGEL

Court of Appeals of Kentucky, 473 S.W.2d 124 (Ky. 1971).

Edward P. HILL, Jr., Judge.

This is an appeal from an order granting appellees summary judgment on the trial of appellant's appeal to the Jefferson Circuit Court from the order of the Jefferson County Court probating a will of Clarence W. Vaughn and refusing to appoint the appellant administratrix of the estate of Clarence W. Vaughn.

The will of Clarence W. Vaughn, regular on its face, was dated January 23, 1963. It left the estate of deceased to a friend and neighbor who was no relation to him.

On July 16, 1966, appellant and the deceased journeyed to the state of Ohio, where common-law marriages are recognized and registered at a motel as Mr. and Mrs. Clarence W. Vaughn. They were at that time residents of Kentucky.

Appellant says they exchanged mutual vows in marriage without witnesses or solemnization. On the following day, they returned to Kentucky with the appellant regaled in the customary diamond ring and wedding band. Until the death of Clarence, they lived and held themselves out as man and wife.

The chancellor considered only the pleadings and answers to interrogatories addressed to appellant and her attorney. But they established beyond a question that the parties to the so-called attempted marriage in question here were "visitors in Ohio" during the less than 24-hour period of their stay in that state.

We could spend considerable time and space in a prolonged discussion of common-law marriage and related questions which may be interesting and beneficial to students of the law, but preferring to leave those questions to the text writers and others, we simply say that this state does not recognize common-law marriage within the boundary lines of this state, but may recognize one legalized by another state. But it takes more than riding across the Ohio River to make one legal.

In Kennedy v. Damron, Ky., 268 S.W.2d 22, 24 (1954), this court wrote these lines which fit the facts and provide the legal answer to the instant case:

> "Upon the evidence in the case before us, the chancellor was justified in concluding that Mr. Damron and Eula Mae were merely visitors in Ohio, with no abode by which they established themselves as members of the community. It is true they occupied a dwelling for a time, but only in the character of transients, and their holding themselves out as man and wife, in Ohio, was principally as to tradesmen with whom they had casual dealings. They did not become an established part of the community."

. . . It is concluded that the claim of common-law marriage fails. It follows that the judgment denying appellant letters of administration is correct and is affirmed.

All concur.

Clark's (1968: 57–58) defense of common law provisions is of interest to social workers because of its humanitarian implications:

> Common law marriage seems to be an unpopular institution today. It is easy to find criticisms of it, not only in judicial opinions, but in the writings of social scientists. They say that common law marriage encourages fraud and vice, that it debases conventional marriage. But this depends on the position from which one looks at common law marriage. The sociologist who condemns common law marriage seems to assume that a man and woman about to be married will make a conscious choice between a ceremony or common law marriage. Of course, if that is the situation they would be well advised to contract a ceremonial marriage in order to avoid future doubts or disputes. It seems more likely that people drift into common law marriage either because one of the parties persuades the other that they can really be married in this fashion, or because the customs of their social class sanction this kind of union. In any event they will have no contact with the law until one of them dies or sues for divorce, at which point the real issues will be financial or property issues. If the courts insist

upon objective evidence that the parties have lived openly as man and wife for a substantial period, as most courts do, there is no greater danger of fraud or imposition on the court here than in the trial of any other question of fact. The argument that common law marriage encourages fraud rests on the false premise that the courts, using the established legal rules, will be unable to separate fraudulent from legitimate claims of marriage.

The assertion that common law marriage encourages vice is also fallacious, since common law marriage has precisely the opposite effect. Recognizing non-ceremonial unions gives them status and to that extent reduces vice. Parties who pretend that a meretricious relationship is a common law marriage are usually found out, which certainly does not encourage such relationships.

As for debasing conventional marriage, there is no evidence that common law marriage has this effect. Quite the contrary. We debase the entire institution of marriage when we place conclusive significance on the occurrence of a ceremony. When a woman has performed the obligations of a wife for thirty-five years and then is brutally deprived of all the financial benefits of marriage on the sole ground that the relationship was not signalized by some sort of a ceremony, this debases marriage. It is far better in such cases to hold that the parties were married.

In short, most of the objections to common law marriage mistake its purpose. As a doctrine it has little or no effect at the outset of the parties' relationship. It comes into play after that relationship has existed for some time, for the purpose of vindicating the parties' marital expectations. There are other legal devices having the same purpose, but common law marriage plays an important part. Without it there would be more injustice and suffering in the world than there is with it. This is particularly true among those social and economic classes who have not accepted middle class standards of marriage. Certainly American marriage law should tolerate this much cultural diversity.

PROXY MARRIAGES

Section 206(b) of the Uniform Marriage and Divorce Act (9A U.L.A. 107 [1973]), provides for proxy marriages:

> If a party to a marriage is unable to be present at the solemnization he may authorize in writing a third person to act as his proxy. If the person solemnizing the marriage is satisfied that the absent party is unable to be present and has consented to the marriage, he may solemnize the marriage by proxy. If he is not satisfied, the parties may petition the [——] court for an order permitting the marriage to be solemnized by proxy.

Social workers may occasionally have to help arrange proxy marriages when a man and woman live apart but desire to marry because of pregnancy. Proxy marriages are most common in time of war.

Proxy marriages are invalid in states that require the presence of both parties when obtaining the marriage license or at the wedding ceremony. A few states have held proxy marriages valid as common law but not as ceremonial marriages, an interpretation based on evidence of previous cohabitation.

BIGAMY AND SUCCESSIVE MARRIAGES

In Western cultures a person may have only one spouse at any one time. Any subsequent marriage is **null and void** if either party is undivorced and has a living spouse. Not only that, but bigamy is a felony. Bigamy most commonly results from defects in divorces. However, suits contesting the validity of a second marriage are often lost because the second marriage is presumed to be valid. Parker v. American Lumber Corp., 56 S.E.2d 214 (Va. 1949), provides an illustration:

The decided weight of authority, and we think the correct view, is that where two marriages of the same person are shown, the second marriage is presumed to be valid; that such presumption is stronger than and overcomes the presumption of the continuance of the first marriage, so that a person who attacks a second marriage has the burden of producing evidence of its invalidity. Where both parties to the first marriage are shown to be living at the time of the second marriage, it is presumed in favor of the second marriage that the first was dissolved by divorce. These presumptions arise, it is said, because the law presumes morality and legitimacy, not immorality and bastardy. [Citations omitted]

In Reynolds v. United States, 98 U.S. 145 (1878), the Supreme Court sustained a finding of bigamy against a Mormon:

We think it may safely be said there never has been a time in any State of the Union when polygamy has not been an offence against society, cognizable by the civil courts and punishable with more or less severity. In the face of all this evidence, it is impossible to believe that the constitutional guaranty of religious freedom was intended to prohibit legislation in respect to this most important feature of social life. Marriage, while from its very nature a sacred obligation, is nevertheless, in most civilized nations, a civil contract, and usually regulated by law. Upon it society may be said to be built, and out of its fruits spring social relations and social obligations and duties, with which government is necessarily required to deal. In fact, according as monogamous or polygamous marriages are allowed, do we find the principles on which the government of the people, to a greater or less extent, rest. Professor Lieber says, polygamy leads to the patriarchal principle, and which, when applied to large communities, fetters the people in stationary despotism, while that principle cannot long exist in connection with monogamy. Chancellor Kent observes that this remark is equally striking and profound. An exceptional colony of polygamists under an exceptional leadership may sometimes exist for a time without appearing to disturb the social condition of the people who surround it; but there cannot be a doubt that, unless restricted by some form of constitution, it is within the legitimate scope of the power of every civil government to determine whether polygamy or monogamy shall be the law of social life under its dominion. . . .

The only question which remains is, whether those who make polygamy a part of their religion are excepted from the operation of the statute. If they are, then those who do not make polygamy a part of their religious belief may be found guilty and punished, while those who do, must be acquitted and go free. This would be introducing a new element into criminal law. Laws are made for the government of actions, and while they cannot interfere with mere religious belief and opinions, they may with practices. Suppose one believed that human sacrifices were a necessary part of religious worship, would it be seriously contended that the civil government under which he lived could not interfere to prevent a sacrifice? Or if a wife religiously believed it was her duty to burn herself upon the funeral pile of her dead husband, would it be beyond the power of the civil government to prevent her carrying her belief into practice?

With the exception of Mormons of an earlier era, most bigamous Americans have been involved in successive marriages and have not lived with multiple spouses at the same time.

COMMUNAL LIVING

The development of communes provides an example of attacks on monogamy as the sole mandated form of family life. Many non-Western societies make legal provisions for polygamy. A Supreme Court case, Village of Belle Terre v. Boraas,

416 U.S. 1 (1974), has implications for communes because it upheld an ordinance limiting the concept of a "single household unit" to two people:

VILLAGE OF BELLE TERRE v. BORAAS

Supreme Court of the United States, 1974. 416 U.S. 1 (1974).

Mr. Justice DOUGLAS delivered the opinion of the Court.

Belle Terre is a village on Long Island's north shore of about 220 homes inhabited by 700 people. Its total land area is less than one square mile. It has restricted land use to one-family dwellings excluding lodging houses, boarding houses, fraternity houses, or multiple-dwelling houses. The word "family" as used in the ordinance means, "[o]ne or more persons related by blood, adoption, or marriage, living and cooking together as a single housekeeping unit, exclusive of household servants. A number of persons but not exceeding two (2) living and cooking together as a single house-keeping unit though not related by blood, adoption, or marriage shall be deemed to constitute a family."

Appellees, the Dickmans, are owners of a house in the village and leased it in December 1971 for a term of 18 months to Michael Truman. Later Bruce Boraas became a co-lessee. Then Anne Parish moved into the house along with three others. These six are students at nearby State University at Stony Brook and none is related to the other by blood, adoption, or marriage. When the village served the Dickmans with an "Order to Remedy Violations" of the ordinance, the owners plus three tenants thereupon brought this action under 42 U.S.C.A. § 1983 for an injunction declaring the ordinance unconstitutional. . . .

The present ordinance is challenged on several grounds: that it interferes with a person's right to travel; that it interferes with the right to migrate to and settle within a State; that it bars people who are uncongenial to the present residents; that it expresses the social preferences of the residents for groups that will be congenial to them; that social homogeneity is not a legitimate interest of government; that the restriction of those whom the neighbors do not like trenches on the newcomers' rights of privacy; that it is of no rightful concern to villagers whether the residents are married or unmarried; that the ordinance is antithetical to the Nation's experience, ideology, and self-perception as an open, egalitarian, and integrated society.

We find none of these reasons in the record before us. It is not aimed at transients. It involves no procedural disparity inflicted on some but not on others such as was presented by *Griffin v. Illinois*. It involves no "fundamental" right guaranteed by the Constitution, such as voting; the right of association; the right of access to the courts; or any rights of privacy. We deal with economic and social legislation where legislatures have historically drawn lines which we respect against the charge of violation of the Equal Protection Clause if the law be "'reasonable, not arbitrary'" (quoting *F.S. Royster Guano Co. v. Virginia*) and bears "a rational relationship to a [permissible] state objective." *Reed v. Reed* [p. 278.] [Citations omitted.]

It is said, however, that if two unmarried people can constitute a "family," there is no reason why three or four may not. But every line drawn by a legislature leaves some out that might well have been included. That exercise of discretion, however, is a legislative, not a judicial, function.

It is said that the Belle Terre ordinance reeks with an animosity to unmarried couples who live together. There is no evidence to support it; and the provision of the ordinance bringing within the definition of a "family" two unmarried people belies the charge.

The ordinance places no ban on other forms of association, for a "family" may, so far as the ordinance is concerned, entertain whomever it likes.

The regimes of boarding houses, fraternity houses, and the like present urban problems. More people occupy a given space; more cars rather continuously pass by; more cars are parked; noise travels with crowds.

A quiet place where yards are wide, people few, and motor vehicles restricted are legitimate guidelines in a land-use project addressed to family needs. This goal is a permissible one within *Berman v. Parker*, supra. The police power is not confined to elimination of filth, stench, and unhealthy places. It is ample to lay out zones where family values, youth values, and the blessings of quiet seclusion and clean air make the area a sanctuary for people.

Mr. Justice MARSHALL, dissenting.

This case draws into question the constitutionality of a zoning ordinance of the incorporated village of Belle Terre, New York, which prohibits groups of more than two unrelated persons, as distinguished from groups consisting of any number of persons related by blood, adoption or marriage, from occupying a residence within the confines of the township. Lessor-appellees, the two owners of a Belle Terre residence, and three unrelated student tenants challenged the ordinance on the ground that it establishes a classification between households of related and unrelated individuals, which deprives them of equal protection of the laws. In my view, the disputed classification burdens the students' fundamental rights of association and privacy guaranteed by the First and Fourteenth Amendments. Because the application of strict equal protection scrutiny is therefore required, I am at odds with my Brethren's conclusion that the ordinance may be sustained on a showing that it bears a rational relationship to the accomplishment of legitimate governmental objectives. . . .

The freedom of association is often inextricably entwined with the constitutionally guaranteed right of privacy. The right to "establish a home" is an essential part of the liberty guaranteed by the Fourteenth Amendment. [Citations omitted]. The choice of household companions—of whether a person's "intellectual and emotional needs" are best met by living with family, friends, professional associates or others—involves deeply personal considerations as to the kind and quality of intimate relationships within the home. That decision surely falls within the ambit of the right to privacy protected by the Constitution. [Citations omitted].

The instant ordinance discriminates on the basis of just such a personal lifestyle choice as to household companions. It permits any number of persons related by blood or marriage, be it two or twenty, to live in a single household, but it limits to two the number of unrelated persons bound by profession, love, friendship, religious or political affiliation, or mere economics who can occupy a single home. Belle Terre imposes upon those who deviate from the community norm in their choice of living companions significantly greater restrictions than are applied to residential groups who are related by blood or marriage, and compose the established order within the community. The town has, in effect, acted to fence out those individuals whose choice of lifestyle differs from that of its current residents.

HOMOSEXUAL
MARRIAGE

The classic case attempting to gain approval for homosexual marriage is Baker v. Nelson, 191 N.W.2d 185 (Minn. 1971).

BAKER v.
NELSON

Supreme Court of
Minnesota,
191 N.W.2d 185
(Minn. 1971).

PETERSON, Justice.

Petitioners, Richard John Baker and James Michael McConnell, both adult male persons, made application to respondent, Gerald R. Nelson, clerk of Hennepin County District Court, for a marriage license, pursuant to Minn.St. 517.08. Respondent declined to issue the license on the sole ground that petitioners were of the same sex, it being undisputed that there were otherwise no statutory impediments to a heterosexual marriage by either petitioner.

The trial court, quashing an alternative writ of mandamus, ruled that respondent was not required to issue a marriage license to petitioners and specifically directed that a marriage license not be issued to them. This appeal is from those orders. We affirm.

1. Petitioners contend, first, that the absence of an express statutory prohibition against same-sex marriages evinces a legislative intent to authorize such marriages. We think, however, that a sensible reading of the statute discloses a contrary intent.

Minn.St. c. 517, which governs "marriage," employs that term as one of common usage, meaning the state of union between persons of the opposite sex. It is unrealistic to think that the original draftsmen of our marriage statutes, which date from territorial days, would have used the term in any different sense. The term is of contemporary significance as well, for the present statute is replete with words of heterosexual import such as "husband and wife" and "bride and groom" (the latter words inserted by L.1969, c. 1145, § 3).

We hold, therefore, that Minn.St. c. 517 does not authorize marriage between persons of the same sex and that such marriages are accordingly prohibited.

2. Petitioners contend, second, that Minn.St. c. 517, so interpreted, is unconstitutional. There is a dual aspect to this contention: The prohibition of a same-sex marriage denies petitioners a fundamental right guaranteed by the Ninth Amendment to the United States Constitution, arguably made applicable to the states by the Fourteenth Amendment, and petitioners are deprived of liberty and property without due process and are denied the equal protection of the laws, both guaranteed by the Fourteenth Amendment.

These constitutional challenges have in common the assertion that the right to marry without regard to the sex of the parties is a fundamental right of all persons and that restricting marriage to only couples of the opposite sex is irrational and invidiously discriminatory. We are not independently persuaded by these contentions and do not find support for them in any decisions of the United States Supreme Court.

The institution of marriage as a union of man and woman, uniquely involving the procreation and rearing of children within a family, is as old as the book of Genesis. . . . This historic institution manifestly is more deeply founded than the asserted contemporary concept of marriage and societal interests for which petitioners contend. The due process clause of the Fourteenth Amendment is not a charter for restructuring it by judicial legislation.

Griswold v. Connecticut, . . . upon which petitioners rely, does not support a contrary conclusion. . . . The basic premise of that decision, however, was that the state, having authorized marriage, was without power to intrude upon the right of privacy inherent in the marital relationship. . . . In a separate opinion for three justices, Mr. Justice Goldberg similarly abhorred this state disruption of "the traditional relation of the family—a relation as old and as fundamental as our entire civilization." 381 U.S. 496, 85 S.Ct. 1688, 14 L.Ed.2d 522.

The equal protection clause of the Fourteenth Amendment, like the due process clause, is not offended by the state's classification of persons authorized to marry. There is no irrational or invidious discrimination. Petitioners note that the state does not impose upon heterosexual married couples a condition that they have a proved capacity or declared willingness to procreate, posing a rhetorical demand that this court must read such condition into the statute if same-sex marriages are to be prohibited. Even assuming that such a condition would be neither unrealistic nor offensive under the Griswold rationale, the classification is no more than theoretically imperfect. We are reminded, however, that "abstract symmetry" is not demanded by the Fourteenth Amendment.

Loving v. Virginia, 388 U.S. 1 (1967), upon which petitioners additionally rely, does not militate against this conclusion. . . . Loving does indicate that not all state restrictions upon the right to marry are beyond reach of the Fourteenth Amendment. But in commonsense and in a constitutional sense, there is a clear distinction between a marital restriction based merely upon race and one based upon the fundamental difference in sex.

We hold, therefore, that Minn.St. c. 517 does not offend the First, Eighth, Ninth, or Fourteenth Amendments to the United States Constitution.

Affirmed.

The principals finally formalized their relationship through adoption. Later they tried unsuccessfully to adopt a child.

A New York state court in 1984 refused to permit a homosexual couple to use adoption as a means to give recognition to their relationship, holding that such a procedure was contrary to the purpose of adoption.

LIVING TOGETHER WITHOUT MARRIAGE

Although the philosophy on which cohabitation without marriage is based may differ greatly from that of traditional common law unions, common law provisions do provide some protection for these couples in those states where they apply. Since so few states provide common law statutes, the legal rights of couples living together without marriage should be well understood. While most young people do not seriously consider the possibility of a partner's death, in the event this should occur the survivor may encounter many problems in claiming ownership of joint possessions or custody of children. Unless couples make wills to explicitly clarify these issues, both material possessions and custody of children may pass to the parents of the deceased rather than to the surviving partner.

A much publicized case, Marvin v. Marvin, 557 P. 2d 106 (Cal. 1976), involved three decisions. First, the California Supreme Court held that a woman could enforce an oral contract under which she was entitled to half the property acquired as well as to support payments. The opinion held that the court should enforce express contracts between nonmarried partners except when the contract is explicitly founded on the consideration of meretricious sexual services, that is, prostitution:

> We base our opinion on the principle that adults who voluntarily live together and engage in sexual relations are nonetheless as competent as any other persons to contract respecting their earnings and property rights. Of course, they cannot lawfully contract to pay for the performance of sexual services, for such a contract is, in essence, an agreement for prostitution and unlawful for that reason. But they may agree to pool their earnings and to hold all property acquired during the relationship in accord with the law governing community property; conversely they may agree that each partner's earnings and the property acquired from those earnings remains the separate property of the earning partner. So long as the agreement does not rest upon illicit meretricious consideration, the parties may order their economic affairs as they choose, and no policy precludes the courts from enforcing such agreements.
>
> In the present instance, plaintiff alleges that the parties agreed to pool their earnings, that they contracted to share equally in all property acquired, and that defendant agreed to support plaintiff. The terms of the contract as alleged do not rest upon any unlawful consideration. We therefore conclude that the complaint furnishes a suitable basis upon which the trial court can render declaratory relief.

The court recognizes the precedence and general acceptance of nonmarriage and of living together as a means to test out the basis of possible marriage:

> We believe that the prevalence of nonmarital relationships in modern society and the social acceptance of them, marks this as a time when our courts should by no means apply the doctrine of the unlawfulness of the so-called meretricious relationship to the instant case. As we have explained, the nonenforceability of agreements expressly providing for meretricious conduct rested upon the fact that such conduct, as the word suggests, pertained to and encompassed prostitution. To equate the nonmarital relationship of today to such a subject matter is to do violence to an accepted and wholly different practice.
>
> We are aware that many young couples live together without the solemnization of marriage, in order to make sure that they can successfully later undertake marriage. This trial period, preliminary to marriage, serves as some assurance that the marriage will not subsequently end in dissolution to the harm of both parties. We are aware, as we have stated, of the pervasiveness of nonmarital relationships in other situations.
>
> The mores of the society have indeed changed so radically in regard to cohabitation that we cannot impose a standard based on alleged moral considerations that have apparently been so widely abandoned by so many. Lest we be misunderstood, however, we take this occasion to point out that the structure of society itself largely depends upon the institution of marriage, and nothing we have said in this opinion should be taken to derogate from that institution. The joining of the man and woman in marriage is at once the most socially productive and individually fulfilling relationship that one can enjoy in the course of a lifetime.

Following this ruling, the superior court made a monetary award to Michelle Marvin:

The court is aware that Footnote 25, *Marvin v. Marvin*, supra, p. 684, urges the trial court to employ whatever equitable remedy may be proper under the circumstances. The court is also aware of the recent resort of plaintiff to unemployment insurance benefits to support herself and of the fact that a return of plaintiff to a career as a singer is doubtful. Additionally, the court knows that the market value of defendant's property at time of separation exceed $1,000.00.

In view of these circumstances, the court in equity awards plaintiff $104,000 for rehabilitation purposes so that she may have the economic means to re-educate herself and to learn new, employable skills or to refurbish those utilized, for example, during her most recent employment and so that she may return from her status as companion of a motion picture star to a separate, independent but perhaps more prosaic existence. [Citations omitted.]

A California appeals court sustained Lee Marvin's appeal, 176 Cal. Rptr. 555 (1981), and held that a rehabilitation award was not a part of the pleadings to the court on Michelle's behalf and that no basis existed in equity or in law for the award. Thus Michelle Marvin ultimately lost the case. It did not significantly advance the claim of a cohabitant for so-called palimony.

DOMESTIC VIOLENCE

Spouse abuse can be treated as a topic within marriage or as a cause of divorce, depending on the outcomes. The last decade has seen increasing attention to wife abuse with the establishment of shelters for women and children who have been the victims of domestic violence. Laws generally require assault charges when criminal actions are desired. Cases are complicated by ambivalence and self-blame on the part of the abused person. The social worker is a key resource in such cases. The few police departments that employ social workers utilize them to counsel the principals in domestic violence.

A particularly interesting question concerns rape of a spouse by the husband. The women's movement stresses remedying statutes that prohibit such suits. An unpublished Oregon case, *Rideout v. Rideout*, which found the husband innocent of spousal rape, received national publicity and apparently motivated other states to change their laws to provide better protection of spouses who were raped.

By 1985, seventeen states had held that marital rape was no longer within the law. Nine states still give husbands complete immunity from marital rape prosecutions.

ANNULMENT

Historically, annulment was the prerogative of ecclesiastical courts, and only gradually did it become part of secular court procedure. Annulment has been replaced in large degree by divorce. Some people who want an ecclesiastical annulment feel that a civil annulment will strengthen their case with the church. The Uniform Marriage and Divorce Act deals with annulment in Section 208, 9A U.L.A. 109 (1982):

Section 208. Declaration of Invalidity.

(a) The [————] court shall enter its decree declaring the invalidity of a marriage entered into under the following circumstances:

(1) a party lacked capacity to consent to the marriage at the time the marriage was solemnized, either because of mental incapacity or infirmity or because of the influence of alcohol, drugs, or other incapacitating substances, or a party was induced to enter into a marriage by force or duress, or by fraud involving the essentials of marriage;

(2)   a party lacks the physical capacity to consummate the marriage by sexual intercourse, and at the time the marriage was solemnized the other party did not know of the incapacity.

(3)   a party [was under the age of 16 years and did not have the consent of his parents or guardian and judicial approval or] was aged 16 or 17 years and did not have the consent of his parents or guardian or judicial approval; or

(4)   the marriage is prohibited.

(b) A declaration of invalidity under subsection (a)(1) through (3) may be sought by any of the following persons and must be commenced within the times specified, but in no event may a declaration of invalidity be sought after the death of either party to the marriage:

(1)   for a reason set forth in subsection (a)(1), by either party or by the legal representative of the party who lacked capacity to consent, no later than 90 days after the petitioner obtained knowledge of the described condition;

(2)   for the reason set forth in subsection (a)(2), by either party, no later than one year after the petitioner obtained knowledge of the described condition;

(3)   for the reason set forth in subsection (a)(3), by the underaged party, his parent or guardian, prior to the time the underaged party reaches the age at which he could have married without satisfying the omitted requirement.

Alternative A
   [(c) A declaration of invalidity for the reason set forth in subsection (a)(4) may be sought by either party, the legal spouse in case of a bigamous marriage, the [appropriate state official], or a child of either party, at any time prior to the death of one of the parties.]

Alternative B
   [(c) A declaration of invalidity for the reason set forth in subsection (a)(4) may be sought by either party, the legal spouse in case of a bigamous marriage, the [appropriate state official] or a child of either party, at any time, not to exceed 5 years following the death of either party.]

   (d) Children born of a marriage declared invalid are legitimate.

   (e) Unless the court finds, after a consideration of all relevant circumstances, including the effect of a retroactive decree on third parties, that the interests of justice would be served by making the decree not retroactive, it shall declare the marriage invalid as of the date of the marriage. The provisions of this Act relating to property rights of the spouses, maintenance, support, and custody of children on dissolution of marriage are applicable to non-retroactive decrees of invalidity.

Nature and Jurisdiction   Annulment indicates that no valid marriage occurred due to an *impediment* existing at the time of the ceremony. Impediments range from impotence to having a spouse already. While annulment and divorce may seem quite different inasmuch as divorce is used to terminate a valid existing marriage, the two often overlap in their treatment of alimony and for child support orders. Confusion would be eliminated if divorce and annulment statutes were consistent. Previously, when the grounds for divorce in New York were limited to adultery, people sought annulment as a means to terminate a marriage. On liberalization of New York divorce laws, annulment actions became rare, and nationally they now account for less than 3 percent of all marital dissolutions.

   Annulment that is freely available makes it possible to clarify promptly the status of doubtful marriages. Generally, jurisdiction for annulment is determined by the couple's domicile, although some states allow the suit to be filed where the marriage celebration took place. In some instances annulment is unnecessarily complicated by the requirement of *personal* rather than *constructive* service—delivery of written notice of the action to the person named therein, rather than mailing or publishing the notice. The defendant whose whereabouts are unknown cannot possibly be served personally. Requirements for both annulment and divorce should include the option of mailing or publishing the notice rather than only personal service.

For proof in annulment actions, clear and convincing evidence rather than a mere preponderance of the evidence is generally required. Some states also require corroboration of the evidence presented by the plaintiff.

Bases for Annulment   Some bases for annulment imply that the marriage is *void*. Others imply that it is *voidable* and thereby require an inquiry into any previously existing imperfection sufficient to declare the marriage void. Defenses to annulment include allegations that the plaintiff was aware of the alleged defect prior to entry into the marriage. In addition, states frequently provide statutes of limitation for annulment suits. Another defense involves **res judicata**, by which a marriage that has already been substantiated by the courts cannot later be challenged by anyone; the first action stands.

Forbidden Degrees of Relationship.   We have seen that provisions governing marriage of persons within a family differ from state to state. Marriages involving persons with certain nuclear family relationships are clearly void, for example, marriages between siblings or parents and children. There is similar agreement on the invalidity of marriage between an aunt and a nephew or an uncle and a niece, but states differ on whether first cousins may marry. The current trend is to allow it. Stepchildren and adopted children cannot usually marry each other by virtue of their having grown up together as siblings in the same family. One purpose of the Uniform Marriage Evasion Act was to prevent marriages that violate state laws and are therefore subject to annulment. The law may also deny survivor's benefits to a person who went to another state to marry a first cousin. Legal attacks on long-standing marriages are particularly troublesome.

Age Requirements.   A marriage may be challenged if the principals are under age. Two requirements are relevant: the minimum age for marriage and parental consent. Provisions for marriage with consent have differed from age twelve for females and fourteen for males in Massachusetts to age eighteen for females and twenty-one for males in California. Pregnancy is often a basis for waiving age requirements, although a completely valid marriage may not necessarily result. Such unions may be marriages for a limited purpose, where the only intent is to give the child a name.

If a couple marries in violation of age standards, the underage party may file for annulment. Some states also permit the parent to bring such action. Underage marriages should be considered *voidable* rather than *void* and should no longer be subject to challenge once the underage person reaches the age of consent. Thereafter, that partner should be precluded from filing for annulment because the person is no longer under age and therefore cannot use nonage as a defense. *Laches* (i.e., delay) is also a defense. The longer a couple has maintained a marital relationship, the stronger the assumption of validity of the marriage. This problem is clarified by statutes of limitations, whereby annulment actions must be filed within a specified time after the marriage.

Health Problems. Many states require proof that both parties are free from venereal disease as a condition for issuing the marriage license. Absence of such proof may be a ground for annulment. This requirement may be waived in the case of pregnancy. Although several states consider epilepsy a disqualification for marriage, public education has led to a relaxation of the sanction.

Impotence. The inability to engage successfully in sexual intercourse provides a ground for annulment, while sterility or inability to have children do not. Although impotence makes a marriage voidable, annulment depends on proof that the plaintiff was unaware of the condition at the time of the marriage.

Miscegenation. Marriage between the races was illegal in a number of states until the U.S. Supreme Court decision in Loving v. Commonwealth of Virginia, 388 U.S. 1 (1967). At one time as many as thirty states prohibited interracial marriage. The *Loving* decision found such statutes to be violations of both the equal protection clause and the due process clause of the Fourteenth Amendment. In writing the unanimous decision of the Court, Justice Earl Warren said in part:

> There can be no doubt that restricting the freedom to marry solely because of racial classifications violates the central meaning of the Equal Protection Clause. . . . These statutes also deprive the Lovings of liberty without due process of law in violation of the Due Process Clause of the Fourteenth Amendment. The freedom to marry has long been recognized as one of the vital personal rights essential to the orderly pursuit of happiness of free men. (388 U.S. at 12)

States that have had such laws have often left them on the books even though they have been invalidated by the U.S. Supreme Court.

Mental Incompetence. Statutes governing annulment provide much less protection on the issue of mental incompetence than those regulating divorce. The key concept in both is a person's capacity to consent consciously to the marriage contract. Standards defining such capacity differ widely from state to state. Marriages of legally incompetent persons may be either void or voidable, depending on statutory provisions. In some states only the incompetent party can sue for annulment based on the requirement of mental competence for entry into the marriage contract. Other states allow either spouse to bring legal action.

Duress. If the plaintiff was unable to act as a free agent at the time of the marriage, the use of force constitutes grounds for annulment. For example, threats of a suit for seduction or bastardy are sometimes used to bring about a marriage. Although there may be some hope for a lasting marriage under such circumstances, the frequent result is that once a child conceived out of wedlock is given a name the parents terminate their relationship.

Fraud. In cases of alleged fraud, pregnancy may be involved. The plaintiff may contract marriage with a woman who is pregnant by another man; or the woman may either conceal pregnancy or insist that the plaintiff is the father. Less often the wife may claim to be pregnant when she is not. Fraud may also result from other physical misrepresentations, such as concealment of venereal disease, impotence, homosexuality, drug addiction, or alcoholism. Misrepresentation of religion can also be considered fraud, as in Bilowit v. Dolitsky, 304 A.2d 774 (N.J. Super. 1973).

Misrepresentation of Intent.   If the defendant has no intention of consummating the marriage or having children, that may be a basis for annulment.

Marriage for a Limited Purpose.   Couples who want to marry to give a baby a name but who do not intend to live together may not be able to obtain an annulment. See Schibi v. Schibi, 69 A.2d 831 (Conn. 1949). Marriage for a limited purpose has also commonly been entered into for purposes of immigration. A foreign national can more easily gain U.S. citizenship by marrying an American. Immigration authorities may deport persons who use sham marriage for this type of subterfuge (United States v. Diogo, 320 F.2d 898 [2d Cir. 1963]).

Special Problems

The *status of children* in marriages terminated by annulment is complicated by legitimacy statutes. In virtually all states, children of an annulled marriage are considered legitimate. If this were not so, divorce would be the better alternative for such couples. The best "remedy" for illegitimacy is found in the statutes of the fourteen states that have adopted the Uniform Parentage Act, which considers every child to be the legitimate offspring of his or her natural parents. The states are Alabama, California, Colorado, Delaware, Hawaii, Illinois, Minnesota, Montana, Nevada, New Jersey, North Dakota, Rhode Island, Washington, and Wyoming.

The question of *alimony* in annulment is also controversial. If no marriage existed, it was traditionally considered inconsistent to grant alimony. Nevertheless, temporary alimony is frequently awarded for the protection of the female partner, and permanent alimony is becoming more common. Arguments in favor of alimony in annulment are the same as in a divorce action.

A classic problem may result when a couple gets a divorce, the wife receives alimony and the husband finds he cannot afford to remarry and still pay. His first wife remarries, and he remarries too, but for some reason the first wife's marriage is annulled. Do the alimony payments have to be resumed? The legal question is whether annulment and divorce decrees should be binding on third parties in accordance with *res judicata*. The third party in this instance is the first husband. The validity of the second marriage is presumed. Otherwise the husband might never remarry because of fear that he would be required to resume the obligation of alimony. Gaines v. Jacobsen, 124 N.E.2d 290 (N.Y. 1954), Sefton v. Sefton, 291 P.2d 439 (Cal. 1955), and McConkey v. McConkey, 215 S.E.2d 640 (Va. 1975), below, have dealt with the question with similar results.

McCONKEY v. McCONKEY

Supreme Court of Virginia,
215 S.E.2d 640
(Va. 1975).

COCHRAN, Justice.

The question for our determination in this appeal is whether a wife, upon annulment of a voidable second marriage, is entitled to reinstatement of the alimony awarded her when she was divorced from her first husband.

Clara Johnson McConkey and Edward Cecil McConkey, her husband, were divorced by final decree entered September 23, 1968, by the trial court, which ordered Edward to pay Clara the sum of $200 per month as alimony. On October 16, 1971, Clara married Calvin D. Sykes. On November 5, 1971, Clara filed her bill of complaint against Sykes in the Circuit Court of the City of Norfolk seeking in the alternative an annulment of their marriage on the ground of Syke's fraud or a divorce on the ground of his desertion. By final decree entered January 3, 1973, the marriage was annulled and declared to be "null, void and of no effect.". . . .

Clara contends that, as her second marriage was declared void retrospectively, she should be restored to the same position and standing she enjoyed before she went through the second marriage ceremony. We do not agree.

Section 20-110 of the Code of 1950, as amended, provides: "If any person to whom alimony has been awarded shall thereafter marry, such alimony shall cease as of the date of such marriage.". . .

It has been generally held that annulment of a voidable second marriage does not entitle the wife to reinstatement of alimony payments from her first husband, where there is a statute providing that alimony shall terminate upon the recipient's remarriage. . . . Other jurisdictions have followed this rule even in the absence of such a statute. . . . and in New York, where there is now a statute authorizing the court, in annulment proceedings, to order the payment of alimony, it is held, that the wife is no longer entitled to reinstate alimony upon annulment of a voidable marriage. . . .

We hold that where the divorced wife enters into a subsequent voidable marriage she thereby forfeits her right to alimony from her former husband. The husband has a right to assume the validity of the second marriage and to arrange his affairs accordingly. When his former wife voluntarily accepts the risk of a subsequent marriage, he should not be held accountable for her gullibility, mistake or misfortune. A voidable marriage may not be annulled for years. Indeed, in the present case the decree of annulment was entered more than a year after the marriage ceremony. To require the former husband to proceed during this period at his peril in making financial commitments that could be suddenly disrupted, through no fault of his, would be to penalize him for events beyond his control. We decline to do so.

The trial court did not err in denying Clara's petition and the judgment order is affirmed.

When public funds are used for the wife's support, such as Social Security or worker's compensation benefits, annulments have usually been made retroactive and payments resumed. This solution does not represent a hardship for an individual, as would the requirement that a first husband resume payment. Folsom v. Pearsall, 245 F.2d 562 (9th Cir. 1957), for example, resulted in the conclusion that, since annulment in California confirmed that no valid marriage existed, payments for Social Security benefits should be reinstated. However, when the spouse had the chance to claim alimony, Social Security benefits were denied in Nott v. Flemming, 272 F.2d 380 (2d Cir. 1959).

We believe that the congressional purpose in terminating a widow's eligibility for Social Security benefits upon her remarriage is reasonably clear. A widow of a wage earner is made eligible for benefits in order that she may be assured of the continuance of that minimal level of support which the Social Security system is designed to provide; but by the act of remarriage she elects to accept the financial support of her second husband and Congress apparently concluded that she should not be entitled thereafter to supplemental support from the Social Security Fund. Thus reference to state law is necessary, but only for the narrow purpose of determining whether the widow has entered into a relationship that will entitle her under state law to support from her second husband. It is clear that in New York a female participant in a ceremonial marriage is entitled to support from her ostensible husband not only during the official existence of the marriage but also after its formal dissolution. Under section 1140-a of the New York Civil Practice Act (enacted Sept. 1, 1940) the court awarding an annulment decree may affix such directions for support "as justice requires." This provision has been authoritatively construed to permit even the "guilty" party to receive alimony. Johnson v. Johnson, 68 N.E.2d 499 (1946). As the district court pointed out below, it is still possible for Mrs. Nott by petition to the New York courts to obtain alimony from Louis Klein.

PROPERTY RIGHTS IN MARRIAGE

If one wishes to have an egalitarian marriage, the principle of community property achieves this goal. It is especially advantageous to the rights of the woman who chooses full-time homemaking rather than employment. Eight states have community property laws: Arizona, California, Idaho, Louisiana, Nevada, New Mexico, Texas, and Washington. The others follow a separate, "common law" system. Weitzman (1981: 28–29) contrasts the two systems:

> In the separate property jurisdictions, a spouse retains all the property he or she brought into the marriage, and all the property he or she earns or inherits during the course of the marriage. The other spouse has no legal right or interest in his or her partner's income or separate property. Since each is the sole owner of his or her earnings, each has also the sole right to contract with regard to those earnings, to obtain credit based on them, and to manage and control them. Thus, in a separate property system a wife who is a full-time homemaker has no right to her husband's income—or to any of the property he acquires; they are his alone. Her sole economic right is to be supported by her husband.
>
> In the eight community property states, each spouse retains separately all the property he or she had before marriage, and any property inherited during marriage. Once married, however, the earnings of each party, together with all other uninherited property acquired during the marriage, become "community property." Each spouse has one-half interest in this community property—and thus in any property or income the other spouse earns during the marriage. In some states the earnings produced by separate property are also community property.

Community property systems do not deal adequately with career assets—the value of an education or a medical practice or pension benefits that have been accrued by the spouses during the term of the marriage. These assets are figuring increasingly in current divorces, although a U.S. Supreme Court decision has denied the former spouse a financial interest in railroad and military benefits provided under federal regulations that were held to prohibit such interests (Hisquierdo v. Hisquierdo, 439 U.S. 572 [1979]), and (McCarty v. McCarty, 453 U.S. 210 [1981]).

MARRIAGE CONTRACTS

Couples often try to clarify their own values and reach an understanding through detailed discussions before marriage. One example of an early written agreement is given in Exhibit 10.2. While this contract deals mainly with emotional elements, other contracts are oriented toward fiscal assets. A special effort is made in the contract in Exhibit 10.2 to deal with issues that arose in the premarital phase of the couple's relationship.

In the preceding sample contract, many of the factual statements do not specify contractual obligations but merely state facts. The validity of such contracts depends on the conditions under which they are drawn and their contents. Often they are not properly witnessed. The preceding example apparently was not. Provisions in Article IV, for example, may also be held invalid because they may be considered

EXHIBIT 10.2
EXAMPLE OF A MARRIAGE CONTRACT

MEMORANDUM OF UNDERSTANDING AND INTENT made this twenty-eighth day of July, 1972, between Donald Brown, residing at 1142 Damon Avenue, City of Chicago, Cook County and State of Illinois, herein called Donald and Ina Jones, residing at 1602 North State Parkway, City of Chicago, Cook County, and State of Illinois, herein called Ina.

WHEREAS the parties about to marry desire to make full and fair disclosures to each other of significant facts and circumstances concerning their lives; and

WHEREAS the parties desire to make full and fair disclosures of their attitudes and expectations concerning their marital future and the future of any children born to them from the pending marriage; and

WHEREAS the parties desire to determine and fix by this antenuptial agreement the rights and claims that will accrue to each of them in the estate and property of the other by reason of the marriage,

IT IS MUTUALLY AGREED AS FOLLOWS:

ARTICLE I

Declaration of marital intention

(a) Donald and Ina each declares to the other the intention to marry in the City of Chicago, Cook County, State of Illinois, on or before September thirtieth, 1972.

(b) This marriage is freely and voluntarily being entered into out of mutual love and respect held by the parties for each other. Neither party has agreed to enter this marriage under any threats, emotional or otherwise, nor has any relative of either of the parties exercised any undue influence upon either Donald or Ina.

(c) Each party assures the other that he or she has had sufficient time and information to make the decision to marry in accordance with the terms of this MEMORANDUM.

ARTICLE II

Historical representation

Donald hereby warrants to Ina and guarantees that she may act in reliance upon the following representations:

(a) He is twenty-nine years old. He attended the University of Chicago from which he graduated in 1965 with a bachelor of science degree and with acceptable but unexceptional grades.

(b) His mother and father are living; until February 1963 he resided with them and contributed toward their support. He still occasionally contributes toward their support and intends to continue to the extent that he is able during marriage. Donald's parents react favorably to the contemplated marriage. Donald's parents have not been divorced, nor has his sister, but his older brother has been divorced twice.

(c) Donald was previously married in April 1963, and that marriage ended in a divorce in June 1970. There is one child of that marriage, Michael, age six. The decree of divorce was handed down by the Supreme Court, Cook County. It awarded custody of Michael to Donald's former wife, granted her alimony and child support in the sum of $140 weekly, and granted Donald visitation privileges every other weekend, holidays, and two weeks in summertime with Michael. A copy of the divorce decree has been shown to and read by Ina.

(d) There is no known history of mental illness in Donald's family. There are no hereditary or other diseases prevalent in Donald's family, and Donald is in excellent physical health.

(e) There is no history of any arrest or conviction of Donald for any criminal behavior, nor is there any history of compulsive addiction to drugs, alcohol, or gambling.

(f) Donald is presently employed as an assistant sales manager for Rugby Electronics Company at a salary of $20,500 annually, including bonuses and exclusive of certain travel and entertainment expenses, which are made available to him by his employer. His salary during the three previous years was as follows: 1969—$14,500, 1970—$17,500, 1971—$18,500.

(g) The relationship of Donald with his parents, his brothers, and sister has been explained fully to Ina.

Donald and Ina have discussed at length his family's "tradition" of a two-week sojourn every year at the Brown residence in Michigan and Donald's desire to continue that tradition. Ina has expressed a reluctance to adhere to the tradition but agrees to be bound by Donald's wishes. Donald has agreed that he will make no arrangements for other familial visitations without the consent of Ina and that such visitations should be no more frequent than twice monthly.

(h) Donald has disclosed to Ina that his relationship with his past wife continues to be strained. He has disclosed to her that on at least two prior occasions he and his former wife have been involved in legal proceedings relating to the custody and amount of support of

EXHIBIT 10.2 (cont'd)

Michael. The nature of such proceedings, the reasons therefore, and all other questions of Ina's concerning them have been fully explored by the parties.

Donald's relationship with Michael has been fully explored by the parties. It is Donald's present feeling that the time may arise when he would wish to gain custody of Michael. Ina is reluctant, however, to consider Donald having custody during the first two years of their marriage. It has been agreed by Donald and Ina that, barring an emergency, no attempt will be made by Donald to obtain such custody for two years from the date of marriage.

Donald has made known to Ina his concern over Michael's hostility toward her. Both parties have agreed that, while the welfare of Michael should continue to be a paramount consideration of both parties, the relationship between Donald and Ina should not be affected by Michael's attitude nor should their marriage be delayed by it. It has been agreed that the parties will make clear to Michael that his hostility will not be tolerated as a wedge between Donald and Ina and that his conduct will have to be reasonably acceptable to both Donald and Ina. The parties have agreed that in the event they cannot cope successfully with this problem they will seek professional guidance to help them overcome it.

(i) There has been nothing in the past sex life of Donald that requires further disclosure. There are no sexual acts that are important to him or an essential part of the sex life contemplated by him that are not presently practiced by the parties. Donald has been able to express himself sexually in all the ways important to the parties, and such issues as frequency of intercourse, desire for periods of sexual abstention, positions of intercourse, etc., have all been explored to Donald's satisfaction.

Ina hereby warrants to Donald and guarantees that he may act in reliance upon the following representations.

(a) She is twenty-one years old. She attended, but did not graduate from, the University of Michigan, which she left after her junior year in 1970. At that time her grades were passing but below average. The circumstances under which she left college and the reasons therefore have been fully explained to Donald.

(b) Her mother and father are divorced, and she has no brothers or sisters. Until October 1970 she lived with her mother. She rarely sees her father, with whom she has an extremely disagreeable relationship. Ina's relationship with her mother is unusually close, and she visits with her as often as three or four times weekly. Ina and Donald have had many conversations concerning what Donald has protested to be far too close a relationship between mother and daughter. He has sought, but has been refused, permission from Ina to discuss the matter directly with her mother. Ina's view that her mother has been left "out on a limb" by her father and that Ina, as a consequence, has an obligation to her mother to visit more frequently than is customary, has been rejected by Donald. Although Ina has agreed to limit her visits to her mother to two afternoons weekly and has agreed that joint visitations with her mother by her and Donald be limited to twice monthly, Ina feels such concessions should not have been asked of her.

Donald has expressed considerable hostility toward Ina's mother and has openly displayed such hostility. For his part, he has agreed to discontinue such practices.

Each party agrees that the "mother-in-law" issue has not been fully resolved between them, but they agree that their marital relationship could have priority over the relationship between Ina and her mother.

(c) Ina's physical and mental condition is excellent, and there is no history of hereditary or mental diseases in the Jones family.

(d) During 1969 Ina had an illegal abortion under circumstances that have been fully disclosed to Donald. During Ina's senior year of high school she was suspended for three weeks after she and a group of fellow students were detained by juvenile authorities for the possession of marijuana cigarettes.

(e) There has been nothing in the past sex life of Ina that requires further disclosure. There are no sexual acts that are important to her or an essential part of the sex life contemplated by her that are not presently practiced by the parties. Ina has been able to express herself sexually in all the ways important to the parties, and such issues as frequency of intercourse, desire for periods of abstention, positions of intercourse, etc., have been explored to Ina's satisfaction.

(f) Ina is presently employed as an assistant interior decorator for Bon Marché Department Store, and her salary this past year was $6,300.

(g) There is no history of compulsive addiction to drugs, alcoholic beverages, or gambling.

ARTICLE III

Future expectations

(a) Donald and Ina have discussed fully where they propose to reside during the course of their marriage. They agree that considerations relating to the location of their respective

EXHIBIT 10.2 (cont'd)

families should play no part in such determination. They agree their primary consideration shall be proximity to Donald's place of business. That factor should govern regardless of where Ina may be employed and regardless of whose earnings are greater.

(b) Neither party to this Memorandum holds any formal religious beliefs that should in any way interfere with the marriage. Neither insists on, or has even expressed any preference concerning, the other's adherence to any particular religious belief. Neither will, without the consent of the other, impose any religious belief upon any children of the marriage.

(c) It is the parties' present intention that Ina continue to work, health permitting, until such time as she may become pregnant. The parties have no exact intentions concerning the employment of Ina after the birth of any child or children, although Ina has expressed the feeling that simply caring for children would not be sufficiently stimulating to her. Donald's inclination at the present time is that he would prefer for Ina to discontinue any full-time employment if she had a child, but he would not insist upon it.

Both parties agree that any subsequent employment of Ina after the birth of a child should be such that it would permit her to spend reasonable periods of time with the child and that it should not entail any evening or weekend hours.

(d) Both Donald and Ina have expressed opposition to adultery. Donald has stated he would immediately divorce Ina if such an act occurred on her part, regardless of the circumstances. Ina has said that, although she does not wish to solicit such conduct on the part of Donald, nevertheless she is unable to determine her attitude toward adultery on Donald's part in advance of knowing what the circumstances might be. If the act were an isolated "meaningless" episode, Ina's opinion is that she would rather not know of it because she does not know how it would affect her relationship with Donald.

Both parties have agreed that in the event either engages in any serious or prolonged affair with anyone else, he or she is under an obligation to disclose that fact to the other.

Both Donald and Ina believe that their sex life together is sufficiently pleasurable and knowledgeable at present so that no serious adjustment need be made by either. Ina has expressed the belief that her sex life with Donald will become more pleasurable, and somewhat less tense, after marriage and after each party has had more "experience" with each other. She denied, however, having any apprehension concerning future sexual relations with Donald.

(e) The parties intend to have two or three children of their own. It is their desire to have such children sometime after the next two years, although the possibility of having a child prior to that time does not cause any particular anxiety in either of them. In the event Ina becomes accidentally pregnant, the parties' present inclination is to have such a child and not seek an abortion. Both parties feel, however, that any decision on abortion should be left entirely to the discretion of Ina.

(f) Donald and Ina have discussed and have rejected the following notions: marriage of limited duration, separate vacations, separate beds, divorce by reason of the physical incapacity of the other, divorce by reason of the inability of Ina to bear children.

(g) In the event Ina is unable to bear children, the parties are in conflict over whether or not to adopt a child. It would be Ina's desire under such circumstances to adopt, but it is Donald's strong feeling that he would not want to. Although the parties agree that this eventually would be of considerable importance to them, they feel it is better to leave resolution of the question of adoption undetermined prior to its arising.

ARTICLE IV

Future support

(a) In the event that either party desires a separation (by mutual agreement or legal decree) or a divorce during the first five years of marriage, provided there is no surviving child born of the marriage neither party will request support from the other unless he or she is in dire need thereof, and then only for such temporary periods as may be deemed necessary in accordance with Article VIII hereof.

(b) If either party desires to separate after the first five years of marriage or if, at the time of a request for separation during the first five years, a child of the marriage is alive, either party may request support, which shall be granted or denied by arbitration in accordance with Article VIII hereof. In determining whether or not to grant support and, if so, in what amount, the arbitrator shall consider the following: the length of the marriage, the number of children, their ages, the ages and health of the parties; the ability of Ina to work, the number of years that Ina has been unemployed, the reasons therefore, and Ina's realistic chances of being productively employed; the disparity between the parties' incomes and income-earning potentials; the amount of property to be divided between them in accordance with this agreement; the question of which party desires such separation or divorce and the reasons therefore; Donald's legal obligations to his former wife and to his son, Michael; and the parties' preseparation standard of living, provided such standard was reasonable. No factor shall be con-

EXHIBIT 10.2 (cont'd)

clusive, and the award of support, if any, should be such as to do substantial justice between the parties after consideration of all factors.

ARTICLE V
Division of property

(a) Donald presently has a checking account at the First National Bank of Chicago, One First National Plaza, the present balance of which is $1,685.50. He maintains a savings account at the same bank, (Account No. 104F–003), the balance of which is $3,750.

(b) Ina presently has a checking account in her own name at the Continental National Bank and Trust Company, 231 South La Salle Street, the present balance of which is $385. She maintains a savings account at the same bank (Account No. 1A24–72), the present balance of which is $950.

(c) Donald owns four hundred shares of Great Western United Corporation, which is traded on the New York Stock Exchange, having a present value of approximately $4,000; he owns no other securities. Donald is also the owner of a 1970 Buick Riviera, on which $650 in installment obligations is presently due.

(d) Ina owns no securities and does not own an automobile.

(e) Neither party presently owns any real property.

ARTICLE VI
Future ownership of property

(a) Donald and Ina have agreed that all property now standing in the name of either shall continue to be held in the individual names of the parties owning such property.

(b) Upon the marriage of Donald and Ina, they will create a joint-checking account and a joint-savings account to which each shall contribute in the same proportion as their earnings shall bear to each other. In the event that either party decides to seek a separation or divorce within a period of thirty-six months from the date of their marriage or at any time prior to the birth of a child, the proceeds of such checking and savings accounts shall be divided in the same proportion in which such funds were contributed by the parties. If either party seeks a separation or divorce after the birth of a child or at the end of said thirty-six-month period, whichever is earlier, such proceeds shall be divided between the parties equally.

(c) In the event that Ina is unable to find employment or is involuntarily unemployed or is unable to work during a period of maternity or illness, her contributions to the joint funds during the period of such unemployment, illness, or maternity shall be deemed to have been made in direct proportion to the contributions previously made by her during the period immediately preceding such unemployment, illness, or maternity.

(d) All questions concerning the investment of the joint funds of Donald and Ina in securities or real estate shall be decided jointly by the parties, and the ownership and division of such real or personal property should be made in accordance with paragraphs (a) and (c) hereof.

(e) The parties do not contemplate a different division of property, real or personal, whether or not either or both may later be guilty of any marital misconduct as defined by the laws of the State of Illinois. Any property not held in accordance with the terms of this article by either of the parties shall be deemed to be held in trust for the other party, and no additional private or oral understanding between the parties concerning the division of property between them is to be deemed valid until agreed to in writing in accordance with paragraph (f) hereof.

(f) In the event that either Donald or Ina subsequently wishes to change the rules by which their property shall be divided, the party desiring such change shall notify the other in writing and by registered mail at least one hundred and twenty days prior to such proposed change. If the other party does not wish to make such change, he or she may notify the other party in writing within the one hundred and twenty days. The matter shall be resolved by arbitration in accordance with the terms of Article VIII hereof. In making a determination the arbitrator shall fully inquire into the facts and circumstances surrounding the reasons for the proposed change. No modification of existing financial arrangements shall be made if it is determined that a substantial reason for such proposed change is that the party seeking modification has the imminent expectation of coming into a sudden period of prosperity from which the other party is to be excluded. The arbitrator may consider such other factors as he wishes in order to do substantial justice between the parties, but he may not order that any modification of the rules by which the parties have agreed to divide the property be made retroactive to the period preceding the written request for modification.

EXHIBIT 10.2 (cont'd)

ARTICLE VII
Matters of estate

After thirty-six months of marriage each party agrees to leave the other at least 40 per cent of his or her entire estate, and each agrees to make no attempt to assign, transfer, or otherwise dispose of, without valuable consideration, any portion of his or her estate with the intention of depriving the other of the benefits of this agreement.

ARTICLE VIII
Arbitration

Any dispute that arises under the terms of this Memorandum shall be resolved in accordance with the rules and regulations then obtaining of the American Arbitration Association, and such arbitration shall be held in the City of Chicago, Cook County, State of Illinois, unless at the time of dispute both parties reside in some other state, in which event arbitration shall take place in that state.

ARTICLE IX
Modification

This Memorandum may not be changed or modified except in writing, signed by the party against whom such change or modification is sought.

IN WITNESS WHEREOF, the parties hereto have signed their hands and seals this 28th day of July, 1972.

Source: Normal Shoeshy and Marya Mannes, "A Radical Guide to Wedlock," *Saturday Review* 55 (1972):33–38.

---

to anticipate separation or divorce. Mention of the topics may serve to aid and abet such a result and therefore could be invalidated.

Weitzman (1981) has researched marriage contracts, concluding that marital partners have lost the traditional privileges of status and at the same time have been deprived of the freedom that contracts could provide. The traditional marriage contract creates an unconstitutional invasion of marital privacy; it discriminates on a gender basis by assigning one set of rights and obligations to husbands and another to wives. The law imposes a single family form on everyone, denying the diversity and heterogeneity in our pluralistic society. The traditional assumption is that people marry when they are young and stay married all their lives.

The proposed contract model would devise a structure appropriate for individual needs and values. Contracts are suitable instruments for establishing egalitarian relationships, not only for couples who marry but also for unwed cohabitants who may reject marriage but want to join together in a legal partnership. They are also useful for homosexuals, who are barred from legal marriage.

Because provisions for alimony may be said to create an expectation of divorce, they may invalidate the entire contract in some states. Language should be checked against state law, or there should be a statement that illegality of any one provision invalidates that portion only and does not affect the rest of the contract.

One of ten contracts presented by Weitzman, that between an already married husband and wife, is shown in Exhibit 10.3.

MARRIAGE AND SOCIAL CHANGE

The legal purposes of marriage provide a responsible framework for satisfying sexual needs and for the protection and nurturance of children. Reliable methods of contraception affect both these goals and tend to make marriage less necessary.

Thus far the law does not deal adequately with life-styles that deny the need for marriage or that regard the birth of children as undesirable. The law has assumed

EXHIBIT 10.3
A CONTRACT BETWEEN AN ALREADY MARRIED HUSBAND AND WIFE

CONTRACT

Barbara and Robert Sloan, husband and wife, are both 42 years old. They have been married for 21 years and have two children: Steven, age 20, and Susan, age 18. For the first 16 years of this marriage Barbara was a full-time housewife and mother. Four years ago she returned to school. After completing her college degree she obtained a job as a keypunch operator for a computer company. Robert Sloan is a life insurance agent employed by a large company, a job he has held for the past 22 years. When Barbara returned to school she continued to manage the household while carrying a full college course load. Although Robert and the children tried "to help" she still bore the major burden and her resentment grew.

At the same time, Robert began to resent Barbara's outside activities and started seeing another woman. He now realizes that his involvement with the other woman was aimed at making his wife jealous and getting her to pay more attention to him. He also hoped to prevent her new interests from usurping the central place he had always held in her life. After filing for divorce, the couple decided to see a marriage counselor for the children's sake, and in the course of counseling they realized they really wanted to stay together and try to reconstruct their marriage.

Their contract, the result of months of discussion, was written to affirm their new understanding of their relationship. Although their children are not parties to this contract, they participated in the discussions, and both of them have agreed to support and honor the spirit of this contract.

The excerpts presented below focus on their interpersonal relationship.

Living in partnership

Barbara and Robert desire to continue their marriage and to make it a full and equal partnership. The parties share a commitment to the process of negotiations and compromise that will continue to strengthen their equality in the partnership. Decisions will be made with respect for individual needs and equality. The parties hope to maintain such mutual decision-making so that the daily decisions affecting their lives will not become a struggle between the parties for power, authority, and dominance.

Therefore, the parties agree that such a process, while sometimes time-consuming and fatiguing, is a good investment in the future of their relationship and their continued love and esteem for each other.

Names

The parties do not ascribe to the concept of ownership implied by the woman's adoption of the man's name. However, since Barbara has used Robert's name for the past 21 years and is known to all her friends at work by this name, it would not be practical for her to resume her birth name at this time. Therefore, the parties agree to retain and use the family name of Sloan.

Careers

Barbara and Robert value the importance and integrity of their respective careers and acknowledge the demands that their jobs place on them as individuals and on their partnership. Although commitment to their work will sometimes place stress on the relationship, they believe that their experiences at work contribute to individual self-fulfillment and thereby strengthen the partnership.

Relationships with others, jealousy, and trust

1. The parties acknowledge their desire to retain a monogamous sexual relationship. They, therefore, agree to be sexually faithful to each other.

2. Barbara freely acknowledges her jealousy and insecurity when Robert is involved with persons of the opposite sex. Robert acknowledges that he would be equally upset if Barbara became involved with someone else.

3. Therefore, the parties agree to discuss plans for activities that involve persons of the opposite sex when the other party is not involved, and when such activities are not directly a part of one's work.

4. They also agree to allow each other the power to veto such activities for a six-month period. Thus, if Robert's activities cause Barbara undue anxiety (even if they are innocent and/or helpful to his work), he will change his plans. The parties feel that they are currently in a financial position to forgo some of Robert's extra commissions if, in order to obtain them, he has to engage in social activities that make Barbara uncomfortable. At the same time, Barbara

EXHIBIT 10.3 (cont'd)

will try to become a more trusting person. However, since she has been deeply hurt by Robert's affair, this trust will have to be built over a period of time.

5. Realizing that trust is built by practical plans as well as by good intentions, the parties also agree to set aside one evening during each week and one evening each weekend to spend alone together. In addition, they will spend one evening each week at some social activity as a couple. The choice of what to do will be made on a weekly rotation basis, with one partner determining the weekday evening and the other the weekend and social activity each week. A calendar will be posted two months in advance. Both parties will enter their plans on the large calendar in the kitchen.

Care and use of the home

1. The partners reject the concept that the responsibility for housework rests with the woman while the duties of home maintenance and repair rest with the man. They also reject the notion that children should be taken care of instead of sharing home maintenance tasks.

2. Therefore, the parties agree that all household tasks, including cooking and meal management, laundry, cleaning, gardening, car repair, shopping, etc., will be shared by *all* members of the household. The household work schedule now in effect (which assigns household tasks to us, our daughter Susan and our son Steven—until he goes to college in the fall) will be attached as a modifiable amendment to this agreement.

3. Because Robert has higher standards of cleanliness and home neatness than Barbara (and Susan and Steven), and because in the past conflicts have arisen over the condition of the home, the parties agree to continue their current practice of assigning one person the task of inspecting household work for cleanliness and neatness. Once a month, when Robert is inspector, we will conform to his standards. We will conform to the standards set by the three other inspectors on their weeks.

4. Each party has a room in the house for a study and/or bedroom and all matters regarding the care and activities within that room shall be the party's private concern.

Financial arrangements

1. Barbara and Robert intend that their accumulation of assets and liabilities, wages, salaries, and other incomes during their 21 years of marriage represent an economic partnership of two equal partners. This shall be reflected in the ownership of property, and in the control of their income.

2. The parties therefore agree that these articles of their marriage contract shall replace the property laws of the state whereby Robert alone would be the sole owner of most of their property except the house, which is in joint tenancy.

3. To accomplish these aims all current (and future) property, wages, salaries, and other income, tangible and intangible assets (with the exception of inheritances), and liabilities will be transferred to and held in joint tenancy with the right of survivorship.

4. The parties agree that all debts and loans against the joint assets will be mutually agreed upon, and co-signed by both parties.

5. The parties agree to designate each other full beneficiary of any benefits which they now own or may acquire during this marriage in insurance, retirement funds, or other co-signed benefits, with the exception of the following clause.

6. The parties have established trust funds for the college education of each of their children, Steven and Susan. These funds should be sufficient to cover tuition, books and basic room and board for four years. The student will be expected to cover other expenses through part-time or summer work. The children are also the beneficiaries of life insurance policies of $100,000 on Robert's life and $100,000 on Barbara's life.

7. The parties agree that in case of divorce the original sum of any inheritance will become the sole property of the inheritor. Any further profits or losses realized from an inheritance will be considered to be owned jointly and will be equally divided between the two parties.

8. Further, the parties agree that all other properties jointly owned and managed by the partnership will be equally divided in case of divorce.

Renewal and resolving conflicts

1. We agree to an annual review of the provisions of the contract, including the work schedule appendix, on or about the anniversary date of the execution of the contract.

2. We agree that if we have unresolved conflicts over any provisions of the contract, we will seek assistance from R.S., a licensed social worker and marriage counsellor, who has helped us to understand each other's point of view and to work things out in the past.

Source: Lenore J. Weitzman, *The Marriage Contract: Spouses, Lovers, and The Law* (New York: Free Press, 1981).

traditional goals and traditional sex roles. That the male should marry at an older age than the female because he will be the provider is only one illustration.

When marriages do not maintain themselves through the child-rearing period and family members are less likely to assume care of the child, the state's role in child care is crucial but foster homes and other substitute care systems are not ideal alternatives either.

The law is not able to deal well with a succession of extralegal affiliations. Common law provisions assume a degree of continuity not found in short-term cohabitation. Polygamous communes receive the least acceptance from the courts.

In a permissive society there are few difficulties with alternate life-styles until special problems related to economic need, pregnancy, illness, or death develop. Eligibility standards of social service systems are often value-laden. Current attitudes of the society toward divorce are much better reflected in law reform than are attitudes toward marriage. We will examine those provisions in Chapter 14.

Questions for Review

1. What concept of engagement would justify a breach-of-promise suit?

2. What is the most frequent reason for drafting a prenuptial contract concerning property rights?

3. Explain presumptions that support the validity of marriage.

4. What are the tests of a common law marriage?

5. Why do relatively few states recognize common law marriages?

6. Define *annulment*. Is annulment now of great interest to social workers?

7. Why is the method of serving notice important in actions concerning marital status?

8. Illustrate *res judicata* in a situation involving possible annulment.

9. How does it apply to annulment?

10. What is the difference between a *void* marriage and a *voidable* marriage?

11. How have differential age requirements for marriage been affected by the women's movement?

12. What rights were violated by miscegenation statutes?

13. How are social workers likely to be involved with the issue of marriage for a limited purpose?

14. Why are annulments more likely to be retroactive when public funds are involved than when they lead to claims against a former spouse?

Questions for Debate and Discussion

1. How might marriage provisions differ if marriage were regulated by ecclesiastical courts?

2. Defend or challenge the following statement: The failure of a state to recognize common law unions tends to discourage them.

3. Some states permit all sexual activities between consenting adults. How does this relate to *Baker v. Nelson?*

4. What legal safeguards should be taken by couples who are living together without marriage?

5. Although *Loving v. Virginia* was decided in 1967, why do many states still have laws on the books prohibiting miscegenation?

6. Analyze the three decisions in *Marvin v. Marvin.* Why do you agree or disagree with the final result?

Selected Readings

Butler, Edgar W. *Traditional Marriage and Emerging Alternatives.* New York: Harper & Row, 1979.

Crutchfield, Charles F. "Nonmarital Relationships and Their Impact on the Institution of Marriage." *Journal of Family Law* 19 (1981): 247–261.

Glendon, Maryann. "Modern Marriage Law and Its Underlying Assumptions: The New Marriage and the New Property." *Family Law Quarterly* 13 (1980): 441–460.

Riga, Peter J. *Marriage and Family Law: Historical, Constitutional, and Practical Perspectives.* Port Washington, N.Y.: Associated Faculty Press, 1983.

——. "The Supreme Court's View of Marriage: Tradition or Transition." *Journal of Family Law* 18 (1979–80): 301–330.

Wardel, Lynn D. "Rethinking Marital Age Restrictions." *Journal of Family Law* 22 (1983–84): 1–57.

Wiersma, G. E. *Cohabitation: An Alternative to Marriage.* Hingham, Mass.: Kluwer Academic Press, 1983.

CHAPTER

11

Human Reproduction

Three changes over the past twenty years have significantly affected fertility and sexual practices: (1) the development of oral contraceptives, which require no direct preparation for sexual intercourse and no inconvenient or unaesthetic postcoital procedures, and the increased use of vasectomy and tubal ligation by couples who are certain they want no more children; (2) the availability of legal abortion in settings providing improved protection to the patient; (3) and the development of more successful techniques to overcome infertility. All these developments have both influenced the women's movement and been influenced by it.

Contraception and abortion have brought about conflicts between church and state. Opposition of religious bodies has been most explicit in the case of abortion. While U.S. Supreme Court decisions on abortion reflect the past twenty years of social change, decisions in the lower courts on such issues as artificial insemination have been problematic.

DEFINITIONS   Birth control, population control, contraception, family planning, and child spacing need to be differentiated.

Birth control implies preventing the birth of children and includes both contraception and abortion. At the societal level, **population control** is the deliberate regulation of population size. As yet, only India and China have attempted population control as a matter of public policy. **Contraception** generally emphasizes precluding pregnancy by preventing fertilization of the ovum.

Family planning has been a popular term in programs designed for the poor because its intent is not to prevent people from having children but to permit them to have the number they want. Family planning may involve contraception or treatment for infertility. **Child spacing** involves controlling the interval between births. For the family that has already achieved the number of children desired, family planning and birth control are synonymous. Data indicate that such couples have fewer contraceptive errors than those who want children but are trying to space them (Ryder and Westoff, 1977).

Increasing societal concern about curbing population growth makes the need for control more apparent. If couples consciously choose childlessness, **birth control** becomes the goal. While the women's movement has challenged some laws with little effect, the right of a woman to control her own reproductive functions was recognized by the U.S. Supreme Court over a decade ago. Roe v. Wade, 410 U.S. 113 (1973), gave women the right to choose abortion as long as the choice is made early in the pregnancy.

INVOLUNTARY
STERILIZATION

Both mental defectives and felons have been considered candidates for involuntary sterilization. The intent of sterilization in such cases is to safeguard the quality of the population by making reproduction impossible. The right to procreate was established in Skinner v. State of Oklahoma, 316 U.S. 535 (1942), in which a state law that permitted involuntary sterilization of persons found guilty of repeated larceny but not of repeated embezzlement was held unconstitutional by the U.S. Supreme Court. The right to procreate was termed "one of the basic civil rights of man," a "basic liberty."

Fifteen years earlier, in Buck v. Bell, 274 U.S. 200 (1927), the Court had ruled that the police power of the government may be used to compel sterilization as long as the requirements of legal due process were followed. Such requirements included medical evidence that any child parented by the individual to be sterilized would necessarily be an imbecile or feebleminded. The state could resort to involuntary sterilization in order to prevent the birth of "degenerate offspring." Fifteen states had sterilization statutes in 1920. By 1942 the number had risen to thirty-two; however, at least eight states have since repealed those statutes, and in many of the remainder the laws are rarely invoked. Courts have invalidated these laws more frequently for criminals than for mental defectives.

Given the modern emphasis on civil rights, involuntary sterilizations are now much less common. Written, informed consent is required of all individuals to be sterilized under federally funded programs (42 C.F.R. §50.204). Mandatory referral to a court is included. The court acts on the recommendation of a committee of at least six people who represent both sexes and are competent to deal with the medical, legal, social, and ethical issues involved; at least two members of the committee must represent the population served by the agency. A waiting period of seventy-two hours between consent and sterilization is required. In addition, a specific definition of "informed consent" was devised:

> (d) "Informed consent" means the voluntary, knowing assent from the individual on whom any sterilization is to be performed after he has been given (as evidenced by a document executed by such individual) (1) a fair explanation of the procedures to be followed; (2) a description of the attendant discomforts and risks; (3) a description of the benefits to be expected; (4) an explanation concerning appropriate alternative methods of family planning and the effect and impact of the proposed sterilization including the fact that it must be considered to be an irreversible procedure; (5) an offer to answer any inquiries concerning the procedures; and (6) an instruction that the individual is free to withhold or withdraw his or her consent to the procedure at any time prior to the sterilization without prejudicing his or her future care and without loss of other project or program benefits to which the patient might otherwise be entitled. (42 C.F.R. §50.204)

Compulsory sterilization evokes a strong negative response from social workers. Many would like to see involuntary sterilization outlawed entirely.

CONTRACEPTION

The right to employ contraceptive methods is derived from the right to procreate. Religious doctrine has often restricted contraception. Some state laws have limited the sale of contraceptives, either to all persons or specifically to minors. Commercial display of contraceptives has also been held illegal.

In Griswold v. State of Connecticut, 381 U.S. 479 (1965), the Planned Parenthood League of Connecticut had been fined one hundred dollars for providing married persons with "information, instruction, and medical advice" on means of preventing conception. The U.S. Supreme Court decision, written by Justice William O. Douglas, emphasized the principle of privacy:

> The present case, then, concerns a relationship lying within the zone of privacy created by several fundamental constitutional guarantees. And it concerns a law which, in forbidding the *use* of contraceptives rather than regulating their manufacture or sale, seeks to achieve its goal by means having a maximum destructive impact on that relationship. Such a law cannot stand in light of the familiar principle, so often applied by this court, that a "governmental purpose to control or prevent activities constitutionally subject to state regulation may not be achieved by means which sweep unnecessarily and thereby invade the area of protected freedoms." . . . "Would we allow the police to search the sacred precincts of marital bedrooms for telltale signs of use of contraceptives? The very idea is repulsive to the notions of privacy surrounding the marrriage relationship."
>
> "We deal with a right of privacy older than the Bill of Rights—older than our political parties, older than our school systems. Marriage is a coming together for better or worse, hopefully enduring, and intimate to the degree of being sacred. It is an association that promotes a way of life, not causes; a harmony in living, not political faith; a bilateral loyalty, not commercial or social projects. Yet it is an association for as noble a purpose as any involved in our prior decisions." (381 U.S. at 485–486)

The finding in *Griswold v. State of Connecticut* illustrates the importance of earlier dissents in Supreme Court cases on major decisions. For instance, Justice John Harlan, in Poe v. Ullman, 367 U.S. 497 (1961), had indicated:

> Of this whole "private realm of family life," it is difficult to imagine what is more private or intimate than a husband and wife's marital relationships. We would indeed be straining at a gnat and swallowing a camel were we to show concern for the niceties of property law . . . and yet fail at least to see any substantial claim here. (367 U.S. at 552)

Eisenstadt v. Baird, 405 U.S. 438 (1972), involved an appeal from a Massachusetts conviction for giving away "any drug, medicine, instrument or article whatever for the prevention of conception" except by medical prescription to married couples. Citing the equal protection clause of the Fourteenth Amendment to the Constitution, the Court concluded that no grounds existed for differential treatment of married and unmarried persons under the Massachusetts law. "Whatever the rights of the individual to access to contraceptives may be, the rights must be the same for the unmarried and the married alike."

Justice Douglas concurred, but followed a simpler line of reasoning—that the action against a lecturer for giving away contraceptives was a violation of the First Amendment: "I do not see how we can have a Society of the Dialogue, which the First Amendment envisages, if the time-honored teaching techniques are barred to those who give educational lectures."

An area not well charted by court decisions involves contraceptives for sexually active minors—prevention of unwanted pregnancies over and against parental involvement that might threaten the effectiveness of a contraceptive service. When the minor seeks birth control, the dependency or parental authority has already ceased. Minors have traditionally experienced difficulty in obtaining nonprescription contraceptives, including condoms, which are still technically distributed "for the prevention of disease." In Carey v. Population Services International, 431 U.S.

678 (1977), the Supreme Court struck down a New York statute that made it a crime "(1) for any person to sell or distribute any contraceptive of any kind to a minor under the age of 16 years; (2) for anyone other than a licensed pharmacist to distribute contraceptives to persons over 16; and (3) for anyone, including licensed pharmacists, to advertise or display contraceptives."

In 1983 a proposed Department of Health and Human Services regulation that programs receiving federal funds must inform parents when adolescents sought contraceptive services was invalidated by a federal court. The proposed regulation is included in chapter 2 of this book, pp. 39–42.

Arizona has a liberal statute that provides "family planning and adoption services and supplies that consist of any medically approved means including diagnosis, treatment, drugs, supplies, devices and related counseling which are furnished or prescribed by or under the supervision of a physician for individuals of child-bearing age, including minors who can be considered to be sexually active for purposes of enabling such individuals freely to determine the number and spacing of their children" (Arizona Rev. Stat. § 36-125.04).

Tort of Unwanted Life

Civil damages for "unwanted life" were allowed in Troppi v. Scarf, 187 N.W.2d 511 (Mich. App. 1971). An award of $250,000 was sought because a pharmacist negligently supplied the wrong drug to a married woman who had ordered an oral contraceptive. As a consequence, she became pregnant and delivered a normal, healthy, eighth child. One of the major questions was whether a healthy child constitutes major benefit. The appeals court responded: "There is a growing recognition that the financial services which parents can expect from their offspring are largely illusory. Cases decided when the "loss of companionship" was a compensable item of damage . . . reveal no tendency to value companionship so highly as to outweigh expenses in every foreseeable case." Subsequent to the ruling of the court, on retrial the Scarfs accepted a $12,000 out of court settlement.

ABORTION— BASIC COURT DECISIONS

Roe v. Wade, 410 U.S. 113 (1973), was concerned with the constitutionality of state criminal abortion statutes. A Texas statute prohibited all abortions, with the exception of those necessary for preservation of the mother's life, without regard to the stage in a woman's pregnancy or other interests involved. Such statutes were held to violate the due process clause of the Fourteenth Amendment:

> (a) For the stage prior to approximately the end of the first trimester, the abortion decision and its effectuation must be left to the medical judgment of the pregnant woman's attending physician.
> (b) For the stage subsequent to approximately the end of the second trimester, the State in promoting its interest in the health of the mother, may if it chooses, regulate the abortion procedure in ways that are reasonably related to maternal health.
> (c) For the stage subsequent to viability, the State in promoting its interest in the potentiality of human life may, if it chooses, regulate, and even proscribe, abortion except where it is necessary, in appropriate medical judgment, for the preservation of the life or health of the mother. (410 U.S. at 164)

Some people were surprised that the Court chose to deal with the viability issue. However, the emphasis on privacy is appropriate to the attitudinal stance of conservative justices. In an earlier section, the decision affirmed the right of privacy

> whether it be founded in the Fourteenth Amendment's concept of personal liberty and restrictions upon state action, as we feel it is, or, as the District Court determined,

in the Ninth Amendment's reservation of rights to the people; it is broad enough to encompass a woman's decision whether or not to terminate her pregnancy. The detriment that the State would impose upon the pregnant woman by denying this choice altogether is apparent. Specific and direct harm medically diagnosable even in early pregnancy may be involved. Maternity, or additional offspring, may force upon a woman a distressful life and future. Psychological harm may be imminent. Mental and physical health may be taxed by child care. There is also the distress, for all concerned associated with the unwanted child, and there is the problem of bringing a child into a family already unable, psychologically and otherwise, to care for it. In other cases, as in this one, the additional difficulties and continuing stigma of unwed motherhood may be involved. All these are factors the woman and her responsible physician necessarily will consider in consultation. (410 U.S. at 153)

At the time of *Roe v. Wade*, only four states (Alaska, Hawaii, New York, and Washington) remained unaffected by the decision. Fifteen states had relatively modern laws, while those of the other thirty-one states were thoroughly invalidated by the decision. A Uniform Abortion Act was devised to carry out the intent of the Supreme Court decisions.

After the *Roe* decision, a growing demand developed for passage of a "right to life" constitutional amendment as a means to prohibit abortions. One proposal by such proponents is to extend the due process and equal protection clauses by a constitutional amendment "to any human being from the moment of conception."

In Doe v. Bolton, 410 U.S. 179 (1973), a Georgia resident had sought an abortion after eight weeks of pregnancy. The request was denied because of failure to meet three conditions specified in Georgia law: that the abortion be performed in a hospital accredited by the Joint Commission on Accreditation of Hospitals, that the procedure be approved by the hospital staff abortion committee, and that the performing physician's judgment be confirmed by independent examinations of the patient by two other licensed physicians. The U.S. Supreme Court held that these conditions violated the Fourteenth Amendment because they are restrictive of patients' rights and because the law's residence requirement denied protection to persons who enter Georgia to obtain medical services.

In July 1976 the U.S. Supreme Court ruled on four issues related to abortion: written consent requirements applying to the pregnant woman, spousal consent, parental consent requirements for pregnant minors, and the statutory prohibition of saline amniocentesis after the first twelve weeks of pregnancy. The major decision was Planned Parenthood of Central Missouri v. Danforth, 428 U.S. 52 (1976), ruling that written consent from the woman could be required for abortion as for other types of surgery:

It seems manifest that, ideally, the decision to terminate a pregnancy should be one concurred in by both the wife and her husband. No marriage may be viewed as harmonious or successful if the marriage partners are fundamentally divided on so important and vital an issue. But it is difficult to believe that the goal of fostering mutuality and trust in a marriage, and of strengthening the marital relationship and the marriage institution, will be achieved by giving the husband a veto power exercisable for any reason whatsoever or for no reason at all. Even if the State had the ability to delegate to the husband a power it itself could not exercise, it is not at all likely that such action would further, as the District Court majority phrased it, the "interest of the state in protecting the mutuality of decisions vital to the marriage relationship." 392 F.Supp. at 1370.

We recognize, of course, that when a woman, with the approval of her physician but without the approval of her husband, decides to terminate her pregnancy, it could be said that she is acting unilaterally. The obvious fact is that when the wife and the husband disagree on the decision, the view of only one of the two marriage partners can prevail. Since it is the woman who physically bears the child and who is the more directly and immediately affected by the pregnancy, as between the two, the balance weighs in her favor. (Cf. Roe v. Wade, 410 U.S. at 153)

This decision continues to leave the major decision-making responsibility to the pregnant woman and her physician. The husband cannot prevent her going ahead with an abortion.

Parental consent was also at issue in another case decided the same day, Bellotti v. Baird, 428 U.S. 132 (1976), as well as in *Danforth*. The decision invalidated any blanket provision for parental consent for an unmarried minor during the first twelve weeks of pregnancy. The portion of the decision below is from *Danforth*:

> We agree with appellants and with the courts whose decisions have just been cited that the State may not impose a blanket provision, such as § 3(4), requiring the consent of a parent or person *in loco parentis* as a condition for abortion of an unmarried minor during the first 12 weeks of her pregnancy. Just as with the requirement of consent from the spouse, so here, the State does not have the constitutional authority to give a third party an absolute, and possibly arbitrary, veto over the decision of the physician and his patient to terminate the patient's pregnancy, regardless of the reason for withholding the consent.
>
> Constitutional rights do not mature and come into being magically only when one attains the state-defined age of majority. Minors, as well as adults, are protected by the Constitution and possess constitutional rights. The Court indeed, however, long has recognized that the State has somewhat broader authority to regulate the activities of children than of adults. It remains, then, to examine whether there is any significant state interest in conditioning an abortion on the consent of a parent or person *in loco parentis* that is not present in the case of an adult.
>
> One suggested interest is the safeguarding of the family unit and of parental authority. 392 F.Supp. at 1370. It is difficult, however, to conclude that providing a parent with absolute power to overrule a determination made by the physician and his minor patient to terminate the patient's pregnancy will serve to strengthen the family unit. Neither is it likely that such veto power will enhance parental authority or control where the minor and the nonconsenting parent are so fundamentally in conflict and the very existence of the pregnancy already has fractured the family structure. Any independent interest the parent may have in the termination of the minor daughter's pregnancy is no more weighty than the right of privacy of the competent minor mature enough to have become pregnant.
>
> We emphasize that our holding that § 3(4) is invalid does not suggest that every minor, regardless of age or maturity, may give effective consent for termination of her pregnancy. See *Bellotti v. Baird*, post. The fault with § 3(4) is that it imposes a special consent provision, exercisable by a person other than the woman and her physician, as a prerequisite to a minor's termination of her pregnancy and does so without a sufficient justification for the restriction. It violates the strictures of *Roe* and *Doe*.

The Court also ruled in *Danforth* that saline amniocentesis could not be outlawed as a method of abortion for use after the twelfth week of pregnancy, as the Missouri law had provided.

As a result of these decisions, groups opposed to abortion have increased their efforts for a constitutional amendment prohibiting abortions without therapeutic justification.

RECENT COURT DECISIONS ON ABORTION RIGHTS

A Utah statute requiring a physician to notify, "if possible," the parent or guardian on whom an abortion is to be performed while she is an unmarried minor living with and dependent on her parents was found not to violate the guarantees of the Constitution in H.L. v. Matheson, 450 U.S. 398 (1981). The decision held that the appellant lacked standing to challenge the Utah statute since she was neither mature or emancipated, and that the Utah statute serves important state interests by providing an opportunity for parents to supply essential and other medical information to a physician. "An adequate medical and psychological case history is important to the physician" (450 U.S. at 411). The Supreme Court did not find that the Utah law gave the parents veto power over the minor's decision to have an abortion.

Abortion decisions by the Supreme Court in 1983 reinforced the positions the Court had taken beginning ten years earlier. The most comprehensive decision was Akron v. Akron Center for Reproductive Health, 462 U.S. 416 (1983), in which the Court invalidated four provisions of an Akron ordinance: (1) All abortions in the second trimester must be performed in a hospital; (2) physicians could not perform abortions on unmarried minors under fifteen years of age without parental consent; (3) a detailed list of risks of abortion had to be presented to pregnant women seeking abortions; and (4) there was to be a twenty-four-hour waiting period before the abortion could be performed.

On the same day, a similar decision on a hospital requirement for second-trimester abortion was made in Planned Parenthood of Kansas City, Missouri v. Ashcroft, 462 U.S. 476, on the basis that the requirement "unreasonably infringes upon a woman's constitutional right to obtain an abortion." The parental consent provisions in Missouri's law were found to be constitutional as part of the state's interest in protecting immature minors.

In Simopoulos v. Virginia, 462 U.S. 506 (1983), however, the Court held that the state requirement that second-trimester abortions be performed in licensed outpatient clinics is not an unreasonable means of protecting a woman's health.

PAYMENT OF ABORTION COSTS

In Maher v. Roe, 432 U.S. 464 (1977), the U.S. Supreme Court decided that the scope of personal constitutional freedom recognized in *Roe v. Wade* did not include an entitlement to Medicaid payments for abortions that are not medically necessary. Previous abortion decisions did not prevent the state of Connecticut from making a value judgment favoring childbirth over abortion and allocating public funds on that basis. The regulation was unrelated to possible indigency of a client.

The Hyde Amendment, P.L. 94-439, 90 Stat 1434 (1976) attached to an appropriations bill for the Department of Health, Education, and Welfare prohibited the use of federal funds for abortions where the mother's health was not in danger.

The Supreme Court dealt with the use of state funds for medically necessary abortions in Harris v. McRae, 448 U.S. 297 (1980). In its decision it stated that Medicaid regulations in Title XIX of the Social Security Act do not require a participating state to pay for those medically necessary abortions for which federal reimbursement is unavailable under the Hyde Amendment: "Nothing in Title XIX . . . suggests that Congress intended to recognize a participating state to assume the full costs of any health service in its Medicaid plan." The Court also declared that the Hyde Amendment places no governmental obstacle in the path of a woman who chooses to terminate her pregnancy and that the amendment does not violate the equal protection component of the due process clause of the Fifth Amendment to the U.S. Constitution. According to the Court, a woman's freedom of choice does not carry with it a constitutional right to financial resources to avail herself of the full range of protected services. The Hyde Amendment is related to a legitimate governmental interest, since by encouraging childbirth except in the most urgent circumstances it is rationally related to the legitimate governmental objectives of protecting potential life.

ABORTION—IMPLICATIONS FOR SOCIAL WORK

The recent Supreme Court decisions have greatly enlarged the options open to women who seek termination of pregnancy. Much pre-abortion counseling is done by social workers. Given the controversial nature of the subject, it is difficult to summarize the prevailing opinions of the profession. The National Association of Social Workers has recognized that different groups have different value systems, so that organization does not take a position concerning the morality or immorality of abortion. The association has not issued a position statement since 1975. That statement provides:

> The profession's position concerning abortion service is based upon the principle of self-determination. Every individual (within the context of his or her value system) must be free to participate in or refrain from abortion counseling.
>
> In the event a woman chooses to consider terminating a pregnancy with abortion the following services should be available to her: (a) patient counseling and referral provided by professionally trained staff who are knowledgeable of the social and psychological dynamics of unwanted pregnancy and abortion; (b) safe, surgical care including pre- and post-operative services; (c) contraceptive counseling regarding the use of contraception and the prevention of further unwanted pregnancies; (d) provision of appropriate contraception; delivery of services to all women.
>
> The social worker is expected to extend all options and support services (for example, pre- and post-abortion counseling, post-natal counseling, counseling for single parents and adoption counseling for women at all economic levels), and insure their availability to those women who wish to keep their child, place for adoption, and/or other alternatives they desire.
>
> In the event a social worker chooses not to participate in abortion counseling, it is his or her responsibility to provide meaningful referral services to assure that this option is available to clients. In addition, the profession supports the development of public education and information services designed to inform people about the current legal, medical and social aspects of abortion. A system for reporting services provided is also supported.

In sum, abortion is a right for those who desire it, and a social worker has the responsibility to facilitate obtaining the service for such a client or making a referral to someone else who will do so.

Artificial Insemination

Physicians have observed a similar level of anxiety in people who think they are pregnant and do not want to be and in those who fear they are unable to become pregnant. In the latter case, artificial insemination is one way to achieve pregnancy. The husband's semen alone may be used (AIH); this procedure is not common and presents no legal problem if conception results. However, the semen of a donor may be used (AID). It may also be mixed with that of the husband. Generally, legal questions arise only when successful donor insemination is followed by marital breakdown. Otherwise, the particulars of artificial insemination will remain unknown and the offspring will enjoy the status of any other child. Unfortunately, when paternity has been challenged in the case of artificial insemination by donor, the child has tended to be found illegitimate. Donor insemination may also provide grounds for divorce on the basis of adultery unless the husband's consent has been obtained. While fullest legal protection would be assured if the husband were to adopt any child born as the result of AID, this precaution is rarely taken.

In People v. Sorensen, 437 P.2d 495 (Cal. 1968), the California Supreme Court held that Sorenson must support a child born after consensual AID.

> A reasonable man who, because of his inability to procreate, actively participates and consents to his wife's artificial insemination in the hope that a child will be produced whom they will treat as their own, knows that such behavior carries with it the legal responsibilities of fatherhood and criminal responsibility for nonsupport. One who consents to the production of a child cannot create a temporary relation to be assumed and disclaimed at will, but the arrangement must be of such a character as to impose an obligation of supporting those for whose existence he is directly responsible.

The child was not considered the product of an adulterous relationship, nor was he considered illegitimate. This ran counter to Gursky v. Gursky, 242 N.Y.S.2d 406 (1963), in which the court found an implied promise on the part of the husband to support the child and equitable estoppel in view of his consent to the AID procedures. The court held that the child could not be considered the legitimate issue of the husband. In contrast to this finding, In re Adoption of Anonymous, 345 N.Y.S.2d 430 (1973), concluded that the stepfather could not adopt the AID child when the mother's previous husband refused to give consent. The decision recognized the child as the husband's legitimate offspring.

The most obvious conclusion from these cases is that AID should be limited to stable marriages. Unfortunately, marital stability is difficult to predict successfully.

The Uniform Parentage Act (§3, 9A U.L.A. 589 [1980]) deals with the issue of artificial insemination:

> (a) If, under the supervision of a licensed physician and with the consent of her husband, a wife is inseminated artificially with semen donated by a man not her husband, the husband is treated in law as if he were the natural father of the child thereby conceived.
> . . .
>   (b) The donor of semen provided to a licensed physician for use in artificial insemination of a married woman other than the donor's wife is treated in law as if he were not the natural father of the child thereby conceived.

SOCIAL WORK AND REPRODUCTIVE RIGHTS

Since the social worker may help clients make decisions about contraception, abortion, and/or artificial insemination, respect for the client's own values and the principle of self-determination are most important. The wishes of the young pregnant woman in a marginal economic position may be particularly hard to determine, because she will be subjected to many influences and may lack the autonomy to express her own preferences.

Questions for Review

1. What major legal changes concerning contraception and abortion have occurred in the last two decades?

2.   Differentiate between *birth control* and *population control*.

3.   How common is sterilization in federally supported clinics?

4.   What dissent was a forerunner of *Griswold v. Connecticut*? Why is it important to review dissenting opinions on issues that have implications for social policy?

5.   What was the finding in *Griswold v. Connecticut*?

6.   What was the original charge in *Eisenstadt v. Baird*? What was the basis for the Supreme Court decision?

7.   What was the legal issue in *Troppi v. Scarf*? What was the outcome?

8.   Following *Roe v. Wade*, how does the interest of the state differ in each trimester of pregnancy?

9.   What was the contribution of *Doe v. Bolton* to the abortion question?

10.   According to the Supreme Court, what rights has the father concerning abortion?

11.   Compare the Supreme Court decisions on parental notification about abortion and formulate a policy statement that embodies the Court's position.

12.   What avenues are available to people who want abortion services but are unable to pay for them? How does the Hyde Amendment affect their situation?

13.   Why is a baby conceived by AID considered illegitimate in some jurisdictions?

14.   Given the secrecy surrounding AID, how could the child unknowingly become involved in incest when he or she marries?

15.   What is the main point of the section of the Uniform Parentage Act on artificial insemination?

Questions for Debate and Discussion

1.   Debate the decision in *Carey v. Population Services*. Should parents be informed of contraceptive services requested by minors?

2.   Why have some states provided contraceptive information to minors receiving welfare but not to other minors? Evaluate this policy.

3.   Evaluate the policy of the National Association of Social Workers on abortion. Identify any inconsistencies.

4.   Why is client self-determination most important in dealing with human reproduction?

Selected Readings   Bickett, Paula. "Federal Funding of Abortion." *Arizona State Law Journal* 1980 (1980): 160–205.

Buchanan, Elizabeth. "The Constitution and the Anomaly of the Pregnant Teenager." *Arizona Law Review* 24 (1982): 553–610.

Cates, Willard, Jr. "Legal Abortion: Public Health Record." *Science* 215 (1982): 1586–1590.

Frohock, Fred M. *Abortion: A Case Study in Law and Morals*. Westport, Conn.: Greenwood Press, 1983.

Jost, Kenneth. "The Right to a Life of Misery (Baby Doe)." *New Jersey Law Journal* 112 (1983): 7.

Katz, Sanford, "Rewriting the Adoption Story." *Family Advocate* 5 (1982): 8–10.

Petchesky, Rosalind P. *Abortion and Woman's Choice: the State, Sexuality, and the Conditions of Reproductive Freedom*. New York: Longman, 1983.

Rebone, Joseph W. "Personhood and the Contraceptive Right." *Indiana Law Journal* 57 (1982): 579–604.

Roth, Paul A. "Personhood, Property Rights, and the Permissibility of Abortion." *Law and Philosophy* 2 (1983): 163–191.

Schneider, Carl, and Morris Vinovskis. *The Law and Politics of Abortion.* Lexington, Mass.: Lexington Books, 1980.

"Squealing on Kids: HHS's Controversial New Regulation on Confidentiality and Contraception." *Children's Legal Rights Journal* 4 (1983): 8–12.

CHAPTER
12

Unmarried Parents and Illegitimacy

The legal system has dealt with unmarried parents and illegitimate children with only limited understanding. Our culture has been particularly harsh with what it considers sexual misconduct, although gradually the stigma of an illegitimate birth has been reduced. Before the birth, social services are most important to answer the basic questions about whether to marry, keep the child, release the child for adoption, or have an abortion. Only recently have services been made available to the males involved.

The law becomes important if the couple does not marry and financial support is needed, or if child placement becomes the plan of choice. This chapter summarizes parentage provisions, cases dealing with the legal rights of illegitimate children, and other law reforms.

OPTIONS RELATED TO PREGNANCY

To what extent has society been willing to change its attitudes toward illegitimacy? The illegitimate child has been at a disadvantage in English law. Originally, a bastard was denied both maternal and paternal inheritance and was known as *filius nullius*—the child of no one. Illegitimacy was irremediable unless the parents married prior to the child's birth.

Traditionally, children of annulled marriages did not attain legitimacy, since the defect in the marriage was usually determined after the woman had become pregnant or given birth to the child. Annulment could make a person a bastard retroactively. Now children of annulled marriages are considered legitimate.

The welfare and legal rights of single mothers and their children are of major relevance for social workers, especially for those working with mothers who are young, poor, or both. The offspring of unmarried parents have been the major source of children for adoption. With societal changes, the sexually active woman now has many more options from which to choose. Effective birth control methods will usually prevent unwanted pregnancies. The woman who does become pregnant can elect not to carry the child to term by having an abortion within the first trimester of pregnancy. Most women who choose to bear a child out of wedlock prefer to keep the infant rather than release him or her for adoption. Social workers may be involved in helping such women elect the best alternative for their own and the child's welfare. They may also help the mother who decides to keep her child resolve housing, familial, and employment problems related to single parenthood.

PATERNAL RIGHTS AND RESPONSIBIL- ITIES

Social workers are becoming increasingly involved in ascertaining the legal rights and responsibilities of fathers of illegitimate children. An attempt to obtain the father's consent is required prior to release of such children for adoption, and when a mother decides to keep the child, the putative father's ability and responsibility to contribute economic support becomes a major issue.

The issue of paternal responsibility for child support is the subject of federal legislation, which has provided for blood tests to determine paternity. Child support enforcement is included in Title XX of the Social Security Act as a means to strengthen family responsibility and control public welfare costs. In order to receive benefits, AFDC (Aid to Families with Dependent Children) mothers are obliged to reveal the identity of their children's father. Social workers have been skeptical of both the philosophical and monetary advantages of such a policy because of the financial stress it imposes on the mother and the limited income potential of the fathers involved, but the program is apparently cost-effective. The father's acknowledgment of paternity also gives the child the legal right to claim residual social insurance entitlements on the father's death or disablement.

ACKNOWLEDG- MENT AND PROOF OF PATERNITY

Acknowledgment of paternity is one means to legitimate a child. Generally paternity must be acknowledged in some public manner. The most elaborate legitimation procedure is followed in California, where not only is the father's acknowledgment of paternity necessary, but also proof that he received the child into his home with the consent of his wife. Consent of the wife is mandatory even if the couple lives apart.

Statutes of limitations are important in paternity proceedings. The Uniform Parentage Act (§§1-30, 9AULA 579–622 [1973]) stipulates a three-year period during which parents or others may bring action. In the interest of fairness, however, the child is allowed a period of twenty-one years in which to bring a paternity action on his or her own behalf.

Factors admissible in court as evidence of paternity include resemblance of the child to the putative father, testimony from other family members, and admissions of paternity by the father himself. In proving paternity, some states require the same standards of evidence as in a criminal proceeding—proof beyond reasonable doubt—while others are satisfied with a preponderance of evidence. In some states the mother's testimony must be corroborated also.

Blood tests are increasingly important in determining paternity. The Human Leukocyte Antigen (HLA) test makes it possible to determine paternity on an inclusive basis. Previous blood-typing procedures could exclude only the father. In 1983, HLA tests were admissible in thirty-five states and the District of Columbia. The details of the test and its acceptability in each state are presented by Kolko (1983).

Putative fathers may be required to submit to a blood test. The U.S. Supreme Court held in a case involving drunken driving, Schmerber v. State of California, 384 U.S. 757 (1966), that the Fifth Amendment protection from self-incrimination was not violated by an involuntary blood test, nor was the taking of blood an unlawful search and seizure under the Fourth Amendment.

In some cases, multiple factors can be used to deny paternity, as in *Beck v. Beck*, 304 N.E.2d 541 (Ind. Ct. App. 1973).

BECK v. BECK

Court of Appeals of
Indiana,
Third District 304
N.E.2d 541 (Ind. Ct.
App. 1973).

HOFFMAN, Chief Judge.

. . . The law presumes that a child born during wedlock is legitimate. Although at common-law this presumption was conclusive, it is now well-established that it may be overcome by evidence which is direct, clear and convincing. Thus, on appeal, reviewing the evidence most favorable to the appellee, the question becomes one of whether the trial court could find that the evidence was direct, clear and convincing.

In Phillips v. State, ex rel. (1925), 82 Ind.App. 356, at 360, 145 N.E. 895, at 897, it was stated that,

> "[T]he presumption could be overcome by proof that the husband was impotent; or that he was entirely absent so as to have had no access to the mother; or was entirely absent at the time the child in the course of nature must have been begotten; or was present only under such circumstances as to afford clear and satisfactory proof that there was no sexual intercourse."

The existing exceptions to the presumption of legitimacy . . . have been regarded as being susceptible to expansion. For example, . . . sterility of the husband, if conclusively shown, might also overcome the presumption. . . .

Thus, where the appellee denied having sexual relations with his wife during the possible period of conception; where the wife traveled to another town with a man other than her husband; where the wife had been in taverns with other men; where the husband consistently denied being the father of his wife's child; where the parties did not live together after the time when the wife disclosed her pregnancy; and where the results of blood tests showed that the husband was excluded as being the father of the child; the trial court did not err in finding that all of the evidence, considered together, constituted direct, clear and convincing proof that Joseph Ray Beck was not the father of his wife's child.

In Watts v. Watts (337 A.2d 350 [N.H. 1975]), a husband was denied the right to introduce a blood test as evidence of nonpaternity after acknowledging paternity of the children for fifteen years.

WATTS v. WATTS

Supreme Court of New
Hampshire,
Hillsborough, 337 A.2d
350 (N.H. 1975).

KENISON, Chief Justice.

The question presented by this action is whether a husband may escape liability for support of two minor children by attempting to disprove paternity through blood tests where he has acknowledged the children since their birth. . . .

Barbara and Milton Watts were married October 28, 1950. During the marriage four children were born: Alice, George, Dianne and Walter. In September 1971, Barbara filed for divorce on the ground of irreconcilable differences, requesting support as well as custody of the minor children Alice, Dianne and Walter. Milton retained custody of George. By a temporary order dated October 29, KELLER, C. J., granted plaintiff custody of the three children and ordered defendant to pay support in the amount of $45 per week. . . .

Based on the pleadings and on the trial court's ruling of August 28, 1972, DUNFEY, J., denied defendant's motion for blood tests dated March 23, 1973, in which he once again denied paternity of Dianne and Walter Watts. . . .

Basically, defendant contends that RSA 522:1 furnishes express statutory authority permitting him to request blood tests in order to rebut the presumption that Alice and Walter are his children. RSA 522:1 provides that in a civil action in which paternity is a relevant fact the court may order the mother, child or alleged father to submit to blood tests. While the prevailing rules permit both common law and statutory presumptions to be rebutted by blood tests, those rules do not apply in a situation such as this one where defendant has acknowledged the children as his own without challenge for over fifteen years.

To allow defendant to escape liability for support by using blood tests would be to ignore his lengthy, voluntary acceptance of parental responsibilities. Although there is neither a New Hampshire statute nor case in point, the policy of the law in this State does not permit defendant to abandon his parental responsibilities at this late date. An analogous result is required by RSA 457:42 (Legitimation of Children, Marriage of Parents) which provides that if "parents of children born before marriage afterwards intermarry, and recognize such children as their own, such children shall be legitimate and shall inherit equally with their other children. . . ." . . . The obligation to support inheres no less where a father has consistently recognized children as his own for a period of over fifteen years. The trial court's findings and rulings are supported by the record and are sustained.

If the defendant is found guilty in a paternity action, the court determines the amount he must pay toward the mother's expenses, including attorney's fees, and child support. Traditionally the level of support in such awards has been minimal. There is no reason these awards should not be based on the child's needs and the father's resources, just as in any other case involving child support. Imprisonment has been used to enforce such orders, but it is counterproductive because it reduces the father's capacity to pay by depriving him of his income and perhaps his job. Enforcement of paternity judgments by courts across state lines has also been especially problematical. Children generally have not received the full benefits of the Uniform Enforcement of Support Act.

DEFENSES IN PATERNITY PROCEEDINGS

Generally our society defends a strong presumption of legitimacy. Clark (1974: 172–173) observes that impotence, evidence of a convincing nature that the husband and wife were never together under circumstances in which sexual intercourse was possible, or a blood test with negative findings are the main facts sufficient to rebut the presumption of paternity.

A major question is whether the mother's promiscuity (*exceptio plurium concumbentium*) may constitute a defense. Under this principle, proof that the mother engaged in sexual relations with men other than the defendant at about the time of conception assures that he cannot be found to be the father. This defense is rarely successful because it depends on the mother's admission of multiple acts of sexual intercourse. If she makes such an admission, the court can only weigh her word against that of men subpoenaed as witnesses on the defendant's behalf. In some countries, all men who testify to having intercourse with a woman have been held liable for child support.

RIGHTS OF CUSTODY

Until recently the mother has been accorded the primary right to the child's custody as well as the primary duty of support. Paternal rights traditionally resulted from voluntary acknowledgment or a positive finding in a paternity proceeding. Stanley v. Illinois, 405 U.S. 645 (1972), recognized the claims of putative fathers to a hearing on their fitness before they can be denied custody of their children. As a result of this decision, a release must be secured from the putative father and the mother before the child can be placed in adoption. The major problem is that many fathers have no interest in such children and do not even know that they were conceived. A search for the father under such circumstances delays placement proceedings unnecessarily.

THE UNIFORM PARENTAGE ACT

A model act is of value in specifying and publicizing goals in the extension of rights to unmarried mothers and their children. The Uniform Parentage Act, §§ 1–29, 9 A U.L.A. 587–622 (1973), published in 1974, provides the process for determining paternity.

The Parent-Child Relationship

States could eliminate the distinction between legitimacy and illegitimacy by enacting the Uniform Parentage Act, which accomplishes the purpose in its first two sections:

> **Section 1.   Parent and Child Relationship Defined**
> As used in this Act, "parent and child relationship" means the legal relationship existing between a child and his natural or adoptive parents incident to which the law confers or imposes rights, privileges, duties, and obligations. It includes the mother and child relationship and the father and child relationship.
>
> **Section 2.   Relationship Not Dependent on Marriage**
> The parent and child relationship extends equally to every child and to every parent, regardless of the marital status of the parents.

Children born as a result of maternal insemination by donor present a complex legal situation. As indicated in Chapter 11, some states hold that such a child is illegitimate since the husband is not the donor. This problem is frequently dealt with by mixing the sperm of the donor with that of the husband so that paternity can more easily be attributed to the latter. Section 5 of the Uniform Parentage Act requires the husband's written consent to donor insemination, thereby assuring that he will legally be treated as the natural father of a child so conceived.

Jurisdiction

Legal jurisdiction over the putative father is required for a paternity action. The Uniform Parentage Act states: "A person who has sexual intercourse in this state thereby submits to the jurisdiction of the courts of this state as to any action brought under the act with respect to a child who might have been conceived by that act of intercourse." Jurisdiction over the alleged father may or may not be based on the child's conception and/or birth in that state. Personal jurisdiction is provided by personal service of summons or by registered mail with proof of actual receipt. The action may be brought in the county in which the child or the alleged father resides or is found.

Parties to the Action   The child shall be made a party to the paternity action and be represented by his or her general guardian or a guardian ad litem. The natural mother and each man presumed or alleged to be the natural father shall also be made parties to the suit.

Procedure   The Uniform Parentage Act provides for an informal hearing from which the public will be barred. Blood tests may be required by the court and are relied on as a major means by which to encourage voluntary settlement. Section 12 outlines evidence relating to paternity:

1.   evidence of sexual intercourse between the mother and alleged father at any possible time of conception;

2.   an expert's opinion concerning the statistical probability of the alleged father's paternity based upon the duration of the mother's pregnancy;

3.   blood test results, weighted in accordance with evidence, if available, of the statistical probability of the alleged father's paternity;

4.   medical or anthropological evidence relating to the alleged father's paternity of the child based on tests performed by experts. If a man has been identified as a possible father of the child, the court may, and upon request of a party shall, require the child, the mother, and the man to submit to appropriate tests; and

5.   all other evidence relevant to the issue of paternity of the child.

A pretrial hearing may result in agreement on one of the three recommendations outlined in Section 13 of the act (note the opportunity for compromise contained in the second provision):

Section 13.   Pre-trial Recommendations

(a) On the basis of the information produced at the pretrial hearing, the judge [or referee] conducting the hearing shall evaluate the probability of determining the existence or non-existence of the father and child relationship in a trial and whether a judicial declaration of their relationship would be in the best interest of the child. On the basis of the evaluation, an appropriate recommendation for settlement shall be made to the parties, which may include any of the following:

(1)   that the action be dismissed with or without prejudice;

(2)   that the matter be compromised by an agreement among the alleged father, the mother, and the child, in which the father and child relationship is not determined but in which a defined economic obligation is undertaken by the alleged father in favor of the child and, if appropriate, in favor of the mother, subject to approval by the judge [or referee] conducting the hearing. In reviewing the obligation undertaken by the alleged father in a compromise agreement, the judge [or referee] conducting the hearing shall consider the best interest of the child, in the light of the factors enumerated in Section 15(e), discounted by the improbability, as it appears to him, of establishing the alleged father's paternity or non-paternity of the child in a trial of the action. In the best interest of the child, the court may order that the alleged father's identity be kept confidential. In that case, the court may designate a person or agency to receive from the alleged father and disburse on behalf of the child all amounts paid by the alleged father in fulfillment of obligations imposed on him; and

(3)   that the alleged father voluntarily acknowledge his paternity of the child.

(b) If the parties accept a recommendation made in accordance with Subsection (a), judgment shall be entered accordingly.

(c) If a party refuses to accept a recommendation made under Subsection (a) and blood tests have not been taken, the court shall require the parties to submit to blood tests, if practicable. Thereafter the judge [or referee] shall make an appropriate final recommendation. If a party refuses to accept the final recommendation, the action shall be set for trial.

(d) The guardian ad litem may accept or refuse to accept a recommendation under this Section.

(e) The informal hearing may be terminated and the action set for trial if the judge [or referee] conducting the hearing finds it unlikely that all parties would accept a recommendation he might make under Subsection (a) or (c).

When none of the procedures contained in Section 13 can be agreed on by the interested parties, the paternity action will be set for trial:

Section 14. Civil Action; Jury

(a) An action under this Act is a civil action governed by the rules of civil procedure. The mother of the child and the alleged father are competent to testify and may be compelled to testify. Subsections (b) and (c) of Section 10 and Sections 11 and 12 apply.

(b) Testimony relating to sexual access to the mother by an unidentified man at any time or by an identified man at a time other than the probable time of conception of the child is inadmissible in evidence, unless offered by the mother.

(c) In an action against an alleged father, evidence offered by him with respect to a man who is not subject to the jurisdiction of the court concerning his sexual intercourse with the mother at or about the probable time of conception of the child is admissible in evidence only if he has undergone and made available to the court blood tests the results of which do not exclude the possibility of his paternity of the child. A man who is identified and is subject to the jurisdiction of the court shall be made a defendant in the action.

[(d) The trial shall be by the court without a jury.]

The drafters of the act explain Section 14:

> Subsection (a) makes it clear that the action to establish paternity is a civil action. A number of states have continued to view the action as criminal or quasi-criminal, although a majority of states now treat the paternity action as a civil proceeding.
>
> Subsections (b) and (c) deal with the problem of the *exceptio plurium concumbentium* and, more specifically, the problem of perjured testimony concerning alleged sexual access to the mother offered by other men on behalf of the alleged father. It is recognized that in rare cases, these provisions may result in the exclusion of "honest" evidence. However, the Committee concluded that this is outweighed by the need for closing the door to the wanton attacks on the mother's character that characterize too many paternity suits under present laws.
>
> The use of a jury is not desirable in the emotional atmosphere of cases of this nature. The clause eliminating the jury is bracketed only because of some states constitutions may prevent elimination of a jury trial in this context.

Child Support   Section 15 of the act provides detailed guidelines for determining the amount of child support to be paid:

Section 15. Judgment or Order

(a) The judgment or order of the court determining the existence or non-existence of the parent and child relationship is determinative for all purposes.

(b) If the judgment or order of the court is at variance with the child's birth certificate, the court shall order that [an amended birth registration be made] [a new birth certificate be issued] under Section 23.

(c) The judgment or order may contain any other provision directed against the appropriate party to the proceeding, concerning the duty of support, the custody and guardianship of the child, visitation privileges with the child, the furnishing of bond or other security for the payment of the judgment, or any other matter in the best interest of the child. The judgment or order may direct the father to pay the reasonable expenses of the mother's pregnancy and confinement.

(d) Support judgments or orders ordinarily shall be for periodic payments which may vary in amount. In the best interest of the child, a lump sum payment or the purchase of an annuity may be ordered in lieu of periodic payments of support. The court may limit the father's liability for past support of the child to the proportion of the expenses already incurred that the court deems just.

(e) In determining the amount to be paid by a parent for support of the child and the period during which the duty of support is owed, a court enforcing the oblibation of support shall consider all relevant facts, including (1) the needs of the child; (2) the standard of living and circumstances of the parents; (3) the relative financial means of the parents; (4) the earning ability of the parents; (5) the need and capacity of the child for education, including higher education; (6) the age of the child; (7) the financial resources and the earning ability of the child; (8) the responsibility of the parents for the support of others; and (9) the value of services contributed by the custodial parent.

Release for Adoption   In view of the special interest of social agencies in issues related to adoption, Section 24 of the Uniform Parentage Act and the drafters' comments thereto are included below in their entirety. This section deals with the rights accorded putative fathers in the release of their children for adoption. These provisions are consistent with the Supreme Court decision in Stanley v. Illinois, 405 U.S. 645 (1972).

Section 24. Custodial Proceedings

(a) If a mother relinquishes or proposes to relinquish for adoption a child who has (1) a presumed father under Section 4(a), (2) a father whose relationship to the child has been determined by a court, or (3) a father as to whom the child is a legitimate child under prior law of this State or under the law of another jurisdiction, the father shall be given notice of the adoption proceeding and have the rights provided under [the appropriate State statute] [the Revised Uniform Adoption Act], unless the father's relationship to the child has been previously terminated or determined by a court not to exist.

(b) If a mother relinquishes or proposes to relinquish for adoption a child who does not have (1) a presumed father under Section 4(a), (2) a father whose relationship of the child has been determined by a court, or (3) a father as to whom the child is a legitimate child under prior law of this State or under the law of another jurisdiction, or if a child otherwise becomes the subject of an adoption proceeding, the agency or person to whom the child has been or is to be relinquished, or the mother or the person having custody of the child, shall file a petition in the [   ] court to terminate the parental rights of the father, unless the father's relationship to the child has been previously terminated or determined not to exist by a court.

(c) In an effort to identify the natural father, the court shall cause inquiry to be made of the mother and any other appropriate person. The inquiry shall include the following: whether the mother was married at the time of conception of the child or at any time thereafter; whether the mother was cohabiting with a man at the time of conception or birth of the child; whether the mother has received support payments or promises of support with respect to the child or in connection with her pregnancy; or whether any man has formally or informally acknowledged or declared his possible paternity of the child.

(d) If, after the inquiry, the natural father is identified to the satisfaction of the court, or if more than one man is identified as a possible father, each shall be given notice of the proceeding in accordance with Subsection (f). If any of them fails to appear or, if appearing, fails to claim custodial rights, his parental rights with reference to the child shall be terminated. If the natural father or a man representing himself to be the natural father, claims custodial rights, the court shall proceeed to determine custodial rights.

(e) If, after the inquiry, the court is unable to identify the natural father or any possible natural father and no person has appeared claiming to be the natural father and claiming custodial rights, the court shall enter an order terminating the unknown natural father's parental rights with reference to the child. Subject to the disposition of an appeal, upon the expiration of [6 months] after an order terminating parental rights is issued under this subsection, the order cannot be questioned by any person, in any manner, or upon any ground, including fraud, misrepresentation, failure to give any required notice, or lack of jurisdiction of the parties or of the subject matter.

(f) Notice of the proceeding shall be given to every person identified as the natural father or a possible natural father [in the manner appropriate under rules of civil procedure for the service of process in a civil action in this state, or] in any manner the court directs. Proof of giving the notice shall be filed with the court before the petition is heard. [If no person has been identified as the natural father or a possible father, the court, on the basis of all information available, shall determine whether publication or public posting of notice of the proceedings is likely to lead to identification and, if so, shall order publication or public posting at times and in places and manner it deems appropriate.]

The drafters comment:

Subsection (a) provides that a father whose identity is presumed under Subsection 4 or whose paternity has been formally ascertained, must be given notice of an adoption proceeding relating to his child.

Subsection (b) deals with the case in which the father has not been formally ascertained and the mother seeks to surrender the child for adoption. In the light of the U.S. Supreme Court's decisions in Stanley v. Illinois, 405 U.S. 645, 1208 (1972); Rothstein v. Lutheran Social Services of Wisconsin and Upper Michigan, 405 U.S. 1051 (1972), and Vanderlaan v. Vanderlaan, 405 U.S. 1051 (1972), and related state court decisions, it is considered essential that the unknown or unascertained father's potential rights be terminated formally in order to safeguard the subsequent adoption.

Subsections (c) through (f) provide a procedure by which the court may ascertain the identity of the father and permit speedy termination of his potential rights *if he shows no interest in the child*. If, on the other hand, the natural father or a man representing himself to be the natural father claims custodial rights, the court is given authority to determine custodial rights. It is contemplated that there may be cases in which the man alleging himself to be the father is so clearly unfit to take custody of the child that the court would proceed to terminate his potential parental rights without deciding whether the man actually is the father of the child. If, on the other hand, the man alleging himself to be the father and claiming custody is prima facie fit to have custody of the child, an action to ascertain paternity is indicated, unless a voluntary acknowledgment can be obtained in accordance with Section 4(a)(5) of this Act.

Subsection (e) raises serious constitutional questions in that it attempts to cut off after a given period any claim seeking to reopen a judgment terminating parental rights. While of questionable constitutionality, such a provision is not without precedent. A similar provision is contained in Section 15(b) of the revised Uniform Adoption Act, approved by the Commissioners on Uniform State Laws in 1969, and other similar provisions are contained in the adoption acts of a number of states. Moreover, it must be considered that the case of adoption differs from other situations. The parent's claim to his child can hardly be compared to a person's claim to property. The Supreme Court itself recognized that the interest of the child is heavily involved in these cases when remanding the *Rothstein* case to the Wisconsin Supreme Court, requiring that the court give "due consideration [to] the completion of the adoption proceedings and the fact that the child has apparently lived with the adoptive family for the intervening period of time." Cf. Armstrong v. Manzo, 380 U.S. 545 (1965).

Subsection (f) seeks to conform to the following footnote in Stanley v. Illinois: "We note in passing that the incremental cost of offering unwed fathers an opportunity for individualized hearings on fitness appears to be minimal. If unwed fathers, in the main, do not care about the disposition of their children, they will not appear to demand hearings. If they do care, under the scheme here held invalid, Illinois would admittedly at some later time have to afford them a properly focused hearing in a custody or adoption proceeding.

"Extending opportunity for hearing to unwed fathers who desire and claim competence to care for their children creates no constitutional or procedural obstacle to foreclosing those unwed fathers who are not so inclined. The Illinois law governing procedure in juvenile cases . . . provides for personal service, notice by certified mail or for notice by publication when personal or certified mail service cannot be had or when notice is directed to unknown respondents under the style of 'all whom it may concern.' Unwed fathers who do not promptly respond cannot complain if their children are declared wards of the State. Those who do respond retain the burden of proving their fatherhood."

This footnote *might* be interpreted to require publication in all cases in which a child with unascertained paternity is surrendered for adoption. The Committee considered, however, that there will be many such cases in which it will be highly probable that publication will not lead to the identification of the father. In view of that and the fact that in nearly all cases publication will lead to substantial embarrassment for the mother, the Committee thought it appropriate to allow the court to determine whether, in the particular circumstances of each case, publication would be likely to lead to the identification of the father. One serious consequence that might result from an indiscriminate publication requirement is that some mothers may be caused to withhold their children from adoption even where adoption would be in the child's best interest.

EQUAL RIGHTS FOR ILLEGITIMATE CHILDREN

Attempts at achieving the goal of equal rights for all children and parents, regardless of parental marital status, have been greatly enhanced by several U.S. Supreme Court decisions.

Two decisions found Louisiana's wrongful death statute unconstitutional: Levy v. Louisiana, 391 U.S. 68 (1968), and Glona v. American Guarantee and Liability Insurance Co., 391 U.S. 73 (1968). The former excluded illegitimate children from recovery for the wrongful death of their mother.

LEVY v. LOUISIANA

Supreme Court of the United States, 391 U.S. 68 (1968).

Mr. Justice DOUGLAS delivered the opinion of the Court.

Appellant sued on behalf of five illegitimate children to recover under a Louisiana statute (La.Civ.Code Ann. Art. 2315 [Supp. 1967]) for two kinds of damages as a result of the wrongful death of their mother: (1) the damages to them for the loss of their mother, and (2) those based on the survival of a cause of action which the mother had at the time of her death for pain and suffering. Appellees are the doctor who treated her and the insurance company.

We assume in the present state of the pleadings that the mother, Louise Levy, gave birth to these five illegitimate children and that they lived with her; that she treated them as a parent would treat any other child; that she worked as a domestic servant to support them, taking them to church every Sunday and enrolling them, at her own expense, in a parochial school. The Louisiana District Court dismissed the suit. The Court of Appeals affirmed, holding that "child" in Article 2315 means "legitimate child," the denial to illegitimate children of "the right to recover" being "based on morals and general welfare because it discourages bringing children into the world out of wedlock." 192 So.2d 193, 195. The Supreme Court of Louisiana denied certiorari. . . .

The case is here on appeal . . . and we noted probable jurisdiction, . . . the statute as construed having been sustained against challenge under both the Due Process and Equal Protection Clauses of the Fourteenth Amendment.

We start from the premise that illegitimate children are not "nonpersons." They are humans, live, and have their being. They are clearly "persons" within the meaning of the Equal Protection Clause of the Fourteenth Amendment.

While a State has broad power when it comes to making classifications . . . , it may not draw a line which constitutes an invidious discrimination against a particular class. . . . Though the test has been variously stated, the end result is whether the line drawn is a rational one. . . .

In applying the Equal Protection Clause to social and economic legislation, we give great latitude to the legislature in making classifications. Even so, would a corporation, which is a "person," for certain purposes, within the meaning of the Equal Protection Clause . . . be required to forego recovery for wrongs done its interests because its incorporators were all bastards? However that might be, we have been extremely sensitive when it comes to basic civil rights . . . and have not hesitated to strike down an invidious classification even though it had history and tradition on its side. . . . The rights asserted here involve the intimate, familial relationship between a child and his own mother. When the child's claim of damage for loss of his mother is in issue, why, in terms of "equal protection," should the tortfeasors go free merely because the child is illegitimate? Why should the illegitimate child be denied rights merely because of his birth out of wedlock? He certainly is subject to all the responsibilities of a citizen, including the payment of taxes and conscription under the Selective Service Act. How under our constitutional regime can he be denied correlative rights which other citizens enjoy?

Legitimacy or illegitimacy of birth has no relation to the nature of the wrong allegedly inflicted on the mother. These children, though illegitimate, were dependent on her; she cared for them and nurtured them; they were indeed hers in the biological and in the spiritual sense; in her death they suffered wrong in the sense that any dependent would.

We conclude that it is invidious to discriminate against them when no action, conduct, or demeanor of theirs is possibly relevant to the harm that was done the mother.

Reversed.

In Glona v. American Guarantee and Liability Insurance Company (391 U.S. 73 [1968]) a mother sued following the wrongful death of her illegitimate son.

GLONA v. AMERICAN GUARANTEE & LIABILITY INSURANCE CO.

Supreme Court of the United States, 391 U.S. 73 (1968).

Mr. Justice DOUGLAS delivered the opinion of the Court.

This suit was brought in the Federal District Court under the head of diversity jurisdiction to recover for a wrongful death suffered in an automobile accident in Louisiana. The plaintiff, a Texas domiciliary, was the mother of the victim, her illegitimate son. Had the Texas wrongful death statute been applicable, it would, as construed, have authorized the action. But summary judgment was granted on the ground that under Louisiana law the mother had no right of action for the death of her illegitimate son. The Court of Appeals affirmed, rejecting the claim that the discrimination violated the Equal Protection Clause of the Fourteenth Amendment. 379 F.2d 545. We granted the petition for a writ of certiorari . . . in order to hear the case along with *Levy v. Louisiana*. . . .

Louisiana follows a curious course in its sanctions against illegitimacy. A common-law wife is allowed to sue under the Louisiana wrongful death statute. When a married woman gives birth to an illegitimate child, he is, with a few exceptions, conclusively presumed to be legitimate. Louisiana makes no distinction between legitimate children and illegitimate children where incest is concerned. A mother may inherit from an illegitimate child whom she has acknowledged and vice versa. If the illegitimate son had a horse that was killed by the defendant and then died himself, his mother would have a right to sue for the loss of that property. If the illegitimate son were killed in an industrial accident at his place of employment, the mother would be eligible for recovery under the Louisiana Workmen's Compensation Act, if she were a dependent of his. Yet it is argued that since the legislature is dealing with "sin," it can deal with it selectively and is not compelled to adopt comprehensive or even consistent measures. In this sense the present case is different from the *Levy* case, where by mere accident of birth the innocent, although illegitimate child was made a "nonperson" by the legislature, when it came to recovery of damages for the wrongful death of his mother.

Yet we see no possible rational basis for assuming that if the natural mother is allowed recovery for the wrongful death of her illegitimate child, the cause of illegitimacy will be served. It would, indeed, be farfetched to assume that women have illegitimate children so that they can be compensated in damages for their death. A law which creates an open season on illegitimates in the area of automobile accidents gives a windfall to tortfeasors. But it hardly has a causal connection with the "sin," which is, we are told, the historic reason for the creation of the disability. To say that the test of equal protection should be the "legal" rather than the biological relationship is to avoid the issue. For the Equal Protection Clause necessarily limits the authority of a State to draw such "legal" lines as it chooses.

Opening the courts to suits of this kind may conceivably be a temptation to some to assert motherhood fraudulently. That problem, however, concerns burden of proof. Where the claimant is plainly the mother, the State denies equal protection of the laws to withhold relief merely because the child, wrongfully killed, was born to her out of wedlock.

[Justices Harlan, Black, and Stewart dissented in *Levy v. Louisiana*, and *Glona v. American Guarantee and Liability Ins. Co.*]

Weber v. Aetna Casualty & Surety Company, 406 U.S. 164 (1972), determined that dependent, unacknowledged, illegitimate children are eligible for receipt of worker's compensation benefits on the death of their father.

WEBER v. AETNA CASUALTY & SURETY CO.

Supreme Court of the United States, 406 U.S. 164 (1972).

Mr. Justice POWELL delivered the opinion of the Court.

The question before us, on writ of certiorari to the Supreme Court of Louisiana, concerns the right of dependent unacknowledged, illegitimate children to recover under Louisiana workmen's compensation laws benefits for the death of their natural father on an equal footing with his dependent legitimate children. We hold that Louisiana's denial of equal recovery rights to dependent unacknowledged illegitimates violates the Equal Protection Clause of the Fourteenth Amendment.

On June 22, 1967, Henry Clyde Stokes died in Louisiana of injuries received during the course of his employment the previous day. At the time of his death Stokes resided and maintained a household with one Willie May Weber, to whom he was not married. Living in the household were four legitimate minor children, born of the marriage between Stokes and Adlay Jones Stokes, who was at the time committed to a mental hospital. Also living in the home was one unacknowledged illegitimate child born of the relationship between Stokes and Willie Mae Weber. A second illegitimate child of Stokes and Weber was born posthumously.

On June 29, 1967, Stokes' four legitimate children, through their maternal grandmother as guardian, filed a claim for their father's death under Louisiana's workmen's compensation law. The defendant employer and its insurer impleaded Willie May Weber, who appeared and claimed compensation benefits for the two illegitimate children. . . .

The trial judge awarded the four legitimate children the maximum allowable amount of compensation and declared their entitlement had been satisfied from the tort suit settlement. Consequently, the four legitimate children dismissed their workmen's compensation claim. Judgment was also awarded to Stokes' two illegitimate offspring to the extent that maximum compensation benefits were not exhausted by the four legitimate children. Since such benefits had been entirely exhausted by the amount of the tort settlement, in which only the four dependent legitimate offspring participated, the two dependent illegitimate children received nothing.

For purposes of recovery under workmen's compensation, Louisiana law defines children to include "only legitimate children, stepchildren, posthumous children, and illegitimate children acknowledged under the provisions of Civil Code Articles 203, 204 and 205." Thus legitimate children and acknowledged illegitimates may recover on an equal basis. Unacknowledged illegitimate children, however, are relegated to the lesser status of "other dependents" under § 1232(8) of the workmen's compensation statute and may recover *only* if there are not enough surviving dependents in the preceding classifications to exhaust the maximum allowable benefits. Both the Louisiana Court of Appeal and a divided Louisiana Supreme Court sustained these statutes over appellants' constitutional objections, holding that our decision in *Levy*, supra, was not controlling.

We disagree. . . .

The court below sought to distinguish *Levy* as involving a statute which absolutely excluded *all* illegitimates from recovery, whereas in the compensation statute in the instant case acknowledged illegitimates may recover equally with legitimate children and "the unacknowledged illegitimate child is not *denied* a right to recover compensation, he being merely relegated to a less favorable position as are other dependent relatives such as parents." . . . Stokes v. Aetna Casualty and Surety Co., 257 La. 424, 433–434, 242 So.2d 567, 570 (1970). The Louisiana Supreme Court likewise characterized *Levy* as a tort action where the tortfeasor escaped liability on the fortuity of the potential claimant's illegitimacy, whereas in the present action full compensation was rendered, and no "tortfeasor goes free because of the law." Id., at 434, 242 So.2d, at 570.

We do not think *Levy* can be disposed of by such finely carved distinctions. The Court in *Levy* was not so much concerned with the tortfeasor going free as with the equality of treatment, under the statutory recovery scheme. Here, as in *Levy*, there is impermissible discrimination. An unacknowledged illegitimate child may suffer as much from the loss of a parent as a child born within wedlock or an illegitimate later acknowledged. So far as this record shows, the dependency and natural affinity of the unacknowledged illegitimate child for her father were as great as those of the four legitimate children whom Louisiana law has allowed to recover. (The affinity and dependency on the father of the posthumously born illegitimate child is, of course, not comparable to that of offspring living at the time of their father's death. This fact, however, does not alter our view of the case. We think a posthumously born illegitimate child should be treated the same as a posthumously born legitimate child, which the Louisiana statutes fail to do.) The legitimate children and the illegitimate child all lived in the home of the deceased and were equally dependent upon him for maintenance and support. It is inappropriate, therefore, for the court below to talk of relegating the unacknowledged illegitimate "to a less favorable position as are other dependent relatives such as parents." The unacknowledged illegitimate is *not* a parent or some "other dependent relative"; in this case she is a *dependent child*, and as such is entitled to rights granted other *dependent children*.

Respondent contends that our recent ruling in Labine v. Vincent . . . controls this case. In *Labine*, the Court upheld against constitutional objections, Louisiana intestacy laws which had barred an acknowledged illegitimate child from sharing equally with legitimate children in her father's estate. That decision reflected, in major part, the traditional deference to a State's prerogative to regulate the disposition at death of property within its borders. . . . The Court has long afforded broad scope to state discretion in this area. Yet the substantial state interest in providing for "the stability of . . . land titles and in the prompt and definitive determination of the valid ownership of property left by decedents," Labine v. Vincent, 229 So.2d 449, 452 (La.App. 1969), is absent in the case at hand.

Moreover, in *Labine* the intestate, unlike deceased in the present action, might easily have modified his daughter's disfavored position. . . .

Such options, however, were not realistically open to Henry Stokes. Under Louisiana law he could not have acknowledged his illegitimate children even had he desired to do so. The burdens of illegitimacy, already weighty, become doubly so when neither parent nor child can legally lighten them.

Both the statute in *Levy* and the statute in the present case involve state-created compensation schemes, designed to provide close relatives and dependents of a deceased a means of recovery for his often abrupt and accidental death. Both wrongful death statutes and workmen's compensation codes represent outgrowths and modifications of our basic tort law. The former alleviated the harsh common-law rule under which "no person could inherit the personal right of another for tortious injuries to his body"; the latter removed difficult obstacles to recovery in work-related injuries by offering a more certain, though generally less remunerative compensation. In the instant case, the recovery sought under the workmen's compensation statute was in lieu of an action under the identical death statute which was at issue in *Levy*. Given the similarities in the origins and purposes of these two statutes, and the similarities of Louisiana's pattern of discrimination in recovery rights, it would require a disregard of precedent and the principles of *stare decisis* to hold that *Levy* did not control the facts of the case before us. It makes no difference that illegitimates are not so absolutely or broadly barred here as in *Levy*; the discrimination remains apparent.

Having determined that *Levy* is the applicable precedent, we briefly reaffirm here the reasoning which produced that result. The tests to determine the validity of state statutes under the Equal Protection Clause have been variously expressed, but this Court requires, at a minimum, that a statutory classification bear some rational relationship to a legitimate state purpose. . . . Though the latitude given state economic and social regulation is necessarily broad, when state statutory classifications approach sensitive and fundamental personal rights, this Court exercises a stricter scrutiny. . . . The essential inquiry in all the foregoing cases is, however, inevitably a dual one: What legitimate state interest does the classification promote? What fundamental personal rights might the classification endanger?

The Louisiana Supreme Court emphasized strongly the State's interest in protecting "legitimate family relationships," 257 La., at 433, 242 So.2d, at 570, and the regulation and protection of the family unit has indeed been a venerable state concern. We do not question the importance of that interest; what we do question is how the challenged statute will promote it. As was said in *Glona*: "We see no possible rational basis . . . for assuming that if the natural mother is allowed recovery for the wrongful death of her illegitimate child, the case of illegitimacy will be served. It would indeed be farfetched to assume that women have illegitimate children so that they can be compensated in damages for their death." . . . Nor can it be thought here that persons will shun illicit relations because the offspring may not one day reap the benefits of workmen's compensation.

It may perhaps be said that statutory distinctions between the legitimate and illegitimate reflect closer family relationships in that the illegitimate is more often not under care in the home of the father nor even supported by him. The illegitimate, so this argument runs, may thus be made less eligible for the statutory recoveries and inheritances reserved for those more likely to be within the ambit of familial care and affection. Whatever the merits elsewhere of this contention, it is not compelling in a statutory compensation scheme where dependency on the deceased is a prerequisite to anyone's recovery, and where to the acknowledgment so necessary to equal recovery rights may be unlikely to occur or legally impossible to effectuate even where the illegitimate child may be nourished and loved.

Finally, we are mindful that States have frequently drawn arbitrary lines in workmen's compensation and wrongful death statutes to facilitate potentially difficult problems of proof. Nothing in our decision would impose on state court systems a greater burden in this regard. By limiting recovery to dependents of the deceased, Louisiana substantially lessens the possible problems of locating illegitimate children and of determining uncertain claims of parenthood. Our decision fully respects Louisiana's choice on this matter. It will not expand claimants for workmen's compensation beyond those in a direct blood and dependency relationship with the deceased and avoids altogether diffuse questions of affection and affinity which pose difficult probative problems. Our ruling requires equality of treatment between two classes of persons and genuineness of those claims the State might in any event be required to determine.

The state interest in legitimate family relationships is not served by the statute; the state interest in minimizing problems of proof is not significantly disturbed by our decision. The inferior classification of dependent unacknowledged illegitimates bears, in this instance, no significant relationship to those recognized purposes of recovery which workmen's compensation statutes commendably serve.

The status of illegitimacy has expressed through the ages society's condemnation of irresponsible liaisons beyond the bonds of marriage. But visiting this condemnation on the head of an infant is illogical and unjust. Moreover, imposing disabilities on the illegitimate child is contrary to the basic concept of our system that legal burdens should bear some relationship to individual responsibility or wrongdoing. Obviously, no child is responsible for his birth and penalizing the illegitimate child is an ineffectual—as well as an unjust—way of deterring the parent. Courts are powerless to prevent the social opprobrium suffered by these hapless children, but the Equal Protection Clause does enable us to strike down discriminatory laws relating to status of birth where—as in this case—the classification is justified by no legitimate state interest, compelling or otherwise.

Reversed and remanded.

Mr. Justice BLACKMUN, concurring in the result.

Mr. Justice REHNQUIST, dissenting:

This case is distinguishable from Levy v. Louisiana, 391 U.S. 68 (1968), and could be decided the other way on the basis of this Court's more recent decision in *Labine v. Vincent*. . . . Yet I certainly do not regard the Court's decision as an unreasonable drawing of the line between *Levy* and *Labine*, and would not feel impelled to dissent if I regarded *Levy* as rightly decided. I do not so regard it. I must agree with Mr. Justice Harlan's dissenting opinion, which described *Levy* and its companion case, Glona v. American Guarantee & Liability Insurance Co., 391 U.S. 73 (1968), as "constitutional curiosities," and called the Court's method of reaching the result "a process that can only be described as brute force."

The Supreme Court, in Gomez v. Perez (409 U.S. 535 [1973]), decided that an illegitimate child is guaranteed the right of support from the father. This decision affects many more children than the wrongful death cases.

GOMEZ v. PEREZ

Supreme Court of the
United States,
409 U.S. 535. (1973).

PER CURIAM.

The issue presented by this appeal is whether the laws of Texas may constitutionally grant legitimate children a judicially enforceable right to support from their natural fathers and at the same time deny that right to illegitimate children.

In 1969, appellant filed a petition in Texas District Court seeking support from appellee on behalf of her minor child. After a hearing, the state trial judge found that appellee is "the biological father" of the child, and that the child, "needs the support and maintenance of her father," but concluded that because the child was illegitimate "there is no legal obligation to support the child and the Plaintiff take nothing." The Court of Civil Appeals affirmed this ruling over the objection that this illegitimate child was being denied equal protection of law. 466 S.W.2d 41. The Texas Supreme Court refused application for a Writ of Error, finding "No reversible error." We noted probable jurisdiction. 408 U.S. 920, 92 S.Ct. 2479, 33 L.Ed.2d 331.

In Texas, both at common law and under the statutes of the State, the natural father has a continuing and primary duty to support his legitimate children. That duty extends even beyond dissolution of the marriage, and is enforceable on the child's behalf in civil proceedings and, further, is the subject of criminal sanctions. . . . The duty to support exists despite the fact that the father may not have custody of the child. . . . The Court of Civil Appeals has held in this case that nowhere in this elaborate statutory scheme does the State recognize any enforceable duty on the part of the biological father to support his illegitimate children and that absent a statutory duty to support, the controlling law is the Texas common law rule that illegitimate children, unlike legitimate children, have no legal right to support from their fathers.

It is also true that fathers may set up illegitimacy as a defense to prosecutions for criminal nonsupport of their children.

In this context, appellant's claim, on behalf of her daughter, that the child has been denied equal protection of the law is unmistakably presented. Indeed, at argument here, the attorney for the State of Texas, appearing as *amicus curiae*, conceded that but for the fact that this child is illegitimate she would be entitled to support from appellee under the laws of Texas.

We have held that under the Equal Protection Clause of the Fourteenth Amendment a State may not create a right of action in favor of children for the wrongful death of a parent and exclude illegitimate children from the benefit of such a right. *Levy v. Louisiana* . . . . Similarly, we have held that illegitimate children may not be excluded from sharing equally with other children in the recovery of workmen's compensation benefits for the death of their parent. *Weber v. Aetna Casualty & Surety Co.* . . . Under these decisions, a State may not invidiously discriminate against illegitimate children by denying them substantial benefits accorded children generally. We therefore hold that once a State posits a judicially enforceable right on behalf of children to needed support from their natural fathers there is no constitutionally sufficient justification for denying such an essential right to a child simply because her natural father has not married her mother. For a State to do so is "illogical and unjust," *Weber v. Aetna Casualty & Surety Co.* . . . We recognize the lurking problems with respect to proof of paternity. Those problems are not to be lightly brushed aside, but neither can they be made into an impenetrable barrier that works to shield otherwise invidious discrimination.

The judgment is reversed and the case remanded for further proceedings not inconsistent with this opinion.

It is so ordered. . . .

Mr. Justice STEWART, with whom Mr. Justice REHNQUIST joins, dissenting.

Right to support for illegitimate children is clearer than the rights to inheritance. The three Supreme Court decisions on this latter subject are narrowly drawn, based on technical details in the laws of Louisiana, Illinois, and New York, respectively, and do not provide the basis for a general principle on inheritance rights of this class of person.

In Labine v. Vincent, 401 U.S. 532 (1971), the Supreme Court ruled that the Louisiana law of succession for inheritance was not violative of the rights of the illegitimate child:

> Louisiana also has a complex set of rules regarding the rights of illegitimate children. Children born out of wedlock and who are never acknowledged by their parents apparently have no right to take property by intestate succession from their father's estate. In some instances, their father may not even bequeath property to them by will. Illegitimate children acknowledged by their fathers are "natural children." Natural children can take from their father by intestate succession "to the exclusion only of the State." They may be bequeathed property by their father only to the extent of either one-third or one-fourth of his estate and then only if their father is not survived by legitimate children or their heirs. Finally, children born out of wedlock can be legitimated or adopted, in which case they may take by intestate succession or by will as any other child.

Trimble v. Gordon, 430 U.S. 762 (1977), involved inheritance rights of an illegitimate child for whom a paternity order had been issued. The father had been making regular support payments when he became a homicide victim. The asset at issue was an automobile with a value of $2,500. The U.S. Supreme Court held that Section 12 of the Illinois Probate Act, which allows illegitimate children to inherit by intestate succession only from their mothers, violated the equal protection clause of the Fourteenth Amendment.

Lalli v. Lalli, 439 U.S. 259 (1978), was consistent with *Labine*. The New York statute under attack provided:

> An illegitimate child is the legitimate child of his father so that he and his issue inherit from his father if a court of competent jurisdiction has, during the lifetime of the father, made an order of filiation declaring paternity in a proceeding instituted during the pregnancy of the mother or within two years from the birth of the child.

The Court decided that this requirement did not violate the equal protection clause of the Constitution.

Weyrauch and Katz (1983: 598–599) present an interesting comparison of the decisions of individual justices in the *Labine* and *Trimble* cases.

Two recent decisions have dealt with time requirements to bring paternity suits. In Mills v. Habluetzel, 456 U.S. 91 (1982), a Texas statute providing that a paternity suit must be brought before the child is one year old was invalidated because it denies illegitimate children the equal protection of law. The period for obtaining support must be of sufficient duration to present a reasonable opportunity for those with an interest in such children to assert claims on their behalf.

A similar requirement by the state of Tennessee was considered by the U.S. Supreme Court in Pickett v. Brown, 462 U.S. 1 (1983). Although Tennessee allowed two years to file a paternity suit, the court came to the same conclusion as it did in *Mills*.

While we have considered unmarried mothers and illegitimate children in traditional terms in this chapter, our major concern has been single mothers. Children are also born to people who live together but who are not married. This situation is quite different from traditionally unmarried parenthood. Clarification to assure the legal status of children born to parents who are cohabiting is needed.

Questions for Review

1. What are the current options related to pregnancy? How does this affect the number of children available for adoption?

2. Given the current decisions of unmarried mothers to keep their babies, why is enforcement of child support especially necessary?

3. In a strict sense, what do blood tests prove concerning paternity?

4. Who sets the financial responsibility of the father once paternity is established?

5. Why is such a long period provided for the child to bring a paternity action?

6. Explain promiscuity as a defense against paternity.

7. How have several states eliminated the distinction between "legitimate" and "illegitimate"?

8. How does the Uniform Parentage Act deal with donor insemination?

9. How is personal jurisdiction provided in the Uniform Parentage Act?

10. Explain the compromise provisions in Section 13 of the Uniform Parentage Act.

11. Evaluate the criteria for the amount of child support enumerated in Section 15 of the Uniform Parentage Act.

12. Which of the decisions extending rights to illegitimate children affects the largest number?

13. What is meant by wrongful death? What rights do illegitimate children have in such cases?

14. Contrast the findings in *Labine v. Vincent* and in *Trimble v. Gordon*.

Questions for Debate and Discussion

1. *Stanley v. Illinois* has been criticized because much effort is made to find fathers who have no interest in their children. Do you agree with the criticism? What remedies would you suggest?

2. Do you agree that the illegitimacy concept no longer serves a useful purpose?

3. Gather data for your state on the success of the federal program emphasizing parental support enforcement.

Selected Readings

Burden, Dianne S., and Lorraine V. Klerman. "Teenage Parenthood: Factors That Lessen Economic Dependence." *Social Work* 29 (1984): 11–16.

Kolko, S. Joel. "Admissibility of HLA Test Results to Determine Paternity." *Family Law Reporter* 9 (1983): 4009–4018.

Krause, Harry. *Illegitimacy: Law and Social Policy*. Indianapolis: Bobbs-Merrill, 1971.

———. "Uniform Parentage Act." *Family Law Quarterly* 8 (1974): 1–25.

Teichman, Jenny. *Illegitimacy: An Examination of Bastardy*. Ithaca, N.Y.: Cornell University Press, 1982.

CHAPTER
13

Adoption

There are two steps in adoption: (1) legal termination of a child's rights and responsibilities toward his or her natural parents and (2) substitution of similar rights and responsibilities toward the adoptive parents.

In voluntary termination of parental rights, biological parents relinquish their child and give statutory consent to adoption. Involuntary termination of parental rights occurs as the consequence of a dependency or neglect proceeding in court.

Both children and adults (including married people) may be adopted. Adult adoptions are rare but are occasionally used to designate heirs. They require no social work intervention. The procedures and cases discussed in this chapter concern the adoption of children because this is a major social work endeavor. Social workers serve biological parents and select and counsel adoptive applicants in nonrelative placements.

The adoption literature is mainly concerned with placement of infants surrendered by their mothers and placed with nonrelatives. In the last decade, however, the number of infant placements has decreased sharply because of effective contraceptive techniques, the availability of legal abortion, and the increasing number of single mothers who decide to keep their children. Today, the typical child available for nonrelative adoption is beyond infancy and will have had some experience with foster care. For such a child, the preferred plan is to encourage the foster parents to adopt the child, because that option provides continuity for the child. Because there is such a small number of infants available for adoption, more applicants are advertising to obtain children outside of social agencies.

TYPES OF ADOPTION

There are three types of adoption: agency adoptions, independent adoptions, and stepparent adoptions.

Agency Adoptions

In agency-sponsored adoptions, social workers obtain consent from the biological parents or seek involuntary termination of their rights and then proceed to select and investigate adoptive applicants. Recommendations are subsequently made to the court. In addition, social workers provide casework services to the biological and adoptive parents and to children to be placed.

Independent Adoptions

Approximately 25 percent of nonrelative adoptions are termed independent or private adoptions, in which placement is arranged between the biological and adoptive parents, sometimes through a doctor or an attorney who serves as broker. The identified biological parent is typically an unwed mother, and the adoptive parents generally pay for her expenses related to childbirth. Some states prohibit independent adoptions, others require a confirmatory investigation by the court staff or a social agency to ensure that the child will have a suitable home.

Illegal adoptions involve the sale of babies for profit. Some lawyers who arrange such adoptions charge exorbitant fees, a small portion of which may be paid to the biological mother. While such adoptions are illegal in all states, recent reports indicate that the current scarcity of white infants available for adoption has led to an increase in illegal placements.

Research indicates that both independent and agency-sponsored adoptive placements of infants are successful (Meezan et al., 1978). Special studies of older children and minorities of color (e.g., Kadushin, 1970; Fanshel, 1972) have yielded similar results, although the National Association of Black Social Workers and other groups representing minorities of color have challenged such reports.

Stepparent Adoptions

About half of all adoptions are by relatives. The most typical cases involve a stepfather's adoption of his wife's children. While relative adoptions are handled by many courts routinely, social workers tend to feel that such petitions should also be subject to social investigation. Affinity is not necessarily a guarantee of effective parenthood. However, stepparent adoption may simply be legally recognizing the child's ongoing living situation.

JURISDICTION AND THE ADOPTION

Courts generally have authority to grant adoptions in the county where the prospective parents reside, where the child is physically present, or where the agency is located. Ideally, the applicants should file in their county of residence where they are best known and where information about them can be most easily verified. States generally recognize each other's adoption decrees as long as jurisdiction has been established.

A court hearing determines whether consents by the biological parents are valid and whether the agency investigatory report supports the petition of the adoptive applicants. If so, an **interlocutory (temporary) decree** is granted, typically running for six months to a year. During this time the adoptive parents or the agency may decide to terminate the placement. If this "supervision period" is successful, a final decree is granted and the child is issued a new birth certificate in the name of the adoptive parents.

Adoption proceedings and records are confidential. They may not be examined without a court order. This procedure is intended primarily to prevent the biological and adoptive parents from learning each other's identity, although it also prevents adopted children from learning the name of their biological parents. These procedures are being increasingly questioned, especially by persons who have been adopted. They argue that they are the only parties to the adoption who did not have a voice in the decision.

CONSENT AND REVOCATION

Consent to adoption is invalid if obtained fraudulently or by coercion. The decision to give up a biological child for adoption often causes emotional stress. Most states require that a valid consent be executed forty-eight to seventy-two hours after the birth. If a consent is taken before birth, the mother often changes her mind after she sees the child. British law requires the mother to wait a minimum of six weeks after birth before consenting to her child's adoption, to assure that she is physically and psychologically able give up the child; West Germany mandates that three months must elapse between birth and consent. The Revised Uniform Adoption Act (1971) speaks to the issue of consent.

Section 5. Persons Required to Consent to Adoption

(a) Unless consent is not required under section 6, a petition to adopt a minor may be granted only if written consent to a particular adoption has been executed by:

(1)   the mother of the minor;

(2)   the father of the minor, if the father was married to the mother at the time the minor was conceived or at any time thereafter, the minor is his child by adoption, or [he has otherwise legitimated the minor according to the laws of the place in which the adoption proceeding is brought]

(3)   any person lawfully entitled to custody of the minor or empowered to consent;

(4)   the court having jurisdiction to determine custody of the minor, if the legal guardian or custodian of the person of the minor is not empowered to consent to the adoption;

(5)   the minor, if more than [10] years of age, unless the Court in the best interest of the minor dispenses with the minor's consent; and

(6)   the spouse of the minor to be adopted.

(b) A petition to adopt an adult may be granted only if written consent to adoption has been executed by the adult and the adult's spouse.

Section 6. Persons as to Whom Consent and Notice Not Required

(a) Consent to adoption is not required of:

(1)   a parent who has [deserted a child without affording means of identification, or who has] abandoned a child;

(2)   a parent of a child in the custody of another, if the parent for a period of at least one year has failed significantly without justifiable cause (i) to communicate with the child or (ii) to provide for the care and support of the child as required by law or judicial decree;

(3)   the father of a minor if the father's consent is not required by section 5(a)(2);

(4)   a parent who has relinquished his right to consent under section 19;

(5)   a parent whose parental rights have been terminated by order of court under section 19;

(6)   a parent judicially declared incompetent or mentally defective if the Court dispenses with the parent's consent;

(7)   any parent of the individual to be adopted, if (i) the individual is a minor [18] or more years of age and the Court dispenses with the consent of the parent or (ii) the individual is an adult;

(8)   any legal guardian or lawful custodian of the individual to be adopted, other than a parent, who has failed to respond in writing to a request for consent for a period of [60] days or who, after examination of his written reasons for withholding consent, is found by the Court to be withholding his consent unreasonably; or

(9)   the spouse of the individual to be adopted, if the failure of the spouse to consent to the adoption is excused by the Court by reason of prolonged unexplained absence, unavailability, incapacity, or circumstances constituting an unreasonable withholding of consent.

(b) Except as provided in section 11, notice of a hearing on a petition for adoption need not be given to a person whose consent is not required or to a person whose consent or relinquishment has been filed with the petition.

Section 7.   How Consent Is Executed

(a) The required consent to adoption shall be executed at any time after the birth of the child and in the manner following:

(1)   if by the individual to be adopted, in the presence of the court;

(2)   if by an agency, by the executive head or other authorized representative, in the presence of a person authorized to take acknowledgments;

(3)   if by any other person, in the presence of the Court [or in the presence of a person authorized to take acknowlegments];

(4)   if by a court, by appropriate order or certificate.

(b) A consent which does not name or otherwise identify the adopting parent is valid if the consent [is executed in the presence of the Court and] contains a statement by the person whose consent it is that the person consenting voluntarily executed the consent irrespective of disclosure of the name or other identification of the adopting parent.

Section 8.   Withdrawal of Consent

(a) A consent to adoption cannot be withdrawn after the entry of a decree of adoption.

(b) A consent to adoption may be withdrawn prior to the entry of a decree of adoption if the Court finds, after notice and opportunity to be heard is afforded to petitioner, the person seeking the withdrawal, and the agency placing a child for adoption, that the withdrawal is in the best interest of the individual to be adopted and the Court orders the withdrawal.

The much publicized "Baby Lenore" case, People ex rel. Scarpetta v. Spence-Chapin Adoption Service, 269 N.E.2d 787 (N.Y. 1971), dealt with the mother's withdrawal of consent prior to entry of the final adoption decree but well after the child's placement with the adoptive parents and the issuance of an interlocutory decree. Note the court's summary of the laws of various states.

PEOPLE EX REL. SCARPETTA v. SPENCE-CHAPIN ADOPTION SERVICE

Court of Appeals of New York, 269 N.E.2d 787 (N.Y. 1971).

This appeal involves the return of an out-of-wedlock infant to its natural mother after she had executed a purported surrender of the child to an authorized adoption agency. The case does not involve the undoing of an adoption or the return of an adopted child to its natural parent. Nor does the case involve the undoing of a surrender by the natural mother on her mere say-so, but rather the undoing is based on a finding of fact that for various reasons, some obvious, the surrender was not made by her with such stability of mind and emotion that the surrender should not be undone for improvidence. On the other hand, there is not the slightest suggestion that the adoption agency was unfair or guilty of any overreaching in obtaining the surrender. . . . The infant child was born on May 18, 1970, to Olga Scarpetta, who was unmarried and 32 years old. She had become pregnant in her native Colombia by a married Colombian in the summer of 1969. Seeking to minimize the shame of an out-of-wedlock child to herself and her family, Miss Scarpetta came to New York for the purpose of having her child. . . .

Four days after the birth of the child, she placed the infant for boarding care with Spence-Chapin Adoption Service, an agency authorized by statute to receive children for adoption. Ten days later, a surrender document was executed by Miss Scarpetta to the agency, and on June 18, 1970, the baby was placed with a family for adoption. Five days later, on June 23, 1970, the mother repented her actions and requested that the child be returned to her.

After several unsuccessful attempts to regain her child from the agency, the mother commenced this habeas corpus proceeding. Before the surrender, the mother had had a number of interviews with representatives of the adoption agency. On the other hand, shortly before or after the birth of the child, her family in Colombia, well-to-do, and devout in their religion, were shocked that she should put out her child for adoption by strangers. They assured her of their support and backing and urged her to raise her own child.

Special Term, "[a]fter considering all the facts, concluded "that the child should be forthwith returned to petitioner, its natural mother." Following unanimous affirmance by the Appellate Division, . . . we granted leave to appeal. . . . [References omitted.]

The resolution of the issue of whether or not a mother, who has surrendered her child to an authorized adoption agency, may regain the child's custody, has received various treatment by the legislatures and courts in the United States. At one extreme, several jurisdictions adhere to the rule that the parent has an absolute right to regain custody of her child prior to the final adoption decree. On the other hand, some jurisdictions adhere to the rule that the parent's surrender is final, absent fraud or duress. The majority of the jurisdictions, however, place the parent's right to regain custody within the discretion of the court—the position which, of course, our Legislature has taken. The discretionary rule allows the court leeway to approve a revocation of the surrender when the facts of the individual case warrant it and avoids the obvious dangers posed by the rigidity of the extreme positions.

In New York, a surrender executed by a mother, in which she voluntarily consents to a change of guardianship and custody to an authorized agency for the purpose of adoption, is expressly sanctioned by law. . . .

. . . [T]he sole issue before us on this appeal is whether there is any evidence in the record to establish that the interest of the child will be promoted by returning the child to the natural mother.

It has repeatedly been determined, insofar as the best interests of the child are concerned, that "[t]he mother or father has a right to the care and custody of a child, superior to that of all others, unless he or she has abandoned that right or is proved unfit to assume the duties and privileges of parenthood." . . . It has been well said that "the status of a natural parent" is so important "that in determining the best interests of the child, it may counterbalance, even outweigh, superior material and cultural advantages which may be afforded by adoptive parents. . . .

. . . Nor do we perceive any distinction, in principle, between the effect of a surrender to an authorized agency and of a surrender to an individual. "The policy urged that, if surrender may be undone, authorized agencies will be inconvenienced or even frustrated in their placement of children is not a sufficient counterweight. The fact of relationship between a natural parent and child ought not to be subordinated to such considerations, important as they are." . . .

Consequently, to give the fundamental principle meaning and vitality, we have explicitly declared that "[e]xcept where a nonparent has obtained legal and permanent custody of a child by adoption, guardianship or otherwise, he who would take or withhold a child from mother or father must sustain the burden of establishing that the parent is unfit and that the child's welfare compels awarding its custody to the nonparent." . . .

Another significant factor to be considered is the "motivation of the mother in seeking return of the child. It is recognized that very often there is a substantial risk of improper motivation. In such case the authorized agency and the court must be especially alert not to permit the improper motivation to endanger the interests of the child or lead to any other noxious consequence. As important as this factor is, however, it is also true that the change of mind by a natural mother is not an evil thing. Instead, the change of mind is to be accorded great sympathy, and, in a proper case, encouragement and favorable action." . . .

In no case, however, may a contest between a parent and nonparent resolve itself into a simple factual issue as to which affords the better surroundings, or as to which party is better equipped to raise the child. . . . It may well be that the prospective adoptive parents would afford a child some material advantages over and beyond what the natural mother may be able to furnish, but these advantages, passing and transient as they are, cannot outweigh a mother's tender care and love unless it is clearly established that she is unfit to assume the duties and privileges of parenthood.

We conclude that the record before us supports the finding by the courts below that the surrender was improvident and that the child's best interests—moral and temporal—will be best served by its return to the natural mother.

Within 23 days after the child had been given over to the agency, and only 5 days after the prospective adoptive parents had gained provisional custody of the child, the mother sought its return. If the matter had been resolved at that time, much heartache and distress would have been avoided. However, since the child was not returned, the mother had no alternative but to commence legal proceedings to regain its custody, and this she did without delay.

In revoking the surrender and directing the return of the child to the mother, the trial court held that the mother was "motivated solely by her concern for the well-being of her child." Moreover, the evidence fully supports the conclusion that the mother "has adequately stabilized her own relationships and has become stable enough in her own mind to warrant the return of the child to her." No finding of present or prospective unfitness has been made against the mother. On the contrary, the record discloses that she is well educated, financially secure, and in a position to properly assume the care, training and education of her child.

It cannot be doubted that the public policy of our State is contrary to the disclosure of the names and identities of the natural parents and prospective adoptive parents to each other. . . .

Similarly, we find no merit to the contention that the failure to allow the prospective adoptive parents to intervene in the instant proceeding deprived them of due process of law so as to render the court's determination awarding custody of the child to the mother, constitutionally invalid. The prospective adoptive parents do not have legal custody of the baby. Spence-Chapin, the adoption agency, by virtue of the mother's surrender, was vested with legal custody. . . . In not being permitted to intervene, they are not deprived of a protected interest, as contemplated by the Constitution.

The order of the Appellate Division should be affirmed, without costs.. . .

Baby Lenore's adoptive parents moved with her to Florida, where they were granted custody despite the New York ruling. New York subsequently passed legislation limiting withdrawal of consent to thirty days after initiation of adoption proceedings.

INVOLUNTARY TERMINATION OF PARENTAL RIGHTS

A child may be freed for adoption without the consent of biological parents for several reasons, as specified in Section 7 of the Uniform Adoption Act:

(c) In addition to any other proceeding provided by law, the relationship of parent and child may be terminated by a court order issued in connection with an adoption proceeding under this Act on any ground provided by other law for termination of the relationship, and in any event on the ground (1) that the minor has been abandoned by the parent, (2) that by reason of the misconduct, faults, or habits of the parent or the repeated and continuous neglect or refusal of the parent, the minor is without proper parental care and control, or subsistence, education, or other care or control necessary for his physical, mental, or emotional health or morals, or by reason of physical or mental incapacity the parent is unable to provide necessary parental care for the minor, and the court finds that the conditions and causes of the behavior, neglect, or incapacity are irremediable or will not be remedied by the parent, and that by reason thereof the minor is suffering or probably will suffer serious physical, mental, moral, or emotional harm, or (3) that in the case of a parent not having custody of a minor, his consent is being unreasonably withheld contrary to the best interest of the minor.

(d) For the purpose of proceeding under this Act, a decree terminating all rights of a parent with reference to a child or the relationship of parent and child issued by a court of competent jurisdiction in this or any other state dispenses with the consent to adoption proceedings of a parent whose rights or parent and child relationship are terminated by the decree and with any required notice of an adoption proceeding other than as provided in this section.

Previously, only the unwed mother's consent or involuntary termination of her rights were required to release a child legally for adoption. Stanley v. Illinois, 405 U.S. 645 (1972), stipulated that the unwed father's consent also be required under law.

STANLEY v. ILLINOIS

Supreme Court of the United States, 405 U.S. 645 (1972).

Mr. Justice WHITE delivered the opinion of the Court.

Joan Stanley lived with Peter Stanley intermittently for 18 years during which time they had three children. When Joan Stanley died, Peter Stanley lost not only her but also his children. Under Illinois law the children of unwed fathers become wards of the State upon the death of the mother. Accordingly, upon Joan Stanley's death, in a dependency proceeding instituted by the State of Illinois, Stanley's children were declared wards of the State and placed with court appointed guardians. Stanley appealed, claiming that he had never been shown to be an unfit parent and that since married fathers and unwed mothers could not be deprived of their children without such a showing, he had been deprived of the equal protection of the laws guaranteed him by the Fourteenth Amendment. The Illinois Supreme Court accepted the fact that Stanley's own unfitness had not been established but rejected the equal protection claim, holding that Stanley could properly be separated from his children upon proof of the single fact that he and the dead mother had not been married. Stanley's actual fitness as a father was irrelevant. In re Stanley, 45 Ill.2d 132, 256 N.E.2d 814 (1970). . . .

Stanley presses his equal protection claim here. The State continues to respond that unwed fathers are presumed unfit to raise their children and that it is unnecessary to hold individualized hearings to determine whether particular fathers are in fact unfit parents before they are separated from their children. We granted certiorari [citation omitted]. . . .

. . . Stanley's claim in the state courts and here is that failure to afford him a hearing on his parental qualifications while extending it to other parents denied him equal protection of the laws. We have concluded that all Illinois parents are constitutionally entitled to a hearing on their fitness before their children are removed from their custody. It follows that denying such a hearing to Stanley and those like him while granting it to other Illinois parents is inescapably contrary to the Equal Protection Clause.

The judgment of the Supreme Court of Illinois is reversed and the case is remanded to that court for proceedings not inconsistent with this opinion. It is so ordered.

Reversed and remanded.

It has been argued that *Stanley* should not be applied to all adoptions since the case approximated a common law marriage more than the typical adoptive situation. Because most agency adoptions concern illegitimate children, the *Stanley* decision requiring notice to alleged fathers has served to delay placements, when only very few fathers are interested in requesting a hearing.

Quilloin v. Walcott, 434 U.S. 246 (1978), involved a father's objection to the adoption of an eleven-year-old child who had lived with a stepparent for nine years when adoption proceedings were begun. The U.S. Supreme Court affirmed the lower court decision granting the adoption:

QUILLOIN v. WALCOTT

Supreme Court of the United States, 434 U.S. 246 (1978).

The child was born in December 1964 and has been in the custody and control of his mother, appellee Ardell Williams Walcott, for his entire life. The mother and the child's natural father, appellant Leon Webster Quilloin, never married each other or established a home together, and in September 1967 the mother married appellee Randall Walcott. In March 1976 she consented to adoption of the child by her husband, who immediately filed a petition for adoption. Appellant attempted to block the adoption and to secure visitation rights, but he did not seek custody or object to the child's continuing to live with appellees. Although appellant was not found to be an unfit parent, the adoption was granted over his objection. . . .

. . . Appellant did not petition for legitimation of his child at any time during the 11 years between the child's birth and the filing of Randall Walcott's adoption petition. However, in response to Walcott's petition, appellant filed an application for a writ of habeas corpus seeking visitation rights, a petition for legitimation and an objection to the adoption. Shortly thereafter, appellant amended his pleadings by adding the claim that §§ 74-203 and 74-403(3) were unconstitutional as applied to his case, insofar as they denied him the rights granted married parents, and presumed unwed fathers to be unfit as a matter of law.

This is not a case in which the unwed father at any time had, or sought, actual or legal custody of his child. Nor is this a case in which the proposed adoption would place the child with a new set of parents with whom the child had never before lived. Rather, the result of the adoption in this case is to give full recognition to a family unit already in existence, a result desired by all concerned, except appellant. Whatever might be required in other situations, we cannot say that the State was required in this situation to find anything more than that the adoption, and denial of legitimation, were in the "best interests of the child." . . .

. . . We think appellant's interests are readily distinguishable from those of a separated or divorced father, and accordingly believe that the State could permissibly give appellant less veto authority than it provides to a married father.

Although appellant was subject, for the years prior to these proceedings, to essentially the same child-support obligation as a married father would have had, . . . he has never exercised actual or legal custody over his child, and thus has never shouldered any significant responsibility with respect to the daily supervision, education, protection, or care of the child. Appellant does not complain of his exemption from these responsibilties and, indeed, he does not even now seek custody of his child. In contrast, legal custody of children is, of course, a central aspect of the marital relationship, and even a father whose marriage has broken apart will have borne full responsibility for the rearing of his children during the period of the marriage. Under any standard of review, the State was not foreclosed from recognizing this difference in the extent of commitment to the welfare of the child.

We conclude that §§ 74-203 and 74-403(3), as applied in this case, did not deprive appellant of his asserted rights under the Due Process and Equal Protection Clauses. The judgment of the Supreme Court of Georgia is accordingly, Affirmed.

In Caban v. Mohammed, 441 U.S. 380 (1979), concerning gender-based rights, the parents had lived together until the oldest child was four years old and had shared custody afterward, so the oldest child was seven by the time adoption petitions were filed. The Court held that the father's rights had to be considered.

CABAN v. MOHAMMED

Supreme Court of the United States, 441 U.S. 380 (1979).

. . . Abdiel Caban and appellee Maria Mohammed lived together in New York City from September 1968 until the end of 1973. During this time Caban and Mohammed represented themselves as being husband and wife, although they never legally married. Indeed, until 1974 Caban was married to another woman, from whom he was separated. While living with the appellant, Mohammed gave birth to two children: David Andrew Caban, born July 16, 1969, and Denise Caban, born March 12, 1971. Abdiel Caban was identified as the father on each child's birth certificate and lived with the children as their father until the end of 1973. Together with Mohammed, he contributed to the support of the family.

In December 1973, Mohammed took the two children and left the appellant to take up residence with appellee Kazim Mohammed, whom she married on January 30, 1974. For the next nine months, she took David and Denise each weekend to visit her mother, Delores Gonzales, who lived one floor above Caban. Because of his friendship with Gonzales, Caban was able to see the children each week when they came to visit their grandmother.

In September 1974, Gonzales left New York to take up residence in her native Puerto Rico. At the Mohammeds' request, the grandmother took David and Denise with her. According to appellees, they planned to join the children in Puerto Rico as soon as they had saved enough money to start a business there. During the children's stay with their grandmother, Mrs. Mohammed kept in touch with David and Denise by mail; Caban communicated with the children through his parents, who also resided in Puerto Rico. In November 1975, he went to Puerto Rico, where Gonzales willingly surrendered the children to Caban with the understanding that they would be returned after a few days. Caban, however, returned to New York with the children. When Mrs. Mohammed learned that the children were in Caban's custody, she attempted to retrieve them with the aid of a police officer. After this attempt failed, the appellees instituted custody proceedings in the New York Family Court, which placed the children in the temporary custody of the Mohammeds and gave Caban and his new wife, Nina, visiting rights.

In January 1976, appellees filed a petition under § 110 of the New York Domestic Relations Law to adopt David and Denise. In March, the Cabans cross-petitioned for adoption. After the Family Court stayed the custody suit pending the outcome of the adoption proceedings, a hearing was held on the petition and cross petition before a law assistant to a New York Surrogate in Kings County, N.Y. At this hearing, both the Mohammeds and the Cabans were represented by counsel and were permitted to present and cross-examine witnesses.

The Surrogate granted the Mohammeds' petition to adopt the children, thereby cutting off all of appellant's parental rights.

. . . Adoption by Abdiel was held to be impermissible in the absence of Maria's consent, whereas adoption by Maria could be prevented by Abdiel only if he could show that the Mohammeds' adoption of the children would not be in the children's best interests. Accordingly, it is clear that § 111 treats unmarried parents differently according to their sex.

III

Gender-based distinctions "must serve important governmental objectives and must be substantially related to achievement of those objectives" in order to withstand judicial scrutiny under the Equal Protection Clause. The question before us, therefore, is whether the distinction in § 111 between unmarried mothers and unmarried fathers bears a substantial relation to some important state interest. Appellees assert that the distinction is justified by a fundamental difference between maternal and paternal relations—that "a natural mother, absent special circumstances, bears a closer relationship with her child . . . than a father does."

Contrary to appellees' argument and to the apparent presumption underlying § 111, maternal and paternal roles are not invariably different in importance. Even if unwed mothers as a class were closer than unwed fathers to their newborn infants, this generalization concerning parent-child relations would become less acceptable as a basis for legislative distinctions as the age of the child increased. The present case demonstrates that an unwed father may have a relationship with his children fully comparable to that of the mother. Appellant Caban, appellee Maria Mohammed, and their two children lived together as a natural family for several years. As members of this family, both mother and father participated in the care and support of their children. There is no reason to believe that the Caban children— aged 4 and 6 at the time of the adoption proceedings—had a relationship with their mother unrivaled by the affection and concern of their father. We reject, therefore, the claim that the broad, gender-based distinction of § 111 is required by any universal difference between maternal and paternal relations at every phase of a child's development.

As an alternative justification . . . appellees argue that the distinction between unwed fathers and unwed mothers is substantially related to the State's interest in promoting the adoption of illegitimate children. Although the legislative history of § 111 is sparse, the New York Court of Appeals identified as the legislature's purpose in enacting § 111 the furthering of the interests of illegitimate children, for whom adoption often is the best course. The court concluded:

> "to require the consent of fathers of children born out of wedlock . . . or even some of them, would have the overall effect of denying homes to the homeless and of depriving innocent children of the other blessings of adoption. The cruel and undeserved out-of-wedlock stigma would continue its visitations. At the very least, the worthy process of adoption would be severely impeded."

The court reasoned that people wishing to adopt a child born out of wedlock would be discouraged if the natural father could prevent the adoption by the mere withholding of his consent. Indeed, the court went so far as to suggest that "marriages would be discouraged because of the reluctance of prospective husbands to involve themselves in a family situation where they might only be a foster parent and could not adopt the mother's offspring."

The court noted that if unwed fathers' consents were required before adoption could take place, in many instances the adoption would have to be delayed or eliminated altogether, because of the unavailability of the natural father.

The State's interest in providing for the well-being of illegitimate children is an important one. We do not question that the best interests of such children often may require their adoption into new families who will give them the stability of a normal, two-parent home. Moreover, adoption will remove the stigma under whiich illegitimate children suffer. But the unquestioned right of the State to further these desirable ends by legislation is not in itself sufficient to justify the gender-based distinction of § 111. Rather, under the relevant cases applying the Equal Protection Clause it must be shown that the distinction is structured reasonably to further these ends. As we repeated in Reed v. Reed, 404 U.S. at 76, 92 S.Ct. at 254, such a statutory "classification 'must be reasonable, not arbitrary, and must rest upon some ground of difference having a fair and substantial relation to the object of the legislation, so that all persons similarly circumstanced shall be treated alike.' "

We find that the distinction in § 111 between unmarried mothers and unmarried fathers as illustrated by this case does not bear a substantial relation to the State's interest in providing adoptive homes for its illegitimate children. This impediment to adoption usually is the result of a natural parental interest shared by both genders alike; it is not a manifestation of any profound difference between the affection and concern of mothers and fathers for their children. Neither the State nor the appellees have argued that unwed fathers are more likely to object to the adoption of their children than are unwed mothers; nor is there any self-evident reason why as a class they would be.

[7–10] The New York Court of Appeals in *In re Malpica-Orsini*, supra, suggested that the requiring of unmarried fathers' consent for adoption would pose a strong impediment for adoption because often it is impossible to locate unwed fathers when adoption proceedings are brought, whereas mothers are more likely to remain with their children. Even if the special difficulties attendant upon locating and identifying unwed fathers at birth would justify a legislative distinction between mothers and fathers of newborns, these difficulties need not persist past infancy. When the adoption of an older child is sought, the State's interest in proceeding with adoption cases can be protected by means that do not draw such an inflexible gender-based distinction as that made in § 111. In those cases where the father never has come forward to participate in the rearing of his child, nothing in the Equal Protection Clause precludes the State from withholding from him the privilege of vetoing the adoption of that child. Indeed, under the statute as it now stands the surrogate may proceed in the absence of consent when the parent whose consent otherwise would be required never has come forward or has abandoned the child. But in cases such as this, where the father has established a substantial relationship with the child and has admitted his paternity, a State should have no difficulty in identifying the father even of children born out of wedlock. Thus, no showing has been made that the different treatment afforded unmarried fathers and unmarried mothers under § 111 bears a substantial relationship to the proclaimed interest of the State in promoting the adoption of illegitimate children.

In sum, we believe that § 111 is another example of "overbroad generalizations" in gender-based classifications. The effect of New York's classification is to discriminate against unwed fathers even when their identity is known and they have manifested a significant paternal interest in the child. The facts of this case illustrate the harshness of classifying unwed fathers as being invariably less qualified and entitled than mothers to exercise a concerned judgment as to the fate of their children. Section 111 both excludes some loving fathers from full participation in the decision whether their children will be adopted and, at the same time, enables some alienated mothers arbitrarily to cut off the paternal rights of fathers. We conclude that this undifferentiated distinction between unwed mothers and unwed fathers, applicable in all circumstances where adoption of a child of theirs is at issue, does not bear a substantial relationship to the State's asserted interests.

The judgment of the New York Court of Appeals is
Reversed.

In his dissent, Justice John Paul Stevens emphasized the effect of the decision on the legitimacy of the child:

> This case involves a dispute between natural parents over which of the two may adopt the children. If both are given a veto, as the Court requires, neither may adopt and the children will remain illegitimate. If, instead of a gender-based distinction, the veto were given to the parent having custody of the child, the mother would prevail just as she did in the state court. Whether or not it is wise to devise a special rule to protect the natural father who (a) has a substantial relationship with his child, and (b) wants to veto an adoption that a court has been found to be in the best interests of the child, the record in this case does not demonstrate that the Equal Protection Clause requires such a rule.
>
> I have no way of knowing how often disputes between natural parents over adoption of their children arise after the father "has established a substantial relationship with the child and [is willing to admit] his paternity," ante, at 1769, but has previously been unwilling to take steps to legitimate his relationship. I am inclined to believe that such cases are relatively rare. But whether or not this assumption is valid, the far surer asssumption is that in the more common adoption situations, the mother will be the more, and often the only, responsible parent, and that a paternal consent requirement will constitute a hindrance to the adoption process. Because this general rule is amply justified in its normal application, I would therefore require the party challenging its constitutionality to make some demonstration of unfairness in a significant number of situations before concluding that it violates the Equal Protection Clause. That the Court has found a violation without requiring such a showing can only be attributed to its own "stereotyped reaction" to what is unquestionably, but in this case justifiably, a gender-based distinction.

RIGHTS OF DIVORCED FATHERS

Sheehan (1981) notes that although *Quilloin* appears to give greater power to divorced fathers to bar adoption than to unwed fathers, state courts often apply identical standards. Payment or sincere offers of financial support refused by the mother determined the veto power of divorced fathers in Oklahoma and Iowa cases (Matter of Darren Todd H.'s Adoption, 615 P.2d 287 [Okl. 1980]; In re Adoption of Vogt, 219 N.W.2d 529 [Iowa 1974]). However, a Georgia court permitted a divorced father who had not paid child support the previous year, with the approval of the mother, to prevent adoption by the stepfather (Kriseman v. Kenmore, 238 S.E.2d 585 [1977]).

A New Jersey appellate court held that a divorced father whose visitation rights were being frustrated by the children's mother could prevent stepfather adoption (Matter of Adoption by J.P.P., 419 A.2d 1135 [N.J. 1980]). The father had deposited support payments in a bank account rather than paying the mother and had provided life insurance policies for the children.

THE REMEDY OF THE UNIFORM PARENTAGE ACT

In the Uniform Parentage Act, adopted by thirteen states by 1985, notice is given to the unwed or divorced father only if he is: "(1) a presumed father under Section 4(a), (2) a father whose relationship to the child has been determined by a court, or (3) a father as to whom the child is a legitimate child under prior law of this State or under the law of another jurisdiction. . . ."

(c) In an effort to identify the natural father, the court shall cause inquiry to be made of the mother and any other appropriate person. The inquiry shall include the following: whether the mother was married at the time of conception of the child or at any time thereafter; whether mother was cohabiting with a man at the time of conception or birth of the child; whether the mother has received support payments or promises of support with respect to the child or in connection with her pregnancy; or whether any man has formally or informally acknowledged or declared his possible paternity of the child.

(d) If, after the inquiry, the natural father is identified to the satisfaction of the court, or if more than one man is identified as a possible father, each shall be given notice of the proceeding in accordance with Subsection (f). If any of them fails to appear or, if appearing, fails to claim custodial rights, his parental rights with reference to the child shall be terminated. If the natural father or a man representing himself to be the natural father, claims custodial rights, the court shall proceed to determine custodial rights.

(e) If, after the inquiry, the court is unable to identify the natural father or any possible natural father and no person has appeared claiming to be the natural father and claiming custodial rights, the court shall enter an order terminating the unknown natural father's parental rights with reference to the child. . . .

(f) Notice of the proceeding shall be given to every person identified as the natural father or a possible natural father [in the manner appropriate under rules of civil procedure for the service of process in a civil action in this state, or] in any manner the court directs. Proof of giving the notice shall be filed with the court before the petition is heard. [If no person has been identified as the natural father or a possible father, the court, on the basis of all information available, shall determine whether publication or public posting of notice of the proceeding is likely to lead to identification and, if so, shall order publication or public posting at times and in places and manner it deems appropriate.]

[The Uniform Parentage Act provides the following explanatory note.]

Subsections (c) through (f) provide a procedure by which the court may ascertain the identity of the father and permit speedy termination of his potential rights *if he shows no interest in the child*. If, on the other hand, the natural father or a man representing himself to be the natural father claims custodial rights, the court is given authority to determine custodial rights. It is contemplated that there may be cases in which the man alleging himself to be the father is so clearly unfit to take custody of the child that the court would proceed to terminate his potential parental rights without deciding whether the man actually is the father of the child. If, on the other hand, the man alleging himself to be the father and claiming custody is *prima facie* fit to have custody of the child, an action to ascertain paternity is indicated, unless a voluntary acknowledgment can be obtained in accordance with Section 4(a)(5) of this Act.

Subsection (e) raises serious constitutional questions in that it attempts to cut off after a given period *any* claim seeking to reopen a judgment terminating parental rights. While of questionable constitutionality, such a provision is not without precedent. A similar provision is contained in Section 15(b) of the revised Uniform Adoption Act, approved by the Commissioners on Uniform State Laws in 1969, and other similar provisions are contained in the adoption acts of a number of states. Moreover, it must be considered that the case of adoption differs from other situations. The parent's claim to his child can hardly be compared to a person's claim to property. The Supreme

Court itself recognized that the interest of the child is heavily involved in these cases when remanding the *Rothstein* case to the Wisconsin Supreme Court, requiring that the court give "due consideration [to] the completion of the adoption proceedings and the fact that the child has apparently lived with the adoptive family for the intervening period of time." Cf. Armstrong v. Manzo, 380 U.S. 545 (1965).

Subsection (f) seeks to conform to the following footnote in *Stanley v. Illinois*:

"We note in passing that the incremental cost of offering unwed fathers an opportunity for individualized hearings on fitness appears to be minimal. If unwed fathers, in the main, do not care about the disposition of their children, they will not appear to demand hearings. If they do care, under the scheme here held invalid, Illinois would admittedly at some later time have to afford them a properly focused hearing in a custody or adopting proceeding.

"Extending opportunity for hearing to unwed fathers who desire and claim competence to care for their children creates no constitutional or procedural obstacle to foreclosing those unwed fathers who are not so inclined. The Illinois law governing procedure in juvenile cases . . . provided for personal service, notice by certified mail or for notice by publication when personal or certified mail service cannot be had or when notice is directed to unknown respondents under the style of "all whom it may concern." Unwed fathers who do not promptly respond cannot complain if their children are declared wards of the State. Those who do respond retain the burden of proving their fatherhood."

PLACEMENT AND ADOPTION

The legal process required for adoption is specified by the Uniform Adoption Act:

Section 9. Petition for Adoption

(a) A petition for adoption shall be signed and verified by the petitioner, filed with the clerk of the Court, and state:

(1)   the date and place of birth of the individual to be adopted, if known;

(2)   the name to be used for the individual to be adopted;

(3))   the date [petitioner acquired custody of the minor and] of placement of the minor and the name of the person placing the minor;

(4)   the full name, age, place and duration of residence of the petitioner;

(5)   the marital status of the petitioner, including the date and place of marriage, if married;

(6)   that the petitioner has facilities and resources, including those available under a subsidy agreement, suitable to provide for the nurture and care of the minor to be adopted, and that it is the desire of the petitioner to establish the relationship of parent and child with the individual to be adopted;

(7)   a description and estimate of value of any property of the individual to be adopted; and

(8)   the name of any person whose consent to the adoption is required, but who has not consented, and facts or circumstances which excuse the lack of his consent normally required to the adoption.

(b) A certified copy of the birth certificate or verification of birth record of the individual to be adopted, if available, and the required consents and relinquishments shall be filed with the clerk. . . .

Section 10. Report of Petitioner's Expenditures

(a) Except as specified in subsection (b), the petitioner in any proceeding for the adoption of a minor shall file, before the petition is heard, a full accounting report in a manner acceptable to the Court of all disbursements of anything of value made or agreed to be made by or on behalf of the petitioner in connection with the adoption. The report shall show any expenses incurred in connection with:

(1)   the birth of the minor;

(2)   placement of the minor with petitioner;

(3)   medical or hospital care received by the mother or by the minor during the mother's prenatal care and confinement; and

(4)   services relating to the adoption or to the placement of the minor for adoption which were received by or on behalf of the petitioner, either natural parent of the minor, or any other person.

(b) This section does not apply to an adoption by a step-parent whose spouse is a natural or adoptive parent of the child.

(c) Any report made under this section must be signed and verified by the petitioner. . . .

Section 11.   Notice of Petition, Investigation, and Hearing

(a) After the filing of a petition to adopt a minor, the Court shall fix a time and place for hearing the petition. At least 20 days before the date of hearing, notice of the filing of the petition and of the time and place of hearing shall be given by the petitioner to. . . . [All interested parties are named.]

(b) An investigation shall be made by the [Public Welfare Department] or any other qualified agency or person designated by the Court to inquire into the conditions and antecedents of a minor sought to be adopted and of the petitioner for the purpose of ascertaining whether the adoptive home is a suitable home for the minor and whether the proposed adoption is in the best interest of the minor.

(c) A written report of the investigation shall be filed with the Court by the investigator before the petition is heard.

(d) The report of the investigation shall contain an evaluation of the placement with a recommendation as to the granting of the petition for adoption and any other information the Court requires regarding the petitioner or the minor.

(e) Unless directed by the Court, an investigation and report is not required in cases in which an agency is a party or joins in the petition for adoption, a step-parent is the petitioner, or the person to be adopted is an adult. In other cases, the Court may waive the investigation only if it appears that waiver is in the best interest of the minor and that the adoptive home and the minor are suited to each other. The [Public Welfare Department] which is required to consent to the adoption may give consent without making the investigation. . . .

Section 12.   Required Residence of Minor

A final decree of adoption shall not be issued and an interlocutory decree of adoption does not become final, until the minor to be adopted, other than a stepchild of the petitioner, has lived in the adoptive home for at least 6 months after placement by an agency, or for at least 6 months after the [Public Welfare Department] or the court has been informed of the custody of the minor by the petitioner, and the department or Court has had an opportunity to observe or investigate the adoptive home. . . .

Section 13.   Appearance; Continuance; Disposition of Petition

(a) The petitioner and the individual to be adopted shall appear at the hearing on the petition, unless the presence of either is excused by the Court for good cause shown.

(b) The Court may continue the hearing from time to time to permit further observation, investigation, or consideration of any facts or circumstances affecting the granting of the petition.

(c) If at the conclusion of the hearing the Court determines that the required consents have been obtained or excused and that the adoption is in the best interest of the individual to be adopted, it may (1) issue a final decree of adoption; or (2) issue an interlocutory decree of adoption which by its own terms automatically becomes a final decree of adoption on a day therein specified, which day shall not be less than 6 months nor more than one year from the date of issuance of the decree, unless sooner vacated by the Court for good cause shown.

(d) If the requirements for a decree under subsection (c) have not been met, the court shall dismiss the petition and determine the person to have custody of the minor, including the petitioners if in the best interest of the minor. In an interlocutory decree of adoption the Court may provide for observation, investigation, and further report on the adoptive home during the interlocutory period. . . .

Section 16. Hearings and Records in Adoption Proceedings; Confidential Nature

Notwithstanding any other law concerning public hearings and records,

(1) all hearings held in proceedings under this Act shall be held in closed Court without admittance of any person other than essential officers of the court, the parties, their witnesses, counsel, persons who have not previously consented to the adoption but are required to consent, and representatives of the agencies present to perform their official duties; and

(2) all papers and records pertaining to the adoption whether part of the permanent record of the court or of a file in the [Department of Welfare] or in an agency are subject to inspection only upon consent of the Court and all interested persons; or in exceptional cases, only upon an order of the Court for good cause shown; and

(3) except as authorized in writing by the adoptive parent, the adopted child, if [14] or more years of age, or upon order of the court for good cause shown in exceptional cases, no person is required to disclose the name or identity of either an adoptive parent or an adopted child.

Section 17. Recognition of Foreign Decree Affecting Adoption

A decree of court terminating the relationship of parent and child or establishing the relationship by adoption issued pursuant to due process of law by a court of any other jurisdiction within or without the United States shall be recognized in this state and the rights and obligations of the parties as to matters within the jurisdiction of this state shall be determined as though the decree were issued by a court of this state.

. . .

Section 18. Application for New Birth Record

Within 30 days after an adoption decree becomes final, the clerk of the court shall prepare an application for a birth record in the new name of the adopted individual.

. . .

Investigations required by the court are conducted by social workers, who interview the applicants to determine:

- How interest in adoption developed.
- Motivation for adoption
- Attitude toward childlessness and infertility
- Understanding of children and experiences with children
- History of the marriage and current patterns of marital interaction
- Developmental history
- Educational and employment history
- Patterns of social participation
- Attitude of extended family toward adoption
- Attitude toward illegitimacy and the out-of-wedlock child

- Problems anticipated in adoption and how they must be handled
- Attitudes toward working with the agency

WHO MAY ADOPT

According to the Revised Uniform Adoption Act, the following individuals may adopt:

- A husband and wife together, even though one or both are minors
- An unmarried adult
- The unmarried father or mother of the individual to be adopted
- A married individual without the other spouse joining as a petitioner, if the individual to be adopted is not his or her spouse, and if (1) the other spouse is a parent of the individual to be adopted and consents to the adoption; (2) the petitioner and the other spouse are legally separated; or (3) the failure of the other spouse to join in the petition or to consent to the adoption is excused by the court for prolonged unexplained absence, unavailability, incapacity, or circumstances constituting an unreasonable withholding of consent.

RIGHTS OF GRANDPARENTS

Old age and ill health hinder grandparents who want to adopt, even if they have been caring for the child. Sheehan (1981) notes that because states do not recognize by law a right of grandparents to adopt their grandchildren, practice varies considerably from case to case. One court reviewed the grandparents' age, health, home environment, ability to prevent interference from the biological parents, potential trauma if the child legally becomes the sibling of a biological parent, and the separation trauma in removing the child from the grandparents' home in deciding to permit them to adopt (In re Tachick's Adoption, 210 N.W.2d 865 [1973]).

Adoptive applicants who are about the same age as the birth parents are sought to make it more likely that the parents will be alive throughout the child's minority. Age was the main issue in In re Haun, 277 N.E.2d 258 (Ohio 1971).

IN RE HAUN

Probate Court of
Cuyahoga County,
Ohio,
277 N.E.2d 258 (Ohio
1971).

This proceeding was commenced on September 3, 1971, by the filing of a petition by Charles Haun and his wife (petitioners) seeking a decree of adoption of Julie (sometimes called Sheila) an infant of three years.

The petition has been opposed by Children's Services, a community supported child welfare agency in Cleveland. . . . [Citation omitted.] Children's Services has custody of the child by reason of a permanent surrender executed by the child's mother on April 20, 1970. . . .

The full impact of the contention urged in the motion of Children's Services is that in the absence of consent by Children's Services, however its decision to withhold consent be arrived at, the court is helpless to exercise its primary and plenary powers to grant or deny an application for adoption, or indeed to conduct hearings pursuant to a petition for adoption. . . .

On these premises, all parties in interest being before the court, the court decided to conduct a full hearing on the petition for adoption which included considerable testimony and evidence bearing on the decision of Children's Services to withhold its consent to adoption of the child by the petitioners. . . .

The facts adduced by the parties at the hearing are not contrary in any material respects.

Petitioners, Charles Haun and his wife, are 68 and 55 years old, respectively, and are in excellent health. They have resided in their Olmsted Falls, Ohio, home, valued at Twenty-eight Thousand Dollars for twenty-two years, and in the course of their married life have had four children, one adopted, and have, upon arrangement started in 1959 with Children's Services, been foster parents of thirty-four children of whom Julie, now aged three, is one. Mr. Haun, retired, receives a Railroad Retirement pension from the Federal Government of Four Hundred Ninety-two Dollars per month. This pension will continue to be paid Mrs. Haun in the event of the prior decease of her husband. The family homestead is unencumbered and the Hauns have cash savings of Twenty-one Thousand Six Hundred Dollars of which Sixteen Hundred Dollars was banked between February 4, and October 7, 1971, attesting to the thrift and financial sagacity of petitioners. Insurance in a modest sum is paid up. Petitioners have no long term obligations.

Julie, born December 4, 1968, has been continuously in the Haun home, except for short periods of hospitalization, since she was fifteen days old. Premature at birth, Julie was legally placed by Children's Services with petitioners in their home because of their previously demonstrated expertise in the care of premature babies. Julie's mother was in labor sixteen hours and it was suspected that the child suffered some brain damage although "at the time they couldn't know how serious." . . .

. . . Presently Julie is happily characterized as a normal healthy child having an IQ of 112. Without doubt the improvement over somewhat cloudy beginnings is due to the care, affection, attention and love accorded by petitioners. In turn love and affection are exhibited by Julie toward the Hauns. On this all are agreed.

This productive, continuing placement found by this court to be exceptionally beneficial to the child, has been put in jeopardy for the future by the threatened withdrawal of Julie from the care and home of petitioners. . . .

In terms of placement of children, Children's Services first concern is the need of the specific child, emotional, physical, and otherwise. When considering the acceptability of an adoption couple, Children's Services looks for (1) maturity, (2) stability (3) financial ability to carry additional responsibilty, and (4) love of children. These factors or standards were found to be met by petitioners except that Children's Services urges that physical and emotional stability diminish as age increases, and that the second factor, stability, may not be present during the later years of Julie's minority. To the court this is a matter of conjecture. But certainly the evidence is clear that presently, and at least for the near term, and probably for the entire intervening period until the child's maturity, the factor of stability, in addition to the other stated factors, is satisfied by petitioners. . . .

The best interests of Julie are inextricably interwoven with her special needs in view of her physical history. This case differs from the bulk of adoption proceedings because of the child's medical background and the lurking hazard of regression. Medical guidance is most cogent in determining the child's needs. Fortunately the medical guidance available to us is both unambiguous and meaningful.

Among the exhibits is a memorandum of October 4, 1971, addressed to whom it may concern from the physician in charge of the Child Neurology Clinic, University Hospitals of Cleveland, who is also an assistant professor of neurology and pediatrics and the consultant to Children's Services staff physician in this case. . . .

The court is moved especially by the language—". . . we would respectfully submit that continuation of the care received from Mrs. Haun would be highly desirable for this delightful child." . . .

. . . The opinion of the neurologist supports another previously expressed opinion (September 1, 1971) of a physician attached to the Nourse Clinic of Children's Services. This physician, Mrs. Haun testifies, ". . . just threw up his hands in the air and he said "what the hell is the matter with those people downtown, don't they know that they can't move this baby?" To run counter to such medical opinions would constitute reckless disregard of the child's best interest and future welfare.

These professional judgments are unrebutted and in the opinion of the court are to be accorded maximum weight and cogency. To the court they are practically conclusive—they clinch the case for petitioners.

Children's Services would move Julie from the care of the Hauns to new parents yet to be chosen. The testimony of Children's Services is that skill is required on the part of case workers in helping foster families to have a successful and uncomplicated move, that skill and patience are needed in working with the family to enable them to understand the child, "to hold their hand while they are being adjusted to each other." . . . It is apparent to the court that in this case if skill and patience fail, as they do all too frequently, Julie's future well being becomes speculative in contrast to the certain stability and peace obtaining should her environment remain as at present. . . . The risk is uncalled for and unnecessary in these circumstances; it is vital that the present stance be maintained.

The position of Children's Services evidenced by withholding of consent in this case does not have its source in the facts and professional judgments available to it and the court. The court discerns no justification for withholding consent nor warrant for an order other than one granting the petition.

RELIGIOUS CONSIDERATIONS

Most states require that, whenever practical, a child be placed with adoptive parents of the same religion as the biological parents. This means that applicants without any formal religious affiliation will sometimes not be approved as adoptive applicants. In re Adoption of "E," 279 A.2d 785 (N.J. 1971), illustrates a successful appeal on this question.

IN RE ADOPTION OF "E"

Supreme Court of New Jersey,
279 A.2d
785 (N.J. 1971).

The county court denied plaintiffs' application for a final decree of adoption. The court held that plaintiffs' lack of belief in a Supreme Being rendered them unfit to be adoptive parents. The plaintiffs appealed to the Appellate Division, and prior to argument there, we certified the case on our own motion. We reverse.

On June 27, 1969, the plaintiffs, John and Cynthia Burke, received custody of the baby girl "E" from the Children's Aid and Adoption Society of New Jersey (Society). On May 23, 1970, the Burkes, having received the consent of the Society, filed an application for adoption with the county court. The Society filed a report with the court recommending that the application be granted. . . .

The facts are undisputed. Cynthia Burke, holder of a Ph.D. in Psychology, is a past Associate Professor at Seton Hall University. Her husband, John, holder of a Master's Degree in Speech Pathology, is currently working toward his Doctorate at Southern Illinois University. In 1965, the Burkes applied to the New Jersey Bureau of Children's Services for assistance in the adoption of a child. They were informed that, pursuant to a department regulation, they would be required to demonstrate some church affiliation before they could be considered suitable applicants. Since they could not demonstrate such an affiliation, they were denied the opportunity to adopt a child, and they instituted a suit for declaratory judgment seeking resolution of the question whether such "a religious qualification" might properly be required as a prerequisite to an adoption. The suit was dismissed by stipulation, however, when the Bureau of Children's Services revised its regulations which now provide in pertinent part:

"Opportunity for religious or spiritual and ethical development of the child should receive full consideration in the selection of adoptive homes. Lack of religious affiliation or of a religious faith, however, should not be a bar to consideration of any applicants for adoption."

In July of 1967, after the regulations had been amended, the Society placed a baby boy (David) with the Burkes. With the recommendation of the Society, the county court granted final adoption on September 28, 1968. David has been living with the Burkes ever since and there is no dispute that he has been well cared for.

On June 27, 1969, the Society placed a three week old baby girl, "E", with the Burkes and she has been with them continuously since that date. On May 23, 1970, plaintiffs filed a complaint seeking adoption of the child. After conducting an investigation, the Society compiled and filed a report recommending the adoption. The report noted that both Cynthia and John Burke were in excellent health, intelligent, well educated, attentive to their children, and able to provide a physically suitable home. The report also noted that ". . . the Burkes' attitude toward the children is one that is healthy, and one that is full of warmth and love. . . . Mr. and Mrs. Burke have no church affiliation; however the agency has found them to be people of high moral and ethical standards."

At the hearing, the trial judge focused on the area of religion. He directed almost all of his questions to the plaintiffs' lack of church affiliation and their lack of belief in the existence of a Supreme Being. John Burke testified that he had had formal religious training as a Catholic and Cynthia testified that she had been raised as a Protestant. Both said they were now unaffiliated with any church and did not believe in a Supreme Being. Both articulated their humanistic views of morality and ethics, and their views of the type of ethical training they thought necessary to proper child rearing. The following colloquies with John Burke are illustrative:

THE COURT: Let's see now, an atheist doesn't believe in God at all and an agnostic does what? Can you tell me what you are? Are you an agnostic or an atheist, Mr. Burke?

> MR. BURKE: Labels such as these have connotations that are unpalatable to some people. I wouldn't call myself an agnostic or an atheist.
> THE COURT: Well, tell me what you are.
> MR. BURKE: I am a humanist, I suppose. I believe in people. I believe in the goodness of morality in that what we need to learn in life is being good to one another and that the perception, the true perception of the Juda-Christian way of life are what make us good and this is the morality that obviously I haven't been able nor did I desire to throw off the teaching of my childhood. . . .
> MR. BURKE: I do not believe in the existence of a Supreme Being.
> THE COURT: I am a little perturbed . . . the man is outspoken. He could have lied about it and the fact that he didn't lie about it is so much in his favor.

Cynthia Burke, who said her views were the same as her husband's, responded similarly to inquiries by the court:

> THE COURT: Well, tell me your views about a Supreme Being.
> MRS. BURKE: It would be very difficult for me to give you a description of what I believe a Supreme Being to be. I believe in the power of life. I am very much in awe of the creating of power of life. But, I do not believe in a Supreme Being who is in any way personified.
> THE COURT: All right. You don't believe in religion as such, do you?
> MRS. BURKE: I do not believe that any one religion is any more preferable to any other.
> THE COURT: Do you believe in any religion?
> MRS. BURKE: I do not subscribe to any religion, no. I am not a practicing member. . . .
> THE COURT: Mrs. Burke, do you have any definite plans as far as raising these children in reference to a particular religious training or religious training per se?
> MRS. BURKE: Well, religious training involves, as far as I am concerned, a great many things. It involves standards of morality or a way of life which I feel involves honesty, regard of others, responsibility for one's own faith. I have already begun to teach my child [David] these things, both by teaching him the things that I think a three-year-old boy is capable of learning and I expect to teach him these things by example. As far as philosophy and the more abstract ideas involved in religion and philosophy, I suspect that my children will end up knowing more about Christianity than the average child who goes to Sunday School. . . .
> THE COURT: Maybe I am old-fashioned, Mr. Burke, maybe I am old-fashioned. If you are Jewish, you are a good Jew. If you be a Protestant, you be a good Protestant. If you are Catholic, you are a good Catholic. It doesn't mean that people are good or that people are as good as you are.

In his written opinion, the trial judge recognized that a court should be loath to intervene in matters of religion. . . . [H]e held that the best interests of the child "E" would not be served by granting the application. . . . In effect, held that the plaintiffs were unfit to assume the responsibility of adoptive parents. Accordingly, he denied the adoption and ordered that the child "E" be returned to the Society.

The trial court's decision rested solely on the grounds that plaintiffs, through their own testimony, did not believe in a Supreme Being or belong to a church of a recognized religion. . . .

. . . We believe that the trial court's decision and the suggestion of the court appointed amicus curiae both run counter to state and federal law. . . .

The "best interests of the child" standard is flexible and leaves a great deal of discretion to the trial judge. . . . In the present case, the question is whether the trial court misused its discretion in denying an adoption solely because the applicants did not believe in a Supreme Being and were not affiliated with a church.

There are no prior reported decisions in this state holding that an adoption may be denied solely because the prospective adoptive parents were nonbelievers. . . .

Although there are no decisions in this state which are directly on point, the cases demonstrate that generally our courts have been most reluctant to intervene in religious matters. . . .

On the other hand, religion has in some circumstances been one of the factors considered in determining the best interests of the child in both custody disputes and adoption proceedings. . . . In our efforts to protect the best interests of the child, we may afford religion special significance in certain cases, as, for example, where the natural parents object to the religion of the adoptive parents, . . . where the prior religious training of the child cannot be pursued because of the environment, *T. v. H.,* supra (Jewish children raised in rural Idaho where there were no available religious facilities and no other persons of the same faith); or where a child has had some religious training and a court finds that the granting of custody to persons of a different religious persuasion would cause emotional difficulties for the child. And, of course, we have not hesitated to intervene to protect a child where the religious beliefs of the parents threaten the physical well being of the child. None of these factors operate against the adoption in this case.

It is implicit in our decisions as well as those of other states that religion may be viewed as a relevant factor in determining custody or adoption but, without other factual support, the religious factor is not controlling. . . .

Summarizing, while religion when coupled with other considerations may be a factor to be weighed by the court in determining the advisability of granting an adoption of a child, that factor barring special circumstances such as those referred to above, is not and cannot be controlling. Since the trial court denied the adoption solely because of the Burkes' lack of a religious belief, he misused his discretion and erred as a matter of law.

The lower court's decision is also defective in that it runs afoul of the First Amendment of the United States Constitution. . . .

The First Amendment provides in pertinent part:

"Congress shall make no law respecting an establishment of religion, or prohibiting the free exercise thereof. . . ."

This freedom of religion provision is applicable to the states through the Fourteenth Amendment. . . . It applies to the judiciary as well as the executive and legislative branches of the government. . . . The provision consists of two separate but related clauses, the Establishment Clause and the Free Exercise Clause. The Establishment Clause bars a state from placing its official support behind a religious belief, while the Free Exercise Clause bars a state from interfering with the practice of religion by its citizens. . . .

. . . We, as judges, regardless of our own personal beliefs and religious affiliations, cannot take the position that children may be placed only in the homes of believers until they are able to choose for themselves which course to pursue. Under the First Amendment we are incompetent to do so. Should we invade the province of religion in this instance, the religious beliefs of every citizen would be imperiled. We cannot forget that many of our forebears fled to this country to escape religious persecution for professing beliefs which were unpopular in their homeland. It was for this very reason that the Amendment was adopted, and if it is to have any meaning, it must protect minority rights in this area. . . .

Finally, the court appointed amicus curiae suggests that the likelihood that a child of nonbelievers will be ostracized serves as a valid secular reason for denying adoptions to them. Even assuming that nonbelievers are shunned by some elements of the populace, most minority groups suffer or in the past have suffered the same penalty. Yet, absent special circumstances, no one would contend that members of a minority group should be denied the opportunity to adopt a child on that basis. . . .

The judgment of the trial court is reversed. Since the sole ground for denying the adoption was the Burkes' beliefs regarding religion and it is clear from the record that they are otherwise fit, we grant the adoption in the exercise of our original jurisdiction. . . .

An opposite finding on religion is found in Dickens v. Ernesto (281 N.E. 2d 153 [N.Y. 1972]).

DICKENS v. ERNESTO

Court of Appeals of New York, 281 N.E.2d 153 (N.Y. 1972).

FULD, Chief Judge.

On December 22, 1969, the petitioners, Robert and Anne Dickens, sought to file an application as adoptive parents with respondent Erie County Department of Social Services. Refused permission to do so by respondent department solely on the ground that they did not have a religious affiliation, they brought this article 78 proceeding for a judgment (1) declaring that the challenged constitutional and statutory provisions offend against certain provisions contained in the Federal Constitution and (2) directing the respondent to immediately "process . . . [their] application as adoptive parents." The courts below decided that there was no violation of petitioners' constitutional rights but directed the respondent to accept and process their application. From that determination, the petitioners appeal as of right, urging that the provisions in question "create an establishment of religion" and deny them "their freedom of religion" under the First Amendment and also deny them equal protection of the laws under the Fourteenth Amendment. . . .

In dealing with the petitioners' contention that New York, by Constitution and legislation, has created an establishment of religion, we note that "No perfect or absolute separation [of government and religion] is really possible; the very existence of the Religion Clauses is an involvement of sorts." . . . A number of criteria have been developed, however, to determine when a law is violative of the Establishment Clause. "[T]o withstand the strictures of [that] Clause," the Supreme Court has observed, "there must be a secular legislative purpose and a primary effect that neither advances nor inhibits religion." . . . More, such legislation "must not foster 'an excessive government entanglement with religion.' . . ."

Legislation which provides for the placement of a child with adoptive parents of the same religion "so far as consistent with the best interests of the child, and where practicable" (Family Ct. Act. § 116, subd. [g]), undoubtedly fulfills a "secular legislative purpose" and certainly reflects and preserves a "benevolent neutrality" toward religion. . . .

Certainly subdivision (e) of section 116 of the Family Court Act, relied upon by the petitioners, does not support their claim of unconstitutionality. Insofar as relevant, that statute provides that "The words 'when practicable' . . . shall be interpreted as being without force or effect if there is a proper or suitable person of the same religious faith . . . as that of the child available . . . or . . . if there is a duly authorized . . . society or institution under the control of persons of the same religious faith or persuasion as that of the child, at the time available and willing to assume the responsibility for the custody of or control over any such child." As indicated in the new subdivision (g) of section 116 of the Family Court Act, subdivision (e) must be deemed to require that the "religious wishes" of the natural parent or parents be given effect "so far as consistent with the best interests of the child." And subdivision (g) provides that, in expressing their "religious wishes," the parents themselves may authorize the placement of the child with adoptive parents of a different religion, express their "indifference to religion" as a prerequisite to adoption or make religion a "subordinate consideration." Accordingly, the court, in applying subdivision (e) in the light of the strictures of subdivision (g), still retains discretion to determine whether a particular placement is in the best interests of the child, taking into account both religious and secular considerations.

Nor is the petitioners' First Amendment right to the "free exercise of religion" violated by the religious "matching" requirements. They argue that they are forced to choose between their right to profess no religion and their right to adopt because there are many more prospective parents than adoptive children and because all the natural parents in the Erie County area require their children to be placed with adoptive parents of one of the "predominant" religions. However, there have been instances, as the court below found, in which natural parents have indicated "their indifference to the religious placement of their child." Adoptive parents without religious affiliations would, as the courts below have indicated, be eligible to adopt such a child or a child whose religious background is unknown. Moreover, there is no indication that the petitioners are limited to the Erie County area in their search for an adoptive child. Under these circumstances, religious conformity provisions which serve a valid secular purpose may not be said to discriminate against or penalize the petitioners because they do not have a religious affiliation, nor are they thereby placed under an obligation to assume a religious faith in order to be able to adopt a child. [Citation omitted.]

Likewise without substance is the petitioners' equal protection argument. They urge that the religious conformity provisions, since they are not reasonably related to the purpose of the adoption laws, create an arbitrary classification which denies them equal protection of the laws. In point of fact, their real quarrel is not with the religious conformity provisions—which quite properly allow surrendering parents to express a religious preference . . .

—but, rather, with the shortages of adoptive children and surrendering parents without religious affiliation or preference.

The order appealed from should be affirmed, without costs.

Classification of children on the basis of religion has apparently resulted in racial discrimination and in some cases limited their access to adoption.

> Why then is there this near unanimity on maintaining religious identity between natural parents and adoptive parents? It clearly has nothing to do with the child's welfare except in those cases where an older child is adopted. The only explanation which seems to fit the facts is that the statutes impose a truce upon proselytizing by maintaining the status quo during adoption. The ultimate purpose is to avoid conflict between religious groups through the historically respectable device of the legal fiction, the fiction that in this context the child's religion is that of his parent. (Larr, 1968, p. 64)

Sectarian agencies may limit adoptive services to persons of their faith. Such a limitation encourages independent adoptions when a sharp discrepancy exists between the religion of adoptive applicants and the supply of children available.

TRANSRACIAL ADOPTIONS

Transracial adoptions have always been controversial. Because of statutes against interracial marriages in many states, both agencies and courts hardly considered the possibility of such placements until the late 1960s.

For a brief period following the acceptance of such placements, they flourished. However, the black community objected to transracial adoptions on the basis that children had a need for racial identity. Resources were sought to aid in recruitment of black adoptive parents and to help adoptive parents meet the cost of care. In spite of these efforts, the supply of black homes does not meet the demand. Native Americans, Asians, and other minorities have objected to transracial placements on much the same basis.

While there have been studies of transracial placements, the strong opposition to them from minorities will be more forceful than research data which substantiate their general success. The problems with placement of Vietnamese refugee children illustrates the difficulties implicit in a mass program carried out under crisis conditions.

A major question about transracial placements remains: Is a transracial adoptive placement better than leaving a child to grow up in an institution or a series of foster homes? Minority group members differ in their individual answers to this question, but they stress that provision of adequate placement resources would make that question obsolete.

In 1981 the California Department of Social Services proposed the following policy regarding transracial/transethnic placements.

CALIFORNIA DEPARTMENT OF SOCIAL SERVICES PROPOSED POLICY ON TRANSRACIAL PLACEMENTS

Racial background and ethnic identification are factors of prime importance in the placement of children for foster care and adoption. Each child's opportunity to be placed with a family that reflects his own racial or ethnic heritage should be maximized by the following priority order of placement preference:

1. In the home of a relative
2. With a family of the same racial or ethnic identification
3. With a family of a different racial or ethnic identification

Placements with foster or adoptive parents of a different racial or ethnic background should only be considered when agencies can demonstrate:

1. That proximity of the natural parents to the foster care placement is necessary so as to facilitate visitation and family reunification, or

2. That they have made extensive outreach efforts and there are no foster or adoptive parents of the same or similar background available to the child, or

3. That the child has established a significant family relationship with a foster or adoptive parent of a different background and it would be detrimental to the child to be removed from the family, or

4. That the birth parents have expressly requested that factors other than race or ethnic background, such as religious preference, nonrelative placement, etc., be considered as the prime placement criteria in adoptive placement and the agency can demonstrate that outreach efforts have failed to locate adoptive families of the same or similar racial or ethnic background that meet the birth parents' expressed placement criteria

In implementing this policy, agencies should observe the following additional principles:

1. If a child is of mixed racial background, placement should be with parents of the same background, if possible, or if not, with a family of either background.

2. Adoptive outreach efforts for a specific child should be time limited (90 days from the time the child is legally free for adoption) in order to ensure that a child does not remain in foster care for an excessive period of time.

3. A transracial placement should be made based on the needs of the child, not the desire of the adoptive parents for a child of a particular race, or on an expedience for the agency.

4. Permanent care in a home, not of the child's background, is preferable to institutionalization or extended temporary foster care.

5. In some instances, long-term foster care in a home of the child's same background where strong emotional ties have developed is preferable to adoption by a family that is not of the child's background.

6. Recruitment efforts should be initiated to develop a pool of minority families as placement resources.

7. Agencies should use state and region-wide exchanges to locate approved minority families for adoptive placements.

8. Agencies should document their efforts to find parents of the same racial background or ethnic identification as the child.

9. Before making a transracial adoptive placement, agencies should have documentation in the child's case record from the statewide exchange system and from the regional exchanges, including the minority components of such exchanges.

INHERITANCE AND ADOPTION

Adoptive parents wish to assure their children the right to inherit from their estate.

Intestate Succession

In the absence of a will, an adopted child inherits from adoptive parents in the same way as any biological child. Generally the adopted child also shares in the intestate estate of persons related to the adoptive parents. An adopted child also still inherits from biological relatives in about one-quarter of the states.

Wills and Trusts

Do wills and trusts naming "children" include an adopted child? A strong trend is evident in both cases and statutes to include the adopted child in the class unless the testator's intent not to include him clearly appears from the instrument. The Revised Uniform Adoption Act states:

. . . [T]he adopted individual thereafter is a stranger to his former relatives for all purposes including inheritance and the interpretation or construction of documents, statutes, and instruments, whether executed before or after the adoption is decreed, which do not expressly include the individual by name or by some designation not based on a parent and child or blood relationship; and

(2) to create the relationship of parent and child between petitioner and the adopted individual, as if the adopted individual were a legitimate blood descendant of the petitioner, for all purposes including inheritance and applicability of statutes, documents, and instruments, whether executed before or after the adoption is decreed, which do not expressly exclude an adopted individual from their operation or effect. . . .

Equitable, De Facto, or Common Law Adoption

Many courts allow children to inherit from persons who treated them in all ways as though they were their own but failed to complete the legal adoption process. This situation frequently arises when a child is left in the care of a family that rears him or her without any formal agreement. Recognition of the de facto adoptive status is especially important when the parents have left no will because it would assure the child's right to receive Social Security benefits and to share in the estate.

ATTACK ON ADOPTION DECREES

Biological parents may attempt to have an adoption decree set aside on the basis of alleged fraud, duress, or inadequate notice. The best interests of the child require that adoption decrees be final and irrevocable. The Revised Uniform Adoption Act provides:

> Subject to the disposition of an appeal, upon the expiration of [one] year after an adoption decree is issued the decree cannot be questioned by any person including the petitioner, in any manner upon any ground, including fraud, misrepresentation, failure to give any required notice, or lack of jurisdiction of the parties or of the subject matter.

Gottesman (1981) has noted that a number of states are considering requiring judicial process each time parental rights are terminated, even if termination is voluntary, in order to guard against coercion.

SUBSIDIZED ADOPTIONS

Subsidized adoption is available in more than forty states. Its purpose is to help poorer persons become adoptive parents, and it is especially helpful in providing special-needs children with homes. The Model State Subsidized Adoption Act states that a child would be eligible for subsidized adoption either because the child "has established significant emotional ties with prospective adoptive parents while in their care as a foster child" or because of physical or mental disability, emotional disturbance, recognized high risk of physical or mental disease, age, sibling relationship, racial or ethnic factors, or any combination of these conditions.

Certifying a child as eligible for subsidy is a new concept. The focus is on the child and his or her needs rather than on the financial ability of the adoptive parents to meet those needs. Many state statutes currently refer to the financial status of prospective adoptive parents; however, the model act provides for three types of subsidy: the special service subsidy, the time-limited subsidy, and the long-term subsidy.

Special Service Subsidy

The special service subsidy is limited to the time span of the necessary service. It may be a one-time payment for an anticipated expense when there is no other resource. It may include, among other costs, (a) legal and court costs of adoption;

(b) other costs incidental to adoptive placement, e.g., preplacement visits; (c) special medical costs; or (d) costs of other special services, including physio-, psycho-, or occupational therapy, remedial education, rehabilitation training, extraordinary corrective dental treatment, speech and hearing therapy, wheelchairs, braces, crutches, prostheses, day care, transportation, and any other expenses related to the care and treatment of the child under "medical costs." According to the Model State Subsidized Adoption Act,

> In the case of a child with a known medical condition which will require treatment or surgery after placement for adoption or after the adoption decree, investigation must be made of the adopting family's medical insurance and of other public and voluntary community services (such as Crippled Children's Services and Medicaid) to determine whether the costs of the treatment and related costs can be covered by one or more of them. Where costs for treatment and related expenses cannot be covered or can be only partially covered by insurance and by other community services, the subsidy agreement shall provide for the necessary funds for the treatment required after adoptive placement or after the adoption decree. If, because of genetic background or other medical history there is a recognized high risk that physical or mental disease may later develop, the agreement shall include provision of funds, if not otherwise available, for treatment of such disease.

Time-limited Subsidy

The time-limited subsidy is a payment for a specified time after placement or after legal adoption. Its purpose is to help with expenses of integrating the child into the family or to provide needed funds for a specified length of time.

Long-term Subsidy

Long-term subsidy is designed for cases where children cannot be adopted unless their long-term financial needs are met. Payments may continue until the child reaches majority or, in some cases, beyond if other appropriate resources are absent and if state regulations are met. The model act states that the amount of time-limited and long-term subsidies is not to exceed the prevailing rate paid to foster family homes.

Howe (1983) notes that the Adoption Assistance and Child Welfare Act of 1980 removed the state disincentive to the adoption of foster children by providing continuing federal adoption subsidies. The Economic Recovery Act of 1981 allowed deduction of up to $1,500 of adoption expenses of a special-needs child.

MODEL LEGISLATION FOR SPECIAL-NEEDS CHILDREN

Draft model legislation for adoption of children with special needs was proposed by the Department of Health and Human Services in the final Model Act for Adoption of Children with Special Needs, published in the *Federal Register*, October 8, 1981.

Despite omission of sections of the preliminary draft alluding to putative fathers, revocation of relinquishment, and unlicensed adoption placement, and insertion of sections increasing the emphasis on eliminating barriers to adopting special-needs children and maintaining the privacy of biological parents, both the National Conference of Commissioners on Uniform State Laws and the family law section of the American Bar Association (ABA) opposed the final model act (Howe, 1983). The ABA family law section's Adoption Committee was directed to recast its own initial drafts of model legislation for adoption of children with special needs, eliminating any preference for either agency or private adoptions.

THE SEARCH FOR NATURAL FAMILY MEMBERS

The quest for identity is a psychological or physical search for biological parents that adopted children may initiate on reaching adolescence or at the birth of their own first child. The search has recently called into serious question one of the basic legal assumptions of adoption. In order to prevent embarrassment and interference between the parties or hindrance of the adoptive process, neither the child nor the adoptive parents were traditionally to know the identity of the biological parents. However, medical information has increasingly been revealed in response to a growing recognition of genetic concerns.

Social workers have recommended that adoption records be opened to adopted persons to provide all information regarding the biological parents except possibly their names. However, the quest for identity has led adult adoptees to form such organizations as the Adoptees Liberty Movement Association and Yesterday's Children to lobby for the right to learn the identity of their biological parents. Organizations of adoptive parents have formed to oppose open records. As of 1984, adoptees could inspect their original birth certificates without restriction in three states. Several other states permit adoptive parents to request that no new birth certificate be issued. According to a survey by Pierce (1984), five states had legal provisions for obtaining the consent of the birth parents, and ten states provided registries where persons directly involved in adoptions could register their willingness to meet. Thus the trend has been to provide more access to information. West European nations also allow adult adoptees access to their original birth records. After Great Britain opened records in 1975, fewer than 2 percent exercised their rights. Data from Minnesota showed a high interest when that state agreed to open its records (Weidell, 1980).

Gitlin (1981) notes that courts have gone both ways in interpreting the "good cause" exception to provisions for sealed records. In the District of Columbia (In re Adoption of Female Infant, 105 D. Wash L. Rptr. 245 [1977]) and South Carolina (Bradey v. Children's Bureau of S. Carolina, 274 S.E.2d 418 [1981]), courts have held that enhancing the adoptee's psychological welfare was good cause. However, New York (In the Matter of In re Linda F.M. v. Department of Health of the City of New York, 418 N.E.2d 236 [N.Y. 1981]) and Illinois (In re Roger B., 418 N.E.2d 751 [Ill. 1981]) courts ruled that simply attaining the age of majority or wanting to know the identity of biological parents was not good cause to order sealed records opened.

Adoptees hoped that their right to inherit from biological parents who die without a will would be a compelling reason to open records to aid the search, but this issue was raised unsuccessfully in an Illinois court (Aimone v. Finley, 447 N.E.2d 868 [Ill. 1983]).

The highest New York court ruled in 1985 that heirs of the late Mayor James J. Walker were not entitled to receive copies of the adoption decrees among their father's property. Such papers were expected to be helpful in the search that was being conducted by Mayor Walker's daughter.

While courts have been reluctant to open records to adoptees, social agencies have also used a legal basis to refuse access to their records. Actually only four states prohibit agencies from giving information to searchers. The adopted person's needs rather than those of the biological or natural parents should be accorded primacy from the agency.

At least agencies should not continue to promise confidentiality to natural parents and adoptive applicants who are involved in current adoptive placements.

One approach is to provide "open" adoptions, in which biological parents intent on maintaining contact would be matched with adoptive parents who are agreeable to such an arrangement.

SURROGATE MOTHERS

Surrogate mothers are a countertrend toward infant adoptions with questions not adequately addressed by existing law. Fertilization of a human egg after it has been removed from the body, followed by its placement in a uterus and subsequent birth, is increasingly prevalent (Annas and Elias, 1983).

Although this technology is new, the legal issues are similar to those involved in artificial insemination by a donor. However,

> the sperm donor is merely turning over a gamete (as would a female donating an egg), while the surrogate is relinquishing her rights to a living individual. Even if the surrogate mother were not viewed as selling a child, donating sperm is just not comparable to providing nine months of prenatal care and childbearing. The former could be characterized as a product, sold at a uniform price, while the latter is a personalized service. The surrogate is, in effect, entering into an employment contract. (Andrews, 1981: 24–25)

Howe (1983: 196) asks the legal and psychological questions:

> If there is some mishap with a surrogate birth, who bears responsibility for the child— the surrogate mother, the adoptive parent, or the state? If adoptees have suffered anguish in the past attempting to unravel the mysteries of their birth, what new psychic traumas await the child for whom no birth parents can be identified? It has been asserted that learning begins even before birth, and that the fetus responds to changes in the mother's mental and physical condition. If that be so, what may be the long-run impact on the fetus carried by a surrogate mother whose mind-set is that she is only carrying a "product" for another, so that when birth occurs she suffers no loss in giving up the child?

In a worst-case example of the above drawn from recent events, a child with microcephaly was born to a surrogate mother, Judy Stiver, after which neither she and her husband nor Alexander Malahoff, the man who had contracted with her to bear the child in order to persuade his own wife to return to him, wanted the infant. Laboratory test results that the child was not Malahoff's were announced on a national television talk show with the Stivers, Malahoff, and their attorneys present. The surrogate mother contract had required that the Stivers not have sexual intercourse for thirty days after insemination but made no provision for beforehand.

In discussing legal remedies for situations of this sort, Annas and Elias (1983: 219) recommended that "two interrelated concerns should be paramount in any legislative or regulatory scheme: the best interests of the child, and the minimization of commercial aspects of the transaction." They give as an example of the first instance that the child might be given a contractual right at the age of majority to learn the identity of the surrogate mother. The second instance recalls concerns with selling babies for profit. Michigan courts have upheld the provision of that state's adoption code prohibiting payment to surrogate mothers (Doe v. Attorney General, 307 N.W. 2d 438, 441 [1981]).

Apparently contracts involving surrogate mothers are not legally enforceable. If the surrogate mother changes her mind and wants to keep the child or if the adoptive parents do not want the child, how can the best interests of the child be determined?

The two steps in the adoption process are useful to remember here: (1) legal termination of the relationship with the biological parents and (2) creation of a new relationship with the adoptive parents. Andrews (1981) notes that adoption laws preventing valid consent on the part of the mother until after the child is born void any surrogate mother contract made before or during pregnancy, and that accepting a fee after the birth is child-selling and therefore illegal.

ADOPTION IN THE 1980s

Despite the traditional view of adoption as involving mostly infants, a perspective renewed by the issues stemming from surrogate motherhood, adoption today more typically involves older children. Katz (1982: 9) summarizes the current situation:

> Today [nonrelative] adoption is usually the end of a process that began as a child neglect or abuse proceeding. While there are still some newborns being placed for adoption, the typical profile of the adoptive child in the 80s is a three- to five-year-old youngster who has lived with his or her birth mother, then with a series of foster parents, and has lacked a permanent home for at least a year. The birth mother usually has failed to rehabilitate herself, and the most likely candidates to adopt the child are the child's foster parents.

Permanency planning through adoption for children in foster care involves programs staffed by social workers. The need for legal and psychological knowledge in order to serve these children, their biological parents, and potential adoptive parents has never been greater.

Questions for Review

1. What are the two steps in the adoptive process?
2. What are the different purposes of child adoption and adult adoption?
3. What are the primary social work roles in the adoptive process?
4. Differentiate between independent and illegal adoptions.
5. How is jurisdiction determined?
6. Why is revocation of consent an important issue?
7. Distinguish *Stanley v. Illinois* and *Caban v. Mohammed* from *Quilloin v. Walcott* in terms of the developed parent-child relationship.
8. What is the purpose of agency investigations? What factors are considered?
9. What is the impact of marital status, age, race, and sex on adoptive applicants? Should grandparents have the right to adopt their grandchildren?
10. Summarize *In re Adoption of "E"* and *Dickens v. Ernesto*. What is the role of religion in adoption?
11. Why do minority groups object to transracial adoption?
12. Explain de facto adoption. What is the impact of adoption on inheritance when the birth parents have no will?

13.   Why are adoption decrees occasionally attacked by biological parents?

14.   Why are fewer infants available for adoption currently than in the past?

15.   Who are the special-needs children?

16.   What is the purpose of subsidized adoption?

Questions for Debate and Discussion

1.   Should all biological fathers be required to consent before a child is adopted? If not, why not?

2.   How can legal reforms help adopted children in their search for identity? How can agencies be helpful?

3.   A number of agencies are bringing approved applicants and birth mothers together on several occasions to encourage communication. Is this a desirable practice?

4.   In view of the favorable outcomes of adoptive placements, have too many societal resources been invested in selection of adoptive parents?

5.   What modifications would you propose in the processing of relative adoptions?

6.   Should foster parents who are going to become adoptive parents be subject to any additional evaluation? Should they receive long-term subsidies if they need the extra income?

Selected Readings   Canado, Eugene R. *Marriage, Divorce, and Adoption*. Binghamton, N.Y.: Guild Publications, 1979.

Chaloff, Miriam B. "Grandparents' Statutory Visitation Rights and the Rights of Adoptive Parents." *Brooklyn Law Review* 49 (1982): 149–171.

"Children's Rights." *Clearinghouse Review* 16 (1983): 751–756.

Howe, Ruth-Orlene W. "Adoption Practice: Issues and Laws (1958–1983)." *Family Law Quarterly* 17 (1983): 173–197.

Klein, Rona. "Putative Fathers: Unwed But No Longer Unprotected." *Hofstra Law Review* 8 (1980): 425–449.

Leavy, Morton L. *Law of Adoption*. Dobbs Ferry, N.Y.: Oceana Publications, 1979.

Miller, Suzanne. "Protecting Parents and Children Through Adoption Proceedings." *Juvenile Law* 7 (1983): 212–227.

Ricciardello, Carol G. "Adoptees' Right to Identity." *South Dakota Law Review* 27 (1981): 122–136.

Rucher, Cynthia. "Texas Adoption Laws and Adoptees' Rights of Access to Confidential Records." *St. Mary's Law Journal* 15 (1983): 53–113.

Sparks, Nancy. "Adoption: Sealed Records Laws." *Oklahoma Law Review* 35 (1982): 1805–1820.

Unruh, Maurice C. "Adoptees' Equal Protection Rights." *UCLA Law Review* 28 (1981): 1314–1364.

CHAPTER 14

Divorce

Marriage often leads to divorce. Longer life expectancy has increased the need for divorce. People do not want to be partners in an unrewarding marriage for many years. A higher standard of living has also made it less necessary for couples to remain married for economic reasons. Divorce is no longer considered evidence of failure in human relations. It no longer conveys a clear stigma.

People may seek counseling to save a marriage or to facilitate divorce. Because divorce affects family structure, economics, and child-rearing arrangements, it often involves social work services.

As a result of the universal acceptance of no-fault legislation, divorce has undergone more changes between 1975 and 1985 than any other topic in this book. By 1984 only South Dakota still required adversary grounds for divorce.

DEFINITION AND HISTORY

Divorce means the legal termination of a valid marriage. While divorce has been available in many places for centuries, legal tradition in the United States has taken the view that it should be difficult to obtain.

England gave ecclesiastical courts exclusive jurisdiction over marriages until 1857. Divorce was most likely to involve permission to live apart but not to remarry (divorce *a mensa et thoro*, i.e., from bed and board). Under these circumstances the wife was given support out of the husband's estate. Total divorce (*a vinculo matrimonii*) was almost impossible in England, although there were bases for annulment. In 1857 divorce was transferred to the civil courts, and the innocent party could bring action in case of adultery. In 1937 modern grounds such as desertion and cruelty were added to English law.

Divorce has been more easily obtainable in the United States than in England. It is firmly established as a judicial function, although some state legislatures have passed divorce bills. Relatively recent developments include alimony, property divisions, and child support and custody. Divorces are now more easily obtained as long as both parties agree to the divorce and to the terms of settlement. Compulsory counseling and cooling-off periods to discourage divorce have met with little success; they occur too late to effect a reconciliation.

Increases in the divorce rate have been paralleled by a growing rate of remarriage. Consequently, in order to protect their freedom to remarry, couples seek final divorces rather than legal separations, and the courts have been increasingly willing to comply. Divorce settlements may commit the assets of a former spouse and thus reduce the standard of living of a second family, but this has not been a deterrent to second marriages.

JURISDICTION   The federal courts do not have the jurisdiction to grant divorces, but they do hear appeals related to divorce. Several of the decisions presented in this chapter came from the U.S. Supreme Court.

Domicile   All states have statutes governing jurisdiction to grant divorces. Generally, at least one of the parties in the divorce is required to have a **domicile**, that is, legal residence, in the state in which the divorce is sought for a specified period—as little as six weeks in Nevada and Idaho and ninety days in Colorado. A one-year residence requirement in the state of Iowa was affirmed by the U.S. Supreme Court in 1975 (Sosna v. Iowa, 419 U.S. 393). In their dissenting opinion, Justices Thurgood Marshall and William Brennan considered the residence requirement a penalty on interstate travel.

SOSNA v. IOWA

Supreme Court of the United States, 419 U.S. 393 (1975).

Mr. Justice REHNQUIST delivered the opinion of the Court.

Appellant Carol Sosna married Michael Sosna on September 5, 1964, in Michigan. They lived together in New York between October 1967 and August 1971, after which date they separated but continued to live in New York. In August 1972, appellant moved to Iowa with her three children, and the following month she petitioned the District Court of Jackson County, Iowa, for a dissolution of her marriage. Michael Sosna, who had been personally served with notice of the action when he came to Iowa to visit his children, made a special appearance to contest the jurisdiction of the Iowa court. The Iowa court dismissed the petition for lack of jurisdiction, finding that Michael Sosna was not a resident of Iowa and appellant had not been a resident of the State of Iowa for one year proceeding filing of her petition. In so doing the Iowa court applied the provisions of Iowa Code §598.6 requiring that the petitioner in such an action be "for the last year a resident of the state." . . .

The durational residency requirement under attack in this case is a part of Iowa's comprehensive statutory regulation of domestic relations, an area that has long been regarded as a virtually exclusive province of the States. Cases decided by this Court over a period of more than a century bear witness to this historical fact. In Barber v. Barber, 62 U.S. (21 How.) 582, 584 (1859), the Court said that "[w]e disclaim altogether any jurisdiction in the courts of the United States upon the subject of divorce. . . ." In Pennoyer v. Neff, 95 U.S. 714, 734–735 (1877), the Court said: "The State . . . has absolute right to prescribe the conditions upon which the marriage relation between its own citizens shall be created, and the causes for which it may be dissolved," and the same view was reaffirmed in Simms v. Simms, 175 U.S. 162, 167 (1899).

The statutory scheme in Iowa, like those in other States, sets forth in considerable detail the grounds upon which a marriage may be dissolved and the circumstances in which a divorce may be obtained. Jurisdiction over a petition for dissolution is established by statute in "the county where either party resides," . . . and the Iowa courts have construed the term "resident" to have much the same meaning as is ordinarily associated with the concept of domicile. . . . Iowa has recently revised its divorce statutes, incorporating the no-fault concept, but it retained the one-year durational residency requirement.

The imposition of a durational residency requirement for divorce is scarcely unique to Iowa, since 48 States impose such a requirement as a condition for maintaining an action for divorce. As might be expected, the periods vary among the States and range from six weeks to two years. The one-year period selected by Iowa is the most common length of time prescribed.

Appellant contends that the Iowa requirement of one year's residence is unconstitutional for two separate reasons: *first*, because it establishes two classes of persons and discriminates against those who have recently exercised their right to travel to Iowa, thereby contravening the Court's holdings in Shapiro v. Thompson, 394 U.S. 618 (1969), Dunn v. Blumstein, 405 U.S. 330 (1972), and Memorial Hospital v. Maricopa County, 415 U.S. 250 (1974); and *second*, because it denies a litigant the opportunity to make an individualized showing of bona fide residence and therefore denies such residents access to the only method of legally dissolving their marriage. Vlandis v. Kline, 412 U.S. 441 (1973) ; Boddie v. Connecticut [p. 812].

State statutes imposing durational residence requirements were of course invalidated when imposed by States as a qualification for welfare payments, *Shapiro*, supra, for voting, *Dunn*, supra, and for medical care, *Maricopa County*, supra. But none of those cases intimated that the States might never impose durational residency requirements, and such a proposition was in fact expressly disclaimed. What those cases had in common was that the durational residency requirements they struck down were justified on the basis of budgetary or record-keeping considerations which were held insufficient to outweigh the constitutional claims of the individuals. . . .

Iowa's residency requirement may reasonably be justified on grounds other than purely budgetary considerations or administrative convenience. Cf. Kahn v. Shevin [p. 280]. A decree of divorce is not a matter in which the only interested parties are the State as a sort of "grantor," and a plaintiff such as appellant in the role of "grantee." Both spouses are obviously interested in the proceedings, since it will affect their marital status and very likely their property rights. Where a married couple has minor children, a decree of divorce would usually include provisions for their custody and support. With consequences of such moment riding on a divorce decree issued by its courts, Iowa may insist that one seeking to initiate such a proceeding have the modicum of attachment to the State required here.

Such a requirement additionally furthers the State's parallel interests in both avoiding officious intermeddling in matters in which another State has paramount interest, and in minimizing the susceptibility of its own divorce decrees to collateral attack. A State such as Iowa may quite reasonably decide that it does not wish to become a divorce mill for unhappy spouses who have lived there as short a time as appellant had when she commenced her action in the state court after having long resided elsewhere. Until such time as Iowa is convinced that appellant intends to remain in the State, it lacks the "nexus between person and place of such permanence as to control the creation of legal relations and responsibilities of the utmost significance." Williams v. North Carolina, 325 U.S. 226,229 (1945). Perhaps even more importantly, Iowa's interests extend beyond its borders and include the recognition of its divorce decrees by other States under the Full Faith and Credit Clause of the Constitution, Art. IV, § 1. For that purpose, this Court has often stated that "judicial power to grant a divorce—jurisdiction, strictly speaking—is founded on domicile." *Williams*, supra. Where a divorce decree is entered after a finding of domicile in *ex parte* proceedings, this Court has held that the finding of domicile is not binding upon another State and may be disregarded in the face of "cogent evidence" to the contrary. *Williams*, supra, at 236. For that reason, the State asked to enter such a decree is entitled to insist that the putative divorce plaintiff satisfy something more than the bare minimum of constitutional requirements before a divorce may be granted. The State's decision to exact a one-year residency requirement as a matter of policy is therefore buttressed by a quite permissible inference that this requirement not only effectuates state substantive policy but likewise provides a greater safeguard against successful collateral attack than would a requirement of bona fide residence alone. This is precisely the sort of determination that a State in the exercise of its domestic relations jurisdiction is entitled to make.

We therefore hold that the state interest in requiring that those who seek a divorce from its courts be genuinely attached to the State, as well as a desire to insulate divorce decrees from the likelihood of collateral attack, requires a different resolution of the constitutional issue presented than was the case in *Shapiro*, supra, *Dunn*, supra, and *Maricopa County*, supra.

Nor are we of the view that the failure to provide an individualized determination of residency violates the Due Process Clause of the Fourteenth Amendment. Vlandis v. Kline, 412 U.S. 441 (1973), relied upon by appellant, held that Connecticut might not arbitrarily invoke a permanent and irrebuttable presumption of non-residence against students who sought to obtain in-state tuition rates when that presumption was not necessarily or universally true in fact. But in *Vlandis* the Court warned that its decision should not "be construed to deny a State the right to impose on a student, as one element in demonstrating bona fide residence, a reasonable durational residency requirement." 412 U.S., at 452. . . . An individualized determination of physical presence plus the intent to remain, which appellant apparently seeks, would not entitle her to a divorce even if she could have made such a showing. For Iowa requires not merely "domicile" in that sense, but residence in the State for a year in order for its courts to exercise their divorce jurisdiction.

In Boddie v. Connecticut [p. 812] this Court held that Connecticut might not deny access to divorce courts to those persons who could not afford to pay the required fee. Because of the exclusive role played by the State in the termination of marriages, it was held that indigents could not be denied an opportunity to be heard "absent a countervailing state interest of overriding significance." But the gravamen of appellant Sosna's claim is not total deprivation, as in *Boddie,* but only delay. . . .

Affirmed.

Mr. Justice MARSHALL, with whom Mr. Justice Brennan joins, dissenting. . . .

The Court omits altogether what should be the first inquiry: whether the right to obtain a divorce is of sufficient importance that its denial to recent immigrants constitutes a penalty on interstate travel. In my view, it clearly meets that standard. The previous decisions of this Court make it plain that the right of marital association is one of the most basic rights conferred on the individual by the State. The interests associated with the marriage and divorce have repeatedly been accorded particular deference, and the right to marry has been termed "one of the vital personal rights essential to the orderly pursuit of happiness by free men." Loving v. Virginia [p. 10]. In Boddie v. Connecticut [p. 812], we recognized the right to seek dissolution of the marital relationship was closely related to the right to marry, as both involve the voluntary adjustment of the same fundamental human relationship. Without further laboring the point, I think it is clear beyond cavil that the right to seek dissolution of the marital relationship is of such fundamental importance that denial of this right to the class of recent interstate travelers penalizes interstate travel within the meaning of *Shapiro, Dunn,* and *Maricopa County.*

Having determined that the interest in obtaining a divorce is of substantial social importance, I would scutinize Iowa's durational residency requirement to determine whether it constitutes a reasonable means of furthering important interests asserted by the State. The Court, however, has not only declined to apply the "compelling interest" test to this case, it has conjured up possible justifications for the State's restriction in a manner much more akin to the lenient standard we have in the past applied in analyzing equal protection challenges to business regulations. . . . I continue to be of the view that the "rational basis" test has no place in equal protection analysis when important individual interest with constitutional implications are at stake. . . . But whatever the ultimate resting point of the current readjustments in equal protection analysis, the Court has clearly directed that the proper standard to apply to cases in which state statutes have penalized the exercise of the right to interstate travel is the "compelling interest" test. . . .

I conclude that the course Iowa has chosen in restricting access to its divorce courts unduly interferes with the right to "migrate, resettle, find a new job, and start a new life." Shapiro v. Thompson, 394 U.S., at 629. I would reverse the judgement of the District Court and remand for entry of an order granting relief if the court finds that there is a continuing controversy in this case.

Migratory Divorces   Differing residence requirements have led to so-called **migratory divorces**—moving to a state with a brief residence requirement, such as Nevada, in order to obtain a divorce sooner than the state of origin would allow. More liberal divorce laws and practices in most states have made migratory divorces less common. A classic case of migratory divorce was the subject of two U.S. Supreme Court decisions three years apart: Williams v. State of North Carolina, 317 U.S. 287 (1942) and Williams v. State of North Carolina, 325 U.S. 226 (1945). First, North Carolina was ordered to credit a Nevada divorce; in the second decision the claim of domicile on which the Nevada divorce took place was found defective because the couple had gone there solely to obtain a divorce. The second decision, then, limited the degree to which a state had to give full faith and credit to minimum domicile requirements of another state.

Until 1971, divorces could be obtained in Mexico in one day. If they were obtained by mail order, they were considered invalid by U.S. courts. If only the plaintiff appeared in a Mexican court, domicile was subject to question, but, when both plaintiff and defendant appeared together, the divorce was likely to be considered valid. Haiti and the Dominican Republic still offer quick divorces that are of questionable validity in some jurisdictions in the United States.

Res Judicata Sherrer v. Sherrer (334 U.S. 343 [1948]) provides an example of the application of *res judicata*, finality of the judgment, in divorce. The wife went from Massachusetts to Florida and sued for divorce. The husband appeared personally and the divorce was granted. The U.S. Supreme Court held that the husband could not later attack the validity of the decree in Massachusetts because he had personally appeared and been party to the divorce action in Florida:

> It is one thing to recognize as permissible the judicial reexamination of findings of jurisdictional fact where such findings have been made by a court of a sister State which has entered a divorce decree in ex parte proceedings. It is quite another thing to hold that the vital rights and interests involved in divorce litigation may be held in suspense pending the scrutiny by courts of sister States of findings of jurisdictional fact made by a competent court in proceedings conducted in a manner consistent with the highest requirements of due process and in which the defendant has participated. We do not conceive it to be in accord with the purposes of the full faith and credit requirement to hold that a judgment rendered under the circumstances of this case may be required to run the gantlet of such collateral attack in the courts of sister States before its validity outside of the State which rendered it is established or rejected. That vital interests are involved in divorce litigation indicates to us that it is a matter of greater rather than lesser importance that there should be a place to end such litigation. And where a decree of divorce is rendered by a competent court under the circumstances of this case, the obligation of full faith and credit requires that such litigation should end in the courts of the State in which the judgment was rendered. (334 U.S. at 355–356)

The *Sherrer* rule was applied in Lorant v. Lorant, 318 N.E.2d 830 (Mass. 1974):

> The husband with an air of pious repentance comes forward in the present suit to say that in fact he had not resided in Georgia for the required six months before filing his petition for divorce and that he had not in any event the intention to remain in the State that could support a finding of domicile; therefore, he claims, Georgia did not have judicial jurisdiction to grant the divorce, and the divorce decree crashes. The Probate judge correctly stated in his report of material facts that "[a]s to the question of whether the libellant [husband] acquired a domicile in Georgia, I am not free to find whether he did or not."
>
> The adjudication by the Georgia court that it had jurisdiction to enter the decree (an adjudication implicit in making the decree, but rendered explicit in the present case by the decree's recitals) is, as between the parties, entitled under the full faith and credit clause to the same res judicata effects in Massachusetts that it would be accorded by Georgia, provided only the parties appeared in the Georgia court and there was an actual contest of the issue of jurisdiction or a fair opportunity to contest it; it does not matter that such an opportunity was foregone, as in the present case, by an admission or acknowledgment that jurisdiction existed.
>
> The only question left is what res judicata effects Georgia would accord. The parties have briefed the question. It is reasonably clear that Georgia would not allow a "collateral" attack, analogous to the attack made here, on the 1965 divorce decree regular on its face, for any such alleged reason as that the husband had not in fact resided in Georgia for six months or had not acquired a domicile there. The same

would doubtless hold as to a claim that grounds for divorce had not in fact existed. With the *Sherrer* rule controlling, it adds nothing for the husband to charge that the parties "colluded" or acted "fraudulently" in using the Georgia court to procure the divorce. . . . So the Georgia decree must be considered valid, as the judge below held, and it follows that the occasion did not arise for the husband to exercise an option to void the separation agreement.

If need be, another basis could be offered for holding that the Georgia decree may not be impeached, namely, that the husband is "estopped" from questioning it in the sense that it would be conspicuously unfair and inequitable for him to do so at this stage. . . . A case where the spouse who himself initiated the divorce proceeding and obtained the divorce decree seeks much later to repudiate it in order to avoid obligations incident to or dependent on it invites defensive use of estoppel—a matter, we should note, that appears to be governed by Massachusetts not Georgia law.

As is evident in the final paragraph of *Lorant v. Lorant*, the person who obtained a divorce cannot later attack the divorce on jurisdictional grounds. After a person has had a chance to present his or her case, the decision is viewed as final. Furthermore, anyone who successfully persuades a married person to obtain a divorce is estopped from later attacking the decree. A woman's acceptance of alimony would also estop her from attacking the divorce later. These situations illustrate the court's reluctance to upset existing relationships, especially those formed in good faith.

Bifurcated Divorce The divorce action and the property settlement may be handled in two separate actions, with the divorce being granted first, but some courts insist that the divorce require an agreed-on settlement involving money and property, child custody and visitation, and child support and maintenance.

Divisible Divorce Full faith and credit requires that the divorce decree be recognized by all states but does not end the wife's right to claim alimony payments under the laws of her domicile. Her right to alimony and/or child support cannot be terminated by an *ex parte*, one-party, divorce action in which she is not served personally. Problems frequently arise in collecting such awards from a husband domiciled in another state, in spite of the Uniform Reciprocal Enforcement of Support Act. Title XX of the Social Security Act, which includes provisions to encourage more aggressive enforcement of support awards, will be discussed later in this chapter.

Separate Maintenance A spouse occasionally sues for separate maintenance as a prelude to divorce in order to assure financial support. Some couples do not proceed beyond separate maintenance because they have no desire to remarry or because there may be tax advantages to this agreement. A permanent separate maintenance arrangement has the same effect as divorce *a mensa et thoro*.

TRADITIONAL GROUNDS— MARITAL FAULT What is the cause of marital breakdown? Traditionally it was necessary to have both an offender and an aggrieved party in order to obtain a divorce, with the grievance constituting grounds for the action.

Cruelty or **mental cruelty** were generally typical adversary grounds for divorce. Cruelty was previously limited to serious physical assault and was used mainly to protect the spouse from harm. The ground generally required only mild maltreatment, although such terms as *extreme* or *repeated* cruelty may be employed. Withdrawal of marital companionship, quarreling, refusal of sexual intercourse or excessive sexual demands, refusal to speak to the spouse, and a series of unkind acts can be considered cruelty. Cruelty usually must extend over time, but a single act, such as an attempt to shoot the spouse, is adequate to qualify. In addition, cruelty is usually alleged to have had an adverse effect on the health of the plaintiff. Mental cruelty has been the most popular ground and may involve anything that creates stress or unhappiness.

Desertion or **abandonment** involves voluntary separation without consent or justification and with no intent to resume cohabitation. Courts usually require such separation to have lasted from one to five years, depending on state statutes. When spouses maintain joint residence but stop associating with each other or refuse to engage in sexual intercourse, case law is inconsistent on whether desertion can be claimed. Some states find the wife guilty of desertion if her husband changes the family domicile and she refuses to move. Desertion is an inappropriate ground if it is shown that the departure was a justified response to the plaintiff's conduct. The term *constructive desertion* is used for that situation.

Subsequent to modernization of New York divorce laws, **adultery**—voluntary sexual intercourse by a married person with someone other than the spouse—is rarely used as a ground for divorce. Although adultery is common, other grounds are usually chosen in order to avoid the difficulties of corroboration and the negative effect of publicizing the action. Adultery is a crime in some states, and other states have erroneously considered artificial insemination by a donor adulterous behavior on the part of the wife.

Conviction of a felony, drunkenness, drug addiction, insanity, and **gross neglect of duty** are among other grounds for divorce. The social worker should not try to provide clients with detailed counsel on possible grounds for divorce, but he or she may suggest that some of the avenues discussed in this section be explored in detail with a lawyer.

The decision in Odom v. Odom, 273 N.E.2d 623 (Ill. App. 1971), illustrates the complexities involved in divorce actions and the differences in how the parties perceive the facts.

ODOM v. ODOM

Appellate Court of Illinois, First District, Fifth Division, 273 N.E.2d 623 (Ill. App. 1971).

DRUCKER, Justice.

This is an appeal from a decree granting a divorce to defendant. On appeal plaintiff's main contention is that there was insufficient evidence for the trial court to find that she committed extreme and repeated acts of physical cruelty against the defendant.

Plaintiff originally filed a complaint for divorce; defendant filed a cross-complaint and an amended cross-complaint for divorce and plaintiff filed an amended complaint for separate maintenance.

The evidence of plaintiff in the trial for separate maintenance disclosed that the parties were married on November 24, 1962; that a daughter was born in 1967; that in 1966 plaintiff had filed for separate maintenance charging physical violence in February and March 1966; that defendant left the home on January 15, 1969, without cause and that the parties lived separate and apart since then. Defendant was called by plaintiff as an adverse witness under Section 60 and testified that he started packing to leave home about the 1st of January, 1969, had applied for an apartment on January 6 and that he told her "it would be best to get a divorce under the circumstances we were living." When asked what these circumstances were, he replied, "many acts of violence by my wife or by myself." He described her as five feet three or four inches tall weighing 120 pounds. He was six feet one and one-half inches tall and weighed 154 pounds. He left the apartment on January 14, 1969.

At the conclusion of plaintiff's evidence the court found plaintiff had established a prima facie case for separate maintenance. Defendant was granted leave to proceed on his cross-complaint for divorce with the evidence thereunder to stand as his defense to the separate maintenance action.

Defendant testified that plaintiff committed the following acts of cruelty:

1. May 1964—struck defendant with a decanter—no bruise or mark.

2. March 1966—pulled a knife—no injury.

3. July 1966—pulled a gun—bit the defendant.

4. March 1968—After a heated discussion about bills struck defendant's arm with a mirror.

5. August 1968—pointed gun and "something struck him above left eye." (This incident is not alleged in defendant's cross-complaint.)

6. November 6, 1968—struck defendant's left wrist with doorknob—no medical treatment.

7. January 14, 1969—After a heated discussion about money, struck defendant with boot on left elbow; had X-ray a day or two thereafter and took a day and a half from work. (Defendant's witness, Amanda Norman, testified that about January 27, 1969, defendant was given a heat treatment for a bruise on his arm from a shoe.)

Defendant also testified that while he lived in the home until he moved out on January 15, 1969, he last slept with his wife in August 1968. (As a witness for plaintiff under Section 60 in the separate maintenance action defendant first testified that they cohabited until January 1969; later he stated that there were no sexual relations between him and his wife after March 1968.)

Plaintiff testified that sexual relations continued until January 7, 1969, and that she never pointed a gun at defendant, never struck her husband with a mirror, doorknob or boot. She also denied the other alleged incidents. She further testified that in August 1968 defendant pulled his gun and threatened to kill her; that plaintiff's Exhibit 10 represented a carbon copy of a complaint she signed based on this incident; and that she dropped the charges a few days later. (In the separate maintenance trial defendant first testified that he never owned a gun; on being shown a gun registration form he admitted applying for it on June 26, 1968.)

The court granted defendant a divorce on his amended countercomplaint and dismissed plaintiff's amended complaint for separate maintenance with prejudice.

In Levy v. Levy, 388 Ill. 179, 184, 57 N.E.2d 366, 369, the court stated:

"Our statute requires proof of 'extreme and repeated cruelty' and obviously 'slight acts of violence' are not extreme as to a normal person whether husband or wife."

The court further stated:

> "It is true that the physical condition of the parties involved must be taken into account and each case considered upon its own facts."

In the instant case plaintiff was five feet three inches tall weighing 120 pounds while defendant was six feet one and one-half inches tall and weighed 154 pounds. He testified that:

> "I've never struck my wife in anger. I am a fighter and know my wife is no competition for me. I was a Golden State Boxing Champion for 3 years, National Boxing Champion, Michigan State College, for 2 years, and AAU Boxing Champion for 2 years."

Under all the circumstances of this case we cannot agree with a finding that extreme and repeated cruelty was proven.

We therefore find that the court erred in granting defendant a divorce on his cross-complaint and in dismissing the amended complaint for separate maintenance with prejudice.

The judge found at the conclusion of plaintiff's evidence that plaintiff had proved a prima facie case for separate maintenance. Although defendant's evidence on his cross-complaint was to stand at his defense to the separate maintenance action, we find no evidence therein to rebut plaintiff's evidence. Defendant testified that he had decided to move out in August 1968, started moving on January 1, 1969, and applied for his own apartment on January 6, 1969.

The judgment of May 27, 1969, is reversed and the cause remanded with directions to vacate the decree granting the divorce and dismissing the amended complaint for separate maintenance; to enter a decree in favor of plaintiff for separate maintenance incorporating the provisions of the divorce decree relating to child custody and child support and for further hearings in regard to the amount, if any, for her maintenance and attorney's fees.

NO-FAULT DIVORCE

Divorce reform has eliminated adversary procedures in favor of a "no-fault" approach. To the uninvolved layperson, grounds may seem very important as the legal basis for a divorce action, but most divorces are based on consent of the partners, and more than nine out of ten are uncontested. The facts of marital conflict and the formal grounds bear little resemblance to each other. After the couple agrees to the desirability or inevitability of divorce, they choose grounds from among those allowed by the laws of the state. States now offer grounds for divorce which eliminate fault, and marriage may be terminated with a minimum of delay, scandal, or publicity. The *Family Law Reporter* provides periodic reviews of changes in each state.

Marriage Breakdown

More than thirty states specify **irretrievable breakdown** as the basis for no-fault divorce proceedings. **Irreconcilable differences** have been recognized by at least six states. Twenty include varying periods of separation as a basis. A 1972 California statute was the first to legally incorporate the concept of marital breakdown. Sections

302 and 305 of the Uniform Marriage and Divorce Act include a similar concept by implying that mutual agreement on the need for divorce should constitute legal grounds for the action. The Uniform Act indicates that the court may continue the case not less than thirty or more than sixty days while the partners decide whether they really want the divorce. Eight states have modeled their laws on this act.

At least two other grounds may be based on no-fault, although fault can also be alleged. **Incompatibility** is recognized in at least eight states. It was first adopted by the Virgin Islands. The Virgin Islands defines incompatibility as "conflicts in personalities and dispositions so deep as to be irreconcilable and to render it impossible for the parties to continue a normal marital relationship with each other. . . . The disharmony of the spouses in their common life must be so deep and intense as to be irremediable" (16 V.I.C. 104).

Living separate and apart need not involve fault. Unlike desertion, it makes no mention of justification for the departure, but only requires the couple to have been separated during a specified period—sometimes as long as three to five years. A divorce action on this basis is especially appropriate after a separation decree because it explicitly recognizes separation as confirmation that the marriage is dead. The most permissive statutory provision grants divorce on fulfillment of the prescribed time. However, the courts sometimes attach so many conditions to this ground that its straightforwardness is lost.

SUMMARY DIVORCE

California has provided for **summary divorce**, designed to simplify the procedure for marriages of short duration with no children and little property. It also recognizes the effect of inflation by adjusting the specified dollar amounts:

Section 4550. Summary Dissolution

A marriage may be dissolved by the summary dissolution procedure specified in this chapter when all of the following conditions exist at the time the proceeding is commenced:

(a) Either party has met the jurisdictional requirements of Sections 4530 and 4531 with regard to dissolution of marriage.

(b) Irreconcilable differences have caused the irremediable breakdown of the marriage and the marriage should be dissolved.

(c) There are no children of the relationship of the parties born before or during the marriage or adopted by the parties during the marriage, and the wife, to her knowledge, is not pregnant.

(d) The marriage is not more than five years in duration at the time the petition is filed.

(e) Neither party has any interest in real property wheresoever situated, with the exception of the lease of a residence occupied by either party, if it does not include an option to purchase, and if it terminates within one year from the date of the filing of the petition.

(f) There are no unpaid obligations in excess of three thousand dollars ($3,000) incurred by either or both of the parties after the date of their marriage, excluding the amount of any unpaid obligation with respect to an automobile.

(g) The total fair market value of community property assets, excluding all encumbrances and automobiles, is less than ten thousand dollars ($10,000) and neither party has separate property assets, excluding all encumbrances and automobiles, in excess of ten thousand dollars ($10,000).

(h)   The parties have executed an agreement setting forth the division of assets and the assumption of liabilities of the community, and have duly executed any documents, title certificates, bills of sale, or other evidence of transfer necessary to effectuate the agreement.

(i)   The parties waive any rights to spousal support.

(j)   The parties, upon entry of final judgment of dissolution of marriage, irrevocably waive their respective rights to appeal, their rights to request findings of fact and conclusions of law, and their rights to move for a new trial.

(k)   The parties have read and understand the summary disolution brochure provided for in Section 4556.

(l)   The parties desire that the court dissolve the marriage.

Commencing January 1, 1983, and on January 1 of each odd-numbered year thereafter, the amounts in subdivisions (f) and (g) shall be adjusted to reflect any change in the value of the dollar. The adjustments shall be made by multiplying the base amounts by the percentage change in the California Consumer Price Index as compiled by the Department of Industrial Relations, with the result rounded to the nearest thousand dollars. The Judicial Council shall compute and publish the amounts.

Summary divorce does not require the services of an attorney. It is possible to represent oneself in other states as well, but the courts do not usually look kindly on it. Attorneys in several states have published do-it-yourself kits that contain suggestions and the necessary forms to file for divorce, but some states have ruled that publication of the kits is unethical.

DEFENSES IN DIVORCE

Defenses refer not to the testimony given by one of the principals to justify his or her behavior but to certain situations in which the courts are precluded from granting a divorce. These defenses stem from the strong ecclesiastical tradition of maintaining marriage at almost any cost. No-fault laws generally include repeal of the defenses.

Recrimination

The strangest defense, **recrimination**, is based on the principle that the law may not help a wrongdoer. When both spouses have been guilty of misconduct constituting grounds for divorce, the "clean hands" principle is applied, and neither party can obtain the divorce. The law should provide one of two logical alternatives: either grant the divorce to the least guilty party (comparative rectitude) or award the divorce to both parties, as is the case in no-fault divorce.

Provocation

The defendant may allege that the plaintiff's conduct provoked the defense. **Provocation** could be an appropriate defense if a husband withdrew from home because his wife kept seventy-five dogs and cats notwithstanding their children's allergic reaction to animals.

Condonation

Forgiveness of a spouse for an action of the other partner precludes that action from forming a basis for divorce. **Condonation** usually involves knowledge of a spouse's adultery followed by resumption of sexual intercourse. The courts are inconsistent on whether condonation is final or conditional. Can adultery be revived conditionally as a ground if the party who is forgiven later becomes the agent of "mental cruelty"?

Connivance

The term **connivance** implies that a spouse not only seeks termination of the marriage but also is active in developing the grounds for divorce. For example, the plaintiff may have persuaded a friend to seduce the other spouse and thereby create an opportunity for adultery.

Collusion   Collusion occurs when one spouse agrees to commit an offense in order for the other to obtain divorce, or when one agrees to sue and the other to make no defense. It is interesting that collusion is usually brought to the court's attention only **after** a divorce, when one of the parties is unhappy with some aspect of its provisions. Collusion should probably be allowable as a defense only when the alleged marital offense did not actually occur, as in the case of the faked adultery scenes that took place in New York prior to 1957 before other grounds for divorce were permitted.

The law has traditionally been opposed to divorce by consent, even though in reality most divorces occur this way. A broader definition of collusion would threaten most of the current uncontested fault divorces in which grounds are developed with full knowledge of both spouses and the defendant either agrees to challenge no statements made or to be absent from the hearing. A no-fault approach based on marital breakdown is a more honest way to carry out divorce proceedings because it recognizes the contribution of both partners to an unsuccessful marriage and does not require the independent development of specific adversarial grounds.

PARTIES TO DIVORCE   Social workers have a particular concern with protecting the welfare of children when parents divorce. Ideally, minor children should be made a party to their parents' divorce action and be represented by counsel whose sole responsibility is to defend the children's rights. Unfortunately, this ideal is rarely realized. About half the jurisdictions maintain a ritual of designating a public officer as party to the divorce action in undefended or uncontested cases. The officer is sometimes expected to take into account the interests of the children. While married minors may bring and defend divorce actions, a *guardian ad litem* may be required to represent them unless the jurisdiction accords full legal capacity to married minors.

A defendant's insanity creates a number of complex problems, although it does not automatically preclude the divorce action. A conservator or guardian should be appointed to safeguard the defendant's interests. The divorce may be denied if it is proved that the defendant was insane at the time of the alleged misconduct and thus incapable of exercising an intent to injure the plaintiff. As Clark (1968:383) observed, the law's response to the wife whose husband beats her is, "We are sorry, but since your husband is insane and therefore not able to form a specific intent to hurt you, you must continue living with him as his wife."

Neither an insane person nor his or her guardian may bring a divorce action as plaintiff. The law considers an insane person incapable of sufficient voluntary exercise of will to make the decision to terminate a marriage—a decision that is too important and personal to be made by anyone else.

Finally, death of one of the parties to a divorce terminates the action unless the case has already been fully adjudicated and the final decree given.

EVIDENCE   Some type of hearing must be held in every divorce action. Corroboration of any evidence is often required in fault divorce to prevent collusion. In no-fault situations, this requirement is unnecessary. Divorce testimony is not seriously affected by interspousal privilege, since the nature of the action often requires one spouse to testify against the other. Similarly, confidential communications between spouses are generally admissible as evidence in divorce actions.

The court may mandate a social work investigation in order to determine the physical and emotional conditions of the couple's children and the relative fitness of each parent to assume custody. Illinois has amended its law in Section 605 to authorize such investigations in custody proceedings. The report may be used as evidence as long as it is submitted to both parents. In addition, the social worker and others who contributed to the report must be available to testify if necessary. However, divorcing parents may be particularly hostile to social workers' reports.

METHODS OF ENCOURAGING RECONCILIATION

Social workers have sometimes been involved in compulsory marriage counseling as a means to prevent divorce. The results of such counseling have been dismal. The service is usually offered too late, and a couple's unsuccessful attempt at reconciliation may make it necessary for them to seek new grounds in order to resume the divorce action. In addition, counseling resources are inadequately distributed; many communities have no services at all, while others have more than they can use.

Cooling-off periods and interlocutory decrees whereby the divorce is finalized only after a stated time has elapsed have similarly failed to discourage divorces and have created the same types of legal problems. These approaches are based on the assumption that most divorces are entered into hastily with little serious attempt at reconciliation, an assumption that is probably fiction.

ALIMONY AND DIVISION OF PROPERTY

Alimony, now commonly called maintenance, is intended to protect the divorced couple's children, to prevent the wife from becoming a financial burden on society, to ease the transition from married to single status, to compensate the wife for services rendered, and to give tangible form to moral judgments on a spouse's fault. Alimony payments can be allowed both husbands and wives, depending on the circumstances of the divorce and the relative financial means of each partner. This principle was defined by the U.S. Supreme Court in Orr v. Orr, 440 U.S. 268 (1979); ten states already had such a provision. The basis for the decision is presented in Chapter 18.

Greater egalitarianism has reduced the likelihood of alimony. Five considerations influence alimony awards: the husband's ability to pay, the wife's need, the wife's capacity to earn, child-rearing responsibilities that reduce the wife's capacity to be self-supporting, and possible damages for wrongdoing. When the fault lies with the wife, and the husband has no adequate means of support, he may be awarded alimony.

Childless marriages of brief duration in which both partners are employable may offer little reason for alimony. Considerations of age, health, and earning capacity strengthen the case for alimony. It is increasingly likely that the wife's own assets will also be taken into account in determining an award.

Temporary alimony may be provided while a divorce action is pending. Sometimes an accusation of fault will invalidate that party's claim for temporary alimony, but should have no effect on the award of child support.

Formerly, attorney's fees were usually awarded to the wife, but now if she has her own income she is likely to pay her own fee. The husband may be expected to pay the attorney's fees if an alimony or child support award is modified later.

Few states permit a wife who is present at the divorce action and neglects to sue for alimony to do so later. In an *ex parte* divorce obtained by the husband in the wife's absence, her alimony claims generally survive under the divisible divorce principle. In Hudson v. Hudson, 344 P.2d 295 (Cal. 1959), California courts concluded that they had the right to order the wife's support following an Idaho divorce obtained by the husband. This finding is consistent with two U.S. Supreme Court cases, Estin v. Estin, 334 U.S. 541 (1948), and Vanderbilt v. Vanderbilt, 354 U.S. 416 (1957). Both affirmed the New York courts' determination that the wife had a right to support. In *Estin* a judgment for support was made prior to, and in *Vanderbilt* after, a Nevada divorce.

A 1909 Supreme Court decision, Sistare v. Sistare, 218 U.S. 1, established that full faith and credit applies to all alimony decrees; i.e., they must be enforced by the courts of other states. The Uniform Reciprocal Enforcement of Support Act is intended to cover awards for alimony and child support on an interstate basis. Its provisions now apply in all states.

Modification of Alimony

Several factors may affect modification of alimony:

1. The wife's remarriage usually terminates alimony.

2. Remarriage of the husband may reduce alimony to place both wives on equal footing. However, most courts required continued payment at the original level.

3. Changes in the wife's needs may decrease or increase alimony, as in the case of an inheritance or a serious illness.

4. Alimony payments may be reduced if the husband has experienced financial reverses, but they are less likely to be increased if his income increases.

5. The husband's death generally terminates alimony payments, although in some cases provision will have been made for payments to continue from his estate.

6. Modifications are sometimes sought based on the wife's subsequent misconduct.

Both alimony and child support awards have been problematic because of inflation. New Hampshire has recognized the problem by limiting alimony awards to three-year periods, after which they are reviewed, modified, and extended for another three years.

O'Connor Bros. Abalone Co. v. Brando, involving a celebrity, is an example of termination of alimony because of the woman's conduct following annulment of the marriage.

O'CONNOR BROS. ABALONE CO. v. BRANDO

Court of Appeal, Second District, Division 2, 114 Cal.Rptr. 773 (Cal. App. 1974).

COMPTON, Associate Justice.

In July of 1968, in connection with the annulment of their marriage, Marlon and Movita Brando executed a written agreement purporting to settle certain financial matters and child custody rights.

As a part of that agreement Marlon undertook to make monthly payments of $600 for the support of the minor children and monthly payments of $1400 for the support of Movita. Only the latter payments to Movita are at issue here. . . .

The resolution of this dispute turns on whether, under the terms of the agreement between Marlon and Movita, her conduct was such as to terminate Marlon's obligation to make further payments. The crucial provision in the agreement is as follows:

> "(a) Defendant agrees to pay or cause to be paid to Plaintiff, the amount of $1,400.00 per month commencing on the first day of the calendar month next succeeding the month in which this Agreement is executed and continuing for a period of one-hundred fifty-six (156) months, *or until she remarries or dies, whichever occurs sooner. For the purposes of this Agreement, 'remarriage' shall include, without limitation, Plaintiff's appearing to maintain a marital relationship with any person, or any ceremonial marriage entered into by Plaintiff even though the same may later be annulled or otherwise terminated or rendered invalid.*" [Emphasis added.]

In reliance on this "remarriage" clause, Marlon ceased to make the payments in April 1971. He contends that in 1968, Movita entered into a relationship with one James Ford which relationship was within the provisions of the term "remarriage" as defined in the Agreement.

The evidence in the trial left little doubt that Movita and Ford enjoyed a relationship of substantial duration, which relationship bore the objective indicia of marriage. By their own admission they engaged in frequent sexual intercourse. Ford kept his clothes at the residence in Coldwater Canyon; he ate meals there many of which he prepared. Ford frequently purchased the groceries for their meals by charging them to Movita's account at the market. He drove her cars and was authorized to use her charge account at one of the major department stores.

Additionally, Ford on significant occasions gave the Coldwater Canyon address as his own. He used that address in applying for a driver's license and in reporting to his probation officer. The two were often in company together and in company with Movita's children in public.

The trial court's finding that they "lived" together is well supported. The further finding that such relationship could not be reasonably interpreted as indicating that Ford and Movita were in fact married apparently flowed from the absence of any evidence that they told anyone they were married. . . .

We here summarize the position of the respective parties. O'Connor contends, and the trial court concluded, that the phrase "appearing to maintain a marital relationship" means a holding out by Movita that she was in fact married or conduct on her part that would imply a marriage in fact. According to this version, a meretricious relationship, no matter how intimate and enduring, would not terminate the obligation for support payments so long as it was made clear to the world that Movita and her paramour were *not* married. This interpretation would place a premium on the persistence with which Movita publicized the illicit nature of the relationship.

On the other hand, Marlon contends that the Agreement was designed to prevent Movita from maintaining a relationship with a male companion as a result of which the latter appeared to enjoy the usual rewards of marriage without assuming the obligations which flow from a ceremony of marriage. According to Marlon the Agreement means a "marital type" relationship and such interpretation is necessary to avoid what he sought to avoid, i.e., the possibility that Movita's male companion, in sharing Movita's shelter, bed and board, would also benefit from the support payments which Marlon was providing. . . .

The final Agreement evolved from two previously written drafts. The first draft simply used the phrase "until she remarries" without further definition. To this Marlon objected. The second draft defined remarriage as "cohabitation by plaintiff with any person." To this Movita objected.

Mr. Garey testified that Movita's attorney indicated that the objection to "cohabitation" was based on a fear that the word might apply to so-called "one night stands.". . .

Clearly the purpose of the Agreement was not to circumscribe Movita's sexual activity per se as she was free to engage in sexual intercourse with other men. The Agreement sought to embrace actual ceremonial marriages on the one hand and on the other, relationships which were not marriages but which had the attributes of marriage such as companionship of substantial duration, the sharing of habitation, eating together and sexual intimacy. The characterization of such a relationship as "marital" does not depend on whether third persons are led to believe the existence of a ceremonial marriage. In fact, public belief that Movita and Ford were actually married would be less demeaning to Marlon than their conduct of "living" together while disavowing an actual marriage.

What is important here from the standpoint of the objectives of the Agreement is that such a relationship creates the strong probability that the male partner will derive benefit from the support payments. And that, in fact, is what occurred here. O'Connor contends in its brief that there was no common financial or economic relationship between Ford and Movita and that this detracts from the "marital" character of the relationship. Interestingly enough, however, in respondent's support of this argument it is admitted that Movita paid for the upkeep of her cars which Ford drove. She paid for the groceries which Ford charged, and she paid for the department store purchases which Ford charged. It appears without contradiction that Movita paid for the maintenance of the house in which they lived.

We interpret the phrase "appearing to maintain a marital relationship" as including the appearance of "living together" under circumstances such as existed here, whether or not there is the appearance of marriage in fact. This appears to us to be the only possible reasonable interpretation of the Agreement.

Division of property also involves more emphasis on equality. The family home used to go automatically to the wife, who reared the children, but provision is now often made for sale of the home with division of the proceeds. Sale may be delayed until the children reach majority. Settlements are more likely to include a fifty-fifty division of marital property, with each spouse retaining his or her property held at the time of the marriage. In states with community-property laws, the even division is required.

CHILD CUSTODY Child custody following divorce is a problem complicated by parents living apart at great distances. Chapter 8 considered the problems of child visitation and kidnapping by noncustodial parents. By 1984 all states had enacted the Uniform Child

Custody Jurisdiction Act, which denies jurisdiction to another state if a spouse has removed a child from the custodial parent without that parent's permission. The seriousness of the situation was also recognized at the federal level in P.L. 96-611, the Parental Kidnapping Act of 1980.

CHILD SUPPORT

As in alimony, the amount of child support is set by the court, and the same criteria apply. The duty of child support exists by statute and is usually imposed on the father. If he cannot supply support, the duty falls on the mother. Child support will be necessary if the parents live apart, whether they are divorced or not. Support orders are based on personal jurisdiction of the father. When mothers are employed, they are likely to be required to contribute their share to child support. Cash payments may be required from them when the father is awarded custody.

Res judicata is important to child support. If paternity has been decided affirmatively, the husband cannot try to terminate child support payments simply because the child is not really his. Conversely, if a paternity action fails, the wife is precluded from relitigating the question, although the child may do so on his or her own behalf.

Social workers are often involved with mentally or physically handicapped children who may require financial support well into their majority. Parents may generally be expected to support a severely disabled child beyond age eighteen or twenty-one.

The costs of a college education are increasingly likely to be a part of divorce settlements, especially if the child meets academic admission requirements and the father is financially able to provide a college education. However, with eighteen years as the age of majority this claim is sometimes rejected. Modifications in child support orders are made when each child reaches majority or marries. Otherwise, the reasons for modification are the same as for alimony.

Enforcement of support orders may be sought through a contempt action, as in the case of alimony. Attachment, garnishment, sequestration (seizure of property), and assignment of wages are means of collecting support payments from recalcitrant fathers. Title XX of the Social Security Act mandates support enforcement efforts by the states:

Section 452

(a) The Secretary shall establish, within the Department of Health, Education, and Welfare a separate organizational unit, under the direction of a designee of the Secretary, who shall report directly to the Secretary and who shall—

(1) establish such standards for State programs for locating absent parents, establishing paternity, and obtaining child support as he determines to be necessary to assure that such programs will be effective;

(2) establish minimum organizational and staffing requirements for State units engaged in carrying out such programs under plans approved under this part;

(3) review and approve State plans for such programs;

(4) evaluate the implementation of State programs established pursuant to such plan, conduct such audits of State programs established under the plan approved under this part as may be necessary to assure their conformity with the requirements of this part, and, not less often than annually, conducted a complete audit of the programs established under such plan in each State and determine for the purposes of the penalty

provision of section 403(h) whether the actual operation of such programs in each State conforms to the requirements of this part;"

Section 454 (As Amended)
A State plan for child support must—

(1) provide that it shall be in effect in all political subdivisions of the State;

(2) provide for financial participation by the State;

(3) provide for the establishment or designation of a single and separate organizational unit, which meets such staffing and organizational requirements as the Secretary may by regulation prescribe, within the State to administer the plan;

(4) provide that such State will undertake—

(A) in the case of a child born out of wedlock with respect to whom an assignment under section 402(a)(26) of this title is effective, to establish the paternity of such child (unless the agency administering the plan of the State under part A of this title determines in accordance with the standards prescribed by the Secretary pursuant to section 402(a)(26)(B) that it is against the best interests of the child to do so); and

(B) in the case of any child with respect to whom such assignment is effective, to secure support for such child from his parent (or from any other person legally liable for such support), utilizing any reciprocal arrangements adopted with other States, unless the agency administering the plan of the State under part A of this title determines in accordance with the standards prescribed by the Secretary pursuant to section 402(a)(26)(B) that it is against the best interests of the child to do so, except that when such arrangements and other means have proven ineffective, the State may utilize the Federal courts to obtain or enforce court orders for support;

(5) provide that, in any case in which child support payments are collected for a child with respect to whom an assignment under section 402(a)(26) is effective, such payments shall be made to the State for distribution pursuant to section 457 and shall not be paid directly to the family except that this paragraph shall not apply to such payments (except as provided in section 457(c)) for any month in which the amount collected is sufficient to make such family ineligible for assistance under the State plan approved under part A;

Under the provisions of Title XX, states may be reimbursed for 75 percent of their expenses in locating and collecting from fathers.

ELEMENTS IN A FINANCIAL SETTLEMENT

Financial settlements in divorce have recognized two new principles. The wife is likely to be able to claim some of the value of the pension credits accrued by the spouse, especially if the pension is assured through vesting. Professional education will also usually be given a monetary value in the settlement if a partner contributed financially to the aid of a student-spouse.

Courts differ on whether the income from a pension or the cash value of the plan at the time of divorce should be used in calculating the settlement. In McCarty v. McCarty, 453 U.S. 210 (1981), the U.S. Supreme Court held that the former wife could not receive benefits from the military retirement pay of the former husband, but this decision was quickly rejected by Congress with the passage of the Uniformed Services Former Spouses Protection Act in 1982.

FEDERAL TAX LIABILITY

People contemplating divorce are especially interested in the effect of a divorce on liability for federal income taxes. Since 1954, alimony payments are subject to tax for the wife and are a deduction for the husband. Child support payments are not deductible. For tax purposes, child support payments must be specifically identified and separated from alimony. Installment payments for the wife's support are clearly taxable to her. Payments that are indefinite in either amount or duration are neither taxable to the wife nor deductible by the husband.

If the separation agreement or alimony decree requires that life insurance policies be kept in force, premium payments are deductible by the husband and must be reported as income by the wife.

AVAILABILITY OF DIVORCE TO THE INDIGENT

Although the divorce rate is higher among the poor, many poor people lack economic means to pay the legal costs of divorce. This disability was partially eliminated by the U.S. Supreme Court decision in Boddie v. Connecticut, 401 U.S. 371, in 1972. The state of Connecticut held that parties to a divorce action must pay approximately $60 for the court and administrative costs attendant to the action regardless of their ability to do so. The state contended that the mandatory fee would serve to prevent "frivolous litigation," assure appropriate allocation of scarce state resources, and maintain a balance between the defendant's right to notice and the plaintiff's right to action. The decision, written by Justice John Harlan, held that "none of these considerations is sufficient to override the interests of these plaintiff-appellants in having access to the only avenue open for dissolving their allegedly untenable marriages" (401 U.S. at 381). The decision extended the right of due process to persons seeking access to the judicial system. It cited the finding concerning criminal procedure in Griffin v. People of the State of Illinois, 351 U.S. 12 (1956), in which it was determined that charging a fee for a transcript beyond the means of an indigent person blocked access to the judicial process.

In his concurring opinion, Justice William O. Douglas said, "Under Connecticut law divorces may be denied or granted solely on the basis of wealth. . . . Affluence does not pass muster under the Equal Protection Clause for determining who must remain married and who shall be allowed to separate" (407 U.S. at 386). Nevertheless, the scope of the decision was quite limited, as indicated in its final paragraph:

> In concluding that the Due Process Clause of the Fourteenth Amendment requires that these appellants be afforded an opportunity to go into court to obtain a divorce, we wish to re-emphasize that we go no further than necessary to dispose of the case before us, a case where the *bona fides* of both appellants' indigency and desire for divorce are here beyond dispute. We do not decide that access for all individuals to the courts is a right that is, in all circumstances, guaranteed by the Due Process Clause of the Fourteenth Amendment so that its exercise may not be placed beyond the reach of any individual, for, as we have already noted, in the case before us this right is the exclusive precondition to the adjustment of a fundamental human relationship. (401 U.S. at 382–383)

Since divorce is often a necessary means of dealing with serious family problems, this decision is significant for social workers. While *Boddie* did not require states to pay lawyers' fees for the indigent, the indigent may use legal aid services to keep costs at a minimum.

The question of legal fees was raised in In Re Smiley, 330 N.E.2d 53 (N.Y. 1975). The New York Court of Appeals held that representation by counsel is not required in order to obtain access to the courts and that counties need not provide litigants with counsel or compensate counsel. Judge Fuchsberg's dissent provides a clear statement on the need of the indigent for legal counsel.

IN RE SMILEY

**Court of Appeals of New York,
330 N.E.2d 53
(N.Y. 1975).**

BREITEL, Chief Judge.

The issue on this appeal is whether an indigent plaintiff wife in a divorce action and an indigent defendant wife in a similar action are entitled, as a matter of constitutional right, to have the County of Tompkins provide them with counsel or compensate counsel retained by them. . . .

As a practical matter, representation of private litigants, too poor to retain their own lawyers, has been accomplished through the discretionary assignment of uncompensated counsel by the courts, and in more populated areas by voluntary legal aid and charitable organizations. . . . Then, too, there are the more recent Federally-funded legal services programs for the poor. . . .

Petitioners, on the basis of *Boddie v. Connecticut*, . . . seek to extrapolate a constitutional principle mandating the provision and compensation of counsel in matrimonial matters. Assuming momentarily that the *Boddie* case could be so used to mandate the provision or compensation or counsel, it and the cases establishing the right to assigned counsel in criminal matters could not be used to mandate compensation by public funding. Even in expending the criminal right to assigned counsel the courts, Federal and State, never presumed to direct the appropriation and expenditure of public funds. . . .

The *Boddie* case does not support, or by rationale imply, an obligation of the State to assign, let alone compensate, counsel as a matter of constitutional right. The *Boddie* case held narrowly that because the State's regulation of marriage and divorce, in the generic sense, is an assumption of governmental power, the State could not deny access to its courts in matrimonial actions by exacting a court fee from indigent matrimonial suitors. In Deason v. Deason, 32 N.Y.2d 93, 343, N.Y.S.2d 321, 296 N.E.2d 229, this court extended the *Boddie* rationale to apply to the State's requirement that in certain circumstances costly service by publication of process could not be imposed as a precondition to an indigent bringing a matrimonial action. It was thus held that, under the constitutional principles articulated in the *Boddie* case, the State or its subdivisions would be required to pay the cost of such access to the courts, if such costly service of process were the only alternative.

On no view of the matter is counsel required in a matrimonial action as a condition to access to the court. Of course, counsel is always desirable, and in complicated matrimonial litigation would be essential. But however desirable or necessary, representation by counsel is not a legal condition to access to the courts. . . . Access to the courts was the only problem to which the *Boddie* and *Deason* cases were addressed. . . .

None of this is to say that the need and burden of representing indigent matrimonial suitors will not currently overtax voluntary private resources and the voluntary services available from the Bar on a noncompensated basis. The need and burden may become even greater in the future, especially with liberalized divorce laws. All of this, however, is a problem to be addressed to the Legislature which has the power to appropriate the funds required for publicly-compensated counsel. . . .

In the meantime, courts and litigants must make do with what exists and with what lies within the powers and capacity of the courts and the Bar. The courts have a broad discretionary power to assign counsel without compensation in a proper case. . . .Voluntary organizations and Federally-funded programs play their role. As for the Bar they follow, as they are obliged to do, the canons of their profession in performing obligations to the indigent and duties imposed by assignment of the courts. If more is required, the relief must be provided by the Legislature. The fundamental is that the courts constitute but one branch of government. The absence of appropriated funds and legislation to raise taxes under our State constitutional system, as in the rest of the Union, is not a judicially-fillable gap.

JONES, Judge (dissenting). . . .

The Supreme Court of the United States, in *Boddie v. Connecticut*, held: "that, given the basic position of the marriage relationship in this society's hierarchy of values and the concomitant state monopolization of the means for legally dissolving this relationship, due process does prohibit a State from denying, solely because of inability to pay, access to its courts to individuals who seek judicial dissolution of their marriages." In *Deason v. Deason*, . . ., we joined in recognition of this fundamental principle. I can only interpret the position taken by the majority today as a significant and in my opinion an impermissible retreat from that position. . . .

FUCHSBERG, Judge (dissenting).

Is denial of the right to counsel a real barrier to access to court for litigants, wither in civil cases generally or in divorce actions in particular? Unfortunately, in our complex society, it is. As Mr. Justice Sutherland said in *Powell v. Alabama*, "The right to be heard would be, in many cases, of little avail if it did not comprehend the right to be heard by counsel. Even the intelligent and educated layman has small and sometimes no skill in the science of law." (287 U.S. 45, 68, 69, 53 S.Ct. 55, 64, 77 L.Ed. 158) . . .

With this in mind, courts have recently been applying the reasoning of Gideon v. Wainwright, 372 U.S. 335, 83 S.Ct. 792, 9 L.Ed.2d 799, to some "civil" matters where important issues of liberty or property were at stake. For instance, . . . our court ruled that an indigent parent, threatened in a neglect proceeding with termination of the right to custody of a minor child, had the right to be provided with counsel. . . .

However, it is one thing to state that the denial of counsel is an obstruction to access to courts in the civil litigation of matters of consequence to people generally and another to apply that principle to divorce actions in particular. Therefore, a closer examination of divorce litigation is necessary to determine whether lack of counsel is a genuine obstacle in such cases.

In the State of New York, many divorce cases are extremely simple. In a very large percentage of divorces involving indigents, there exists no legal dispute whatsoever; the court performs an essentially ministerial function either because the parties have executed and complied with a one-year separation agreement under subdivision (6) of section 170 of the Domestic Relations Law, or because the parties have agreed to a dissolution on grounds of cruelty, and one party appears in court to give summary unchallenged testimony of abuse. In such divorces, it is probable that many uncounseled litigants would be able to process the litigation by themselves, perhaps with the assistance of Bar-approved manuals for the layman or of trained paraprofessionals, or with the aid of court clerks who, aware of the shortage of legal services for the poor, are usually extremely helpful in explaining procedures to unrepresented parties, and should be encouraged to assist them.

In addition, a substantial number of contested divorces involve no disagreement about the decision to end the marriage, but only difficulty in resolving issues of custody or support. Even where custody and support are initially contested, the Supreme Court may refer those ancillary services to the Family Court, whose mediation services may resolve the dispute without requiring counsel. . . .

But indigents are also parties to divorces where the dissolution of the marriage itself is contested, or where issues of custody and support are not capable of informal mediation. In such cases, if the spouses ultimately disagree about any of these three issues—ending the marriage, support of a spouse, or custody and child support—in my view, the assistance of counsel is essential, because lay persons are generally incapable of effectively meeting their legal burdens where such issues are disputed. For example, a party seeking, against a spouse's will, to terminate a marriage, must first decide whether it is preferable to obtain a divorce or an annulment. If the former, the party must select the best ground for obtaining the divorce (e.g., abandonment, mental cruelty, adultery, or other grounds). . . . It is also necessary to marshal evidence, and abide by technical requirements of proof. . . . Also, as in any civil case, a command of the rules of procedure and skill in presenting facts are essential. . . . The party opposing divorce must have a similar command of the legal intricacies. For example, where adultery is charged, the defendant may need technical assistance to identify and offer the relevant defenses of insanity, condonation, recrimination, procurement, collusion or Statute of Limitations. . . .

Also, if there is a dispute over support, pretrial investigative tools may be essential for discovering resources. Refusing counsel to an indigent party can, therefore, jeopardize that party's right to obtain support from a solvent spouse. And, if custody is disputed, the need for counsel is most apparent; children's futures will depend upon the outcome of the case, necessitating factual inquiries beyond the competence of the lay person. Frequently, expert witnesses must be examined. The Judge must often depend on counsel for the effective investigation, organization and presentation of the facts since the law's only guide is the vaguely worded standard of the "best interests of the child." . . .

Accordingly, I would hold that because of the importance of the rights involved, indigent matrimonial litigants are entitled, under the due process clauses of the Fourteenth Amendment to the Federal Constitution and section 6 of Article 1 of the New York State Constitution, to be supplied with counsel whenever counsel is essential to the effective exercise of their right of access to the court. This right should attach whenever the courts finds that indigent parties are incapable of preparing and presenting matrimonial actions *pro se*, including all divorce actions in which the dissolution is contested or in which property, support and custody issues cannot readily be resolved through mediation. While my view has obvious implications for other types of civil judicial proceedings, it would not need to be determined at the present time what other interests, if any, are sufficiently fundamental to require that counsel be provided when they are threatened. I would note only that the Supreme Court, which has been faced with this question in a filing fee case under the Federal Constitution, is in the process of distinguishing between those types of actions that involve "basic necessities" or "fundamental interests" and those that do not. . . .

PROTECTING WOMEN AND CHILDREN

Weitzman (1981) presents several proposals for meeting the needs of women and children who need protection in divorce actions: (1) an expanded definition of community property to include career assets; (2) legislative presumption in favor of maintaining the family residence for minor children and their custodian; (3) realistic child support schedules that allow children to maintain the same standard of living as the wealthier parent; cost of living escalation; and automatic wage assignments for child support; (4) opportunities for younger divorced women to develop a satisfactory earning capacity through more generous and protracted support awards; (5) opportunities for the older divorced women to equalize their net income with that of the spouse; and (6) economic and social supports for the custodial parent.

DIVORCE TRENDS AND SOCIAL SERVICES

Social agencies have traditionally offered marriage counseling directed at reconciliation, but since couples usually seek counseling too late to achieve successful reconciliation, such counseling increasingly serves to help them decide about the advisability of divorce rather than the preservation of an untenable marital relationship. Divorce mediation that involves social workers and lawyers in a team relationship has become increasingly popular. It has been questioned, however, because it may involve social workers in the unauthorized practice of law (Silberman, 1981).

A realistic use of limited social services is to assign highest priority to premarital and early marital counseling, especially for those involved in prospective second (or subsequent) marriages. Couples who have experienced marital adversity are motivated to make a new relationship work rather than try to repair an old one. The popularity of second and subsequent marriages and the couple's recognition of potential postmarital failure suggest the usefulness of intensive efforts with this client group. Neither a feeling of responsibility toward one's children nor the effect of divorce on one's reputation is sufficient to deter most unhappy people from divorce. Counseling oriented toward future success can help couples use their past experience constructively and make therapy more promising.

Questions for Review

1. Explain "migratory divorce" and evaluate its current importance.

2. What are the main issues concerning jurisdiction in divorce?

3. Explain and indicate the importance of divisible divorce.

4. Evaluate the importance of grounds in divorce. What possible hazards does no-fault divorce have?

5. What is the difference between *desertion* and *living separate and apart?* What is *constructive desertion?*

6. Explain why the wife who is beaten by her insane husband may have no grounds for getting a divorce on the basis of cruelty.

7. What was the purpose of corroboration in divorce actions?

8. Why would a lawyer advise a person in South Dakota who is contemplating divorce not to undertake reconciliation?

9. What is the usual effect of remarriage on alimony payments? On division of property?

10. Explain the rulings in *Estin* and *Vanderbilt*.

11. On what basis may alimony sometimes be reduced following the husband's remarriage?

12. What parental financial responsibilities may extend beyond the age of some children's majority?

13. Why does enforcement of support orders on an interstate basis constitute a major problem? What is the effect of mobility on collection of support?

14. Explain how retirement benefits become involved in a divorce settlement.

15. How would you determine the value of a professional education at the time of divorce?

16. Will a former husband pay income tax on alimony payments of $400 per month? On child support payments of $600? On what amount will the former wife pay taxes?

Questions for Debate and Discussion

1. Does no-fault divorce actually increase the number of divorces granted?

2. How would you explain the decrease in divorce rates seen for the first time in 1983?

3. Why are more divorces being granted without alimony?

4. Some advocates of women's rights consider no-fault divorce undesirable. Why would they take this position?

5. Under what circumstances will persons seeking a divorce have the greatest success in representing themselves in court?

Selected Readings   Allers, Robert D. *Divorce, Child, and the School.* Princeton, N.J.: Princeton Book Co., 1982.

Cherlin, Andrew. *Marriage—Divorce—Remarriage.* Cambridge, Mass.: Harvard University Press, 1981.

Cochran, Robert F., Jr., and Paul C. Vitz. "Child Protective Divorce Laws: A Response to the Effects of Parental Separation on Children." *Family Law Quarterly* 17 (1983): 327–363.

Halem, Lynne C. *Divorce Reform: Changing Legal and Social Perspectives.* New York: Free Press, 1980.

Haynes, John M. *Divorce Mediation: A Practical Guide for Therapists and Counselors.* Springfield, Ill.: Thomas, 1981.

Kahn, Lawrence E. *When Couples Part: How the Legal System Can Work for You.* New York: Watts, 1981.

Katz, Sanford N. "Humanizing the Divorce Process." *Family Advocate* 4 (1981): 63.

Kenneth, D., and Betty Sell. *Divorce in the United States, Canada, and Great Britain: A Guide to Information Sources.* Detroit: Gale Press Co., 1979.

McEvary, Margaret D. *A Woman Lawyer Talks About Divorce.* Reston, Va.: Dean Company of Washington, 1981.

Mitnick, Harold. *How to Handle Your Divorce Step by Step.* Chicago: Lone Oak Books, 1981.

Wheeler, Michael. *Divided Children: A Legal Guide for Divorcing Parents.* New York: Penguin Books, 1980.

Winks, Patricia L. "Divorce Mediation: A Non-adversary Procedure for the No-Fault Divorce." *Journal of Family Law* 19 (1981): 615–653.

CHAPTER
15

Rights of Children and Youth

Laws dealing with youths are characterized by paradoxes and inconsistencies. For example, until the 1970s, eighteen-year-old males were required to register for the draft but could not marry without parental permission or vote. Adolescents may not engage in certain specified hazardous occupations or buy liquor. In some states, youths are restricted from attending X-rated movies but may be tried as adults for alleged crimes and be sentenced to adult correctional facilities if found guilty. Juveniles are generally allowed little control over their property or person. Failure to attend school or respect a curfew is sufficient ground for detention.

Since youths were traditionally presumed incapable of assuming responsibility for their actions, minors have usually been able to disavow contracts. By emancipation or marriage, minors may prematurely obtain such adult responsibilities as self-support, support of a wife, and the legal responsibility to fulfill contracts with creditors. Older adolescents have gained other rights. Their needs have influenced the legal framework to reduce the age of majority and to eliminate legal age distinctions between the sexes.

Obligatory military service for eighteen-year-old males provided a strong impetus for establishment of eighteen as the minimum voting age. However, according other privileges to youths, such as the right to purchase liquor, has incurred strong opposition. The lower age of majority may also reduce parental responsibility for the support and continued education of a child.

LEGAL ASSUMPTIONS ABOUT CHILDREN Laws to protect children have been based on several assumptions: (1) that America is a familial, child-centered society in which parents are responsible for their own children and maintain primary control over them; (2) that the adult community, usually represented by the state, will not assume responsibility for any child until the parents are unable or refuse to do so or until the child has broken the law; (3) that officials of a child-loving society consider it their duty to intervene when necessary in promoting the child's "best interest"; (4) that the parents and state have the primary role in making decisions that affect children's lives. (Rodham, 1973:4)

Previously, persons under twenty-one were legally labeled infants, children, or minors. This age has generally been lowered to eighteen years. Because minors are assumed to exercise only limited judgment, they are accorded more protections and fewer liberties than adults. Custody and guardianship grant parents or other adults the legal right to make most decisions for children, although minors themselves are gradually granted more rights as they grow older. Adults retain the right to determine with whom a small child shall live and to restrict the liberty of a child whose behavior is clearly contrary to adult norms.

The primary responsibility for supervising children and providing them with the necessities of life resides in their biological parents as natural guardians. When parents are unable to assume this responsibility through no fault of their own, as in the case of parental physical or mental illness, their children may be alleged to be dependent. As a consequence of dependency or neglect, transfer in guardianship often results. (See chapters 7 and 8.)

Children are often charged with status offenses. That is, minors who disobey their parents or are habitually truant from school may be alleged to be *delinquent* or *in need of supervision* even though their actions would not consitute a crime if committed by an adult (see chapter 6). Application of these labels may result in restrictions or loss of a youth's liberty. The same due process safeguards that are already available to delinquents are needed for neglected, dependent, or incorrigible children and their parents.

CHILDREN'S BILL OF RIGHTS Because of their physical and mental immaturity, children have unique needs. These needs have been expressed in several bills of rights for children, including the U.N. Declaration of the Rights of the Child (United Nations, 1960).

UNITED NATIONS DECLARATION OF THE RIGHTS OF THE CHILD
Principle 1
The child shall enjoy all the rights set forth in this Declaration. All children, without any exception whatsoever, shall be entitled to these rights, without distinction or discrimination on account of race, color, sex, language, religion, political or other opinion, national or social origin, property, birth or other status, whether of himself or of his family.
Principle 2
The child shall enjoy special protection, and shall be given opportunities and facilities, by law and by other means, to enable him to develop physically, mentally, morally, spiritually and socially in a healthy and normal manner and in conditions of freedom and dignity. In the enactment of laws for this purpose the best interest of the child shall be the paramount consideration.
Principle 3
The child shall be entitled from his birth to a name and a nationality.
Principle 4
The child shall enjoy the benefits of social security. He shall be entitled to grow and develop in health; to this end special care and protection shall be provided both to him and to his mother including adequate pre-natal and post-natal care. The child shall have the right to adequate nutrition, housing, recreation and medical services.
Principle 5
The child who is physically, mentally or socially handicapped shall be given the special treatment, education and care required by his particular condition.
Principle 6
The child, for the full and harmonious development of his personality, needs love and understanding. He shall, wherever possible, grow up in the care and under the responsibility of his parents, and in any case in an atmosphere of affection and of moral and material security; a child of tender years shall not, save in exceptional circumstances, be separated from his mother. Society and the public authorities shall have the duty to extend particular care to children without a family and to those without adequate means of support. Payment of state and other assistance toward the maintenance of children of large families is desirable.
Principle 7
The child is entitled to receive education, which shall be free and compulsory, at least in the elementary stages. He shall be given an education which will promote his general culture, and enable him on a basis of equal opportunity to develop his abilities, his individual judgment,

and his sense of moral and social responsibility, and to become a useful member of society.

The best interests of the child shall be the guiding principle of those responsible for his education and guidance; that responsibility lies in the first place with his parents.

The child shall have full opportunity for play and recreation, which should be directed to the same purposes as education; society and the public authorities shall endeavor to promote the enjoyment of this right.

Principle 8

The child shall in all circumstances be among the first to receive protection and relief.

Principle 9

The child shall be protected against all forms of neglect, cruelty and exploitation. He shall not be the subject of traffic, in any form.

The child shall not be admitted to employment before an appropriate minimum age; he shall in no case be caused or permitted to engage in any occupation or employment which would prejudice his health or education, or interfere with his physical, mental or moral development.

Principle 10

The child shall be protected from practices which may foster racial, religious and any other form of discrimination. He shall be brought up in a spirit of understanding, tolerance, friendship among peoples, peace and universal brotherhood and in full consciousness that his energy and talents should be devoted to the service of his fellow men.

The Joint Commission on Mental Health of Children (1970:3–4) compiled the following list of children's rights:

- The right to be wanted

- The right to be born healthy

- The right to live in a healthy environment

- The right to satisfaction of basic needs

- The right to continuous loving care

- The right to acquire the intellectual and emotional skills necessary to achieve individual aspirations and to cope effectively in our society

- The right to receive care and treatment through facilities which are appropriate to their needs and which keep them as closely as possible within their normal social setting

The first bill of rights for children and youth of the National Association of Social Workers (1975:27–28) included representation, legal protection, and advocacy.

BILL OF RIGHTS FOR CHILDREN AND YOUTH
NATIONAL ASSOCIATION OF SOCIAL WORKERS
Preface

Historically, children have been considered as property with laws governing the relationship between parent and child relegating the child to little more than chattel. Nineteenth century reformers challenged this philosophy and initiated legislation to protect children from undue hardship and provide for more basic developmental needs. Despite the advances made on behalf of children, children too often remain second class citizens.

It is essential that public social policy recognize the child as an individual with rights, including the right to be a part of a family. The well-being of the child is most frequently advanced by public social policy which supports the well-being of the family. Children's needs as dependent persons requiring nurture must be reconciled with the protection of children's basic human rights and civil liberties.

The guarantee of such protection should not deny children greater participation in society. In the past, basic rights extended for adults have not applied to children. This has resulted in circumstances of gross injustice and isolation. Rather than keeping youth "infants until sudden adulthood," emancipation from dependency should be a gradual process from greater protection to greater participation and responsibility at key stages of maturity.

I. The right to sound preparation for life

Children are entitled to a good beginning. This is based upon being wanted and cared for. This shall include adequate family planning to assist potential parents in the decision of when it is best to have a child. Potential parents voluntarily should have access to genetic information to evaluate the probabilities of transmitting hereditary diseases. It shall also include the right of availability of adequate prenatal care and protection from trauma during the birth process.

II. The right to individuality

The child has the right to be a child, which includes the opportunity for spontaneity, curiosity, and the right to play, as a foundation for development of mastery and competence.

III. The right to a positive social identity

Law should consider the child as a person, not property. The child has the right to develop a positive social identity. Identity as a person should include pride in racial and ethnic characteristics, family and national culture, unique and individual differences. Such identity can only be achieved when the child is free from discrimination because of racial or ethnic origins; language; political or social origins; sexual preferences or origin of birth. Children should be permitted: to express such individuality by exercising the right to speak other than English freely and without derision; to express social and ethnic characteristics in dress; and when age-appropriate, should have freedom of choice of religion, including the option of none.

IV. The right to a good parenting experience

Every child has a right to continuous nurturing care and consistent parental controls and expectations. This is based upon the expectations that parents receive sufficient preparations and supports in family living so that the family experience can be conducive to healthy development. Where there is a decision to be made about who the child's parents may be, the child is entitled to participation in the decision, appropriate to age and capacity to understand the situation. The child's family should be determined by who the psychological parents are, not necessarily by the biological or legal parentage, current physical or legal custody, nor by arbitrary community definitions of adequate parents. This does not deny the rights of natural parents.

V. The right to a healthy environment

The child should have access to the following rights of all persons: freedom from want; adequate housing; safety; and security. Children shall receive environmental supports conducive to health and development. Children should have freedom from pollution of air, water, and food. Provision of recreational space and beautification of the environment are vital to aesthetic development and to a sense of respect for self, other persons, and the environment.

VI. The right to health

Children have a right to total health care at all critical stages of development from conception to maturity. They have a right to adequate nutrition and to health care which prevents and treats potentially handicapping diseases and disabilities. Comprehensive care includes: care appropriate at various age categories, physical and mental health, and information about their own bodies.

VII. The right to a relevant education

Children shall be guaranteed the access to quality education from preschool to maturity in order to develop to their fullest potential. Access to education, mental health, handicap, or social class. Such education shall meet the standards of sufficient preparation for maturity, employment, parenthood, and citizenship in a changing and complex society. Education is a highly individualized process within which each child has the right to participate in the design of his own learning experiences. The atypical child must have opportunities geared to specific needs including the opportunity to participate with normal children to the maximum of ability.

VIII. The right to participatory citizenship

Children have a right to a socially recognized and sanctioned role in society. Responsible participation by children in society includes opportunities for interaction between generations that contribute to development of self-identity, role acquisition, and career possibilities. Gradual, age-appropriate participation in social institutions which affect their lives provides developing individuals with preparatory experiences in citizenship.

IX. The right to representation

Children have the right to have their interests represented by children and youth on decision-making bodies directly affecting their lives. While adult advocates or representatives may appropriately continue efforts on behalf of children, they are not a substitute for representatives who are, themselves, minors. Children and youth, within reasonable limits of age and personal competence, as is true of the adult population, are entitled and able to be representatives of other minors. The process of selection and representation procedures so as to encourage the building of competence should be observed. Wherever possible, such representation should include voting power on school boards, city planning councils, health and social service boards, legislative panels, and task forces at every level of government.

X. The right to legal status, legal protection, and legal redress

Children shall have all the safeguards and protections of due process as guaranteed to adults by the Fourteenth Amendment, Bill of Rights and Statutory Law. This includes the right to protection from physical and psychological violence and cruel punishment. Children have the right to redress of grievances against both parents and social institutions that are damaging or interfering with their welfare or rights. Children have a right to appropriate representation in judicial and quasi-judicial proceedings in which their interests may be directly affected. This includes custody proceedings.

Children should have: freedom from incarceration for offenses which, if committed by an adult, would not be considered criminal acts; freedom from incarceration with adult offenders; and freedom from incarceration beyond minimum length and conditions necessary for their safety and the safety of others.

Children have the same right to privacy and confidentiality afforded to adults, in addition to special provisions to protect minors.

XI. The right to service

Children, who are dependent upon society for care and protection or who have special needs, must be given the opportunity to achieve the highest level of social functioning of which they are capable. Service must be legislatively mandated, with input from knowledgeable citizens and professionals, and must establish a comprehensive integrated system of services for families with children and for children separated from their families.

XII. The right to advocacy

The professional social worker must advocate for all clients, especially those who cannot advocate for themselves. Therefore, we as a professional association must reaffirm our professional responsibility of advocating for children to insure that the rights of children herein defined become a reality. Children must have the right to advocacy services to provide assurance that they will be guaranteed full benefit of the legal rights established by our society for the protection and well-being of all citizens.

Statements by various organizations professing recognition of rights for children have called attention to unmet needs, but they have not significantly increased enforceable rights. Since none of these statements has been implemented in law, the rights presented are unenforceable. Such statements are composed mainly of adults' obligations to children. They do not significantly increase children's freedom. Rodham (1973:10) has reviewed additional needs statements and concluded that "most claims based on psychological and even physical needs are not yet considered legal rights." A U.S. Supreme Court decision, San Antonio Independent School District v. Rodriguez, 411 U.S. 1 (1973), substantiates this view by denying that the educational needs of children are a constitutionally protected right. The Court supported its opinion by noting that more important needs than education, such as adequate food, clothing, and housing, are not constitutionally protected rights.

A MODEL CHILD PLACEMENT STATUTE   A model statute to legally protect the needs of children for continuous care by adults may be more useful than general bills of rights (Goldstein, Freud, and Solnit, 1973:97–101). The proposed placement statute suggests that the concept of the "psychological parent" be adopted as a legal guideline in all child custody decisions to promote fulfillment of the child's need for continuous loving care.

EXCERPTS FROM A MODEL CHILD PLACEMENT STATUTE
Article 10. Definitions

10.1 Biological parents. The biological parents are those who physically produce the child.

10.2 Wanted child. A wanted child is one who receives affection and nourishment on a continuing basis from at least one adult and who feels that he or she is and continues to be valued by those who take care of him or her.

10.3 Psychological parent. A psychological parent is one who, on a continuing, day-to-day basis, through interaction, companionship, interplay, and mutuality, fulfills the child's psychological needs for a parent, as well as the child's physical needs. The psychological parent may be a biological (para. 10.1), adoptive, foster, or common-law (para. 10.4) parent, or any other person. There is no presumption in favor of any of these after the initial assignment at birth (para. 20).

10.4 Common-law parent-child relationship. A common-law parent-child relationship is a psychological parent (para. 10.3)-wanted child (para. 10.2) relationship which developed outside of adoption, assignment by custody in separation or divorce proceedings, or the initial assignment at birth of a child to his or her biological parents (para. 20.1).

10.5 Child's sense of time. A child's sense of time is based on the urgency of his or her instinctual and emotional needs and thus differs from an adult's sense of time, as adults are better able to anticipate the future and thus to manage delay. A child's sense of time changes as he or she develops. Intervals of separation between parent and child that would constitute important breaks in continuity at one age might be of reduced significance at a later age.

10.6 Least detrimental available alternative. The least detrimental available alternative is that child placement and procedure for child placement which maximizes, in accord with the child's sense of time (para. 10.5), the child's opportunity for being wanted (para. 10.2) and for maintaining on a continuous, unconditional, and permanent basis a relationship with at least one adult who is or will become the child's psychological parent (para 10.3.)

Article 20. Initial Placement

20. Placement of child. At birth, a child is placed with his biological parents (para. 10.1). Unless other adults assume or are assigned the role, they are presumed to become the child's psychological parents (para. 10.3).

Article 30. Intervention to Alter a Child's Placement

30.1 State policy of minimizing disruption. It is the policy of this state to minimize disruptions of continuing relationships between a psychological parent (para. 10.3) and the child. The child's developmental needs are best served by continuing unconditional and permanent relationships. The importance of a relationship's duration and the significance of a disruption's duration vary with the child's developmental stage.

30.2 Intervenor. An intervenor is any person (including the state, institutions of the state, biological parents, and others) who seeks to disrupt a continuing relationship between psychological parent (para. 10.3) and child or seeks to establish an opportunity for such a relationship to develop. Upon such interventions the court's decision must secure for the child the least detrimental available alternative (para. 10.6).

30.3 Burden on the intervenor. A child is presumed to be wanted (para 10.2) in his or her current placement. If the child's placement is to be altered, the intervenor, except in custody disputes in divorce or separation, must establish both (i) that the child is unwanted, *and* (ii) that the child's current placement is not the least detrimental available alternative (para. 10.6).

In custody disputes in divorce or separation, the intervenor, that is the adult seeking custody, must establish that he or she is the least detrimental available alternative (para. 10.6).

30.4 Child's party status. Whenever an intervenor seeks to alter a child's placement the child shall be made a party to the dispute. The child shall be represented by independent counsel.

30.5 Final unconditional disposal. All placements shall be unconditional and final, that is, the court shall not retain continuing jurisdiction over a parent-child relationship or establish or enforce such conditions as rights of visitation.

30.6 Timely hearing and appeal. Trials and appeals shall be conducted as rapidly as is consistent with responsible decisionmaking. The court shall establish a timetable for hearing, decision, and review on appeal which, in accord with the specific child's sense of time (para. 10.5), shall maximize the chances of all interested parties to have their substantive claims heard while still viable, and shall minimize the disruption of parent-child relationships (para. 30.1).

Tapp (1978:378) criticized the model child placement statute:

> The authors adopted the "least detrimental alternative" because the courts have inadequate knowledge of the psychological needs of the child and are incompetent to supervise human development adequately; the result was embarrassingly devoid of extensive or "hard" evidence and impressively rich with proposed guidelines based primarily on singular cases from professional experience with an absence of systematic empirically based analysis and a distinct psychoanalytic orientation.

However., the least detrimental alternative would appear to provide a useful "do no harm" guideline until further empirical research can add to our knowledge of the needs of children.

THE AGE OF MAJORITY

The age of majority has shifted from twenty-one to eighteen in most states. The right to vote in national elections at age eighteen is guaranteed by the Twenty-sixth Amendment to the Constitution, adopted in 1971. Permitting eighteen-year-olds to serve on juries and as executors or administrators of estates has also been a statutory innovation. The new age of majority coincides better with legal termination of parental authority and the transfer of control from juvenile to adult courts, which were already fixed at age eighteen.

In addition, adult rights are now more likely to be granted to males and females at the same age by virtue of a U.S. Supreme Court decision disallowing an age differential based on sex in a Utah statute that specified a greater age of majority for males than for females in the context of parental support obligations (Stanton v. Stanton, 421 U.S. 7 [1975]). Other state laws, such as those allowing females to marry at an earlier age than males, have also been held unconstitutional.

Minors and Contracts

Generally, children may make and enforce contracts, but they may also disaffirm such agreements before reaching majority or within a reasonable time thereafter. Contracts made between adults and children are binding on the adult but not on the child, except where so provided by statutory exception. If two children make a contract, either may disaffirm it.

When a child disaffirms a contract, anything received from the other party must usually be returned, unless it has been lost, dissipated, or damaged, in which case the child is not normally required to make restitution. Statutory exceptions may occur occasionally when the other party to the transaction has made a fair contract in good faith or when a child has fraudulently misrepresented age. The case of Adams v. Barcomb, 216 A.2d 648 (Vt. 1966), concerned the right of a minor to rescind a contract.

ADAMS v. BARCOMB

Supreme Court of Vermont, 216 A.2d 648 (Vt. 1966).

SHANGRAW, Justice. This is a civil action to recover the consideration paid under a contract made by plaintiff. . . . Findings of fact were made by the trial court and judgment entered in favor of the defendant. The plaintiff has appealed. . . .

The plaintiff, Rose Adams, was born August 6, 1943, and became twenty-one years of age on August 6, 1964.

In May of 1964 while the plaintiff was working in Burlington she contacted the defendant, Leonard Barcomb, concerning the purchase of an automobile. As a result she purchased a 1960 Impala two door convertible Chevrolet. For said car she traded in a 1959 Opel and paid $975 in cash. Said sale was consummated on May 28, 1964.

The plaintiff operated the purchased Chevrolet for approximately two weeks and was dissatisfied with it.

. . . The defendant told her that he would not return the money and the plaintiff then contacted an attorney, and suit for the return of the money was instituted by writ dated July 15, 1964.

. . . It has always been the law in this state that contracts made by a minor during infancy, if not for necessaries, may be avoided by him if disaffirmed within a reasonable time after arriving at full age.

The plaintiff became of age on August 6, 1964, and was within her rights in disaffirming the contract while under age. . . .

After disaffirmance, she was entitled to the return of the consideration paid for the automobile.

. . . It is contended by the defendant that it was a prerequisite that the plaintiff first return the automobile purchased of the defendant if liability under the contract was to be avoided by her. As a general rule, if an infant avoids his contract, he must restore the consideration that he received. . . . The defendant refused to return the money which he had received as part of payment therefor. This refusal on the part of the defendant excused the plaintiff from tendering the return of the automobile purchased by the plaintiff. The law does not require the doing of a useless act or the doing of that which would be only a vain and idle ceremony. . . .

Such use of the automobile by the plaintiff during the pendency of this action to recover what she had paid for the vehicle, after the defendant had flatly rejected her prior disaffirmance, does not constitute a ratification of the original contract as a matter of law. . . .

Judgment reversed and cause remanded for an appropriate judgment order in favor of the plaintiff.

The case of *Robertson v. King* also took up the question of whether a contract entered into by a minor can be rescinded by that minor.

ROBERTSON v. KING

Supreme Court of Arkansas, 280 S.W.2d 402 (Ark. 1955).

ROBINSON, Justice. The principal issue here is whether [defendant], a minor, may rescind a contract to purchase a pick-up truck. On the 20th day of March, 1954, L. D. Robertson, a minor, entered into a conditional sales agreement whereby he purchased from Turner King and J. W. Julian, doing business as the Julian Pontiac Company, a pick-up truck for the agreed price of $1,743.85. On the day of the purchase, Robertson was 17 years of age, and did not have his 18th birthday until April 8th. Robertson traded in a passenger car for which he was given a credit of $723.85 on the purchase price, leaving a balance of $1,020 payable in 23 monthly installments of $52.66 plus one payment of $52.83. He paid the April installment of $52.66. . . . It appears that Robertson had considerable trouble with the wiring on the truck. He returned it to the automobile dealers for repairs, but the defective condition was not remedied. On May 2nd, the truck caught fire and was practically destroyed. He notified the automobile concern and they stated that they would send the insurance man to see him. It appears that the insurance representative, upon finding out that Robertson was only 17 years of age, refused to deal with him.

On June 7th, [plaintiffs] filed suit to replevy the damaged truck from Robertson. By his father and next friend, Robertson filed a cross-complaint in which he alleged that he is a minor and asked that the contract of the purchase be rescinded and sought to recover that part of the purchase price he had paid. . . . There was a judgment for King and Julian on the complaint and the cross-complaint. On appeal, Robertson contends that he was 17 years of age at the time of the alleged purchase and that he has a right under the law to rescind the contract and to recover the portion of the purchase price he has paid.

[Plaintiffs] also contend that . . . a minor cannot rescind a contract of purchase without reimbursing the seller for any loss that he may have sustained by reason of such rescission. This statute deals with situations where a minor is 18 years of age at the time of making a purchase. The statute is not applicable here because according to the undisputed evidence Robertson was only 17 years of age at the time of entering into the purchase agreement. . . .

The automobile dealers have disposed of the car they received in the trade, and cannot restore it to the minor. In a situation of this kind, the weight of authority is that the actual value of the property given as part of the purchase price by the minor is the correct measure of damages. Neither side is bound by the agreement reached as to the value of the car at the time the trade was made. . . . Hence, the court erred in finding for the automobile dealers, and the cause is therefore reversed and remanded for a new trial.

Contracts to perform as actors or athletes, educational loans, and certain other business contracts may be binding on minors. Common law allows children to make certain contracts when they are not living with a parent who is furnishing them necessities. Necessities are defined as such indispensable articles as food, clothing, housing, and medical attention. Statutes often prevent children from disaffirming commitments made under these situations.

In Gastonia Personnel Corp. v. Rogers, 172 S.E.2d 19 (N.C. 1970), a married minor was not allowed to disaffirm a contract with an employment agency because such service was found to be a necessity.

GASTONIA PERSONNEL CORP. v. ROGERS

Supreme Court of North Carolina, 172 S.E.2d 19 (N.C. 1970)

Defendant had graduated from high school in 1966. On May 29, 1968, he was nineteen years old, emancipated and married. He needed only "one quarter or 22 hours" for completion of the courses required at Gaston Tech for an A.S. degree in civil engineering. His wife was employed as a computer programmer at First Federal Savings and Loan. He and she were living in a rented apartment. They were expecting a baby in September. Defendant had to quit school and go to work.

For assistance is obtaining suitable employment, defendant went to the office of plaintiff, an employment agency, on May 29, 1968. After talking with Maurine Finley, a personnel counselor, defendant signed a contract containing, inter alia, the following: "If I ACCEPT employment offered me by an employer as a result of a lead (verbal or otherwise) from you within twelve (12) months of such lead even though it may not be the position originally discussed with you, I will be obligated to pay you as per the terms of the contract." Under the contract, defendant was free to continue his own quest for employment. He was to become obligated to plaintiff only if he accepted employment from an employer to whom he was referred by plaintiff.

After making several telephone calls to employers who might need defendant's services as a draftsman, Mrs. Finley called Spratt-Seaver, Inc., in Charlotte, North Carolina. It was stipulated that defendant, as a result of his conversation with Mrs. Finley, went to Charlotte, was interviewed by Spratt-Seaver, Inc., and was employed by that company on June 6, 1968, at an annual salary of $4,784. The contract provided that defendant would pay plaintiff a service charge of $295 if the starting salary of accepted employment was as much as $4,680. . . .

Plaintiff sued to recover a service charge of $295. In his answer, defendant admitted he had paid nothing to plaintiff; alleged he was not indebted to plaintiff in any amount; and, as a further answer and defense, pleaded his infancy. . . .

BOBBITT, Chief Justice. . . .

In general, our prior decisions are to the effect that the "necessaries" of an infant, his wife and child, include only such necessities of life as food, clothing, shelter, medical attention, etc. In our view, the concept of "necessaries" should be enlarged to include such articles of property and such services as are reasonably necessary to enable the infant to earn the money required to provide the necessities of life for himself and those who are legally dependent upon him.

. . . To hold, as a matter of law, that such a person cannot obligate himself to pay for services rendered him in obtaining employment suitable to his ability, education and specialized training, enabling him to provide the necessities of life for himself, his wife and his expected child, would place him and others similarly situated under a serious economic handicap.

In the effort to protect "older minors" from improvident or unfair contracts, the law should not deny to them the opportunity and right to obligate themselves for articles of property or services which are reasonably necessary to enable them to provide for the proper support of themselves and their dependents. The minor should be held liable for the reasonable value of articles of property or services received pursuant to such contract.

Applying the foregoing legal principles, which modify *pro tanto* the ancient rule of the common law, we hold that the evidence offered by plaintiff was sufficient for submission to the jury for its determination of issues substantially as indicated below.

To establish liability, plaintiff must satisfy the jury by the greater weight of the evidence that defendant's contract with the plaintiff was an appropriate and reasonable means for the defendant to obtain suitable employment. If this issue is answered in plaintiff's favor, plaintiff must then establish by the greater weight of the evidence the reasonable value of the services received by defendant pursuant to the contract. Thus, plaintiff's recovery, if any, cannot exceed the reasonable value of its services to defendant.

Accordingly, the judgment of the Court of Appeals is reversed and the cause is remanded to that Court with direction to award a new trial to be conducted in accordance with the legal principles stated herein.

Error and remanded.

MINORS AND TORTS

A **tort** is "a private or civil wrong or injury independent of contract." Children may both sue and be sued, but in either case, they are represented by an adult. Children are generally liable for tortious acts. More lenient standards of intent or negligence may be applied to them than to adults. Suit may be brought by a guardian or "next friend," who is allowed to prosecute on the child's behalf without being appointed guardian. Suits are usually defended by a **guardian ad litem**, who represents the child for the purpose of litigation only. Lee v. Comer, 224 S.E.2d 721 (W. Va. 1976), illustrates the current status of parental immunity from torts brought by the child:

> The doctrine of parental immunity was introduced into American jurisprudence by the Mississippi Supreme Court in Hewlett v. George, 9 So. 885 (1891), and rapidly spread throughout the various jurisdictions of our country. In recent years, this doctrine has begun to recede as rapidly as it had once spread. There has been a landslide trend toward the abrogation or limitation of the doctrine. This court perceives no reason why minor children should not enjoy the same right to legal redress for wrongs done to them as others enjoy. The need for and value of family tranquility must not be discounted, but to hold that a child's pains must be endured for the peace of the family is something of a mockery.
>
> American common law permits a minor child to maintain an action against his parent for matters of contract and property. It is unreasonable to say that our law should protect the property and contract rights of a minor more zealously than the rights of his person. This court does not here advocate the total abrogation of the parental immunity doctrine. It does, however, abrogate totally that doctrine in cases where a child is injured in an automobile accident as a result of his parent's negligence. In the realm of automobile accident cases, the court cannot brush aside or ignore the almost universal existence of liability insurance. Where such insurance exists, the domestic tranquillity argument is no longer valid, for the real defendant is not the parent but the insurance carrier.
>
> One objection to the abrogation of parental immunity is the fear that such action will turn the family into a legal battleground. Where insurance exists, an action against the parent is beneficial rather than detrimental to the family relationship. Where there

is no insurance, a child will rarely sue. But if a child does sue a parent knowing that he is without liability insurance, it then becomes very evident that family tranquillity was nonexistent prior to the suit. Certainly, a tort action between parent and child as true adversaries will not spawn any more acrimony or disharmony than would a contract or property action between the same parties, and such actions, as heretofore noted, have long been permitted at common law.

Another objection is the possibility of collusion between parent and child with the goal of securing an unjustified recovery from an insurance carrier. The possibility of collusion exists to a degree in the trial of any case. Even though some collusive claims may succeed, this possibility does not justify the continuation of a doctrine designed to deprive minors of the right to maintain an action in such cases.

MINORS AND PROPERTY

Children may acquire, own, and convey real and personal property. A guardian of the estate may be appointed to make binding contracts concerning the child's property under court supervision. Most states have adopted the Uniform Gifts to Minors Act, whereby children may be given lands or property without the need for mandatory appointment of a guardian of the estate. Instructions concerning administration of the property are given to a designated custodian instead.

WORK AND EARNINGS

Child labor laws prohibit hazardous work and regulate conditions of permissible employment before age sixteen or eighteen. Common law held that parents were entitled to their child's earnings. Modern case law has determined that parents waive this right by consenting to employment outside the home and allowing the child to keep any earnings. A parent who abandons a child has no claim to the child's earnings.

EMANCIPATION

Emancipation is the legal term for surrender of parental authority and duties concerning a child, including custody, care, and entitlement to earnings. Children in at least twenty-five states may become emancipated upon marriage or demonstration of their ability to live alone and be self-supporting. Emancipation may be partial, as when a parent abandons a child. In this situation, the child may be able to choose a legal residence while the parent is still required to provide support.

Emancipation is a label used to describe a situation that already exists. The duties of parents concerning custody and support and of children regarding obedience should be selectively removed when circumstances no longer indicate a need for such a relationship. California law, for example, permits emancipation as early as age fourteen and provides both for partial emancipation, in which the parents retain a duty to support, and for recision of emancipation status.

PARENTAL CONSENT TO MEDICAL TREATMENT

Children typically must receive the permission of their guardian for medical treatment, except on rare occasions when older children are allowed to consent to their own surgical operations. Exception is also made in some states for children seeking birth control and family planning information or treatment for venereal disease or drug addiction. In such cases, guardians need not consent or even be notified.

Abortion   Planned Parenthood of Central Missouri v. Danforth, 428 U.S. 52 (1976), took
up children's rights generally in dealing with parental consent for abortion:

**PLANNED
PARENTHOOD OF
CENTRAL
MISSOURI v.
DANFORTH**

Supreme Court of the
United States, 428 U.S.
52 (1976).

. . . [Missouri Law] Section 3(4) requires, with respect to the first 12 weeks
of pregnancy, where the woman is unmarried and under the age of 18 years,
the written consent of a parent or person in loco parentis unless, again, "the
abortion is certified by a licensed physician as necessary in order to preserve
the life of the mother." It is to be observed that only one parent need consent.

The appellees defend the statute in several ways. They point out that
the law properly may subject minors to more stringent limitations than are
permissible with respect to adults, and they cite, among other cases, Prince
v. Massachusetts, 321 U.S. 158 (1944), and McKeiver v. Pennsylvania, 403
U.S. 528 (1971). Missouri law, it is said, "is replete with provisions reflecting
the interest of the state in assuring the welfare of minors," citing statutes
relating to a guardian ad litem for a court proceeding, to the care of delinquent and neglected children, to child labor, and to compulsory education.
Brief for Appellees 42. Certain decisions are considered by the state to be
outside the scope of a minor's ability to act in his own best interest or in the
interest of the public, citing statutes proscribing the sale of firearms and
deadly weapons to minors without parental consent, and other statutes
relating to minors' exposure to certain types of literature, the purchase by
pawnbrokers of property from minors, and the sale of cigarettes and alcoholic beverages to minors. It is pointed out that the record contains testimony
to the effect that children of tender years (even ages 10 and 11) have sought
abortions. Thus, a State's permitting a child to obtain an abortion without
the counsel of an adult "who has responsibility or concern for the child would
constitute an irresponsible abdication of the State's duty to protect the welfare of minors." Id., at 44. Parental discretion, too, has been protected from
unwarranted or unreasonable interference from the State, citing Meyer v.
Nebraska, 262 U.S. 390 (1923); Pierce v. Society of Sisters, 268 U.S. 510
(1925); Wisconsin v. Yoder, 406 U.S. 205 (1972). Finally, it is said that § 3
(4) imposes no additional burden on the physician because even prior to
the passage of the Act the physician would require parental consent before
performing an abortion on a minor.

The appellants, in their turn, emphasize that no other Missouri statute
specifically requires the additional consent of a minor's parent for medical
or surgical treatment, and that in Missouri a minor legally may consent to
medical services for pregnancy (excluding abortion), venereal disease, and
drug abuse. Mo.Laws 1971, pp. 425–426, H.B. No. 73, §§ 1–3. The result
of § 3 (4), it is said, "is the ultimate supremacy of the parents' desires over
those of the minor child, the pregnant patient." Brief for Appellants 93. It is
noted that in Missouri a woman who marries with parental consent under
the age of 18 does not require parental consent to abort, and yet her contemporary who has chosen not to marry must obtain parental approval.

The District Court majority recognized that, in contrast to § 3(3), the
State's interest in protecting the mutuality of a marriage relationship is not
present with respect to § 3(4). It found "a compelling basis," however, in
the State's interest "in safeguarding the authority of the family relationship."

392 F.Supp., at 1370. The dissenting judge observed that one could not seriously argue that a minor must submit to an abortion if her parents insist, and he could not see "why she would not be entitled to the same right of self-determination now explicitly accorded to adult women, provided she is sufficiently mature to understand the procedure and to make an intelligent assessment of her circumstances with the advice of her physician." Id., at 1376. . . .

We agree with appellants and with the courts whose decisions have just been cited that the State may not impose a blanket provision, such as § 3 (4), requiring the consent of a parent or person in loco parentis as a condition for abortion of an unmarried minor during the first 12 weeks of her pregnancy. Just as with the requirement of consent from the spouse, so here, the State does not have the constitutional authority to give a third party an absolute, and possibly arbitrary, veto over the decision of the physician and his patient to terminate the patient's pregnancy, regardless of the reason for withholding the consent.

Constitutional rights do not mature and come into being magically only when one attains the state-defined age of majority. Minors, as well as adults, are protected by the Constitution and possess constitutional rights. The Court indeed, however, long has recognized that the State has somewhat broader authority to regulate the activities of children than of adults. It remains, then, to examine whether there is any significant state interest in conditioning an abortion on the consent of a parent or person in loco parentis that is not present in the case of an adult.

One suggested interest is the safeguarding of the family unit and of parental authority. 392 F.Supp., at 1370. It is difficult, however, to conclude that providing a parent with absolute power to overrule a determination, made by the physician and his minor patient, to terminate the patient's pregnancy will serve to strengthen the family unit. Neither is it likely that such veto power will enhance parental authority or control where the minor and the nonconsenting parent are so fundamentally in conflict and the very existence of the pregnancy already has fractured the family structure. Any independent interest the parent may have in the termination of the minor daughter's pregnancy is no more weighty than the right of privacy of the competent minor mature enough to have become pregnant.

We emphasize that our holding that § 3 (4) is invalid does not suggest that every minor, regardless of age or maturity, may give effective consent for termination of her pregnancy. The fault with § 3 (4) is that it imposes a special consent provision, exercisable by a person other than the woman and her physician, as a prerequisite to a minor's termination of her pregnancy and does so without a significant justification for the restriction. It violates the strictures of *Roe* and *Doe*.

In 1981 the U.S. Supreme Court upheld a Utah parental notification statute for unemancipated minors seeking abortion (H.L. v. Matheson, 450 U.S. 398). The decision included the following facts:

A Utah statute requires a physician to "notify, if possible," the parents or guardian of a minor upon whom an abortion is to be performed. H.L., while an unmarried minor living with and dependent on her parents, became pregnant. A physician advised her that an abortion would be in her best medical interest but, because of the statute, refused to perform the abortion without first notifying her parents. The appellant instituted a suit in state court seeking a declaration that the statute is unconstitutional and an injunction against its enforcement. She sought to represent a class consisting of unmarried minors "who are suffering unwanted pregnancies and desire to terminate the pregnancies but may not do so" because of their physicians' insistence on complying with the statute. The trial court upheld the statute as not unconstitutionally restricting a minor's right of privacy to obtain an abortion or to enter into a doctor-patient relationship. The Utah Supreme Court affirmed the trial court's decision.

The Court indicated that the appellant lacked standing to challenge the statute and held that the statute was narrowly drawn to serve important state interests involving unemancipated minors: "Although a state may not constitutionally leg-islate a blanket, unreviewable power of parents to veto their daughter's abortion, a statute setting out a 'mere requirement of parental notice' does not violate the constitutional rights of an immature, dependent minor."The Court stated, further, that

> The Utah statute does not give parents veto power over the minor's abortion decision. As applied to immature and dependent minors, the statute serves important consid-erations of family integrity and protecting adolescents as well as providing an oppor-tunity for parents to supply essential medical and other information to the physician. The statute is not unconstitutional for failing to specify what information parents may furnish to physicians, or to provide for a mandatory period of delay after the physician notifies the parents; or because the state allows a pregnant minor to consent to other medical procedures without formal notice to her parents if she carries the child to term; or because the notice requirement may inhibit some minors from seeking abortions.

In 1983 the U.S. Supreme Court invalidated an Akron ordinance that pro-hibited physicians from performing abortions on unmarried minors under the age of fifteen without parental consent (City of Akron V. Akron Center for Reproductive Health, 462 U.S. 416 [1983]). The Court also upheld a Missouri parental consent statute (Planned Parenthood Association v. Ashcroft, 103 S.Ct. 2517 [1983]):

> A State's interest in protecting immature minors will sustain a requirement of a consent substitute, either parental or judicial. It is clear, however, that "the State must provide an alternative procedure whereby a pregnant minor may demonstrate that she is suf-ficiently mature to make the abortion decision herself or that, despite her immaturity, an abortion would be in her best interests." *City of Akron*, ante, at 21–22. The issue here is one purely of statutory construction:.whether Missouri provides a judicial alternative that is consistent with these established legal standards.
>
> The Missouri statute, § 188.028.2, in relevant part, provides "(4) In the decree, the court shall for good cause: (a) Grant the petition for majority rights for the purpose of consenting to the abortion; or (b) Find the abortion to be in the interests of the minor and give judicial consent to the abortion, setting forth the grounds for so finding; or (c) Deny the petition, setting forth the grounds on which the petition is denied. On its face, § 188.028.2(4) authorizes juvenile courts to choose among any of the alternatives outlined in the section. The Court of Appeals concluded that a denial of the petition permitted in subsection (c) "would initially require the court to find that the minor was not emancipated and was not mature enough to make her own decision and that an abortion was not in her best interests." 655 F.2d, at 858. Plaintiffs contend that this interpretation is unreasonable. We do not agree.

Where fairly possible, courts should construe a statute to avoid a danger of unconstitutionality. The Court of Appeals was aware, if the statute provides discretion to deny permission to a minor for *any* "good cause," that arguably it would violate the principles that this Court has set forth. Ibid. It recognized, however, that before exercising any option, the juvenile court must receive evidence on "the emotional development, maturity, intellect and understanding of the minor." Mo. Rev. Stat. § 188.028.2(3) (Supp. 1982). The court then reached the logical conclusion that "findings and the ultimate denial of the petition must be supported by a showing of 'good cause.' " 655 F.2d, at 858. The Court of Appeals reasonably found that a court could not deny a petition "for good cause" unless it first found—after having received the required evidence—that the minor was not mature enough to make her own decision. See Bellotti II, 443 U.S., at 643–644, 647–648 (plurality opinion). We conclude that the Court of Appeals correctly interpreted the statute and that § 188.028, as interpreted, avoids any constitutional infirmities.

Both case law and statutes in some states do not require parental consent for medical treatment when an emergency exists or if the minor is "mature" (close to the age of majority), emancipated, or the treatment is determined by a court to be in the best interests of the child. However, policies are fragmented and fail to meet the needs for medical care as defined in the bills of rights presented earlier.

In view of the minor's general right to disaffirm contracts and the question of ability to pay, physicians usually favor the requirement that parental consent be obtained prior to medical intervention. In addition, physicians are also subject to the possibility of tort liability if the minor is physically touched without parental consent, whether the results of treatment are beneficial or not.

Wilkins (1975) proposed a Uniform Medical Consent Statute that avoids the need for parental consent.

UNIFORM MEDICAL CONSENT STATUTE
Section 1

(a) Any person, regardless of age or marital status, may consent to the furnishing of any lawful diagnostic, recuperative, counseling, surgical, rehabilitative, post mortem procedure, and related hospital services directed to the medical, dental, and emotional needs of such person.

(b) If the occasion for the furnishing of the services enumerated in subsection (a) above arises under emergency circumstances and the person empowered to consent by that subsection is unable to consent to those services, emergency treatment may be rendered by professional persons duly licensed under the laws of this state without consulting any other person if, within a reasonable degree of medical certainty, delay in obtaining such consultation would endanger the health of the ill or injured person.

Section 2

(a) If the person empowered to consent by section 1(a) above is a minor, and the rendering of the services permitted by that section would create a substantial risk of harm to the physical or mental well-being of such person, the facts of such person's request for such services, and the nature and consequences of such services shall be communicated to the parents or legal guardian of such person by the treating professional or professionals prior to, or if an emergency exists within a reasonable time after, the rendering of such services.

(b) Where full confidentiality of the information referred to in subsection 2(a) above would not, to a reasonable degree of medical certainty, be detrimental to the physical or mental well-being of the person or a member of the person's family, or to the health and safety of the public, such information shall not be divulged without the express consent of the person to whom the services were rendered.

Section 3

The consent of a minor for the furnishing of the services enumerated in subsection 1(a) above shall, notwithstanding any other provision of law, be as valid and effective for all purposes as if such minor had reached the age of majority, and shall not be subject to later avoidance by the minor, the minor's spouse, parents, legal guardian or other custodian, heirs, executors and administrators by reason of having given such consent while below the age of majority.

Section 4

(a) All persons receiving services under this act shall assume full legal responsibility for payment for such services, except those persons who are proven unable to pay, who receive the services in public institutions, or, if a minor and the spouse, parents, legal guardian, or other custodian of such minor has expressly or impliedly agreed to accept financial responsibility under the provisions of subsection 4(b) below.

(b) If the person receiving such services is a minor, the spouse, parents, legal guardian, or other custodian of such minor shall not incur legal responsibility for payment for such services unless an express or implied agreement to pay for such services has been made by the spouse, parents, legal guardian, or other custodian. It shall be sufficient evidence of an implied agreement under this act that the services were rendered at the direction, request, or suggestion of the spouse, parents, legal guardian, or other custodian.

(c) If the person receiving such services or otherwise agreeing to accept legal responsibility for payment of such service is a minor, full disclosure of the nature of the financial responsibility of such person shall be made by the professional person or agency rendering the services prior to the rendering of such services where feasible, and upon such full disclosure, the legal responsibility for payment for such services, notwithstanding any other provision of law, shall not be subject to disaffirmance by reason of the minority of such person.

Section 5

Professional persons or agencies, or persons acting at the direction of such professional persons or agencies shall incur no civil liability by reason of rendering the services or providing the information authorized or required by the sections above except for negligent acts or omissions in rendering such services or providing such information.

(b) Nothing in this act shall be construed to permit or relieve professional persons or agencies or persons acting at the direction of such professional persons and agencies of liability for treatment of a minor that is not, as corroborated by substantial medical evidence, reasonably calculated to arrest or correct an existing medical, dental, or emotional condition, illness or injury suffered by such minor.

PARENTAL COMMITMENT TO A MENTAL HOSPITAL

Parental commitment of a minor to a state mental hospital is permitted under a U.S. Supreme Court decision (Parham v. J.R., 442 U.S. 584 [1979]), which held that states do not have to accord due process rights to minors hospitalized by their parents. It emphasized that parents and mental health professionals tend to act in the best interests of children. Details on *Parham* will be found in Chapter 24, on mental health.

Most states provide more safeguards of children's rights than those described in *Parham*. For example, a California Supreme Court decision, In Re Roger S., 569 P.2d 1286 (Cal. 1977), provides due process protection for minors whose parents seek to commit them to a state mental hospital:

> We conclude . . . that no interest of the state or of a parent sufficiently outweighs the liberty interest of a minor old enough to independently exercise his right to due process to permit the parent to deprive him of that right . . .
>
> Due process forbids the arbitrary deprivation of liberty (Goss v. Lopez, supra, 419 U.S. 565, 574) and, in the context of commitment to a mental hospital, requires at least "that the nature and duration of commitment bear some reasonable relation to the purpose for which the individual is committed" (Jackson v. Indiana [1972] 406

U.S. 715, 738). Thus, the focus of our attention must be to delineate procedures that will ensure the child a fair opportunity to establish that (1) he is not mentally ill or disordered, or that (2) even if he is, confinement in a state mental hospital is unnecessary to protect him or others and might harm rather than improve his condition. Procedures designed to establish these facts are necessary to accommodate both the parent's right to control his child's development and the state's interest in limiting parental control when parental action may harm the physical or mental health of the child.

When the state participates in deprivation of a person's right to personal liberty, even a conditional liberty, due process requires that the facts justifying that action be reliably established. To that end the United States Supreme Court has suggested that, at a minimum, due process requires that the person receive a hearing after adequate written notice of the basis for the proposed action; an opportunity to appear in person and to present evidence in his own behalf; the right to confrontation by, and the opportunity to cross-examine, adverse witnesses; a neutral and detached decision maker; findings by a preponderance of the evidence; and a record of the proceeding adequate to permit meaningful judicial or appellate review. Inasmuch as a minor may be presumed to lack the ability to marshal the facts and evidence, to effectively speak for himself and to call and examine witnesses, or to discover and propose alternative treatment programs, due process also requires that counsel be provided for the minor.

Rights of School Pupils

A major topic, rights of school pupils, is discussed in Chapter 22 on education. Major topics include rights to school attendance, freedom of expression and searches of pupils, especially for drugs. On the latter issue, Chapter 24 includes consideration of a New Jersey case, New Jersey v. T.L.O. (53 U.S.L.W. 4083) decided in 1985 by the U.S. Supreme Court. It authorizes warrantless searches of pupils under reasonable circumstances and does not require the Fourth Amendment test involving probable cause.

CHILD ADVOCACY

Wilkins (1975) suggests that the best protection of minors' interests in receiving medical treatment is a child advocacy program. He accepts a definition of advocacy from Kahn, Kamerman, and McGowan (1973: 117–118) emphasizing systems change to make social institutions work for children rather than against them.

> Child advocacy's main concern is intervention into secondary institutions such as schools, juvenile courts, health programs, child welfare programs, and the like. The target may be the total institution or some of its functions, policies, professional processes, programs, or personnel.
>
> Child advocacy is a shorthand term for advocacy on behalf of families and children. The stakes of family and child are often intertwined, and efforts on behalf of the family as a whole (with regard to income supports and housing, for example) are usually necessary steps in providing for children's welfare. However, child advocacy also encompasses concern for children who live in substitute or surrogate families, e.g., in foster homes, institutions, or adoptive homes. In addition, it has a mission related to adolescents and other children who may see their interests as conflicting with those of their parents and on occasion are right.

Another formulation on advocacy achieves a basic goal of social workers in that it makes *all* needs of children legally enforceable rights:

> 1. *Advocacy assumes people have, or ought to have, certain basic rights.* . . . This is essentially a philosophical position that forms the basis of many legal and non-legal advocacy strategies. Sometimes, as noted earlier in regard to welfare law, it leads to questions

of procedural due process. In other instances, it leads to the expansion of substantive rights. Most often, it leads to efforts to strengthen by pragmatic or administrative changes due process procedures and services afforded to people. For children, who have traditionally been considered non-persons in the eyes of the law, taking this premise seriously implies reexamining and redefining the legal framework as it affects the children. Since children are in some ways different from, and in other ways the same as, adults, this in turn poses some difficult psychological, legal, and social dilemmas. Rodham, in a thoughtful discussion, delineated two directions in the efforts to reassess the legal framework: (1) efforts to ensure to all children all the rights adults now have, and (2) efforts to carve out a set of rights that derive from the special nature of childhood. The latter implies that children have access to appropriate developmental opportunities, and raises many issues for child advocates.

2. *Advocacy assumes rights are enforceable by statutory, administrative, or judicial procedures.* . . . Acceptance of this assumption is critical to effective advocacy, for without a commitment to developing and enforcing procedures to ensure rights, the claims of advocacy and rhetoric can readily become indistinguishable. Emphasis on the enforcement of rights is particularly significant in relation to children, who are especially vulnerable to decision making on the basis of an individualistic and arbitrary interpretation of the child's best interest. For too long, and with severe consequences to children and families, we have relied upon the assumption that adults with power to intervene in the child's life care about children and inevitably make the right decision. (Knitzer, 1976:204)

Advocacy may focus on all children in a given geographic area, all children with a particular status or characteristic, or a combination of the two. Strategies may include any or all of the following: case advocacy, class litigation, monitoring of existing services, and legislative advocacy.

Other important topics concerning the rights of young people may be targets for social work advocacy. In this book, chapters on marriage, contraception and abortion, paternity and support obligations, adoption, neglect and abuse, placement and guardianship, and divorce and custody all discuss aspects of children's rights. Rights are also basic in such social concerns as poverty, delinquency, and education.

Questions for Review

1. Laws to protect children are based on what assumptions?

2. What is a major criticism of bills of rights for children? What is the value of such bills of rights?

3. How can the needs expressed in children's bills of rights be made enforceable rights?

4. Define "psychological parent." What persons may fit this role?

5. What is the criticism of the "least detrimental alternative" concept?

6. What is the age of majority in most states?

7. What types of contracts tend to be binding for minors?

8. What is the status of minors when it comes to ownership of property?

9. What are the principal provisions of child labor laws?

10. Summarize tort law concerning minors. What is the current status of parental immunity from torts brought by a child?

11.   Define emancipation. What circumstances provide evidence for emancipation?

12.   When can minors receive medical treatment without the consent of the parent or guardian? Summarize the law concerning parental consent or notification when a minor seeks an abortion.

13.   What protections are provided under the *Parham* case for minors whose parents attempt to commit them to a mental hospital?

14.   Why do physicians generally favor obtaining consent? How would the proposed Uniform Medical Consent Statute allay these concerns without requiring parental consent?

15.   What are the main concerns of child advocacy? What are two basic assumptions of advocacy?

Questions for Debate and Discussion

1.   If you were age sixteen and sold a bicycle to a twenty-four-year-old acquaintance who agreed to pay $10 per month until the $50 balance was paid, could you disaffirm the contract? Would you ever be likely to do so?

2.   If you bought a car as a minor and falsified your age, then damaged the car, could you disaffirm the contract? Why or why not?

3.   Do you find children's bills of rights to be helpful in child advocacy? Suggest additional issues that they might cover.

4.   How can children's rights and parental responsibilities be reconciled?

Selected Readings

Agostinelli, Marie. *On Wings of Love: The United Nation's Declaration on the Rights of Children.* New York: Philomel, 1981.

Asquith, Stewart. *Children and Justice.* New York: Columbia University Press, 1982

Ayers, Albert L., and John M. Rejan. *The Teenager and the Law.* West Hanover, Mass.: Christopher Publishing House, 1978.

Cohen, Howard. *Equal Rights for Children.* Totowa, N.J.: Littlefield, Adams & Co., 1980.

Gottesman, Roberta. *The Child and the Law.* St. Paul, Minn.: West Publishing Co., 1981.

Hogan, John C., and Norbert D. Schwartz. *Children's Rights.* Lexington, Mass.: Lexington Books, 1984.

Shatten, Deborah A., and Robert S. Chabon. "Decision-making and the Right to Refuse Lifesaving Treatment for Newborns." *Journal of Legal Medicine* 3 (1982): 59–79.

Squealing on Kids: HHS's Controversial New Regulation on Confidentiality and Contraception. *Children's Legal Rights Journal* 4 (1983): 8–12.

Taub, Sheila. "Treatment for Defective Newborns Law." *Law, Medicine, and Health Care* 10 (1982): 4–10.

Westman, Jack C. *Child Advocacy.* New York: Free Press, 1979.

Wringe, Colin. *Children's Rights.* London: Routledge & Kegan Paul, 1981.

Legal Problems of the Aged

More than 20 million people, or one in ten, are over age sixty-five. This proportion could rise to 25 percent by the end of the twentieth century. With an increase both in numbers and in proportion of the elderly, the legal needs of the aged will receive increased attention.

The elderly have many of the problems of other groups. If they have special financial problems, they are identified with the poor. With more health problems than younger people, they are conspicuous among the ill. They tend to lose their jobs more frequently or to be retired, so they are numbered among the unemployed. The major issue in organization of services for the aged concerns whether there should be special programs for the elderly or whether their needs should be met in programs for adults in general. For example, are the problems of the aged unique enough that they need specialized legal services? Do social welfare, guardianship, and employment problems justify creating specialized agencies or programs restricted to the aged within a larger agency framework? Because senior citizens feel they do not get their share of resources, they may demand special consideration.

The literature on aging differentiates the young-old and the old-old (over age 80). The latter group—the so-called frail elderly—is more likely to be poor and to have extensive medical needs.

This chapter will discuss federal programs for the aged and consider relevant legislation and court decisions dealing with civil rights, health, housing, and the legal needs of the elderly.

FEDERAL PROGRAMS FOR THE AGED

Many advocates of older U.S. citizens hoped that the Administration on Aging under the Department of Health and Human Services would eventually be replaced by a new cabinet-level department to serve the needs of the elderly, but such a department to represent the needs of any specific age group is unlikely.

Basic legislation for the aged is contained in the Older Americans Act of 1965. The act has ten objectives for this age-group:

1. An adequate income
2. The best possible physical and mental health
3. Suitable housing
4. Full restorative services
5. Opportunity for employment without age discrimination
6. Retirement in health, honor, and dignity

7.　Pursuit of meaningful activity

8.　Efficient community services when needed

9.　Immediate benefit from proven research knowledge

10.　Freedom, independence, and the free exercise of individual initiative (Butler, 1975)

The Older Americans Comprehensive Services Amendments of 1973 established a Federal Council on the Aging composed of fifteen members appointed by the President for three-year terms with the advice and consent of the Senate. At least five members of the committee were to be older persons, and the Secretary of Health, Education, and Welfare and the Commissioner on Aging were ex officio members. The amendments were designed to increase the capacity of state and area agencies on aging to promote coordination and development of services. The Title III program gives special emphasis to geographic areas with significant concentrations of low-income and minority persons age sixty and over. Research and demonstration grants are provided by Title IV. Title VII includes a nutrition program to serve low-cost hot meals to the elderly at least five days a week. Transportation and supportive social services are also authorized.

The Administration on Aging appropriation in fiscal 1985 was a total of $700 million, covering community services, training and research, nutrition programs, multidisciplinary geriatric centers, and multipurpose service centers.

Since the political significance of older persons has become more apparent, more effective organization on behalf of social action for the aged is being achieved.

LEGAL COMMITMENT AND COMPETENCE

With the aging process often come loss of memory and other problems resulting in referral to mental health facilities. The rights to freedom and to treatment are fundamental to older people.

The aged are especially vulnerable to being railroaded into mental hospitals by family members, neighbors, and public officials. Commitment may result simply because no more appropriate facilities are available. Even though the elderly are frequently vulnerable or confused, this does not justify their confinement or institutionalization.

Many hospital admissions for the mentally ill are involuntary. How can the older person's right to refuse such care be exercised? Only a few states guarantee the legal rights of mental patients. In Texas, Idaho, and Alabama, an emergency admission to a mental institution must be accompanied by a judge's warrant ordering apprehension and custody of the patient. However, in most states the warrant may be issued on the basis of an affidavit without seeing the patient. At the very least, and regardless of one's ability to pay, the committed person should be guaranteed access to the services of a lawyer and to judicial review.

For the aged, a distinction should be made between commitment for mental illness and incompetency to manage one's business affairs. Mental illness and incompetency have very different implications, but several states equate the two concepts (Colorado, Indiana, New Hampshire, Ohio, Oklahoma, Michigan, and Washington). Involuntary patients in these states are prohibited from exercising such rights as making contracts, managing their estates, marrying, voting, and holding a driver's license. Such persons also may not sustain legal relations with others. Commitment renders their signatures worthless. Georgia, Illinois, and Texas specifically recognize that mental illness and incompetence are not synonymous.

Need for hospitalization is usually based on one's being dangerous to self or others. This does not necessarily mean that one is incompetent or unable to manage one's business affairs. Incompetency proceedings should require proper notice and representation by counsel. Issues relative to the right to treatment will be considered in Chapter 23, but the aged are of particular concern here because they are commonly assigned low priority in the allocation of scarce treatment resources and have consequently tended to receive custodial care. As an illustration, one important decision concerning patients' rights, Lake v. Cameron (364 F.2d 657 [D.C. Cir. 1966]), involved a sixty-year-old woman who was detained by the police and later committed. She was diagnosed as having chronic brain syndrome with arteriosclerosis, but she was not found to need psychiatric services, nor was total deprivation of her liberty required. Judge David Bazelon said in part:

> Deprivation of liberty solely because of dangers to the ill persons themselves should not go beyond what is necessary for their protection. The court's duty to explore alternatives in such a case as this is related also to the obligation of the state to bear the burden of exploration of possible alternatives an indigent cannot bear.

Acceptable alternatives to hospitalization might include out-patient treatment, halfway houses, foster care, day hospitals, or nursing homes. Notwithstanding the court's decision in this case, the patient was reinstitutionalized for want of any feasible alternatives for her care. The incongruous outcome of Lake demonstrates the need for adequate facilities for the elderly.

EMPLOYMENT

The Age Discrimination in Employment Act took effect in 1967, but the law applied only to those under the age of sixty and to employers of over twenty-five workers and employment agencies. The same employment benefits must be offered to employees irrespective of age.

Continuing education and retraining of the elderly are essential in order for them to remain employable. Conflicts between the needs of older workers and corporate demands for maximum productivity suggest the need to develop a more viable system of evaluating employment efficiency to remunerate elderly employees who continue to work.

Under pressure from senior citizen groups, Congress raised the retirement age from sixty-five to seventy in 1978, but few people have stayed on to take advantage of the law. Government work programs provide older workers with employment alternatives through public service jobs. Foster grandparents, the Service Corps of Retired Executives, the Peace Corps, and Vista provide a range of opportunities. While volunteer activities provide the elderly with an opportunity to remain productive in old age, most older people require income, as well as outlets for their creativity and effort.

ADEQUATE INCOME

Three public programs operate on behalf of the elderly in the United States: social insurance (Social Security), social assistance ("welfare"), and means-tested pensions for special needs (Supplemental Security Income). Through social insurance a large number of participants can pool their resources and balance their risks over extended periods of time. Social assistance refers to the availability of benefits to persons who can prove need. Pensions under SSI are an unconditional minimum-income guarantee for individuals who reach a specified age.

The Social Security Act of 1935 was designed to provide a social-insurance program aimed at partially replacing job income lost through retirement, disability, or death. The United States was one of the last industrial nations to establish such a contributory earnings-related system. Social Security initially began as a trust fund made up exclusively by equal "contributions"—from workers and their employers.

Technically, old age and survivors' benefits under Social Security are not insurance. Payments into the system are not returned to the credit of each individual beneficiary; instead, current payments are used to meet current benefits due those who are already retired or disabled. Benefits on this pay-as-you-go basis make deductions a payroll tax rather than insurance.

The Social Security system continues to represent the main source of pension income for most retired workers. In 1980, only 22 percent of retired workers received private pension benefits, accounting for 7 percent of their total income.

Many low-income families pay considerably more for Social Security taxes than for personal income taxes. The same rate is levied on all employment income up to a given ceiling, without any modification for people in poverty. Accounting for 4 percent of federal revenues in 1949 and 33 percent in 1982, these taxes have grown faster than any others.

The Social Security system imposes an unfair penalty on those who work for wages beyond the age at which they would be eligible for benefits. In 1984, people under age seventy who earned over $6,960 a year were penalized; for those under 65, the exempt amount was $5,160. However, no reduction in benefits is incurred by those who receive income from stocks and bonds or from insurance annuities or rents.

Widows and widowers may be discouraged from getting married because the Social Security benefits paid to married couples are less than the sum total of their benefits as single persons. Older couples are consequently encouraged to follow the pattern of an increasing number of young people and just live together without marriage.

In order to provide beneficiaries protection against inflation, an escalator clause went into effect in 1975. Social Security benefit levels are reviewed each year and adjusted to reflect increases in prices or wage rates. Consequently, increases will always lag behind the true cost-of-living level.

Notwithstanding the intent of the escalator clause, it is applicable solely to changes in the cost-of-living index and in no way reflects fluctuation in the gross national product. As a result, older Americans are excluded from participation in the nation's growth and improved standard of living.

The 1983 Social Security Amendments were designed mainly to increase revenues or reduce expenditures for the OASDI. They included:

1. More federal employees required to participate in the system

2. Coverage of employees of nonprofit organizations and refusal to permit state, local, and nonprofit groups to terminate coverage

3. Cost-of-living adjustments on an annual rather than a six-month's basis

4. Inclusion of up to 50 percent of Social Security benefits in the taxable income of higher-income beneficiaries

5. Revision upward in Social Security tax rates including the self-employed

6. Gradual increase of the age of eligibility for full benefits to age 66 in 2009 and to age 67 in 2027.

HEALTH-CARE PROVISIONS   The majority of the elderly are unable to afford proper medical care. Health personnel are rarely trained to deal with older people, doctors are frequently inaccessible, and the elderly have been allocated low status as patients. Yet a person over age sixty-five spends three times as much for health care as one under sixty-five. The health needs of the elderly are many, ranging from such daily problems as chronic complaints and multiple ailments to the leading causes of death among the elderly—heart disease, cancer, strokes, and accidents. Many major problems faced by the elderly arise from a failure to treat reversible brain syndromes caused by such factors as malnutrition and anemia, congestive heart failure, infection, drugs, head trauma, alcohol, cerebrovascular accidents, dehydration, and reaction to surgery. Older people often have serious problems in obtaining transportation to hospital services and are frequently given large doses of drugs as a means of pacification.

Medicare and Medicaid are the major health programs included under the Social Security Act. Medicare is of special interest here because it applies only to the aged. Both programs are discussed in detail in Chapter 23.

Butler (1975: 220–222) suggested sixteen specific improvements in the Medicare system which still have not been implemented.

1. Part B of the Medicare system—covering outpatient doctor's costs—should be automatic; and the monthly premium and the 20 percent co-insurance feature should be eliminated. Part B should be brought under Social Security through use of general-revenue funds.

2. There should be an end to the deductibles in Medicare which in fact deduct only from the care of the patient.

3. There should be expanded coverage for drugs and prosthetics, so that those prescribed on an outpatient basis are included. Dentures, eyeglasses, hearing aids, and foot care should be covered.

4. Medicare should be extended to cover all diagnostic and treatment services, both inside and outside the hospital. This would greatly reduce the incentive for unnecessary hospitalization, which has proved to be so expensive under existing law. It would also encourage preventive-care practices by financing periodic check-ups and multiphasic screening examinations.

5. Nearly 5 million people have no telephone or other communicative contact with the outside world. For many, a telephone to summon medical aid is a necessity. On the doctor's prescription, the cost of a telephone should be an added Medicare benefit. A telephone can be both a more effective and a less expensive instrument to allay anxiety than a tranquilizer. We cannot underestimate the disruptive effects of loneliness and anxiety on the physical and mental health of the isolated person.

6. There should be a realistic broadening of coverage of the "home health visit" to many additional forms of home care, as a means of reducing institutionalization. Thus escort, homemaker, and housekeeper services and other types of personal care would be covered.

7. At present, Medicare coverage for psychiatric disorders is unrealistically lim-

ited. These limitations must be brought into line with those respecting physical illness.

8. Social services should be covered.

9. Medicare should pay for blood transfusions. Medicare requires that the beneficiary pay for the cost of the first three pints of blood or provide replacement. Older people do not have the money and all too frequently have no friends or family to call on for replacement.

10. Medicare should operate wherever the beneficiary is living or traveling. Although travel is highly touted as one of the rewards of retirement, Medicare does not fully cover service outside the United States or its territories.

11. Medicare should cover advisory collateral visits to the doctor by family members, when indicated, to offer a medical history and to aid in the treatment and care of the patient.

12. Dental care should be provided.

13. Expansion of coverage for rehabilitation, from physical medicine to occupational and activities therapy, is essential.

14. Perhaps food should be a legislated Medicare prescription—until we have assured adequate income for all so that the elderly are no longer poorly nourished owing to lack of funds.

15. A fixed percentage of Social Security and Medicare trust funds should be used in research and development studies that would improve income security and health delivery for the elderly. The National Institutes of Health should also be providing leadership and direction to programs designed to improve the health of the older people of the United States. Basic and clinical research and training in the causes, diagnosis, prevention, and cure of diseases of old age are needed.

16. Physicians should have special training in geriatric medicine to be eligible for Medicare reimbursement.

MENTAL HEALTH PROVISIONS

Two program strategies have been used in providing for the daily needs of the elderly: referral to community mental health centers and transfer from mental hospitals to nursing homes. The use of drugs has made it possible for many older people to remain outside the mental hospital.

Community mental health centers serve the aged in significant numbers. Less than one-fifth of the centers maintain special geriatric programs, and persons over age sixty-five constitute less than 5 percent of their caseloads. Financial inducements serve as strong motivators in encouraging the transfer of elderly patients from mental hospitals to other facilities.

More of the institutionalized aged now live in commercial nursing homes. Nursing home scandals are well known. Comprehensive federal standards for nursing homes were established in 1974. Federal responsibility for nursing homes is divided among a half-dozen agencies. Confusion can result from such widely shared responsibility:

> In the House of Representatives the Committee on Ways and Means has jurisdiction over the Medicare and Medicaid programs. The Committee on Interstate and Foreign Commerce is concerned with health facilities, planning and funding for construction. The Banking and Currency Committee deals with the sections of the National Housing

Act which provide mortgage insurance for various types of nursing homes and other facilities for the care of the aged. The Committee on Veterans Affairs is interested in providing nursing-home care for veterans in private nursing homes. The Committee on Government Operations is concerned with the quality of administration of nursing-home programs and the effectiveness of federal and state government relationships in carrying out such programs.

At the executive-administrative level, too, there is not only the participation of the Department of Housing and Urban Development, and of Health [and Human Services] but the Small Business Administration, which has its own criteria for making loans for nursing-home construction.

Moreover, the government has divided its responsibilities in nursing homes between housing and health. The Department of Housing and Urban Development provides monies through the Federal Housing Administration to build health facilities—for instance, insuring 90 percent mortgages. The Department of Health [and Human Services] provides the Medicare and Medicaid funds. This division leads to confusion in standards. (Butler 1975: 288–289)

Another major question concerns the right to treatment. The number of patients to be served and the low priority of elderly patients as the medical profession sees it make it unlikely that older people will receive their proportionate share of treatment services in either inpatient or outpatient facilities.

HOUSING

A traumatic aspect of aging centers around the sale of the family dwelling. Although some people sell their homes on completion of child-rearing, for many others a forced change in housing comes at retirement. High real estate taxes that cannot be met without a full income frequently prompt such a move. Some states make concessions to home owners in the form of homestead exemptions that usually cover a small portion of the current assessed valuation.

Proposals have been made to help older people retain their homes through a combination home sale and annuity plan whereby the older person would retain a life interest in his or her home and receive the proceeds gradually throughout retirement years. A government corporation could help administer such a program.

Elderly people have been denied mortgages because of a common requirement that the age of a borrower plus the term of the mortgage total less than eighty years. The Department of Housing and Urban Development (HUD) has provided funds to guarantee direct mortgage loans to build housing for the elderly. Some state welfare laws have required that people in need of old-age assistance sign over their homes to the state with a provision for final title transference on their death. This has been a deterrent to older people in applying for assistance.

The older person in search of rental housing faces even more problems than the home owner. Given their limited income, the elderly are more likely to obtain substandard housing. Federal housing programs have been disappointing. Even if the 120,000 units per year proposed by the Senate Special Committee on Aging were built, more than twenty years would be required to replace inadequate units.

Housing for the elderly must take into account the need for nursing services, congregate meal facilities, and housing designs that eliminate architectural barriers for those confined to wheelchairs. Some students of aging call particular attention to the housing problems of the rural poor, which are accentuated by the movement of farmers from the land. Mobile homes have been particularly appealing to the elderly, but problems created by poor construction and rapid depreciation may outweigh their advantages. New federal standards for mobile homes will help this situation.

Although nearly 40 percent of public housing has been designated for the elderly, only about 20 percent of existing units are occupied by older people. Problems are created by the current requirement that new public housing projects must cover 85 percent of their operating costs from rents. This excludes the poorest families, who need a greater rent subsidy. The public housing situation is especially perplexing because projects occupied by the elderly have the fewest problems, but there is inadequate interest in the needed expansion of units.

REMARRIAGE

Older married couples are now more likely to remarry or live together, whether they are widowed or divorced. Two special legal problems evolve: (1) for the widow or widower, the use of prenuptial contracts to assure compliance with the wishes of a remarried person who wishes to bequeath material assets to the first family; and (2) in the case of divorce, adequate financial provisions for the former wife. Whether the older couple merely lives together or marries often depends on the effect marriage will have on their pension benefits. The inequity of the situation would be eliminated by allowing older people to figure their pension benefits in two ways, on both a single and a married basis, and to opt for the higher of the two totals.

Prenuptial contracts have frequently been invalidated because they encourage divorce, inasmuch as they provide the plan for property settlement if the marriage is terminated. On prenuptial contracts, Foster (1975: 465) comments:

> Older people contemplating marriage may have especially compelling needs to fix the economic character of their relationship by an antenuptial contract. The prospective spouses often have children as well as grandchildren by a prior marriage, and it is understandable that they would desire to allocate their wealth to their first family. Generally, protection of the first family's expectancy against the claims of a second spouse works no serious inequity. In all probability, each spouse's assets antedated their relationship, and there is no economic reason to force upon either spouse an interest in the property of the other merely because they are married. Moreover, older marriages do not involve the career building partnership and division of labor which ordinarily occur in the case of young couples and thus their marriage is not centered on economic considerations.

Foster stresses the need to recognize the economic requirements wrought by divorce on the elderly wife, who is frequently incapable of employment and self-support. The age, work history, and health of the wife must be considered in awarding alimony. Foster recommends that, in addition to alimony, the wife be made irrevocable beneficiary of a life insurance policy on the husband's death. Automatic, no-fault divorces, which are increasingly common, may inadequately provide for the needs of an elderly wife.

LEGAL SERVICES

The elderly need legal help in managing their business affairs and in obtaining their entitlements from such sources as Medicare and Medicaid. They are frequently targets for fraud in purchase of dancing lessons, travel cruises, or hearing aids or in obtaining companions to overcome loneliness.

In settlement of their estates, older people may be better served by a public guardian or conservator than by family members. Probate procedures should be reformed to provide for quick and fair estate settlements. The elderly require legal defense against age discrimination. Class action suits may be the most effective weapons against such discrimination.

Unfortunately, some legal services have allocated their resources almost exclusively to problems of younger families and neglected concerns of the elderly. In view of the recent nursing home scandals, quality of institutional care should have the highest priority legal action.

THE RIGHT TO DIE

Until In the Matter of Quinlan, 355 A.2d 647 (N.J. 1976), authorized withdrawing life supports, the right to die received little attention. The question is particularly important for the aged, who are likely to face painful and perhaps incurable illnesses and general loss of functioning. Questions are raised about life supports in a medical setting as well as the individual's control over this decision under other circumstances.

California was the first state to pass a "Natural Death Act," which took effect at the start of 1977 (1976 Statutes, Ch. 1439). The legislature affirmed the adult's fundamental right to control decisions relating to the rendering of his or her own medical care, including having life-sustaining procedures withheld or withdrawn for a terminal condition because "modern medical technology has made possible the prolongation of life beyond natural limits." The act recognizes the right of an adult to make a written directive to the physician (Exhibit 16.1) to withhold or withdraw life-sustaining procedures in such conditions. The directive is effective for five years unless it is revoked earlier by the declarant.

The law provides that such a withholding or withdrawal of life-sustaining procedures does not constitute a suicide or impair or invalidate life insurance. The making of such a directive is not to restrict, inhibit, or impair the sale, procurement, or issuance of life insurance or modify existing life insurance. Health insurance carriers cannot require execution of a directive as a condition for being insured for, or receiving, health care services. The directive is to be signed in the presence of two witnesses. The form is provided in the statute:

EXHIBIT 16.1
CALIFORNIA STATUTE'S DIRECTIVE TO PHYSICIANS CONCERNING LIFE-SUSTAINING PROCEDURES

DIRECTIVE TO PHYSICIANS

Directive made this ———— day of ———— (month, year).

I ————, being of sound mind, willfully, and voluntarily make known my desire that my life shall not be artificially prolonged under the circumstances set forth below, do hereby declare:

1. If at any time I should have an incurable injury, disease, or illness certified to be a terminal condition by two physicians, and where the application of life-sustaining procedures would serve only to artificially prolong the moment of my death and where my physician determines that my death is imminent whether or not life-sustaining procedures are utilized, I direct that such procedures be withheld or withdrawn, and that I be permitted to die naturally.

2. In the absence of my ability to give directions regarding the use of such life-sustaining procedures, it is my intention that this directive shall be honored by my family and physician(s) as the final expression of my legal right to refuse medical or surgical treatment and accept the consequences from such refusal.

3. If I have been diagnosed as pregnant and that diagnosis is known to my physician, this directive shall have no force or effect during the course of my pregnancy.

4. I have been diagnosed and notified at least 14 days ago as having a terminal condition by _____, M.D., whose address is _____, and whose telephone number is _____. I understand that if I have not filled in the physician's name and address, it shall be presumed that I did not have a terminal condition when I made out this directive.

5. This directive shall have no force or effect five years from the date filled in above.

6. I understand the full import of this directive and I am emotionally and mentally competent to make this directive.

Signed _____

City, County and State of Residence _____
The declarant has been personally known to me and I believe him or her to be of sound mind.
Witness _____
Witness _____

Similar legislation has been enacted in half the states, and many people have signed "living wills" that make such a declaration, even though it cannot be enforced without statutory authorization. A declaration would not have been helpful in the *Quinlan* instance, since the patient could not execute the document.

Delgado (1975) believes that decisions concerning death deserve constitutional protection by virtue of the right of privacy:

> In recent years, successive holdings by the Supreme Court of the United States have drawn a protective mantle of privacy about certain decisions that fundamentally affect the human life cycle. This cycle may be viewed as a kind of trajectory, whose peak between birth and death represents the capacity for productivity and independent action. The Court has included many of the choices that determine the shape of that trajectory within the right of privacy. Thus, it has been held that decisions regarding marriage, contraception, procreation, and the raising and educating of children are protected. One critical choice that has, so far, escaped inclusion in the list of protected decisions is the choice of the terminus of that trajectory—the moment and manner of one's death. Today, suicide is treated as a crime in only a small minority of American jurisdictions. Still, aiding and abetting suicide is often punished as a felony, and affirmative acts, even the acts of a physician in response to the requests of a competent, terminally ill patient, designed to hasten the arrival of death, constitute the crime of first-degree murder. The Supreme Court has yet to review a case involving euthanasia or mercy killing. . . .
>
> Those for whom life continues to hold the promises of family, friends, and self-worth cherish existence as an ultimate value. For others, terminal disease may guarantee only an agonizing wait for death. Most of us fall into the former category, never, until our own final moments, appreciating death's haven. Our insensitivity to the needs of the dying, our bias toward the maintenance of life at all costs, permits legislatures to turn a deaf ear to the pleas of the dying for final relief. So long as this is so, courts will need to exercise their traditional function of interceding on behalf of politically impotent minorities. In carrying out this function, the right of privacy enunciated in recent Supreme Court opinions offers itself as a ready instrument for safeguarding the integrity of individual choice. (P. 474)

The 1980s have seen increased interest in authorization to withdraw life supports. Many hospitals have review committees, and the state of New York appointed a panel to review the issue in 1985.

SOCIAL WORK ROLES Work with the aged and medical social work are two of the most rapidly growing fields for social workers. So far, programs for the aged have stressed helping persons who are ill, poor, and without families. The need will increase to assist the aged who function better but who still wish to enhance their own situations. Social workers can do much to add life to the years through counseling, activity programs, and other supportive services. Counseling that stresses the acceptability of marrying again and of sex in old age can enhance enjoyment and overcome loneliness. Meanwhile, adequate incomes and basic civil rights for the aged require sustained attention. Finally, in the years ahead decisions relating to death may be as controversial and perplexing as the development of policies toward abortion.

Questions for Review

1. Which objectives of the Older Americans Act are most difficult to achieve? Which are closest to realization?

2. What is the difference between legal commitment and incompetency proceedings? Why is it undesirable that one action always imply the other?

3. What was the major finding in *Lake v. Cameron?*

4. What federal legislation covers age discrimination for persons over age sixty-five?

5. What is the difference in the position under Social Security of the fully retired person who has income from stocks and bonds and the sixty-seven-year-old who still earns $20,000 annually?

6. Why are Social Security provisions a deterrent to marriage for people over age sixty-five?

7. What feature in Social Security has been added to deal with changes in the cost of living?

8. Why do many people give up the family dwelling at retirement?

9. What must be considered in designing housing for the elderly?

10. What kinds of ventures often involve defrauding older people?

Questions for Debate and Discussion

1. Why are Social Security old age and survivors' benefits correctly considered a payroll tax rather than insurance?

2. Given the financial crisis in Social Security, what changes in old age benefits would you propose?

3. What is the appropriate role of the federal government in improving nursing home services?

4. Should senior citizens have specialized legal service agencies?

5. Why have so few people chosen to continue to work until age seventy?

6. What safeguards are needed for incompetent older people concerning family members serving as guardians?

Selected Readings   Brown, Robert. *The Rights of Older Persons.* New York: Avon Books, 1979.

"Developments in Senior Citizens Law." *Clearinghouse Review* 16 (1983): 769–775.

Hasko, John, Alan Holoch, and Nancy Long. "Gerontology and the Law: A Selected Bibliography." *Southern California Law Review* 56 (1982): 289–459.

Levin, Jack, and William Levin. *Agism: Prejudice and Discrimination Against the Elderly.* Belmont, Calif.: Wadsworth, 1980.

Lockett, Betty A. *Aging, Politics and Research: Setting the Federal Agenda for Research on Aging.* New York: Springer Publishing Co., 1983.

Parker, Rosetta E. *Housing for the Elderly: The Handbook for Managers.* Chicago: Institute of Real Estate, 1984.

Pollak, Otto, and Nancy L. Kelley. *The Challenges of Aging.* Croton-on-Hudson, N.Y.: North River Press, 1982.

Rones, Philip L. "The Labor Market Problems of Older Workers." *Monthly Labor Review* 106 (1983): 3.

Rose, Edgar A. *Housing Needs and the Elderly.* Brookfield, Vt.: Gower Pub., 1982.

Wershaw, Harold J. *Controversial Issues in Gerontology.* New York: Springer Publishing Co., 1981.

Weshard, William R. *Rights of the Elderly and Retired: A People's Handbook.* San Francisco, Calif.: Craguant Publishers, 1979.

Williamson, John B., et al. *The Politics of Aging: Power and Policy.* Springfield, Ill.: Thomas, 1982.

PART

IV

Major Social Problems

CHAPTER

17

Racism

ORIGINS AND REMEDIES OF INSTITUTIONAL RACISM

Institutional racism is the product of laws, policies, and practices of organizations—not the attitudes of individuals. Individual attitudes may reflect prejudice, but discriminatory practices of official bodies have a far greater effect on human rights.

This chapter will review selected racist laws in U.S. history and recent remedies for those laws. Discrimination against groups composed of persons of color will be reviewed. The movement for voting rights for blacks provides an extended example of efforts to end racism through law. Social work roles in eliminating racism will also be considered.

Slavery is the most blatant example of institutional racism in the United States. A major historical review of the rights of black persons under the U.S. Constitution occurred in Dred Scott v. Sanford, 60 U.S. 393 (1857). Because slaves were not citizens, the opinion held that losing the property rights to slaves whom they brought to a free jurisdiction violated the Fifth Amendment due process rights of slave holders.

Northern states began abolishing slavery as early as 1777, and Lincoln issued the Emancipation Proclamation freeing slaves in Confederate territory in 1863, but until after the Civil War, northern whites were apt to maintain a distinction between granting blacks legal protection—the right to life, liberty, and property—and granting them political and social equality (Litwak, 1961:15).

In the Proclamation, Lincoln stated that emancipation was "a practical war measure to be decided upon according to the advantages or disadvantages it may offer to the suppression of the rebellion." And in a speech in 1858, he stated:

> I will say, then, that I am not, nor ever have been, in favor of bringing about in any way the social and political equality of the White and black races; that I am not, nor ever have been, in favor of making voters or jurors of Negroes, nor of qualifying them to hold office, nor to inter-marry with White people. . . .
>
> And inasmuch as they cannot so live, while they do remain together there must be the position of superior and inferior, and I as much as any other man am in favor of having the superior position assigned to the White race. (Hofstadter, 1948:116)

The impact of *Dred Scott* was nullified by ratification of the Thirteenth Amendment to the U.S. Constitution (1865), abolishing slavery, and the Fourteenth Amendment (1868), making blacks citizens and protecting their rights from abridgment by the states. The Fifteenth Amendment (1870) guaranteed blacks the right to vote. However, social acceptance of blacks and exercise of their political rights did not follow, and the opinion voiced by Lincoln persisted in laws throughout the ensuing century.

DISCRIMINATION AGAINST NATIVE AMERICANS

Dred Scott summarized laws concerning Native Americans (or American Indians) in distinguishing their situation from that of blacks:

> The situation of . . . [blacks] was altogether unlike that of the Indian race. The latter, it is true, formed no part of the colonial communities, and never amalgamated with them in social connections or in government. But although they were uncivilized, they were yet a free and independent people, associated together in nations or tribes, and governed by their own laws. . . . Indian Governments were regarded and treated as foreign Governments, as much so as if an ocean had separated the red man from the white; and their freedom has constantly been acknowledged, from the time of the first emigration to the English colonies to the present day, by the different Governments which succeeded each other. Treaties have been negotiated with them, and their alliance sought for in war; and the people who compose these Indian political communities have always been treated as foreigners not living under our Government. . . . [T]hey may, without doubt, like the subjects of any other foreign Government, be naturalized by the authority of Congress, and become citizens of a State, and of the United States; and if an individual should leave his nation or tribe, and take up his abode among the white population, he would be entitled to all the rights and privileges which would belong to an emigrant from any other foreign people. (60 U.S. at 403, 404)

In 1831, the U.S. Supreme Court held that "American Indians' relation to the United States resembles that of a ward to his guardian" (Cherokee Nation v. State of Georgia, 30 U.S. [5 Pet.] 1). It has been suggested by one author ("Red, White, and Grey," 1969:1236) that American Indian law came out of the movement of white settlers westward onto Indian lands. First it was based on the "separative premise"—Indians were merely moved to other territory. Later, when there was a scarcity of land, the law was based on the "assimilative premise"—the Indians were brought into the white man's private-property system, where they could lose their property through devices such as inflated tax appraisals and long-term leases that returned minimal rents.

Citizenship was not granted to all Indians in the United States until the Indian Citizenship Act of 1924, 43 Stat. 253. The situation today is a compromise between assimilation and separation. Indians now have, at least in theory, the choice of how they will be related to the rest of American society. There are attempts to improve the status of reservation Native Americans and to help in the transition process for those who choose to join the mainstream of American society. Indian groups have also been moving toward greater participation in the national political process. They have advanced claims for land and for mineral rights.

Attempts by several Western tribes to control such assets on their land were dealt a blow by a U.S. Supreme Court decision Northern Cheyenne Tribe v. Hollowbreast, 425 U.S. 649 (1976).

According to the decision, the Northern Cheyenne Allotment Act of 1926

> did not give the allotees of surface lands vested rights in the mineral deposits underlying those lands. This reading of the Act is supported by its legislative history, which indicates a congressional intent to sever the surface estate from the interest in the mineral deposits and thereby relinquish "control and management thereof" as Congress

may deem expedient for the benefit of said Indians. Such conclusion is also supported by the fact that the agency charged with executing the Act construed it as not granting the allotees any vested rights.

The Supreme Court upheld the principle of tribal sovereignty in Bryan v. Itasca, 426 U.S. 373 (1976).

Over half of all Native Americans live outside reservations in urban ghettos in Los Angeles, Chicago, and other cities, forced to move there by a relocation program started in the 1950s or choosing to leave problems on the reservation behind. However, in the cities, language poses a problem, as do alcoholism and suicide. Their rates, high enough on reservations, increase in the cities. Poverty and unemployment are also prevalent. Disagreements between tribes have prevented organization of a successful political coalition. The current status of Native Americans is an example of the effects of institutional racism.

DISCRIMINA- TION AGAINST ASIANS AND PACIFIC ISLANDERS

The Chinese who had immigrated to California were targets of discrimination when the California Supreme Court held in 1854 that persons of color could not give evidence in court concerning a white person (People v. Hall, 4 Cal. 399). From the Chinese Exclusion Act of 1882 until 1965, Asians were subjected to racist immigration laws aimed at restricting their entry into the United States. The Supreme Court determined in United States v. Wong Kim Ark, 169 U.S. 649 (1898), that Chinese persons born in the United States are citizens whether their parents are aliens or not, and Congress granted the right of naturalization to the Chinese in 1943 (57 Stat. 660).

Japanese immigrants were to be prevented from earning a living in agriculture by the alien land laws enacted in 1913 by California, followed by other states. In 1924 the Quota Act (43 Stat. 153) excluded "aliens ineligible to citizenship," also aimed at the Japanese. Soon after the start of World War II, pressure groups, many of them representing western agricultural interests, advocated evacuation of the Japanese. In 1942, President Roosevelt issued executive orders providing for curfew, evacuations, and internment of persons of Japanese ancestry. The Supreme Court upheld the constitutionality of the curfew (Kiyoshi Hirabayashi v. United States, 320 U.S. 81 [1943]) and evacuation (Toyosaburo Korematsu v. United States, 323 U.S. 214 [1944]) and released an interned Japanese on narrow grounds while expressly failing to reach a decision on the constitutionality of internment (Ex parte Mitsuye Endo, 323 U.S. 283 [1944]).

The Japanese lost much of their property while interned, and both California and Oregon attempted to confiscate their property for alleged violation of alien land laws. Since aliens were not to own land, the property should revert to the state for want of an individual competent to inherit, and the common law procedure of escheat. The U.S. Supreme Court held that escheat was unconstitutional because it denied equal protection to the citizen son in whose name the alien father had placed the property (Oyama v. State of California, 332 U.S. 633 [1948]).

In 1948 the Supreme Court held that California could not bar first-generation Japanese immigrants from obtaining commercial fishing licenses because they were "aliens ineligible to citizenship" (Torao Takahashi v. Fish and Game Commission, 334 U.S. 410) as this would violate the equal protection clause of the Fourteenth Amendment. In 1952, Japanese aliens gained the right to citizenship through the Walter-McCarren Act (66 Stat. 163).

Asian Americans from Korea, Burma, Indonesia, Samoa, South Vietnam, and other nations in East Asia were also subjected to immigration laws and quotas. A reversal in post–World War II immigration policy led to acceptance of a large number of Orientals.

DISCRIMINA-TION AGAINST CHICANOS AND HISPANICS

The origins of contemporary racial discrimination against people of Mexican descent may be traced to the invasion and usurpation of Mexican territory by the United States, ratified by both governments in the Treaty of Guadalupe Hidalgo of 1848. The treaty assured the Mexican people who lived in the conquered regions (present-day Arizona, California, Colorado, Nevada, New Mexico, Texas, and Utah) the right of U.S. citizenship and respect for their language and cultural, religious, and property rights. Notwithstanding the promises contained therein, the treaty was soon amended and partially revoked. Lands were confiscated and full civil rights withheld. Present-day advocates of rights for the Spanish-speaking consider the broken treaty to constitute a legal agreement that the U.S. government should be required to uphold. As in the case of the Native American, they would demand retribution in the form of a return of confiscated lands. Many allude to the broken treaty as the major source of continued discrimination and the accordance of near alien status to native-born U.S. citizens of Mexican descent.

In response to government violation of the treaty, the Mexican people opted for an outwardly passive attitude toward white domination. While contributing greatly to industrial and agricultural interests, they have traditionally been denied such rights as the freedom to strike, form unions, and receive Social Security and workmen's compensation. In the 1920s, Mexican-Americans were recruited to the North to work as farm laborers and factory workers. In the South, they constituted the mainstay of the silver, zinc, and copper mining industries and served everywhere as farmhands. Their numbers steadily increased until the Depression years, when thousands were encouraged by the government to deport to Mexico in an effort to reduce the welfare roles. Those who remained in the United States were frequently denied even the most menial employment during these years.

World War II marked a new beginning for Mexican Americans. Service in the armed forces allowed many to learn English and later afforded them the right to receive benefits under the G.I. Bill. The first major Spanish-speaking organization developed in Chicago after the war and was followed by many others aimed at enhancing the Mexican-American's rights to equal education, housing, employment opportunities, and so on. Employment opportunities that had flourished during the war, however, tapered off shortly afterward.

Unemployment, which had always been particularly acute along the U.S. border, was aggravated by governmental policy authorized in 1951—the Mexican Agricultural Workers Importation Act, 65 Stat. 119, whereby Mexican aliens were actively recruited to cross and recross the border daily to take jobs with substandard pay while maintaining residence in Mexico. Although this "Bracero Program" was denounced as detrimental to the employment situation among native-born Mexican-Americans, it was not rescinded until 1964. Partly in response to the government's attitude toward exploitation of cheap Mexican labor, industry followed suit and engaged in such tactics as the "commuter factory," whereby equipment parts were manufactured in the United States, shipped to Mexico for assembly or finishing, and returned to the United States for sale.

On termination of the Bracero Program, growers reverted to other means to recruit cheap Mexican labor. Illegal aliens and aliens with work permits were commonly employed, and would later be used as strike breakers in the 1960s. The Mexicans continued to cooperate with the growers, but they lost the few rights to which they had previously been entitled. While immigration laws require that green-card holders will not adversely affect the wages and working conditions of similarly employed workers in the United States, there are no controls once the green card has been issued.

These policies also resulted in considerable animosity between the Mexican-American and Mexican immigrant or illegal alien, which constitutes a major stumbling block to present-day attempts at unification. Mexicans may still be imported temporarily to meet agricultural needs while being denied the right to remain or become citizens. Immigration laws are strongly enforced in light of a recent concern that Mexican aliens who entered the United States illegally are contributing to the U.S. unemployment rate.

Hispanics—the name given to people from Spanish-speaking backgrounds by the Census Bureau and other agencies—are a fast-growing population in the United States. At the present rate of increase, Latinos (the term most often used by the people themselves) are likely to become the largest racial minority group in the nation. The increase is due both to a high birth rate and to emigration from Mexico and Central and South American countries.

How much of this immigration is illegal? Economic factors such as a 100 percent inflation rate annually in Mexico since 1982 and a high unemployment rate have pressed people from Mexico to cross the border into the United States to look for work. Political unrest and war in a number of Central and South American nations have led people to flee to the United States. Since efforts by the border patrol to prevent illegal immigration along the 2,000-mile southern border have not been successful, a large increase in the budget of the Immigration and Naturalization Service has been proposed. Over half the money would be used to hire additional border patrol agents.

The search for illegal aliens once they have entered the United States has also been intensified. Four cases decided by the U.S. Supreme Court considered the scope of such searches. In 1973 the Court said that the government may not stop cars randomly in order to look for undocumented workers (Almeida-Sanchez v. United States, 413 U.S. 266 [1973]), but in 1975 the Court held that cars may be stopped for less than probable cause if there is a reasonable suspicion that illegal immigrants are inside (United States v. Brignoni-Ponce, 422 U.S. 873).

The Court also held that fixed immigration checkpoints near the border were permissible (United States v. Martinez-Fuerte, 428 U.S. 543, 551–552 [1976]). In the fourth case, in 1984, the Court took up the question of whether searches of factories by Immigrations officials were constitutional (Immigration and Naturalization Service v. Delgado 104 S.Ct. 1758 [1984]). It affirmed the right of the Immigration and Naturalization Service to conduct factory "surveys" of the work force in search of illegal aliens. Interrogation relating to one's identity or a request for identification was not held to violate Fourth Amendment rights. Such questioning does not result in a detention. If mere questioning did not constitute seizure inside the factory, it was no more a seizure when it occurred at the exits. Successful litigation would have required seizure or detention. Justices William Brennan and Thurgood Marshall dissented, commenting that "only through a considerable feat of legerdemain could the individual questioning not be regarded as a seizure."

**Proposed
Legislation** There have been many attempts to amend immigration law through legislation. Since 1980, the Simpson-Mazzoli bill, which provides a comprehensive attempt at immigration reform, has been considered by Congress. Different versions of the bill were passed by the House of Representatives and the Senate in 1984, but the bill died because a conference committee could not agree on a final draft. The bill would have reduced the number of legal immigrants permitted to enter the United States annually. It would have limited judicial review of immigration decisions, and authorized civil and criminal penalties for employers who knowingly hire undocumented workers. The bill proposed to expand the program of temporary foreign labor, primarily migrant farm workers, but subjected it to greater regulation. It provided a general amnesty to illegal aliens who had lived in the United States for a designated number of years in hopes of eliminating a shadow population that is now forced into an underground existence.

According to the Simpson-Mazzoli bill, employers who hire illegal aliens would be asked to verify the legal status of each job applicant, perhaps by calling a toll-free number and having the federal government verify the applicant's Social Security number. The checks are intended to dispel the fear that people who look like they are Spanish-speaking would be discriminated against. However, Social Security cards or any other form of identification can be counterfeited.

Opponents pointed out that the bill would lead an employer not to hire applicants who appear to be Latino in order to be safe. A truly workable system would require a special identification card and a national computerized data bank that could violate the privacy of all people in the United States.

Legislation has been proposed by members of the Hispanic Caucus in Congress to provide for more rigorous enforcement of existing labor laws without employer sanctions, issuing identification cards, or allowing a guest worker program. The potential for racial discrimination is clear. Mexicans make up about 60 percent of the undocumented work force, but at least 90 percent of the arrests.

In the Refugee Act of 1980, 8 U.S.C. 1157–1159, those who claim a "well-founded fear of persecution" in their home country are classified as refugees. The President is to inform Congress each year of "the anticipated allocation of refugee admissions." Refugee applications are processed on a first come, first served basis. People already in the United States who claim a "well-founded fear of persecution" are classified as political asylum applicants, for which there is no numerical ceiling. According to Shapiro and Henderson (1984:171–172), the act "harmonizes American law with international standards in the refugee field for the first time and, in theory at least, both liberalizes and rationalizes America's refugee program. [This legislation] focuses on the individual rather than the country from which the individual is fleeing.

Cubans, Haitians, and Salvadorans have come to the United States for political asylum since the Refugee Act was passed. The current debate over whether the subject of refugees is a foreign policy question or a human rights issue was illustrated by the Reagan administration's detention of some of these groups for more than a year without assurance that they could apply for political asylum.

The racial aspects of immigration law will continue to be debated, for the

United States has never before been faced with such a large-scale migration of nonwhite refugees. The addition of undocumented workers coming into the nation for economic reasons adds to the pressure to amend current immigration law.

DISCRIMINA-
TION AGAINST
BLACKS

Institutional racism against blacks after the Civil War and the Thirteenth, Fourteenth, and Fifteenth Amendments to the Constitution took the form of state laws designed to separate blacks and whites with regard to access to public facilities and to prevent blacks from voting. Belief in the inferiority of blacks was still the predominant point of view throughout the nation so that withdrawal of federal troops from the South attendant to the Hayes-Tilden Compromise of 1876 was viewed as a tolerable concession to national unity, although their removal allowed the states to legislate away black civil rights.

Access to public facilities regardless of race was guaranteed by the Civil Rights Act of 1875 (180 Stat. 337), but the withdrawal of federal troops led to flagrant violations in the South. The act was declared unconstitutional in 1883 by the Supreme Court (The Civil Rights Cases, 109 U.S. 3) on the ground that the Fourteenth Amendment did not allow the redress of private wrongs by federal law. While slavery was outlawed, racial discrimination in access to public facilities was left to the individual states. This ruling led to an increase in segregation statutes because the South had assurance that the federal government would not protect the civil and political rights of blacks.

The constitutionality of segregation statutes was affirmed by the Supreme Court in Plessy v. Ferguson, 163 U.S. 537 (1896). The court held:

> We cannot say that a law which authorizes or even requires the separation of the two races in public conveyances is unreasonable, or more obnoxious to the Fourteenth Amendment than the acts of Congress requiring separate schools for colored children in the District of Columbia, the constitutionality of which does not seem to have been questioned, or the corresponding acts of state legislatures. (163 U.S. at 550–551)

The Supreme Court would not return to this issue for fifty-eight years.

A similar pattern occurred in restricting the voting rights of blacks. Negro suffrage was widespread in the South immediately following the Civil War, but white political dominance was established by 1885. The states of the Old Confederacy again began programs that resulted in disfranchisement of blacks. Between 1890 and 1910, twelve states took steps to make the franchise exclusively white; the most common devices were literacy tests and poll taxes. From 1871 to 1957, however, Congress enacted no legislation to enforce the Fifteenth Amendment.

ENDING RACISM
THROUGH LAW

The 1950s would see the first challenges to legal racism preceding the sweeping civil rights legislation of the 1960s. In Brown v. Board of Education of Topeka, 347 U.S. 483 (1954), the Supreme Court held that segregation statutes for public education led to unconstitutional inequality. The difficulty of implementing *Brown* in school desegregation, as well as the general issue of racism in education, will be discussed at length in Chapter 22. The point here is that the court cited *Brown* in subsequent cases in the 1950s as authority for ending state-sponsored racial segregation of public facilities.

Privately owned public facilities with segregation or exclusionary policies were not within the scope of the court's interpretation of *Brown*. It remained for Title II of the Civil Rights Act of 1964, 42 U.S.C. §2000 (a)(b), to prohibit racial discrimination in any public facility with an "interstate flow of goods and people," as noted by the Supreme Court in establishing the constitutionality of the act in Heart of Atlanta Motel, Inc. v. United States, 379 U.S. 241 (1964).

HEART OF ATLANTA MOTEL, INC. v. UNITED STATES.

Supreme Court of the United States, 379 U.S. 241 (1964)

. . . . Justice CLARK delivered the opinion of the Court.

The appellant contends that Congress in passing this Act exceeded its power to regulate commerce under Art. I, § 8, cl. 3, of the Constitution of the United States; that the Act violates the Fifth Amendment because appellant is deprived of the right to choose its customers and operate its business as it wishes, resulting in a taking of its liberty and property without due process of law and a taking of its property without just compensation; and, finally, that by requiring appellant to rent available rooms to Negroes against its will, Congress is subjecting it to involuntary servitude in contravention of the Thirteenth Amendment. 379 U.S. at 243, 244.

The appellees counter that the unavailability to Negroes of adequate accommodations interferes significantly with interstate travel, and that Congress, under the Commerce Clause, has power to remove such obstructions and restraints; that the Fifth Amendment does not forbid reasonable regulation and that consequential damage does not constitute a "taking" within the meaning of that amendment; that the Thirteenth Amendment claim fails because it is entirely frivolous to say that an amendment directed to the abolition of human bondage and the removal of widespread disabilities associated with slavery places discrimination in public accommodations, beyond the reach of both federal and state laws. Id. at 244.

Title II of the [Civil Rights] Act [of 1964]. This Title is divided into seven sections beginning with § 201(a), which provides that:

> "All persons shall be entitled to the full and equal enjoyment of the goods, services, facilities, privileges, advantages, and accommodations of any place of public accommodation, as defined in this section, without discrimination or segregation on the ground of race, color, religion, or national origin."

There are listed in § 201(b) four classes of business establishments, each of which "serves the public" and "is a place of public accommodation" within the meaning of § 201(a) "if its operations affect commerce, or if discrimination or segregation by it is supported by State action." The covered establishments are:

> "(1) any inn, hotel, motel, or other establishment which provides lodging to transient guests, other than an establishment located within a building which contains not more than five rooms for rent or hire and which is actually occupied by the proprietor of such establishment as his residence;
> "(2) any restaurant, cafeteria . . . . [not here involved];
> "(3) any motion picture house . . . . [not here involved];
> "(4) any establishment . . . . which is physically located within the premises of any establishment otherwise covered by this subsection, or . . . . within the premises of which is physically located any such covered establishment . . . . [not here involved]."

Section 201(c) defines the phrase "affect commerce" as applied to the above establishments. If first declares that "any inn, hotel, motel, or other establishment which provides lodging to transient guests" affects commerce per se. Restaurants, cafeterias, etc., in class two affect commerce only if they serve or offer to serve interstate travelers or if a substantial portion of the food which they serve or products which they sell have "moved in commerce." Motion picture houses and other places listed in class three affect commerce if they customarily present films, performances, etc., "which move in commerce." And the establishments listed in class four affect commerce if they are within, or include within their own premises, an establishment "the operations of which affect commerce." Private clubs are excepted under certain conditions. See § 201(e).

Section 201(d) declares that "discrimination or segregation" is supported by state action when carried on under color of any law, statute, ordinance, regulation or any custom or usage required or enforced by officials of the State or any of its subdivisions.

In addition, § 202 affirmatively declares that all persons "shall be entitled to be free, at any establishment or place, from discrimination or segregation of any kind on the ground of race, color, religion, or national origin, if such discrimination or segregation is or purports to be required by any law, statute, ordinance, regulation, rule, or order of a State or any agency or political subdivision thereof."

Application of Title II to Heart of Atlanta Motel. It is admitted that the operation of the motel brings it within the provisions of § 201(a) of the Act and that appellant refused to provide lodging for transient Negroes because of their race or color and that it intends to continue that policy unless restrained.

The sole question posed is, therefore, the constitutionality of the Civil Rights Act of 1964 as applied to these facts. . . .

The Civil Rights Cases, 109 U.S. 3, 3 S.Ct. 18 (1883), and Their Application. In light of our ground for decision, it might be well at the outset to discuss the Civil Rights Cases, supra, which declared provisions of the Civil Rights Act of 1875 unconstitutional. 18 Stat. 335, 336. We think that decision inapposite, and without precedential value in determining the constitutionality of the present Act. Unlike Title II of the present legislation, the 1875 Act broadly proscribed discrimination in "inns, public conveyances on land or water, theatres, and other places of public amusement," without limiting the categories having a direct and substantial relation to the interstate flow of goods and people, except where state action is involved. Further, the fact that certain kinds of business may not in 1875 have been sufficiently involved in interstate commerce to warrant bringing them within the ambit of the commerce power is not necessarily dispositive of the same question today. Our populace had not reached its present mobility, nor were facilities, goods and services circulating as readily in interstate commerce as they are today. . . . [V]oluminous testimony presents overwhelming evidence that discrimination by hotels and motels impedes interstate travel. Id. at 250, 251, 253. . . .

We, therefore, conclude that the action of the Congress in the adoption of the Act as applied here to a motel which concededly serves interstate travelers is within the power granted it by the Commerce Clause of the Constitution, as interpreted by this Court for 140 years. Id. at 261.

In Evans v. Abney, 396 U.S. 435 (1970), the Supreme Court ruled that the closing of a public park and reversion to testators of the property that had been willed to a city expressly for whites only was constitutional because of lower court decisions "eliminating the park itself, and the termination of the park was a loss shared equally by the white and negro citizens of Macon." Similarly, Jackson, Mississippi, was permitted to close public swimming pools rather than desegregate them (Palmer v. Thompson, 403 U.S. 217 [1971]). The court held that closing the pools to avoid desegregation did not deny blacks equal protection of the law.

Private clubs are excluded from coverage under Title IX of the Civil Rights Act of 1964. This action was sustained by the U.S. Supreme Court in Moose Lodge No. 107 v. Irvis, 407 U.S. 163 (1972).

MOOSE LODGE NO. 107 v. IRVIS

Supreme Court of the United States, 407 U.S. 163 (1972)

Appellee Irvis, a Negro, was refused service by appellant Moose Lodge, a local branch of the national fraternal organization located in Harrisburg, Pennsylvania. Appellee then brought this action under 42 U.S.C. § 1983 for injunctive relief in the United States District Court for the Middle District of Pennsylvania. He claimed that because the Pennsylvania liquor board had issued appellant Moose Lodge a private club license that authorized the sale of alcoholic beverages on its premises, the refusal of service to him was "state action" for the purposes of the Equal Protection clause of the Fourteenth Amendment. He named both Moose Lodge and the Pennsylvania Liquor Authority as defendants, seeking injunctive relief that would have required the defendant liquor board to revoke Moose Lodge's license so long as it continued its discriminatory practices. Appellee sought no damages. . . .

Appellee, while conceding that right of private clubs to choose members upon a discriminatory basis, asserts that the licensing of Moose Lodge to serve liquor by the Pennsylvania Liquor Control Board amounts to such State involvement with the club's activities as to make its discriminatory practices forbidden by the Equal Protection Clause of the Fourteenth Amendment. The relief sought and obtained by appellee in the District Court was an injunction forbidding the licensing by the liquor authority of Moose Lodge until it ceased its discriminatory practices. We conclude that Moose Lodge's refusal to serve food and beverages to a guest by reason of the fact that he was a Negro does not, under the circumstances here presented, violate the Fourteenth Amendment. . . .

The Court has never held, of course, that discrimination by an otherwise private entity would be violative of the Equal Protection Clause if the private entity receives any sort of benefit or service at all from the State, or if it is subject to state regulation in any degree whatever.

VOTING RIGHTS

The Civil Rights Acts of 1957 (71 Stat. 634) and 1960 (74 Stat. 86) authorized the attorney general to act as an advocate for black voting rights. These attempts proved largely unsuccessful, however, and it remained for civil rights protestors to secure the right of blacks to vote.

Between 1961 and 1965, civil rights protestors won virtually all the more than thirty-six sit-in cases heard by the U.S. Supreme Court, but the Court withheld review of convictions involving disorder and upheld convictions for contempt and violation of criminal statutes. After the early 1960s, courts generally held that sit-ins, lie-ins, and similar conduct on private or public premises may be prohibited.

The Civil Rights Acts of 1964 (78 Stat. 241) and 1965 (79 Stat. 437) were enacted as a result of the civil rights movement. The challenge to the constitutionality of the 1965 act in State of South Carolina v. Katzenbach, 383 U.S. 301 (1966), provides a historical review of attempts of blacks to vote from the Fifteenth Amendment forward as well as detailing the provisions of the legislation under attack.

STATE OF SOUTH CAROLINA v. KATZENBACH

Supreme Court of the United States, 383 U.S. 301 (1966).

. . . . Chief Justice WARREN delivered the opinion of the Court.

The Fifteenth Amendment to the Constitution was ratified in 1870. Promptly thereafter Congress passed the Enforcement Act of 1870, which made it a crime for public officers and private persons to obstruct exercise of the right to vote. The statute was amended in the following year to provide for detailed federal supervision of the electoral process, from registration to the certification of returns. As the years passed and fervor for racial equality waned, enforcement of the laws became spotty and ineffective, and most of their provisions were repealed in 1894. The remnants have had little significance in the recently renewed battle against voting discrimination.

Meanwhile, beginning in 1890, the States of Alabama, Georgia, Louisiana, Mississippi, North Carolina, South Carolina, and Virginia enacted tests still in use which were specifically designed to prevent Negroes from voting. Typically, they made the ability to read and write a registration qualification and also required completion of a registration form. These laws were based on the fact that as of 1890 in each of the named States, more than two-thirds of the adult Negroes were illiterate while less than one-quarter of the adult whites were unable to read or write. At the same time, alternate tests were prescribed in all of the named States to assure that white illiterates would not be deprived of the franchise. These included grandfather clauses, property qualifications, "good character" tests, and the requirement that registrants "understand" or "interpret" certain matter.

The course of subsequent Fifteenth Amendment litigation in this Court demonstrates the variety and persistence of these and similar institutions designed to deprive Negroes of the right to vote. Grandfather clauses were invalidated in Guinn v. United States, 238 U.S. 347, and Myers v. Anderson, 238 U.S. 368. Procedural hurdles were struck down in Lane v. Wilson, 307 U.S. 268. The white primary was outlawed in Smith v. Allwright, 321 U.S. 649, and Terry v. Adams, 345 U.S. 461. Improper challenges were nullified in United States v. Thomas, 362 U.S. 58. Racial gerrymandering was forbidden by Gomillion v. Lightfoot, 364 U.S. 339. Finally, discriminatory application of voting tests was condemned in Schnell v. Davis, 336 U.S. 933; Alabama v. United States, 371 U.S. 37; and Louisiana v. United States, 380 U.S. 145.

According to the evidence in recent Justice Department voting suits, the latter strategem is now the principal method used to bar Negroes from the polls. Discriminatory administration of voting qualifications has been found in all eight Alabama cases, in all nine Louisiana cases, and in all nine Mississippi cases which have gone to final judgment. Moreover, in almost all of these cases, the courts have held that the discrimination was pursuant to a widespread "pattern or practice." White applicants for registration have often been excused altogether from the literacy and understanding tests or have been given easy versions, have received extensive help from voting officials, and have been registered despite serious errors in their answers. Negroes, on the other hand, have typically been required to pass difficult versions of all the tests, without any outside assistance and without the slightest error. The good-morals requirement is so vague and subjective that it has constituted an open invitation to abuse at the hands of voting officials. Negroes obliged to obtain vouchers from registered voters have found it virtually impossible to comply in areas where almost no Negroes are on the rolls. . . .

During the hearings and debates on the Act, Selma, Alabama, was repeatedly referred to as the pre-eminent example of the ineffectiveness of existing legislation. In Dallas County, of which Selma is the seat, there were four years of litigation by the Justice Department and two findings by the federal courts of widespread voting discrimination. Yet in those four years, Negro registration rose only from 156 to 383, although there are approximately 15,000 Negroes of voting age in the county. Any possibility that these figures were attributable to political apathy was dispelled by the protest demonstrations in Selma in the early months of 1965. . . .

The Voting Rights Act of 1965 reflects Congress' firm intention to rid the country of racial discrimination in voting. The heart of the Act is a complex scheme of stringent remedies aimed at areas where voting discrimination has been most flagrant. Section 4(a)–(d) lays down a formula defining the States and political subdivisions to which these new remedies apply. The first of the remedies, contained in § 4(a), is the suspension of literacy tests and similar voting qualifications for a period of five years from the last occurrence of substantial voting discrimination. Section 5 prescribes a second remedy, the suspension of all new voting regulations pending review by federal authorities to determine whether their use would perpetuate voting discrimination. The third remedy, covered in §§ 6(b), 7, 9, and 13(a), is the assignment of federal examiners on certification by the Attorney General to list qualified applicants who are thereafter entitled to vote in all elections.

Other provisions of the Act prescribe subsidiary cures for persistent voting discrimination. Section 8 authorizes the appointment of federal poll-watchers in places to which federal examiners have already been assigned. Section 10(d) excuses those made eligible to vote in sections of the country covered by § 4(b) of the Act from paying accumulated past poll taxes for state and local elections. Section 12(e) provides for balloting by persons denied access to the polls in areas where federal examiners have been appointed.

The remaining remedial portions of the Act are aimed at voting discrimination in any area of the country where it may occur. Section 2 broadly prohibits the use of voting rules to abridge exercise of the franchise on racial grounds. Sections 3, 6(a), and 13(b) strengthen existing procedures for attacking voting discrimination by means of litigation. Section 4(e) excuses citizens educated in American schools conducted in a foreign language from passing English-language literacy tests. Section 10(a)–(c) facilitates constitutional litigation challenging the imposition of all poll taxes for state and local elections. Sections 11 and 12(a)–(d) authorize civil and criminal sanctions against interference with the exercise of rights guaranteed by the Act.

. . .[T]he only sections of the Act to be reviewed at this time are §§4(a)–(d), 5, 6(b), 7, 9, 13(a), and certain procedural portions of § 14, all of which are presently in actual operation in South Carolina. . . .

These provisions of the Voting Rights Act of 1965 are challenged on the fundamental ground that they exceed the powers of Congress and encroach on an area reserved to the States by the Constitution. South Carolina and certain of the *amici curiae* also attack specific sections of the Act for more particular reasons. They argue that the coverage formula prescribed in § 4(a)–(d) violates the principle of the equality of States, denies due process by employing an invalid presumption and by barring judicial review of administrative findings, constitutes a forbidden bill of attainder, and impairs the separation of powers by adjudicating guilt through legislation. They claim that the review of new voting rules required in § 5 infringes Article III by directing the District Court to issue advisory opinions. They contend that the assignment of federal examiners authorized in § 6(b) abridges due process by precluding judicial review of administrative findings and impairs the separation of powers by giving the Attorney General judicial functions; also that the challenge procedure prescribed in § 9 denies due process on account of its speed. Finally, South Carolina and certain of the *amici curiae* maintain that §§ 4(a) and 5, buttressed by § 14(b) of the Act, abridge due process by limiting litigation to a distant forum. . . .

The ground rules for resolving this question are clear. The language and purpose of the Fifteenth Amendment, the prior decisions construing its several provisions, and the general doctrines of constitutional interpretation, all point to one fundamental principle. As against the reserved powers of the States, Congress may use any rational means to effectuate the constitutional prohibition of racial discrimination in voting. . . .

Section 1 of the Fifteenth Amendment declares that "[t]he right of citizens of the United States to vote shall not be denied or abridged by the United States or by any State on account of race, color, or previous condition of servitude." This declaration has always been treated as self-executing and has repeatedly been construed, without futher legislative specification, to invalidate state voting qualifications or procedures which are discriminatory on their face or in practice. . . . [Citations omitted.] These decisions have been rendered with full respect for the general rule, reiterated last Term in Carrington v. Rash, 380 U.S. 89, 91, 85 S.Ct. 775, 777, 13 L.Ed.2d 675, that States "have broad powers to determine the conditions under which the right of suffrage may be exercised." The gist of the matter is that the Fifteenth Amendment supersedes contrary exertions of state power. "When a State exercises power wholly within the domain of state interest, it is insulated from federal judicial review. But such insulation is not carried over when state power is used as an instrument for circumventing a federally protected right." Gomillion v. Lightfoot, 364 U.S., at 347, 81 S.Ct., at 130.

South Carolina contends that the cases cited above are precedents only for the authority of the judiciary to strike down state statutes and proce-dures—that to allow an exercise of this authority by Congress would be to rob the courts of their rightful constitutional role. On the contrary, § 2 of the Fifteenth Amendment expressly declares that "Congress shall have power to enforce this article by appropriate legislation." By adding this authori-zation, the Framers indicated that Congress was to be chiefly responsible for implementing the rights created in § 1. "It is the power of Congress which has been enlarged. Congress is authorized to *enforce* the prohibitions by appropriate legislation. Some legislation is contemplated to make the [Civil War] amendments fully effective." Ex parte Virginia, 100 U.S. 339, 345, 25 L.Ed. 676. Accordingly, in addition to the courts, Congress has full remedial powers to effectuate the constitutional prohibition against racial discrimi-nation in voting.

Congress has repeatedly exercised these powers in the past, and its enactments have repeatedly been upheld. On the rare occasions when the Court has found an unconstitutional exercise of these powers, in its opinion Congress has attacked evils not comprehended by the Fifteenth Amend-ment.

The basic test to be applied in a case involving § 2 of the Fifteenth Amendment is the same as in all cases concerning the express powers of Congress with relation to the reserved powers of the States. Chief Justice Marshall laid down the classic formulation, 50 years before the Fifteenth Amendment was ratified:

> "Let the end be legitimate, let it be within the scope of the constitution, and all means which are appropriate, which are plainly adapted to that end, which are not prohibited, but consist with the letter and spirit of the constitution, are con-stitutional." McCulloch v. Maryland, 4 Wheat. 316, 421, 4 L.Ed. 579.

The Court has subsequently echoed his language in describing each of the Civil War Amendments:

> "Whatever legislation is appropriate, that is, adapted to carry out the objects the amendments have in view, whatever tends to enforce submission to the prohibitions they contain, and to secure to all persons the enjoyment of perfect equality of civil rights and the equal protection of the laws against State denial of invasion, if not prohibited, is brought within the domain of congressional power." Ex parte Virginia, 100 U.S., at 345–346. . . .

We therefore reject South Carolina's argument that Congress may ap-propriately do no more than to forbid violations of the Fifteenth Amendment in general terms—that the task of fashioning specific remedies or of applying them to particular localities must necessarily be left entirely to the courts. . . .

Section 5 of the 1965 Civil Rights Act requires that change in election pro-cedures be approved by the courts or the attorney general. This provision protected the rights of blacks to vote in a number of court cases in the late 1960s and early 1970s, including a ruling by the U.S. Supreme Court in 1969 that blacks could not be denied a place on the ballot for failing to comply with Alabama's newly enacted "official declaration of candidacy" statute, which had not been approved.

Congress and the Supreme Court continued to protect the rights of blacks to vote in action subsequent to the 1965 legislation. The Civil Rights Act of 1968, 82 Stat. 73, provided criminal sanctions for intimidation of voters, poll watchers, or other election officials. The Voting Rights Act Amendment of 1970, 84 Stat. 314, extended the ban on literacy tests for prospective voters to all states, the constitutionality of which the Supreme Court determined in Oregon v. Mitchell, 400 U.S. 112 (1970). The Voting Rights Act of 1965 was extended in 1982 until the year 2009. Despite such protections, blacks as well as Latinos are still significantly underrepresented in state and local legislative bodies. Other racial and ethnic minorities have begun to demand an end to discrimination. More groups are now seeking fewer resources, placing blacks in a difficult position.

AFFIRMATIVE ACTION

The U.S. Supreme Court has considered three cases concerning racial criteria for admission to programs or access to resources. In the first, the Court ruled that a medical school need not set aside a specific number of positions in a class for blacks or other minorities only (Regents of University of California v. Bakke, 438 U.S. 265 [1978]). However, the Court did say that race could be a factor in admitting students.

In 1979 the Court held that setting aside half the positions in an employee training program for black workers was permissible (United Steel Workers of America v. Weber, 443 U.S. 193). The Court noted the plan of the Kaiser Steel Company at issue had three important redeeming features: (1) it was not necessary to discharge white workers and replace them by blacks; (2) the advancement of white workers was not barred because half those trained would be white; (3) the plan was only a temporary measure, designed to eliminate an obvious racial imbalance.

In the third case, the Supreme Court held that the Federal Public Works Employment Act of 1977 was constitutional (Fullilove v. Klutznick, 448 U.S. 448 [1980]). This legislation provides that 10 percent of a program that funds state and local capital construction projects must be set aside for contractors who are members of racial minorities.

Affirmative action received a setback in a U.S. Supreme Court decision in 1984 in Firefighters v. Stotts, 104 S.Ct. 2576. The Memphis Fire Department announced that it had to reduce city employees because of budget deficits. The District Court issued an order enjoining the fire department from following its seniority system in determining who should be laid off. A layoff plan was presented and approved, providing that white employees with more seniority were to be laid off while black employees were to be retained. The court held that the layoff plan could not be justified. Title VII of the 1964 Civil Rights Act protects bona fide seniority systems. A court can avoid competitive seniority only when the beneficiary of the award has been a victim of illegal discrimination, which had not been so in this instance.

The Reagan administration moved away from enforcement of civil rights in the areas of school desegregation and voting rights. It also held that the Internal Revenue Service should extend tax-exempt status to racially segregated schools. However, the U.S. Supreme Court held that the Internal Revenue Service was correct to deny tax-exempt status to segregated schools because of the nation's "fundamental and overriding interest in eradicating racial discrimination in education" (Bob Jones University v. United States, 461 U.S. 574 [1983]).

INTERRACIAL MARRIAGE AND CHILD CUSTODY

Social workers and lawyers were both surprised when a case came before the U.S. Supreme Court in 1984 in which the lower courts had refused child custody to a mother who subsequently married a black man, citing the possible effect of social stigmatization on the child (Palmore v. Sidoti 104 S.Ct. 1879 [1984]). The Supreme Court, in one of the shortest and most rapid decisions in its history, ruled: "The effects of racial prejudice, however real, cannot justify a racial classification removing an infant child from the custody of its natural mother found to be an appropriate person to have such custody."

LINDA SIDOTI PALMORE v. ANTHONY J. SIDOTI

Supreme Court of the United States, 104 S.Ct. 1879 (1984).

Chief Justice Burger delivered the opinion of the Court.

We granted certiorari to review a judgment of a state court divesting a natural mother of the custody of her infant child because of her remarriage to a person of a different race.

I

When petitioner Linda Sidoti Palmore and respondent Anthony J. Sidoti, both Caucasians, were divorced in May 1980 in Florida, the mother was awarded custody of their three-year-old daughter.

In September 1981 the father sought custody of the child by filing a petition to modify the prior judgment because of changed conditions. The change was that the child's mother was then cohabiting with a Negro, Clarence Palmore, Jr., whom she married two months later. Additionally, the father made several allegations of instances in which the mother had not properly cared for the child.

After hearing testimony from both parties and considering a court counselor's investigative report, the court noted that the father had made allegations about the child's care, but the court made no findings with respect to these allegations. On the contrary, the court made a finding that "there is no issue as to either party's devotion to the child, adequacy of housing facilities, or respect[a]bility of the new spouse of either parent." App. to Pet. for Cert. 24.

The court then addressed the recommendations of the court counselor, who had made an earlier report "in [another] case coming out of this circuit also involving the social consequences of an interracial marriage. Niles v. Niles, 299 So.2d 162." Id., at 25. From this vague reference to that earlier case, the court turned to the present case and noted the counselor's recommendation for a change in custody because "[t]he wife [petitioner] has chosen for herself and for her child, a life-style unacceptable to her father *and to society.* . . . The child . . . is, or at school age will be, subject to environmental pressures not of choice." Record 84 (emphasis added).

The court then concluded that the best interests of the child would be served by awarding custody to the father. The court's rationale is contained in the following:

"The father's evident resentment of the mother's choice of a black partner is not sufficient to wrest custody from the mother. It is of some significance, however, that the mother did see fit to bring a man into her home and carry on a sexual relationship with him without being married to him. Such action tended to place gratification of her own desires ahead of her concern for the child's future welfare. *This Court feels that despite the strides that have been made in bettering relations between the races in this country, it is inevitable that Melanie will, if allowed to remain in her present situation [until she] attains school age and is thus more vulnerable to peer pressures, suffer from the social stigmatization that is sure to come."* App. to Pet. for Cert. 26–27 (emphasis added).

The Second District Court of Appeals affirmed without opinion, thus denying the Florida Supreme Court jurisdiction to review the case. We granted certiorari, ——— U.S. ——— (1983), and we reverse.

II

The judgment of a state court determining or reviewing a child custody decision is not ordinarily a likely candidate for review by this Court. However, the court's opinion, after stating that the "father's evident resentment of the mother's choice of a black partner is not sufficient" to deprive her of custody, then turns to what it regarded as the damaging impact on the child from remaining in a racially-mixed household. App. to Pet. for Cert. 26. This raises important federal concerns arising from the Constitution's commitment to eradicating discrimination based on race.

The Florida court did not focus directly on the parental qualifications of the natural mother or her present husband, or indeed on the father's qualifications to have custody of the child. The court found that "there is no issue as to either party's devotion to the child, adequacy of housing facilities, or respect[a]bility of the new spouse of either parent." Id., at 24. This, taken with the absence of any negative finding as to the quality of the care provided by the mother, constitutes a rejection of any claim of petitioner's unfitness to continue the custody of her child.

The court correctly stated that the child's welfare was the controlling factor. But that court was entirely candid and made no effort to place its holding on any ground other than race. Taking the court's findings and rationale at face value, it is clear that the outcome would have been different had petitioner married a Caucasian male of similar respectability.

A core purpose of the Fourteenth Amendment was to do away with all governmentally-imposed discrimination based on race. Classifying persons according to their race is more likely to reflect racial prejudice than legitimate public concerns; the race, not the person, dictates the category. Such classifications are subject to the most exacting scrutiny; to pass constitutional muster, they must be justified by a compelling government interest and must be "necessary . . . to the accomplishment" of its legitimate purpose, McLaughlin v. Florida, 379 U.S. 184, 196 (1964).

The State, of course, has a duty of the highest order to protect the interests of minor children, particularly those of tender years. In common with most states, Florida law mandates that custody determinations be made in the best interests of the children involved. Fla. Stat. § 61.13(2)(b)(1) (1983). The goal of granting custody based on the best interests of the child is indisputably a substantial governmental interest for purposes of the Equal Protection Clause.

It would ignore reality to suggest that racial and ethnic prejudices do not exist or that all manifestations of those prejudices have been eliminated. There is a risk that a child living with a step-parent of a different race may be subject to a variety of pressures and stresses not present if the child were living with parents of the same racial or ethnic origin.

The question, however, is whether the reality of private biases and the possible injury they might inflict are permissible considerations for removal of an infant child from the custody of its natural mother. We have little difficulty concluding that they are not. The Constitution cannot control such prejudices but neither can it tolerate them. Private biases may be outside the reach of the law, but the law cannot, directly or indirectly, give them effect. "Public officials sworn to uphold the Constitution may not avoid a constitutional duty by bowing to the hypothetical effects of private racial prejudice that they assume to be both widely and deeply held." Palmer v. Thompson, 403 U.S. 217, 260–261 (1971) (White, J., dissenting).

This is by no means the first time that acknowledged racial prejudice has been invoked to justify racial classifications. In Buchanan v. Warley, 245 U.S. 60 (1917), for example, this Court invalidated a Kentucky law forbidding Negroes from buying homes in white neighborhoods.

> "It is urged that this proposed segregation will promote the public peace by preventing race conflicts. Desirable as this is, and important as is the preservation of the public peace, this aim cannot be accomplished by laws or ordinances which deny rights created or protected by the Federal Constitution." Id., at 81.

Whatever problems racially-mixed households may pose for children in 1984 can no more support a denial of constitutional rights than could the stresses that residential integration was thought to entail in 1917. The effects of racial prejudice, however real, cannot justify a racial classification removing an infant child from the custody of its natural mother found to be an appropriate person to have such custody.

The judgment of the District Court of Appeals is reversed.

SOCIAL WORK ROLES IN ELIMINATION OF RACISM

The National Association of Social Workers has defined the elimination of racism as one of two major goals for the profession. Social workers are in a good position to help eliminate racism by serving as advocates for racial equality in legislation and in formulation of national policies to which minority group members are most exposed.

Social workers should also be sensitive to the types of informal discrimination that often occur within the public and private agencies by which they are employed. Henderson and Kim (1975:193-194) provide several examples of institutional racism of which the social work practitioner should be aware:

■ *Quality of service.* In an agency with several branch offices, the less skilled staff members may be assigned to the office serving minority people. The explanation may be that other staff "won't go to that neighborhood."

■ *Administrative policies.* Rules and procedures may be based on racism. An office in one neighborhood may schedule all intake interviews at 9 a.m., resulting in long waits for some people. If a person is late, he has to come back the next day. Other offices may not have such a rule. The racist explanation is that blacks are often late for appointments, and it is necessary to be strict.

■ *Services given.* Blacks, Asians, or Indians may be told what services they need. When a black family needs help to bring a relative into the home because of a crisis, a request for a bus ticket may be denied, but homemaker service may be offered. Yet the presence of a key member may mean more than anything else to the family, and he or she may actually provide more care than a homemaker. Also, minorities may be referred automatically to public services but Whites to private agencies first.

■ *Personal behavior of staff members, especially hard to control* [may affect] *hiring and advancement of staff.* In spite of civil rights laws, many subtle values operate in staff selection. Reasons may be found not to hire minority members who are well qualified. One is that they may be too militant. On the other hand, recent emphasis on providing opportunities for minorities can lead to charges of reverse racism against hiring whites. This is sometimes justified as "making up for past wrongs."

■ *Assignment of duties and work loads.* Minority staff members may get the undesirable assignments. Minority workers may also be given caseloads made up entirely of minority clients. This is considered racist. . . .

■ *Treatment of persons served.* Minority clients complain of curt and rude treatment or condescension from agency staff members. That may or may not be racism. What may be seen as racism can be prejudice against all clients—white and nonwhite—because they are poor, trying to get something for nothing, or too "stupid" to understand the agency forms. Then the attitude of the staff member is hostile but not racist.

Social workers themselves may become subjects of differential treatment based on race. Black social work students in field placement reported that they were apt to be given all-black caseloads, that they were expected to be authorities on blacks and were frequently consulted by other workers, that some white workers considered themselves the experts on black people and accepted no suggestions or ideas, and that when black workers were permitted to develop their own ways of making contact and channeling services, white workers were upset by the departure from the rules (Vargus, 1975). Henderson and Kim (1975:193) recommend several ways to eliminate racism in social work practice and education:

■ Clients are entitled to a general understanding of their culture so they are not served inappropriately out of ignorance.

■ All clients should be served without discrimination or prejudice.

■ Minority clients should have a voice in planning and managing services provided for them.

■ Minority staff members are generally best qualified to serve members of their own group and should be hired to do so.

■ Opportunities for promotion and advancement should be available to minority employees on an equitable basis.

■ Minorities should be accorded special opportunities for professional training. This may mean modification in educational programs.

■ Minority faculty members are essential. Credentials of experience and skill are more important than academic degrees.

Legislation such as the Indian Child Welfare Act of 1978, 92 Stat. 3069, demonstrates the relationship between social work practice and law. This legislation provided procedural safeguards through detailed procedures for child custody and adoption to prevent Native American children from being moved from their homes unnecessarily by social workers.

One effective solution is the development of alternative service delivery models such as that in the Pacific/Asian-American communities (Murase, Egawa, and Tashima, 1981). Passage of well-meaning laws without supporting services is not sufficient.

Legal racism has contributed to the housing, education, and criminal justice policies of the United States, as noted in chapters on those topics. Interracial marriage and transracial adoption are also discussed elsewhere in this volume. Every field of practice in social work must be examined to eliminate the institutional racism that has been a part of the history of the United States.

Questions for Review

1. What was the finding in *Dred Scott?*

2. What is institutional racism?

3. Summarize the legal treatment of Native Americans.

4. Why have immigration laws restricted the entry of the Chinese?

5. What was the purpose of alien land laws? Why were the Japanese interned during World War II?

6. How have Latinos been exploited? What is the relationship between Mexican aliens and U.S. agriculture? According to the U.S. Supreme Court, where can searches for undocumented workers take place? Summarize proposed immigration legislation.

7. Why were the constitutional amendments aimed at the rights of blacks not enforced after the Civil War? Why did the Supreme Court declare the Civil Rights Act of 1875 unconstitutional?

8. Are segregation statutes constitutional? What was the finding in *Plessy v. Ferguson? Brown v. Board of Education?*

9. Trace the development of the Civil Rights Acts. What was the role of civil rights protestors in influencing enforcement of voting and public access provisions?

10. How did the Supreme Court distinguish the constitutionality of the Civil Rights Act of 1964 from its previous ruling regarding the Civil Rights Act of 1875?

11. Is racial discrimination in access to public facilities prohibited? Consider the Supreme Court decisions in *Evans, Palmer,* and *Moose Lodge.*

12. How have the lower courts distinguished *Moose Lodge* from their prohibition of tax exemptions for discriminatory private organizations?

13. What two procedures were implemented by states to prevent blacks from voting? How did the Civil Rights Acts attempt to alleviate interference with black voting?

14. Summarize affirmative action decisions by the U.S. Supreme Court in *Bakke, Weber* and *Fullilove.*

15. How has racism been manifested in social work practice? What methods have been recommended for its elimination?

Questions for Debate and Discussion

1.   In recent years, minority groups have used few activist techniques to obtain their goals. How can this be explained? Has the lack of activity had any effect on legal decisions on behalf of social justice?

2.   Should the use of school busing to achieve racial balance be prohibited?

3.   Given the needs of minorities, do you consider assigning minority social workers to serve them to be racist? Are there situations in which minority clients actually prefer white social workers?

Selected Readings

"Affirmative Action and Electoral Reform." *Yale Law Journal* 90 (1981): 1811–1832.

Brandenbrenner, Martin. "Hyphenated Americans—Economic Aspects." *Law and Contemporary Problems* 45 (1982):9–27.

Calmore, John O. "Exploring the Significance of Race and Class in Representing the Black Poor." *Oregon Law Review* 61 (1982):201–244.

Days, Drew. "Racial Justice," in Norman Dorsen (ed.) *Our Endangered Rights*. New York: Pantheon, 1984.

Dillard, Edward. "The Emancipation Proclamation in the Perspective of Time." *Law in Transition* 23 (1963):95–100.

Draper, Thomas. *Human Rights*. New York: Wilson, 1982.

Eisenberg, Theodore. *Civil Rights Legislation*. Indianapolis: Bobbs-Merrill, 1981.

Hutchinson, E. P. *Legislative History of American Immigration Policy*. Philadelphia: U. of Pa. Press, 1981.

Kramer, David C. *Comparative Civil Rights and Liberties*. Lanham, Md.: University Press of American, 1982.

McNeely, R. L. and Mary Kenny Bodomi. "Inter-racial Communication in School Social Work." *Social Work* 29(1984):22–27.

Shapiro, Stephen, and Wade Henderson. "Justice for Aliens," in Norman Dorsen (ed.) *Our Engangered Rights*. New York: Pantheon, 1984.

Sindler, Allan P. *Bakke, DeFunis and Minority Admissions*. New York: Longman, 1978.

CHAPTER

18

Sex-based Discrimination

Sex-based discrimination is a major problem in our society, along with racial, ethnic, and age discrimination. This subject is particularly relevant to social work— one of the few professions in which females significantly outnumber males. In the National Association of Social Workers, for example, women comprised 73 percent of the membership in 1982.

CONSTITU-TIONAL GUARANTEES AGAINST SEX DISCRIMINA-TION

Constitutional guarantees against discrimination are contained in the first two sections of the Fourteenth Amendment to the U.S. Constitution, which assure equal protection to all American citizens. However, the second section, concerning voting and selection of state representatives, defines citizens as males twenty-one years of age or older. These provisions are of particular interest in light of recent emphasis on women's rights. The Fourteenth Amendment reads:

> Section 1. All persons born or naturalized in the United States, and subject to the jurisdiction thereof, are citizens of the United States and of the State wherein they reside. No State shall make or enforce any law which shall abridge the privileges or immunities of citizens of the United States; nor shall any State deprive any person of life, liberty, or property, without due process of law; nor deny to any person within its jurisdiction the equal protection of the laws.
>
> Section 2. Representatives shall be apportioned among the several States according to their respective numbers, counting the whole number of persons in each State, excluding Indians not taxed. But when the right to vote at any election for the choice of electors for President and Vice President of the United States, Representatives, in Congress, the executive and judicial officers of a State, or the members of the Legislature thereof, is denied to any of the male inhabitants of such State, being twenty-one years of age, and citizens of the United States, or in any way abridged except for participation in rebellion, or other crime, the basis of representation therein shall be reduced in the proportion which the number of such male citizens shall bear to the whole number of male citizens twenty-one years of age in such State.

TRADITIONAL MALE SUPREMACY

Sex lines were commonly drawn and enforced in nearly all aspects of public and private life until 1971, when the U.S. Supreme Court began to reverse the trend. An early decision denying females the right to practice law, Bradwell v. State of Illinois, 83 U.S. 130 (1873), illustrates the traditional stance of the courts. Note Justice Joseph Bradley's concurring opinion, in which he pleads for preservation of the family organization instituted on the basis of divine ordinance:

The claim that, under the fourteenth amendment of the Constitution, which declares that no State shall make or enforce any law which shall abridge the privileges and immunities of citizens of the United States, the statute law of Illinois, or the common law prevailing in that State, can no longer be set up as a barrier against the right of females to pursue any lawful employment for a livelihood (the practice of law included), assumes that it is one of the privileges and immunities of women as citizens to engage in any and every profession, occupation, or employment in civil life. (83 U.S. at 140)

It certainly cannot be affirmed, as an historical fact, that this has ever been established as one of the fundamental privileges and immunities of the sex. On the contrary, the civil law, as well as nature herself, has always recognized a wide difference in the respective spheres and destinies of man and woman. Man is, or should be, woman's protector and defender. The natural and proper timidity and delicacy which belongs to the female sex evidently unfits it for many of the occupations of civil life. The constitution of the family organization, which is founded in the divine ordinance, as well as in the nature of things, indicates the domestic sphere as that which properly belongs to the domain and functions of womanhood. The harmony, not to say identity, or interests and views which belong, or should belong, to the family institution is repugnant to the idea of a woman adopting a distinct and independent career from that of her husband. So firmly fixed was this sentiment in the founders of the common law that it became a maxim of that system of jurisprudence that a woman had no legal existence separate from her husband, who was regarded as her head and representative in the social state and, notwithstanding some recent modifications of this civil status, many of the special rules of law flowing from and dependent upon this cardinal principle still exist in full force in most States. One of these is, that a married woman is incapable, without her husband's consent, of making contracts which shall be binding on her or him. This very incapacity was one circumstance which the Supreme Court of Illinois deemed important in rendering a married woman incompetent fully to perform the duties and trusts that belong to the office of an attorney and counsellor. (Id. at 141) . . .

It is the prerogative of the legislator to prescribe regulations founded on nature, reason, and experience for the due admission of qualified persons to professions and callings demanding special skill and confidence. This fairly belongs to the police power of the State; and, in my opinion, in view of the peculiar characteristics, destiny, and mission of woman, it is within the province of the legislature to ordain what offices, positions, and callings shall be filled and discharged by men, and shall receive the benefit of those energies and responsibilities, and that decision and firmness which are presumed to predominate in the sterner sex. (Id. at 142)

This was the era of God-given male and female roles and God-given male supremacy.

In 1924, women were accorded the right to vote under the Nineteenth Amendment: "The right of citizens of the United States to vote shall not be denied or abridged by the United States or by any State on account of sex." Compare this wording with the text of the Fifteenth Amendment, ratified in 1870: "The right of citizens of the United States to vote shall not be denied or abridged by the United States or by any State on account of race, color, or previous conditions of servitude."

Another historic issue has concerned the protection of both women and children from unjust working hours and conditions. Women's hours were the issue in Muller v. State of Oregon, 208 U.S. 412 (1908), which established the right to limit the length of the workday to a maximum of ten hours for women working in a laundry. The decision was based on inherent differences between males and females:

It is undoubtedly true, as more than once declared by this court, that the general right to contract in relation to one's business is part of the liberty of the individual, protected by the Fourteenth Amendment to the Federal Constitution; yet it is equally well settled that this liberty is not absolute and extending to all contracts, and that a State may, without conflicting with the provisions of the Fourteenth Amendment, restrict in many respects the individual's power of contract. [Citations omitted]. . . . (208 U.S. at 421)

That woman's physical structure and the performance of maternal functions place her at a disadvantage in the struggle for subsistence is obvious. This is especially true when the burdens of motherhood are upon her. Even when they are not, by abundant testimony of the medical fraternity continuance for a long time on her feet at work, repeating this from day to day, tends to injurious effects upon the body, and as healthy mothers are essential to vigorous offspring, the physical well-being of woman becomes an object of public interest and care in order to preserve the strength and vigor of the race.

Still again, history discloses the fact that woman has always been dependent upon man. He established his control at the outset by superior physical strength, and this control in various forms, with diminishing intensity, has continued to the present. As minors, though not to the same extent, she has been looked upon in the courts as needing especial care that her rights may be preserved. Education was long denied her, and while now the doors of the school room are opened and her opportunities for acquiring knowledge are great, yet even with that and the consequent increase of capacity for business affairs it is still true that in the struggle for subsistence she is not an equal competitor with her brother. Though limitations upon personal and contractual rights may be removed by legislation, there is that in her disposition and habits of life which will operate against a full assertion of those rights. She will still be where some legislation to protect her seems necessary to secure a real equality of right. Doubtless there are individual exceptions, and there are many respects in which she has an advantage over him; but looking at it from the viewpoint of the effort to maintain an independent position in life, she is not upon an equality. Differentiated by these matters from the other sex, she is properly placed in a class by herself, and legislation designed for her protection may be sustained, even when like legislation is not necessary for men and could not be sustained. . . . The two sexes differ in structure of body, in the functions to be performed by each, in the amount of physical strength, in the capacity for long-continued labor, particularly when done standing, the influence of vigorous health upon the future well-being of the race, the self-reliance which enables one to assert full rights, and in the capacity to maintain the struggle for subsistence. This difference justifies a difference in legislation and upholds that which is designed to compensate for some of the burdens which rest upon her. (Id. at 421–423)

The decision affirming the constitutionality of different standards based on sex is now of interest because of its emphasis on male supremacy. One must remember, however, that in 1906 protections were justifiable in view of the adverse working conditions and long hours prevalent in industry. Not until 1937 were minimum-wage provisions extended to women in West Coast Hotel Co. v. Parrish, 300 U.S. 379. In 1941, wage and hour restrictions were upheld for both sexes in United States v. Darby, 312 U.S. 100.

SEX DIFFERENCES IN JURY SELECTION

Differential methods of jury selection have traditionally been justified on the basis of the woman's homemaking role. Florida law gave women "the privilege to serve" but did not "impose service as a duty." Hoyt v. State of Florida, 368 U.S. 57 (1961), upheld this law:

Appellant, a woman, killed her husband and was convicted in a Florida state court of second-degree murder. She claimed that her trial before an all-male jury violated her rights under the Fourteenth Amendment. A Florida statute provides, in substance, that no woman shall be taken for jury service unless she volunteers for it. *Held*: The Florida statute is not unconstitutional on its face or as applied in this case.

(a) The right to an impartially selected jury assured by the Fourteenth Amendment does not entitle one accused of crime to a jury tailored to the circumstances of the particular case. It requires only that the jury be indiscriminately drawn from among those in the community eligible for jury service, untrammelled by an arbitrary and systematic exclusions.

(b) The Florida statute is not unconstitutional on its face, since it is not constitutional for a State to conclude that a woman should be relieved from jury service unless she herself determines that such service is consistent with her own special responsibilities.

(c) It cannot be said that the statute is unconstitutional as applied in this case, since there is not substantial evidence in the record that Florida has arbitrarily undertaken to exclude women from jury service. . . .

Despite the enlightened emancipation of women from the restrictions and protections of bygone years, and their entry into many parts of community life formerly considered to be reserved to men, woman is still regarded as the center of home and family life. We cannot say that it is constitutionally permissible for a State, acting in pursuit of the general welfare, to conclude that a woman should be relieved from the civic duty of jury service unless she herself determines that such service is consistent with her own special responsibilities.

Florida modified its requirements in 1967 to permit exemption from jury duty for pregnant women and those with children under eighteen who so request.

Louisiana was the last state in which women had to volunteer for jury service. The practice was found to violate the Sixth and Fourteenth Amendments in Taylor v. Louisiana, 419 U.S. 522 (1975). Prior to trial on a kidnapping charge, Taylor sought to invalidate the list from which the jury was to be selected on the basis that women had been systematically excluded from it, thus depriving him of the right to a fair trial by a properly selected jury. The case went to the Louisiana Supreme Court and finally to the U.S. Supreme Court, where Taylor's objection was sustained:

> Accepting as we do, however, the view that the Sixth Amendment affords the defendant in a criminal trial the opportunity to have the jury drawn from venires (jury rosters) representative of the community, we think it is no longer tenable to hold that women as a class may be excluded or given automatic exemptions based solely on sex if the consequence is that criminal jury venires are almost totally male. To this extent we cannot follow the contrary implications of the prior cases, including Hoyt v. Florida. . . . Communities differ at different times and places. What is a fair cross section at one time or place is not necessarily a fair cross section at another time or a different place. Nothing persuasive has been presented to us in this case suggesting that all-male venires in the parishes involved here are fairly representative of the local population otherwise eligible for jury service.

Duren v. Missouri, 439 U.S. 357 (1979), established that women could no longer receive automatic exemptions because the practice interfered with jury lists constituting a cross section of the community.

SEX DISCRIMI-NATION AGAINST MEN

Many statutes apply differentially to the sexes. For example, juvenile jurisdiction has often been retained longer for girls than for boys. The age differential establishing juvenile jurisdiction for boys at age sixteen and for girls at age eighteen was affirmed in Lamb v. State, 475 P.2d 829 (Okl.Cr. App. 1970), but was later found to violate the equal protection clause in Lamb v. Brown, 456 F.2d 18 (10th Cir. 1972). The rationale for sexually based age differences was presented in State v. Chambers, 307 A.2d 78 (N.J. 1973). It was argued that female offenders have been considered better subjects for rehabilitation and that a longer period of detention would generally promote their chance of rehabilitation. These two reasons were found to be inconsistent and discriminatory.

In Wark v. State, 266 A.2d 62 (Me. 1970), the issue concerned differential length of prison sentences in Maine for males and females. Differences were justified by the court in terms of the comparative strength and aggressiveness of men and women:

> The Legislature could on the basis of long experience conclude that women, even those sentenced to the State Prison for serious offenses, tend for the most part to be more amenable to discipline and custodial regulation than their male counterparts and can therefore be effectively confined in an institution which lacks the high walls, armed guards and security precautions of a prison. By the same token the Legislature could reasonably conclude that the greater physical strength, aggressiveness and disposition toward violent action so frequently displayed by a male prisoner bent on escape from a maximum security institution presents a far greater risk of harm to prison guards and personnel and to the public than is the case when escape is undertaken by a woman confined in an institution designed primarily for reform and rehabilitation. Viewing statutory provisions for punishment as in part a deterrent to criminal conduct, the Legislature could logically and reasonably conclude that a more severe penalty should be imposed upon a male prisoner escaping from the State Prison than upon a woman confined at the "Reformatory" while serving a State Prison sentence who escapes from that institution. We conclude that a classification based on sex under these circumstances is neither arbitrary nor unreasonable but is a proper exercise of legislative discretion which in no way violates the constitutional right to equal protection of the law.

Legal provisions setting a later age for males to marry without parental permission based on the male's greater economic responsibility have also been found discriminatory, as Chapter 10 shows.

Weinberger v. Wiesenfeld, 420 U.S. 636 (1975), successfully challenged benefits based on the earnings of a deceased wife and mother under the Social Security Act being barred to the widower. Had the husband died, benefits would have been payable to both the widow and the children. This distinction violated the due process clause of the Fifth Amendment.

WEINBERGER v. WIESENFELD

Supreme Court of the United States, 420 U.S. 636 (1975).

. . . A three-judge District Court for the District of New Jersey held that the different treatment of men and women mandated by § 402 (g) unjustifiably discriminated against women wage-earners by affording them less protection for their survivors than is provided to male employees. . . .

Stephen C. Wiesenfeld and Paula Polatschek were married on November 5, 1970. Paula, who worked as a teacher for five years before her marriage, continued teaching after her marriage. Each year she worked, maximum social security contributions were deducted from her salary. Paula's earnings were the couple's principal source of support during the marriage, being substantially larger than those of appellee.

On June 5, 1972, Paula died in childbirth. Appellee was left with the sole responsibility for the care of their infant son, Jason Paul. Shortly after his wife's death, Stephen Wiesenfeld applied at the Social Security office in New Brunswick, New Jersey for social security survivors' benefits for himself and his son. He did obtain benefits for his son under 42 U.S.C. § 402(d) and received for Jason $206.90 per month until September 1972, and $248.30 per month thereafter. However, appellee was told that he was not eligible for benefits for himself, because § 402(g) benefits were available only to women. If he had been a woman, he would have received the same amount as his son as long as he was not working, . . . and, if working, that amount reduced by $1.00 for every $2.00 earned annually above $2,400. . . .

Appellee filed this suit in February, 1973, claiming jurisdiction under 28 U.S.C. § 1331 . . . on behalf of himself and of all widowers similarly situated. He sought a declaration that § 402 (g) is unconstitutional to the extent that men and women are treated differently, an injunction restraining appellant from denying benefits under 42 U.S.C. § 402(g) solely on the basis of sex, and payment of past benefits commencing with June, 1972, the month of the original application. Cross motions for summary judgment were filed. After the three-judge court determined that it had jurisdiction, it granted summary judgment in favor of appellee, and issued an order giving appellee the relief he sought. . . .

Section 402(g) was added to the Social Security Act in 1939 as one of a large number of amendments designed to "afford more adequate protection to the family as a unit." . . . Monthly benefits were provided to wives, children, widows, orphans, and surviving dependent parents of covered workers. . . . However, children of covered women workers were eligible for survivors' benefits only in limited circumstances, and no benefits whatever were made available to husbands or widowers on the basis of their wives' covered employment.

Underlying the 1939 scheme was the principle that "under a social insurance plan, the primary purpose is to pay benefits in accordance with the *probable needs* of beneficiaries rather than to make payments to the estate of a deceased person regardless of whether or not he leaves dependents." . . . It was felt that "the payment of these survivorship benefits and supplements for the wife of an annuitant are . . . in keeping with the principle of social insurance. . . ." Thus, the framers of the Act legislated on the "then generally accepted presumption that a man is responsible for the support of his wife and child." . . .

Obviously, the notion that men are more likely than women to be the primary supporters of their spouses and children is not entirely without empirical support. . . . But such a gender-based generalization cannot suffice to justify the denigration of the efforts of women who do work and whose earnings contribute significantly to their families' support. . . .

Here Stephen Wiesenfeld was not given the opportunity to show, as may well have been the case, that he was dependent upon his wife for his support, or that, had his wife lived, she would have remained at work while he took over care of the child. Second, in this case social security taxes were deducted from Paula's salary during the years in which she worked. Thus, she not only failed to receive for her family the same protection which a similarly situated male worker would have received, but she also was deprived of a portion of her own earnings in order to contribute to the fund out of which benefits would be paid to others. . . . The Constitution forbids the gender-based differentiation . . . . that results in the efforts of women workers required to pay social security taxes producing less protection for their families than produced by the efforts of men. . . .

It is apparent both from the statutory scheme itself and from the legislative history of § 402(g) that Congress' purpose in providing benefits to young widows with children was not to provide an income to women who were, because of economic discrimination, unable to provide for themselves. Rather, § 402(g), linked as it is directly to responsibility for minor children, was intended to permit women to elect not to work and to devote themselves to the care of children. Since this purpose in no way is premised upon any special disadvantages of women, it cannot serve to justify a gender-based distinction which diminishes the protection afforded to women who do work. . . .

Given the purpose of enabling the surviving parent to remain at home to care for a child, the gender-based distinction of § 402(g) is entirely irrational. The classification discriminates among surviving children solely on the basis of the sex of the surviving parent. Even in the typical family hypothesized by the Act, in which the husband is supporting the family and the mother is caring for the children, this result makes no sense. The fact that a man is working while there is a wife at home does not mean that he would, or should be required to, continue to work if his wife dies. *It is no less important for a child to be cared for by its sole surviving parent when that parent is male rather than female.* [Emphasis added.] And a father, no less than a mother, has a constitutionally protected right to the "companionship, care, custody, and management" of "the children he has sired and raised, (which) undeniably warrants deference and, absent a powerful countervailing interest, protection." Stanley v. Illinois, 405 U.S. 645 (1972). Further, to the extent that women who work when they have sole responsibility for children encounter special problems, it would seem that men with sole responsibility for children will encounter the same child-care related problems. Stephen Wiesenfeld, for example, found that providing adequate care for his infant son impeded his ability to work. . . .

Finally, to the extent that Congress legislated on the presumption that women as a group would choose to forego work to care for children while men would not, the statutory structure, independent of the gender-based classification, would deny or reduce benefits to those men who conform to the presumed norm and are not hampered by their child-care responsibilities. Benefits under § 402(g) decrease with increased earnings. . . . According to the Government the role of male workers would receive no benefits in any event," Brief for Appellant, at 17, because they earn too much. Thus, the gender-based distinction is gratuitous; without it, the statutory scheme would only provide benefits to those men who are in fact similarly situated to the women the statute aids.

> Since the gender-based classification of § 402(g) cannot be explained as an attempt to provide for the special problems of women, it is indistinguishable from the classification held invalid in Frontiero. Like the statutes there, "[b]y providing dissimilar treatment for men and women who are. . . . similarly situated, the challenged section violates the [Due Process] Clause." . . . [Citations omitted.]
> Affirmed.

By virtue of the Court's conclusion that such gender-based classifications violated the Constitution, Social Security benefits to widowers wishing to stay home and rear their children were affirmed.

The question of gender-based discrimination was again dealt with in Califano v. Goldfarb, 430 U.S. 199 (1977), in which the U.S. Supreme Court held that a widower did not have to prove actual dependency in order to qualify for survivors' benefits from Social Security based on earnings of a deceased spouse. Until this decision, under 42 U.S.C. § 402(f)(1)(D) a widow never had to prove such dependency, but the widower had to have been receiving at least half his support to qualify for benefits on the basis of his wife's earnings. The opinion held that the provision violated the due process clause of the Fifth Amendment. This decision drew on the precedents of *Wiesenfeld* and *Frontiero v. Richardson*, 411 U.S. 677 (1973).

TRENDS IN SEX DISCRIMINA-TION DECISIONS

The trend in Supreme Court decisions exemplified by *Weinberger v. Wiesenfeld* began in 1971 with the decision in Reed v. Reed, 404 U.S. 71, which struck down an Idaho law whereby a male was to be preferred in selecting an estate executor, notwithstanding the claims of other persons who "were equally entitled" to assume the executor role.

Following *Reed*, in Eslinger v. Thomas, 476 F.2d 225 (4th Cir. 1973), a female law student who had been denied a job as page in the South Carolina legislature was successful in alleging discrimination solely on the basis of sex:

> When we apply the test of *Reed*, we are compelled to conclude that Section 525 denies equal protection. The "public image" of the South Carolina Senate and of its members is obviously a proper subject of state concern. Apparently, the South Carolina Senate felt that certain functions performed by pages on behalf of senators, e.g., running personal errands, driving senators about in their autos, packing their bags in hotel rooms, cashing personal checks for senators, etc., were "not suitable under existing circumstances for young ladies and may give rise to the appearance of impropriety." . . .
> In their brief, defendants argued that "[i]n placing this restriction upon female pages, the Senate is merely attempting to avoid placing one of its employees in a conceivably damaging position, protecting itself from appearing to the public that an innocent relationship is not so innocent, and maintaining as much public confidence while conducting the business of the people of South Carolina as possible.
> We find this rationale unconvincing. It rests upon the implied premise, which we think false, that "[o]n the one hand, the female is viewed as a pure, delicate and vulnerable creature who must be protected from exposure to criminal influences; and on the other, as a brazen temptress, from whose seductive blandishments the innocent male must be protected. Every woman is either Eve or Little Eva—and either way, she loses." [Citations omitted.] We have only to look at our own female secretaries and female law clerks to conclude that an intimate business relationship, including

travel on circuit, between persons of different sex presents no "appearance of impropriety." In addition, it is interesting to note that South Carolina has had female senators whose associations with male pages have not created any "appearance of impropriety" sufficient to require legislative regulation. This fact alone constitutes a historic precedent sufficient to reverse Section 525. In short, present societal attitudes reject the notion that free business associations between the persons are to be limited, regulated and restricted because of a difference in sex. The last decade has seen many characteristic sex discrimination efforts to correct the attached needs.

DISCRIMINATION IN EMPLOYMENT

Cases dealing with sex-based discrimination in employment are too numerous to cover fully in the space available, but some of the major decisions will demonstrate their variety and indicate problems of discrimination that affect men as well as women.

In Shultz v. Wheaton Glass Co., 421 F.2d 259 (3d Cir. 1970), and Hodgson v. Miller Brewing Company, 457 F.2d 221 (7th Cir. 1972), wage differentials favoring males who performed essentially the same work as females were considered discriminatory. In Sprogis v. United Airlines, 444 F.2d 1194 (7th Cir. 1971), airlines were precluded from discharging stewardesses upon marriage. In Diaz v. Pan American World Airways, 442 F.2d 385 (5th Cir. 1971), passenger preference for female cabin attendants did not constitute an adequate basis for a bona fide occupational qualification permitting only females be hired to fulfill this role.

Wilson v. Sibley Memorial Hospital, 340 F.Supp. 686 (D.C. 1972), led to the finding that a male nurse may attend female patients and that hospitals may not discriminate in nurse selection on the basis of sex.

In Rafford v. Randle Eastern Ambulance Service, Inc., 348 F.Supp. 316 (S.D.Fla. 1972), the court found that men dismissed from service for refusing to trim their mustaches have no basis for alleging sex discrimination on the part of their employer. Since women do not typically have mustaches, dismissal of men who refused to trim their mustaches could not be considered sex discrimination. Hair-length requirements can also be imposed on policemen as a condition of employment as long as there is a rational connection between the regulation and safety of persons and property (Kelley v. Johnson, 425 U.S. 238 [1976]). However, a grooming code stipulating different hair-length standards for the two sexes is discriminatory, according to Willingham v. Macon Telegraph Publishing Co., 482 F.2d 535 (5th Cir. 1973).

Two decisions determined that females could not be excluded from consideration for such specified traditionally male occupations as that of agent telegrapher (Rosenfeld v. South Pacific Co. 444 F.2d 1219 [9th Cir. 1971]) or telephone switchman (Weeks v. Southern Bell Tel. & Tel. Co., 408 F.2d 228 [5th Cir. 1969]). The latter case involved the applicant's physical capacity to lift thirty pounds—an alleged capability of a male but not of a female:

> We conclude that the principle of nondiscrimination requires that we hold that in order to rely on the bona fide occupational qualification exception an employer has the burden of proving that he had reasonable cause to believe, that is, a factual basis for believing, that all or substantially all women would be unable to perform safely and efficiently the duties of the job involved.
>
> Southern Bell has clearly not met that burden here. They introduced no evidence concerning the lifting abilities of women. Rather, they would have us "assume," on the basis of a "stereotyped characterization" that few or no women can safely lift 30

pounds, while all men are treated as if they can. While one might accept arguendo, that men are stronger on the average than women, it is not clear that any conclusions about relative lifting ability would follow. This is because it can be argued tenably that technique is as important as strength in determining lifting ability. Technique is hardly a function of sex. What does seem clear is that using these class stereotypes denies desirable positions to a great many women perfectly capable of performing the duties involved.

CHILD-BEARING AND CHILD-REARING

Two suits involving maternity benefits for teachers were combined and treated as one before the U.S. Supreme Court in Cleveland Board of Education v. LaFleur and Cohen v. Chesterfield County School Board. The Court held in 1974 (414 U.S. 632) that both the Cleveland prohibition on the return of teachers to work until a child was three months old and the Chesterfield requirement that pregnant teachers begin maternity leave when they are five months into the pregnancy violated the due process clause.

The child-care issue came to the attention of the Supreme Court in Phillips v. Martin Marietta Corp., 400 U.S. 542 (1971), where it was alleged that the company's refusal to hire women with preschool children violated Title VII of the Civil Rights Act of 1964.

> Petitioner Mrs. Ida Phillips commenced an action in the United States District Court for the Middle District of Florida under Title VII of the Civil Rights Act of 1964 alleging that she had been denied employment because of her sex. The District Court granted summary judgment for Martin Marietta Corp. (Martin) on the basis of the following showing: (1) in 1966 Martin informed Mrs. Phillips that it was not accepting job applications from women with pre-school-age children; (2) as of the time of the motion for summary judgment, Martin employed men with pre-school-age children; (3) at the time Mrs. Phillips applied 70–75% of the applicants for the position she sought were women; 75–80% of those hired for the position, assembly trainee, were women, hence no question of bias against women as such was presented. (400 U.S. at 543)
>
> Section 703(a) of the Civil Rights Act of 1964 requires that persons of like qualifications be given employment opportunities irrespective of their sex. The Court of Appeals therefore erred in reading this section as permitting one hiring policy for women and another for men—each having pre-school-age children. The existence of such conflicting family obligations, if demonstrably more relevant to job performance for a woman than for a man, could arguably be a basis for distinction under § 703(e) of the Act. But that is a matter of evidence tending to show that the condition in question "is a bona fide occupational qualification reasonably necessary to the normal operation of that particular business or enterprise." The record before us, however, is not adequate for resolution of these important issues (see Kennedy v. Silas Mason Co., 334 U.S. 249, 256, 257 [1948]). Summary judgment was therefore improper and we remand for fuller development of the record and for further consideration. (Id. at 544).
>
> Vacated and remanded.

The concurring opinion of Justice Thurgood Marshall is of particular interest:

> Mr. Justice MARSHALL, concurring.
>
> While I agree that this case must be remanded for full development of the facts, I cannot agree with the Court's indication that a "bona fide occupational qualification reasonably necessary to the normal operation of" Martin Marietta's business could be established by a showing that some women, even the vast majority, with pre-school-

age children have family responsibilities that interfere with job performance and that men do not usually have such responsibilities. Certainly, an employer can require that all of his employees, both men and women, meet minimum performance standards, and he can try to insure compliance by requiring parents, both mothers and fathers, to provide for the care of their children so that job performance is not interfered with.

But the Court suggests that it would not require such uniform standards. I fear that in this case, where the issue is not squarely before us, the Court has fallen into the trap of assuming that the Act permits ancient canards about the proper role of women to be a basis for discrimination. Congress, however, sought just the opposite result.

By adding the prohibition against job discrimination based on sex to the 1964 Civil Rights Act Congress intended to prevent employers from refusing "to hire an individual based on stereotyped characterizations of the sexes." [Citations omitted.] Even characterizations of the proper domestic roles of the sexes were not to serve as predicates for restricting employment opportunity. The exception for a "bona fide occupational qualification" was not intended to swallow the rule. (Id. at 544–545).

The Court apparently supported the idea that "conflicting family obligations" might be the basis for a "bona fide occupational qualification." Justice Marshall's opinion is consistent with the social work view.

While companies provide income replacement for nearly all disabilities, a Supreme Court opinion in December 1976 held that disabilities from pregnancy and childbirth were an exception (General Electric v. Gilbert, 429 U.S. 125). The court held that, since men could not receive disability related to pregnancy benefits, denying such benefits to women is not discriminatory. Previous decisions in lower courts and the policies of the Federal Equal Opportunity Commission had taken the opposite position and considered discrimination against the pregnant worker to be a basic form of sex-based bias.

The women's movement has had a particular interest in the question because improvement in the status of employed women is not likely as long as differential treatment continues. The *General Electric* decision provides a strong argument for passage of the Equal Rights Amendment. The Fourteenth Amendment's equal protection clause apparently has not been adequate to safeguard women's rights.

NONDISCRIMINATION IN EDUCATION

Title IX of the education amendments of 1972 (20 U.S.C. § 1681) was designed to eliminate discrimination on the basis of sex in any education program or activity receiving federal financial assistance and illustrates the extent to which financial sanctions may be applied against noncompliant educational institutions. Federal prohibitions include discrimination on the basis of sex in admissions and recruitment, in educational programs and activities, in financial and employment assistance to students, health and insurance benefits, marital and parental status, athletics, and employment in education programs and activities.

The broad provisions of this title affect the development of facilities, hiring practices related to faculty, and many other areas of school or university life.

DISCRIMINATION IN EXTENSION OF CREDIT

Women have keenly felt discriminatory practices in the extension of credit. Married women often found that their incomes were not considered in determining the family credit standing—mainly because of the possibility of pregnancy that would remove them from the labor market. Divorced women found that they have no credit rating because their privileges had been derived from their husband.

The Equal Credit Opportunity Act of 1975 (16 U.S.S. § 1691) was designed to remedy the problem. Title V set forth the need:

> The Congress finds that there is a need to insure that the various financial institutions and other firms engaged in the extensions of credit exercise their responsibility to make credit available with fairness, impartiality, and without discrimination on the basis of sex or marital status.

The law protects *all* credit applications from such discrimination. You are no longer required to identify sex or marital status when you apply for a credit account in which no collateral is pledged. You may be asked about marital status in terms of unmarried, married or separated, but the term *divorced* cannot appear on the application. You need not disclose income from child support or alimony payments. Information about the spouse is relevant only if he or she will use the account or be relied on for repayment. Unless you were granted credit solely on your spouse's income, a lender may not ask you to reapply when you change your name or your marital status. If you are denied credit or an account is terminated, you are entitled to an explanation in writing.

Since November 1, 1976, credit information of married persons has been reported in the names of both husband and wife. This makes it possible for wife to develop a credit history that she can use independently if necessary. The Equal Credit Opportunity Act does not provide easy credit, but it does make the extension of credit more equitable—especially to women.

Orr v. Orr, 440 U.S. 268 (1979), held that an Alabama statute that imposed alimony obligations on husbands, but not on wives violated the equal protection clause of the Fourteenth Amendment:

> To withstand scrutiny [under the equal protection clause] classifications by gender must serve important governmental objectives and must be substantially related to achievement of those objectives.
>
> The statutes cannot be validated on the basis of the State's preference for an allocation of family responsibilities under which the wife plays a dependent role. "No longer is the female destined solely for the home and the rearing of the family, and only the male for the marketplace and the world of ideas." [Citations omitted.]

Leaders of the women's movement have generally supported the principle that both husbands and wives should be subject to alimony obligations based on their circumstances at the time of divorce.

THE EQUAL RIGHTS AMENDMENT

Critics of discrimination against women were strong supporters of the Equal Rights Amendment (ERA) proposed by the 92nd Congress in 1972. The proposed amendment read:

> Section 1.   Equality of rights under the law shall not be denied or abridged by the United States or by any State on account of sex.
>
> Section 2.   The Congress shall have the power to enforce, by appropriate legislation, the provisions of this article.
>
> Section 3.   This amendment shall take effect two years after the date of ratification.

The basic principle of the Equal Rights Amendment was that sex should not be a factor in determining legal rights, making sex a prohibited classification. It would disallow classifications that disfavor either men or women and would eliminate traditional defenses for differential treatment unless personal privacy or physical characteristics unique to one sex are involved.

Even though Congress extended the time for ratification, the amendment did not receive the necessary two-thirds of the votes from the states, and it died in 1982.

A study by Avner and Greene (1982) indicated that fourteen states had enacted ERA provisions, nine based on the proposed federal amendment and five on the language of the Fourteenth Amendment to the U.S. Constitution. These provisions had demonstrable impact on family law.

Sex-based discrimination is likely to continue as a major theme of litigation in the next decade, despite the fate of the Equal Rights Amendment. Within social work, women's groups are focusing increasing attention on the rights of female clients and female practitioners.

DISCRIMINA-TION IN PENSION BENEFITS

Discrimination in pension benefits has been of concern to women's groups. In Los Angeles Department of Water and Power v. Manhart, 435 U.S. 702 (1978), the U.S. Supreme Court held that Title VII of the Civil Rights Act of 1974 prohibits employers from requiring women to make larger contributions than men in order to obtain the same monthly pension benefits as men. The reason for charging more to women or paying smaller benefits was their longer life expectancy.

In Arizona Governing Committee v. Norris, 463 U.S. 1073 (1983), the court held that Title VII also prohibits an employer from offering employees the option of receiving retirement benefits from one of several companies selected by the employer, all of which pay a woman lower monthly retirement benefits than a man who has made the same contributions. This ruling was narrow and was not retroactive, so its effect is limited. Beneficiaries can apparently still be expected to purchase lump-sum annuities at the time of retirement which have the same discriminatory features built in.

NEWER ISSUES

Sexual harassment related to the work place and comparable worth of differing occupations provide two newer sex-based discrimination issues on which we may expect a body of case law.

Harassment charges are based on Title VII of the Civil Rights Act of 1964, which concerns equal opportunity in employment. Comparable-worth cases typically allege discrimination when women receive inferior pay for work they consider at least as valuable as that performed by men. A female librarian in charge of a branch library, for example, brings suit against the public library because the unionized truck driver who distributes the books among the branches receives a higher salary than she does.

Questions for Review

1. What was considered a major impediment to women practicing law in *Bradwell v. Illinois*?

2.   From what duty were women excused because they are the center of home and family life?

3.   How have men been victims of sex discrimination?

4.   What was the question and the finding in *Weinberger v. Wiesenfeld?* What constitutional safeguard was at issue?

5.   Which of the discrimination-in-employment cases dealt with practices against men, and which concerned women?

6.   Maternity-leave policies in the schools were discriminatory both before and after the birth of the baby. How do the *LaFleur* and *Chesterfield* cases illustrate that statement?

7.   In *Phillips v. Martin Marietta*, on what reasoning did the Supreme Court base its refusal to hire married women with preschool children?

8.   What was the basic principle of the Equal Rights Amendment? What has been the effect of similar provisions in the states?

Questions for Debate and Discussion

1.   Does a profession made up predominantly of women incur less sex-based discrimination than one made up of males? Why or why not?

2.   Should there be any difference in labor laws governing men and women? How would you support an affirmative position based on *Muller v. Oregon?*

3.   How has Title IX of the education amendments affected college athletics? Are additional remedies necessary?

4.   What were the major objections to the Equal Rights Amendment?

Selected Readings   Bethel, Charles A., and Linda R. Singer. "Mediation: A New Remedy for Cases of Domestic Violence." *Vermont Law Review* 7 (1982): 15–32.

Huntington, Jane F. "Powerless and Vulnerable: The Social Experiences of Imprisoned Girls." *Juvenile and Family Courts Journal* 33 (1982): 33–34.

Jain, Harish D., and Peter J. Sloane. *Equal Employment Issues: Race and Sex Discrimination in the United States, Canada, and Britain.* New York: Praeger, 1981.

Lopata, Helen, and Kathleen Fordham. "Changing Commitments of American Women to Work and Family Roles." *Social Security Bulletin* 43 (1980): 3–14.

Munson, P. J. "Protecting Battered Wives: The Availability of Legal Remedies." *Journal of Sociology and Social Welfare* 7 (1980): 586–600.

Player, Mack A. *Cases and Materials on Employment Discrimination Law.* St. Paul, Minn.: West Publishing Co., 1981.

Thomas, Claire S. *Sex Discrimination.* St. Paul, Minn.: West Publishing Co., 1982.

CHAPTER

19

Poverty and Income Maintenance

If social work were not identified with poverty, it would be better understood and better accepted by society. The essence of social work to the lay person has typically been "poor relief." With that responsibility have come concerns about the worthiness of the poor for help, gross assumptions about their willingness to work, and suspicions of fraud.

The American system of income maintenance has been particularly unresponsive to the needs of the working poor. Even with full-time employment, these people cannot make ends meet because of their low income. Yet they are ineligible for the major welfare programs because they are working. Unless they qualify for Medicaid or for food stamps, they get little or no help from public agencies. A guaranteed income is the only proposal that would help them.

WELFARE BENEFITS AND WELFARE REFORMS

The Social Security Act provides cash grants to the needy aged, blind, permanently and totally disabled, and families of dependent children. The first three categories are federally financed and administered with uniform national eligibility conditions and benefit levels. In addition to these four client groups, the federal government also supports Medicaid grants and provides a food stamp program.

Aid to Families with Dependent Children

Aid to Families with Dependent Children (AFDC) is the largest welfare program and is designed to provide care for children and families that are in financial need. Most of the benefits go to single, female parents, but half the states also provide for grants to families that have an unemployed father in the home. Benefit levels are set by the states, and many states do not pay enough to cover the budgeted need of eligible families.

Supplemental Security Income

The Supplementary Security Income (SSI) program (81 Stat. 896) replaced the former federal-state categorical programs of aid to the aged, blind, and permanently and totally disabled in the fifty states and the District of Columbia for the purpose of ensuring a minimum level of income for all eligible individuals. The change became effective January 1, 1974. The federal component of SSI is administered by the Social Security Administration and financed through general funds from the U.S. Treasury. Uniform nationwide eligibility standards and a federal income floor provide more equitable treatment of aged, blind, and disabled persons with limited income and resources. In many cases, payments supplement the basic Social Security benefits. In addition, states may supplement this payment for certain categories of beneficiaries and must supplement it for persons who would otherwise have been adversely affected by the transition to the federal program. Federal administration of a state's supplemental program provided a strong economic incentive for states to adopt SSI.

Medicaid

Welfare recipients and others who cannot pay the cost of medical care are eligible for Medicaid (79 Stat. 343), which is discussed in Chapter 23.

ATTITUDES TOWARD PUBLIC ASSISTANCE

High cost and a widespread feeling that many recipients are unworthy of public funds have made public assistance programs controversial. As a result, many states tried to control expenditures by regulating eligibility through residency and work requirements and also by restricting the personal conduct and life-style of the recipient. These questions led to litigation in the late 1960s.

Major issues identified included: midnight raids on the homes of AFDC recipients and the "man in the house" rule, residence requirements, work requirements, due process, state discretion to set benefit levels to meet only partial financial need, and maximum family grants.

In the 1970s, the U.S. Supreme Court ruled on all these questions, largely because of diligent efforts of Office of Economic Opportunity lawyers interested in law reform. Sometimes, however, the cases appealed were by no means ideal to achieve the goals of the law reformers. In *King v. Smith*, the alleged father substitute was living with a legal spouse as well as the subject of the litigation.

Public assistance litigation decreased in the late 1970s and in the 1980s. Not only did the welfare rights movement lose strength, but support for legal aid declined. Also, legal-aid lawyers became reluctant to bring cases to a conservative Supreme Court for fear the decision would be unfavorable.

SEXUAL CONDUCT AND ELIGIBILITY FOR PUBLIC ASSISTANCE

AFDC grants are intended to benefit needy children, yet eligibility may be conditional on the behavior of the family. King v. Smith, 392 U.S. 309 (1968), recounts attempts to regulate parental sexual behavior as a condition of eligibility. Since Alabama's AFDC program did not include unemployed fathers, the state argued that families with a natural mother and a substitute father should be disqualified in the same way as a family with two natural parents. The substitute father regulation also was intended to discourage illegitimacy and illicit sexual conduct. The goal of AFDC was held by the U.S. Supreme Court to be "protection of children." Consequently, Alabama's AFDC eligibility requirements conflicted with the Social Security Act. The *King* decision also included a legal definition of "dependent child" and affirmed permissible state latitude in determining the level of AFDC benefits.

KING v. SMITH

Supreme Court of the United States, 392 U.S. 309 (1968).

Mr. Chief Justice WARREN delivered the opinion of the Court.

Alabama, together with every other State, Puerto Rico, the Virgin Islands, the District of Columbia, and Guam, participates in the Federal Government's Aid to Families with Dependent Children (AFDC) program, which was established by the Social Security Act of 1935. . . . At issue is the validity of Alabama's so-called "substitute father" regulation which denies AFDC payments to the children of a mother who "cohabits" in or outside her home with any single or married able-bodied man. . . .

. . . The category singled out for welfare assistance by AFDC is the "dependent child," who is defined . . . as an age-qualified "needy child . . . who has been deprived of parental support or care by reason of the death, continued absence from the home or physical or mental incapacity of a parent, and who is living with" any one of several listed relatives. Under this provision, and insofar as relevant here, aid can be granted only if "a parent" of the needy child is continually absent from the home. Alabama considers a man who qualifies as a "substitute father" under its regulation to be a nonabsent within the federal statute. The State therefore denies aid to an otherwise eligible needy child on the basis that his substitute parent is not absent from the home. . . .

. . . Whether the substitute father is actually the father of the children is irrelevant. It is also irrelevant whether he is legally obligated to support the children, and whether he does in fact contribute to their support. What is determinative is simply whether he "cohabits" with the mother. . . .

The State argues that its substitute father regulation simply defines who is a nonabsent "parent" under § 406(a) of the Social Security Act. . . . The State submits that the regulation is a legitimate way of allocating its limited resources available for AFDC assistance, in that it reduces the caseload of its social workers and provides increased benefits to those still eligible for assistance. Two state interests are asserted in support of the allocation of AFDC assistance achieved by the regulation: first, it discourages illicit sexual relationships and illegitimate births; second, it puts families in which there is an informal "marital" relationship on a par with those in which there is an ordinary marital relationship, because families of the latter sort are not eligible for AFDC assistance.

We think it well to note at the outset what is *not* involved in this case. There is no question that States have considerable latitude in allocating their AFDC resources, since each State is free to set its own standard of need and to determine the level of benefits by the amount of funds it devotes to the program. Further, there is no question that regular and actual contributions to a needy child, including contributions from the kind of person Alabama calls a substitute father, can be taken into account in determining whether the child is needy. In other words, if by reason of such a man's contribution, the child is not in financial need, the child would be ineligible for AFDC assistance without regard to the substitute father rule. The appellees here, however, meet Alabama's need requirements; their alleged substitute father makes no contribution to their support; and they have been denied assistance solely on the basis of the substitute father regulation. Further, the regulation itself is unrelated to need, because the actual financial situation of the family is irrelevant in determining the existence of a substitute father.

Also not involved in this case is the question of Alabama's general power to deal with conduct it regards as immoral and with the problem of illegitimacy. This appeal raises only the question whether the State may deal with these problems in the manner that it has here—by flatly denying AFDC assistance to otherwise eligible dependent children.

Alabama's argument based on its interests in discouraging immorality and illegitimacy would have been quite relevant at one time in the history of the AFDC program. However, subsequent developments clearly establish that these state interests are not presently legitimate justifications for AFDC disqualification. Insofar as this or any similar regulation is based on the State's asserted interest in discouraging illicit sexual behavior and illegitimacy, it plainly conflicts with federal law and policy.

A significant characteristic of public welfare programs during the last half of the 19th century in this country was their preference for the "worthy" poor. Some poor persons were thought worthy of public assistance, and others were thought unworthy because of their supposed incapacity for "moral regeneration." . . . This worthy-person concept characterized the mothers' pension welfare programs, which were the precursors of AFDC. . . . Benefits under the mothers' pension programs, accordingly, were customarily restricted to widows who were considered morally fit. . . .

In this social context it is not surprising that both the House and Senate Committee Reports on the Social Security Act of 1935 indicate that States participating in AFDC were free to impose eligibility requirements relating to the "moral character" of applicants. . . . During the following years, many state AFDC plans included provisions making ineligible for assistance dependent children not living in "suitable homes." . . . As applied, these suitable home provisions frequently disqualified children on the basis of the alleged immoral behavior of their mothers. . . .

In the 1940s, suitable home provisions came under increasing attack. Critics argued, for example, that such disqualification provisions undermined a mother's confidence and authority, thereby promoting continued dependency; that they forced destitute mothers into increased immorality as a means of earning money; that they were habitually used to disguise systematic racial discrimination; and that they senselessly punished impoverished children on the basis of their mothers' behavior, while inconsistently permitting them to remain in the allegedly unsuitable homes. In 1945, the predecessor of HEW produced a state letter arguing against suitable-home provisions and recommending their abolition. . . . Although 15 States abolished their provisions during the following decade, numerous other States retained them. . . .

In the 1950s, matters became further complicated by pressures in numerous States to disqualify illegitimate children from AFDC assistance. Attempts were made in at least 18 States to enact laws excluding children on the basis of their own or their siblings' birth status. . . . All but three attempts failed to pass the state legislatures, and two of the three successful bills were vetoed by the governors of the States involved. . . . In 1960, the federal agency strongly disapproved of illegitimacy disqualifications. . . .

Nonetheless, in 1960, Louisiana enacted legislation requiring, as a condition precedent for AFDC eligibility, that the home of a dependent child be "suitable," and specifying that any home in which an illegitimate child had been born subsequent to the receipt of public assistance would be considered unsuitable. Louisiana Acts, No. 251 (1960). In the summer of 1960, approximately 23,000 children were dropped from Louisiana's AFDC rolls. . . .

In disapproving this legislation, then Secretary of Health, Education, and Welfare Flemming issued what is now known as the Flemming Ruling, stating that as of July 1, 1961,

> "*A State plan . . . may not impose an eligibility condition that would deny assistance with respect to a needy child on the basis that the home conditions in which the child lives are unsuitable, while the child continues to reside in the home.* Assistance will therefore be continued during the time efforts are being made either to improve the home conditions or to make arrangements for the child elsewhere."

Congress quickly approved the Flemming Ruling, while extending until September 1, 1962, the time for state compliance. . . . At the same time, Congress acted to implement the ruling by providing, on a temporary basis, that dependent children could receive AFDC assistance if they were placed in foster homes after a court determination that their former homes were, as the Senate Report stated, "unsuitable because of the immoral or negligent behavior of the parent.". . .

In 1962, Congress made permanent the provision for AFDC assistance to children placed in foster homes and extended such coverage to include children placed in child-care institutions. . . . amending § 404(b) of the Act. As amended, the statute permits States to disqualify from AFDC aid children who live in unsuitable homes, provided they are granted other "adequate care and assistance.". . .

Thus under the 1961 and 1962 amendments to the Social Security Act, the States are permitted to remove a child from a home that is judicially determined to be so unsuitable as to "be contrary to the welfare of such child.". . . The States are also permitted to terminate AFDC assistance to a child living in an unsuitable home, if they provide other adequate care and assistance for the child under a general welfare program. . . .The statutory approval of the Flemming Ruling, however, precludes the States from otherwise denying AFDC assistance to dependent children on the basis of their mother's alleged immorality or to discourage illegitimate births.

The most recent congressional amendments to the Social Security Act further corroborate that federal public welfare policy now rests on a basis considerably more sophisticated and enlightened than the "worthy-person" concept of earlier times. State plans are now required to provide for a rehabilitative program of improving and correcting unsuitable homes . . .to provide voluntary family planning services for the purpose of reducing illegitimate births, . . . and to provide a program for establishing the paternity of illegitimate children and securing support for them. . . .

In sum, Congress has determined that immorality and illegitimacy should be dealt with through rehabilitative measures rather than measures that punish dependent children, and that protection of such children is the paramount goal of AFDC. In light of the Flemming Ruling and the 1961, 1962, and 1968 amendments to the Social Security Act, it is simply inconceivable, as HEW has recognized, that Alabama is free to discourage immorality and illegitimacy by the device of absolute disqualification of needy children. Alabama may deal with these problems by several different methods under the Social Security Act. But the method it has chosen plainly conflicts with the Act.

III

Alabama's second justification for its substitute father regulation is that "there is a public interest in a State not undertaking the payment of these funds to families who because of their living arrangements would be in the same situation as if the parents were married, except for the marriage." In other words, the State argues that since in Alabama the needy children of married couples are not eligible for AFDC aid so long as their father is in the home, it is only fair that children of a mother who cohabits with a man not her husband and not their father be treated similarly. The difficulty with this argument is that it fails to take account of the circumstance that children of fathers living in the home are in a very different position from children of mothers who cohabit with men not their fathers: the child's father has a legal duty to support him, while the unrelated substitute father, at least in Alabama, does not. We believe Congress intended the term "parent" in § 406(a) of the Act, 42 U.S.C. § 606(a), to include only those persons with a legal duty of support.

Alabama's substitute father regulation, as written and as applied in this case, requires the disqualification of otherwise eligible dependent children if their mother "cohabits" with a man who is not obligated by Alabama law to support the children. The regulation is therefore invalid because it defines "parent" in a manner that is inconsistent with § 406(a) of the Social Security Act, 42 U.S.C. § 606(a). In denying AFDC assistance to appellees on the basis of this invalid regulation, Alabama has breached its federally imposed obligation to furnish "aid to families with dependent children . . . with reasonable promptness to all eligible individuals. . . ."

States are not barred from judicial determination of unsuitable homes, but they must be sure that needy children receive aid either in their own home or in a more suitable setting. About half the states allow payments to families of needy children when the father is present and able-bodied, as long as he is unemployed. In these states the presence of a male with the legal duty of support would not prevent aid.

The "early morning mass raid" (alluded to in the majority opinion in *Wyman v. James*, 400 U.S. 309 [1971]; later in this chapter) was an unannounced intrusion into recipients' homes to detect a sexual partner as evidence of unreported financial resources. The California Supreme Court, in *Parrish v. Civil Service Commission of Alameda County*, held that this practice violated the Fourth Amendment. Subsequent federal regulations forbade entering a recipient's home during sleeping hours. The case is an example of expectations applied to social workers and AFDC recipients.

PARRISH v. CIVIL SERVICE COMMISSION OF COUNTY OF ALAMEDA

Supreme Court of California, 425 P.2d 223 (1967).

TOBRINER, Justice.

In the present case an Alameda County social worker, discharged for "insubordination" for declining to participate in a mass morning raid upon the homes of the county's welfare recipients, seeks reinstatement with back pay on the ground that such participation would have involved him in multiple violations of rights secured by the federal and state Constitutions. He urges that his superiors could not properly direct him to participate in an illegal activity and that he could not, therefore, be dismissed for declining to follow such directions.

For the reason set forth in this opinion we have decided that the county's failure to secure legally effective consent to search the homes of welfare recipients rendered the mass raids unconstitutional. We have determined further that, even if effective consent had been obtained, the county could not constitutionally condition the continued receipt of welfare benefits upon the giving of such consent. We have therefore held, for these two independently sufficient reasons, that the project in which the county directed the plaintiff to take part transgressed constitutional limitations. In light of plaintiff's knowledge as to the scope and methods of the projected operation, we have concluded that he possessed adequate grounds for declining to participate.

On November 21, 1962, the Board of Supervisors of Alameda County ordered the county welfare director to initiate a series of unannounced early-morning searches of the homes of the county's welfare recipients for the purpose of detecting the presence of "unauthorized males." The searches were to be modeled on a Kern County project popularly known as "Operation Weekend."

Neither in planning nor in executing the searches did the county authorities attempt to secure appropriate search warrants. The social workers who conducted the searches were not required or permitted to restrict them to the homes of persons whom they had probable cause to arrest, or even to the homes of those welfare recipients whose eligibility they had any reason to doubt. Indeed, as will later appear, the majority of persons whose homes were searched were under no suspicion whatever and were in fact subjected to the raid for that very reason. . . .

Since the social workers lacked experience with the techniques employed by the fraud investigators they received special instruction in the procedures to be followed. Their superiors instructed them to work in pairs with one member covering the back door of each dwelling while the recipient's own social worker presented himself at the front door and sought admittance. Once inside, he would proceed to the rear door and admit his companion. Together the two would conduct a thorough search of the entire dwelling, giving particular attention to beds, closets, bathrooms and other possible places of concealment.

Plaintiff was one of the social workers chosen to participate in the first wave of raids. Upon learning the nature of the proposed operation, he submitted a letter to his superior declaring that he could not participate because of his conviction that such searches were illegal. After plaintiff had explained his position to the division chief and the welfare director, he was discharged for insubordination.

"Insubordination can be rightfully predicated only upon a refusal to obey some order which a superior officer is entitled to give and entitled to have obeyed." . . . Plaintiff contends that his superiors were not entitled to compel his participation in illegal searches and urges that such participation might have exposed him to severe penalties under federal law. . . . We conclude that the searches contemplated and undertaken in the course of the operation in the present case must be deemed unconstitutional unless the county can show compliance with the standards which govern searches for evidence of crime. . . .

Our case proceeds far beyond a mere request for admission presented by authorities under color of office. Thus we need not determine here whether a request for entry, voiced by one in a position of authority under circumstances which suggest that some official reprisal might attend a refusal, is itself sufficient to vitiate an affirmative response by an individual who had not been apprised of his Fourth Amendment rights. The persons subjected to the instant operation confronted far more than the amorphous threat of official displeasure which necessarily attends any such request. The request for entry by persons whom the beneficiaries knew to possess virtually unlimited power over their very livelihood posed a threat which was far more certain, immediate, and substantial. These circumstances nullify the legal effectiveness of the apparent consent secured by the Alameda County searchers. Both this court and the Supreme Court of the United States have recently emphasized the heavy burden which the government bears when it seeks to rely upon a supposed waiver of constitutional rights. The county has not sustained that burden here. . . .

In any event the instant operation does not meet the last of the three requirements which it must satisfy: so striking is the disparity between the operation's declared purpose and the means employed, so broad its gratuitous reach, and so convincing the evidence that improper considerations dictated its ultimate scope, that no valid link remains between that operation and its proffered justification. . . . The judgment is reversed and the cause is remanded to the trial court with directions to enter judgment in accordance with this opinion.

Parrish was reinstated in his job and given back pay by Alameda County.

RESIDENCE REQUIREMENTS FOR PUBLIC ASSISTANCE

Residence requirements as long as five years have been used as traditional bars to receipt of aid. Originating from the English poor laws, such requirements were designed to discourage people from intentionally migrating to get on welfare. Restrictions on eligibility have been most important in states with high benefit levels and in states that attract the elderly at the time of retirement.

In Shapiro v. Thompson, 394 U.S. 618 (1969), the Supreme Court held that durational residence requirements deprived recent arrivals of equal protection by restricting the fundamental right of interstate travel. Aid recipients must intend to reside legally within the state, but they need not have lived there for a certain period of time to become eligible for benefits. This decision has led to strong pressure from the states to finance AFDC fully from federal funds. The decision included this rationale:

> Appellants justify the waiting-period requirement as a protective device to preserve the fiscal integrity of state public assistance programs. It is asserted that people who require welfare assistance during their first year of residence in a State are likely to become continuing burdens on state welfare programs. Therefore, the argument runs, if such people can be deterred from entering the jurisdiction by denying them welfare benefits during the first year, state programs to assist long-time residents will not be impaired by a substantial influx of indigent newcomers. . . .
>
> This Court long ago recognized that the nature of our Federal Union and our constitutional concepts of personal liberty unite to require that all citizens be free to travel throughout the length and breadth of our land uninhibited by statutes, rules, or regulations which unreasonably burden or restrict this movement.

In Graham v. Richardson, 403 U.S. 365 (1971), the eligibility requirement that AFDC recipients be U.S. citizens and the imposition of a durational residential requirement on aliens was held to be invalid.

Also under the law, individuals are not eligible for SSI during any month they are outside the United States—defined as the fifty states and the District of Columbia. The U.S. Supreme Court upheld the rule that recipients who went to Puerto Rico were thereby disqualified for SSI. The decision included the observations that benefits otherwise would be superior to those available to residents of Puerto Rico and that a state would be responsible for paying benefits indefinitely once a person had resided there (Califano v. Torres, 435 U.S. 1 [1978]).

In Harris v. Rosario, 446 U.S. 651 (1980), inferior AFDC assistance grants provided by Puerto Rico compared with the states were held not to violate equal protection provisions. Puerto Rican residents do not contribute to the U.S. Treasury, the cost of treating Puerto Rico as a state for this purpose would be high, and a greater AFDC benefit would disrupt the Puerto Rican economy.

WORK REQUIREMENTS AND PUBLIC ASSISTANCE

Federal AFDC eligibility requirements state that caretakers of needy dependent children must be evaluated as to employability. If certified employable, they must register for training and employment in order to qualify for aid. The Work Incentive (WIN) Program (42 U.S.C. 8630) has been designed to provide work training. Failure to cooperate results in exclusion of the caretaker in determination of the benefit level. Failure to participate in the training program may harm the children by decreasing the amount of money available to the AFDC household.

State work requirements for AFDC caretakers stricter than those required by the federal government were the issue in New York State Department of Social Services v. Dublino, 413 U.S. 405 (1973).

NEW YORK STATE DEPARTMENT OF SOCIAL SERVICES v. DUBLINO

Supreme Court of the United States, 413 U.S. 405 (1973).

The question before us is whether the Social Security Act of 1935, 49 Stat. 620, as amended, bars a State from independently requiring individuals to accept employment as a condition for receipt of federally funded aid to families with dependent children. More precisely, the issue is whether that part of the Social Security Act known as the Federal Work Incentive Program (WIN) preempts the provisions of the New York Social Welfare Law, McKinney's Consol Laws, c. 55, commonly referred to as the New York Work Rules. . . .

. . . The Work Rules establish a presumption that certain recipients of public assistance are employable and require those recipients to report every two weeks to pick up their assistance checks in person; to file every two weeks a certificate from the appropriate public employment office stating that no suitable employment opportunities are available; to report for requested employment interviews; to report to the public employment office the result of a referral for employment; and not to fail willfully to report for suitable employment when available. In addition to establishing a system of referral for employment in the private sector of the economy, the Work Rules permit the establishment of public works projects in New York's social service districts. Failure of "employable" persons to participate in the operation of the Work Rules results in a loss of assistance.

In the court below, appellees, New York public assistance recipients subject to the Work Rules, challenged those Rules as violative of several provisions of the Constitution and as having been preempted by the WIN provisions of the Federal Social Security Act. The three-judge District Court rejected all but the last contention. . . . On this point, it held that "for those in the AFDC program WIN preempts" the New York Work Rules. . . . We now reverse this holding. . . .

New York . . . has attempted to operate the Work Rules in such a manner as to avoid friction and overlap with WIN. Officials from both the State Department of Labor and a local Social Service Department testified below that every AFDC recipient appropriate for WIN was first referred there, that no person was to be referred to the state program who was participating in WIN, and that only if there was no position available for him under WIN, was a recipient to be referred for employment pursuant to state statute. Where coordinate state and federal efforts exist within a complementary administrative framework, and in the pursuit of common purposes, the case for federal pre-emption becomes a less persuasive one. . . .

We thus reverse the holding below that WIN pre-empts the New York Work Rules. Our ruling establishes the validity of a state work program as one means of helping AFDC recipients return to gainful employment. . . .

In Lavine v. Milne, 424 U.S. 577 (1976), the Court ruled that New York could properly exclude home benefits for seventy-five days if anyone terminates employment or reduces earning capacity voluntarily, unless the applicants could establish that they did not leave employment to qualify for benefits. The burden of proof for eligibility is on the applicant.

Townsend v. Swank, 404 U.S. 282 (1971), curtailed state discretion regarding eligibility of older children for AFDC:

> Under the Illinois statute and regulation needy dependent children 18 through 20 years of age who attend high school or vocational training school are eligible for benefits under the federally assisted Aid to Families with Dependent Children program (AFDC) . . . but such children who attend a college or university are not eligible. Section 406(a)(2) of the Social Security Act, on the other hand, defines "dependent child" to include a child " . . . (B) under the age of twenty-one and (as determined by the State in accordance with standards prescribed by the Secretary) a student regularly attending a school, college, or university, or regularly attending a course of vocational or technical training designed to fit him for gainful employment." . . . We hold that the Illinois statute and regulation conflict with § 406(a)(2)(B) and for that reason are invalid under the Supremacy Clause, 404 U.S. at 283–285.

The Supreme Court also limited state discretion regarding work requirements in Shea v. Vialpando, 416 U.S. 251 (1974). Colorado's attempt to establish a standard income disregard when calculating work expenses for an employed AFDC recipient was held invalid because it served as a maximum. The Court held that a standard disregard must provide for individual expenses beyond the standard.

Maher v. Gagne, 448 U.S. 122 (1980), gave AFDC recipientss the right to deduct actual work expenses in excess of state allowances, when they could be proved, and to collect attorney feess for the appeal.

Two cases dealt with unemployment compensation. In Philbrook v. Glodgett, 421 U.S. 707 (1975), AFDC applicants could be excluded from AFDC benefits only for those weeks in which unemployment compensation was actually received. States could also deny AFDC benefits to participants in a labor dispute (Batterton v. Francis, 432 U.S. 416 [1977]).

THE RIGHT TO ADMINISTRA-TIVE HEARINGS

Applicants denied AFDC benefits have a right to an administrative hearing, but they are not permitted to obtain benefits in the interim pending the outcome of their appeal. Termination of aid requires a prior hearing on the authority of Goldberg v. Kelly, 397 U.S. 254 (1970).

GOLDBERG v. KELLY

Supreme Court of the United States, 397 U.S. 254 (1970).

Mr. Justice BRENNAN delivered the opinion of the Court.

The question for decision is whether a State that terminates public assistance payments to a particular recipient without affording him the opportunity for an evidentiary hearing prior to termination denies the recipient procedural due process in violation of the Due Process Clause of the Fourteenth Amendment.

This action was brought in the District Court for the Southern District of New York by residents of New York City receiving financial aid under the federally assisted program of Aid to Families with Dependent Children (AFDC) or under New York State's general Home Relief program. Their complaint alleged that the New York State and New York City officials administering these programs terminated, or were about to terminate, such aid without prior notice and hearing, thereby denying them due process of law. At the time the suits were filed there was no requirement of prior notice or hearing of any kind before termination of financial aid. However, the State and city adopted procedures for notice and hearing after the suits were brought, and the plaintiffs, appellees here, . . . then challenged the constitutional adequacy of those procedures.

. . . A caseworker who has doubts about the recipient's continued eligibility must first discuss them with the recipient. If the caseworker concludes that the recipient is no longer eligible, he recommends termination of aid to a unit supervisor. If the latter concurs, he sends the recipient a letter stating the reasons for proposing to terminate aid and notifying him that within seven days he may request that a higher official review the record, and may support the request with a written statement prepared personally or with the aid of an attorney or other person. If the reviewing official affirms the determination of ineligibility, aid is stopped immediately and the recipient is informed by letter of the reasons for the action. Appellees' challenge to this procedure emphasizes the absence of any provisions for the personal appearance of the recipient before the reviewing official, for oral presentation of evidence, and for confrontation and cross-examination of adverse witnesses. However, the letter does inform the recipient that he may request a post-termination "fair hearing." This is a proceeding before an independent state hearing officer at which the recipient may appear personally, offer oral evidence, confront and cross-examine the witnesses against him, and have a record made of the hearing. If the recipient prevails at the "fair hearing" he is paid all funds erroneously withheld. . . .

The constitutional issue to be decided, therefore, is the narrow one whether the Due Process Clause requires that the recipient be afforded an evidentiary hearing *before* the termination of benefits. . . .

. . . We agree with the District Court that when welfare is discontinued, only a pre-termination evidentiary hearing provides the recipient with procedural due process. . . .

We also agree with the District Court, however, that the pre-termination hearing need not take the form of a judicial or quasi-judicial trial. We bear in mind that the statutory "fair hearing" will provide the recipient with a full administrative review. Accordingly, the pre-termination hearing has one function only: to produce an initial determination of the validity of the welfare department's grounds for discontinuance of payments in order to protect a recipient against an erroneous termination of his benefits. . . .

The opportunity to be heard must be tailored to the capacities and circumstances of those who are to be heard. It is not enough that a welfare recipient may present his position to the decision maker in writing or second-hand through his caseworker. Written submissions are an unrealistic option for most recipients, who lack the educational attainment necessary to write effectively and who cannot obtain professional assistance. Moreover, written submissions do not afford the flexibility of oral presentations; they do not permit the recipient to mold his argument to the issues the decision maker appears to regard as important. Particularly where credibility and veracity are at issue, as they must be in many termination proceedings, written submissions are a wholly unsatisfactory basis for decision. The second-hand presentation to the decision maker by the caseworker has its own deficiencies; since the caseworker usually gathers the facts upon which the charge of ineligibility rests, the presentation of the recipient's side of the controversy cannot safely be left to him. Therefore a recipient must be allowed to state his position orally. Informal procedures will suffice; in this context due process does not require a particular order of proof or mode of offering evidence. . . .

. . . Welfare recipients must . . . be given an opportunity to confront and cross-examine the witnesses relied on by the department.

. . . We do not say that counsel must be provided at the pre-termination hearing, but only that the recipient must be allowed to retain an attorney if he so desires. . . .

Federal regulations issued in light of *Goldberg* required a prior hearing in cases of proposed reduction of benefits as well as termination. Following the single administrative hearing, the decision rendered by the state agency may be reviewed by a state or federal court, as applicable.

Other important pertinent rulings concerning the right to receive benefits include

■ In Maine v. Thiboutot, 448 U.S. 1 (1980), attorney's fees were allowed for successful appeals for retroactive benefits.

POVERTY AND INCOME MAINTENANCE 429

■ In Edelman v. Jordan, 415 U.S. 651 (1974), the Court determined that while new applicants who were refused benefits had the right to appeal, the applicants were not entitled to retroactive payments even if the appeals were successful.

■ In Quern v. Jordan, 440 U.S. 332 (1979), the Court ruled that initial applicants for aged, blind, or disabled benefits from federal sources whose applications were denied may use administrative procedures to receive a determination of entitlement to past benefits from state sources.

HOME VISITS AND ELIGIBILITY

Home visits were considered an important tool in the helping process at the time they were challenged by welfare clients. Since then, payments have been administered by one group of social workers, and social services have been administered by another group. Because clients no longer are required to receive social services, the need for home visits has been reduced. Physical danger to public assistance workers has also led to the reduction of home visits. Protection from danger has become a subject of union contracts entered into by the workers.

Federal and state regulations require initial and periodic determination of eligibility for AFDC. Most states include home visits for initial determination and periodic subsequent visits to assure continued eligibility as determined by regulations or the discretion of the welfare worker. The constitutionality of home visit requirements as a condition of receiving aid was challenged. Wyman v. James, 400 U.S. 309 (1971), reversed the lower court decision.

WYMAN v. JAMES

Supreme Court of the United States, 400 U.S. 309 (1971).

Mr. Justice BLACKMUN delivered the opinion of the Court.

This appeal presents the issue whether a beneficiary of the program for Aid to Families with Dependent Children (AFDC) may refuse a home visit by the caseworker without risking the termination of benefits. . . .

The District Court majority held that a mother receiving AFDC relief may refuse, without forfeiting her right to that relief, the periodic home visit which the cited New York statutes and regulations prescribe as a condition for the continuance of assistance under the program. The beneficiary's thesis, and that of the District Court majority, is that home visitation is a search and, when not consented to or when not supported by a warrant based on probable cause, violates the beneficiary's Fourth and Fourteenth Amendment rights. . . .

Plaintiff Barbara James is the mother of a son, Maurice, who was born in May 1967. They reside in New York City. Mrs. James first applied for AFDC assistance shortly before Maurice's birth. A caseworker made a visit to her apartment at that time without objection. The assistance was authorized.

Two years later, on May 8, 1969, a caseworker wrote Mrs. James that she would visit her home on May 14. Upon receipt of this advice, Mrs. James telephoned the worker that, although she was willing to supply information "reasonable and relevant" to her need for public assistance, any discussion was not to take place at her home. The worker told Mrs. James that she was required by law to visit in her home and that refusal to permit the visit would result in the termination of assistance. Permission was still denied.

On May 13 the City Department of Social Services sent Mrs. James a notice of intent to discontinue assistance because of the visitation refusal. The notice advised the beneficiary of her right to a hearing before a review officer. The hearing was requested and was held on May 27. Mrs. James appeared with an attorney at that hearing. They continued to refuse permission for a worker to visit the James home, but again expressed willingness to cooperate and to permit visits elsewhere. The review officer ruled that the refusal was a proper ground for the termination of assistance. His written decision stated:

> "The home visit which Mrs. James refuses to permit is for the purpose of determining if there are any changes in her situation that might affect her eligibility to continue to receive Public Assistance, or that might affect the amount of such assistance, and to see if there are any social services which the Department of Social Services can provide to the family."

A notice of termination issued on June 2.

Thereupon, without seeking a hearing at the state level, Mrs. James, individually and on behalf of Maurice, and purporting to act on behalf of all other persons similarly situated, instituted the present civil rights suit under 42 U.S.C. § 1983. She alleged the denial of rights guaranteed to her under the First, Third, Fourth, Fifth, Sixth, Ninth, Tenth, and Fourteenth Amendments, and under Subchapters IV and XVI of the Social Security Act and regulations issued thereunder. She further alleged that she and her son have no income, resources, or support other than the benefits received under the AFDC program. She asked for declaratory and injunctive relief. A temporary restraining order was issued on June 13, James v. Goldberg, . . . and the three-judge District Court was convened. . . .

> "Whenever the State agency has reason to believe that any payments of aid . . . made with respect to a child are not being or may not be used in the best interests of the child, the State agency may provide for such counseling and guidance services with respect to the use of such payments and the management of other funds by the relative . . . in order to assure use of such payments in the best interests of such child, and may provide for advising such relative that continued failure to so use such payments will result in substitution therefor of protective payments . . . or in seeking the appointment of a guardian . . . or in the imposition of criminal or civil penalties. . . ."

III

When a case involves a home and some type of official intrusion into that home, as this case appears to do, an immediate and natural reaction is one of concern about Fourth Amendment rights and the protection which that Amendment is intended to afford. Its emphasis indeed is upon one of the most precious aspects of personal security in the home: "The right of the people to be secure in their persons, houses, papers, and effects. . . ." This Court has characterized that right as "basic to a free society." And over the years the Court consistently has been most protective of the privacy of the dwelling.

In *Camara*, Mr. Justice White, after noting that the "translation of the abstract prohibition against 'unreasonable searches and seizures' into workable guidelines for the decision of particular cases is a difficult task," went on to observe:

"Nevertheless, one governing principle, justified by history and by current experience, has consistently been followed: except in certain carefully defined classes of cases, a search of private property without proper consent is 'unreasonable' unless it has been authorized by a valid search warrant." 387 U.S., at 528–529, 87 S.Ct., at 1730–1731.

He pointed out, too, that one's Fourth Amendment protection subsists apart from his being suspected of criminal behavior. . . .

IV

This natural and quite proper protective attitude, however, is not a factor in this case, for the seemingly obvious and simple reason that we are not concerned here with any search by the New York social service agency in the Fourth Amendment meaning of that term, . . . the visitation itself is not forced or compelled, and that the beneficiary's denial of permission is not a criminal act. If consent to the visitation is withheld, no visitation takes place. The aid then never begins or merely ceases, as the case may be. There is no entry of the home and there is no search.

There are a number of factors that compel us to conclude that the home visit proposed for Mrs. James is not unreasonable:

1. The public's interest in this particular segment of the area of assistance to the unfortunate is protection and aid for the dependent child whose family requires such aid for that child. The focus is on the *child* and, further, it is on the child who is *dependent*. There is no more worthy object of the public's concern. The dependent child's needs are paramount, and only with hesitancy would we relegate those needs, in the scale of comparative values, to a position secondary to what the mother claims as her rights.

2. The agency, with tax funds provided from federal as well as from state sources, is fulfilling a public trust. The State, working through its qualified welfare agency, has appropriate and paramount interest and concern in seeing and assuring that the intended and proper objects of that tax-produced assistance are the ones who benefit from the aid it dispenses. Surely it is not unreasonable, in the Fourth Amendment sense or in any other sense of that term, that the State have at its command a gentle means, of limited extent and of practical and considerate application, of achieving that assurance.

3. One who dispenses purely private charity naturally has an interest in and expects to know how his charitable funds are utilized and put to work. The public, when it is the provider, rightly expects the same. It might well expect more, because of the trust aspect of public funds, and the recipient, as well as the caseworker, has not only an interest but an obligation.

4. The emphasis of the New York statutes and regulations is upon the home, upon "close contact" with the beneficiary, upon restoring the aid recipient "to a condition of self-support," and upon the relief of his distress. The federal emphasis is no different. It is upon "assistance and rehabilitation," upon maintaining and strengthening family life, and upon "maximum self-support and personal independence consistent with the maintenance of continuing parental care and protection . . ." 42 U.S.C. § 601 (1964 ed. Supp. V); Dandridge v. Williams, 397 U.S. 471, 479, 90 S.Ct. 1153, 1158, 25 L.Ed.2d 491 (1970), and id., at 510, 90 S.Ct., at 1174 (Marshall, J., dissenting). It requires cooperation from the state agency upon specified

standards and in specified ways. And it is concerned about any possible exploitation of the child.

5. The home visit, it is true, is not required by federal statute or regulation. But it has been noted that the visit is "the heart of welfare administration"; that it affords "a personal, rehabilitative orientation, unlike that of most federal programs"; and that the "more pronounced service orientation" effected by Congress with the 1956 amendments to the Social Security Act "gave redoubled importance to the practice of home visiting." Note, Rehabilitation, Investigation and the Welfare Home Visit. . . . The home visit is an established routine in States besides New York.

6. The means employed by the New York agency are significant. Mrs. James received written notice several days in advance of the intended home visit. The date was specified. Section 134-a of the New York Social Services Law, effective April 1, 1967, and set forth in n. 2, supra, sets the tone. Privacy is emphasized. The applicant-recipient is made the primary source of information as to eligibility. Outside informational sources, other than public records, are to be consulted only with the beneficiary's consent. Forcible entry or entry under false pretenses or visitation outside working hours or snooping in the home are forbidden. HEW Handbook of Public Assistance Administration, pt. IV. . . . All this minimizes any "burden" upon the homeowner's right against unreasonable intrusion.

7. Mrs. James, in fact, on this record presents no specific complaint of any unreasonable intrusion of her home and nothing that supports an inference that the desired home visit had as its purpose the obtaining of information as to criminal activity. She complains of no proposed visitation at an awkward or retirement hour. She suggests no forcible entry. She refers to no snooping. She describes no impolite or reprehensible conduct of any kind. She alleges only, in general and nonspecific terms, that on previous visits and, on information and belief, on visitation at the home of other aid recipients, "questions concerning personal relationships, beliefs and behavior are raised and pressed which are unnecessary for a determination of continuing eligibility." Paradoxically, this same complaint could be made of a conference held elsewhere than in the home, and yet this is what is sought by Mrs. James. The same complaint could be made of the census taker's questions.

What Mrs. James appears to want from the agency that provides her and her infant son with the necessities for life is the right to receive those necessities upon her own informational terms, to utilize the Fourth Amendment as a wedge for imposing those terms, and to avoid questions of any kind.

8. We are not persuaded, as Mrs. James would have us be, that all information pertinent to the issue of eligibility can be obtained by the agency through an interview at a place other than the home, or, as the District Court majority suggested, by examining a lease or a birth certificate, or by periodic medical examinations, or by interviews with school personnel. 303 F.Supp. at 943. Although these secondary sources might be helpful, they would not always assure verification of actual residence or of actual physical presence in the home, which are requisites for AFDC benefits, or of impending medical needs. And, of course, little children, such as Maurice James, are not yet registered in school.

9. The visit is not one by police or uniformed authority. It is made by a caseworker of some training whose primary objective is, or should be, the welfare, not the prosecution, of the aid recipient for whom the worker has profound responsibility. As has already been stressed, the program concerns dependent children and the needy families of those children. It does not deal with crime or with the actual or suspected perpetrators of crime. The caseworker is not a sleuth but rather, we trust, is a friend to one in need.

10. The home visit is not a criminal investigation, does not equate with a criminal investigation, and despite the announced fears of Mrs. James and those who would join her, is not in aid of any criminal proceeding. If the visitation serves to discourage misrepresentation or fraud, such a by-product of that visit does not impress upon the visit itself a dominant criminal investigative aspect. And if the visit should, by chance lead to the discovery of fraud and a criminal prosecution should follow, then even assuming that the evidence discovered upon the home visitation is admissible, an issue upon which we express no opinion, that is a routine and expected fact of life and a consequence no greater than that which necessarily ensues upon any other discovery by a citizen of criminal conduct.

11. The warrant procedure, which the plaintiff appears to claim to be so precious to her, even if civil in nature, is not without its seriously objectionable features in the welfare context. If a warrant could be obtained (the plaintiff affords us little help as to how it would be obtained), it presumably could be applied for ex parte, its execution would require no notice, it would justify entry by force, and its hours for execution would not be so limited as those prescribed for home visitation. The warrant necessarily would imply conduct either criminal or out of compliance with an asserted governing standard. Of course, the force behind the warrant argument, welcome to the one asserting it, is the fact that it would have to rest upon probable cause, and probable cause in the welfare context, as Mrs. James concedes, requires more than the mere need of the caseworker to see the child in the home and to have assurance that the child is there and is receiving the benefit of the aid that has been authorized for it. In this setting the warrant argument is out of place.

It seems to us that the situation is akin to that where an Internal Revenue Service agent, in making a routine civil audit of a taxpayer's income tax return, asks that the taxpayer produce for the agent's review some proof of a deduction that taxpayer has asserted to his benefit in the computation of his tax. If the taxpayer refuses, there is, absent fraud, only a disallowance of the claimed deduction and a consequent additional tax. The taxpayer is fully within his "rights" in refusing to produce the proof, but in maintaining and asserting those rights a tax detriment results and it is a detriment of the taxpayer's own making. So here Mrs. James has the "right" to refuse the home visit, but a consequence in the form of cessation of aid, similar to the taxpayer's resultant additional tax, flows from that refusal. The choice is entirely hers, and nothing of constitutional magnitude is involved.

VII

Our holding today does not mean, of course, that a termination of benefits upon refusal of a home visit is to be upheld against constitutional challenge under all conceivable circumstances. The early morning mass raid upon homes of welfare recipients is not unknown. But that is not this case. Facts of that kind present another case for another day.

We therefore conclude that the home visitation as structured by the New York statutes and regulations is a reasonable administrative tool; that it serves a valid and proper administrative purpose for the dispensation of the AFDC program; that it is not an unwarranted invasion of personal privacy; and that it violates no right guaranteed by the Fourth Amendment.

Reversed and remanded with directions to enter a judgment of dismissal. . . .

Mr. Justice Douglas, dissenting.

We are living in a society where one of the most important forms of property is government largesse which some call the "new property." The payrolls of government are but one aspect of that "new property." Defense contracts, highway contracts, and the other multifarious forms of contracts are another part. So are subsidies to air, rail, and other carriers. So are disbursements by government for scientific research. So are TV and radio licenses to use the air space which of course is part of the public domain. Our concern here is not with those subsidies but with grants that directly or indirectly implicate the *home life* of the recipients.

In 1969 roughly 127 billion dollars were spent by the federal, state, and local governments on "social welfare." To farmers alone almost four billion dollars were paid, in part, for not growing certain crops. Almost 129,000 farmers received $5,000 or more, their total benefits exceeding $1,450,000,000. Those payments were in some instances very large, a few running a million or more a year. But the majority were payments under $5,000 each.

Yet almost every beneficiary whether rich or poor, rural or urban, has a "house"—one of the places protected by the Fourth Amendment against "unreasonable searches and seizures." The question in this case is whether receipt of largesse from the government makes the *home* of the beneficiary subject to access by an inspector of the agency of oversight, even though the beneficiary objects to the intrusion and even though the Fourth Amendment's procedure for access to one's *house* or *home* is not followed. The penalty here is not, of course, invasion of the privacy of Barbara James, only her loss of federal or state largesse. That, however, is merely rephrasing the problem. Whatever the semantics, the central question is whether the government by force of its largesse has the power to "buy up" rights guaranteed by the Constitution. But for the assertion of her constitutional right Barbara James in this case would have received the welfare benefit. . . . Is a search of her home without a warrant made "reasonable" merely because she is dependent on government largesse? . . . If the welfare recipient was not Barbara James but a prominent, affluent cotton or wheat farmer receiving benefit payments for not growing crops, would not the approach be different? Welfare in aid of dependent children, like social security and unemployment benefits, has an aura of suspicion. There doubtless are frauds in every sector of public welfare whether the recipient be a Barbara James or someone who is prominent or influential. But constitutional rights—here the privacy of the *home*—are obviously not dependent on the poverty or on the affluence of the beneficiary. It is the precincts of the *home* that the Fourth Amendment protects; and their privacy is as important to the lowly as to the mighty. . . .

I would place the same restrictions on inspectors entering the *homes* of welfare beneficiaries as are on inspectors entering the *homes* of those on the payroll of government, or the *homes* of those who work for those having government contracts. The values of the *home* protected by the Fourth Amendment are not peculiar to capitalism as we have known it; they are equally relevant to the new form of socialism which we are entering. Moreover, as the numbers of functionaries and inspectors multiply, the need for protection of the individual becomes indeed more essential if the values of a free society are to remain. . . .

The bureaucracy of modern government is not only slow, lumbering, and oppressive; it is omnipresent. It touches everyone's life at numerous points. It pries more and more into private affairs, breaking down the barriers that individuals erect to give them some insulation from the intrigues and harassments of modern life. Isolation is not a constitutional guarantee; but the sanctity of the sanctuary of the *home* is such—as marked and defined by the Fourth Amendment. . . . I would sustain the judgment of the three-judge court in the present case. . . .

UNBORN CHILDREN AND ELIGIBILITY

The Supreme Court, in Burns v. Alcala, 420 U.S. 575 (1975), concerning AFDC eligibility, held that states could deny benefits to pregnant women for their unborn children even though they would qualify after the children were born.

BURNS v. ALCALA

Supreme Court of the United States, 420 U.S. 575 (1975).

Mr. Justice POWELL delivered the opinion of the Court.

The question presented by this case is whether States receiving federal financial aid under the program of Aid to Families with Dependent Children (AFDC) must offer welfare benefits to pregnant women for their unborn children. As the case comes to this Court, the issue is solely one of statutory interpretation.

I

Respondents, residents of Iowa, were pregnant at the time they filed this action. Their circumstances were such that their children would be eligible for AFDC benefits upon birth. They applied for welfare assistance but were refused on the ground that they had no "dependent children" eligible for the AFDC program. Respondents then filed this action against petitioners, Iowa welfare officials. On behalf of themselves and other women similarly situated, respondents contended that the Iowa policy of denying benefits to unborn children conflicted with the federal standard of eligibility under § 406(a) of the Social Security Act, as amended, 42 U.S.C. § 606(a), and resulted in a denial of due process and equal protection under the Fourteenth Amendment. The District Court certified the class and granted declaratory and injunctive relief. The court held that unborn children are "dependent children" within the meaning of § 406(a) and that by denying them AFDC benefits Iowa had departed impermissibly from the federal standard of eligibility. The District Court did not reach respondents' constitutional claims. Alcala v. Burns, 362 F.Supp. 180 (S.D.Ia.1973). The Court of Appeals for the Eighth Circuit affirmed. We granted certiorari to resolve the conflict among the federal courts that have considered the question. We conclude that the statutory term "dependent child" does not include unborn children, and we reverse.

Respondents contend, citing dictionary definitions, that the word "child" can be used to include unborn children. This is enough, they say, to make the statute ambiguous and to justify construing the term "dependent child" in light of legislative purposes and administrative interpretation. They argue that both factors support their position in this case. First, paying benefits to needy pregnant women would further the purpose of the AFDC program because it would enable them to safeguard the health of their children through prenatal care and adequate nutrition. Second, for over 30 years the Department of Health, Education, and Welfare (HEW) has offered States an option to claim federal matching funds for AFDC payments to pregnant women. . . .

Our analysis of the Social Security Act does not support a conclusion that the legislative definition of "dependent child" includes unborn children. Following the axiom that words used in a statute are to be given their ordinary meaning in the absence of persuasive reasons to the contrary . . . and reading the definition of "dependent child" in its statutory context, we conclude that Congress used the word "child" to refer to an individual already born, with an existence separate from its mother.

As originally enacted in 1935, the Social Security Act made no provision for the needs of the adult taking care of a "dependent child." It authorized aid only for the child and offered none to support the mother. The Act expressly contemplated that the first eligible child in a family would receive greater benefits than succeeding children, recognizing the lower per capita cost of support in families with more than one child, id., § 403(a), but the Act included no similar provision recognizing the incremental cost to a pregnant woman of supporting her "child." The Act also spoke of children "living with" designated relatives, id., § 406(a), and referred to residency requirements dependent on the child's place of birth. Id., at § 402(b). These provisions would apply awkwardly, if at all, to pregnant women and unborn children. The failure to provide explicitly for the special circumstances of pregnant women strongly suggests that Congress had no thought of providing AFDC benefits to "dependent children" before birth. . . .

Congress did not ignore the needs of pregnant women or the desirability of adequate prenatal care. In Title V of the Social Security Act, now codified as 42 U.S.C. §§ 701–708, Congress provided federal funding for prenatal and postnatal health services to mothers and infants, explicitly designed to reduce infant and maternal mortality. See S.Rep. No. 661, supra, at 20. In selecting this form of aid for pregnant women, Congress had before it proposals to follow the lead of some European countries that provided "maternity benefits" to support expectant mothers for a specified period before and after childbirth. Hearings on S. 1130 before the Senate Committee on Finance, 74th Cong., 1st Sess., at 182, 965–971 (1935). If Congress had intended to include a similar program in the Social Security Act, it very likely would have done so explicitly rather than by relying on the term "dependent child," at best a highly ambiguous way to refer to unborn children. . . .

Burns demonstrated the degree to which the court shifted in its attitude regarding eligibility from the decisions of the late 1960s and early 1970s. The courts have become more responsive to agency functions and interpretations that constrict rather than expand eligibility.

BENEFIT LEVEL   *Determination of Need Standard*   As noted above in *King v. Smith*, "Each state is free to set its own standard of need and to determine the level of benefits by the amount of funds it devotes to the program." The level may be independent of the cost of living and federal poverty standards. States may set the level where they please.

   Maximum Grant   As discussed in *King v. Smith*, recipients may be paid less than the standard of need established by their state. Dandridge v. Williams, 397 U.S. 471 (1970), permitted states to adopt a maximum grant that put a ceiling on public assistance grants for large families. Some states reduce the benefit levels by a fixed percentage of determined need, which appears to be a more equitable method of allocating limited resources than imposing a maximum grant. Other states use both methods in combination.

   Ratable Reduction   In Jefferson v. Hackney, 406 U.S. 535 (1972), the Supreme Court dealt with the methods of determining benefits when a state paid only a percentage of need. The decision was based on the following rationale:

> Texas, like many other States, first applies the percentage reduction factor to the recipient's standard of need, thus arriving at a reduced standard of need that the State can guarantee for each recipient within the present budgetary restraints. After computing this reduced standard of need, the State then subtracts any nonexempt income in order to arrive at the level of benefits that the recipient needs in order to reach his reduced standard of need. This is the amount of welfare the recipient is given.
>
> Under an alternative system used by other States, the order of computation is reversed. First, the outside income is subtracted from the standard of need, in order to determine the recipient's "unmet need." Then, the percentage reduction factor is applied to the unmet need, in order to determine the welfare benefits payable.
>
> The two systems of accounting for outside income yield different results. Under the Texas system all welfare recipients with the same needs have the same amount of money available each month, whether or not they have outside income. Since the outside income is applied dollar for dollar to the reduced standard of need, which the welfare department would otherwise pay in full, it does not result in a net improvement in the financial position of the recipient. Under the alternative system, on the other hand, any welfare recipient who also has outside income is in a better financial position because of it. The reason is that the percentage-reduction factor there is applied to the "unmet need," after the income has been subtracted. Thus, in effect, the income-earning recipient is able to "keep" all his income, while he receives only a percentage of the remainder of his standard of need.
>
> Each of the two systems has certain advantages. Appellants note that under the alternative system there is a financial incentive for welfare recipients to obtain outside income. The Texas computation method eliminates any such financial incentive, so long as the outside income remains less than the recipient's reduced standard of need. However, since Texas' pool of available welfare funds is fixed, any increase in benefits paid to the working poor would have to be offset by reductions elsewhere. Thus, if Texas were to switch to the alternative system of recognizing outside income, it would be forced to lower its percentage-reduction factor, in order to keep down its welfare budget. Lowering the percentage would result in less money for those who need the

welfare benefits the most—those with no outside income—and the State has been unwilling to do this.

The Court held that states could use either method in dealing with percentage benefits and outside income.

SEX DISCRIMI-NATION AND ELIGIBILITY

Unemployment of the father had made families eligible for AFDC benefits in states choosing that optional benefit. Califano v. Westcott, 443 U.S. 76 (1979), extended the same eligibility in cases where the mother is unemployed. The discretionary gender-based distinction had been defended on the basis that unemployed fathers were made eligible in order to deter real or pretended desertion to obtain benefits.

SPOUSAL FINANCIAL RESPONSIBILITY

Two cases were heard by the Supreme Court concerning use of spousal income to meet medical expenses: Schweiker v. Grey Panthers, 453 U.S. 34 (1981), and Herweg v. Ray, 455 U.S. 265 (1982). In *Schweiker*, the Court held that the income of one spouse may be "deemed" available to the other for determining eligibility for Medicaid benefits. The funds referred to those left over after the spouse had deducted a sum on which to live. "Deeming" the funds to be available means that the spouse would be assessed for the portion of the cost of care he or she is able to pay. In *Herweg*, the Court held that the "deeming" principle forbids a state from considering the husband's income as available after one month from the time the couple had ceased to live together (in this instance the wife was institutionalized).

RECENT ISSUES IN INCOME MAINTENANCE

In his 1982 State of the Union Speech, President Ronald Reagan proposed that the principal entitlement programs be divided between the federal government and the states, with the federal government assuming full responsibility for Medicaid (presently financed at about fifty-fifty between the states and the federal government) and the states taking responsibility for AFDC (another fifty-fifty program) and food stamps (presently a federal program). This proposal in effect said to the governors, "If you take the nation's poor, I'll take the sick." The governors rejected the offer, arguing that any division between the sick and the poor was illogical, that all entitlement programs should be nationalized, and that the President himself had endorsed the concept of a uniform national "safety net" in his State of the Union message. (Babbitt, 1983: 13)

The governors countered with a proposal that the states would fully finance AFDC if there were uniform national eligibility and benefit levels. This proposal was not acceptable to the Reagan administration. This "new federalism" would have provided federal funding for the preferred poor—elderly and disabled people and Social Security recipients—while leaving to the states the nonpreferred poor, "the unemployed, mothers and children, and those displaced by skill, general health, or conditions of the economy from full employment." (Emling, 1983: 23)

Because of cuts initiated by the Reagan administration beginning with the fiscal year 1981 budget, many American families on public assistance are worse off as of 1983. The administration put a ceiling on AFDC payments, a four-month limit on the modified earnings disregard, a more stringent ceiling on work expenses and child-care costs, and a new cap on food stamp eligibility. In addition, income supplementation for the working poor was rejected by the Reagan administration. (Kahn and Kamerman, 1983: 30)

California pays the second highest AFDC benefits in the United States, after Alaska, and California's SSI payments are the highest in the nation (Clancy, 1984). Even so, Californians with dependent children could afford only two-thirds of a family's basic needs, as defined by the federal government (Clancy, 1984: 3). This is despite California's having adjusted public assistance benefit levels for inflation.

Because of President Reagan's welfare cuts, almost 500,000 families have become ineligible for AFDC, and many of those households lost Medicaid and food stamps as well. The Center for the Study of Social Policy concluded that the 1981 welfare reductions "pushed more families into poverty and made families who were poor even poorer" (see Clancy, 1984: 3). Census Bureau figures show that the poverty rate was 15 percent in 1982, the highest since 1965. Changes in the rate of federal taxation harmed the working poor while benefiting households earning above-average incomes. "Under the Reagan administration, the war on poverty has been reduced to attacks upon the poor." (Clancy, 1984: 3)

SOCIAL WORK ROLES

Eliminating poverty is a major goal of the National Association of Social Workers. Social workers have been active in the development and advocacy of welfare reform proposals.

Welfare workers who determine the eligibility of applicants for income from the AFDC program or for social services identify with the social work profession, although most do not have a social work degree. Social workers are often blamed for "the welfare mess," a term that may refer to inadequate funding, lack of work incentives, no aid to the working poor, or fraud by recipients.

Many social work clients do not have sufficient income. Poverty affects most client groups with whom social work has become concerned. Healthy single persons, childless couples, and families with a poorly paid, full-time worker in the family are ineligible for AFDC in its present form. The United States is the only major industrial nation not to enact a uniform children's allowance to replace the variable level of benefits provided by AFDC programs in the states.

Questions for Review

1. Why is SSI a model for AFDC reform?

2. What was the finding in *King v. Smith?* What is the definition of a dependent child for purposes of the AFDC program?

3. Why are durational residence requirements unconstitutional?

4. How are needy dependent children affected if their parents refuse to participate in a work program?

5. What is the right to hearing concerning denial, reduction, and termination of AFDC benefits? Is the initial hearing administrative or judicial? Must an attorney be provided to represent the applicant?

6. What are the purposes of home visits cited in *Wyman v. James?*

7. What are the problems concerning welfare workers as social control agents in *Parrish?* How is consent by recipients open to coercion?

8.   What discretion is permitted states regarding determination of need and level of benefits in the AFDC program?

9.   Explain "income disregard" when calculating available resources. What is the intended effect on work incentives?

10.   Why is the percentage of poor people in the population increasing?

11.   What is the effect of *Califano, Schweiker,* and *Herweg* on economic assistance and family relationships?

Questions for Debate and Discussion

1.   Evaluate the food stamp program and suggest proposals for reform.

2.   Although living costs have gone up, activities of welfare recipients for higher benefits have decreased. Discuss the reasons for the change.

3.   Why would states rather let mothers of young children stay home than pay for day care for their children?

4.   What is the major prerogative of the states in relation to AFDC? How does it result in unequal treatment?

5.   How has the composition of the U.S. Supreme Court influenced reform of poverty law?

Selected Readings   Babbitt, Bruce. "The New Federalism Debate." *Public Welfare* 41 (1983): 9–15.

Cloward, Richard, and Frances Piven. "Toward a Class-Based Realignment of American Politics: A Movement Strategy." *Social Policy* 13 (1983): 3.

Emling, Diana. "The Reagan Scheme as Welfare Reform." *Public Welfare* 41 (1983): 22–16.

Munger, Jerald. "Medicare and Medicaid: The Failure of the Present Health Care System for the Elderly." *Arizona Law Review* 17 (1975): 527–530.

Ozawa, Martha N. "The 1983 Amendments to the Social Security Act: The Issue of Intergenerational Equity." *Social Work* 29 (1984): 131–138.

Samford, Frank P. "The Burger Court and Social Welfare Cases." *University of Detroit Journal of Urban Law* 57 (1980): 813–830.

Wellman, Carl. *Welfare Rights.* Toowa, N.J.: Rowman & Littlefield, 1982.

CHAPTER

20

Consumer Protection

Consumer protection is of special interest to social workers because of the effects of economics on human behavior, life-style, and well-being. Low-income consumers can least afford to withstand improper business or professional practices, yet they are most likely to be victimized by them. Higher income does not guarantee immunity from being taken advantage of. Middle-class families also use credit to obtain costly items such as automobiles and furniture. When the cost of credit is high or the quality of goods is poor, the economic equilibrium is upset regardless of level of income.

Purchases based on credit frequently entail contractual obligations that extend over several years. The purchaser who defaults on payments faces possible garnishment of wages, seizure of personal assets not covered by the contract, or liens against his or her home. Small wonder credit problems often contribute to loss of a job, personal health problems, or a broken marriage.

THE POOR AS CONSUMERS

The poor are particularly susceptible to unethical business practices by virtue of their inability to pay with cash and their desperate need for credit. The poor are also subject to other impediments to consumer protection which the social worker can help overcome.

Lack of Established Credit

Low income makes it impossible for a person to qualify for credit through regular channels. Without a credit rating, the customer is labeled a "high risk." Credit extended under such circumstances usually has unfavorable terms and conditions. In some cases, the required down payment represents almost the full and true worth so that the vendor is assured of a profit before installments are paid. Automobiles and appliances frequently break down long before they are paid for, but the buyer is still responsible for the full amount of the contract.

Lack of Understanding and Language Barriers

Credit contract provisions have been difficult for the well educated to understand and impossible for people who have limited education or who do not read English. Some states now require that a contract be drawn in the buyer's native language or at least be available in Spanish as well as English. However, this does not preclude the possibility that a person will sign the document without reading it or be hopelessly confused by the technical language.

Lack of Mobility

The poor are often limited in their freedom to seek the best prices even when they are able to pay cash. There are few large supermarkets or furniture or appliance stores in ghettos. Residents may have to hire a taxi to go to do their buying, or patronize small neighborhood stores, where prices are higher.

Lack of Money   The poor are caught up in a vicious circle of dependence. It takes money to save money. Many families are unable to take advantage of sales or to buy in quantity because of a need to pay past debts or meet present immediate needs. Postponing gratification successfully on a marginal income is difficult, especially when funds are depleted soon after payday. Shopkeepers are familiar with the struggle of public-assistance recipients toward the end of the month. The need for credit may invite higher prices.

Lack of Storage Facilities   Even if a person is able to shop in quantity and pay lower prices, housing facilities may not provide adequate space to store food safely. With a quantity of food, family members may eat it too soon and then have to go hungry. This negates the economy of quantity buying. Also, rats and mice or lack of refrigeration often make it inadvisable to have much food on hand.

The most effective consumer protection would be eradication of poverty. Consumer protection also includes elimination of unfair sales techniques, legal regulation of consumer credit, and unfair contractual provisions, as well as control over debt collection methods.

QUESTIONABLE SALES TECHNIQUES   Three sales tactics suggest the need for consumer protection. **Bait and switch** involves enticing customers with the promise of low prices. Once in the store, customers are led to believe that the advertised merchandise is really junk and are convinced to purchase a much more expensive product. In the **turnover** technique, a customer is passed from a salesperson to an assistant manager to a manager, each of whom offers a more incredible deal. In the **chain referral** approach, the customer is told he or she can get repaid for a purchase by providing the names of other customers. The original client is promised a rebate from the purchases made by each additional customer provided.

Schrag (1973: 1009) illustrated detailed training materials for door-to-door vacuum cleaner salespeople. While they are trained to insist to the customer that they are not selling anything, their ultimate goal is to sell an overpriced vacuum cleaner.

Increasingly common is a statutory provision providing that any contract signed with a door-to-door salesperson may be canceled without penalty within 72 hours of purchase. The delay ensures that the customer has time to reevaluate the wisdom of such a purchase.

Caplovitz (1963: 25) discusses a special kind of merchandising directed at the poor:

> Characteristic of the comparatively traditional and personal form of the low-income economy is the important role played in it by the door-to-door credit salesman, the customer peddler. The study of merchants found that these peddlers are not necessarily competitors of the store-owners. Almost all merchants make use of peddlers in the great competition for customers. The merchants tend to regard peddlers as necessary evils who add greatly to the final cost of purchases. But they need them because in their view, customers are too ignorant, frightened, or lazy to come to the store themselves. Thus, the merchants' apparent contempt for the peddler does not bar them from employing outdoor salesmen (or "canvassers," as they describe the peddlers who work for one store or another). Even the merchants who are themselves reluctant to hire canvassers find they must do so in order to meet the competition. The peddler's main function for the merchant, then, is getting the customer to the store and, if he

will not come, getting the store to the customer. But this is not his only function.

Much more than the storekeeper, the peddler operates on the basis of a personal relationship with the customer. By going to the customer's home, he gets to know the entire family; he sees the condition of the home and he comes to know the family's habits and wants. From this vantage point he is better able than the merchant to evaluate the customer as a credit risk. Since many of the merchant's potential customers lack the standard credentials of credit, such as having a permanent job, the merchant needs some other basis for discriminating between good and bad risks. If the peddler, who has come to know the family, is ready to vouch for the customer, the merchant will be ready to make the transaction. In short, the peddler acts as a fiduciary agent, a Dun and Bradstreet for the poor, telling the merchant which family is likely to meet its obligations and which is not.

One way to eliminate many consumer abuses would be to outlaw any door-to-door selling involving over fifty dollars.

MAJOR CONSUMER CREDIT PROBLEMS

Consumer credit may involve four common problems: excessive interest rates, unclear credit terms, loss of consumer protection when a contract is sold to a third party, and unfair contract provisions.

Interest Rates

General usury laws have been on the books for many years, prohibiting excessive interest rates. The laws go back to the biblical principle of prohibiting profit from someone else's distress. Legal limits generally ranged from 6 to 12 percent interest on loans. However, such rates have been raised because they were not profitable. The consumer will find that interest rates should be calculated on the unpaid balance. A flat rate of 18 percent a year on the total loan actually costs 27.7 percent when one-twelfth of the loan is paid back each month.

Small loan services have developed outside the scope of the usury law. Until the passage of state statutes to control them, interest rates ran as high as 33.3 percent per month on small loans. States permit small loans to be made at higher rates than larger loans covered by general usury statutes. The average maximums are about 3 percent per month for smaller sums and may decrease for loans over $300. These statutes control almost all consumer borrowing except for home mortgages. Recent economic trends have involved general inflation in interest rates and pressure to raise the interest ceilings. Rate problems are especially complex in interstate commerce where the rate of the seller's state differs from that in the buyer's state. A national bank, for example, can charge the highest rate of the state in which it is located.

Social workers should be familiar with small loan provisions in their own state, both to help clients obtain credit at the best terms and to determine whether clients are being overcharged.

Interest rates are not of major importance if laws permit merchandise purchased on credit to be sold at a higher price than it would be if purchased for cash. Since the difference between the credit price and the regular cash price is not considered an interest charge, both the dealer and the finance company can profit. The former obtains a higher price for the article and also receives a commission for drawing up the time payment contract. The latter buys the contract and profits from interest income.

Those who wish to buy on credit may borrow at a regular bank and use their savings account as collateral, borrow from a commercial bank at perhaps 18 percent interest, or obtain a cheaper loan at a credit union. Other alternatives include the use of a credit card at over 20 percent interest, or the signing of a conditional sales contract. The store may in turn sell the contract to a finance company. Obviously, these options are not generally available to the poor.

To extend credit to the poor, the government could act as guarantor of loans, a suggestion more feasible for Federal Housing Authority (FHA) home mortgages and for educational loans than for small credit transactions.

Truth in Lending

Truth in lending requires written disclosure of the amount of finance charges and the percentage rate as a proportion of the balance due on a consumer credit agreement. The provisions constitute Title I of the Consumer Credit Protection Act of 1968 (82 Stat. 146), which passed after a long battle in Congress. The act applied to states having no comparable provisions in their own statutes. A Truth-in-Lending Simplification and Reform Act passed and signed in 1980 resulted in a truth-in-lending statement that was easier to read and provided a model form that creditors could use to be sure they complied fully with the law.

According to one study, two out of five Americans knew the rate they were being charged for installment credit, while only one out of seven had been aware before the truth-in-lending law took effect. Users of department store accounts and credit cards—middle-class customers—were found to be the most knowledgeable about interest provisions.

Disclosure provisions are obviously more protective of middle-class customers than poorer customers. Many people never even understand that they have to pay a finance charge. Others know that costs are high, but they must have credit. A vendor can increase the price of an article but lower the finance charges, resulting in the same level of profit. The Uniform Credit Code, the model law for such transactions, requires that vendors charge the same price to all customers.

Three important titles have been added to the Consumer Credit Protection Act. In 1970 the Fair Credit Reporting Act regulated the contents and confidentiality of reports of "consumer reporting agencies" and provided for consumer access to such reports. Consumers have the right to see the information about themselves that is in the reporting agency's file. When a consumer is denied credit, the user of the report must provide the consumer with the name and address of the reporting agency.

The Equal Credit Opportunity Act of 1979 prohibited discrimination based on sex or marital status in extension of credit. In the same year, the Fair Credit Billing Act required creditors to provide consumers with the opportunity to make complaints about billing errors.

The Selling of Contracts

Only about 15 percent of credit instruments are held by the original seller. Until 1976, selling of contracts to finance companies under "holder in due course" made it difficult for the purchaser of merchandise to bring action against the seller. Since May 1976, the Federal Trade Commission has required of the purchaser of credit contracts the same liability as the original seller of the merchandise. This was a major consumer reform. Until then, if the contract included the provision that the buyer waives all claims and defenses against innocent third-party purchasers, the original seller was freed of any obligation by selling the contract instrument to a third party, who in turn was also liability-free by virtue of such a contract provision.

The following example (Schrag, 1973: 1084) illustrates the problem:

> If a man purchased a food freezer or a vacuum cleaner from a door-to-door salesman, and signed such a note, he would soon learn that the note had been sold to a bank, and he would be told to make his monthly payments to that institution. However, the man might stop making his payments when he discovered that he'd been cheated by the salesman's fraudulent statements about the nature of the merchandise. In a suit by the bank on the note, the buyer would not be permitted to assert defenses . . . provided that the bank took the note in good faith, for value, and without notice of the buyer's defenses. If the seller deliberately lied to the buyer about the goods, if the merchandise was unmerchantable, or even if the goods were never delivered . . . the buyer would still have to pay.

Since the buyer had little idea of whether a contract would be sold, subsequent product liability was in doubt.

Under the current rule, the finance company is subject to the consumer's defenses against the seller of the goods. The rule does not cover agricultural or real estate transactions.

The Federal Trade Commission provided that the contract include the following language (in large bold type):

> This credit contract finances a purchase. All legal rights which the buyer has against the seller arising out of this transaction, including all claims and defenses, are also valid against any holder of this contract. The right to recover money from the holder under this provision is limited to the amount paid by the buyer under this contract.
>
> A claim is a legally valid reason for suing the seller. A defense is a legally valid reason for not paying the seller. A holder is anyone trying to collect for the purchase.

When you use a credit card and pay a bank, the bank has some liability for the transaction. If you have a dispute with the seller, you may be entitled to withhold payment until the dispute is resolved. Unauthorized use of lost or stolen credit cards may be only a fifty-dollar obligation. The issuers must fulfill five requirements: (1) the card must have been "accepted" by the person named on it; (2) adequate notice of potential liability must have been furnished to the cardholder; (3) the card issuer must have provided an addressed notification statement which the cardholder may return in the event of loss or theft of a credit card; (4) the unauthorized use must have occurred before the cardholder notified the card issuer of the loss or theft; (5) the card issuer must have provided a method by which the user of a card can be identified as the person unauthorized to use it (e.g., signature on card).

Unfair Contract Provisions *Black's Law Dictionary* defines an **unconscionable contract** as "one which no man in his sense, not under delusion, would make, on the one hand, and which no fair and honest man would accept on the other." Under the Uniform Credit Code, courts may refuse to enforce such a contract, enforce all but the unconscionable clause, or limit application to avoid any unconscionable result. The basic test of a contract is whether the clauses are so one-sided as to be unconscionable at the time it was made.

The difficulties involved in unconscionable contracts are illustrated in Williams v. Walker-Thomas Furniture Company (350 F.2d 445 [D.C. Cir. 1964]). The contract had "add-on" provisions stipulating that "all payments now and hereafter made . . . shall be credited proportionally on all outstanding leases, bills, and accounts due the company by the purchaser at the time each payment is made." The debt was secured by the right to repossess all items previously bought. Each new item automatically became subject to a security interest arising out of previous dealings. The U.S. Court of Appeals clearly indicated that lower courts had the power to refuse to enforce such contracts.

Prices and terms may also be considered unconscionable. In American Home Improvement, Inc., v. MacIver (201 A.2d 886 [N.H. 1964]) the sale of storm windows valued at $959 plus a sales commission of $800 and carrying charges of $809.60, resulted in such a finding.

Home freezer contracts that include food purchase plans, or home improvements, furniture, and automobile contracts, have been especially detrimental to consumers. Unfortunately, consumers are often frightened by vendors' threats and pay up without seeking legal remedies because they lack the knowledge or funds to litigate.

PRODUCT LIABILITY

Laws governing product liability have made manufacturers and suppliers responsible for any injury or negative consequences caused by their products. Manufacturers must comply with all safety regulations issued by the government, use due care in the design of products, and employ the best available safety devices. They are likewise required to warn users of unavoidable dangers.

The responsibility of the retailer is less clear. Sellers have been held liable when product misrepresentation has caused injury to customers, but some decisions have freed them from liability even though imminent danger could have been discovered by inspecting the product. Others hold them responsible for discovering and disclosing any defects that may be found by inspection alone. A practical illustration involves a retailer's responsibility for injury to a client caused by a tack protruding through the sole of a shoe. The courts researched opposite decisions concerning retailer liability in Lindsey v. International Shoe Company (233 So.2d 507 [Ala. App. 1970]) and Santise v. Martins, Inc. (17 N.Y.S.2d 741 [App. Div. 1940]). Safety problems with automobiles requiring recall of thousands of units present a more serious problem. More than half the consumers notified usually do not have the work done.

When injury to a client results, strict tort is the simplest legal recourse because it requires only that the product be defective at the time it leaves the defendant's hands and that the defect be the cause of the plaintiff's harm. Defectiveness must be proven and shown to have a clear causal relationship to the injury.

Warranties have provided a major problem in consumer protection. Improvements in warranties came mainly in the 1970s.

The Magnusson-Moss Warranty–Federal Trade Commission Act of 1975, 15 U.S.C. § 2301, helped solve warranty problems. Its provisions include rules governing contents of warranties, full and conspicuous disclosure of terms and conditions, and additional requirements for contents:

(a) In order to improve the adequacy of information available to consumers, prevent deception, and improve competition in the marketing of consumer products any warrantor warranting a consumer product to a consumer by means of a written warranty shall, to the extent required by rules of the Commission, fully and conspicuously disclose in simple and readily understood language the terms and conditions of such warranty. Such rules may require inclusion in the written warranty of any of the following items among others:

(1) The clear identification of the names and addresses of the warrantors

(2) The identity of the party or parties to whom the warranty is extended

(3) The products or parts covered

(4) A statement of what the warrantor will do in the event of a defect, malfunction, or failure to conform with such written warranty—at whose expense—and for what period of time

(5) A statement of what the consumer must do and expenses he must bear

(6) Exceptions and exclusions from the terms of the warranty

(7) The step-by-step procedure which the consumer should take in order to obtain performance of any obligation under the warranty, including the identification of any person or class of persons authorized to perform the obligation set forth in the warranty

(8) Information respecting the availability of any informal dispute settlement procedure offered by the warrantor and a recital where the warranty so provides, that the purchaser may be required to resort to such procedure before pursuing any legal remedies in the courts

(9) A brief, general description of the legal remedies available to the consumer

(10) The time at which the warrantor will perform any obligations under the warranty

(11) The period of time within which, after notice of a defect, malfunction, or failure to conform with the warranty, the warrantor will perform any obligations under the warranty

(12) The characteristics of properties of the products, or parts thereof, that are not covered by the warranty

(13) The elements of the warranty in words or phrases which would not mislead a reasonable, average consumer as to the nature or scope of the warranty

The law provides that either the U.S. attorney general or the Federal Trade Commission may file injunctive proceedings to restrain any manufacturer from issuing a deceptive warranty with respect to a consumer product. Consumers may also file for damages, costs, and expenses if they have been negatively affected by violations of the act. The manufacturer or dealer must be given the opportunity to make repairs or replacement, and informal settlement procedures must be attempted before the consumer may sue. The consumer may recover costs of litigation if the suit is successful.

PACKAGING Since packaging itself has strong "sales appeal," the manner in which an article is packaged or labeled can mislead the customer regarding the quality of merchandise contained therein. Consumer deception is also practiced in packaging. Some control is furnished by the Fair Packaging and Labeling Act, passed by Congress in 1966 (80 Stat. 1296), requiring packages to demonstrate unambiguous statements of quantities and measurements and prohibiting such terms as "jumbo half-quart" for a pint container.

DEBTORS IN DEFAULT The typical debtor who has problems of default has marginal income, low occupational status, and is more likely to be a member of a racial or ethnic minority.

Customers frequently default on payments for products purchased on credit because of a sudden reduction or loss in income or difficulties with a defective product. In many cases, consumer default may be defended by evidence that the product has fallen apart, that it can be bought at one-third the price somewhere else, or that other merchandise had been substituted for that originally purchased. The customer who defaults on payments is frequently subjected to a series of threats followed by repossession and personal suit, garnishment of wages or salary, and action against real estate, personal property, or bank accounts. Consumer remedies are spelled out in Section 9 of the Uniform Commercial Code.

Repossession

Under a conditional sales contract, the creditor may reclaim the merchandise when the debtor becomes delinquent in payments. Repossession is used when an article has substantial value. Automobiles are frequently repossessed by the creditor's simply driving them away from the street in front of the debtor's residence. This is called "self-help" repossession. The debtor usually thinks the car has been stolen.

In 1972 the Supreme Court ruled in Fuentes v. Shevin (407 U.S. 67) that debtors were entitled to due process of law and had to be given advance notice in replevin (repossession) actions:

> We hold that the Florida and Pennsylvania prejudgment replevin provisions work a deprivation of property without due process of law insofar as they deny the right to a prior opportunity to be heard before chattels are taken from their possessor. Our holding, however, is a narrow one. We do not question the power of a State to seize goods before a final judgment in order to protect the security interests of creditors so long as those creditors have tested their claim to the goods through the process of a fair prior hearing. The nature and form of such prior hearings, moreover, are legitimately open to many potential variations and are a subject, at this point, for legislation— not adjudication. Since the essential reason for the requirement of a prior hearing is to prevent unfair and mistaken deprivations of property, however, it is axiomatic that the hearing must provide a real test. "[D]ue process is afforded only by the kinds of 'notice' and 'hearing' that are aimed at establishing the validity, or at least the probable validity, of the underlying claim against the alleged debtor *before* he can be deprived of his property. . . ." [Citations omitted]. (407 U.S. at 96, 97)

With the powerlessness of the debtor and the difficulties of preventing illegal actions, the decision has not prevented self-help repossessions.

Deficiency Judgments

Repossession does not end the debtor's responsibility. One of the major abuses of consumers occurs in the repossession of automobiles in which a deficiency judgment is filed against the client if at the time of default the value of the car is insufficient to satisfy the vendor's claim.

A car sold for $2,764 was repossessed by the finance company when the purchaser defaulted after total payments of $1,716, making the debt $1,048. The finance company reported that the original dealer bought the car back from it for $450, making the net obligation $598. A deficiency judgment was entered for that amount. The dealer then sold the car to another customer for $1,500. By buying the car back at an abnormally low price, the dealer was able to make a huge profit (Russell Pontiac, Inc., v. Loveless No. CV-16-6712–6836 [16th Cir.Ct., Conn. 1967]). The debtor should have sold the car and paid off the loan. (Schrag 1973: 1106)

Collusion between the finance company and the dealer involved undervaluing the repossessed item and then selling it later for the true market price.

Garnishments

The debtor may get an order making it possible for him to claim up to 25 percent of the wages from the employer to satisfy a debt. Costs of the action are added to the amount owed. Just threatening garnishment is often all that is necessary, because the debtor knows it will reveal financial difficulties to the employer and threaten the debtor's job. Garnishments are usually short term. In Michigan, new applications must be made against every paycheck—a real nuisance for an employer.

While the federal government prohibits garnishment of income of federal employees, creditors contact the employer frequently to put pressure on the employee to settle. Paradoxically, loss of a job would defeat the creditor's purpose.

The Consumer Credit Protection Act limits garnishment to 25 percent of a person's weekly disposable earnings (salary less deductions) or the amount by which such earnings exceed thirty times the minimum wage, whichever is less. The 25 percent covers all garnishments. Alimony and child support claims will be given priority over commercial claims. The act also prohibits an employer from discharging an employee because of garnishments.

Confession of Judgment

Some states will permit a "cognovit" clause in contracts, in which the debtor agrees to a judgment to be entered against him or her in case of default without institution of legal proceedings. The buyer confesses that he or she is at fault in whatever action arises between buyer and seller. Creditors or collectors need not even tell the buyer they are taking the case to court.

Social workers need to be familiar with the consequences of default. Until recently, debtors were denied recourse if the product was not satisfactory because the contract will have been sold to a "holder in due course," the purchase could be repossessed if it had any value, additional money would be due after repossession, and the amount owed was likely to be deducted from wages, leading to problems with the employer. In addition, the debtor may have confessed to fault in advance, so he or she has no legal recourse. But the debtor's position has improved. Repossession and garnishment are likely to be the most common means of recourse against a debtor. Holder in due course has been eliminated, and confession of judgment is limited to a few states. The debtor has access to the courts and to legal counsel, but often has to spend more in legal fees than the amount of the claim. Whether the product was defective, payments had been made but not credited, or attempts were made to overcharge, it is easier to pay than to fight.

Now the courts tend to act primarily as collection agents for creditors. Process servers who collect a fee for serving the papers may not present the summons. They falsely swear they have delivered it to the debtor. Then when a consumer case comes up, the defendant does not appear and a default judgment is issued.

Neighborhood courts are needed to handle credit matters near the debtor's place of residence. Arbitration would reduce the impersonal character of credit actions. Wherever there is a personal relationship, the outcome is improved.

OTHER CONSUMER REMEDIES

Remedies against illicit sales and credit practices are provided by consumer protection agencies that are generally part of a state's attorney general's office. While such programs have grown rapidly, they are typically underfinanced and lack significant enforcement powers. Class action suits against vendors are important, but they have little impact on the routine abuses to which poorer clients are regularly subjected.

For relief of individual consumer grievances, legal service lawyers are a potential resource. However, credit litigation has relatively low priority in legal services offices, compared to such issues as welfare and landlord-tenant relations. Voluntary arbitration procedures and small-claims courts are other means of dealing with consumer problems, but their availability is limited. In addition, small claims courts often have a low limit, making it impossible to obtain a hearing on cases involving major appliances or automobile repairs.

CONSUMER PROTECTION AGENCIES The Federal Trade Commission and the federal Food and Drug Administration have already been mentioned as traditional protective agencies. Better Business Bureaus are identified as possible sources of help, but they have not worked aggressively on behalf of the consumer because they are sponsored by the business community. Ecology movements have fostered new organizations and new emphases. Generally, the fate of the low-income consumer has not improved measurably. The social worker must often resolve consumer-related economic difficulties before being able to help families in other ways.

Questions for Review

1. If interest rates are legally regulated, how can a seller still increase his or her return on a product?

2. What is an unconscionable contract?

3. What is meant by truth in lending?

4. How has selling of credit instruments made consumer protection difficult? Is this still a serious problem?

5. What is involved in the "bait and switch" sales technique?

6. Give an example of product liability. Would the manufacturer and the dealer be equally liable in case of injury?

7. What are the requirements for a strict tort approach to product liability?

8. Explain the purposes of the Equal Credit Opportunity Act.

9. Explain what is meant by consumer class actions.

10. Of the undesirable practices discussed in this chapter, which is most typically used in the selling of storm windows, siding, or other home improvements?

Questions for Debate and Discussion

1. Why are the poor in special need of consumer protection?

2. Explain why lack of transportation can be a consumer protection problem.

3. With what types of businesses are Better Business Bureaus most likely to provide effective consumer protection? When will they be less effective?

4. Gather data on recent attempts at federal legislation on behalf of consumers. Why is less interest being shown in such laws?

5. Poll your class on their experiences with automobile and other product recalls. Do they consider such a protective mechanism helpful?

Selected Readings

Consumer Law, Student Text. St. Paul, Minn.: Changing Times Education Service, 1982.

Hemphill, Charles F., Jr. *The Consumer Protection Handbook.* Englewood Cliffs, N.J.: Prentice-Hall, 1981.

Lester, Paul A. "The Magnuson-Moss Warranty Act: The Courts Begin to Talk." *Uniform Commercial Code Law Journal* 16 (1983): 119–146.

Spanogle, John A., and Ralph J. Rohner. *Consumer Law Cases and Materials.* St. Paul, Minn.: West Publishing Co., 1979.

Sprotzer, Ira. "A Survey of Federal Consumer Credit Legislation." *Ohio State Business Administration Reporter* 53 (1980): 2061.

Turner, R. J. *Consumer's Guide to the Mortgage Maze.* New York: St. Martin's Press, 1983.

CHAPTER
21

Housing

SOCIAL WORKERS' ROLES IN HOUSING

Social workers are expected to be skilled in helping people modify the environment and improve their life situations. Inadequate housing is a major factor contributing to family problems in which social workers are asked to intervene. Choice of housing is instrumental in determining not only the home environment but also the neighborhood facilities available to the family. Aaron (1972:5) showed the broad implications of housing for other aspects of living:

> When a homeowner or renter chooses a house or apartment, he purchases not only housing services, but also a wide range of goods and services—public schools, stores, parks, public transportation, neighbors, and other amenities. Though they cost him nothing beyond the price of housing and attendant property taxes, his satisfaction—indeed his welfare—depends on these conditions as much as on his housing.
>
> The residents of poor neighborhoods are victims of high prices, inferior merchandise, high interest rates, and aggressive and deceptive sales practices. They pay for the cost of doing business where pilferage and default risks are above average. Costs are averaged over all customers so that reliable households suffer from living where high costs customers are particularly numerous. Such extra costs of living are among costs of residential services that affect the price people will pay for housing services. Another social cost that varies by neighborhood is the probability of crime. The major market response the individual can make to differences in crime rates is to alter the price he is willing to pay for housing.

Social workers are often involved in obtaining better housing for their clients. As advocates on behalf of tenants both individually and in groups, social workers encounter many opportunities to deal constructively with housing problems beyond the traditional role of relocating people in better shelter. They may help tenants take legal action against landlords because of violations of housing codes, or encourage rent withholding and rent strikes to force landlords to bring properties up to standard. Legal-aid lawyers are often social workers' most effective partners. In order to deal effectively with housing problems, social workers must command a thorough knowledge of the laws and administrative codes on which law enforcement efforts must be based.

TENANTS' RIGHTS

What are tenants' rights under common law? According to Berger (1973:631):

> The tenant often faces a Hobson's choice: either endure the interference or move into other quarters not as desirable as those left behind—a situation that cannot change

while decent housing for the poor remains desperately short. Moreover, before the tenant can establish that his quiet enjoyment has been disrupted, he must first show that the landlord is legally required to halt the interference. To illustrate: tenant complains of a drunken, noisy upstairs neighbor. Courts have said that landlord has no duty to stop the disturbance; therefore, landlord has not himself interfered with tenant's enjoyment. (One might argue that any occupant who is regularly allowed to behave disruptively derives authority for his acts from the landlord.) To give a second— and more common—illustration: the tenant complains that his apartment is rat infested. At common law, courts have held that the landlord need not warrant that the premises are habitable. In the absence of this antecedent duty, tenant cannot prove that landlord's inaction has caused a substantial interference with his enjoyment. Similarly, the common law has exacted no duty from the landlord that he repair and maintain the premises; therefore unheated quarters resulting from a landlord's refusal to fix a broken boiler do not legally deny that tenant quiet enjoyment. Finally, even where landlord has expressly agreed to maintain the premises, many courts have advanced the principle of independent covenants, that is, the landlord's duty to repair is independent from the tenant's duty to pay rent. This has meant that the tenant may not treat the breach of a repair covenant as equivalent to a breach of a covenant of quiet enjoyment permitting tenant to vacate the premises and rescind the lease if his use has been substantially impaired. Instead the tenant has had to look to his rights in damages.

This description illustrates how tenants have traditionally lacked a strong legal basis on which to claim recognition of their rights. Tenants have frequently had no alternative other than to move out of unsuitable housing in search of alternative facilities. However, the poor usually encounter similar problems regardless of where they move, suggesting the need for solutions to curtail the continual exodus of families.

Leases have been frequent sources of conflict between owners and tenants. An improved lease form developed by the Chicago Council of Lawyers to eliminate ambiguities and sources of conflict is included herein (Exhibit 21.1).

ZONING

The alleged purpose of zoning is to maintain the "quality" of neighborhoods, but it may seriously restrict the options of people seeking housing. Zoning rules vary widely in that they are designed predominantly by individual municipalities and townships. One common means of controlling population density is to regulate the size of parcels of land. For example, some estate areas are zoned for five-acre parcels in order to limit construction to luxury housing. Large-size lots, a house of at least a certain area, and exclusion of multiple dwellings and mobile homes have been used to control population density. Consequently, zoning may result in a conflict between the desire to maintain property values and the desire to protect broader human freedoms. A more serious aspect of this zoning problem for social workers will be considered later in this chapter.

PROVISIONS OF HOUSING CODES

Effective recognition of tenants' rights developed concurrently with the evolution of housing codes. Until 1954, only fifty-six housing codes were in existence. However, when the federal government began to require such codes as a condition for receipt of federal funds, new housing codes were widely enacted. While most of these were devised by municipalities, Connecticut, Iowa, Massachusetts, Mich-

EXHIBIT 21.1
SAMPLE LEASE

GEORGE E. COLE
LEGAL FORMS

NO. L-19
MAY 1977

CHICAGO COUNCIL OF LAWYERS
STANDARD FORM LEASE

NOTICE TO USERS: This lease is designed to be supplemented, changed, completed and negotiated by lessor and tenant as agreed. Some provisions may not apply to the leasing of certain properties and should be changed by lessor and tenant; read before signing.

APARTMENT LEASE AGREEMENT

LEASE SUMMARY

DATE OF LEASE	TERM OF LEASE		TOTAL RENT FOR TERM	PAYABLE MONTHLY	SECURITY DEPOSIT*	DECORATING ALLOWANCE*
	BEGINNING	ENDING				
	12:01 A.M.	MIDNIGHT				
	_____, 19___	_____, 19___				

IF NONE, WRITE "NONE"

TENANT		LESSOR	
NAME(s) ●		NAME ●	
APARTMENT ●			
ADDRESS OF PREMISES ●		BUSINESS ADDRESS ●	
TELEPHONE ●		TELEPHONE ●	

This Agreement is made and entered into on the date first shown above by and between Lessor and Tenant. Lessor and Tenant agree together:

ADDITIONAL AGREEMENTS between Lessor and Tenant (if any)

1. **THE PREMISES.** Lessor hereby leases to Tenant the apartment shown above (called the "premises") located at the address above, under the terms and conditions set forth below.

2. **TERM OF LEASE AND RENT.** Tenant shall be entitled to occupy the premises for the term shown in the Lease Summary above and for a total rent as shown in the Lease Summary, payable by Tenant to Lessor on the premises in equal monthly installments beginning on the first day of occupancy. Lessor shall give Tenant a written rent receipt for rent paid whenever requested.

3. **UTILITIES.** Lessor agrees to furnish the following services to Tenant free of charge: electricity (in the common areas); gas; water; heat; trash and garbage removal. Lessor will not be responsible for failure to furnish such services by reason of any cause beyond his control. For use on the premises of the following utilities Tenant will be billed directly and make payment to the utility company: (specify) telephone _____.

4. **REPAIRS.** Lessor acknowledges that the following conditions or items (specify, if any) are in need of repair and agrees to satisfactorily repair them by _____, 19___, with allowance for delays beyond the control of Lessor.

5. **FIXTURES.** All cabinets, drapes, blinds and shutters, plumbing fixtures, electrical fixtures, refrigerators, ovens, stoves and all following fixtures and furniture now on the premises (specify, if any) are part of the premises and leased at no extra charge to Tenant with the premises: _____.

6. **PARKING.** Lessor hereby leases to Tenant garage or parking space number _____for the storage of automotive vehicles, automotive supplies and other property of Tenant at no charge for the term of this Agreement.

7. **STORAGE.** Tenant, at his sole risk, and without any liability or responsibility of Lessor, may exclusively use at no charge for the term of this Agreement, the storage area described or identified as follows: _____. Tenant agrees not to put in the storage area any items that would create a danger to other tenants or to Lessor's property.

8. **OPTIONS.** Lessor hereby grants to Tenant the exclusive option to occupy the premises for the additional term beginning at the expiration of the initial hereof and ending _____months later, under the same terms and conditions except that rent shall be $ _____ per month for said additional term, which option shall be exercised by Tenant giving written notice of exercise of Lessor not less than 60 days prior to expiration.

9. **HEATING AND HOT WATER.** Lessor shall furnish to and for the use of Tenant, in fixtures on the premises provided for such purpose by Lessor and no other fixtures, hot and cold water and from September 15 to June 1, in radiators or other fixtures on the premises, a reasonable amount of heat at reasonable hours at least as required by the applicable municiple code.

10. **USE OF PROPERTY.** Tenant shall use the premises for residential purposes only, except for incidental use in a trade or business (such as telephone solicitation of sales orders), so long as such incidental use does not violate zoning laws, interfere with other tenants or substantially impede Lessor's ability to obtain fire or liability insurance or increase the cost thereof.

11. **WARRANTY.** Lessor hereby expressly warrants that the premises are adequately fit for human habitation and comply with all applicable municipal housing, building and zoning codes.

12. **DECORATING ALLOWANCE.** Lessor grants to Tenant a decorating allowance equal to the decorating allowance shown in the Lease Summary, which allowance may be deducted from rent due during the term of this Agreement, provided Tenants hall have first provided Lessor with receipts or other written evidence of Tenant's expenditures of an amount not less than such deduction. The decorating allowance shall be used on the premises for the following purposes only: painting or the application of other protective substances, plastering, replacement or repair of fixtures, wallpapering or remodeling.

13. **SECURITY DEPOSIT.** Upon execution of this Agreement, Tenant shall pay Lessor a security deposit equal to the security deposit shown in the Lease Summary. Lessor's signature on this Agreement is evidence of Lessor's receipt of said deposit. The deposit may be applied by Lessor toward reimbursement for any cost incurred because of Tenant's violation of this Agreement, including nonpayment of rent. Lessor shall inspect the premises during the week prior to termination of this Agreement and, before Tenant vacates, shall give Tenant a written, itemized statement of needed repairs, repairs already made by Lessor and the costs. Within two weeks after Tenant vacates the premises, Lessor shall return to Tenant his security deposit, with accrued interest at the rate of 5% per annum, less any deductions Lessor is entitled to make, provided, however, that deductions for repairs shall be made only for repairs listed in the written statement required by the prior sentence and for which there are receipts.

14. **ENTRY BY LESSOR.** Lessor shall have the right to enter the premises only after advance notice of at least 24 hours to Tenant of the date, purpose and approximate time of the entry and only for the purposes of:
    a. Inspecting the premises for damage or needed repairs or improvement without intruding into Tenant's personal effects.
    b. Making necessary repairs or improvements.
    c. Exhibiting the premises to prospective purchases, tenants (only during the last 60 days of term) or mortgagees.

Unless Tenant agrees otherwise in writing, such entry may be made only between the hours of 9:00 a.m. and 6:00 p.m. Entry may be made without prior notice if Lessor reasonably believes that there exists an emergency, such as a fire or broken water pipe, that requires immediate entry without notice.

15. **ADDITIONAL TENANT OBLIGATIONS.** Tenant shall:
    a. Not use or store on the premises any inflammable or explosive substances or, except as permitted in paragraph 6 hereof, gasoline.
    b. Pay for any damage to the premises, and for any damage to, or loss of, the appliances and fixtures therein, caused by any act or neglect of Tenant, excepting damage due to ordinary and reasonable wear and tear.
    c. Place garbage and refuse inside containers provided by Lessor.
    d. Refrain from acts or practices which unreasonably disturb neighbors.
    e. Keep the premises in a clean and sanitary condition.
    f. Prevent the premises from being occupied by, or sublet to, persons not in Tenant's family for more than 30 days total during the term of this Agreement unless Lessor consents otherwise, which consent shall not be withheld unreasonably, providing such occupancy does not violate any applicable municipal housing, building or zoning code.
    g. Notify Lessor of any condition on the premises or Lessor's property which Tenant believes to be dangerous to the health or safety of tenants.

16. **ADDITIONAL LESSOR OBLIGATIONS.** Subject to paragraph 15 above. Lessor shall be responsible for the following duties in addition to those set forth elsewhere herein, without additional cost to Tenant:
    a. Maintaining an extermination service for the premises and Lessor's property which shall include the elimination of all vermin and rodents from all rooms, apartments and common areas.
    b. Installing and maintaining good locks on all doors leading from the premises to the outside or to the common areas and leading from the common areas to the outside.
    c. Installing and maintaining adequate illumination in the common areas.
    d. Providing and installing screens, storm windows (between October 1 and May 1) and window shades, or their equivalents, in good condition for all windows on the premises.

e. Keeping in repair all doors, windows and stairs on Lessor's property.

f. Installing and maintaining a private, secure mail box for Tenant. (Failure to perform this duty shall not of itself make Lessor liable for the loss of any mail box contents.)

g. Maintaining the premises and common areas in accordance with all applicable municipal housing, building and zoning code standards.

h. Providing closed garbage containers within 100 feet walking distance of the premises and providing garbage and refuse collection service at least once a week.

i. Maintaining the common areas in a neat, clean and sanitary condition.

j. Maintaining security on the premises and Lessor's property.

k. Maintaining in good working order any and all fixtures and appliances furnished by Lessor.

l. Maintaining Lessor's property in substantially the same condition and providing the same services as existed on the date of this Agreement.

17. **ALTERATIONS.** No alteration or addition shall be made by Tenant in or to the premises without the prior written consent of Lessor. Such consent shall not be withheld unreasonably and may be conditioned upon Tenant's agreeing to restore the premises to its former condition upon moving out.

18. **BANKRUPTCY.** In the event Tenant is adjudicated bankrupt or makes an assignment for benefit of creditors, this Agreement at the option of Lessor and upon 30 days notice to Tenant shall terminate and the premises shall be surrendered to Lessor. In the event Lessor is adjudicated bankrupt or makes an assignment for the benefit of creditors, this Agreement at the option of Tenant and upon 30 days notice to lessor, shall terminate.

19. **SELF-HELP.** In addition to all other remedies available to Tenant, if Lessor fails to perform as agreed in paragraphs 3, 4, 9 and 16 above, then Tenant may, after 20 days have elapsed since Lessor's first knowledge of his failure to perform, remedy the failure of performance by engaging a qualified serviceman to remedy the condition and by purchasing necessary materials. The reasonable cost to Tenant of any such remedy, to the extent evidenced by bills or receipts, shall be deducted from Tenant's rent due or to come due under this Agreement. However, if repair of defective locks, windows, exterior doors, mailboxes or exterior lighting necessary to the safety and security of Tenant or his property is not begun within 36 hours of Tenant's notice to Lessor, Tenant may remedy the failure and deduct the cost from rent as above. Tenant shall permit Lessor to copy the key for any new lock installed pursuant to this paragraph.

20. **TENANT'S TERMINATION FOR GOOD CAUSE.** Upon 90 days' written notice to Lessor, Tenant may terminate this Agreement due to the involuntary change of the place of employment to another community or the involuntary loss of the main source of income used to pay rent.

21. **SUBORDINATION.** This Agreement is subject to all present or future mortgages or trust deeds affecting the premises and Tenant hereby appoints Lessor as Attorney-in-Fact to execute and deliver any and all necessary documents to subordinate this Agreement to any present or future mortgage or trust deed affecting the premises.

22. **ACCESS AND COMMON AREAS.** Lessor hereby grants to Tenant and his business and social guests the right to use all vestibules, stairways, corridors, passenger elevators, if any, and paths on Lessor's property for passage when necessary to gain access to or from the street or other public way. Lessor hereby grants to Tenant the right to use in common with all other tenants on Lessor's property the following areas: basement, lounge, lawn and laundry room; such areas together with vestibules, stairways, corridors, elevators, paths and other public areas are collectively called the "common areas." (As used in this Agreement, "Lessor's property" means all Lessor's buildings and grounds contiguous to the premises.)

23. **RENEWAL.** Lessor shall not arbitrarily refuse to renew Tenant's occupancy of the premises under the same terms and conditions (except for nondiscriminatory rent changes); and Lessor shall not refuse to renew Tenant's occupancy of the premises for the reason that the premises are being converted to a cooperative or condominium form of ownership without 12 months' prior written notice to Tenant of an intention to so convert.

24. **PLURALS; SUCCESSORS.** The words "Lessor" and "Tenant" herein shall be construed to mean "Lessors" and "Tenants" in case more than one person constitutes either party to this Agreement and all the agreements herein contained shall be binding upon, and inure to, Lessor's and Tenant's respective successors, heirs, executors, administrators and assigns, and Tenant's immediate family. Where applicable, "his" shall mean "its" or "hers."

25. **REGULATIONS.** The following regulations shall be a part of this Agreement. Tenant agrees to follow them and Lessor agrees to enforce and follow them. As a condition to Tenant's agreeing to follow these regulations, Lessor hereby warrants that all tenants residing on Lessor's property shall be and are bound by the same regulations.

a. No animals are permitted without a leash in the common areas.

b. Except for lawns, benches, lounges and other areas set aside for special use, the common areas shall not be obstructed or be used for children's play or for any other purpose than for access to or from Lessor's property or apartments.

c. All furniture shall be delivered through the rear or service entrance, stairway or elevator.

d. Carriages, bicycles, sleds and the like are to be stored only in places designated for their storage by Lessor.

e. No sign, signal, illumination, notice or any other lettering or equipment shall be exhibited or exposed on or at any door or window or on any part of the outside of the premises or Lessor's property without the prior written consent of Lessor, except for occasional civic or political posters.

f. Sinks, toilets, bathtubs and other plumbing fixtures shall not be used to any purpose other than for those for which they were designed; no sweepings, rubbish, rags or other improper articles shall go into the water pipes. Any damages resulting from misuse of such fixtures shall be paid for by Tenant.

g. No nails, spikes or hooks shall be driven into the woodwork of the premises without the consent of Lessor, and except as may be provided in paragraph 19 above. Tenant shall not alter any lock or install a new lock or a knocker or other attachment on any door of the premises without the consent of Lessor.

h. No furniture filled with a liquid or semi-liquid substance shall be used on the premises unless contained in proper frame and liner.

i. No waste receptacles, supplies, footwear, umbrellas or other articles shall be placed in the common areas, nor shall anything be hung or shaken from the windows or placed upon the outside window sills or balconies.

WITNESS the signature of the parties hereto, as of the first date appearing above.

LESSOR _____

TENANT _____

NOTE: Both Lessor and Tenant should initial each paragraph that has been changed or supplemented as well as each page of any typed or handwritten attachments to this agreement, and each party should retain one fully executed initialed copy of this Agreement.

GUARANTEE

For value received, the undersigned hereby guarantees the payment of the rent and the performance of the convenants by Tenant in this Agreement.

WITNESS _____ signature this _____ day of _____, 19_____.

_____

---

igan, Minnesota, New Jersey, and Pennsylvania enacted state codes. Although California and New York instituted extensive state legislation, more stringent codes are permitted at the local level.

State laws are especially important because they convey the power necessary to enforce housing codes and to require landlords to improve substandard housing. State law also conveys the power to make repairs and impose their cost as a lien on the property and the legal authority to withhold rent.

Housing codes, then, encompass the entire body of state and local law prescribing and authorizing enforcement of housing standards. Exhibit 21.2 gives the city of Chicago's guide to landlord and tenant responsibilities and obligations based on its housing code.

Housing regulations are valid as long as they bear a demonstrable relationship to public health, safety, and welfare and do not deprive the landlord of property interests without due process of law. Housing codes may clearly be retroactive—

EXHIBIT 21.2
CHICAGO'S GUIDE TO LANDLORD AND TENANT RESPONSIBILITIES

A Landlord must . . .

Maintain the exterior of the building including the yard. This includes all brickwork, mortar, siding or frame shingle, cornices, roofs and gutters, porches, outside steps and stairways, fire escapes, canopies, exterior doors, windows and screens. In the yard, grass, trees and shrubs should be cared for so as not to become a nuisance to tenants or neighbors. No rubbish or debris may be left in the yard.

Maintain all public areas within the building. All corridors, exit ways, stairways and stair-wells, basements and areas under stairwells must be kept clean and cleared of any debris, rubbish or any objects which would hinder movement in those areas or produce a health and fire hazard. All carpeting or tile in the corridors and vestibule must be kept in good repair and walls, lobby and ceilings must be kept clean and in good repair. Halls must be free of holes, cracks, loose, warped, protruding or rotting boards. Stair treads must be uniform in height and securely fastened.

Supply Smoke Detectors in three story buildings containing six or more units and in all four story or higher buildings with one or more dwellings. The detectors must be in each dwelling unit within 15 feet of any room or rooms used for sleeping purposes and also at the top (ceiling) of each interior stairway. Buildings that are type I (fire resistant) construction or fully sprinklered are exempt.

Supply heat in all dwellings from September 15 through June 1. Minimum Fahrenheit temperature required is 60 degrees at 6:30 A.M., 65 degrees at 7:30 A.M. and 68 degrees from 8:30 A.M. through 10:30 P.M. From 10:30 P.M. until 6:30 A.M. a minimum of 55 degrees must be maintained.

Supply hot water with a minimum temperature of 120 degrees to all required outlets in the building. This includes outlets in bathtubs, showers, lavatories and kitchen sinks. Hot water must be available to all residents between the hours of 6 A.M. to 10:30 P.M.

A Landlord must . . .

Repair and maintain all equipment he is required to supply. This includes all major appliances such as stoves, ovens, refrigerators and washing and drying machines *if* provided by the owner. Also included would be garbage cans, fire extinguishers, plumbing fixtures, most light fixtures, smoke detectors, heating systems and devices.

Supply and maintain refuse facilities. The property owner must supply all refuse containers or facilities such as garbage chutes. *In some cases, according to lease, the tenant may be required to carry garbage and waste to suitable containers in alleys, but whether this is agreed upon or not, the owner is responsible for the removal of all garbage and waste from the physical premises of the building and lot.* If the building contains more than four dwelling units, the owner must hire a private scavenger to remove garbage. If the building contains four dwelling units or less, the City will remove the garbage. Refuse should always be placed in containers which must be located to make pickup convenient. *No garbage containers may be left in corridors and hallways.*

Exterminate insects and rodents, if more than one dwelling unit in the building is infested, or if the public areas or shared parts of the structure such as hallways, corridors, lobbies, vestibules or basement are infested.

Provide proper lighting in the public areas of the building. All halls, stairways, corridors, lobbies and vestibules must be adequately lighted at all times. How light the public areas of the building should be is mainly a matter of common sense. But there must be enough light for anyone to be able to see well. Lights must also be provided in the basement of buildings.

A Landlord must . . .

Provide electrical service adequate to take care of the needs of the building. The electrical service of an apartment building must be able to handle all modern appliances and electrical devices which could normally be used in day-to-day living.

Provide adequate plumbing service for the building. Every family unit in an apartment building containing apartments more than 500 square feet in size or more than two habitable rooms must be provided with a room containing a flush water closet, a bathtub or shower and a wash basin. Each family unit must also have a kitchen sink. In a building containing two-room apartments or apartments with less than 500 square feet, a bathroom can be shared by occupants from two apartments provided that the occupants of each family unit have access to the bathroom without passing through any other family unit and provided the two apartments sharing the bathroom are on the same floor. In a building specifically designated as a rooming house, one complete bathroom (water closet, bathtub or shower and wash basin) must be provided for each ten occupants. In a rooming house shared by both sexes, all bathroom facilities must be completely separate for each sex. All plumbing facilities, including piping, sewers, gutters, traps, drains and fixtures must be maintained and replaced when worn out.

Adhere to all provisions of the building code and zoning ordinance relating to structure, exits, size of rooms, number of dwelling units, ventilation. The owner must make sure he or she obtains permits from the Department of Inspectional Services for any type of work on the building which requires a permit. Outside of normal maintenance and painting, most work requires a permit. No building may be altered or changed in use or size or number of apartments without a permit. Sometimes changes of various kinds require rulings from the Zoning Board of Appeals or from the City Council.

A Tenant must . . .

Keep the apartment or room he or she occupies and controls in a clean, sanitary and safe condition. Everyone has an obligation to keep his or her premises clean. As long as the property owner supplies the basic needs of the building it is up to the tenant to take care of the area rented to him or her. For an apartment to be clean, sanitary and safe requires only normal and regular cleaning and maintenance on the part of the tenant.

Keep all plumbing fixtures in a clean and sanitary condition, and use reasonable care in the use of the plumbing facilities. All plumbing fixtures and facilities are supplied by the building owner, but it is up to the tenant to take care of those facilities. Don't throw large or hard objects into the toilets and drains in sinks and bathtubs. Children must not be allowed to tamper with piping or plumbing facilities which can be easily broken.

Exterminate any insects, rodents or other pests in the apartment if it is the only apartment in a multiple family building which is so infested. In most buildings, an extermination service is supplied by the landlord, and the tenant should allow exterminators into his or her apartment.

Not place on the premises any furniture, equipment or material which harbors insects, rodents or pests. Vermin can't survive unless they are fed and there is a general condition of filth. It is up to the tenant to make sure garbage is sealed and placed in tight, covered containers provided, and that food is not left open. Filthy furniture and materials of many kinds harbor insects, and each tenant must make sure his furniture and household items are clean and free of insects and vermin. Insecticides can be applied carefully and safely by tenants if necessary. The chances are good that there will be no vermin and few insects, if any, in a building if tenants keep their apartments clean and free of garbage.

A Tenant must . . .

Dispose of all garbage and other refuse only in the proper containers or garbage chutes provided for that purpose. In certain small apartment buildings, tenants may be required to carry refuse to containers in the back yard for pick up. Garbage disposal facilities must be provided by the building owner, but the tenant must use those facilities. The tenant must never under any circumstances leave garbage open in hallways, stairways, back porches or basements.

Hang and remove all screens required for the apartment unless the owner has agreed to supply this service. Screens are required for windows and doors opening to the outside from April 15 through November 15. However, screens are not required for apartments above the fourth floor of an apartment building unless required by the Department of Inspectional Services when unusual circumstances of insect prevalence exist. In most cases building owners will provide the service of supplying and hanging or placing screens in doors and windows.

Not place on the premises any material which causes a fire hazard or otherwise endangers the health or safety of any resident in the building. All inflammable type materials such as kerosene, gasoline, window sprays, insect sprays must be carefully stored if kept on the premises. The tenant must not let rags and papers accumulate. All materials which may be poisonous should be kept under lock. All extra furniture, tables and household items should be stored in storage rooms provided by the building owner. There should be no storage in hallways or under stairs, on stairs, in lobbies, vestibules or exit ways.

A Tenant must . . .

Not permit his apartment or room to be so occupied as to violate any of the provisions of the housing code. A tenant may not subdivide his apartment or lease any part of it. A family dwelling unit is for the tenant who should make sure he or she does not overcrowd the apartment and the building by leasing or renting out any portion of the apartment he or she controls. If a tenant moves out of the apartment prior to the time the lease is up, he may sublease the apartment only with the permission of the building owner. A family unit must contain a minimum of 450 square feet of floor area to accommodate four persons. For each additional occupant, there must be a minimum of 75 square feet. An apartment occupied by two persons must contain at least 250 square feet. A room used only for sleeping purposes by one person must contain at least 70 square feet of floor area and every room occupied for sleeping purposes by more than one person must contain 50 square feet of floor area for each person twelve years of age or over and 35 square feet of floor area for each person twelve years of age.

Make use of all the property and its facilities in a careful, decent and safe manner. The building owner is legally responsible for the public areas of the building, but these areas cannot possibly be kept up if tenants or their children are destructive or careless.

COMPLAINTS OF BUILDING CODE VIOLATIONS

Filing a complaint

To report Municipal Code violations to the Department of Inspectional Services, phone 744-3420 or write to:

Complaint Section
Department of Inspectional Services
City Hall, Room 803C
121 North LaSalle Street
Chicago, Illinois 60602

When a complaint is received by the Department of Inspectional Services it is assigned to a code enforcement inspector who will inspect the property. If he or she finds any violations of the Municipal Building Code the Inspectional Services Department will make immediate use of one of three tools geared to bring about compliance.

Compliance board

If minor violations are found, the responsible parties are sent a list of the violations and are directed to appear before the Compliance Board of the Department of Inspectional Services. There they are given the opportunity to explain when and how they will correct the violations. If their plan of action is acceptable and the time required is reasonable, they will be allowed adequate time to comply. At the end of this period the property will be reinspected to determine whether it is now in compliance with the Building Code. If not, the Department of Inspectional Services will initiate legal action against those responsible.

When the seriousness of the violations warrants it, the Department will bypass the Compliance Board hearing and take the case directly to Municipal or Circuit Court.

Municipal court

When the reinspection which follows a Compliance Board hearing determines that the violations have not been corrected, the Inspectional Services Department will refer the case to the Municipal Court System of Chicago. In the Municipal Court fines may be imposed for each violation of the Building Code.

It should be noted that even after paying fines, the responsible parties are still required to correct all violations. If they do not, the Inspectional Services Department will return the case directly to Municipal Court where additional fines will be assessed. This process will be continued until the violations have been corrected.

Municipal Court action may be directed at anyone contributing to or responsible for Building Code violations. Such a person need not be the legal owner of the property.

Circuit court

In the case of more serious violations, the Department of Inspectional Services can file a complaint against the owner of the property in the Circuit Court of Cook County. This Court can exercise broad powers by: issuing injunctions, mandatory orders, and contempt citations; placing substandard property into receivership; and ordering dilapidated, dangerous, or abandoned buildings to be vacated and demolished.

---

old buildings that were in conformity with the codes when they were first built may have to be upgraded and improved in accordance with contemporary standards.

ENFORCEMENT OF HOUSING CODES   Enforcement depends both on the content of the laws and on the number of inspectors available to assure implementation of the laws. Improvements required by the codes are not likely to be made unless landlords are able to finance their cost. It is frequently more economical for a landlord to abandon or demolish a building than to invest in making necessary improvements. If housing is scarce and a building is in good condition, abandonment or demolition can create a hardship on tenants who have few housing alternatives from which to choose.

Coercive measures against nonconforming landlords were used extensively during the 1960s but were not very successful. Governmental departments instituted to enforce building codes forced landlords to vacate unfit buildings or make repairs; tenants were encouraged to seek legal remedies, sometimes with the help of legal-aid attorneys. In addition, landlords were offered such inducements as financing and tax advantages to rehabilitate their properties.

Housing violations are typically dealt with indecisively in the courts. Suits are typically marked by many delays because they are considered criminal actions requiring the defendants' physical presence in court. Should the parties to the action fail to appear, the case can be postponed repeatedly.

Injunctions

Court orders proscribing specific conduct have proved effective in forcing landlords to improve housing conditions. Injunctions often prompt them to comply with the law in the future. This approach has been widely used in Chicago, where more than two hundred injunctions have been issued in a year. The courts have insisted on retaining jurisdiction over a landlord until the housing controversy at hand has been settled, since preliminary (temporary) injunctions are relatively easy to obtain, while permanent injunctions often require considerable time.

REMEDIAL HOUSING PROGRAMS

Government housing programs have sought to remedy situations where a large number of dwellings are abandoned and/or in need of extensive repair. These programs included government improvement and repair of such dwellings, receivership programs, and repair by tenants with corresponding deductions from rent.

Government Repair Programs

A revolving fund of $1,000,000 was appropriated in New York City for the repair of dwellings requiring immediate action. If owners refused to pay the cost of such repairs, the city would do so and seek reimbursement from rents paid by tenants. After one and a half years of operation, the program had collected only $21,500—half of which came from landlord payments and half from rents. This return represented only about 2 percent of the program's expenditures on housing improvements. Very few liens on property had been secured, many structures had been abandoned, and the city had not obtained title to them. Consequently New York was forced to discontinue the program.

Receivership

The court may appoint a receiver to collect rents and apply them toward repairs and rehabilitation. Receivership served as a threat to landlords who otherwise might not have made needed improvements. Although a few states provide the statutory authority for receivership, it was used most extensively in Chicago for several thousand buildings in the 1970s, but here again the difficulty in implementation was economic. Costs of rehabilitation were so high that they could not be recovered from rents paid by low-income families. An additional economic drawback includes the high administrative costs of the program.

Repair and Offset

The tenant makes repairs, deducts them from the rent payment, and forwards the difference together with the receipts for work done to the landlord. In Marini v. Ireland, 265 A.2d 526 (N.J. 1970), the court found:

[If a landlord] fails to make repairs and replacements of vital facilities necessary to maintain the premises in a livable condition for a period of time adequate to accomplish such repair and replacements, the tenant may cause the same to be done and deduct the cost thereof from future rents. The tenants' recourse to such self-help must be preceded by timely and adequate notice to the landlord of the faulty condition in order to accord him the opportunity to make the necessary replacement or repair. If the tenant is unable to give such notice after a reasonable attempt, he may nonetheless proceed to repair or replace. This does not mean that the tenant is relieved from the payment of rent so long as the landlord failed to repair. The tenant has only the alternative remedies of making the repairs or removing from the premises upon such a constructive eviction.

We realize that the foregoing may increase the trials and appeals in landlord and tenant dispossess cases and thus increase the burden of the judiciary. By way of warning, however, it should be noted that the foregoing does not constitute an invitation to obstruct the recovery of possession by a landlord legitimately entitled thereto. It is therefore suggested that if the trial of the matter is delayed the defendant may be required to deposit the full amount of unpaid rent in order to protect the landlord if he prevails. Also, an application for a stay of an order of removal on appeal should be critically analyzed and not automatically granted.

RENT WITHHOLDING

Rent withholding in response to unfit housing conditions involving code violations has been successfully used by both individuals and welfare departments to pressure landlords to improve their properties. In any case, rent withholding has been sanctioned by the courts. In Javins v. First National Realty Corp., 428 F.2d 1071 (D.C. Cir. 1970) the court held:

In the present cases, the landlord sued for possession for nonpayment of rent. Under contract principles, however, the tenant's obligation to pay rent is dependent upon the landlord's performance of his obligations, including his warranty to maintain the premises in habitable condition. In order to determine whether any rent is owed to the landlord, the tenant must be given an opportunity to prove the housing code violations alleged as breach of the landlord's warranty.

The Spiegel Law, providing rent withholding, was enacted by New York in 1962 to protect welfare tenants living in buildings that contain a violation of the law "which is dangerous, hazardous, or detrimental to life or health" (Social Services Law §143-b). The law was challenged in Farrell v. Drew, 227 N.E.2d 824 (N.Y. 1967), by a landlord who contended that rent abatement provisions work a "denial of equal protection of the laws, a deprivation of property without due process and an unconstitutional impairment of contractual rights." The court held:

Welfare recipients have even less freedom than other tenants of deteriorated buildings in selecting a place to live, and . . . the landlords of welfare recipients secure in their receipt of rents directly from public funds have even less incentive than other landlords to make repairs.

The remedial legislation challenged in the case before us is reasonably aimed at correcting the evil of substandard housing and may not be stricken as unconstitutional even though the means devised to accomplish that result may, to some extent, impair the obligation of the landlord's contract.

Rent withholding has its shortcomings. It is useful primarily for giving publicity to adverse housing conditions, but such strikes do not necessarily facilitate necessary repairs or rehabilitation, create an adequate supply of low-cost housing, or lead to effective cooperation between landlord and tenant—a condition necessary for long-term housing improvement. On the other hand, rent withholding can be effective if it involves enough housing units and strong financial pressure consistently and rationally applied. When a lease expires, however, there is no way for a rent withholder to maintain tenancy. A thirty-day notice from the landlord ordering removal from the premises is sufficient to terminate the tenancy.

RETALIATORY EVICTION

Tenants who complain about housing conditions are frequently subject to retaliatory eviction by their landlords. McQueen v. Druker, 438 F.2d 781 (1st Cir. 1971), illustrates the unsuccessful attempt of a landlord to evict tenants "because of many confrontations" with them. The landlord in this case was restrained by the U.S. Court of Appeals. Similar evictions have occurred in public housing projects. A resident of North Carolina received notice to vacate within twenty-four hours after having been elected president of a tenant union.

In Escalera v. New York City Housing Authority, 425 F.2d 853 (2d Cir. 1970), termination for nondesirability was found deficient because the tenant was inadequately informed as to the nature of evidence against him. He was denied access to information compiled on him by the plaintiff agency, as well as the right to cross-examine and confront persons who has supplied such data. The actions taken were not based on legal rules for fair hearings established by the Supreme Court in Goldberg v. Kelly, 397 U.S. 254 (1970).

PUBLIC HOUSING

Although public housing projects have been criticized as encouraging large concentrations of people with social problems, such housing units have been in demand because the rents charged make them a good bargain. However, only a small proportion of applicants for public housing can be accommodated. The differential between supply and demand has promoted court actions by applicants who were allegedly subjected to unfair selection procedures. Federal law contains few specific guidelines on eligibility, but holds that public housing agencies are not to "discriminate against families, otherwise eligible for admission to public housing, because their incomes are derived in whole or in part from public assistance" (42 U.I.C. §81402). Full consideration is also to be given applicants who are veterans. Since tenant selection is usually controlled by the housing authorities themselves, one of the major selections in both northern and southern cities has involved de facto segregation—a problem beyond the control of housing project managers.

Eligibility and administrative procedures were challenged in Holmes v. New York City Housing Authority in 1968 (398 F.2d 262 [2d Cir.]). Thirty-one plaintiffs joined in a class action suit claiming many deficiencies in admissions policies and practices. Among their specific complaints were that regulations were not made available to prospective tenants, that applications were not processed chronologically, that all applications expired after the end of two years, and that an application for contract renewal was given no preference. In addition, no waiting list was provided, and ineligible applicants were neither so notified nor provided with reasons for their ineligibility. These procedures allegedly deprived applicants of due process of law. The U.S. Court of Appeals concluded:

> Clearly there is sufficient in the complaint to state a claim for relief under section 1983 and the due process clause. One charge made against the defendant, which has merit

is that it [the Housing Authority] failed to establish the fair and orderly procedure for allocating its scarce supply of housing which due process requires. Due process requires that selections among applicants be made in accordance with "ascertainable standards" and in cases where many candidates are equally qualified that further selections be made in some reasonable manner such as by lot or on the basis of chronological order of application.

The U.S. District Court ruled in Thomas v. Housing Authority of City of Little Rock, 282 F.Supp. 575 (E.D.Ark. 1967), on the authority's policy excluding unwed mothers from public housing

[An authority] may not exclude from the benefit of public housing a low income family merely because of the incidence of illegitimacy within the family group. Such a policy simply has no place in the low rent housing program, and in that sense is arbitrary and capricious. . . . an indiscriminate denial of access to public housing to families unfortunate enough to have or acquire one or more illegitimate children would be to deprive of the real or supposed benefits of the program many of the very people who need it most—the poorest and most ignorant of the poor. An administrative policy which involves such a denial does not square with the humane purpose of the low rent housing program.

On the other hand, many decisions have upheld the power of housing authorities to deny undesirable persons public housing. In one case, adjudication on several occasions as a youthful offender and repeated involvement in criminal activity constituted a proper basis to deny eligibility (Manigo v. New York City Housing Authority, 273 N.Y.S.2d 1003 [1966]).

Berger (1973:787–788) suggests the attitudes appropriate for public housing. Note the inconsistencies of items a and b with c and g:

a. The right to decent housing is everyone's right. There are neither deserving nor undeserving poor.

b. Families who are denied public housing as problem-ridden may benefit most from a fresh start in a decent housing environment.

c. A public landlord should be as discriminating as a private landlord. The housing authority must respect the well-being of all tenants in a project and attempt to screen out those applicants likeliest to disrupt or discomfort other occupants.

d. Public housing projects maintain a delicate financial balance. Therefore, housing authorities should be able to reject any applicant if they doubt he will pay his rent or if they believe he may cause excessive physical damage to his apartment.

e. Public and congressional approval of public housing is essential to the program's financial support. Therefore, housing projects should be run as model communities; this means model tenants and highly selective admission practices.

f. Problem families are least able to compete for suitable housing in the private market. Therefore, they should be given special consideration as applicants for public housing.

g. No one should be denied eligibility on the prediction that he will be an undesirable tenant. There is time enough to terminate his benefits if he is undesirable in fact.

Established residents strongly oppose construction of public housing for low-income families in their neighborhoods. In James v. Valtierra, 402 U.S. 137 (1971), provisions operative in California since 1950 were upheld, with the stipulation "No low-rent housing project should be developed, constructed, or acquired in any manner by a state public body until the project was approved by a majority of those voting at a community election." Plaintiffs who brought such suits were eligible for public housing in localities where the referenda had been defeated. The equal protection and supremacy clauses were major issues.

> The people of California have also decided by their own vote to require referendum approval of low-rent public housing projects. This procedure ensures that all the people of a community will have a voice in a decision which may lead to large expenditures of local governmental funds for increased public services and to lower tax revenues. It gives them a voice in decisions that will affect the future development of their own community. This procedure for democratic decision-making does not violate the constitutional command that no State shall deny to any person the equal protection of the laws.

In the dissenting opinion, Justice Thurgood Marshall observed that "singling out the poor to bear a burden not placed on any other class of citizens tramples the values that the Fourteenth Amendment was designed to protect."

TRENDS IN HOUSING LAW

New trends in housing law include decisions on public housing in the white suburbs, court-ordered zoning for the poor, and life-style and communal living restrictions.

Public Housing in the White Suburbs

The principal U.S. Supreme Court decision on racial discrimination in locating public housing was Hills v. Gautreaux, 425 U.S. 284 (1976). Black tenants had challenged the Chicago housing pattern in which all the sites approved for family public housing had been "within the areas known as the Negro ghetto." The Supreme Court held that the District Court had the authority to direct HUD to engage in remedial efforts to deal with the pattern of segregation in public housing by involving the metropolitan area outside the city limits of Chicago. Since the decision, there has been little public housing built in Cook County, Illinois.

Court-ordered Zoning for the Poor

A New Jersey superior court in Middlesex County ruled in May 1976 that the zoning ordinances of eleven municipalities were unconstitutional (Urban League of Greater New Brunswick v. Mayor and Council of Borough of Carteret, 359 A.2d 526 [N.J. 1976]). The court ordered the communities to plan a total of over 11,000 low- and moderate-income housing units by 1985. The judge gave them ninety days to develop regulations to enable them to provide their fair share of such housing as indicated by regional needs.

Eleven other communities originally named previously agreed to amend their ordinances in a manner satisfactory to the plaintiffs, who filed the class action suit on behalf of minorities and low-income families. Specific quotas were assigned to each community. The court based its decision in part on *Hills v. Gautreaux.*

Housing and Life-styles

In a 1974 decision reported in Chapter 10, Village of Belle Terre v. Boraas, 416 U.S. 1, the U.S. Supreme Court upheld an ordinance of Long Island limiting a single housekeeping unit to two unrelated persons living and cooking together. The ordinance was challenged by college students and the owners of a house they had rented. In the dissent, Justice Thurgood Marshall raised the life-style issue. Apparently the ordinance had been intended mainly to contest communal living.

HOUSING THE HOMELESS

Serving the homeless in the mid-1980s reminds one of descriptions of the depression a half-century earlier. The homeless are often young; a considerable number are family units; some of them are women; many are mentally ill.

New York courts, unlike those in most other states, have mandated state and city agencies to provide shelter (e.g., Callahan v. Carey (New York State Supreme Court #42582/79) and Eldredge v. Koch (New York Supreme Court #41494/82)). Because many of the single room occupancy hotels (SROs) were torn down the former occupants found themselves on the streets.

Many of the homeless refuse to go to shelters. In the winter of 1984–85, Chicago, Philadelphia, and New York police were ordered to pick up homeless people, against their will if necessary, to protect them against life-threatening cold. Los Angeles city officials considered declaring the city a disaster area because of the influx of homeless in the same year.

ZONING AS A SOCIAL WORK CONCERN

The original purpose of zoning was to enhance the general welfare through providing restrictions on the exploitation of an owner's property. Zoning divides a community into various districts or zones and assigns certain land uses to each one. The concept of zoning laws is highly restrictive. Zoning concerns social workers because it effectively excludes certain groups of people from particular residential areas.

Land-use controls such as those in *Belle Terre v. Boraas* become a problem for social workers who seek to establish homelike facilities in residential areas for small numbers of mentally retarded or emotionally disturbed children, juvenile offenders, released prisoners, or the aged. From the community's viewpoint, the right to exclude dissimilar people from relatively homogeneous neighborhoods may be more important than an individual's right to find a pleasant place to live.

More than two decades ago, in Rogers v. Association for the Health of Retarded Children, 120 N.Y.S.2d 329, aff'd 123 N.E.2d 806 (N.Y. 1954), an attempt had been made to enjoin the association from developing a school for retarded children on its property. It was alleged that the health, welfare, and safety of the neighboring community would be adversely affected by the presence of large numbers of mentally retarded children. The court found, in part:

> The health, welfare and safety of the plaintiffs were not adversely affected by the defendant's use of the premises; that the presence of mentally retarded children on the defendant's property did not cause hardship to the families of the plaintiffs; that the method of education afforded by the defendant to mentally retarded children did not disturb the peace and quiet of the neighborhood, nor did those children cause damage to plaintiff's property or bodily harm to anyone in the neighborhood.

Fears of having mentally retarded children in the community were not sufficient to threaten the general welfare and justify an exclusion. Persons with a history of antisocial behavior or those who have had a psychiatric label applied to them, however, are less acceptable than the mentally retarded. Groups of persons of both sexes who adopt unusual communal life-styles and those who are known to be homosexual are likewise suspect.

Zoning laws may include restrictive definitions of family, ranging from a household unit related by blood, marriage, or adoption, to the inclusion of collateral relatives, to specifying maximum numbers of unrelated persons such as "a group not exceeding four persons living as a single housekeeping unit."

Ordinances that limit residential structures to single-family use potentially exclude the development of group homes for social work clientele, including children and adults. For example, individuals living in a group residence for the mentally retarded are generally unrelated to each other. Therefore the claim may be made under the ordinance that these people cannot be considered a family.

As Chandler and Ross (1976) indicate, state legislation will probably provide the most effective action for the mentally retarded. Legislation should stress both the need to normalize the lives of mentally handicapped persons and the proposition that integration into residential areas is required to meet the need. Legislation should cover all political subdivisions, including cities with home rule privileges. Such residences should be a permitted use in all nonindustrial zones. If a maximum number of occupants is specified, it should agree with state licensing provisions for such institutions. Chandler and Ross (1976:311) provide a statement of legislative intent asserting that "mentally and physically handicapped persons are entitled to share with non-handicapped individuals the benefits of normal residential surroundings and should not be excluded therefrom because of their disability." Zoning ordinances and their regulations should not deny this right.

Counterarguments stress that social costs of group homes are imposed on the neighbors. The atmosphere "is not normal, in the sense that the neighborhood will not reflect the ordinary composition of the community." Provisions should recognize the social costs and include:

(1) standards for the site and facility that ensure reasonable privacy to neighbors, (2) effective neighborhood participation in the management of the facility, and (3) a mechanism which guarantees that a residence will not be located in a neighborhood which has become "impacted" by other similar desirable nonresidential social uses. (Deutch, 1976: 347–348)

In the 1984–85 term, the U.S. Supreme Court is expected to rule on a Texas zoning ordinance case involving exclusion of group homes for the retarded from certain neighborhoods (484–468 City of Cleburne v. Cleburne Living Center, 52 L.W. 2515).

FEDERAL HOUSING PROGRAMS

The 1982 program summary of the Department of Housing and Urban Development lists over thirty housing programs and seven programs for policy development and research. They are summarized in Table 21.1.

Current priority areas in federal housing policy include:

■ Implementation of urban economic development activities to increase employment and help revitalize neighborhoods.

■ Actions to reduce costs of housing including mechanisms and construction technologies.

■ Analysis of the strategy of private management of public housing projects.

■ Analysis of: (1) the relationship between tax policies and housing; (2) housing finance mechanisms, such as mortgage instruments; (3) financial institution regulation and reform; and (4) financial incentives for housing.

■ Development and dissemination of information about better methods for city management and delivery of local government services.

■ Formulation of public-private neighborhood partnership.

TABLE 21.1
HUD'S MORTGAGE INSURANCE AND OTHER HOUSING PROGRAMS

Mortgage Insurance	
	Section of National Housing Act, P.L. 73-479
For commercial lenders to facilitate construction and house ownership.	203
For low- and moderate-income home-buyers	235
To increase home ownership opportunities for low- and moderate-income families, especially those displaced by urban renewal	221(d)(2)
To rehabilitate housing in older, declining urban areas	223(e)
For special credit risks	237
For condominium housing	234
For cooperative housing projects	213
To finance purchase of manufactured mobile homes	Title I, Section 1
For construction or rehabilitation of mobile home parks	207
For construction or rehabilitation of multifamily rental housing	207
For purchase or refinancing of existing apartment projects	223
For multifamily rental housing for low- and moderate-income families	221(d)(3) & (4)
For housing the elderly	231
To finance rehabilitation of one- to four-family properties	(203 (d,c)

Other Programs	
	Legislation
Lower-income rental assistance	Section B, Housing Act of 1937.
Low-income public housing	Housing Act of 1937
Public housing modernization	Section 14, Housing Act of 1937
Public housing operating subsidies	Section 9, Housing Act of 1937
Direct loans for housing the elderly	Section 202, Housing Act of 1959
Federal loan insurance to finance home improvements	Title I, Section 2, Housing Act of 1934
Federal loan insurance to finance improvements to multifamily rental housing and health care facilities	Section 241, Housing Act of 1934
Indian housing	Housing Act of 1937
Counseling for home buyers and tenants of all HUD-assisted housing	Housing Act of 1934
Mobile home construction and safety standards	Housing and Community Development Acts of 1974 and 1977
Real estate settlement procedures to control apartments and kickbacks	Real Estate Settlement Procedures Act of 1974

Questions for Review

1. What are the major roles of social workers in dealing with housing problems?

2. Characterize the tenant's rights under common law. What development has bettered the tenant's position?

3. In addition to legal sanctions, on what does effective enforcement of housing regulations depend?

4. What typical problems have been experienced in dealing with housing violations through the courts?

5. What is the effect of a court injunction?

6. What problems have resulted from the use of government repair programs to deal with building violations?

7. Explain receivership. What has been the main problem of receivership as a practical means of upgrading housing quality?

8. Who initiates the repairs in *repair and offset* remedies?

9. Explain the finding on the constitutionality of the Spiegel Law.

10. Explain retaliatory eviction.

11. Characterize requirements for tenant selection procedures. What are the major possible abuses?

12. Why is mortgage insurance the dominant emphasis in federal housing programs?

13. Review the Real Estate Settlement Procedures Act and summarize its provisions.

Questions for Debate and Discussion

1. What aspects of life space and life-style are determined by a person's selection of housing? Do people consider these issues in selecting a neighborhood?

2. The Little Rock Housing Authority defended its "unmarried mother rule" as a means of controlling prostitution and promiscuity. Discuss their position.

3. Analyze current federal housing programs in terms of meeting the needs of the poor.

4. What types of social service facilities are likely to encounter neighborhood opposition and conflict with zoning laws? What means can be used to get public acceptance of residential facilities for special clientele—children, recovering mental patients, and the aged?

Selected Readings   Bloom, Howard S., and Susan E. P. Bloom. "Household Participation in the Section Eight Existing Housing Program." *Evaluation Review* 5 (1981):167–188.

Burke, Gill. *Housing and Social Justice.* New York: Longman, 1981.

Lindamood, Suzanne, and Sherman D. Hanna. *Housing, Society, and Consumers: An Introduction.* St. Paul, Minn.: West Publishing Co., 1979.

Montgomery, Roger, and Dale R. Marshall. *Housing Policy for the 1980s.* Lexington, Mass.: Lexington Books, 1980.

Pynoos, Jon (ed.), *Housing Urban America.* Hawthorne, N.Y.: Aldine, 1980.

Schwemm, Robert G. *Housing Discrimination Law.* Washington, D.C.: Bureau of National Affairs, 1983.

Struyk, Raymond, J. *Housing Policies for the Urban Poor.* Washington, D.C.: Urban Institute, 1978.

Zais, James P., et al. *Housing Assistance for Older Americans: The Reagan Prescription.* Washington, D.C.: Urban Institute, 1982.

CHAPTER

22

Education

This chapter deals with the rights of students to receive an education and ultimately to receive an education of an acceptable quality. Court decisions have covered the rights of children of aliens, the relation of religion and education, desegregation of the schools, the right of handicapped children to special services, and permissible student self-expression. The laws have focused especially on handicapped children.

The U.S. Supreme Court has resisted ruling on the internal operation of the schools, considering these issues to be state and local prerogatives. It has not wanted to affect the schools's *in loco parentis* role. When the Court has ruled, the decisions tended to be conservative as, for example, on the issue of corporal punishment in the schools.

The Reagan administration has continued to curtail the activities of the Department of Education created in 1979 by President Jimmy Carter. The budgets of migrant education programs, Native American education, and civil rights training have been cut. A number of national reports on the status of elementary and secondary public schools have expressed concern about the present quality of education. The quality of learning experiences in some public schools is excellent. Elementary and secondary education may be moving toward creation of two groups of students. One group has a teacher for every ten students and instruction in personal computers starting in kindergarten. The other group may graduate from high school without learning basic skills.

RIGHT TO EDUCATION

All states have constitutional or statutory provisions for free public education, including special provisions for mentally or physically handicapped children. Federal courts have held that children may not be excluded from school simply because they are labeled mentally retarded, emotionally disturbed, hyperactive, or apt to be behavior problems. Compulsory school attendance laws stress that education is an obligation, that it is not a right to be exercised or ignored, as in the case of the right to vote.

Plyler v. Doe, 457 U.S. 202 (1982) took up the right to free public education of school-age children who are illegal aliens. In 1975 the Texas legislature voted to withhold state funds for the education of children who had not been "legally admitted" into the United States. They also authorized local school districts to deny enrollment to such children.

The Supreme Court concluded that the state could not take such action.

If the State is to deny a discrete group of innocent children the free public education that it offers to other children residing within its borders, that denial must be justified by showing that it furthers some substantial state interest. No such showing was made here.

The children who are plaintiffs in these cases are special members of this underclass. Persuasive arguments support the view that a State may withhold its beneficence from those whose very presence within the United States is the product of their own unlawful conduct. These arguments do not apply with the same force to classifications imposing disabilities on the minor *children* of such illegal entrants. At the least, those who elect to enter our territory by stealth and in violation of our law should be prepared to bear the consequences, including, but not limited to, deportation. But the children of those illegal entrants are not comparably situated. Their "parents have the ability to conform their conduct to societal norms," and presumably the ability to remove themselves from the State's jurisdiction, but the children who are plaintiffs in these cases "can affect neither their parents' conduct nor their own status." . . .

In addition to the pivotal role of education in sustaining our political and cultural heritage, denial of education to some isolated group of children poses an affront to one of the goals of the Equal Protection Clause: the abolition of governmental barriers presenting unreasonable obstacles to advancement on the basis of individual merit. Paradoxically, by depriving the children of any disfavored group of an education, we foreclose the means by which that group might raise the level of esteem in which it is held by the majority. . . .

It is difficult to understand precisely what the State hopes to achieve by promoting the creation and perpetuation of a subclass of illiterates within our boundaries, surely adding to the problems and costs of unemployment, welfare, and crime. It is thus clear that whatever savings might be achieved by denying these children an education, they are wholly insubstantial in light of the costs involved to these children, the State, and the Nation.

The justices expressed disparate views in the majority, concurring, and dissenting opinions. While all agreed on the importance of education, some would grant strict scrutiny to any denial of access to the public schools. Others would allow state legislatures to discriminate between groups of children.

The issues that gave rise to the Plyler case reflect a national concern. Schools in such states as Texas, as well as Florida and California, are trying to work out a policy for educating children whose first language is not English. Some programs provide students with subjects in their first language throughout their education. Other schools attempt to transfer them into English-speaking classes as soon as possible. Even after such a transition, some programs provide language courses to enable students to continue to converse in their native tongue. In ethnically diverse school districts such a policy would mean teaching in several different languages, which is expensive. While some critics of bilingual education argue that teaching children in their first language prevents them from mastering English, studies have shown the advantages of knowing two languages and particularly of teaching younger children in their first language.

In the Plyler decision the Court commented:

Whatever his status under the immigration laws, an alien is surely a "person" in any ordinary sense of that term. Aliens, even aliens whose presence in this country is unlawful, have long been recognized as "persons" guaranteed due process of law by the Fifth and Fourteenth Amendments. Indeed, we have clearly held that the Fifth Amendment protects aliens whose presence in this country is unlawful from invidious discrimination by the Federal Government. . . .

In appellants' view, persons who have entered the United States illegally are not "within the jurisdiction" of a State even if they are present within a State's boundaries and subject to its laws. Neither our cases nor the logic of the Fourteenth Amendment supports that constricting construction of the phrase "within its jurisdiction." . . .

Sheer incapability or lax enforcement of the laws barring entry into this country, coupled with the failure to establish an effective bar to the employment of undocumented aliens, has resulted in the creation of a substantial "shadow population" of illegal migrants—numbering in the millions—within our borders. This situation raises the spector of a permanent caste of undocumented resident aliens, encouraged by some to remain here as a source of cheap labor, but nevertheless denied the benefits that our society makes available to citizens and lawful residents. The existence of such an underclass presents most difficult problems for a Nation that prides itself on adherence to principles of equality under law.

RACIAL SEGREGATION

In 1896 the Supreme Court ruled in Plessy v. Ferguson, 163 U.S. 537, that public schools could be racially segregated as long as they were substantially equal. This "separate but equal" doctrine remained in effect until 1954, when the Court held in Brown v. Board of Education of Topeka, Shawnee County, Kansas, 347 U.S. 483, that:

. . . in the field of public education the doctrine of "separate but equal" has no place. Separate educational facilities are inherently unequal. Therefore, we hold that the plaintiffs and others similarly situated for whom the actions have been brought are, by reason of the segregation complained of, deprived of the equal protection of the laws guaranteed by the Fourteenth Amendment. (347 U.S. at 495)

This apparently straightforward ruling was hampered by problems of implementation. In a reargument of Brown on immediacy of relief, the Court requested that a "good faith start" be initiated and completed with "all deliberate speed" (Brown v. Board of Education of Topeka, Kansas, 349 U.S. 294 [1955]). One lower court considered mere cessation of discrimination to constitute adequate compliance until desegregation would be achieved generally. The Supreme Court used stronger language when it called for desegregation "at once" in Green v. County School Board of New Kent County, 391 U.S. 430 (1968). In Alexander v. Holmes County Board of Education, 396 U.S. 19 (1969), the Court held:

. . . [C]ontinued operation of segregated schools under a standard of allowing "all deliberate speed" for desegregation is no longer constitutionally permissible. Under explicit holdings of this Court the obligation of every school district is to terminate dual school systems at once and to operate now and hereafter only unitary schools. (396 U.S. at 20)

Both the difficulties of desegregation of the schools and communities' resistance to desegregation orders are illustrated in the number of plans that cities have had to develop in response to the courts over the past thirty years to be in compliance with the Brown decision.

Students who are familiar with the language of the decision will find it enlightening to review it in the light of subsequent controversies.

In Swann v. Charlotte-Mecklenburg Board of Education, 402 U.S. 1 (1971), the Supreme Court more explicitly defined the scope of the duty of school authorities and district courts in implementing Brown by:

(1) the rejection of geographic proximity (neighborhood schools) as a criterion for school assignments where such policy fails to bring about a 'unitary nonracial school system';

(2) the creation of an evidentiary presumption that segregated school patterns are the result of past discriminatory conduct; (3) the requirement that school boards take all feasible steps to eliminate segregation, including massive, long-distance transportation programs; (4) The validation of using race in student assignments to achieve school desegregation (Fiss, 1971: 700). . .

Lower courts have cited *Swann* in ordering busing to achieve racial balance in schools, and the Supreme Court upheld such an order in 1976 by refusing to review court-ordered busing in Boston.

In Milliken v. Bradley, 418 U.S. 717 (1974), the Supreme Court imposed limitations whereby busing across school districts and counties is considered improper unless district lines were deliberately drawn on the basis of race. The Court also held in Pasadena City Board of Education v. Spangler, 423 U.S. 1335 (1975), that:

since the shifts in the racial makeup of some of the schools resulted from changes in the demographics of Pasadena's residential pattern due to a normal pattern of people moving into, out of, and around the school system, and were not attributable to any segregative action on the school officials' part, neither the school officials nor the District Court "were constitutionally required to make year-by-year adjustments of racial composition of student bodies once the affirmative duty to desegregate has been accomplished and racial discrimination through official action is eliminated from the system."

The principle that discriminatory intent must be proven was repeated by the Court in remanding a plan to desegregate Indianapolis schools by busing black students to suburban districts to the appeals court that had previously approved it (Metropolitan School District v. Buckley, 429 U.S. 1068 [1977]).

Busing across district lines has been condemned by public opinion polls and government officials as well as by a prominent former supporter of busing, James Coleman, whose 1966 study on the salutory effects of integration had been influential in court decisions. Coleman registered his opposition to court-ordered busing before a Senate Judiciary Committee hearing in 1975 on the ground that it causes whites to move, thus "resegregating" blacks. Congress received four proposals for a constitutional amendment to ban busing for the purpose of desegregating schools in 1976. Thirty years after *Brown,* school desegregation remains an issue.

Desegregation efforts have been hampered by lack of government funding. In 1983, President Reagan vetoed legislation that would have provided $20 million to assist in desegregation of the Chicago school system. Settlement of a long court fight in San Francisco over desegregating the city's schools was threatened when the governor vetoed the spending of $8 million to implement the plan. However, lawyers for the National Association for the Advancement of Colored People (NAACP) argued that the school district should put the plan into action and then seek reimbursement from the state, just as other school districts in California with school desegregation plans had done. The settlement had provided for desegregation training for teachers, buying almost $1 million worth of computer equipment, and assigning pupils to schools in order to follow the guideline that no single ethnic group exceed 45 percent of a school's student body.

Another case involving pupil assignments and busing to achieve racial desegregation was decided by the U.S. Supreme Court in 1982 (Crawford v. Los Angeles Board of Education, 458 U.S. 527). The issue was whether a state could pass a referendum to require state courts to do no more to accomplish desegregation than a federal court would require. The Court decided that Proposition I, passed by the state to accomplish that purpose, was constitutional. Proposition I "simply forbids state courts from ordering pupil school assignment or transportation in the absence of a Fourteenth Amendment violation. The benefit it seeks to confer—neighborhood schooling—is made available regardless of race in the discretion of school boards."

RELIGION AND EDUCATION

States may require children to attend school regardless of the wishes of their parents (Prince v. Commonwealth of Massachusetts, 321 U.S. 158 [1944]). However, parents may provide alternative equivalent education in private settings, including church-operated schools (Pierce v. Society of the Sisters of the Holy Names of Jesus and Mary, 268 U.S. 510 [1925]). The Supreme Court's most definitive decision, Wisconsin v. Yoder, 406 U.S. 205 (1972), struck a balance between state interest in universal education and parental freedom of religion.

The Wisconsin Supreme Court had held that members of Amish churches were justified in not sending their children to school after graduation from eighth grade.

The respondents defended their action on the basis that Wisconsin's compulsory attendance laws violated their rights under the First and Fourteenth amendments. They alleged that their children's attendance at high school was contrary to the Amish religion and way of life. By sending their children to high school, they would expose themselves to danger of censure by the church community and also endanger their own salvation and that of their children.

Amish objection to formal education beyond the eighth grade is firmly grounded in these central religious concepts. They object to the high school, and higher education generally, because the values they teach are in marked variance with Amish values and the Amish way of life; they view secondary school education as an impermissible exposure of their children to a "worldly" influence in conflict with their beliefs. The high school tends to emphasize intellectual and scientific accomplishments, self-distinction, competitiveness, worldly success, and social life with other students. Amish society emphasizes informal learning-through-doing; a life of "goodness," rather than a life of intellect; wisdom, rather than technical knowledge, community welfare, rather than competition; and separation from, rather than integration with, contemporary worldly society (406 U.S. at 210–211).

Expert witnesses concluded that the modern high school is not equipped to impart the values promoted by Amish society.

The State advances two primary arguments in support of its system of compulsory education. It notes, as Thomas Jefferson pointed out early in our history, that some degree of education is necessary to prepare citizens to participate effectively and intelligently in our open political system if we are to preserve freedom and independence. Further, education prepares individuals to be self-reliant and self-sufficient participants in society. We accept these propositions.

However, the evidence adduced by the Amish in this case is persuasively to the effect that an additional one or two years of formal high school for Amish children in place of their long-established program of informal vocation education would do little to serve those interests. Respondents' experts testified at trial, without challenge, that the value of all education must be assessed in terms of its capacity to prepare the child for life. It is one thing to say that compulsory education for a year or two beyond the eighth grade may be necessary when its goal is the preparation of the child for life in modern society as the majority live, but it is quite another if the goal of education be viewed as the preparation of the child for life in the separated agrarian community that is the keystone of the Amish faith. (id at 221–222)

Justice William O. Douglas dissented in part because the children were given no part in the decision to attend high school. "Where the child is mature enough to express potentially conflicting desires, it would be an invasion of the child's right to permit such an imposition without canvassing his views. . . . On this important and vital matter of education, I think the children should be entitled to be heard." (id at 242).

The majority decision included this comment on the Douglas dissent: "Our holding today in no degree depends on the assertion of the religious interest of the child as contrasted with that of the parents. It is the parents who are subject to prosecution here for failing to cause their children to attend school, and it is their right of free exercise, not that of their children, that must determine Wisconsin's power to impose criminal penalties on the parent." (id at 230–231)

As Justice Douglas emphasized in his dissenting opinion, a precedent exists for affording children of fourteen considerable voice in electing their way of life, as evidenced by allowing them to choose the parent with whom they wish to live after separation or divorce. As a result of *Yoder*, parents' religious beliefs potentially restrict the right of young persons to education and to self-determination.

UNEQUAL FINANCING

Public elementary and secondary education is funded by local property taxes, state revenues, and federal aid for special programs. Reliance on property taxes has resulted in disproportionate funding for education from one school district to another. Taxpayers resist both higher costs of education and tax dollars for poorer children elsewhere. In 1971 the California Supreme Court ruled that reliance on local property taxes for educational financing was unconstitutional (Serrano v. Priest, 487 P.2d 1241 [Cal. 1971]). The court contended that such funding discriminated against the poor because it made the quality of education dependent upon where a child lived. The New Jersey Supreme Court made a similar decision in 1973 (Robinson v. Cahill, 306 A.2d 65 [N.J. 1973]). *Serrano* was reargued and affirmed in 1977.

In 1973 the U.S. Supreme Court reached the opposite conclusion. In San Antonio Independent School District v. Rodriguez, 411 U.S. 1, the Court held that the financing of public education primarily by property taxes is not uncon-stitutional, even though the result is unequal. In addition, the majority opinion stated that there is no explicit right to education under the Constitution, because education is not "essential to the effective exercise of First Amendment freedoms and to the intelligent utilization of the right to vote." Four justices dissented from this ruling, arguing that there is a constitutional right to education and that children in poorer school districts are a "suspect class" and consequently, entitled to strict defense of their rights under the Fourteenth Amendment. The dissenting judges further contend that although education may not be a fundamental right, when provided it must be available to all equally. According to the dissenting justices, property tax financing fails to meet the rationality test of the Fourteenth Amendment. The *Serrano* and *Cahill* decisions are binding in California and New Jersey because of provisions of their respective state laws. State equal protection standards may be higher than federal provisions, and more than half the states have altered their school budgets in response to reform movements (Gifford and Macchiarola, 1981:718).

The mandate of the state supreme court in *Serrano v. Priest* that California's public school districts should equalize their spending has been difficult to achieve. Limits on how much school districts could spend were set as part of this legislation with the intention that districts that spent less could increase their rate of spending faster than districts that spent more. Eventually parity would be reached among all school districts. However, this legislation also allows an exception to the limits. Districts may override their limit by a simple majority vote. Districts that were already spending above average were the ones that passed overrides which maintained the disparity between rich and poor districts.

One school district in the San Francisco Bay area near the Stanford University campus spends $4,054 per pupil each year, while a bordering district spends only $2,811 educating each student (Nakao, 1984). That ten years after *Serrano v. Priest* almost twice as much money could be spent in one school district as in a neighboring one demonstrates the difficulty of achieving parity.

PUBLIC AID TO NONPUBLIC SCHOOLS

State provisions for a free public education do not extend to nonpublic schools. More than 75 percent of nonpublic schools in the United States have religious affiliations. The establishment clause of the First Amendment prohibits governmental involvement in religious activities, including financial support for religion. The Supreme Court, in Roemer v. Board of Public Works of Maryland, 426 U.S. 736 (1976), relied upon a three-part test developed in Lemon v. Kurtzman, 403 U.S. 602 (1971), that state aid have a secular purpose, a primary effect other than the advancement of religion, and no tendency to entangle the state excessively in church affairs:

> . . . [R]eligious institutions need not be quarantined from public benefits that are neutrally available to all. The Court has permitted the State to supply transportation for children to and from church-related as well as public schools. Everson v. Board of Education, 330 U.S. 1 (1947). It has done the same with respect to secular textbooks loaned by the State on equal terms to students attending both public and church-related elementary schools. . . . 96 S.Ct. at 2344.
>
> In Meek v. Pittenger, 421 U.S. 349 (1975), the Court ruled yet again on a state-aid program for church-related elementary and secondary schools. On the authority of *Allen*, it upheld a Pennsylvania program for lending textbooks to private school students. It found, however, that *Lemon I* required the invalidation of two other forms of aid to the private schools. The first was the loan of instructional materials and equipment. Like the textbooks, these were secular and nonideological in nature. Unlike the textbooks, however, they were loaned directly to the schools. The schools, similar to those in *Lemon I*, were ones in which "the teaching process is, to a large extent, devoted to the inculcation of religious values and belief." Id., at 366. Aid flowing directly to such "religion-pervasive institutions," ibid., had the primary effect of advancing religion. See Hunt v. McNair, supra. The other form of aid was the provision of "auxiliary" educational services: remedial instruction, counseling and testing, and speech and hearing therapy. These also were intended to be neutral and nonideological

and in fact were to be provided by public school teachers. Still, there was danger that the teachers, in such a sectarian setting, would allow religion to seep into their instruction. To attempt to prevent this from happening would excessively entangle the State in church affairs. . . . (Id. at 2348)

The Court ruled in *Roemer* that Maryland's statutory provision for annual "noncategorical" grants to private colleges, among them religiously affiliated institutions, subject only to the restrictions that the funds not be used for "sectarian purposes" does not violate the establishment clause.

The U.S. Supreme Court approved Minnesota's provision for deduction of educational expenses from state income tax in Mueller v. Allen, 463 U.S. 388 (1983), reasoning that this deduction is available to all parents, whether their children attend public schools, private church-related schools, or nonsectarian private schools.

MUELLER v. ALLEN

Supreme Court of the United States, 463 U.S. 388 (1983).

Minnesota, by a law originally enacted in 1955 and revised in 1976 and again in 1978, permits state taxpayers to claim a deduction from gross income for certain expenses incurred in educating their children. The deduction is limited to actual expenses incurred for the "tuition, textbooks and transportation" of dependents attending elementary or secondary schools. A deduction may not exceed $500 per dependent in grades K through six and $700 per dependent in grades seven through twelve. Minn. Stat. § 290.09. . . .

Petitioners—certain Minnesota taxpayers—sued in the United States District Court for the District of Minnesota claiming that § 290.09(22) violated the Establishment Clause by providing financial assistance to sectarian institutions. . . . The general nature of our inquiry in this area has been guided, since the decision in Lemon v. Kurtzman, 403 U.S. 602 (1971), by the "three-part" test laid down in that case:

> "First, the statute must have a secular legislative purpose; second, its principal or primary effect must be one that neither advances nor inhibits religion . . . ; finally, the statute must not foster 'an excessive government entanglement with religion.' " Id., at 612–613. . . .

A state's decision to defray the cost of educational expenses incurred by parents—regardless of the type of schools their children attend—evidences a purpose that is both secular and understandable. An educated populace is essential to the political and economic health of any community, and a state's efforts to assist parents in meeting the rising cost of educational expenses plainly serves this secular purpose of ensuring that the state's citizenry is well-educated. Similarly, Minnesota, like other states, could conclude that there is a strong public interest in assuring the continued financial health of private schools, both sectarian and non-sectarian. By educating a substantial number of students such schools relieve public schools of a correspondingly great burden—to the benefit of all taxpayers. In addition, private schools may serve as a benchmark for public schools, in a manner analogous to the "TVA yardstick" for private power companies. . . .

Other characteristics of § 290.09(22) argue equally strongly for the provision's constitutionality. Most importantly, the deduction is available for educational expenses incurred by *all* parents, including those whose children attend public schools and those whose children attend non-sectarian private schools or sectarian private schools.

The dissent by Justice Thurgood Marshall indicates that although this financial assistance is available to all parents, the primary beneficiaries will be those sending their children to private schools, most of which are church-related. Apart from the religious issue concerning the establishment clause, some social policy analysts fear both tuition tax credits for private school expenses and educational voucher plans. Perhaps only families with above-average incomes will be able to take advantage of these financial benefits. Such public aid to nonpublic schools could contribute to only low-income children attending public schools, while tax dollars subsidize wealthier parents.

Shanker (1984) has offered a scenario in which both the amount of the deduction and the tuition increase each year. More and more parents are putting their children in private schools. Then governments fall on hard times and no longer offer the deduction, so that only wealthy families can afford to send their children to private schools. However, the public schools have deteriorated.

DUE PROCESS The right to education may be interrupted by suspension or expulsion from school. Under the Fourteenth Amendment, no person may be deprived of "life, liberty, or property without due process of law." Due process refers to established procedures designed to assure the accused fair treatment. The Supreme Court has held that education is a property interest and has equated protection of a student's good name with the protection of liberty. No student may be deprived of these rights without due process of law.

In 1975, the U.S. Supreme court extended due process rights to students in two cases involving different aspects of these rights. In Goss v. Lopez, 419 U.S. 565 (1975), the Court held that prior to a suspension of ten days or less a student has the same due process rights as one who faces longer suspension: oral or written notice of charges against him or her, an attorney, presentation of witnesses, and cross-examination of witnesses. Wood v. Strickland, 420 U.S. 308 (1975), determined that students who believe they have been suspended illegally may sue school officials for damages. This decision contradicts the previous assumption that school officials were not liable for actions taken in good faith in the performance of their official duties.

Students may be suspended for breaking rules or disobeying school officials. Courts are divided over whether off-campus activities may result in suspension. Generally, suspension should not be used unless the student is a danger to himself, to others, to school property or has committed a serious crime. In such cases a hearing should be held before any final decision is made. Because suspension entails extreme consequences for a youth, it should be reserved as a response to behavior that is clearly disruptive and dangerous and should be lifted as soon as the emergency is over (Williams v. Dade County School Board, 441 F.2d 299 [5th Cir. 1971]). The right to education guaranteed by most state constitutions suggests that expulsion or long-term exclusion from public education is illegal. But safety in the public schools is such a concern that the attorney general of California sued the Los Angeles Unified School District for failing to provide a safe setting for learning.

While the court denied the suit, crimes committed on school grounds are a widespread worry. It has often been suggested that lowering the compulsory age of attendance would make it easier for school officials to remove offending students over that age.

School officials have conducted searches of public school children to determine whether they are using illegal drugs or carrying a weapon or other contraband. The use of a dog trained to detect drugs to search children at school was not permissible under the Fourth Amendment (Jones v. Latexo Independent School District, 499 F.Supp. 223 [E.D.Tex. 1980]).

The Supreme Court, in a major opinion on constitutional rights in 1985, upheld the legality of a warrantless search of a New Jersey school pupil to get evidence from her purse on breaking a school rule against smoking in New Jersey v. T.L.O. (53 U.S.L.W. 4083). The opinion rejected the doctrine of *in loco parentis* as a basis for the school's right to search. The court held that Fourth Amendment* protections did apply to school pupils, but that probable cause for illegal activity was too restrictive a standard in the school setting. Rather, a standard of reasonableness was applied in which the individual's "legitimate expectations of privacy" must be balanced against the government's need for "effective methods to deal with breaches of public order."

The following sections of the majority opinion are of interest to social workers concerned with interpreting students' rights:

> Notwithstanding the general applicability of the Fourth Amendment to the activities of civil authorities, a few courts have concluded that school officials are exempt from the dictates of the Fourth Amendment by virtue of the special nature of their authority over schoolchildren. Teachers and school administrators, it is said, act *in loco parentis* in their dealings with students: their authority is that of the parent, not the State, and is therefore not subject to the limits of the Fourth Amendment.
>
> Such reasoning is in tension with contemporary reality and the teachings of this Court. We have held school officials subject to the commands of the First Amendment, and the Due Process Clause of the 14th Amendment. If school authorities are state actors for purposes of the constitutional guarantees of freedom of expression and due process, it is difficult to understand why they should be deemed to be exercising parental rather than public authority when conducting searches of their students.
>
> In carrying out searches and other disciplinary functions pursuant to such policies, school officials act as representatives of the State, not merely as surrogates for the parents, and they cannot claim the parents' immunity from the strictures of the Fourth Amendment.
>
> To hold that the Fourth Amendment applies to searches conducted by school authorities is only to begin the inquiry into the standards governing such searches. Although the underlying command of the Fourth Amendment is always that searches and seizures be reasonable, what is reasonable depends on the context within which a search takes place.

Standard of Reasonableness

The determination of the standard of reasonableness governing any specific class of searches requires balancing the need to search against the invasion which the search entails. On one side of the balance are arrayed the individual's legitimate expectations

---

*AMENDMENT IV: The right of the people to be secure in their persons, houses, papers, and effects, against unreasonable searches and seizures, shall not be violated, and no Warrants shall issue, but upon probable cause, supported by Oath or affirmation, and particularly describing the place to be searched, and the persons or things to be seized.

of privacy and personal security; on the other, the government's need for effective methods to deal with breaches of public order.

We have recognized that even a limited search of the person is a substantial invasion of privacy. A search of a child's person or of a closed purse or other bag carried on her person, no less than a similar search carried out on an adult, is undoubtedly a severe violation of subjective expectations of privacy.

Of course, the Fourth Amendment does not protect subjective expectations of privacy that are unreasonable or otherwise "illegitimate." The State of New Jersey has argued that because of the pervasive supervision to which children in the schools are necessarily subject, a child has virtually no legitimate expectation of privacy in articles of personal property "unnecessarily" carried into a school. This argument has two factual premises: (1) the fundamental incompatibility of expectations of privacy with the maintenance of a sound educational environment; and (2) the minimal interest of the child in bringing any items of personal property into the school. Both premises are severely flawed.

Although this Court may take notice of the difficulty of maintaining discipline in the public schools today, the situation is not so dire that students in the schools may claim no legitimate expectations of privacy.

Privacy and Discipline

Against the child's interest in privacy must be set the substantial interest of teachers and administrators in maintaining discipline in the classroom and on school grounds. Maintaining order in the classroom has never been easy, but in recent years, school disorder has often taken particularly ugly forms: drug use and violent crime in the schools have become major social problems. Accordingly, we have recognized that maintaining security and order in the schools requires a certain degree of flexibility in school disciplinary procedures, and we have respected the value of preserving the informality of the student-teacher relationship.

How, then, should we strike the balance between the schoolchild's legitimate expectations of privacy and the school's equally legitimate need to maintain an environment in which learning can take place? It is evident that the school setting requires some easing of the restrictions to which searches by public authorities are ordinarily subject. The warrant requirement, in particular, is unsuited to the school environment; requiring a teacher to obtain a warrant before searching a child suspected of an infraction of school rules (or of the criminal law) would unduly interfere with the maintenance of the swift and informal disciplinary procedures needed in the schools. We hold today that school officials need not obtain a warrant before searching a student who is under their authority.

The school setting also requires some modification of the level of suspicion of illicit activity needed to justify a search. Ordinarily, a search—even one that may permissibly be carried out without a warrant—must be based upon "probable cause" to believe that a violation of the law has occurred. However, "probable cause" is not an irreducible requirement of a valid search.

Balancing of Interests

The fundamental command of the Fourth Amendment is that searches and seizures be reasonable, and although "both the concept of probable cause and the requirement of a warrant bear on the reasonableness of a search,. . . in certain limited circumstances neither is required." Thus, we have in a number of cases recognized the legality of searches and seizures based on suspicions that, although "reasonable," do not rise to the level of probable cause. Where a careful balancing of governmental and private interests suggests that the public interest is best served by a Fourth Amendment standard of reasonableness that stops short of probable cause, we have not hesitated to adopt such a standard.

We join the majority of courts that have examined this issue in concluding that the accommodation of the privacy interest of schoolchildren with the substantial need of teachers and administrators for freedom to maintain order in the schools does not require strict adherence to the requirement that searches be based on probable cause to believe that the subject of the search has violated or is violating the law.

Rather, the legality of a search of student should depend simply on the reasonableness, under all the circumstances, of the search. Determining the reasonableness of any search involves a twofold inquiry; first, one must consider "whether the . . . action was justified at its inception," second, one must determine whether the search as actually conducted "was reasonably related in scope to the circumstances which justified the interference in the first place."

Under ordinary circumstances, a search of a student by a teacher or other school official will be "justified at its inception" when there are reasonable grounds for suspecting that the search will turn up evidence that the student has violated or is violating either the law or the rules of the school. Such a search will be permissible in its scope when the measures adopted are reasonably related to the objectives of the search and not excessively intrusive in light of the age and sex of the student and the nature of the infraction.

This standard will, we trust, neither unduly burden the efforts of school authorities to maintain order in their schools nor authorize unrestrained intrusions upon the privacy of schoolchildren. By focusing attention on the question of reasonableness, the standard will spare teachers and school administrators the necessity of schooling themselves in the niceties of probable cause and permit them to regulate their conduct according to the dictates of reason and common sense. At the same time, the reasonableness standard should insure that the interests of students will be invaded no more than is necessary to achieve the legitimate end of preserving order in the schools.

Justice William J. Brennan's dissent agreed with the practice of conducting a search without a warrant, but defended the need to adhere to the probable cause standard as the basis for a search.

Justice John Paul Stevens also dissented, drawing a distinction for the authorization of a search when there is reason to believe that the search will uncover evidence that the student "is violating the law or engaging in conduct that is seriously disruptive of school order, or the educational process." His dissent included the observation that the majority opinion authorized searches that may reveal evidence of the most trivial school regulation.

Conditions for searching of school lockers or desks, standards that would apply to searches undertaken at the behest of police, and whether searches have to be based on suspicion of an individual student will probably have to be determined by future rulings by the Court.

CORPORAL PUNISHMENT

Most states and school districts permit corporal punishment of students by school personnel "as a last resort" and in the presence of another school official. Corporal punishment may be excessive if it is unreasonable and unnecessary and if injuries are incurred. Students sustaining excessive physical punishment may sue any school official who has acted wantonly or maliciously. School personnel are apparently subject to child abuse statutes by virtue of their capacity as caretakers to children, although most such state statutes have not been tested.

The Supreme Court upheld the constitutionality of state laws authorizing reasonable physical disciplinary punishment in Baker v. Owen, 423 U.S. 907 (1975). In affirming a lower court decision, the Court approved limitations on

physical punishment of all students, except those whose behavior "is so disruptive . . . as to shock the conscience." The Court required that the student must
(1) be warned in advance as to the type of conduct that would result in physical
punishment, (2) be given a hearing in the presence of another school official, and
(3) have another teacher present if physical punishment is to be administered.

Later, in Ingraham v. Wright, 430 U.S. 651 (1977), the Court refused to
ban spanking even if it is severe, excessive, or medically damaging. Ingraham, a
Florida junior high school student, was struck more than twenty times with a
paddle and missed eleven days of school. He had been "slow to respond to his
teacher's instructions."

The Court held that Eighth Amendment provisions against cruel and inhuman
punishment do not apply to punishment in the schools and that the due process
clause of the Fourth Amendment does not require prior notice and hearing before
imposing corporal punishment—a practice authorized and limited by common law.
For excessive punishment, school officials may be subject to damages or criminal
penalties under existing laws. Court requirements would intrude into the area of
educational responsibility of school authorities.

The decision does not affect local laws restricting corporal punishment, such
as those in New Jersey and Massachusetts. Schools in Washington, D.C., New
York City, Baltimore, and Chicago have also banned spanking. A California law
requires written permission from parents for physical punishment.

The *Goss* and *Ingraham* decisions indicate that the child who is suspended has
more due process rights than the child who receives corporal punishment—a peculiar inconsistency in the Court's logic.

SEX DISCRIMINATION

Some states have laws specifically prohibiting sex discrimination in public schools.
Where such laws have not been enacted, court cases have allowed females to take
courses previously restricted to males—such as woodworking, metalworking, and
auto mechanics (Sanchez v. Baron, Civ. Action No. 69 C 1615 [E.D.N.Y. March
22, 1973]; Della Casa v. South San Francisco Unified School District, Civ. Action
No. 171-673 [San Mateo Sup.Ct.]; and Seward v. Clayton Valley High School
District, Civ. Action No. 134173 [Contra Costa Sup. Ct.]).

Female students have also experienced discrimination in sports programs. However, a recent court decision ruled that females could be barred from male teams
only on the basis of individual capabilities and not on the basis of sex. Some states
permit women to participate in noncontact sports with males, while others allow
their participation only in the absence of an equivalent female program.

Women's sports programs have seldom been truly equivalent to those for men
because they have generally received less money for facilities, equipment, and
scholarships and less interest from potential participants. However, regulations
issued by the Department of Health, Education, and Welfare to implement Title
IX of the Educational Amendments of 1972 (20 U.S.C. 1681) ban sex discrimination in admissions, employment, curriculum, housing, financial aid, and athletics
in all public elementary, secondary, and higher educational programs that receive
federal funds. Most controversy has come from requiring equal opportunities for
women in the funding of sports programs, including scholarships. Nevertheless,
they also hold broad promise for ending sex discrimination in personnel policies
in education. In addition, the Women's Education Equity Act (20 U.S.C. 12)

authorizes funds to end sex discrimination in career counseling, sports education, and other programs.

MARRIAGE, PREGNANCY, AND PARENTHOOD

High school students have the right to continue their education after marriage (Board of Education of Harrodsburg v. Bentley, 383 S.W.2d 677 [Ky.1964]; Carrollton-Farmers Branch Independent School District v. Knight, 418 S.W.2d 535 [Tex.Civ.App.1967]; Anderson v. Canyon Independent School District, 412 S.W.2d 387 [Tex.Civ.App.1967]). While some courts have ruled that pregnant girls may be expelled, they have usually been allowed to remain in regular or special school programs (Ordway v. Hargraves, 323 F.Supp. 1155 [D.Mass.1971]). Court decisions have also held that students who are parents have a right to education including participating in extracurricular activities (Holt v. Shelton, 341 F.Supp. 821 [M.D.Tenn.1972]; Davis v. Meek, 344 F.Supp. 298 [N.D.Ohio 1972]; Wellsand v. Valparaiso Community Schools Corp., Civ. Action No. 71 H122[2] [N.D.Ind.1971]; Moran v. School District No. 7, Yellowstone County, 350 F.Supp. 1180 [D.Mont.1972]; see also Hollon v. Mathis Independent School District, 358 F.Supp. 1269 [S.D.Tex.1973]; and Romans v. Crenshaw, 354 F.Supp. 868 [S.D.Tex.1971]). Courts have allowed students who are married or pregnant or who are parents to leave school prior to attaining the compulsory school age (State v. Priest, 27 So.2d 173 [La.1946]; In re State, 39 So.2d 731 [La.1949]; In re Rogers, 234 N.Y.S.2d 172 [1962]). This approach treats education as a right rather than an obligation and is consistent with the concepts of legal emancipation discussed in Chapter 15.

PERSONAL APPEARANCE

Regulation of students' personal appearance by the school is unconstitutional unless it is aimed at preventing disruption of educational activities. Regulations necessary for general health or safety are also permissible, such as the mandatory use of caps in a swimming pool or sneakers in gym class. Half the states also permit the regulation of personal appearance. Students may face suspension if they violate such rules.

Rules have focused particularly on hair length. Long hair has been alleged by school officials to be "distracting" to other students and to cause discipline problems and lower grades. Court decisions are divided, but each of the above assertions has been successfully refuted in court.

CLASSIFICATION OF STUDENTS

Many public schools have classified students according to their ability or aptitude for the purpose of "tracking" or grouping them in separate classes. Schools also label students as mentally retarded, emotionally disturbed, socially or behaviorally maladjusted, hyperactive, and learning disabled in an attempt to assign them to special education classes.

Three legal concerns with tracking and special education have been identified:

First, the exclusion of "uneducable" children and the assignment of other students to inefficacious special education programs may well embody a denial of equal protection. *Second,* the overrepresentation of minority students in slow learner groups and classes for the mildly handicapped appear to have racially specific harmful effects; unless school officials can demonstrate that the educational benefits somehow outweigh the harm, some modification of present patterns appears constitutionally required. *Third,* it is constitutionally appropriate to protect students against the possibility of misclassification by affording them (and their parents) the right to a due process review of placement recommendations (Kirp 1974).

Tracking on the basis of IQ test results was abolished in the District of Columbia (Hobson v. Hansen, 269 F.Supp. 401 [D.D.C. 1967]):

> Because these tests are standardized primarily on and are relevant to a white middle-class group of students, they produce inaccurate and misleading test scores when given to lower class and Negro students. As a result, rather than being classified according to ability to learn, these students are in reality being classified according to their socioeconomic or racial status—or more precisely—according to environmental and psychological factors which have nothing to do with innate ability.

However, this decision has had little impact. Notwithstanding its abolition of tracking, the Court of Appeals decision permitted a new system of "ability grouping," resulting in a mere change in terminology. School officials could continue to track children as before, under the guise of a new name.

Cases have held the exclusion of children from school because of special education labels to be unconstitutional. In 1971 a federal court ordered the implementation of a consent agreement whereby all mentally retarded children in Pennsylvania are to be given free public education appropriate to their learning abilities (Pennsylvania Association for Retarded Children v. Commonwealth of Pennsylvania, 334 F.Supp. 1257 [E.D.Pa.1971]). The agreement specifies that "placement in a regular public school class is preferable to placement in a special public school class, and placement in a special public school is preferable to placement in any other type of program of education and training." The court required that change in the status of any child alleged to be mentally retarded must be effected in accordance with due process:

> [Parents must be notified of their right] to contest the proposed action at a full hearing . . . in a place and at a time convenient to the parent, before the proposed action may be taken, . . . to be represented at the hearing by legal counsel, to examine before the hearing his child's school records including expert medical, psychological, and educational testimony, and to confront and to cross-examine any school official . . . who may have evidence upon which the proposed action may be based.

This case also assured parents the right to a transcription of the hearing and a decision on the record. Provisions were made for the reevaluation of students placed on homebound instruction every three months and for those placed in special schools, every two years.

A case in the District of Columbia in 1972 expanded the Pennsylvania ruling. The federal court held that all children labeled as mentally, behaviorally, or physically impaired had the right to free and appropriate public education (Mills v. Board of Education of the District of Columbia, 348 F.Supp. 866 [D.D.C.1972]). The court held:

> If sufficient funds are not available to finance all of the services and programs that are needed in the system then the available funds must be expended equitably in such a manner that no child is entirely excluded from a publicly supported education consistent with his needs and ability to benefit therefrom.

This philosophy was translated into law in the Education for All Handicapped Children Act of 1975 (PL94–142), whereby all states are required to have

> programs for the full education of handicapped children; education programs which provide for fulfillment of a full service goal; timetables for reaching this goal; full free education for handicapped children up to age 18 and down to age 3; plans for locating and identifying handicapped children; assurances of consultation with parents or guardians of the children being educated; confidentiality of information about the children; testing which is not racially or culturally discriminatory; and, to the extent possible, the education of handicapped children along side of nonhandicapped children.

The U.S. Supreme Court, in Board of Education v. Rowley, 458 U.S. 176 (1982), reviewed the history of this legislation after school officials denied parents' request that a child with a hearing handicap be provided with a sign language interpreter for all classes. The Court concurred in the denial.

BOARD OF EDUCATION v. ROWLEY

Supreme Court of the United States, 458 U.S. 17 (1982)

This case arose in connection with the education of Amy Rowley, a deaf student at the Furnace Woods School in the Hendrick Hudson Central School District, Peekskill, New York. Amy has minimal residual hearing and is an excellent lipreader. During the year before she began attending Furnace Woods, a meeting between her parents and school administrators resulted in a decision to place her in a regular kindergarten class in order to determine what supplemental services would be necessary to her education. Several members of the school administration prepared for Amy's arrival by attending a course in sign-language interpretation, and a teletype machine was installed in the principal's office to facilitate communication with her parents who are also deaf. At the end of the trial period it was determined that Amy should remain in the kindergarten class, but that she should be provided with an FM hearing aid which would amplify words spoken into a wireless receiver by the teacher or fellow students during certain classroom activities. Amy successfully completed her kindergarten year.

As required by the Education for All Handicapped Children, an IEP [Individualized Educational Plan] was prepared for Amy during the fall of her first-grade year. The IEP provided that Amy should be educated in a regular classroom at Furnace Woods, should continue to use the FM hearing aid, and should receive instruction from a tutor for the deaf for one hour each day and from a speech therapist for three hours each week. The Rowleys agreed with the IEP but insisted that Amy also be provided a qualified sign-language interpreter in all of her academic classes. Such an interpreter had been placed in Amy's kindergarten class for a two-week experimental period, but the interpreter had reported that Amy did not need his services at that time. The school administrators likewise concluded that Amy did not need such an interpreter in her first-grade classroom. They reached this conclusion after consulting the school district's Committee on the Handicapped, which had received expert evidence from Amy's parents on the importance of a sign-language interpreter, received testimony from Amy's teacher and other persons familiar with her academic and social progress, and visited a class for the deaf.

When their request for an interpreter was denied, the Rowleys demanded and received a hearing before an independent examiner. After receiving evidence from both sides, the examiner agreed with the administrators' determination that an interpreter was not necessary because "Amy was achieving educationally, academically, and socially" without such assistance. The examiner's decision was affirmed on appeal by the New York Commissioner of Education on the basis of substantial evidence in the record. Pursuant to the Act's provision for judicial review, the Rowleys then brought an action in the United States District Court for the Southern District of New York, claiming that the administrators' denial of the sign-language interpreter constituted a denial of the "free appropriate public education" guaranteed by the Act. . . .

According to the definitions contained in the Act, a "free appropriate public education" consists of educational instruction specially designed to meet the unique needs of the handicapped child, supported by such services as are necessary to permit the child "to benefit" from the instruction. Almost as a checklist for adequacy under the Act, the definition also requires that such instruction and services be provided at public expense and under public supervision, meet the State's educational standards, approximate the grade levels used in the State's regular education, and comport with the child's IEP. Thus, if personalized instruction is being provided with sufficient supportive services to permit the child to benefit from the instruction, and the other items on the definitional checklist are satisfied, the child is receiving a "free appropriate public education" as defined by the Act. . . .

That the Act imposes no clear obligation upon recipient States beyond the requirement that handicapped children receive some form of specialized education is perhaps best demonstrated by the fact that Congress, in explaining the need for the Act, equated an "appropriate education" to the receipt of some specialized educational services. . . .

Implicit in the congressional purpose of providing access to a "free appropriate public education" is the requirement that the education to which access is provided be sufficient to confer some educational benefit upon the handicapped child. It would do little good for Congress to spend millions of dollars in providing access to a public education only to have the handicapped child receive no benefit from that education. The statutory definition of "free appropriate public education," in addition to requiring that States provide each child with "specially designed instruction," expressly requires the provision of "such . . . supportive services . . . as may be required to assist a handicapped child *to benefit* from special education." § 1401(17) (emphasis added). We therefore conclude that the "basic floor of opportunity" provided by the Act consists of access to specialized instruction and related services which are individually designed to provide educational benefit to the handicapped child.

. . . [T]he District Court found that the "evidence firmly establishes that Amy is receiving an 'adequate' education, since she performs better than the average child in her class and is advancing easily from grade to grade." 483 F.Supp., at 534. In light of this finding, and of the fact that Amy was receiving personalized instruction and related services calculated by the Furnace Woods school administrators to meet her educational needs, the lower courts should not have concluded that the Act requires the provision of a sign-language interpreter. Accordingly, the decision of the Court of Appeals is reversed and the case is remanded for further proceedings consistent with this opinion.

In 1982 the U.S. Department of Education issued proposed regulations that would have weakened the provisions of the Education for all Handicapped Children Act, and then withdrew them in response to considerable public protest.

FREEDOM OF EXPRESSION

In a case involving the applicability of free speech to students, Tinker v. Des Moines Independent Community School District, 393 U.S. 503 (1969), the Supreme Court ruled that students are "persons" under the Constitution and do not "shed their constitutional rights to freedom of speech or expression at the schoolhouse gates." This freedom is guaranteed to students under the First Amendment, except where it "materially disrupts classwork, or involves substantial disorder or invasion of the rights of others." This decision has provided the most important precedent for the protection of the rights of students who wish to wear buttons and armbands as political expression, engage in demonstrations and assemblies, or publish and distribute literature.

The major issue of the 1980s has been school prayer. The Supreme Court is expected to rule in 1985 on the use of a period of silence in lieu of oral prayers that have been barred by earlier decisions. This issue is a key part of the Reagan program.

INFORMATION POLICIES

The U.S. Supreme Court curtailed the authority of local school boards to remove books from junior high and high school libraries in Board of Education v. Rico, 457 U.S. 853 (1982). The Court distinguished books available in the library from texts that all students would be required to read. The decision highlighted availability of knowledge:

"The State may not, consistently with the spirit of the First Amendment, contract the spectrum of available knowledge." Griswold v. Connecticut, 381 U.S. 479, 482 (1965). In keeping with this principle, we have held that in a variety of contexts "the Constitution protects the right to receive information and ideas." Stanley v. Georgia, 394 U.S. 557, 564 (1969); see Kleindienst v. Mandel, 408 U.S. 753, 762–763 (1972) (citing cases). This right is an inherent corollary of the rights of free speech and press that are explicitly guaranteed by the Constitution, in two senses. First, the right to receive ideas follows ineluctably from the *sender's* First Amendment right to send them: "The right of freedom of speech and press, . . . embraces the right to distribute literature. . . . and necessarily protects the right to receive it." Martin v. Struthers, 318 U.S. 141, 143 (1943) (citation omitted). "The dissemination of ideas can accomplish nothing if otherwise willing addressees are not free to receive and consider them. It would be a barren marketplace of ideas that had only sellers and no buyers." Lamont v. Postmaster General, 381 U.S. 301, 308 (1966) (BRENNAN, J., concurring).

More importantly, the right to receive ideas is a necessary predicate to the *recipient's* meaningful exercise of his own rights of speech, press, and political freedom. . . .

Because we are concerned in this case with the suppression of ideas, our holding today affects only the discretion to *remove* books. In brief, we hold that local school boards may not remove books from school library shelves simply because they dislike the ideas contained in those books and seek by their removal to "prescribe what shall be orthodox in politics, nationalism, religion, or other matters of opinion."

The Family Education Rights and Privacy Act of 1974 authorizes access to school records. Federal funding is withheld from any educational institution that denies students or parents the right to inspect and challenge educational records. Access is not granted to medical and psychiatric records, but they may be reviewed by an appropriate professional of the student's or parents' choice.

Regulations addressing students' rights in research, experimental activities, and testing developed by the U.S. Department of Education took effect in 1984 to implement Section 430 of the General Education Provisions Act (20 U.S.C. 1232b). The regulations (49 Federal Register 34321 [1984]) are expected to curtail such activities by requiring parental permission for any testing in which the primary purpose is to reveal information about "political affiliations, mental and psychological problems potentially embarrassing to the student or his or her family; sex behavior and attitudes; illegal and anti-social, self-incriminating, and demeaning behavior; critical appraisals of other individuals with whom respondents have close family relationships; legally recognized privileged and analogous relationships such as those of lawyers, physicians, and ministers; or income (other than that required by law to determine eligibility for participation in a program or for receiving

ACCOUNTABIL-ITY FOR LEARN-ING OUTCOMES

Although there is much discussion in law journals about educational malpractice, few cases have been brought (Funston, 1981). Students have a right to sue for educational malpractice, but Funston suggests that the typical reasons for suing—breach of contract, misrepresentation, violation of constitutional rights, or negligence—are all inadequate or inappropriate. He argues that even if a legally sound basis for such a suit could be developed, courts should leave educational policy to school officials.

Students are also being held accountable for their learning or not learning. A number of states have passed laws requiring functional literacy testing. Students who fail these exams may not receive a high school diploma, only a certificate verifying attendance. Students in Florida filed a class action suit seeking to avoid taking such a test (Debra P. v. Turlington, 474 F.Supp. 244 [M.D.Fla., 1979]). The federal district court delayed implementation of the requirement to provide students with adequate notice taking into account the effect of segregated school districts in that state. However, assignment to a remedial class based on test scores was held to be permissible, even though the result might be resegregation of classes by race.

SOCIAL WORK ROLES IN EDUCATION

School social workers predominantly help individual children with personal problems. They also view the schools as social systems that involve a variety of professional tasks, including,

■ Acting as a pupil advocate, focusing upon the urgent needs of selected groups of pupils.

■ Consulting with the school administrators to jointly identify major problems toward which a planned service approach will be aimed; aid in developing cooperative working relationships with community agencies; and assisting in the formulation of school policy that directly affects the welfare of children and young persons.

■ Consulting with teachers about techniques for creating a climate in which children are freed and motivated to learn by interpreting social and cultural influences in the lives of pupils, facilitating the use of peers to help a troubled child, or assisting in managing relationships within a classroom.

■ Organizing parent and community groups to channel concerns about pupils and school and to improve school and community relations.

■ Developing and maintaining liaison between the school and critical fields of social work—child welfare, corrections, mental health, and legal services for the poor. Such liaison facilitates more effective community services for schoolchildren and their families, assists with planned change in the community's organizational pattern of social welfare programs and resources, and acts as a catalyst to change the pattern of the social structure.

■ Providing leadership in the coordination of interdisciplinary skills among pupil services personnel, e.g., guidance counselors, psychologists, nurses, and attendance officers. (Brieland, Costin, and Atherton, 1985: 288)

Mediating between parents and school officials to resolve disputes about placing children in special education classes requires knowledge of both social work practice and school law (Gallant, 1982). School social workers also must have adequate knowledge of the laws and regulations that affect educational policy in order to serve as effective advocates for students and to modify school policies on their behalf.

Questions for Review

1. Is education more a requirement than a right? What impact does immigration have on education?

2. Summarize the relationship between education and religion as characterized by the Supreme Court. Why did Douglas dissent from the majority opinion in *Yoder*?

3. What is the trend regarding due process for students? What are the rights of students facing suspension?

4. What are the effects of marriage, pregnancy, and parenthood on the right to education? Must students who are married, pregnant, or parents attend school?

5. What is the general principle regarding the regulation of personal appearance by school officials?

6. Summarize the Supreme Court's cases regarding racial segregation in public schools. What are the guidelines in busing to achieve integrated schools?

7. What are the three major sources of funds for public schools?

8. Why do expenditures per pupil vary among school districts?

9. Is there a constitutional right to education? What was the finding in *Rodriguez*? Summarize the dissents from the majority opinion.

10. What is the Supreme Court position regarding public financial aid to non-public schools?

11.   What was the effect of *Tinker* on students' rights? What is the principle permitting regulation of freedom of expression?

12.   What are the legal limitations regarding corporal punishment of students by school officials?

13.   What are three legal concerns with tracking and special education?

14.   What impact does *Rowley* have on the Education for Handicapped Children Act?

15.   What is the predominant role of school social workers? What new roles are suggested?

Questions for Debate and Discussion

1.   What problems lead many public school personnel to question current compulsory attendance laws?

2.   Sweden has much stronger statutes against corporal punishment in the schools and by parents. Are such laws desirable in the United States?

3.   Consider expulsion and suspension policies in your local schools. How are they related to the civil rights of students?

4.   What are the problems of school social workers as change agents?

Selected Readings

Cremins, James C. *Legal and Political Issues in Special Education*. Springfield, Ill. Thomas, 1983.

Lustgarten, Laurence, and Vicky Giles. "State Education and Racial Discrimination." *Urban Law and Policy* 4 (1981): 55–58.

Natkin, H. David. "School Discipline and the Handicapped Child." *Washington and Lee Law Review* 39 (1982): 1453–1467.

Nicholl, Lawry, and Miguel Gomez. *Quality Education for Mexican-American Minorities*. Washington D.C.: University Press of America, 1980.

Pressman, Robert, and Margo Haist Wallach. "Developments in Education Review: 1981." *Clearinghouse Review* 15 (1982): 813–824.

Roberts, Joseph, and Bernice Hank. *Legal Rights Primer for the Handicapped*. Novato, Calif.: Academic Therapy Publications, 1980.

School Social Work and the Law. Washington, D.C.: National Association of Social Workers, 1980.

CHAPTER
23

Health

Health services in the United States are characterized by problems of quality, access, and cost. The 1980s have seen reductions in health entitlements and attention to reducing both hospital admissions and length of hospital stay. Meanwhile, costs of health services have escalated. In this context, limited effort has been expended on disease-prevention programs and promotion of good health.

THE SCOPE OF HEALTH-CARE LAW

This chapter deals with areas not covered in detail elsewhere in this volume: federal authority in the area of health care; state and local authority; licensure, credentialing, and accreditation of personnel and programs; health-care programs, including access and discrimination; cost control; medical records, including rights to information and privacy; malpractice; and environmental and occupational health.

Mental health, human reproduction, and aging involve the rights of individuals to obtain health-related treatment or to refuse it. These rights are especially critical for children, committed mental patients, and the elderly in cases where a guardian has been appointed. Other health-related topics treated elsewhere in this volume include child abuse and neglect; nutrition programs for mothers, infants, and school-age children; maternal and child health; and health care for the aged. Rape, like child abuse, involves the need for medical evidence. The basis for vocational rehabilitation is medical service, a major topic in considering the rights of handicapped persons. Whether clients have the right to refuse medication is important in the management of emotional disorders.

In health law the social worker's principal interest is in programs that implement legislation rather than in case law. At the outset, we must recognize the importance of **administrative law** to the field of health. Administrative law is concerned with the rules and regulations of departments, offices, and agencies that translate statutes into standards—in this case for health services and health care. We have already observed the need for general statutes and for administrative agencies to have the authority to develop specific rules. The authority to make rules carries with it far-reaching power. Agencies not only develop and administer regulations but also initiate and receive complaints from consumers of services. Hearings officers from agencies act in a semi-judicial role when they handle clients' grievances.

Protection of the public is provided by the federal Administrative Procedures Act, enacted in 1946 to specify ground rules for hearings and to provide for public input in the development of federal regulations. Publication of proposed new rules in the *Federal Register*, solicitation of comments and suggestions (sometimes through public hearings), and final publication at least thirty days before the rule goes into effect are required by the act.

The Congress or a state legislature controls the authority of an administrative agency both through definition of its statutory powers and duties and through appropriations. The importance of congressional control is clear in the case of the Food and Drug Administration, which has a large research program that sometimes leads to conflict with commercial firms.

FEDERAL AUTHORITY IN HEALTH CARE

Until the beginning of the twentieth century, the federal government exercised little authority in the area of health. Its constitutional power to regulate interstate commerce gives the federal government authority over the goods that are a part of that commerce. The Pure Food and Drug Act of 1906 is an early example of government use of this authority for health-related purposes. The constitutional power to tax and to spend tax receipts gives the federal government authority to grant state and local governments much-needed dollars when they are willing to abide by conditions set down by the federal government. For example, federal grants for health-related purposes were authorized by the Venereal Disease Act of 1918.

The U.S. Postal Service has the authority to regulate advertising, which includes advertising of questionable health remedies, by denying use of the mails. The federal government also employs its power to provide services for military personnel through its powers to maintain a defense system. This includes a large program of direct hospital and health services in military installations and veterans hospitals.

Since 1965 the federal government has financed two large health care programs—Medicare for the elderly and Medicaid for the poor.

STATE AND LOCAL AUTHORITY IN HEALTH CARE

State and local authority to regulate public health developed earlier than federal authority. State boards of health go back to 1869. By 1909 all states had such boards. Local boards of health were also established to provide such services as communicable disease control, maternal and child health care, and environmental sanitation.

Information is one of the key components of a public health system. Vital statistics based on records of births, marriages, and deaths go back to colonial times. Gradually, public health agencies broadened their reporting activities to include fetal deaths and numbers of adoptions based on issuance of new birth certificates.

Reporting of communicable diseases was added later. The diseases reported and the legally required reporters vary widely from state to state. Underreporting is a common problem. Private practitioners fear that reporting patients' names may affect relationships with patients, especially if a public health or social service authority will use the report as a basis for intervention. Practitioners are reluctant to file reports of child abuse when the law encourages reports based on suspicion rather than only on established fact. Child abuse is more likely to be reported by the relatively impersonal staff of the hospital emergency room than by the family doctor.

LICENSING AND ACCREDITATION

Local and state governments set standards for individuals through various forms of licensure. In the health field, licensure provides authorization to engage in a certain type of practice. Licensing extends well beyond health personnel to include such people as barbers and beekeepers and facilities such as restaurants and mortuaries. Its purpose is to prohibit activities that may have an adverse effect on the health and safety of the public. In licensing, inspection is used to assure conformity to standards.

Licensing involves authority to stop a person from carrying on an activity, such as a medical practice; forbid the use of a title without necessarily forbidding the activity (some states require that a person have certain qualifications to use the designation "clincial psychologist," but anyone may use the term "counselor"); close a restaurant or hospital because of violation of health or safety requirements after due warning and time to take corrective action; embargo a dangerous commodity such as poisoned food or contaminated drugs.

The Tylenol adulteration in 1982 led to the most widespread recall of a drug. The producers of Tylenol were successful in maintaining public confidence through aggressive cooperation with public authorities and full disclosure through public information.

Public health agencies may be involved in secondary licensing. A children's treatment center, for example, may be licensed by a public mental health or child welfare agency, but health authorities inspect its food service and may deny its right to operate for lack of sanitation. A fire marshal in this case may also be required to approve the premises before a license can be granted.

Licensure and Credentialing of Personnel

Licensing of physicians began in Texas in 1873. West Virginia's act of 1882 was challenged and ultimately upheld by the U.S. Supreme Court. It required graduation from a medical school approved by the state board of health, ten years of medical practice preceding the act, or passage of an examination by a state board. At least forty-five health professions are now covered in one or more states. Licensing standards depend mainly on credentials and qualifications rather than performance. Because withdrawal of a license based on lack of skill is rare, licensing is not an effective means of assuring quality.

Physicians are subject to mandatory licensing in all states, but practical nurses, psychologists, social workers, physical therapists, and sanitarians can practice without a license in some states. Also, faculty may teach classroom courses on health-related topics whether they are licensed to practice or not.

Development of health-care professions has involved changes in roles and created new licensing categories, including the nurse-practitioner and the physician's assistant. States do not always define these roles consistently, although professional associations establish standards for them.

Certification and Accreditation

Voluntary certification based on uniform national standards is important as a major screening device for applicants. The licensed physician may practice in all branches of medicine, but certification in a specialty is evidence of additional training and experience. Social workers, by contrast, are offered only generic certification through an arm of the NASW, the Academy of Certified Social Workers.

Accreditation seeks the same goals for institutions as licensing does for personnel. Accreditation includes established standards, a self-study, evaluation by a visiting team of peers, approval by the accrediting body, publication of an approved list of accredited institutions, and periodic reevaluation.

Do licensing, certification, and accreditation serve mainly to protect the public, or do they create a monopoly for a selected subset of individuals or institutions? This question is especially pertinent for social work, because there have been few legal actions against practitioners based on licensing laws.

ACCESS TO HEALTH CARE

Health-care services account for nearly one-tenth of the gross national product and employ 7 million people, 400,000 of them physicians. About 80 percent of the population has coverage for health services through private insurance, through Medicare for the elderly, or through Medicaid for low-income people. These two latter programs together pay more than one-third of the hospital expenditures and nearly one-fourth of physician costs. In 1982 they were responsible for 8.8 percent of the federal budget. About 30 million war veterans are eligible for services from the Veterans Administration (VA). However, about one-third of the poor are not covered in any way. The 1984 federal budget for the three health programs is shown in Table 23.1.

The Social Security Act of 1935 has provided welfare benefits for children, the elderly, the blind, and the disabled. Medicare and Medicaid were enacted in 1965. Both involve federal payments rather than direct operation of health-care programs. Both have been plagued by increasing costs. The Medicare trust fund balances, like the Social Security trust fund, have been nearly depleted because of the increased number of elderly persons.

TABLE 23.1
FEDERAL HEALTH PROGRAMS, 1984 BUDGET LEVELS

	Budget	No. of Beneficiaries
Medicare	$61,486,000,000[a]	29.0 million
Medicaid	20,799,000,000	22.0 million
Veterans Administration	9,188,000,000	1.4 million

[a]Net cost; receipts and collections subtracted.

MEDICARE

Medicare provides health and hospitalization insurance to persons over age sixty-five and to those receiving Social Security disability payments. Persons not covered by Social Security but who are otherwise eligible can purchase the coverage themselves. The provisions of the program presented below are taken from the Medicare handbook published by the U.S. Department of Health and Human Services.

THE MEDICARE PROGRAM

Medicare is a federal health insurance program for people 65 or older and certain disabled people. It is run by the Health Care Financing administration. Local Social Security administration offices take applications for Medicare and provide information about the program.

Medicare has two parts—hospital insurance and medical insurance. Hospital insurance can help pay for inpatient hospital care, inpatient care in a skilled nursing facility, and home health care. Medical insurance can help pay for medically necessary doctors' services, outpatient hospital services, and a number of other medical services and supplies that are not covered by the hospital insurance part of Medicare. Medical insurance also can pay for home health services.

Medicare does not pay the full cost of some covered services. As general health-care costs rise, these amounts may increase. If they do, we will notify you. For people with very low incomes, the Medicaid program in their state may pay the amounts Medicare does not pay and may pay some health-care expenses not covered by Medicare.

Medicare payments are handled by private insurance organizations under contract with the government. Organizations handling claims from hospitals, skilled nursing facilities, and home health agencies are called *intermediaries*. Organizations handling claims from doctors and other suppliers of services covered under the medical insurance part of Medicare are called *carriers*.

Health-care organizations and professionals providing services to Medicare beneficiaries must meet all licensing requirements of state or local health authorities. The organizations and persons shown below also must meet additional Medicare requirements before payments can be made for their services:

- Hospitals
- Skilled nursing facilities
- Home health agencies
- Independent diagnostic laboratories and organizations providing X-ray services
- Organizations providing outpatient physical therapy and speech pathology services
- Ambulance firms
- Chiropractors
- Independent physical therapists (those who furnish services in your home or in their offices)
- Facilities providing kidney dialysis or transplant services
- Rural health clinics

Under the law, Medicare does not cover custodial care or care that is not "reasonable and necessary" for the diagnosis or treatment of an illness or injury.

Care that is custodial

Care is considered custodial when it is primarily for the purpose of meeting personal needs and could be provided by persons without professional skills or training. For example, custodial care includes help in walking, getting in and out of bed, bathing, dressing, eating, and taking medicine. Even if you are in a participating hospital or skilled nursing facility or you are receiving care from a participating home health agency, Medicare does not cover your care if it is mainly custodial.

Care that is not reasonable and necessary

If a doctor places you in a hospital or skilled nursing facility when the kind of care you need could be provided elsewhere, your stay would not be considered reasonable and necessary. So Medicare could not cover your stay. If you stay in a hospital or skilled nursing facility longer than you need to be there, Medicare payments would end when further inpatient care is no longer reasonable and necessary.

To help Medicare decide whether inpatient care is reasonable and necessary, each hospital and skilled nursing facility has a Utilization Review Committee, which is made up of at least two doctors. And in most parts of the country there are peer review organizations, which are made up of local doctors who review the care prescribed by their fellow doctors. If, after a medical review, the doctors on the Utilization Review Committee or in the peer review organization find that inpatient care is not medically necessary, Medicare hospital insurance cannot pay for any days of inpatient care that they decide are unnecessary.

If a doctor (or other practitioner) comes to treat you or you visit him or her for treatment more often than is the usual medical practice in your area, Medicare would not cover the "extra" visits unless there are medical complications. Medicare cannot cover more services than are reasonable and necessary for your treatment. Any decision of this kind is always based on professional medical advice.

Some health-care services and supplies are not generally accepted by the health community as being reasonable or necessary for diagnosis and treatment. This includes acupuncture, histamine therapy, and various kinds of medical equipment. Medicare cannot cover services and supplies unless they are generally recognized as safe and effective by the health community.

Medicare hospital insurance helps pay for three kinds of care. The three kinds of care are (1) inpatient hospital care, (2) medically necessary inpatient care in a skilled nursing facility after a hospital stay, and (3) home health care.

There is a limit on how many days of hospital or skilled nursing facility care Medicare can help pay for in each benefit period.* But, your hospital insurance protection is renewed every time you start a new benefit period.

Medicare hospital insurance will pay for most but not all of the services you receive in a hospital or skilled nursing facility or from a home health agency. There are covered services and non-covered services under each kind of care. Covered services are services and supplies that hospital insurance can pay for.

Medicare hospital insurance can help pay for inpatient hospital care if *all* of the following four conditions are met: (1) a doctor prescribes inpatient hospital care for treatment of your illness or injury, (2) you require the kind of care that can only be provided in a hospital, (3) the hospital is participating in Medicare, and (4) the Utilization Review Committee of the hospital or a peer review organization does not disapprove your stay.

Hospital insurance can help pay for up to 90 days of medically necessary inpatient hospital care in each benefit period.

From the 1st day through the 60th day in each benefit period, hospital insurance pays for all covered services *except the first* [$400 as of 1985].† This is called the hospital insurance deductible. The hospital may charge you the deductible only for your first admission in each benefit period. If you are discharged and then readmitted before the benefit period ends, you do not have to pay the deductible again.

From the 61st through the 90th day in a benefit period, hospital insurance pays for all covered services *except for* [$100] a day.† The hospital may charge you for the [$100] a day. Hospital reserve days can help with your expenses if you ever need more than 90 days of inpatient hospital care in a benefit period.

Hospital insurance does *not* cover your doctor's services even though you receive them in a hospital. Doctors' services are covered under Medicare medical insurance.

Major services covered when you are a hospital inpatient

Medicare hospital insurance can pay for these services:

- A semiprivate room (2 to 4 beds in a room)
- All your meals, including special diets
- Regular nursing services
- Costs of special care units, such as an intensive care unit, coronary care unit, etc.
- Drugs furnished by the hospital during your stay
- Blood transfusions furnished by the hospital during your stay
- Lab tests included in your hospital bill
- X-rays and other radiology services, including radiation therapy, billed by the hospital
- Medical supplies such as casts, surgical dressings, and splints
- Use of appliances, such as a wheelchair
- Operating and recovery room costs, including hospital costs for anesthesia services
- Rehabilitation services, such as physical therapy, occupational therapy, and speech pathology services

Some services not covered when you are a hospital inpatient

Medicare hospital insurance *cannot* pay for these services:

- Personal convenience items that you request such as a television, radio, or telephone in your room
- Private duty nurses
- Any extra charges for a private room, unless it is determined to be medically necessary

Hospital inpatient reserve days

What happens if you have a long illness and have to stay in the hospital for more than 90 days? Medicare hospital insurance includes an extra 60 hospital days you can use if this

---

* A benefit period is a way of measuring your use of services under Medicare hospital insurance. Your first benefit period starts the first time you enter a hospital after your hospital insurance begins. A benefit period ends when you have been out of a hospital or other facility primarily providing skilled nursing or rehabilitation services for 60 days in a row (including the day of discharge). There is no limit to the number of benefit periods you can have.

† These amounts are subject to change and have increased substantially since the inception of Medicare.

ever happens. These extra days are called reserve days. Hospital insurance pays for all covered services *except for $152 a day* for each reserve day you use. You are responsible for this $152. *Once you use a reserve day you never get it back.* Reserve days are *not* renewable like your 90 hospital days in each benefit period.

Since you have only 60 reserve days in your lifetime, you can decide yourself when you want to use them. After you have been in the hospital 90 days, you can use all 60 reserve days at one time if you have to stay in the hospital that long. But you don't have to use your reserve days right away if you don't want to. Maybe you have private insurance that can help pay your hospital bill if an illness keeps you in the hospital for more than 90 days. If you don't want to use your reserve days, you must tell the hospital in writing ahead of time. Otherwise, the extra days you need to be in the hospital will automatically be taken from your reserve days.

Hospital insurance can help pay for *no more than* 190 days of care in a participating psychiatric hospital in your lifetime.

After you have been in a hospital, Medicare hospital insurance can help pay for inpatient care in a participating skilled nursing facility* if your condition still requires daily skilled nursing or rehabilitation services which, as a practical matter, can only be provided in a skilled nursing facility.

Hospital insurance can help pay for care in a skilled nursing facility if *all* of the following five conditions are met: (1) you have been in a hospital at least 3 days in a row (not counting the day of discharge) before you transfer to a participating skilled nursing facility, (2) you are transferred to the skilled nursing facility because you require care for a condition which was treated in the hospital, (3) you are admitted to the facility within a short time (generally within 30 days) after you leave the hospital, (4) a doctor certifies that you need, and you actually receive, skilled nursing or skilled rehabilitation services on a daily basis, and (5) the facility's Utilization Review Committee or a peer review organization does not disapprove your stay.

All five conditions must be met. But it's especially important to remember the requirement that you must need skilled nursing care or skilled rehabilitation services on a daily basis.

Medicare medical insurance

[Medical insurance is Part B of Medicare financed by a premium paid by or on behalf of the member. In 1984 this premium was $14.60 per month.] Medicare medical insurance can help pay for (1) doctors' services, (2) outpatient hospital care, (3) outpatient physical therapy and speech pathology services, (4) home health care, and (5) many other health services and supplies which are not covered by Medicare hospital insurance.

Co-payments, deductibles, and limits on length of care make the Medicare patient bear a substantial proportion of medical costs. Co-payments are likely to be increased because of rising costs. The Medicare Advisory Council proposed in 1983 to delay coverage until age sixty-seven in order to reduce costs.

One of the major deficiencies in Medicare is the lack of protection for long, costly illnesses. The 1984 federal budget presented this example to justify proposed changes in Medicare provisions:

After the 60th day of care in a spell of illness, beneficiaries must pay 25% of the inpatient hospital deductible for 30 days. The hospital deductible will be about $350 in 1984; thus, beneficiaries would have to pay about $88 per day for days 61–90. For subsequent days, beneficiaries would have to pay 50% ($175) per day until they exhaust their 60 lifetime reserve days, at which point they would be liable for whatever the hospital charges. A beneficiary with a 150-day stay, thus, would be liable for over $13,000 if he had not previously used any of his reserve days and for over $24,000 if he had no reserve days left.

The Administration proposal would protect the elderly from the risk of these catastrophic hospital costs. Under this proposal, beneficiaries with a continuous five-

---

* A skilled nursing facility is a specially qualified facility which has the staff and equipment to provide skilled nursing care or rehabilitation services and other related health services. In some facilities, only certain portions participate in Medicare. If you are not sure whether a facility or a particular portion participates in Medicare, ask someone at the facility or call a Social Security office.

month hospital stay in calendar year 1984 will incur maximum out-of-pocket expenditures of $1,530—$11,945 less than under current law. In addition, the Administration is proposing to reduce the maximum out-of-pocket skilled nursing care costs for the elderly under Medicare by $2,100 for each spell of illness: from $3,500 to $1,400. The catastrophic hospital costs proposal will protect about 150,000 Medicare beneficiaries.

MEDICAID Medicaid provides federal funds to help meet the health needs of the poor by guaranteeing payment for medical services to welfare recipients and to others who are medically indigent. The latter are subject to deductibles and co-payments.

Services covered include inpatient and outpatient hospital care, laboratory and X-ray services, physician services, skilled nursing care, and family planning. Prescriptions, dental services, eyeglasses, and care in institutions that do not qualify as skilled nursing homes are allowable as options. The states have tended to curtail Medicaid benefits to reduce costs. The Illinois Department of Public Aid spent $1.5 billion in 1982 for just over a million requests with over 28,000 providers of service. Some 52 percent of the costs were for hospital service. The mandatory services provided by Illinois included:

- Inpatient hospital care
- Outpatient hospital care
- Other laboratory and X-ray services
- Rural health clinic services
- Skilled nursing and home health services for individuals 21 and older
- Early and periodic screening, diagnosis, and treatment for individuals under 21
- Family planning services
- Physicians' services

The optional services provided were:

- Clinic services
- Prescribed drugs
- Dental services
- Prosthetic devices
- Eyeglasses
- Dentures
- Physical therapy
- Occupational therapy
- Speech, hearing, and language therapy
- Diagnostic services
- Preventive services
- Rehabilitative services
- Private duty nursing
- Emergency hospital services

- Skilled nursing facility services for individuals under 21

- Optometrists' services

- Podiatrists' services

- Chiropractors' services

- Other practitioners' services

- Care of individuals 65 or older in TB institutions—inpatient hospital services, skilled nursing facility services, intermediate care facility services

- Care for individuals 65 or older in institutions for mental diseases—inpatient hospital services, skilled nursing facility services, intermediate care facility services

- Care for individuals under 21 in psychiatric hospitals—institutional services in intermediate care facilities, intermediate care for the mentally retarded, personal care

The Illinois Department of Public Aid undertook to reduce Medicaid expenditures by $71 million in 1983. Some $60 million of the saving came from eliminating podiatric, chiropractic, optometric, and dental services for all clients and limiting hospital payments for a general assistance recipient to $500. The latter restriction virtually eliminated hospital services for the group of citizens that already were receiving the lowest benefits—$144 per month.

According to Davis and Schoen (1978), the following groups of people are excluded from Medicaid:

- Widows and other single persons under 65 and childless couples

- Most two-parent families (which constitute 70 percent of the rural poor and almost half the poor families in metropolitan areas)

- Families with a father working at a marginal, low-paying job

- Families with an unemployed father in states that do not extend welfare payments to this group; and unemployed fathers receiving unemployment compensation in other states

- Medically needy families in states that do not voluntarily provide this additional coverage

- Single women pregnant with their first child in the states that do not provide welfare aid or eligibility for the "unborn child"

- Children of poor families not receiving AFDC in states that do not take advantage of the optional Medicaid category called "all needy children under 21"

To reduce costs and to provide better service to Medicaid recipients, enrollment in Health Maintenance Organizations or other plans using case management has been implemented in several states. Dallek and Wulsin (1983: 288–289) have raised the issue of freedom of choice of doctor:

> The length of time a recipient is required to stay in a plan and the procedures for either changing physicians or leaving the plan are important patient rights issues. Several plans require enrollees to stay in the plan at least six months in order to guarantee a stable population base; other[s] permit open enrollment and disenrollment. Some plans permit enrollees to change physicians or groups only "for good cause." Others will not permit a change at all; while still others will allow a change for any reason.

A plan should have a developed grievance and hearing procedure. This allows the patient to air complaints and allows the plan to spot incompetent physicians. It is crucial to the protection of patients that health advocates address all of these patient rights issues on behalf of their clients.

They propose twenty issues concerning patient rights:

1. Availability of transportation
2. Distance to care
3. Bilingual services
4. Availability of emergency care
5. Twenty-four-hour availability of services
6. Adequate walk-in appointments, criteria for use, and assured availability
7. Accessibility for the handicapped
8. Patient education in use of the plan and in good health care
9. Minimal waiting time for well visits and other preventive care
10. Broad and unfettered choice of participating providers
11. Patients' choice between a capitated case-managed system and a fee-for-service system
12. Benefit and eligibility bonuses as incentives for joining the case-management capitated system
13. Adequate state monitoring of quality—e.g., number of patient visits, number of hospital stays, length of hospital stay, and mix of services provided per diagnosis
14. Mixed patient population (not only Medicaid and other low-income patients)
15. Exclusion of poor-quality doctors and poor-quality health systems
16. State role in facilitating informed choice by patient as opposed to arbitrary assignment
17. Extent of choice—participating physicians and plans
18. Controls on marketing practice
    a. State central broker for information on plan
    b. State precensorship of written materials
    c. State oversight of marketing practices
19. Provision of assistance for patients' grievances, hearing rights and remedies, change of manager, change of doctor, change of plan, and change to fee-for-service system
20. State hot-line staffed with ombudsmen and other persons to resolve grievances and, where necessary, to allow patient to opt out of the plan for cause on two-days notice

THE VETERANS ADMINISTRATION (VA) HEALTH PROGRAM

Over 90 percent of federal funds spent in federally operated hospitals and clinics benefit members of the armed services or war veterans and their dependents. VA facilities include over 170 hospitals, 200 outpatient clinics, and 90 nursing homes employing about 190,000 personnel. About 30 million veterans are eligible for service.

While medical services were supplied to veterans beginning in 1917, the Veterans Administration was created by Congress in 1930. The period of rapid expansion came from 1945 to 1955, when the number of veterans hospitals increased from 97 to 173. Public Law 79-293, establishing a Department of Medicine and

Surgery, was enacted in 1946 to provide control by medical personnel and cooperation with medical schools to improve the quality of care. It required the VA to offer "complete medical and hospital service."

The VA program gives priority to service-connected disabilities but also provides services to other veterans when facilities are available. The medical program for veterans and their dependents includes the following provisions.

HOSPITALIZATION
Eligibility—General

Discharge or release from the active military service under conditions other than dishonorable.

General admission priorities

First—Veterans needing hospitalization because of injuries or disease incurred or aggravated in line of duty in active service have top priority for admission for treatment of the service-incurred or service-aggravated disability.

Second—Veterans who were discharged or retired for disability incurred or aggravated in line of duty or who are receiving compensation, or would be eligible to receive compensation, except for receipt of retirement pay, who need treatment for some ailment not connected with their service, will be admitted as beds are available.

Third—Veterans who were not discharged or retired for disability or are not receiving compensation, and who apply for treatment of a nonservice-connected disability may be admitted to a VA hospital (1) if hospitalization is deemed necessary, (2) if they state under oath that they are unable to defray the cost of necessary hospital charges elsewhere and (3) if beds are available. NOTE: The "Inability to Pay" requirement does not apply to any veteran who is 65 years of age or older, is in receipt of VA pension, is eligible for Medicaid, or is rated service-connected.

The VA may provide certain outpatient medical services to prepare a veteran for hospital care, or to obviate the need of hospital admission; and to complete treatment of a veteran who has been furnished hospital care.

MEDICAL CARE FOR DEPENDENTS OR SURVIVORS

The Civilian Health and Medical Program of the Veterans Administration (CHAMPVA) is a medical benefits program through which the VA helps pay for medical services and supplies obtained from civilian sources by eligible dependents and survivors of certain veterans. The following persons are eligible for CHAMPVA provided they are not eligible for medical care under CHAMPUS or Medicare:

■ The spouse or child of a veteran who has a total disability, permanent in nature, resulting from a service-connected disability;

■ The surviving spouse or child of a veteran who dies as a result of a service-connected disability, or who at the time of death had a total disability, permanent in nature, resulting from a service-connected disability;

■ The surviving spouse or child of a person who dies while on active duty. This includes the surviving spouse who remarried and the subsequent marriage was terminated.

Normally, care under the CHAMPVA program will be provided in non-VA facilities. VA facilties may be utilized in rare circumstances for specialized treatment when: (1) they are uniquely equipped to provide the most effective care and (2) use of these facilities does not interfere with care and treatment of veterans.

NURSING HOME CARE
Purpose

To provide skilled or intermediate type nursing care and related medical care in VA or private nursing homes for convalescents or persons who are not acutely ill and not in need of hospital care.

Eligibility

For admission or transfer to VA Nursing Home Care Units, it is essentially the same as for hospitalization. Direct admission to private nursing homes at VA expense is limited to

(1) veterans who require nursing care for a service-connected disability after medical determination by the VA, and (2) any person in an Armed Forces hospital who requires a protracted period of nursing care and who will become a veteran upon discharge from the Armed Forces. VA may transfer hospitalized veterans who need a protracted period of nursing care to a private nursing home at VA expense. Normally VA authorized care may not be provided in excess of six months except for veterans whose hospitalization was primarily for a service-connected disability.

General admission priorities

Veterans in need of care in a VA Nursing Home Care Unit may be admitted or transferred according to the following priorities:

First—Veterans receiving hospital or domiciliary care in VA facilities when transfer is required for service-connected or adjunct disabilities and persons being furnished care in Armed Forces hospitals who will require a protracted period of nursing home care upon release therefrom, and will become veterans on discharge from active military service.

Second—Veterans not hospitalized or domiciled by VA who require nursing home care for service-connected or adjunct disabilities.

Third—Veterans receiving hospital or domiciliary care in VA facilities whose transfer is required for nonservice-connected disabilities.

Fourth—Veterans not hospitalized or domiciled by VA who require nursing home care for nonservice-connected disabilities.

ALCOHOL AND DRUG DEPENDENCE TREATMENT
Eligibility—General

Discharge or release from active military service under conditions other than dishonorable. After hospitalization, veterans who received treatment for alcohol or drug dependence while hospitalized may become eligible for follow-up outpatient care.

OUTPATIENT MEDICAL TREATMENT
Purpose

To provide necessary medical services to eligible veterans on an outpatient basis within the limits of Veterans Administration facilities.

Nature of Benefit

Outpatient medical treatment includes medical examination and related medical services including rehabilitation, consultation, professional counseling, training and mental health services as necessary in connection with treatment of physical and mental disabilities.

As part of outpatient medical treatment, veterans may be eligible for home health services necessary or appropriate for the effective and economical treatment of disabilities, including such home improvements and structural alterations as are determined necessary to assure the continuation of treatment or to provide access to the home or to essential lavatory and sanitary facilities. Cost limitations apply to these improvements and structural alterations.

Eligibility

1. Any veteran, for a service-connected disability.

2. Any veteran discharged or released from the active military, naval or air service for a disability incurred in line of duty, for that disability.

3. Any veteran with a service-connected disability rated at 50 percentum or more, for any medical condition.

4. Any veteran of World War I or the Mexican Border period, or any veteran in receipt of aid and attendance or housebound benefits, for any medical condition.

5. Spanish-American War veteran, for any disability.

6. Certain disabled veterans entitled to or receiving vocational rehabilitation training, for any condition requiring medical care to enable the veteran to begin, continue, or return to such training.

7. Any veteran eligible for hospitalization, for medical services on an ambulatory care basis when such services are reasonably necessary in preparation for, or to the extent facilities are available, to obviate the need of, hospital admission.

8. Any veteran who has been granted hospital care, medical services reasonably necessary to complete treatment incident to such hospital care.

Eligible veterans may be furnished drugs or medicine ordered on prescription.

The system initially stressed hospital-based acute care, but later it developed outpatient programs and long-term care. The number of VA hospital beds was decreased from about 120,000 in 1964 to less than 90,000 in 1979. As outpatient service increased, the priorities were included in the Veterans Omnibus Health Care Act of 1976, which reaffirmed the highest status of service-connected disabilities and assigned the next priority to nonservice-connected patients who were seeking outpatient service to prepare for hospitalization or to complete hospital treatment.

As the veteran population grew older, demand for long-term care grew. Extended-care beds increased from 1,500 in 1967 to over 11,000 at the end of the 1970s. The VA was first authorized in 1964 to operate nursing home facilities and to contract for care in nonfederal nursing homes. Three times as many veterans are served in nonfederal nursing homes as in those homes operated directly but the length of stay in nonfederal homes is shorter.

The VA tends to serve people without other hospital insurance, the majority of whom are poor. About one in five is from a racial minority. Most are older, and over half are unmarried. This group of citizens would place larger demands on Medicaid and Medicare if they did not qualify for VA services.

FREE HEALTH SERVICES

There is no absolute right to health care, but hospitals may not turn away persons in emergencies. The Hospital Survey and Construction Act (the Hill-Burton Act), passed in 1946, required both a pledge of nondiscrimination and a reasonable volume of services to be made available for people who cannot pay.

> Twenty years after completion of construction with Hill-Burton-assisted funds, a hospital must either (a) provide the lesser of 3 percent of operating costs or 10 percent of federal assistance in uncompensated services or (b) have an open-door policy under which no individual will be excluded from admission because of inability to pay. Potential recipients of such uncompensated care must be advised of their possible eligibility when they seek admission.

Hospitals are subject to exemption from federal taxation if they are operated for charitable purposes. Specifically, they must "operate an emergency room open to all persons and provide hospital care for all those persons in the community able to pay the cost thereof either directly or indirectly through third-party reimbursement."

We have already noted the decision in Shapiro v. Thompson outlawing residence requirements for public assistance. A similar decision regarding hospital and medical care for the indigent sick was reached in Memorial Hospital v. Maricopa County (Arizona), 415 U.S. 250 (1974). The decision did not mandate medical programs but held that a state that offers them cannot use residency as an eligibility criterion.

COST CONTROL

Health care costs, have risen faster than most other costs, resulting in attempts at cost control. The Hill-Burton Act of 1946 required an annual construction plan from the states, appointment of a state hospital planning council, and designation of a single state agency to implement plans. The Regional Medical Program (1965) and the Comprehensive Health Planning Program (1966) had similar objectives, but not one of the efforts was successful. Planning agencies were understaffed and lacked authority to enforce recommendations.

In 1974 the National Health Planning and Resources Development Act passed by Congress established 205 health service areas each with a local Health Systems Agency. The agencies had no enforcement powers and were unrelated to Medicare and Medicaid, the principal federal health financing programs.

Rising costs have affected private health insurance rates and have been an incentive for people to enroll in Health Maintenance Organizations (HMOs) that provide the advantages of broader services, including prevention, through prepaid group practice. HMOs will cover at least 10 percent of the population by 1988.

Reviews of Medical Services

Reviews to determine whether patients were receiving only those medical services they actually needed began in 1965, but the Professional Standards Review Organization (PSRO) did not begin until 1972. The PSRO program was aimed at unnecessary surgery and excessive acute hospital stays when outpatient or less costly inpatient services would have been appropriate. Second opinions are also used to reduce unnecessary surgery and have been encouraged by private health insurance companies.

Rate Setting

State agencies and federal programs have affected costs by setting maximum rates that they will pay, but for this measure to be effective, hospitals and physicians must agree to provide the service for the given rate. Otherwise, the patient has to pay the difference. A major method of reducing federal costs is to increase co-payments. Medicare rates will be easier to determine reliably under a new classification system for "diagnostic related groups" (DRG). Resulting from the Tax Equity and Financial Responsibility Act of 1982, this system replaced eighty-three classifications based on causes of disease with twenty-three categories based on the body's organ systems.

Thus far, there has been no effective way to reduce increases in the unit cost of health care. The patient can use means of care other than the hospital, stay fewer days, or pay more of the bill from personal savings, but the cost of services continues to increase at a rate higher than general inflation.

MEDICAL RECORDS

Medical records provide information for staff responsible in patient care and document staff and patient behavior if there is any legal question about treatment. The record is also used in reviews of medical services and for teaching and research.

Records are the property of the physician or the health facility. Their content may be specified in detail in administrative health regulations, but often only completeness or accuracy are required. The records must be completed promptly and signed. State statutes provide that they must be retained for periods ranging from ten to twenty-five years after discharge.

Records may be examined by health personnel involved in care of a patient; other people who examine records for teaching and learning purposes should have permission from the patient. Public unrestricted information usually includes a patient's name, address, and age. Other persons, e.g., third parties, get access by patient permission or court order. Records are most important in court proceedings involving alleged malpractice. In the last decade, patients generally have gained access to their own records, as a result of court decisions and new state regulations. Laws granting patient access still apply in less than half the states.

Health records are covered by the Privacy Act of 1974. Included are medical records from federally supported agencies providing direct care, as well as records of payments on a patient's behalf. If a health-care provider believes that direct disclosure would not be in the best interests of a patient, a physician selected by the patient may examine the record.

A care facility often uses records with the names omitted for medical research. Anonymity is facilitated by using computer data banks, but computerization may increase the risk that a patient's identified record would become accessible to third parties.

The Privacy Protection Study Commission (1978) made the following recommendations about the right to medical records:

- Patients should have access to their records, including the right to copy, amend, and correct them.

- Others should have access based on the need to know.

- Patient-identified information should be disclosed only with patient authorization, except for patient audits or on court order; such disclosures shall be limited to the information needed.

- Disclosures to third parties should be recorded in the record.

- These objectives should be furthered by federal and state legislation and regulations and by voluntary cooperation.

The use of records in research involves an institutional review board that considers the risks to patients and invasions of privacy. Patient-identifiable information should be authorized only when it is clearly necessary and when the research is important enough to justify possible identification.

MEDICAL EXPERIMENTATION

The issues concerning records have not been as crucial as those involving research with medical procedures that may involve additional patient risk. Innovative medical treatment that tends to involve greater risk requires greater safeguards. Risk is often considered to be a function of the frequency with which an innovative procedure has been used—the more novel the procedure, the greater the need for protection. Procedures where a proportion of the patients receive a new treatment and the others receive a placebo are the most difficult to explain to the patient and the most difficult to justify in terms of the patient's best interests. When the innovative procedure is part of institutional research, the institutional review board approval is a major element in protection. When the innovative procedure is an isolated instance of treatment, the judgment of the physician may be the only safeguard.

Innovative Procedures Unrelated to Treatment

Scientific research of no demonstrated value to the patient has been particularly controversial since the German medical experiments during the Third Reich. A code was developed as the by-product of the Nuremburg trials. Experimentation was to be based on voluntary consent only, with full power to give or withhold consent without force, fraud, deceit, or any ulterior form of constraint or coercion. Knowledge and comprehension of the research should be sufficient to form the basis of an understanding and enlightened decision concerning consent.

The cornerstone of protection of subjects since that time has become **informed consent**. This criterion may be difficult to satisfy when the procedures are technical and the risks are still not entirely clear to the researcher.

Department of Health and Human Services regulations applying to research with human subjects that it conducts or funds were issued in 1981. Proposals must be initially examined and approved by a five-member institutional review board and then be subject to its continuing review. One member must be from a non-scientific area and one from outside the institution. The board must enforce the following requirements: (1) minimal risk to subjects, (2) risk that is reasonable in relation to anticipated benefits, (3) equitable selection of subjects, (4) seeking and documenting informed consent, (5) monitoring the data to ensure the safety of subjects, (6) ensuring protection of privacy of subjects and confidentiality of data. If the elements of informed consent are presented orally, there must be a witness to the presentation. A signed consent form is not required when risk is minimal and the procedures would not normally require written consent.

Health research with children is particularly difficult because permission is ordinarily sought from the parents. Standards for legal majority are not particularly helpful, because as the children gradually develop understanding they should have an increasing role in informed consent. The law is generally clear that treatment can be given to children without parental consent in case of emergency, but in experimentation children's rights are relatively obscure.

MALPRACTICE

Although medical malpractice is a popular topic in the literature, malpractice actions are still rare. They are covered by tort law, that is, injury by one person to another, and include both intentional and unintentional injuries. Malpractice usually involves failure to exercise care that would be expected of an ordinarily prudent person. If the practitioner does not act "reasonably," conduct may constitute negligence. The jury in a malpractice case then has to take the rule of a "reasonable person" to decide the merits. The major goal of such actions is to obtain compensation, although such suits also serve to deter undesirable actions. Deterrence involves establishment and maintenance of a reputation that will not serve as a barrier to obtaining patients.

To prove malpractice it must be shown that the defendant did not comply with the duty owed to the plaintiff, that the consequence was real harm, and that the breach of duty actually caused the harm. While malpractice actions are still not often brought against physicians or hospitals, they are even rarer against other medical personnel, including medical social workers. Compared with social work, the goals and the procedures of the physician are more easily described and defined; harmful behavior is more easily identified. There is nothing in social work comparable to leaving a towel inside a patient or prescribing a drug that proves dangerous. Also, more substantial damages can usually be recovered from the physician (or rather from an insurance carrier) than from a social worker.

OCCUPATIONAL AND ENVIRONMENTAL HEALTH

Occupational and environmental health are becoming increasingly important. Social workers in employee-assistance programs deal with workers or other family members who are victims of occupationally induced diseases, injuries, and on-the-job deaths. Social workers generally have been concerned about environmental protection, including the hazards of using nuclear power, nuclear wastes, and nuclear weapons.

Occupational Health

Legal provisions for occupational health have come mainly from workers' compensation laws that have provided limited payments for industrial accidents.

Government involvement increased greatly with the passage of the Occupational Safety and Health Act of 1970, which applies to any person engaged in a business affecting commerce who has employees. Persons excluded are those employed by federal, state, or local governments; those protected by a small number of other federal statutes; those employed in domestic service in a residence, in agriculture on a family owned and operated farm, or in a religious service; and the self-employed.

Enforcement was assigned to the Department of Labor through the Occupational Safety and Health Administration (OSHA). A review commission was created to review contested enforcement actions of OSHA. Medical criteria for standards are the responsibility of the National Institute for Occupational Safety and Health in the Department of Health and Human Services.

An example of needed standards and controls involved cotton dust standards that implied a health risk. OSHA's activities in this area were upheld by the Supreme Court in American Textile Manufacturers Institute v. Donovan, 452 U.S. 490 (1981).

Because the law covers 5 million businesses, OSHA established priorities for inspection, including primarily situations involving danger of death or serious physical harm and investigating of catastrophes, fatalities, and accidents involving five or more employees. Employee complaints are given priority, and personnel can request and participate in an OSHA inspection. The Reagan administration has tended to curtail enforcement activities of OSHA.

Environmental Health

The broad areas of environmental health and nuclear power are highly controversial. In the early stages of the Reagan administration, the Environmental Protection Agency was accused of not carrying out its duties objectively and adequately, and reorganization resulted.

The dangers of nuclear materials have become increasingly clear. More effective governmental activity in both occupational and environmental health should get higher priority.

A SICK-CARE SYSTEM

In its report on access to health care at the end of 1983, the Robert Wood Johnson Foundation held that 28 million Americans were truly medically disadvantaged, including 20 percent of Hispanic adults and 15 percent of black adults. These citizens can neither pay for the medical care they need nor obtain necessary health insurance. Even those who are satisfied with their own health care are critical of the system that provides it. We have a sick-care system that seems to be sick itself. Both the programs created by statute and the policies relating to private care give little reason for optimism about acute health needs, health promotion, or disease prevention.

Questions for Review

1.   Explain how administrative law is important to consumers in health programs.

2.   Identify the two federal programs that involve federal payments for care and service.

3.   Identify the large program for direct health services operated directly by the federal government.

4.   Why may private medical practitioners express reluctance to report data involving their patients, especially when names must be included?

5.   Differenitate clearly between *licensing* and *accreditation*.

6.   What actions may be taken against a practitioner under licensing provisions? Against an agency?

7.   Which health program has the largest federal expenditure?

8.   Differentiate between Medicare and Medicaid in terms of clientele. In which program is there payment of insurance premiums? In which one does the individual state participate in the financing?

9.   What three types of care are covered by Medicare *hospital* insurance?

10.   All states cover medical care of people eligible for public assistance through Medicaid. Do they also all cover people who do not receive public assistance but who cannot meet medical costs?

11.   Does the VA provide medical care for non-service-connected disabilities?

12.   Why is the VA program increasingly involved in long-term care?

13.   What services other than acute hospitalization are offered by the VA?

14.   Are all hospital services paid for by one or more of the following: governmental programs, private insurance, the patient? What is the responsibility of hospitals to offer charitable, i.e., *free*, service?

15.   If a federally supported medical agency does not want a patient to have direct access to a medical record, what procedure is followed?

16.   Summarize the recommendation of the Privacy Protection Study Commission concerning medical records.

17.   Identify the safeguards provided for the patient in medical experimentation, in research that is both related and unrelated to treatment.

18.   Explain informed consent.

19.   What are the requirements to prove medical malpractice?

20.   What situations are accorded top priority by OSHA?

21.   What groups are particularly disadvantaged by the American health system?

Questions for Debate and Discussion

1.   For social workers, hospitals and clinics are considered host settings, i.e., settings under the management of another discipline. How does this situation affect the role of the social worker as an advocate for patients' rights?

2.   Compare the government health programs in the United States with England's National Health Service. Would we be better served if we had also adopted a system of state medicine at the time England did?

3.   Malpractice insurance for social workers involves so few claims that it is not necessary for one to carry it. Evaluate this statement.

4.   Tabulate the private health insurance coverage for members of your class; summarize their experience with claims; consider the adequacy of coverage. Have

any of them received services from the Veterans Administration or through Medicaid?

Selected Readings   Adriani, John, and Allen Eaton. *Law and Health Professionals: Fundamentals of the Law and Malpractice.* St. Louis: Green, 1984.

Checkoway, Barry. "The Empire Strikes Back: More Lessons for Health Care Consumers." *Journal of Health Policy and Law* 7 (1982): 111–124.

Consumer Health Information Source Book. 2d ed. New York: Bowker, 1984.

Kapp, Marshall B. "Protecting the Rights of Nursing Home Patients: Using Federal Law." *Florida Bar Journal* 55 (1981): 212–215.

"Michigan's Bill of Rights for Nursing Home Residents." *Wayne Law Review* 27 (1981): 1203–1227.

Wecht, Cyril H. *Legal Medicine, 1980.* Philadelphia: W. B. Saunders, 1980.

CHAPTER

24

Mental Health and Institutionalized Persons

Laws governing involuntary commitment of persons labeled mentally ill, mentally retarded, sexual deviants, alcoholics, drug addicts, and criminally insane are contained in a wide range of state mental health and criminal statutes. This chapter considers the procedures by which these persons are labeled and institutionalized. Also of major importance is the issue of whether individuals who are committed against their will have a right to expect and receive treatment. Do they have a right to refuse treatment or to refuse medication? Finally, when does the social worker whose client threatens another person have a duty to warn the potential victim?

THE RIGHT TO REFUSE OR TERMINATE HOSPITALIZATION

Mentally ill people may seek treatment voluntarily, or they may be subject to involuntary hospitalization. While this chapter deals mainly with the patient who is legally committed, two facts should be recognized: Most patients are hospitalized voluntarily, but a proportion of them have been told that if they do not sign themselves in voluntarily, legal action will be taken to force hospitalization.

Any one of five major procedures may be followed for involuntary commitment:

1. *Emergency Hospitalization*   Emergency hospitalization can range from twenty-four hours to thirty days, depending on the state. Petitioners other than law enforcement or health officers must obtain either judicial approval or medical certification subsequent to examination of the patient by one or two physicians. Some states also require that medical examinations be performed by the admitting institution. Most involuntary patients are admitted by means of emergency hospitalization.

2. *Temporary or Observational Hospitalization*   Temporary or observational hospitalization is a specified period of commitment for the purpose of diagnosis and treatment of nonemergency cases. The delay normally incurred by formal commitment procedures is avoided.

3. *Judicial Commitment*   For a judicial commitment, a judge and occasionally a jury determines whether a person is sufficiently mentally ill to require hospitalization. Typically, a mental examination by a physician prior to the hearing is required. Under such circumstances, patients are usually hospitalized for an indeterminate period.

4. *Medical Certification* With medical certification, there is an examination by one or two physicians, followed by certification of the patient's mental incompetency. Initial judicial review is limited to determining the validity of certifying documents. Court review of certification is available on demand by the patient, who otherwise will remain hospitalized for an indeterminate period.

5. *Administrative Procedure* In an administrative procedure, a board composed mainly of physicians investigates and holds a hearing regarding the need to commit the patient for an indeterminate period.

Legal criteria for involuntary commitments vary. Some jurisdictions provide for judicial hospitalization based either on need for care and treatment or on danger to self or others; others do so only on the basis of dangerousness; a few states rely solely on the need for treatment, while a few others order commitment based on whether the person should be confined "for his own or others'" welfare.

Stone (1975: 69) suggests that the judge or jury consider the answers to five questions prior to approving an involuntary commitment:

1. Do the psychiatrists make a convincing diagnosis of serious illness?
2. Is the patient suffering?
3. Is treatment available, and how long will it take?
4. Does the patient's objection to treatment seem irrational and based on his illness?
5. Would a reasonable person accept the treatment being offered in that hospital? Might a reasonable person object to a proposed treatment method even though the alternative is more costly to the state and/or less apt to be successful?

These requirements would reject legal criteria for involuntary commitment based on the patient's "need for care" or protection consideration of the "welfare of self or others." Stone views the standards of care developed by professional standards review organizations as a viable vehicle by which to implement his proposal.

Efforts at reforming the laws that govern involuntary civil commitments have moved toward assuring mental patients procedural safeguards similar to those that apply in the criminal process. Lessard v. Schmidt, 349 F.Supp 1078 (1972), provided the decision that most clearly identified the patients rights issues in civil commitment occasioned by the Wisconsin statutes.

LESSARD v. SCHMIDT

United States District Court, Eastern District of Wisconsin, 349 F.Supp. 1078 (1972).

Alberta Lessard was picked up by two police officers in front of her residence in West Allis, Wisconsin, and taken to the Mental Health Center North Division, Milwaukee, on October 29, 1971. At the Center, the police officers, defendants James D. Mejchar and Jack Schneider, filled out a form entitled "Emergency Detention for Mental Observation," following which Miss Lessard was detained on an emergency basis. On November 1, 1971, the same police officers appeared before defendant Judge Christ T. Seraphim, Milwaukee County Court, and restated the allegations contained in the petition for emergency detention. On the basis of this ex parte proceeding, Judge Seraphim issued an order permitting the confinement of Miss Lessard for an additional ten days. Thereafter, on November 4, 1971, defendant Dr. George Currier filed an "Application for Judicial Inquiry" with Judge Seraphim, stating that Miss Lessard was suffering from schizophrenia and recommending permanent commitment. At this time Judge Seraphim ordered two physicians to examine Miss Lessard, and signed a second temporary detention document, permitting Miss Lessard's detention for ten more days from the date of the order. This period was again extended on November 12, 1971. Neither Miss Lessard nor anyone who might act on her behalf was informed on any of these proceedings.

On November 5, 1971, Judge Seraphim held an interview with Miss Lessard at the Mental Health Center. At this interview, Judge Seraphim informed Miss Lessard that two doctors had been appointed to examine her and that a guardian ad litem would be appointed to represent her. He asked her if she wished to have her own doctor examine her. Miss Lessard replied that she had no physician. Miss Lessard was not told of this interview in advance and was given no opportunity to prepare for it. Following the interview, Judge Seraphim signed an order appointing Daniel A. Noonan, an attorney, as guardian ad litem for Miss Lessard.

Miss Lessard, on her own initiative, retained counsel through the Milwaukee Legal Services, on November 9 or 10. On November 15, 1971, at 2:00 p.m., Miss Lessard was notified that a commitment hearing had been scheduled for 8:30 a.m., the following morning. This hearing was adjourned and reset for November 24, 1971, in order to give Miss Lessard's attorney an opportunity to appear. Miss Lessard's request that she be allowed to go home during the interim was denied. At the November 24 hearing before Judge Seraphim, testimony was given by one of the police officers and three physicians and Miss Lessard was ordered committed for thirty additional days. Judge Seraphim gave no reasons for his order except to state that he found Miss Lessard to be "mentally ill." Although the hospital authorities permitted Miss Lessard to go home on an out-patient "parole" basis three days later, the thirty day commitment order has been extended for one month each month since November 24, 1971.

The present suit, brought as a class action on behalf of Miss Lessard and all other persons 18 years of age or older who are being held involuntarily pursuant to any emergency, temporary or permanent commitment provision of the Wisconsin involuntary commitment statute, was filed on November 12, 1971. Jurisdiction was claimed under 42 U.S.C. § 1983. The complaint sought declaratory and injunctive relief against the enforcement of certain portions of Wis.Stat.Ann. §§ 51.02, 51.03 and 51.04, relating to the procedure for involuntary detention and commitment of persons alleged to be suffering from mental illness. The complaint sought a temporary restraining order restraining the officials involved from proceeding further against Miss Lessard or detaining her involuntarily for any additional length of time. A three-judge court was requested. In an order dated December 3, 1971, Judge Reynolds of the federal district court for the Eastern District of Wisconsin denied temporary relief but agreed that the substantial constitutional claims raised by the pleadings required the convening of a three-judge court. 28 U.S.C. § 2281. . . .

We conclude that the Wisconsin civil commitment procedure is constitutionally defective insofar as it fails to require effective and timely notice of the "charges" under which a person is sought to be detained; fails to require adequate notice of all rights, including the right to jury trial; permits detention longer than 48 hours without a hearing on probable cause; permits detention longer than two weeks without a full hearing on the necessity for commitment; permits commitment based upon a hearing in which the person charged with mental illness is not represented by adversary counsel, at which hearsay evidence is admitted, and in which psychiatric evidence is presented without the patient having been given the benefit of the privilege against self-incrimination; permits commitment without proof beyond a reasonable doubt that the patient is both "mentally ill" and dangerous; and fails to require those seeking commitment to consider less restrictive alternatives to commitment. . . .

Although the U.S. Supreme Court vacated the judgment in *Lessard* because the state appellate remedies had not been exhausted, the district court decisions influenced reform of civil commitment laws. Herr, Arons, and Wallace (1983: 83) stated: "*Lessard v. Schmidt* represents what is now settled law across the country: civil commitment is constitutionally permissible only if no appropriate, less restrictive alternative is available."

The reasons and the length of time persons may be involuntarily committed remain questions for court scrutiny, as the case of People v. Superior Court (Dodson), 196 Cal. Rptr. 431 (Cal. App. 1983), demonstrates. In this case a mentally disordered person taken into custody for attacking a psychiatrist contended that the standard of confinement set forth in the California Welfare and Institutions Code violated due process because it looked to past conduct rather than to future behavior. Due process prohibited involuntary confinement except on a showing of "imminent danger." The trial court had dismissed the petition for confinement of the patient because Section 5300 of the California law was unconstitutional.

The appellate decision held that Section 5300 could withstand constitutional scrutiny because the language permitted confinement only of one who has inflicted or threatened harm to others, and then only if "as a result of mental disorder" the person "presented a demonstrated danger of substantial physical harm to others." The statute makes clear that past conduct is relevant only as a prognosticator of probable future behavior, a constitutionally valid evidentiary consideration.

THE RIGHT TO TREATMENT

The major issue related to involuntary commitment is the question of whether institutionalized persons have a right to treatment. Rouse v. Cameron, 373 F.2d 451 (D.C.Cir. 1966), was the first of several such cases.

ROUSE v. CAMERON

United States Court of Appeals, District of Columbia Circuit, 373 F.2d 451 (D.C.Cir.1966).

In this habeas corpus case appellant attacks his confinement in Saint Elizabeth's Hospital. He was involuntarily committed in November 1962 by the Municipal Court, now the Court of General Sessions, upon finding him not guilty by reason of insanity of carrying a dangerous weapon, a misdemeanor for which the maximum imprisonment is one year. The District Court has held a hearing and denied relief in habeas corpus. It refused to consider appellant's contention that he has received no psychiatric treatment. . . .

I

The principal issues raised by this appeal are whether a person involuntarily committed to a mental hospital on being acquitted of an offense by reason of insanity has a right to treatment that is cognizable in habeas corpus, and if so, how violation of this right may be established.

The purpose of involuntary hospitalization is treatment, not punishment. The provision for commitment rests upon the supposed "necessity for treatment for the mental condition which led to the acquittal by reason of insanity." Absent treatment, the hospital is "transform[ed] . . . into a penitentiary where one could be held indefinitely for no convicted offense, and this even though the offense of which he was previously acquitted because of doubt as to his sanity might not have been one of the more serious felonies" or might have been, as it was here, a misdemeanor. . . .

Impressed by the considerable constitutional problems that arise because "institutionalized patients often receive only custodial care," Congress established a *statutory* "right to treatment" in the 1964 [D.C.] Hospitalization of the Mentally Ill Act. The act provides:

> A person hospitalized in a public hospital for a mental illness shall, during his hospitalization, be entitled to medical and psychiatric care and treatment. The administrator of each public hospital shall keep records detailing all medical and psychiatric care and treatment received by a person hospitalized for a mental illness and the records shall be made available, upon that person's written authorization, to his attorney or personal physician.

It appears that this provision, like the one limiting the use of mechanical restraints, was intended to cover persons hospitalized under any statutory authorization. Other sections of the Act apply only to patients "hospitalized pursuant to [the 1964 Act]," or to "mentally ill persons," which term is defined by the Act to exclude persons committed by court order in a criminal proceeding. Since there are no such limitations in the "right to treatment" provision set forth above, that right necessarily extends to involuntary commitment under D.C.Code § 24-301.

Regardless of the statutory authority, involuntary confinement without treatment is "shocking." Indeed, there may be greater need for the protection of the right to treatment for persons committed without the safeguards of civil commitment procedures. Because we hold that the right to treatment provision applies to appellant, we need not resolve the serious constitutional questions that Congress avoided by prescribing this right.

The Group for the Advancement of Psychiatry has urged that "provisions that safeguard the patient's right to good treatment as opposed to simple custody" are an essential element of commitment laws. A right to treatment in some form is recognized by law in many states. The requirement in the 1964 Act that the hospital keep records detailing psychiatric care and treatment and make them available to the patient's attorney reinforces our view that Congress intended to implement the right to treatment by affording a judicial remedy for its violation.

The patient's right to treatment is clear. We now consider how violation of the right may be established.

We think "law and justice require" that we remand for a hearing and finding on whether appellant is receiving adequate treatment, and, if not, the details and circumstances underlying the reason why he is not. The latter information is essential to determine whether there is "an overwhelmingly compelling reason" for the failure to provide adequate treatment.

III

The appellant challenges also the District Court's finding that he has not recovered his mental health. A person involuntarily committed and confined under D.C.Code § 24-301 is entitled to release if he has "recovered his sanity and will not in the reasonable future be dangerous to himself or others." That the "person so confined has some dangerous propensities does not, standing alone, warrant his continued confinement in a government mental institution under § 24-301 D.C.Code. The dangerous propensities . . . must be related to or arise out of an abnormal mental condition." The District Court's findings concerning mental illness and dangerous propensities are not to be disturbed unless they lack support in the record or rest on an erroneous legal principle.

Three psychiatrists gave conflicting testimony. Dr. Economon of Saint Elizabeths testified that appellant was suffering from "antisocial reaction" and described its symptoms. Dr. Marland, in private practice, and Dr. Bunge, of the Commission on Mental Health, testified that appellant was not suffering from mental illness. The judge concluded: "In view of the fact that the original arrest involved a dangerous weapon, an extremely dangerous weapon, with a great deal of ammunition, the Court is not going to undertake to release him unconditionally and would have great hesitancy in releasing him even conditionally." The judge then continued the hearing pending a report from the Commission on Mental Health.

The Commission reported that appellant had "recovered" and that "further confinement would stifle his future development." The hearing resumed with the following colloquy:

> COURT: The court has before it the report of the Commission on Mental Health. Is this the case in which the petitioner was arrested in possession of a .45 caliber revolver?
> MR. SILBERT: With 600 rounds of ammunition, too. This was at 1:45 in the morning at 14th & Harvard Sts. N.W.

The judge then pursued at length with Dr. Bunge, as he had with Dr. Marland, appellant's purpose in possessing a gun and ammunition. At the conclusion of the doctor's testimony the judge said:

> I do want to ask you one question, Doctor. I am going to ask you that question in view of the fact that [petitioner] . . . was caught in the possession of a .45 pistol and 600 rounds of ammunition. My principal interest must be to protect the public. Would he be dangerous to himself or others, in your opinion, if he is released?

Dr. Bunge replied: "I don't believe he would be at this time."

The judge made plain not only this reliance on the offense charged, but also his doubt whether the appellant was mentally ill. He said to Dr. Economon, the only psychiatrist who thought him so:

> . . . That is not a symptom of insanity, Doctor, because many sane people do those things. . . .
> You know, we just couldn't accept any psychiatric testimony or theory to the effect that the commission of a crime is a sign of mental disease because if we accepted that our whole system of criminal law would have to break down. . . .

> Appellant may not be held in custody for an offense of which he was found not guilty. Since, as we have pointed out above, he may not be held unless his dangerous propensities "are related to or arise out of an abnormal mental condition" and since the case is being remanded for a hearing and findings concerning treatment, the District Court may reconsider and clarify its findings concerning illness and dangerous propensities.

Rouse did not include a ruling on whether treatment was given or whether the patient was still dangerous, but it did clearly specify that a person who had recovered was entitled to release.

The next major decision came in response to a class action suit. In *Wyatt v. Stickney*, 344 F.Supp. 373 (M.D.Ala. 1972), the court held that the entire mental health system of the state of Alabama was unconstitutional. This case was not reviewed by the U.S. Supreme Court, but many states adopted the standards set forth therein by the federal district court judge. It is also the first instance in which amicus briefs from the American Psychiatric and American Psychological Associations were used in developing standards for treatment in a mental hospital. The discussion below includes the standards.

WYATT v. STICKNEY

United States District Court, Middle District of Alabama, 344 F.Supp. 373 (1972).

This class action originally was filed on October 23, 1970, in behalf of patients involuntarily confined for mental treatment purposes at Bryce Hospital, Tuscaloosa, Alabama. On March 12, 1971, in a formal opinion and decree, this Court held that these involuntarily committed patients "unquestionably have a constitutional right to receive such individual treatment as will give each of them a realistic opportunity to be cured or to improve his or her mental condition." The Court further held that patients at Bryce were being denied their right to treatment and that defendants, per their request, would be allowed six months in which to raise the level of care at Bryce to the constitutionally required minimum. Wyatt v. Stickney, 325 F.Supp. 781 (M.D.Ala. 1971). In this decree, the Court ordered defendants to file reports defining the mission and functions of Bryce Hospital, specifying the objective and subjective standards required to furnish adequate care to the treatable mentally ill and detailing the hospital's progress toward the implementation of minimum constitutional standards. Subsequent to this order, plaintiffs, by motion to amend granted August 12, 1971, enlarged their class to include patients involuntarily confined for mental treatment at Searcy Hospital and at Partlow State School and Hospital for the mentally retarded.

On September 23, 1971, defendants filed their final report, from which this Court concluded on December 10, 1971, 334 F.Supp. 1341, that defendants had failed to promulgate and implement a treatment program satisfying minimum medical and constitutional requisites. Generally, the Court found that defendants' treatment program was deficient in three fundamental areas. It failed to provide: (1) a humane psychological and physical environment, (2) qualified staff in numbers sufficient to administer adequate treatment and (3) individualized treatment plans. More specifically, the Court found that many conditions, such as nontherapeutic, uncompensated work assignments, and the absence of any semblance of privacy, constituted dehumanizing factors contributing to the degeneration of the patients' self-esteem. The physical facilities at Bryce were overcrowded and plagued by fire and other emergency hazards. The Court found also that most staff members were poorly trained and that staffing ratios were so inadequate as to render the administration of effective treatment impossible. The Court concluded, therefore, that whatever treatment was provided at Bryce was grossly deficient and failed to satisfy minimum medical and constitutional standards. Based upon this conclusion, the Court ordered that a formal hearing be held at which the parties and amici would have the opportunity to submit proposed standards for constitutionally adequate treatment and to present expert testimony in support of their proposals.

Pursuant to this order, a hearing was held at which the foremost authorities on mental health in the United States appeared and testified as to the minimum medical and constitutional requisites for public institutions, such as Bryce and Searcy, designed to treat the mentally ill. At this hearing, the parties and amici submitted their proposed standards, and now have filed briefs in support of them. Moreover, the parties and amici have stipulated to a broad spectrum of conditions they feel are mandatory for a constitutionally acceptable minimum treatment program. This court, having considered the evidence in the case, as well as the briefs, proposed standards and stipulations of the parties, has concluded that the standards set out in Appendix A to this decree are medical and constitutional minimums. Consequently, the Court will order their implementation. In so ordering, however, the Court emphasizes that these standards are, indeed, both medical and constitutional minimums and should be viewed as such. The Court urges that once this order is effectuated, defendants not become complacent and self-satisfied. Rather, they should dedicate themselves to providing physical conditions and treatment programs at Alabama's mental institutions that substantially exceed medical and constitutional minimums.

In addition to asking that their proposed standards be effectuated, plaintiffs and amici have requested other relief designed to guarantee the provision of constitutional and humane treatment. Pursuant to one such request for relief, this Court has determined that it is appropriate to order the initiation of human rights committees to function as standing committees of the Bryce and Searcy facilities. The Court will appoint the members of these committees who shall have review of all research proposals and all rehabilitation programs to ensure that the dignity and the human rights of patients are preserved. The committees also shall advise and assist patients who allege that their legal rights have been infringed or that the Mental Health Board has failed to comply with judicially ordered guidelines. At their discretion, the committees may consult appropriate, independent specialists who shall be compensated by the defendant Board. Seven members shall comprise the human rights committee for each institution, the names and addresses of whom are set forth in Appendix B to this decree. Those who serve on the committees shall be paid on a per diem basis and be reimbursed for travel expenses at the same rate as members of the Alabama Board of Mental Health.

This Court will reserve ruling upon other forms of relief advocated by plaintiffs and amici, including their prayer for the appointment of a master and a professional advisory committee to oversee the implementation of the court-ordered minimum constitutional standards. Federal courts are reluctant to assume control of any organization, but especially one operated by a state. This reluctance, combined with defendants' expressed intent that this order will be implemented forthwith and in good faith, causes the Court to withhold its decision on these appointments. Nevertheless, defendants, as well as the other parties and amici in this case, are placed on notice that unless defendants do comply satisfactorily with this order, the Court will be obligated to appoint a master.

Because the availability of financing may bear upon the implementation of this order, the Court is constrained to emphasize at this juncture that a failure by defendants to comply with this decree cannot be justified by a lack of operating funds. As previously established by this Court:

> "There can be no legal (or moral) justification for the State of Alabama's failing to afford treatment—and adequate treatment from a medical standpoint—to the several thousand patients who have been civilly committed to Bryce's for treatment purposes. To deprive any citizen of his or her liberty upon the altruistic theory that the confinement is for humane therapeutic reasons and then fail to provide adequate treatment violates the very fundamentals of due process." Wyatt v. Stickney, 325 F.Supp. at 785.

From the above, it follows consistently, of course, that the unavailability of neither funds, nor staff and facilities, will justify a default by defendants in the provision of suitable treatment for the mentally ill. . . .

In this case, the Court also specified detailed standards of treatment entered in an appendix to the decision under force of law:

> Standards ordered for both the mental illness and mental retardation facilities include: a provision against uncompensated patient labor; a number of protections to insure a humane psychological environment; minimum staffing standards; detailed physical standards; minimum nutritional requirement; a provision for individualized evaluations of residents; treatment plans and programs; a provision to ensure that residents released from Alabama's institutions will be provided with appropriate transitional care; and a requirement that every mentally impaired person has a right to [the] least restrictive setting necessary for treatment.

Standards presented in the appendix concerning the optimal psychological environment of mental institutions state:

1. Patients have a right to privacy and dignity.

2. Patients have a right to the least restrictive conditions necessary to achieve the purposes of commitment.

3. No person shall be deemed incompetent to manage his affairs, to contract, to hold professional or occupation or vehicle operator's licenses, to marry and obtain a divorce, to register and vote, or to make a will *solely* by reason of his admission or commitment to the hospital.

4. Patients shall have the same rights to visitation and telephone communications as patients at other public hospitals, except to the extent that the Qualified Mental Health Professional responsible for formulation of a particular patient's treatment plan writes an order imposing special restrictions. . . .

5.   Patients shall have an unrestricted right to send sealed mail. Patients shall have an unrestricted right to receive sealed mail from their attorneys, private physicians, and other mental health professionals, from courts, and government officials. Patients shall have a right to receive sealed mail from others, except to the extent that the Qualified Mental Health Professional responsible for formulation of a particular patient's treatment plan writes an order imposing special restrictions on receipt of sealed mail. The written order must be renewed after each periodic review of the treatment plan if any restrictions are to be continued.

6.   Patients have a right to be free from unnecessary or excessive medication. No medication shall be administered unless at the written order of a physician. The superintendent of the hospital and the atttending physician shall be responsible for all medication given or administered to a patient. The use of medication shall not exceed standards of use that are advocated by the United States Food and Drug Administration. Notation of each individual's medication shall be kept in his medical records. At least weekly the attending physician shall review the drug regimen of each patient under his care. All prescriptions shall be written with a termination date, which shall not exceed 30 days. Medication shall not be used as punishment, for the convenience of staff, as a substitute for program, or in quantities that interfere with the patient's treatment program.

7.   Patients have a right to be free from physical restraint and isolation. Except for emergency situations, in which it is likely that patients could harm themselves or others and in which less restrictive means of restraint are not feasible, patients may be physically restrained or placed in isolation only on a Qualified Mental Health Professional's written order which explains the rationale for such action. The written order may be entered only after the Qualified Mental Health Professional has personally seen the patient concerned and evaluated whatever episode or situation is said to call for restraint or isolation. Emergency use of restraints or isolation shall be for no more than one hour, by which time a Qualified Mental Health Professional shall have been consulted and shall have entered an appropriate order in writing. Such written order shall be effective for no more than 24 hours and must be renewed if restraint and isolation are to be continued. While in restraint or isolation the patient must be seen by qualified ward personnel who will chart the patient's physical condition (if it is compromised) and psychiatric condition every hour. The patient must have bathroom privileges every hour and must be bathed every 12 hours.

8.   Patients shall have a right not to be subjected to experimental research without the express and informed consent of the patient, if the patient is able to give such consent, and of his guardian or next of kin, after opportunities for consultation with independent specialists and with legal counsel. . . .

9.   Patients have a right not to be subjected to treatment procedures such as lobotomy, electro-convulsive treatment, adversive reinforcement conditioning or other unusual or hazardous treatment procedures without their express and informed consent after consultation with counsel or interested party of the patient's choice.

10.   Patients have a right to receive prompt and adequate medical treatment for any physical ailments.

11.   Patients have a right to wear their own clothes and to keep and use their own personal possessions except insofar as such clothes or personal possessions may be determined by a Qualified Mental Health Professional to be dangerous or otherwise inappropriate to the treatment regimen.

12.   The hospital has an obligation to supply an adequate allowance of clothing to any patients who do not have suitable clothing of their own. Patients shall have the opportunity to select from various types of neat, clean, and seasonable clothing. Such clothing shall be considered the patient's throughout his stay in the hospital.

13.   The hospital shall make provision for the laundering of patient clothing.

14.   Patients have a right to regular physical exercise several times a week. Moreover, it shall be the duty of the hospital to provide facilities and equipment for such exercise.

15.   Patients have a right to be outdoors at regular and frequent intervals, in the absence of medical considerations.

16.   The rights to religious worship shall be accorded to each patient who desires such opportunities. Provisions for such worship shall be made available to all patients on a nondiscriminatory basis. No individual shall be coerced into engaging in any religious activities.

17.   The institution shall provide, with adequate supervision, suitable opportunities for the patient's interaction with members of the opposite sex.

Wyatt was upheld on appeal and remains the most comprehensive right-to-treatment case.

The Supreme Court's later consideration of O'Connor v. Donaldson, 422 U.S. 563 (1957), three years later, combines elements of the right to treatment with the right to refuse treatment.

O'CONNOR v. DONALDSON

Supreme Court of the United States, 422 U.S. 563 (1975).

The respondent, Kenneth Donaldson, was civilly committed to confinement as a mental patient in the Florida State Hospital at Chattahoochee in January of 1957. He was kept in custody there against his will for nearly 15 years. The petitioner, Dr. J. B. O'Connor, was the hospital's superintendent during most of this period. Throughout his confinement Donaldson repeatedly, but unsuccessfully, demanded his release, claiming that he was dangerous to no one, that he was not mentally ill, and that, at any rate, the hospital was not providing treatment for his supposed illness. Finally, in February of 1971, Donaldson brought this lawsuit under 42 U.S.C. § 1983, in the United States District Court for the Northern District of Florida, alleging that O'Connor, and other members of the hospital staff, named as defendants, had intentionally and maliciously deprived him of his constitutional right to liberty. After a four-day trial, the jury returned a verdict assessing both compensatory and punitive damages against O'Connor and a codefendant. The Court of Appeals for the Fifth Circuit affirmed the judgment, 493 F.2d 507. We granted

O'Connor's petition for certiorari, because of the important constitutional questions seemingly presented.

I

Donaldson's commitment was initiated by his father, who thought that his son was suffering from "delusions." After hearings before a county judge of Pinellas County, Florida, Donaldson was found to be suffering from "paranoid schizophrenia" and was committed for "care, maintenance, and treatment" pursuant to Florida statutory provisions that have since been repealed. The state law was less than clear in specifying the grounds necessary for commitment, and the record is scanty as to Donaldson's condition at the time of the judicial hearing. These matters are, however, irrelevant, for this case involves no challenge to the initial commitment, but is focused, instead, upon the nearly 15 years of confinement that followed.

The evidence at the trial showed that the hospital staff had the power to release a patient, not dangerous to himself or others, even if he remained mentally ill and had been lawfully committed. Despite many requests, O'Connor refused to allow that power to be exercised in Donaldson's case. At the trial, O'Connor indicated that he had believed that Donaldson would have been unable to make a "successful adjustment outside the institution," but could not recall the basis for that conclusion. O'Connor retired as superintendent shortly before this suit was filed. A few months thereafter, and before the trial, Donaldson secured his release and a judicial restoration of competency, with the support of the hospital staff.

The testimony at the trial demonstrated, without contradiction, that Donaldson had posed no danger to others during his long confinement, or indeed at any point in his life. O'Connor himself conceded that he had no personal or secondhand knowledge that Donaldson had ever committed a dangerous act. There was no evidence that Donaldson had ever been suicidal or been thought likely to inflict injury upon himself. One of O'Connor's codefendants acknowledged that Donaldson could have earned his own living outside the hospital. He had done so for some 14 years before his commitment, and immediately upon his release he secured a responsible job in hotel administration.

Furthermore, Donaldson's frequent requests for release had been supported by responsible persons willing to provide him any care he might need on release. In 1963, for example, a representative of Helping Hands, Inc, a halfway house for mental patients, wrote O'Connor asking to release Donaldson to its care. The request was accompanied by a supporting letter from the Minneapolis Clinic of Psychiatry and Neurology, which a codefendant conceded was a "good clinic." O'Connor rejected the offer, replying that Donaldson could be released only to his parents. That rule was apparently of O'Connor's own making. At the time, Donaldson was 55 years old, and, as O'Connor knew, Donaldson's parents were too elderly and infirm to take responsibility for him. Moreover, in his continuing correspondence with Donaldson's parents, O'Connor never informed them of the Helping Hands offer. In addition, on four separate occasions between 1964 and 1968, John Lembcke, a college classmate of Donaldson's and a longtime family friend, asked O'Connor to release Donaldson to his care. On each occasion O'Connor refused. The record shows that Lembcke was a serious and responsible person, who was willing and able to assume responsibility for Donaldson's welfare.

The evidence showed that Donaldson's confinement was a simple regime of enforced custodial care, not a program designed to alleviate or cure his supposed illness. Numerous witnesses, including one of O'Connor's codefendants, testified that Donaldson had received nothing but custodial care while at the hospital. O'Connor described Donaldson's treatment as "milieu therapy." But witnesses from the hospital staff conceded that, in the context of this case, "milieu therapy" was a euphemism for confinement in the "milieu" of a mental hospital. For substantial periods, Donaldson was simply kept in a large room that housed 60 patients, many of whom were under criminal commitment. Donaldson's requests for ground privileges, occupational training, and an opportunity to discuss his case with O'Connor or other staff members were repeatedly denied.

At the trial, O'Connor's principal defense was that he had acted in good faith and was therefore immune from any liability for monetary damages. His position, in short, was that state law, which he had believed valid, had authorized indefinite custodial confinement of the "sick," even if they were not given treatment and their release could harm no one.

The trial judge instructed the members of the jury that they should find that O'Connor had violated Donaldson's constitutional right to liberty if they found that he had

> "confined [Donaldson] against his will, knowing that he was not mentally ill or dangerous or knowing that if mentally ill he was not receiving treatment for his mental illness. . . .
> "Now the purpose of involuntary hospitalization is treatment and not mere custodial care or punishment if a patient is not a danger to himself or others. Without such treatment there is no justification from a constitutional standpoint for continued confinement unless you should also find that [Donaldson] was dangerous either to himself or others."

The trial judge further instructed the jury that O'Connor was immune from damages if he

> "reasonably believed in good faith that detention of [Donaldson] was proper for the length of time he was so confined. . . .
> "However, mere good intentions which do not give rise to a reasonable belief that detention is lawfully required cannot justify [Donaldson's] confinement in the Florida State Hospital."

The jury returned a verdict for Donaldson against O'Connor and a codefendant, and awarded damages of $38,500, including $10,000 in punitive damages.

The Court of Appeals affirmed the judgment of the District Court in a broad opinion dealing with "the far-reaching question whether the Fourteenth Amendment guarantees a right to treatment to persons involuntarily civilly committed to state mental hospitals." The appellate court held that when, as in Donaldson's case, the rationale for confinement is that the patient is in need of treatment, the Constitution requires that minimally adequate treatment in fact be provided. The court further expressed the view that, regardless of the grounds for involuntary civil commitment, a person confined against his will at a state mental institution has "a constitutional right to receive such individual treatment as will give him a reasonable opportunity to be cured or to improve his mental condition." Conversely, the court's opinion implied that it is constitutionally permissible for a State to confine a mentally ill person against his will in order to treat his illness, regardless of whether his illness renders him dangerous to himself or others.

II

We have concluded that the difficult issues of constitutional law dealt with by the Court of Appeals are not presented by this case in its present posture. Specifically, there is no reason now to decide whether mentally ill persons dangerous to themselves or to others have a right to treatment upon compulsory confinement by the State, or whether the State may compulsorily confine a nondangerous, mentally ill individual for the purpose of treatment. As we view it, this case raises a single, relatively simple, but nonetheless important question concerning every man's constitutional right to liberty.

The jury found that Donaldson was neither dangerous to himself nor dangerous to others, and also found that, if mentally ill, Donaldson had not received treatment. . . .

Given the jury's findings, what was left as justification for keeping Donaldson in continued confinement? The fact that state law may have authorized confinement of the harmless mentally ill does not itself establish a constitutionally adequate purpose for confinement. . . . Nor is it enough that Donaldson's original confinement was founded upon a constitutionally adequate basis, if in fact, because even if his involuntary confinement was initially permissible, it could not constitutionally continue after that basis no longer existed. . . .

A finding of "mental illness" alone cannot justify a State's locking a person up against his will and keeping him indefinitely in simple custodial confinement. Assuming that that term can be given a reasonably precise content and that the "mentally ill" can be identified with reasonable accuracy, there is still no constitutional basis for confining such persons involuntarily if they are dangerous to no one and can live safely in freedom.

May the State confine the mentally ill merely to ensure them a living standard superior to that they enjoy in the private community? That the State has a proper interest in providing care and assistance to the unfortunate goes without saying. But the mere presence of mental illness does not disqualify a person from preferring his home to the comforts of an institution. Moreover, while the State may arguably confine a person to save him from harm, incarceration is rarely if ever a necessary condition for raising the living standards of those capable of surviving safely in freedom on their own or with the help of family or friends. . . .

May the State fence in the harmless mentally ill solely to save its citizens from exposure to those whose ways are different? One might as well ask if the State, to avoid public unease, could incarcerate all who are physically unattractive or socially eccentric. Mere public intolerance or animosity cannot constitutionally justify the deprivation of a person's physical liberty. . . .

In short, a State cannot constitutionally confine without more [sic] a nondangerous individual who is capable of surviving safely in freedom by himself or with the help of willing and responsible family members or friends.

Since the jury found, upon ample evidence, that O'Connor, as an agent of the State, knowingly did so confine Donaldson, it properly concluded that O'Connor violated Donaldson's constitutional right to freedom.

III

O'Connor contends that in any event he should not be held personally liable for monetary damages because his decisions were made in "good faith." Specifically, O'Connor argues that he was acting pursuant to state law which, he believed, authorized confinement of the mentally ill even when their release would not compromise their safety or constitute a danger to others, and that he could not reasonably have been expected to know that the state law as he understood it was constitutionally invalid. A proposed instruction to this effect was rejected by the District Court.

The District Court did instruct the jury, without objection, that monetary damages could not be assessed against O'Connor if he had believed reasonably and in good faith that Donaldson's continued confinement was "proper," and that punitive damages could be awarded only if O'Connor had acted "maliciously or wantonly or oppressively." The Court of Appeals approved those instructions. But that court did not consider whether it was error for the trial judge to refuse the additional instruction concerning O'Connor's claimed reliance on state law as authorization for Donaldson's continued confinement. Further, neither the District Court nor the Court of Appeals acted with the benefit of this Court's most recent decision on the scope of the qualified immunity possessed by state officials under 42 U.S.C. § 1983.

Under that decision, the relevant question for the jury is whether O'Connor "knew or reasonably should have known that the action he took within his sphere of official responsibility would-violate the constitutional rights of [Donaldson], or if he took the action with the malicious intention to cause a deprivation of constitutional rights or other injury to [Donaldson]." . . . For purposes of this question, an official has, of course, no duty to anticipate unforeseeable constitutional developments.

Accordingly, we vacate the judgment of the Court of Appeals and remand the case to enable that court to consider, in light of Wood v. Strickland, whether the District Judge's failure to instruct with regard to the effect of O'Connor's claimed reliance on state law rendered inadequate the instructions as to O'Connor's liability for compensatory and punitive damages.

It is so ordered.

Vacated and remanded.

In *Donaldson*, the Supreme Court did not explicitly find a constitutional right to treatment. The Court also declined to rule on whether harmless persons may be held against their will as long as treatment is provided, or whether mentally ill persons who are dangerous have a right to treatment. Nevertheless, *Donaldson* clearly held that mental patients who are involuntarily committed to a state institution and who present no danger to themselves or others have a right to either treatment or release.

A federal court ordered St. Elizabeth's Hospital in Washington, D.C., to submit a plan to correct deficiencies in individual treatment for civilly committed patients in Dixon v. Weinberger, 405 F.Supp. 974 (D.D.C. 1975). Dixon was a sixty-five-year-old man who had spent twelve years in the hospital and eight years in a foster home. He was rehospitalized and sought legal counsel to help him return to a foster home. Although the judge's order required an outline of a plan in forty-five days, it took more than four years to develop it and two more years to implement it fully. The basis for the decision was not the least restrictive alternative, but a District of Columbia statute that promised to provide psychiatric care and treatment to committed patients.

A class action suit on behalf of institutionalized disabled persons (Pennhurst v. Halderman, 451 U.S. 1 [1981]), resulted in the Supreme Court's decision that the Federal Developmentally Disabled Aid Bill of Rights Act (42 U.S.C. Section 6010 [1976]), did not require the least restrictive setting. However, the least restrictive setting order was subsequently reinstated based on state law (Halderman v. Pennhurst 673 F.2d 647 [3d. Cir. 1982]).

The least restrictive alternative principle was also at the heart of a consent decree compelling western Massachusetts to establish a continuum of services (Brewster v. Dukakis, 520 F.Supp. 882 [D.Mass. (1981)]). Under this decree, Massachusetts was obligated to evacuate the Northampton State Hospital over a period of three years and substitute community residential and day-care programs. Herr (1983: 174) considers the *Brewster* decree "a binding blueprint for the creation of a comprehensive system of appropriate, less restrictive treatment, training, and support."

THE RIGHT TO REFUSE CERTAIN TREATMENTS

As of 1984 there have been no decisions on the right to refuse treatment by the U.S. Supreme Court. The Supreme Court of Minnesota reviewed electroshock therapy in terms of patients' rights in Price v. Sheppard, 239 N.W.2d 905 (Minn. 1976).

PRICE v. SHEPPARD

Supreme Court of Minnesota,
239 N.W.2d 905 (1976).

This appeal from a summary judgment entered in the Ramsey County District Court involves an action against the medical director of the Minnesota Security Hospital at St. Peter, Dr. Charles G. Sheppard, for (1) assault and battery, and (2) violation of plaintiff Dwight Price's civil rights under 42 U.S.C.A. § 1983. The claims arise out of the administration of a series of 20 electroshock treatments, given against the express wishes of plaintiff Willa Mae Price, Dwight's mother and natural guardian, while Dwight, a minor, was under involuntary commitment in the Minnesota Security Hospital at St. Peter.

Dwight's condition, upon his admission at St. Peter was diagnosed as simple schizophrenia. He was treated with tranquilizing and antidepressant medication, but apparently failed to respond and continued to be aggressive and assaultive to the staff and other patients. For this reason, Dr. Sheppard prescribed electroshock therapy.

He sought Mrs. Price's consent to administer the electroshock treatments. Through her attorney Mrs. Price arranged for an independent medical examination by Dr. William Chalgren, a Mankato psychiatrist, for the purpose of determining the advisability of the proposed treatment. Dr. Chalgren examined Dwight November 27, 1971, and recommended that drug treatment continue but that if Dwight did not respond favorably, electroshock treatment be given.

Dr. Chalgren's recommendations were followed by the staff at St. Peter, but Dwight's condition did not improve. Accordingly, on December 22, 1971, without the consent of Mrs. Price, electroshock therapy began and was continued to February 11, 1972. Dwight was released from St. Peter June 19, 1972.

The issues raised on this appeal are:

(1) Does the administration of electroshock therapy to an involuntary committed minor patient of a state mental hospital, without the consent of the minor's guardian, violate his rights (a) to be free from cruel and unusual punishment, and (b) of privacy?

(2) Is a state official entitled to immunity from an action for damages for acts performed by him in good faith and which he could not reasonably have known would violate the constitutional rights of another?

1. We do not agree with the claim that the electroshock therapy was cruel and unusual punishment for the reason that the record does not suggest, nor have plaintiffs demonstrated, how those treatments under the circumstances of this case, can be regarded as "punishment." While plaintiffs are certainly correct in the statement that the characterization of electroshock therapy by defendant as "treatment" does not insulate it from Eighth Amendment scrutiny, that alone does not establish that the treatments were "punishment."

It is difficult to perceive, on the record before the court, how the electroshock therapy administered to the plaintiff could be regarded as anything but treatment. The purpose of Dwight's presence in the state's mental hospital system was not to reprimand him or deter him from certain behavior but rather for the treatment of his mental problems and developing chemical dependency. Moreover, the decision to administer electroshock therapy was not triggered by any single incident nor did it involve an isolated treatment, both of which would be more characteristic of punishment. Rather, the decision to administer a series of 20 treatments over a substantial period of time was made after other forms of treatment failed to show any curative effect on Dwight's condition, diagnosed as schizophrenia. . . .

2. Plaintiffs second claimed violation of the minor's civil rights—the right of privacy—is more troublesome, primarily because that emerging right is currently so ill-defined. While its origins are said to date back to the late nineteenth century, its birth as an independent constitutional right, clearly denominated as such, is generally regarded as coming in Griswold v. Connecticut, 381 U.S. 479, 1965), where the court overturned a statute prohibiting the use of contraceptives by married couples. . . .

The question in the case before us is whether the state, consistent with Dwight Price's right of privacy, can assume the decision of whether Dwight, an involuntarily committed mental patient, will undergo psychiatric treatment. We observe that the more fundamental decision, whether he was to undergo hospitalization, was assumed by the state at the commitment proceeding, the validity of which is not contested.

The impact of the decision on the individual is unquestionably great, for the result is the alteration of the patient's personality. The state's interest in assuming the decision is in acting as *parens patriae*, fulfilling its duty to protect the well-being of its citizens who are incapable of so acting for themselves. Under the circumstances of this case, that interest can be articulated as the need for the state to assume the decision-making role regarding the psychiatric treatment for one who, presumptively, based on the fact of commitment on the ground of mental illness, is unable to *rationally* do so for himself. If that interest of the state is sufficiently important to deprive an individual of his physical liberty, it would seem to follow that it would be sufficiently important for the state to assume the treatment decision. We hold that it is. . . .

The more important question, we believe, involved in the state's assumption of the treatment decision is the necessity and reasonableness of the means utilized by the state in treating an involuntarily committed patient. The techniques generally available to treat psychological disorders range in degree of severity and coerciveness from the least intrusive forms such as milieu therapy (behavior changes produced by manipulation of the patient's environment) and psychoanalysis, to drug, aversion, or electroconvulsive therapy, and ultimately to psychosurgery. Some of these techniques require the voluntary participation of the patient in order to be effective, while others can be effective when involuntarily imposed. As the techniques increase in severity, so do the risks of serious and long-lasting psychological or neurological damage.

Whether the administration of electroshock treatments, one of the most intrusive forms of treatment, was necessary and reasonable in the treatment of Dwight Price is a question we cannot reach. We believe, and so hold, that whatever the answer to that question may be, on the record before us the defendant is immune from liability under 42 U.S.C.A. § 1983. . . .

Because the potential impact of the more intrusive forms of treatment is so great, we are reluctant in those cases where the patient or guardian refuse their consent, to leave the imposition of the more intrusive forms of treatment solely within the discretion of medical personnel at our state hospitals. For that reason, we adopt the following procedure for future cases:

(1) If the patient is incompetent to give consent or refuses consent or his guardian other than persons responsible for his commitment also refuses his consent, before more intrusive forms of treatment may be utilized, the medical director of the state hospital must petition the probate division of the county court in the county in which the hospital is located for an order authorizing the prescribed treatment;

(2) the court shall appoint a guardian ad litem to represent the interests of the patient;

(3) in an adversary proceeding, pursuant to the petition, the court shall determine the necessity and reasonableness of the prescribed treatment.

In making that determination the court should balance the patient's need for treatment against the intrusiveness of the prescribed treatment. Factors which should be considered are (1) the extent and duration of changes in behavior patterns and mental activity effected by the treatment, (2) the risks of adverse side effects, (3) the experimental nature of the treatment, (4) its acceptance by the medical community of this state, (5) the extent of intrusion into the patient's body and the pain connected with the treatment, and (6) the patient's ability to competently determine for himself whether the treatment is desirable.

We cannot draw a clear line between the more intrusive forms of treatment requiring this procedural hearing and those which do not. Certainly this procedure is not intended to apply to the use of mild tranquilizers or those therapies requiring the cooperation of the patient. On the other hand, given current medical practice, this procedure must be followed where psychosurgery or electroshock therapy is proposed.

Affirmed.

THE RIGHT TO REFUSE MEDICATION

In Mills v. Rogers, 457 U.S. 291 (1982), the U.S. Supreme Court was asked to consider whether an involuntarily committed mental patient may refuse treatment with antipsychotic drugs. Since the Court remanded the case in light of relevant state law, no binding policy resulted.

Subsequently a federal district court in California responded to a class action suit by approving a consent decree which clearly states that adults involuntarily committed to the largest mental health facility in the state have a right to refuse antipsychotic drugs (Jamison v. Farabee, consent decree no. 780445, 1983). They must be informed of possible side effects and other treatment options. They must give informed consent in order to receive such drugs, and they may revoke their consent at any time. If their physician feels that they cannot give informed consent, a review panel of physicians outside the facility will make a judgment.

MENTAL HEALTH SYSTEMS ACT BILL OF RIGHTS

The right to refuse treatment is part of a larger concern with the rights of involuntarily committed mental patients. In 1980, Congress passed the Mental Health Systems Act (P.L. 96-398, 94 Stat. 1598) to encourage the states to include the following bill of rights in their laws. However, this bill of rights has had little effect on state legislation or litigation.

MENTAL HEALTH SYSTEMS ACT BILL OF RIGHTS

SEC. 501. It is the sense of the Congress that each State should review and revise, if necessary, its laws to ensure that mental health patients receive the protection and services they require; and in making such review and revision should take into account the recommendations of the President's Commission on Mental Health and the following:

(1) A person admitted to a program or facility for the purpose of receiving mental health services should be accorded the following:

(A) The right to appropriate treatment and related services in a setting and under conditions that—

(i) are the most supportive of such person's personal liberty; and

(ii) restrict such liberty only to the extent necessary consistent with such person's treatment needs, applicable requirements of law, and applicable judicial orders.

(B) The right to an individualized, written treatment or service plan (such plan to be developed promptly after admission of such person), the right to treatment based on such plan, the right to periodic review and reassessment of treatment and related service needs, and the right to appropriate revision of such plan, including any revision necessary to provide a description of mental health services that may be needed after such person is discharged from such program or facility.

(C) The right to ongoing participation, in a manner appropriate to such person's capabilities, in the planning of mental health services to be provided such person (including the right to participate in the development and periodic revision of the plan described in subparagraph (B)), and, in connection with such participation, the right to be provided with a reasonable explanation, in terms and language appropriate to such person's condition and ability to understand, of—

(i) such person's general mental condition and, if such program or facility has provided a physical examination, such person's general physical condition;

(ii) the objectives of treatment;

(iii) the nature and significant possible adverse effects of recommended treatments;

(iv) the reasons why a particular treatment is considered appropriate;

(v) the reasons why access to certain visitors may not be appropriate; and

(vi) any appropriate and available alternative treatments, services, and types of providers of mental health services.

(D) The right not to receive a mode or course of treatment, established pursuant to the treatment plan, in the absence of such person's informed, voluntary, written consent to such mode or course of treatment, except treatment—

(i) during an emergency situation if such treatment is pursuant to or documented contemporaneously by the written order of a responsible mental health professional; or

(ii) as permitted under applicable law in the case of a person committed by a court to a treatment program or facility.

(E) The right not to participate in experimentation in the absence of such person's informed, voluntary, written consent, the right to appropriate protections in connection with such participation, including the right to a reasonable explanation of the procedure to be followed, the benefits to be expected, the relative advantages of alternative treatments, and the potential discomforts and risks, and the right and opportunity to revoke such consent.

(F) The right to freedom from restraint or seclusion, other than as a mode or course of treatment or restraint or seclusion during an emergency situation if such restraint or seclusion is pursuant to or documented contemporaneously by the written order of a responsible mental health professional.

(G) The right to a humane treatment environment that affords reasonable protection from harm and appropriate privacy to such person with regard to personal needs.

(H) The right to confidentiality of such person's records.

(I) The right to access, upon request, to such person's mental health care records, except such person may be refused access to—

(i) information on such records provided by a third party under assurance that such information shall remain confidential; and

(ii) specific material in such records if the health professional responsible for the mental health services concerned has made a determination in writing that such access would be detrimental to such person's health, except that such material may be made available to a similarly licensed health professional selected by such person and such health professional may, in the exercise of professional judgment, provide such person with access to any or all parts of such material or otherwise disclose the information contained in such material to such person.

(J) The right, in the case of a person admitted on a residental or inpatient care basis, to converse with others privately, to have convenient and reasonable access to the telephone and mails, and to see visitors during regularly scheduled hours, except that, if a mental health professional treating such person determines that denial of access to a particular visitor is necessary for treatment purposes, such mental health professional may, for a specific, limited, and reasonable period of time, deny such access if such mental health professional has ordered such denial in writing and such order has been incorporated in the treatment plan for such person. An order denying such access should include the reasons for such denial.

(K) The right to be informed promptly at the time of admission and periodically thereafter, in language and terms appropriate to such person's condition and ability to understand, of the rights described in this section.

(L) The right to assert grievances with respect to infringement of the rights described in this section, including the right to have such grievances considered in a fair, timely, and impartial grievance procedure provided for or by the program or facility.

(M) Notwithstanding subparagraph (J), the right of access to (including the opportunities and facilities for private communication with) any available—

(i) rights protection service within the program or facility;

(ii) rights protection service within the State mental health system designed to be available to such person; and

(iii) qualified advocate;

for the purpose of receiving assistance to understand, exercise, and protect the rights described in this section and in other provisions of law.

(N) The right to exercise the rights described in this section without reprisal, including reprisal in the form of denial of any appropriate, available treatment.

(O) The right to referral as appropriate to other providers of mental health services upon discharge.

(2)(A) The rights described in this section should be in addition to and not in derogation of any other statutory or constitutional rights.

(B) The rights to confidentiality of and access to records as provided in subparagraphs (H) and (I) of paragraph (1) should remain applicable to records pertaining to a person after such person's discharge from a program or facility.

(3)(A) No otherwise eligible person should be denied admission to a program or facility for mental health services as a reprisal for the exercise of the rights described in this section.

(B) Nothing in this section should—

(i) obligate an individual mental health or health professional to administer treatment contrary to such professional's clinical judgment;

(ii) prevent any program or facility from discharging any person for whom the provision of appropriate treatment, consistent with the clinical judgment of the mental health professional primarily responsible for such person's treatment, is or has become impossible as a result of such person's refusal to consent to such treatment;

(iii) require a program or facility to admit any person who, while admitted on prior occasions to such program or facility, has repeatedly frustrated the purposes of such admissions by withholding consent to proposed treatment; or

(iv) obligate a program or facility to provide treatment services to any person who is admitted to such program or facility solely for diagnostic or evaluative purposes.

(C) In order to assist a person admitted to a program or facility in the exercise or protection of such person's rights, such person's attorney or legal representatives should have reasonable access to—

(i) such person;

(ii) the areas of the program or facility where such person has received treatment, resided, or had access; and

(iii) pursuant to the written authorization of such person, the records and information pertaining to such person's diagnosis, treatment, and related services described in paragraph (1)(I).

(D) Each program and facility should post a notice listing and describing, in language and terms appropriate to the ability of the persons to whom such notice is addressed to understand, the rights described in this section of all persons admitted to such program or facility. Each such notice should conform to the format and content for such notices, and should be posted in all appropriate locations.

(4)(A) In the case of a person adjudicated by a court of competent jurisdiction as being incompetent to exercise the right to consent to treatment or experimentation described in subparagraph (D) or (E) of paragraph (1), or the right to confidentiality of or access to records described in subparagraph (H) or (I) of such paragraph, or to provide authorization as described in paragraph (3)(C)(iii), such right may be exercised or such authorization may be provided by the individual appointed by such court as such person's guardian or representative for the purpose of exercising such right or such authorization.

(B) In the case of a person who lacks capacity to exercise the right to consent to treatment or experimentation under subparagraph (D) or (E) of paragraph (1), or the right to confidentiality of or access to records described in subparagraph (H) or (I) of such paragraph, or to provide authorization as described in paragraph (3)(C)(iii), because such person has not attained an age considered sufficiently advanced under State law to permit the exercise of such right or such authorization to be legally binding, such right may be exercised or such authorization may be provided on behalf of such person by a parent or legal guardian of such person.

(C) Notwithstanding subparagraphs (A) and (B), in the case of a person admitted to a program or facility for the purpose of receiving mental health services, no individual employed by or receiving any remuneration from such program or facility should act as such person's guardian or representative.

Such lists of rights may falsely suggest that clients' needs are being met. However, according to Herr, Arons, and Wallace (1983: 162):

"It is not enough merely to post lists of rights on facility walls or to distribute booklets. By their own observations of staff, patients will soon learn whether a facility gives concrete form to the concept of human dignity and teaches patients how to respond to the rights and responsibilities in their own lives. For instance, staffs could organize programs to help psychiatric inpatients to vote, to claim their welfare entitlements, or to understand the consequences of bizarre or antisocial behavior that can lead to conflict with the criminal-justice system."

Violations of patient rights are still not uncommon. A summary of a Texas decision, Luna v. Van Zandt (554 F.Supp. 68 [D. Tex. 1982]), from the *Clearinghouse Review* (1983) illustrates statutory problems remedied recently through state courts:

The court held unconstitutional a Texas statute's protective custody provision that permitted involuntary detention without a prior probable cause hearing and without notice of the grounds and authority for the protective custody of persons subject to involuntary commitment proceedings. The protective orders were issued ex parte by the county judge after applications for temporary or indefinite commitment proceedings had been filed. They could be issued only for those persons who posed an immediate threat of harm to themselves or others. Under the statute, subjects of petitions for temporary hospitalization could be held up to 14 days and subjects of indefinite commitment hearings could be held up to 30 days. In ruling, the court considered the question of whether the period of confinement bore a reasonable relationship to the justification for confinement given by the state. Finding none, the court held that the statute violated due process and that the state must provide a probable cause hearing within 72 hours of taking a person into protective custody.

THE DUTY TO WARN OF DANGEROUS-NESS   The rights of mental health clients, whether involuntarily committed or outpatient, must be balanced against the protection of others. Tarasoff v. Regents of University of California, 551 P.2d 334 (Cal.) decided in 1976 by the California Supreme court, has provoked considerable debate between mental health professionals and legal advocates.

TARASOFF v. REGENTS OF UNIVERSITY OF CALIFORNIA

551 P.2d 334 (1976).

On October 27, 1969, Prosenjit Poddar killed Tatiana Tarasoff. Plaintiffs, Tatiana's parents, allege that two months earlier Poddar confided his intention to kill Tatiana to Dr. Lawrence Moore, a psychologist employed by the Cowell Memorial Hospital at the University of California at Berkeley. They allege that on Moore's request, the campus police briefly detained Poddar, but released him when he appeared rational. They further claim that Dr. Harvey Powelson, Moore's superior, then directed that no further action be taken to detain Poddar. No one warned plaintiffs of Tatiana's peril.

Concluding that these facts set forth causes of action against neither therapists and policemen involved, nor against the Regents of the University of California as their employer, the superior court sustained defendants' demurrers to plaintiffs' second amended complaints without leave to amend. . . .

Plaintiffs' complaints predicate liability on two grounds: defendants' failure to warn plaintiffs of the impending danger and their failure to bring about Poddar's confinement. Defendants, in turn assert that they owed no duty of reasonable care to Tatiana.

We shall explain that defendant therapists cannot escape liability merely because Tatiana herself was not their patient. When a therapist determines, or pursuant to the standards of his profession should determine, that his patient presents a serious danger of violence to another, he incurs an obligation to use reasonable care to protect the intended victim against such danger. The discharge of this duty may require the therapist to take one or more of various steps, depending upon the nature of the case. Thus it may call for him to warn the intended victim or others likely to apprise the victim of the danger, to notify the police, or to take whatever other steps are reasonably necessary under the circumstances.

In the case at bar, plaintiffs admit that defendant therapists notified the police, but argue on appeal that the therapists failed to exercise reasonable care to protect Tatiana in that they did not confine Poddar and did not warn Tatiana or others likely to apprise her of the danger. Defendant therapists, however, are public employees. Consequently, to the extent that plaintiffs seek to predicate liability upon the therapists' failure to bring about Poddar's confinement, the therapists can claim immunity. No specific statutory provision, however, shields them from liability based upon failure to warn Tatiana or others likely to apprise her of the danger and Government Code section 820.2 does not protect such failure as an exercise of discretion.

Plaintiffs therefore can amend their complaints to allege that, regardless of the therapists' unsuccessful attempt to confine Poddar, since they knew that Poddar was at large and dangerous, their failure to warn Tatiana or others likely to apprise her of the danger constituted a breach of the therapists' duty to exercise reasonable care to protect Tatiana.

Two significant findings are highlighted in *Tarasoff*:

> Once a therapist does in fact determine, or under applicable professional standards reasonably should have determined, that a patient poses a serious danger of violence to others, he bears a duty to exercise reasonable care to protect the foreseeable victim of that danger. While the discharge of this duty of due care will necessarily vary with the facts of each case, in each instance the adequacy of the therapist's conduct must be measured against the traditional negligence standard of reasonable care under the circumstances. . . .
>
> Within the broad range of reasonable practice and treatment in which professional opinion and judgment may differ, the therapist is free to exercise his or her own best judgment without liability; proof, aided by hindsight, that he or she judged wrongly is insufficient to establish negligence.

Beis (1984: 75) provides the following suggestions on the determination of danger:

> A therapist first must determine whether his or her patient poses a serious danger to an identifiable third party or parties. If such a danger is posed, the therapist then must determine what protective action must be taken. Several factors are relevant to these determinations, among them the seriousness of the threatened harm, the likelihood that the patient will harm the third party, the standards in the therapeutic community for assessing the danger and its likelihood, and the impact of protective action on the third party and the patient.
>
> The more serious the threatened harm, the more likely it is that some action is necessary to protect the third party. A wide difference exists between harm threatened with a dangerous weapon—such as a knife, a revolver, or poison—and a threatened punch in the mouth or slap across the face.
>
> The likelihood of the patient carrying out the threatened harm may require consideration of many factors. Were similar threats of serious harm made in the past carried out? Is there any other history of threats or overt acts of harm? Is the likelihood of harm based solely on the prediction of dangerousness without any recent overt threat or harm as a basis? Is the patient suffering from a delusion involving the third party, upon which he or she may act in a violent way? Other factors that may be relevant are the degree of psychotic manifestations, the patient's cultural background, and whether the patient has a history of being physically assaulted as a child. The more likely the harm, the more likely it is that some protective action will be necessary.

In McIntosh v. Milano, 403 A.2d. 500 (N.J. Super. 1979), a seventeen-year-old patient who had received counseling for two years related his sexual and emotional involvements with a twenty-one-year-old woman who lived next door. He admitted firing a BB gun at her car and her house, but according to the psychiatrist had never threatened to harm her. The patient obtained a pistol and fatally shot the woman. On the day of the murder he stole a prescription form from the psychiatrist. The pharmacist became suspicious and called the psychiatrist, who advised him not to fill the prescription for Seconal. The psychiatrist also tried to telephone the patient. The court found the psychiatrist liable and rejected arguments that he could not accurately predict dangerousness. The court rejected the allegation that duty to warn would interfere with the treatment of a violent patient and increase involuntary hospital admissions.

Research on the impact of *Tarasoff* on clinical social work practice suggests that the court's mandate to warn was not as influential with practitioners as their individual professional and personal ethics (Weil and Sanchez, 1983). After initial concern when the case was decided, many clinicians concluded that the need to exercise professional judgment about dangerousness was not a major problem.

However, a recent case, Hedlund v. Superior Court (669 P.2d 41[Cal. 1983]), appears to expand the duty to warn of dangerousness. In *Hedlund*, the California Supreme Court refused to dismiss an action against two pyschologists after a patient had stated an intent to injure LaNita Wilson and later did so. Her son was injured in the same incident.

> LaNita alleges as her cause of action that petitioners had rendered health care services to herself and to Stephen Wilson in the form of psychotherapy, counseling and treatment; that prior to April 9, 1979, Stephen told petitioners of his intent to commit serious bodily injury upon her, and that from his communications to them petitioners, in the exercise of the professional skill, knowledge, and care possessed by members of their specialty, should have known that Stephen presented a serious danger of violence to her. She further alleges that petitioners owed her and other foreseeable victims a duty to diagnose Stephen's condition, to realize that he presented a serious threat of violence to her, and to recognize that the requirements of their profession required them to notify her of the danger. Allegedly this duty was breached when petitioners failed to warn her of the danger. Thereafter, on April 9, 1979, Stephen used a shotgun to inflict serious bodily injury on LaNita. (669 P.2d at 42–43).
>
> Darryl, incorporating the allegations of LaNita's cause of action by reference, alleges that he was born on June 5, 1976. He was seated next to his mother when she was shot by Stephen. She threw herself over him thereby saving his life and preventing serious physical injury to him, but, as a result of the attack he has suffered serious emotional injuries and psychological trauma. Darryl alleges that because it was foreseeable that Stephen's threats, if carried out, posed a risk of harm to bystanders and particularly to those in close relationship to LaNita, petitioners' duty extended to him, and that this duty was breached when they failed to act to protect LaNita and such foreseeable individuals. (Id at 46).

This decision emphasized that a failure to warn a third person of a danger posed by a patient is an act of omission to act in the provision of professional services for which the provider is licensed. The court held that professional negligence was involved and that the action was not time-barred because the three-year statute of limitations for personal injury actions against health-care providers is applicable under the circumstances. The court held further that the negligence involved a duty to the minor child who may be injured or suffer emotional trauma.

In 1983, California passed two laws intended to protect the public against involuntarily committed patients once they are released. Mental hospital staff may now hold patients for an additional six months if they threaten to injure someone once they are released. Mental hospital officials are now required—if requested to do so—to notify local law enforcement and mental health authorities when a patient is released from involuntary commitment.

The inability of clinicians to predict the future so zealously pointed to by mental health rights advocates makes the emerging duty to warn of the dangerousness of patients even more difficult. This balancing of the rights of the individual with the rights of society, as well as the tension between the legal and mental health professions, suggests that laws related to mental health and institutionalized persons will continue to be controversial.

Dangerous patients also may act out against the therapist. While this issue is not prominent in the legal literature, it is a major practical concern. Considerable risk is also involved in investigative roles for social workers in child abuse cases. Increasing experience with these problems has overcome the reluctance to use police protection.

HOSPITALIZED MINORS

The U.S. Supreme Court has ruled that parents may commit their children to a mental health facility without a judicial hearing that would provide due process procedures (Parham v. J.R., 442 U.S. 584 [1979]). The majority assumed that most parents do what is best for their child. The few who do not would be revealed by requiring an independent assessment by a staff physician.

PARHAM v. J.R.

Supreme Court of the United States, 442 U.S. 584 (1979).

The question presented in this appeal is what process is constitutionally due a minor child whose parents or guardian seek state administered institutional mental health care for the child and specifically whether an adversary proceeding is required prior to or after the commitment.

I

(a) Appellee J.R., a child being treated in a Georgia state mental hospital, was a plaintiff in this class action based on 42 U.S.C. § 1983, in the District Court for the Middle District of Georgia. . . .

. . . Appellee sought a declaratory judgment that Georgia's voluntary commitment procedures for children under the age of 18, Ga. Code §§ 88-503.1, 88-503.2 (1975), violated the Due Process Clause of the Fourteenth Amendment and requested an injunction against their future enforcement.

A three-judge District Court was convened pursuant to 28 U.S.C. §§ 2281 (1970 ed.) and 2284. After considering expert and lay testimony and extensive exhibits and after visiting two of the State's regional mental health hospitals, the District Court held that Georgia's statutory scheme was unconstitutional because it failed to protect adequately the appellees' due process rights. J. L. v. Parham, 412 F.Supp. 112, 139 (1976).

To remedy this violation, the court enjoined future commitments based on the procedures in the Georgia statute. It also commanded Georgia to appropriate and expend whatever amount was "reasonably necessary" to provide nonhospital facilities deemed by the appellant state officials to be the most appropriate for the treatment of those members of plaintiffs' class, n. 2, *supra*, who could be treated in a less drastic, nonhospital environment.

Appellee J.R. was declared a neglected child by the county and removed from his natural parents when he was 3 months old. He was placed in seven different foster homes in succession prior to his admission to Central State Hospital at the age of 7.

Immediately preceding his hospitalization, J.R. received outpatient treatment at a county mental health center for several months. He then began attending school where he was so disruptive and incorrigible that he could not conform to normal behavior patterns. Because of his abnormal behavior, J.R.'s seventh set of foster parents requested his removal from their home. The Department of Family and Children Services then sought his admission at Central State. The agency provided the hospital with a complete sociomedical history at the time of his admission. In addition, three separate interviews were conducted with J.R. by the admission team of the hospital.

It was determined that he was borderline retarded, and suffered an "unsocialized, aggressive reaction of childhood." It was recommended unanimously that he would "benefit from the structured environment" of the hospital and would "enjoy living and playing with boys of the same age."

J.R.'s progress was re-examined periodically. In addition, unsuccessful efforts were made by the Department of Family and Children Services during his stay at the hospital to place J.R. in various foster homes. On October 24, 1975, J.R. (with J.L.) filed his suit requesting an order of the court placing him in a less drastic environment suitable to his needs.

(d) Georgia Code § 88-503.1 (1975) provides for the voluntary admission to a state regional hospital of children such as J.L. and J.R. Under that provision, admission begins with an application for hospitalization signed by a "parent or guardian." Upon application, the superintendent of each hospital is given the power to admit temporarily any child for "observation and diagnosis." If, after observation, the superintendent finds "evidence of mental illness" and that the child is "suitable for treatment" in the hospital, then the child may be admitted "for such period and under such conditions as may be authorized by law."

Georgia's mental health statute also provides for the discharge of voluntary patients. Any child who has been hospitalized for more than five days may be discharged at the request of a parent or guardian. § 88-503.3 (a) (1975). Even without a request for discharge, however, the superintendent of each regional hospital has an affirmative duty to release any child "who has recovered from his mental illness or who has sufficiently improved that the superintendent determines that hospitalization of the patient is no longer desirable." § 88-503.2 (1975).

Georgia's Mental Health Director has not published any statewide regulations defining what specific procedures each superintendent must employ when admitting a child under 18. Instead, each regional hospital's superintendent is responsible for the procedures in his or her facility. There is substantial variation among the institutions with regard to their admission procedures and their procedures for review of patients after they have been admitted. . . .

The children's unit at Central State Regional Hospital in Milledgeville, Ga., was added to the existing structure during the 1970's. It can accommodate 40 children. The hospital also can house 40 adolescents. At the time of suit, the hospital housed 37 children under 18, including both named plaintiffs.

Although Central State is affiliated with community clinics, it seems to have a higher percentage of nonreferral admissions than any of the other hospitals. The admission decision is made by an "admissions evaluator" and the "admitting physician." The evaluator is a Ph.D. in psychology, a social worker, or a mental-health-trained nurse. The admitting physician is a psychiatrist. The standard for admission is "whether or not hospitalization is the more appropriate treatment" for the child. From April 1974 to November 1975, 9 of 29 children applicants screened for admission were referred to noninstitutional settings.

II

In holding unconstitutional Georgia's statutory procedure for voluntary commitment of juveniles, the District Court first determined that commitment to any of the eight regional hospitals constitutes a severe deprivation of a child's liberty. The court defined this liberty interest in terms of both freedom from bodily restraint and freedom from the "emotional and psychic harm" caused by the institutionalization. Having determined that a liberty interest is implicated by a child's admission to a mental hospital, the court considered what process is required to protect that interest. It held that the process due "includes at least the right after notice to be heard before an impartial tribunal." 412 F.Supp., at 137.

In requiring the prescribed hearing, the court rejected Georgia's argument that no adversary-type hearing was required since the State was merely assisting parents who could not afford private care by making available treatment similar to that offered in private hospitals and by private physicians. The court acknowledged that most parents who seek to have their children admitted to a state mental hospital do so in good faith. It, however, relied on one of appellees' witnesses who expressed an opinion that "some still look upon mental hospitals as a 'dumping ground'." Id., at 138. No specific evidence of such "dumping," however, can be found in the record.

The District Court also rejected the argument that review by the superintendents of the hospitals and their staffs was sufficient to protect the child's liberty interest. The court held that the inexactness of psychiatry, coupled with the possibility that the sources of information used to make the commitment decision may not always be reliable, made the superintendent's decision too arbitrary to satisfy due process. The court then shifted its focus drastically from what was clearly a procedural due process analysis to what appears to be a substantive due process analysis and condemned Georgia's "officialdom" for its failure, in the face of a state-funded 1973 report outlining the "need" for additional resources to be spent on nonhospital treatment, to provide more resources for noninstitutional mental health care. The court concluded that there was a causal relationship between this intransigence and the State's ability to provide any "flexible due process" to the appellees. The District Court therefore ordered the State to appropriate and expend such resources as would be necessary to provide nonhospital treatment to those members of appellees' class who would benefit from it.

As medical knowledge about the mentally ill and public concern for their condition expanded, the states, aided substantially by federal grants, have sought to ameliorate the human tragedies of seriously disturbed children. Ironically, as most states have expanded their efforts to assist the mentally ill, their actions have been subjected to increasing litigation and heightened constitutional scrutiny. Courts have been required to resolve the thorny constitutional attacks on state programs and procedures with limited precedential guidance. In this case, appellees have challenged Georgia's procedural and substantive balance of the individual, family, and social interests at stake in the voluntary commitment of a child to one of its regional mental hospitals.

The parties agree that our prior holdings have set out a general approach for testing challenged state procedures under a due process claim. Assuming the existence of a protectable property or liberty interest, the Court has required a balancing of a number of factors:

> "First, the private interest that will be affected by the official action; second, the risk of an erroneous deprivation of such interest through the procedures used, and the probable value, if any, of additional or substitute procedural safeguards; and finally, the Government's interest, including the function involved and the fiscal and administrative burdens that the additional or substitute procedural requirement would entail." Mathews v. Eldridge, 424 U.S. 319, 335 (1976), quoted in Smith v. Organization of Foster Families, 431 U.S. 816, 848–849 (1977).

In applying these criteria, we must consider first the child's interest in not being committed. Normally, however, since this interest is inextricably linked with the parents' interest in and obligation for the welfare and health of the child, the private interest at stake is a combination of the child's and parents' concerns. Next, we must examine the State's interest in the procedures it has adopted for commitment and treatment of children. Finally, we must consider how well Georgia's procedures protect against arbitrariness in the decision to commit a child to a state mental hospital.

(a) It is not disputed that a child, in common with adults, has a substantial liberty interest in not being confined unnecessarily for medical treatment and that the state's involvement in the commitment decision constitutes state action under the Fourteenth Amendment. We also recognize that commitment sometimes produces adverse social consequences for the child because of the reaction of some to the discovery that the child has received psychiatric care.

The state through its voluntary commitment procedures does not "label" the child; it provides a diagnosis and treatment that medical specialists conclude the child requires. In terms of public reaction, the child who exhibits abnormal behavior may be seriously injured by an erroneous decision not to commit. Appellees overlook a significant source of the public reaction to the mentally ill, for what is truly "stigmatizing" is the symptomatology of a mental or emotional illness. The pattern of untreated, abnormal behavior— even if nondangerous—arouses at least as much negative reaction as treatment that becomes public knowledge. A person needing, but not receiving, appropriate medical care may well face even greater social ostracism resulting from the observable symptoms of an untreated disorder.

However, we need not decide what effect these factors might have in a different case. For purposes of this decision, we assume that a child has a protectable interest not only in being free of unnecessary bodily restraints but also in not being labeled erroneously by some persons because of an improper decision by the state hospital superintendent.

(b) We next deal with the interests of the parents who have decided, on the basis of their observations and independent professional recommendations, that their child needs institutional care. Appellees argue that the constitutional rights of the child are of such magnitude and the likelihood of parental abuse is so great that the parents' traditional interests in and responsibility for the upbringing of their child must be subordinated at least to the extent of providing a formal adversary hearing prior to a voluntary commitment.

Our jurisprudence historically has reflected Western civilization concepts of the family as a unit with broad parental authority over minor children. Our cases have consistently followed that course; our constitutional system long ago rejected any notion that a child is "the mere creature of the State" and, on the contrary, asserted that parents generally "have the right, coupled with the high duty, to recognize and prepare [their children] for additional obligations." Surely, this includes a "high duty" to recognize symptoms of illness and to seek and follow medical advice. The law's concept of the family rests on a presumption that parents possess what a child lacks in maturity, experience, and capacity for judgment required for making life's difficult decisions. More important, historically it has recognized that natural bonds of affection lead parents to act in the best interests of their children. . . .

As with so many other legal presumptions, experience and reality may rebut what the law accepts as a starting point; the incidence of child neglect and abuse cases attests to this. That some parents "may at times be acting against the interests of their children" as we stated in Bartley v. Kremens, 402 F.Supp. 1039, 1047–1048 (E.D.Pa. 1975), vacated and remanded 431 U.S. 119 (1977), creates a basis for caution, but is hardly a reason to discard wholesale those pages of human experience that teach that parents generally do act in the child's best interests. The statist notion that governmental power should supersede parental authority in *all* cases because *some* parents abuse and neglect children is repugnant to American tradition.

Nonetheless, we have recognized that a state is not without constitutional control over parental discretion in dealing with children when their physical or mental health is jeopardized. Moreover, the Court recently declared unconstitutional a state statute that granted parents an absolute veto over a minor child's decision to have an abortion. Appellees urge that these precedents limiting the traditional rights of parents, if viewed in the context of the liberty interest of the child and the likelihood of parental abuse, require us to hold that the parents' decision to have a child admitted to a mental hospital must be subjected to an exacting constitutional scrutiny, including a formal, adversary, pre-admission hearing.

Appellees' argument, however, sweeps too broadly. Simply because the decision of a parent is not agreeable to a child or because it involves risks does not automatically transfer the power to make that decision from the parents to some agency or officer of the state. The same characterizations can be made for a tonsillectomy, appendectomy, or other medical procedure. Most children, even in adolescence, simply are not able to make sound judgments concerning many decisions, including their need for medical care or treatment. Parents can and must make those judgments. Here, there is no finding by the District Court of even a single instance of bad faith by any parent of any member of appellees' class. . . .

The fact that a child may balk at hospitalization or complain about a parental refusal to provide cosmetic surgery does not diminish the parents' authority to decide what is best for the child.

Parents in Georgia in no sense have an absolute right to commit their children to state mental hospitals; the statute requires the superintendent of each regional hospital to exercise independent judgment as to the child's need for confinement.

In defining the respective rights and prerogatives of the child and parent in the voluntary commitment setting, we conclude that our precedents permit the parents to retain a substantial, if not the dominant, role in the decision, absent a finding of neglect or abuse, and that the traditional presumption that the parents act in the best interests of their child should apply. We also conclude, however, that the child's rights and the nature of the commitment decision are such that parents cannot always have absolute and unreviewable discretion to decide whether to have a child institutionalized. They, of course, retain plenary authority to seek such care for their children, subject to a physician's independent examination and medical judgment.

(c) The State obviously has a significant interest in confining the use of its costly mental health facilities to cases of genuine need. The Georgia program seeks first to determine whether the patient seeking admission has an illness that calls for inpatient treatment. To accomplish this purpose, the State has charged the superintendents of each regional hospital with the responsibility for determining, before authorizing an admission, whether a prospective patient is mentally ill and whether the patient will likely benefit from hospital care. In addition, the State has imposed a continuing duty on hospital superintendents to release any patient who has recovered to the point where hospitalization is no longer needed.

The State in performing its voluntarily assumed mission also has a significant interest in not imposing unnecessary procedural obstacles that may discourage the mentally ill or their families from seeking needed psychiatric assistance. The *parens patriae* interest in helping parents care for the mental health of their children cannot be fulfilled if the parents are unwilling to take advantage of the opportunities because the admission process is too onerous, too embarrassing, or too contentious. It is surely not idle to speculate as to how many parents who believe they are acting in good faith would forgo state-provided hospital care if such care is contingent on participation in an adversary proceeding designed to probe their motives and other private family matters in seeking the voluntary admission.

The State also has a genuine interest in allocating priority to the diagnosis and treatment of patients as soon as they are admitted to a hospital rather than to time-consuming procedural minuets before the admission. One factor that must be considered is the utilization of the time of psychiatrists, psychologists, and other behavioral specialists in preparing for and participating in hearings rather than performing the task for which their special training has fitted them. Behavioral experts in courtrooms and hearings are of little help to patients.

The amici brief of the American Psychiatric Association et al. points out at page 20 that the average staff psychiatrist in a hospital presently is able to devote only 47% of his time to direct patient care. One consequence of increasing the procedures the state must provide prior to a child's voluntary admission will be that mental health professionals will be diverted even more from the treatment of patients in order to travel to and participate in—and wait for—what could be hundreds—or even thousands—of hearings each year. Obviously the cost of these procedures would come from the public moneys the legislature intended for mental health care.

(d) We now turn to consideration of what process protects adequately the child's constitutional rights by reducing risks of error without unduly trenching on traditional parental authority and without undercutting "efforts to further the legitimate interests of both the state and the patient that are served by" voluntary commitments. We conclude that the risk of error inherent in the parental decision to have a child institutionalized for mental health care is sufficiently great that some kind of inquiry should be made by a "neutral factfinder" to determine whether statutory requirements for admission are satisfied.

Another problem with requiring a formalized, factfinding hearing lies in the danger it poses for significant intrusion into the parent-child relationship. Pitting the parents and child as adversaries often will be at odds with the presumption that parents act in the best interests of their child. It is one thing to require a neutral physician to make a careful review of the parents' decision in order to make sure it is proper from a medical standpoint; it is a wholly different matter to employ an adversary contest to ascertain whether the parents' motivation is consistent with the child's interests.

Moreover, it is appropriate to inquire into how such a hearing would contribute to the successful long-range treatment of the patient. Surely, there is a risk that it would exacerbate whatever tensions already exist between the child and the parents. Since the parents can and usually do play a significant role in the treatment while the child is hospitalized and even more so after release, there is a serious risk that an adversary confrontation will adversely affect the ability of the parents to assist the child while in the hospital. Moreover, it will make his subsequent return home more difficult. These unfortunate results are especially critical with an emotionally disturbed child; they seem likely to occur in the context of an adversary hearing in which the parents testify. A confrontation over such intimate family relationships would distress the normal adult parents and the impact on a disturbed child almost certainly would be significantly greater.

It has been suggested that a hearing conducted by someone other than the admitting physician is necessary in order to detect instances where parents are "guilty of railroading their children into asylums" or are using "voluntary commitment procedures in order to sanction behavior of which they disapprov[e]." Curiously, it seems to be taken for granted that parents who seek to "dump" their children on the state will inevitably be able to conceal their motives and thus deceive the admitting psychiatrists and the other mental health professionals who make and review the admission decision. It is elementary that one early diagnostic inquiry into the cause of an emotional disturbance of a child is an examination into the environment of the child. It is unlikely, if not inconceivable, that a decision to abandon an emotionally normal, healthy child and thrust him into an institution will be a discrete act leaving no trail of circumstances. Evidence of such conflicts will emerge either in the interviews or from secondary sources. It is unrealistic to believe that trained psychiatrists, skilled in eliciting responses, sorting medically relevant facts, and sensing motivational nuances will often be deceived about the family situation surrounding a child's emotional disturbance. Surely a lay, or even law-trained, factfinder would be no more skilled in this process than the professional.

By expressing some confidence in the medical decision-making process, we are by no means suggesting it is error free. On occasion, parents may initially mislead an admitting physician or a physician may erroneously diagnose the child as needing institutional care either because of negligence or an overabundance of caution. That there may be risks of error in the process affords no rational predicate for holding unconstitutional an entire statutory and administrative scheme that is generally followed in more than 30 states. . . .

In general, we are satisfied that an independent medical decisionmaking process, which includes the thorough psychiatric investigation described earlier, followed by additional periodic review of a child's condition, will protect children who should not be admitted; we do not believe the risks of error in that process would be significantly reduced by a more formal, judicial-type hearing. The issue remains whether the Georgia practices, as described in the record before us, comport with these minimum due process requirements.

(e) Georgia's statute envisions a careful diagnostic medical inquiry to be conducted by the admitting physician at each regional hospital. The amicus brief for the United States explains, at pages 7–8:

"[I]n every instance the decision whether or not to accept the child for treatment is made by a physician employed by the State. . . .

"That decision is based on interviews and recommendations by hospital or community health center staff. The staff interviews the child and the parent or guardian who brings the child to the facility . . . [and] attempts are made to communicate with other possible sources of information about the child. . . ."

Focusing primarily on what it saw as the absence of any formal mechanism for review of the physician's initial decision, the District Court unaccountably saw the medical decision as an exercise of "unbridled discretion." 412 F.Supp., at 136. But extravagant characterizations are no substitute for careful analysis, and we must examine the Georgia process in its setting to determine if, indeed, any one person exercises such discretion.

In the typical case, the parents of a child initially conclude from the child's behavior that there is some emotional problem—in short, that "something is wrong." They may respond to the problem in various ways, but generally the first contact with the State occurs when they bring the child to be examined by a psychologist or psychiatrist at a community mental health clinic.

Most often, the examination is followed by outpatient treatment at the community clinic. In addition, the child's parents are encouraged, and sometimes required, to participate in a family therapy program to obtain a better insight into the problem. In most instances, this is all the care a child requires. However, if, after a period of outpatient care, the child's abnormal emotional condition persists, he may be referred by the local clinic staff to an affiliated regional mental hospital.

At the regional hospital an admissions team composed of a psychiatrist and at least one other mental health professional examines and interviews the child—privately in most instances. This team then examines the medical records provided by the clinic staff and interviews the parents. Based on this information, and any additional background that can be obtained, the admissions team makes a diagnosis and determines whether the child will likely benefit from institutionalized care. If the team finds either condition not met, admission is refused.

If the team admits a child as suited for hospitalization, the child's condition and continuing need for hospital care are reviewed periodically by at least one independent, medical review group. For the most part, the reviews are as frequent as weekly, but none are less often than once every two months. Moreover, as we noted earlier, the superintendent of each hospital is charged with an affirmative statutory duty to discharge any child who is no longer mentally ill or in need of therapy.

As with most medical procedures, Georgia's are not totally free from risk of error in the sense that they give total or absolute assurance that every child admitted to a hospital has a mental illness optimally suitable for institutionalized treatment. . . .

Georgia's procedures are not "arbitrary" in the sense that a single physician or other professional has the "unbridled discretion" the District Court saw to commit a child to a regional hospital. To so find on this record would require us to assume that the physicians, psychologists, and mental health professionals who participate in the admission decision and who review each other's conclusions as to the continuing validity of the initial decision are either oblivious or indifferent to the child's welfare—or that they are incompetent. We note, however, the District Court found to the contrary; it was "impressed by the conscientious, dedicated state employed psychiatrists who, with the help of equally conscientious, dedicated state employed psychologists and social workers, faithfully care for the plaintiff children. . . ." 412 F.Supp., at 138.

This finding of the District Court also effectively rebuts the suggestion made in some of the briefs amici that hospital administrators may not actually be "neutral and detached" because of institutional pressure to admit a child who has no need for hospital care. That such a practice may take place in some institutions in some places affords no basis for a finding as to Georgia's program; the evidence in the record provides no support whatever for that charge against the staffs at any of the State's eight regional hospitals. Such cases, if they are found, can be dealt with individually; they do not lend themselves to class-action remedies.

We are satisfied that the voluminous record as a whole supports the conclusion that the admissions staffs of the hospitals have acted in a neutral and detached fashion in making medical judgments in the best interests of the children. The State, through its mental health programs, provides the authority for trained professionals to assist parents in examining, diagnosing, and treating emotionally disturbed children. Through its hiring practices, it provides well-staffed and well-equipped hospitals and—as the District Court found—conscientious public employees to implement the State's beneficent purposes.

Although our review of the record in this case satisfies us that Georgia's general administrative and statutory scheme for the voluntary commitment of children is not per se unconstitutional, we cannot decide on this record whether every child in appellees' class received an adequate, independent diagnosis of his emotional condition and need for confinement under the standards announced earlier in this opinion. On remand, the District Court is free to and should consider any individual claims that initial admissions did not meet the standards we have described in this opinion.

In addition, we note that appellees' original complaint alleged that the State had failed to provide adequate periodic review of their need for institutional care and claimed that this was an additional due process violation. Since the District Court held that the appellees' original confinement was unconstitutional, it had no reason to consider this separate claim. Similarly, we have no basis for determining whether the review procedures of the various hospitals are adequate to provide the process called for or what process might be required if a child contests his confinement by requesting a release. These matters require factual findings not present in the District Court's opinion. We have held that the periodic reviews described in the record reduce the risk of error in the initial admission and thus they are necessary. Whether they are sufficient to justify continuing a voluntary commitment is an issue for the District Court on remand. The District Court is free to require additional evidence on this issue. . . .

V

It is important that we remember the purpose of Georgia's comprehensive mental health program. It seeks substantively and at great cost to provide care for those who cannot afford to obtain private treatment and procedurally to screen carefully all applicants to assure that institutional care is suited to the particular patient. The State resists the complex of procedures ordered by the District Court because in its view they are unnecessary to protect the child's rights, they divert public resources from the central objective of administering health care, they risk aggravating the tensions inherent in the family situation, and they erect barriers that may discourage parents from seeking medical aid for a disturbed child.

On this record, we are satisfied that Georgia's medical factfinding processes are reasonable and consistent with constitutional guarantees. Accordingly, it was error to hold unconstitutional the State's procedures for admitting a child for treatment to a state mental hospital. The judgment is therefore reversed, and the case is remanded to the District Court for further proceedings consistent with this opinion.

Reversed and remanded.

Parham expresses the confidence of the Supreme Court that parents, and particularly professional hospital staff members, will act in the best interests of a child. By and large this is true, but just as adults require due process rights to deal with a few intolerable situations, so do children who are committed to the mental health system by their parents. As noted in Chapter 15, *Parham* does not restrict states from offering due process guarantees to children, and many do so.

The plight of children who are given multiple labels without appropriate treatment is illustrated by In re M., 354 N.Y.S.2d 80 (1974).

IN RE M.

Family Court, City of New York, New York County, 354 N.Y.S.2d 80 (1974).

David M. was born on January 13, 1959. In 1966 he was first referred for professional attention to the New York City Board of Education Bureau of Child Guidance by the principal of his school for "restless, aggressive, destructive and acting out behavior." As his behavior did not improve, David subsequently was admitted on February 15, 1967, to the City Hospital at Elmhurst, Psychiatric Division. A diagnosis of childhood schizophrenia was made at that time. The youngster remained in the hospital, a short term city facility for psychiatric care, until May 5, 1967, when he was discharged to his family to be followed up in a Mental Hygiene Clinic. However, his behavior deteriorated and he was then placed for the first time in Queens Children's Hospital, a psychiatric facility operated by the State of New York for long term placement. The state hospital provided care and treatment for David from February 16, 1968, until November 15, 1971, when he was discharged to his family. Eight days after the state hospital had discharged him, it became necessary to readmit him once again to the City Hospital at Elmhurst, Psychiatric Division.

In the past seven years, according to the youngster's medical records, David has been admitted to the City Hospital at Elmhurst six times and to the Queens Children's Hospital twice. In the past six years, the longest period of time that David has been capable of maintenance outside of either the state or city psychiatric hospitals has been less than one month. In the past five years his I.Q. has dropped from 95 to 77 and the reading ability of this 15-year-old boy is second grade at best. The current psychiatric diagnosis of this child as indicated by the Elmhurst City Hospital is "personality disorder, psychopathic type with minimal brain disfunction. There is an underlying schizophrenic process present."

On January 25, 1972, David was referred for the second time to Queens Children's Hospital for long term psychiatric care and treatment. On May 23, 1973, David escaped from said facility (a feat he had managed before because admittedly it is not a closed institution) and allegedly acting in concert with two others attempted to rob a man on the platform of a subway station. When the man resisted, he was thrown onto the tracks into the path of an oncoming train. These acts if done by an adult would have constituted the crimes of attempted murder, assault and robbery. David was 14 at the time and therefore was taken into custody as an alleged juvenile delinquent.

A Juvenile Delinquency petition was subsequently filed in Family Court. The judge then sitting, recognizing that David was a patient in a mental hospital, referred him back to the hospital where he remained until the hospital discharged him on October 17, 1973, to Family Court for hearing on the Juvenile Delinquency petition. The youngster was then remanded to Spofford Juvenile Center, a secure detention facility maintained by the New York City Commissioner of Social Services to await an adjudicatory hearing.

However, before an adjudicatory hearing could be held, Dr. Guggenheim, the psychiatrist at Spofford Juvenile Center advised the Court on

November 5, 1973, that David urgently needed hospitalization and could not be maintained at Juvenile Center. According to Dr. Guggenheim's report (petitioner's exhibit "C"), "at Juvenile Center he is highly unmanageable, frequently assaultive, markedly inappropriate and very uncomfortable. Attempts to medicate this youngster have been unsuccessful, in part because he refuses medication." Spofford Juvenile Center is a secure detention facility structured to house alleged and adjudicated juvenile delinquents. It is not a facility to house mentally ill children. Inasmuch as David was no longer under the jurisdiction of the Commissioner of Mental Hygiene, it would have been a violation of his civil liberties for anyone at Juvenile Center to force him to take medication. On date of discharge from Queens Children's Hospital the discharge note indicated that Respondent was receiving 100 mgs, of Mellaril three times a day. However, since David was unmanageable without medication, the Court had no other alternative than to remand him to Elmhurst Hospital on November 7, 1973. He remained there until November 29, 1973, when he was again referred to Spofford Juvenile Center following discharge by the hospital.

On December 4, 1973, Dr. Guggenheim again requested hospitalization for David (petitioner's exhibit "D"). . . .

David was again remanded to Elmhurst City Hospital where he remained until January 15, 1974, when he was discharged. A hearing on the Juvenile Delinquency petition was scheduled for January 18, 1974, based on the hospital's assurance that David was ready for a hearing.

On January 16, 1974, Dr. Guggenheim, in an emergency psychiatric report (petitioner's exhibit "E"), reported to the court as follows:

"David M. was returned to Juvenile Center once again discharged from Elmhurst City Hospital. We call attention to the report from Elmhurst Hospital in which [that] the youngster is a danger both to himself and to others is repeatedly emphasized. The hospital reports further indicate his excitability, poor judgement and his obvious progressive deterioration. Indeed the youngster was unable to be contained because of his violence on the Child Psychiatric Ward and had to be transferred by them to the Acute Male Adult Ward. His explosiveness, violence and his poor judgement is a danger to himself and to others were the reasons which led to our recommendation of hospitalization twice previously. We also emphasize that both at Juvenile Center and at the hospital the youngster refuses to accept necessary medication.

"For the above reasons we again, for the third time, respectfully urge the court not to return this youngster to Juvenile Center where he cannot be dealt with appropriately and poses a danger to himself and to others. Injuries both to himself and to others have already taken place as documented previously. In our opinion this youngster is in need of long term hospitalization where appropriate psychiatric treatment and medication are available. This youngster is not suitable for placement at Juvenile Center."

Therefore, the Court had no other alternative than to remand David back to Elmhurst City Hospital, Psychiatric Division and to order a competency hearing to resolve the conflicting psychiatric information in respect to this youngster.

A hearing was held on February 8, 1974, continued on February 15, 1974, and then further continued on March 7, 1974, so that the complete psychiatric history of this youngster was available to the Court.

The Court finds that based upon the testimony and the medical records of City Hospital at Elmhurst and the medical records of Queens Children's Hospital and the Psychiatrist's Reports from Juvenile Center that:

(1)   David M. is presently mentally ill within the definition of Section 1.05(17) of the Mental Hygiene Law and has been mentally ill for the past seven years. . . .

(2)   That David was receiving care and treatment for his illness at Queens Children's Hospital for 16 months prior to the alleged delinquent act that brought him before the Family Court and that he continued to receive care and treatment at that hospital for five months thereafter until his discharge from the hospital to the Court on October 17, 1973.

(3)   That at the time David was discharged to Family Court he was still mentally ill and was still in need of care and treatment and that said discharge to Family Court was premature and that this finding of continuing mental illness is confirmed by the records of the City Hospital at Elmhurst, Juvenile Center, as well as by the records of Queens Children's Hospital.

(4)   That the consensus of psychiatric opinion is that David will not benefit from further hospitalization at this time but now needs "placement in a structured, closed residential institution for the protection of others as well as himself" where he can be given educational and vocational training, medication whenever necessary, and psychotherapy.

(5)   That the State Commissioner of Mental Hygiene pursuant to the Mental Hygiene Law Sections 7.05 and 9.03 has been given the power to provide such a facility or to contract for such a facility for the care and treatment of mentally ill children. . . .

(6)   That the State Commissioner of Mental Hygiene should have exercised those powers and not have discharged a mentally ill youngster to Family Court.

In view of the foregoing, it is hereby

Ordered that David M. be remanded back to the care and custody of the State Commissioner of Mental Hygiene, and it is further

Ordered that pursuant to the powers granted under Section 255 of the Family Court Act that the State Commissioner of Mental Hygiene provide or contract for a proper facility for the care and treatment of this mentally ill child by implementing the recommendations of the psychiatrists for a structured, closed residential setting.

This matter is adjourned until May 17, 1974. At that time the Court is to be advised as to the affirmative plan for care and treatment that has been formulated by the State Commissioner of Mental Hygiene to ensure this youngster's right to treatment.

This Court was impressed by a number of facts that came to light in the course of these proceedings. The expert witnesses who appeared, and who have had professional intercourse with the Respondent seemed sincerely interested in helping him.

It would seem, based on testimony herein, that David is not a proper subject for treatment in an ordinary mental hospital, nor an appropriate subject for placement in an institution for ordinary juvenile delinquents. The experts are at a loss to know what to do with David and say the courts must now bear the responsibility of planning for him. It seems that David's case is not unique and other children are, and have been, in a similarly unfortunate state of limbo. The courts are not an executive agency with power to provide the services required by mentally ill children. That is the exclusive province of the executive branch and specifically the Department of Mental Hygiene. The Commissioner of Mental Hygiene is provided with authority to service a child such as David and a remand to the Commissioner's custody is the most appropriate disposition of this case at this time.

Too many children are successively labeled dependent, neglected, in need of supervision, delinquent, and/or mentally ill by various institutions without receiving adequate care or appropriate services.

THE DEVELOP-MENTALLY DISABLED

In Youngberg v. Romeo, 457 U.S. 307 (1982), the U.S. Supreme Court, in its decision regarding the treatment of a hospitalized thirty-three-year-old mentally retarded patient, drew on its findings in *Parham*. As in *Parham*, the Court strongly emphasized the role of professional judgment in balancing the liberty of the individual and "relevant state interests." The Court denied that Romeo's rights under the Eighth Amendment were violated.

Youngberg v. Romeo

Supreme Court of the United States, 457 U.S. 307 (1982).

The question presented is whether respondent, involuntarily committed to a state institution for the mentally retarded, has substantive rights under the Due Process Clause of the Fourteenth Amendment to (i) safe conditions of confinement; (ii) freedom from bodily restraints; and (iii) training or "habilitation." Respondent sued under 42 U.S.C. § 1983 three administrators of the institution, claiming damages for the alleged breach of his constitutional rights.

I

Respondent Nicholas Romeo is profoundly retarded. Although 33 years old, he has the mental capacity of an eighteen-month old child, with an I.Q. between 8 and 10. He cannot talk and lacks the most basic self-care skills. Until he was 26, respondent lived with his parents in Philadelphia. But after the death of his father in May 1974, his mother was unable to care for him. Within two weeks of the father's death, respondent's mother sought his temporary admission to a nearby Pennsylvania hospital.

Shortly thereafter, she asked the Philadelphia County Court of Common Pleas to admit Romeo to a state facility on a permanent basis. Her petition to the court explained that she was unable to care for Romeo or control his violence. As part of the commitment process, Romeo was examined by a physician and a psychologist. They both certified that respondent was severely retarded and unable to care for himself. On June 11, 1974, the Court of Common Pleas committed respondent to the Pennhurst State School and Hospital, pursuant to the applicable involuntary commitment provision of the Pennsylvania Mental Health and Mental Retardation Act, Pa. Stat. Ann. tit. 50 § 4406.

At Pennhurst, Romeo was injured on numerous occasions, both by his own violence and by the reactions of other residents to him. Respondent's mother became concerned about these injuries. After objecting to respondent's treatment several times, she filed this complaint on November 4, 1976, in the United States District Court for the Eastern District of Pennsylvania as his next friend. The complaint alleged that "[d]uring the period July, 1974 to the present, plaintiff has suffered injuries on at least sixty-three occasions." The complaint originally sought damages and injunctive relief from Pennhurst's director and two supervisors; it alleged that these officials knew, or should have known, that Romeo was suffering injuries and that they failed to institute appropriate preventive procedures, thus violating his rights under the Eighth and Fourteenth Amendments.

Thereafter, in late 1976, Romeo was transferred from his ward to the hospital for treatment of a broken arm. While in the infirmary, and by order of a doctor, he was physically restrained during portions of each day. These restraints were ordered by Dr. Gabroy, not a defendant here, to protect Romeo and others in the hospital, some of whom were in traction or were being treated intravenously.

Although respondent normally would have returned to his ward when his arm healed, the parties to this litigation agreed that he should remain in the hospital due to the pending lawsuit. Nevertheless, in December 1977, a second amended complaint was filed alleging that the defendants were restraining respondent for prolonged periods on a routine basis. The second amended complaint also added a claim for damages to compensate Romeo for the defendants' failure to provide him with appropriate "treatment or programs for his mental retardation." All claims for injunctive relief were dropped prior to trial because respondent is a member of the class seeking such relief in another action.

An eight-day jury trial was held in April 1978. Petitioners introduced evidence that respondent participated in several programs teaching basic self-care skills. A comprehensive behavior-modification program was designed by staff members to reduce Romeo's aggressive behavior, but that program was never implemented because of his mother's objections. Respondent introduced evidence of his injuries and of conditions in his unit.

At the close of the trial, the court instructed the jury that "if any or all of the defendants were aware of and failed to take all reasonable steps to prevent repeated attacks upon Nicholas Romeo," such failure deprived him of constitutional rights. The jury also was instructed that if the defendants shackled Romeo or denied him treatment "as a punishment for filing this lawsuit," his constitutional rights were violated under the Eighth Amendment. Finally, the jury was instructed that only if they found the defendants "deliberately indifferent to the serious medical [and psychological] needs" of Romeo could they find that his Eighth and Fourteenth Amendment rights had been violated. The jury returned a verdict for the defendants, on which judgment was entered.

The Court of Appeals for the Third Circuit, sitting en banc, reversed and remanded for a new trial. The court held that the Eighth Amendment, prohibiting cruel and unusual punishment of those convicted of crimes, was not an appropriate source for determining the rights of the involuntarily committed. Rather, the Fourteenth Amendment and the liberty interest protected by that amendment provided the proper constitutional basis for these rights. In applying the Fourteenth Amendment, the court found that the involuntarily committed retain liberty interests in freedom of movement and in personal security. These were "fundamental liberties" that can be limited only by an "overriding non-punitive" state interest. It further found that the involuntarily committed have a liberty interest in habilitation designed to "treat" their mental retardation.

The en banc court did not, however, agree on the relevant standard to be used in determining whether Romeo's rights had been violated. Because physical restraint "raises a presumption of a punitive sanction," the majority of the Court of Appeals concluded that it can be justified only by "compelling necessity." A somewhat different standard was appropriate for the failure to provide for a resident's safety. The majority considered that such a failure must be justified by a showing of "substantial necessity." Finally, the majority held that when treatment has been administered, those responsible are liable only if the treatment is not "acceptable in the light of present medical or other scientific knowledge."

Chief Judge Seitz, concurring in the judgment, considered the standards articulated by the majority as indistinguishable from those applicable to medical malpractice claims. In Chief Judge Seitz's view, the Constitution "only requires that the courts make certain that professional judgment in fact was exercised." He concluded that the appropriate standard was whether the defendants' conduct was "such a substantial departure from accepted professional judgment, practice or standards in the care and treatment of this plaintiff as to demonstrate that the defendants did not base their conduct on a professional judgment."

We granted the petition for certiorari because of the importance of the question presented to the administration of state institutions for the mentally retarded. 451 U.S. 982 (1981).

II

We consider here for the first time the substantive rights of involuntarily-committed mentally retarded persons under the Fourteenth Amendment to the Constitution. In this case, respondent has been committed under the laws of Pennsylvania, and he does not challenge the commitment. Rather, he argues that he has a constitutionally protected liberty interest in safety, freedom of movement, and training within the institution; and that petitioners infringed these rights by failing to provide constitutionally required conditions of confinement.

The mere fact that Romeo has been committed under proper procedures does not deprive him of all substantive liberty interests under the Fourteenth Amendment. Indeed, that state concedes that respondent has a right to adequate food, shelter, clothing, and medical care. We must decide whether liberty interests also exist in safety, freedom of movement, and training. If such interests do exist, we must further decide whether they have been infringed in this case.

A

Respondent's first two claims involve liberty interests recognized by prior decisions of this Court, interests that involuntary commitment proceedings do not extinguish. The first is a claim to safe conditions. In the past, this Court has noted that the right to personal security constitutes an "historic liberty interest" protected substantively by the Due Process Clause. And that right is not extinguished by lawful confinement, even for penal purposes. If it is cruel and unusual punishment to hold convicted criminals in unsafe conditions, it must be unconstitutional to confine the involuntarily committed—who may not be punished at all—in unsafe conditions.

Next, respondent claims a right to freedom from bodily restraint. In other contexts, the existence of such an interest is clear in the prior decisions of this Court. Indeed, "[l]iberty from bodily restraint always has been recognized as the core of the liberty protected by the Due Process Clause from arbitrary governmental action." This interest survives criminal conviction and incarceration. Similarly, it must also survive involuntary commitment.

B

Respondent's remaining claim is more troubling. In his words, he asserts a "constitutional right to minimally adequate habilitation." This is a substantive due process claim that is said to be grounded in the liberty component of the Due Process Clause of the Fourteenth Amendment. The term "habilitation," used in psychiatry, is not defined precisely or consistently in the opinions below or in the briefs of the parties or the amici. As noted previously, the term refers to "training and development of needed skills." Respondent emphasizes that the right he asserts is for "minimal" training, see Brief of Respondent at 34, and he would leave the type and extent of training to be determined on a case-by-case basis "in light of present medical or other scientific knowledge."

In addressing the asserted right to training, we start from established principles. As a general matter, a State is under no constitutional duty to provide substantive services for those within its border.

When a person is institutionalized—and wholly dependent on the State—it is conceded by petitioner that a duty to provide certain services and care does exist, although even then a State necessarily has considerable discretion in determining the nature and scope of its responsibilities. Nor must a State "choose between attacking every aspect of a problem or not attacking the problem at all."

Respondent, in light of the severe character of his retardation, concedes that no amount of training will make possible his release. And he does not argue that if he were still at home, the State would have an obligation to provide training at its expense. The record reveals that respondent's primary needs are bodily safety and a minimum of physical restraint, and respondent clearly claims training related to these needs. As we have recognized that there is a constitutionally protected liberty interest in safety and freedom from restraint, training may be necessary to avoid unconstitutional infringement of those rights. On the basis of the record before us, it is quite uncertain whether respondent seeks any "habilitation" or training unrelated to safety and freedom from bodily restraints. In his brief to this Court, Romeo indicates that even the self-care programs he seeks are needed to reduce his aggressive behavior. And in his offer of proof to the trial court, respondent repeatedly indicated that, if allowed to testify, his experts would show that additional training programs, including self-care programs, were needed to reduce Romeo's aggressive behavior. If, as seems the case, respondent seeks only training related to safety and freedom from restraints, this case does not present the difficult question whether a mentally retarded person, involuntarily committed to a state institution, has some general constitutional right to training *per se*, even when no type or amount of training would lead to freedom.

Chief Judge Seitz, in language apparently adopted by respondent, observed:

> "I believe that the plaintiff has a constitutional right to minimally adequate care and treatment. The existence of a constitutional right to care and treatment is no longer a novel legal proposition."

Chief Judge Seitz did not identify or otherwise define—beyond the right to reasonable safety and freedom from physical restraint—the "minimally adequate care and treatment" that appropriately may be required for this respondent. In the circumstances presented by this case, and on the basis of the record developed to date, we agree with his view and conclude that respondent's liberty interests require the State to provide minimally adequate or reasonable training to ensure safety and freedom from undue restraint. In view of the kinds of treatment sought by respondent and the evidence of record, we need go no further in this case.

III

A

We have established that Romeo retains liberty interests in safety and freedom from bodily restraint. Yet these interests are not absolute; indeed to some extent they are in conflict. In operating an institution such as Pennhurst, there are occasions in which it is necessary for the State to restrain the movement of residents—for example, to protect them as well as others from violence. Similar restraints may also be appropriate in a training program. An institution cannot protect its residents from all danger of violence if it is to permit them to have any freedom of movement. The question then is not simply whether a liberty interest has been infringed but whether the extent or nature of the restraint or lack of absolute safety is such as to violate due process.

In determining whether a substantive right protected by the Due Process Clause has been violated, it is necessary to balance "the liberty of the individual" and "the demands of an organized society."

Accordingly, whether respondent's constitutional rights have been violated must be determined by balancing his liberty interests against the relevant state interests. If there is to be any uniformity in protecting these interests, this balancing cannot be left to the unguided discretion of a judge or jury. We therefore turn to consider the proper standard for determining whether a State adequately has protected the rights of the involuntarily-committed mentally retarded.

B

We think the standard articulated by Chief Judge Seitz affords the necessary guidance and reflects the proper balance between the legitimate interests of the State and the rights of the involuntarily committed to reasonable conditions of safety and freedom from unreasonable restraints.

At the same time, this standard is lower than the "compelling" or "substantial" necessity tests the Court of Appeals would require a state to meet to justify use of restraints or conditions of less than absolute safety. We think this requirement would place an undue burden on the administration of institutions such as Pennhurst and also would restrict unnecessarily the exercise of professional judgment as to the needs of residents.

Moreover, we agree that respondent is entitled to minimally adequate training. In this case, the minimally adequate training required by the Constitution is such training as may be reasonable in light of respondent's liberty interests in safety and freedom from unreasonable restraints. In determining what is "reasonable"—in this and in any case presenting a claim for training by a state—we emphasize that courts must show deference to the judgment exercised by a qualified professional. By so limiting judicial review of challenges to conditions in state institutions, interference by the federal judiciary with the internal operations of these institutions should be minimized. Moreover, there certainly is no reason to think judges or juries are better qualified than appropriate professionals in making such decisions.

For these reasons, the decision, if made by a professional, is presumptively valid; liability may be imposed only when the decision by the professional is such a substantial departure from accepted professional judgment, practice or standards as to demonstrate that the person responsible actually did not base the decision on such a judgment. In an action for damages against a professional in his individual capacity, however, the professional will not be liable if he was unable to satisfy his normal professional standards because of budgetary constraints; in such a situation, good-faith immunity would bar liability.

IV

In deciding this case, we have weighed those post-commitment interests cognizable as liberty interests under the Due Process Clause of the Fourteenth Amendment against legitimate state interests and in light of the constraints under which most state institutions necessarily operate. We repeat that the state concedes a duty to provide adequate food, shelter, clothing and medical care. These are the essentials of the care that the state must provide. The state also has the unquestioned duty to provide reasonable safety for all residents and personnel within the institution. And it may not restrain residents except when and to the extent professional judgment deems this necessary to assure such safety or to provide needed training. In this case, therefore, the state is under a duty to provide respondent with such training as an appropriate professional would consider reasonable to ensure his safety and to facilitate his ability to function free from bodily restraints. It may well be unreasonable not to provide training when training could significantly reduce the need for restraints or the likelihood of violence.

Respondent thus enjoys constitutionally protected interests in conditions of reasonable care and safety, reasonably non-restrictive confinement conditions, and such training as may be required by these interests. Such conditions of confinement would comport fully with the purpose of respondent's commitment. In determining whether the state has met its obligations in these respects, decisions made by the appropriate professional are entitled to a presumption of correctness. Such a presumption is necessary to enable institutions of this type—often, unfortunately, overcrowded and understaffed—to continue to function. A single professional may have to make decisions with respect to a number of residents with widely varying needs and problems in the course of a normal day. The administrators, and particularly professional personnel, should not be required to make each decision in the shadow of an action for damages.

In this case, we conclude that the jury was erroneously instructed on the assumption that the proper standard of liability was that of the Eighth Amendment. Accordingly, we vacate the decision of the Court of Appeals and remand for further proceedings consistent with this decision.

THE AGED

Older persons may face institutionalization as their need for physical care increases and they begin to exhibit behaviors that some may view as mental illness. Until recently, nearly 40 percent of the state hospital population was over age sixty-five. Now the elderly are more likely to live in nursing homes than to be involuntarily committed to state mental hospitals. Notwithstanding changes in treatment setting, the issues of whether institutionalization is necessary and the right of institutionalized persons to treatment remain.

A major drawback in attempts to resolve these issues has been a lack of available services other than institutions.

In Lake v. Cameron, 364 F.2d 657 (D.C. Cir. 1966), the Court held:

> The entire spectrum of services should be made available, including out-patient treatment, foster care, halfway houses, day hospitals, nursing homes, etc. The alternative course of treatment or care should be fashioned as the interest of the person and of the public require. . . . Deprivations of liberty solely because of the dangers to the ill persons themselves should not go beyond what is necessary for their protection.

Unfortunately, exploration of alternatives to placement mandated by *Lake* resulted in recommitment of the elderly woman in question because of a lack of existing alternatives. In addition, the superintendent of St. Elizabeth's Hospital testified that only half their patients were in need of mental treatment and that the primary need of most older persons was for physical care.

Public guardianship has been suggested as a means to aid the elderly to obtain supportive services and avoid institutionalization. However, the purpose of most existing state laws is that, on determination of mental incompetency, a guardian is appointed primarily to manage the ward's property rather than his or her person.

SEX OFFENDERS

State standards for offenses differ widely. The exclusion of sexual offense charges for activities between consenting adults simplifies the basis for litigation, but many states have not adopted this standard.

In the 1930s states began to enact statutes imposing longer sentences for sexual crimes and providing treatment for such offenders. Most states provide for an indeterminate commitment of one day to life for any person found guilty of sexual behavior resulting from mental illness. The problem of definition is a major concern:

> All sex offenders are not sexually deviated; all sex deviations do not become sexual offenses; some nonsexual offenses are motivated by sexual conflict; there are nonsexual conflicts that stimulate sexual deviance or offence; there are a variety of psychiatric conditions and dynamic factors which go into producing any one of the sex offenses. (Stone, 1975: 183)

As part of the trend toward extending procedural safeguards to civil proceedings, the Supreme Court held in Specht v. Patterson, 386 U.S. 605 (1967), that persons facing commitment as sexual psychopaths are entitled to a hearing with full due process rights. The Court had previously upheld provisions for civil commitment of sexual offenders in State of Minnesota ex rel. Pearson v. Probate Court of Ramsey County, 309 U.S. 270 (1940).

ALCOHOL ABUSERS

State statutes include many varied approaches to the treatment of alcoholism. Some require that persons arrested for drunkenness be jailed or fined, while others refer them for mandatory treatment in clinics or hospitals. Nearly thirty states provide for involuntary civil commitment of chronic alcoholics for an indeterminate period as part of statutes governing the mentally ill. One important court case, Driver v. Hinnant, 356 F.2d 761 (4th Cir. 1966), viewed chronic alcoholism as a disease that causes the involuntary act of public drunkenness:

> The defendant was sentenced to be imprisoned for two years by a North Carolina court for the crime of public intoxication, having been convicted for the same offense over 200 times during his adult life of about 40 years; he had already spent most of his life incarcerated for chronic alcoholism. On this occasion the defendant pleaded that it was cruel and unusual punishment in violation of the Eighth Amendment to penalize him for chronic alcoholism which he argued was a disease effectively destroying the power of free will. His case was appealed through the various state courts until it reached the Federal Circuit Court of Appeals which upheld his argument. (Tancredi, Lief, and Slaby, 1975: 106)

One drawback of the treatment approach is the impossibility of objectively defining the degree of alcoholism that requires involuntary commitment. Determination of the level of alcoholism and the nature of treatment may both be highly discretionary on the part of institutional officials.

Decriminalization statutes providing that police may escort an intoxicated person home or to a volunteer treatment center provide less restrictive alternatives and are becoming widely accepted. Such statutes are favored by alcoholic treatment groups, even though police may use them to ignore public drunkenness. This may lead to death from cold and exposure—especially for homeless persons.

DRUG ABUSERS

In Robinson v. State of California, 370 U.S. 660 (1962), the Supreme Court held that drug addiction was an illness that should not be criminally punished. As with chronic alcoholism, the mental illness statutes of over thirty states provide for involuntary commitment of narcotics addicts. The problem of determining the degree of addiction for mandatory treatment is likewise troublesome:

Some states rely strictly on a medical definition of an addict, i.e., one who has habitually used a drug to the point of developing a tolerance for the drug and there is not a health need that he be on such medication. Others define an addict in terms of societal safety; for example, the Oregon statute states that a person can be committed who habitually uses a habit-forming drug and who as a result endangers the public health, safety or morals. Maryland in contrast defines an addict as one who uses specific drugs such as cocaine or morphine to the degree that he is deprived of "reasonable self-control."

Involuntary commitment of the mentally ill is similar to the drug addict, particularly in that he may lose important rights when he has been involuntarily committed. This could include the right to form contracts, as well as the right to conduct other private, personal affairs. In addition the drug addict, since he has most likely been committed through a judicial proceeding, finds it very difficult to terminate his commitment. The court may have the final word in deciding whether the addict should be released from the hospital. An addict may be released in a relatively short time if he has entered a suitable program that specializes in withdrawing addicts from narcotics; if because of limited facilities he finds himself in a state mental institution he may be confined for an inappropriately long period of time. (Tancredi, Lief, and Slaby, 1975: 102)

Recently, marijuana use has less often been equated with drug addiction, and state statutes are reflecting this view. Most states recommend a conditional discharge for a first offense of possession of small quantities of marijuana.

EMPLOYEES

Employee groups frequently receive social services through employee assistance programs sponsored by employees or labor unions. Many of the problems involve alcoholism, substance abuse, or other mental stress that present legal issues. Since 1983 the *EAP Digest* has had a column dealing with legal issues in the workplace. For example, Lehr (1983: 15) considered reinstatement rights after voluntary resignation: An arbitrator concluded that the grievant could not have his job back because he was aware of what he was doing and, while he was "a sick human being deserving some compassion," the company was free to grant or withhold compassion. Ironically, the more confused and severely disturbed the employee, the greater the likelihood that he will prevail when seeking reinstatement.

In reviewing a Texas Supreme Court decision, Otis Engineering Corporation v. Clark 668 S.W. 2d 307 [Tex. 1983]), involving employer liability for damages caused by an employee who was sent home by his supervisor for being obviously intoxicated, Lehr (1984: 12) offers three suggestions for decision-making: (1) an obviously intoxicated employee should not be permitted to leave the workplace driving a vehicle; (2) the employer should request that the employee remain at the workplace and make other arrangements for transportation; and (3) the employer should consider suspending the employee's driving privileges pending an investigation. These actions would be responsive to the concern of the Texas court: "When because of an employee's incapacity, the employer exercises control over the employee, the employer has a duty to take such action as a reasonable, prudent employer, under the same similar circumstances, would take to prevent the employee from causing unreasonable risk of harm to others." (668 S.W. 2d at 311)

ALLEGED CRIMINALS

Persons accused of a crime who are considered unable to understand the nature of the charges against them, to consult an attorney, and to participate in their defense will be judged incompetent to stand trial. Stone (1975: 200) points out:

The potential consequences for the defendant are: (a) he may be denied bail, (b) he may be incarcerated for a period longer than the maximum sentence for the crime he is alleged to have committed, (c) he may be placed in an institution that combines the worst elements in jails and hospitals, and (d) any pretrial mental examination poses serious questions about the fifth amendment rights of the defendant.

In the past, persons found incompetent sometimes spent the rest of their lives in institutions for the criminally insane. However, the Supreme Court remedied this situation in Jackson v. Indiana, 406 U.S. 715 (1972).

JACKSON v. INDIANA

Supreme Court of the United States, 406 U.S. 715 (1972).

We are here concerned with the constitutionality of certain aspects of Indiana's system for pretrial commitment of one accused of crime. Petitioner, Theon Jackson, is a mentally defective deaf mute with a mental level of a pre-school child. He cannot read, write, or otherwise communciate except through limited sign language. In May 1968, at age 27, he was charged in the Criminal Court of Marion County, Indiana, with separate robberies of two women. The offenses were alleged to have occurred the preceding July. The first involved property (a purse and its contents) of the value of four dollars. The second concerned five dollars in money. The record sheds no light on these charges since, upon receipt of not-guilty pleas from Jackson, the trial court set in motion the Indiana procedures for determining his competency to stand trial. Ind.Ann.Stat. § 9-1706a (Supp.1971), now Ind.Code 35-5-3-2 (1971).

As the statute requires, the court appointed two psychiatrists to examine Jackson. A competency hearing was subsequently held at which petitioner was represented by counsel. The court received the examining doctors' joint written report and oral testimony from them and from a deaf-school interpreter through whom they had attempted to communicate with petitioner. The report concluded that Jackson's almost nonexistent communication skill, together with his lack of hearing and his mental deficiency, left him unable to understand the nature of the charges against him or to participate in his defense. One doctor testified that it was extremely unlikely that petitioner could ever learn to read or write and questioned whether petitioner even had the ability to develop any proficiency in sign language. He believed that the interpreter had not been able to communicate with petitioner to any great extent and testified that petitioner's "prognosis appears rather dim." The other doctor testified that even if Jackson were not a deaf mute, he would be incompetent to stand trial, and doubted whether petitioner had sufficient intelligence ever to develop the necessary communication skills. The interpreter testified that Indiana had no facilities that could help someone as badly off as Jackson to learn minimal communication skills.

On this evidence, the trial court found that Jackson "lack[ed] comprehension sufficient to make his defense," § 9-1706a, and ordered him committed to the Indiana Department of Mental Health until such time as that Department should certify to the court that "the defendant is sane."

Petitioner's counsel then filed a motion for a new trial, contending that there was no evidence that Jackson was "insane," or that he would ever attain a status which the court might regard as "sane" in the sense of competency to stand trial. Counsel argued that Jackson's commitment under these circumstances amounted to a "life sentence" without his ever having been convicted of a crime, and that the commitment therefore deprived Jackson of his Fourteenth Amendment rights to due process and equal protection, and constituted cruel and unusual punishment under the Eighth Amendment made applicable to the States through the Fourteenth. The trial court denied the motion. On appeal the Supreme Court of Indiana affirmed, with one judge dissenting, 253 Ind. 487, 255 N.E.2d 515 (1970). Rehearing was denied with two judges dissenting. We granted certiorari, 401 U.S. 973, 91 S.Ct. 1203, 28 L.Ed.2d 322 (1971).

We hold that a person charged by a State with a criminal offense who is committed solely on account of his incapacity to proceed to trial cannot be held more than the reasonable period of time necessary to determine whether there is a substantial probability that he will attain that capacity in the foreseeable future. If it is determined that this is not the case, then the State must either institute the customary civil commitment proceeding that would be required to commit indefinitely any other citizen, or release the defendant. . . .

This ruling limits abuses of the incompetency determination processes. However, one problem remains. Few persons confined for thirty to ninety days during pretrial evaluation are found incompetent to stand trial. Consequently, in the majority of cases, confinement serves only to have a devastating effect on their personal lives.

Historically, the law has established the *insanity defense*. It has held that a person must have the capacity for free choice in order to be held criminally responsible for his or her actions. In considering a "not guilty by reason of insanity" plea, a judge or jury must generally make "an assessment of the offender's intellectual capacities to determine right from wrong and to comply with societal and legal sanctions, an assessment of his volition from the standpoint of whether he desired to commit the crime, and a consideration of his emotional capacity to control his own behavior (Tancredi, Lief, and Slaby [1975: 9]).

Despite considerable literature on the subject of mental incapacity, successful pleas of not guilty by reason of insanity are rare—fewer than 1 in 1,000 arrests (Panel, 1983). Some 60 to 80 percent of these persons are psychotic, and most of their cases are settled through plea-bargaining. Those exculpated from criminal action on the basis of insanity may be confined in mental institutions under a treatment rationale for as long, if not longer, [as] they would have been confined had they been judged guilty and placed in the prison system. In nearly one-third of the states, subsequent hospitalization is automatic, while in half the states the court decides whether the offense is likely to be repeated and whether release is indicated.

The major reason for renewed interest in the insanity defense is that John W. Hinckley, Jr., shot the President of the United States in 1981. The shooting was videotaped, and millions of viewers repeatedly saw President Reagan attacked through replays. Hinckley was acquitted on the grounds that he was insane at the time of the attempted assassination (United States v. Hinckley, 525 F.Supp. 1342 [D.D.C. 1981]). This decision prompted a number of attempts to limit the insanity defense. Winslade and Ross (1983: 201) advocate an elimination of the insanity defense, elimination of most psychiatric testimony by psychiatrists about the defendant's state of mind, adoption of the "guilty but mentally ill" plea, and the separation of the guilt and penalty phases of a trial when the defendant pleads mental illness.

The National Mental Health Association convened a national commission on the insanity defense after the Hinckley verdict. They recommended a "not responsible by reason of insanity" verdict because it is difficult for an average person to accept that a defendant is not guilty if it is clear that they did commit the alleged action. However, this would be only a semantic change, with the same legal meaning as not guilty by reason of insanity. This commission also recommended "retaining the insanity defense in all jurisdictions; shifting the burden of proof to the defendant by a preponderance of the evidence; rejecting 'guilty but mentally ill' verdicts; adopting strong dispositional statutes; and prohibiting mental health expert witnesses from testifying about legal issues."

The major change in the insanity defense came in the Comprehensive Crime Act of 1984, which shifted the burden of proof of insanity to the defendant. This change is also noted in Chapter 5.

Jones v. United States, 463 U.S. 354 (1983), dealt with the question of release after a finding of not guilty by reason of insanity for Jones, who had attempted to steal a coat in a department store. The Supreme Court said that Jones was not entitled to be released from the hospital even though he had been hospitalized for a period longer than he would have served had he been convicted of the theft. The nature and duration of the commitment must bear some reasonable relation to the purpose for which the individual is committed. Commitment can continue until such time as the patient has regained his or her sanity or is no longer a danger to self or society. Justice William Brennan, in his dissent, commented that the state must "shoulder the burden of proof by clear and convincing evidence that such additional confinement is appropriate."

An indigent Oklahoma defendant who was tried for killing two people was not provided a psychiatrist to prepare his defense because of the expense to the state. The U.S. Supreme Court held that he was deprived of due process. His single defense was insanity (Ake v. Oklahoma, USLW [1985]. The Supreme Court's opinion emphasized that future dangerousness of the defendant was a significant factor at the sentencing phase and recounted his bizarre behavior at the time of the trial. Courts in over 40 states specifically provide indigent defendants in such cases with a psychiatrist.

Questions for Review

1. What is the most frequently used procedure for involuntary commitment? What are the legal criteria for such commitments?

2. Summarize *Lessard*. Do procedural safeguards constitute sufficient reform? How does *Dodson* illustrate problems of looking to past conduct in predicting future behavior?

3. What was the basis for the right to treatment ruling in *Rouse?*

4. Summarize *Wyatt*. Are the standards of treatment enforceable? How have subsequent cases followed *Wyatt?*

5. On what basis did the U.S. Supreme Court find for the institutionalized person in *Donaldson?*

6.   Does the administration of electroshock therapy to an involuntarily committed minor patient without the consent of the minor's guardian violate the rights (a) to be free from cruel and unusual punishment and (b) to privacy in light of *Price v. Sheppard?* Why or why not? Why is this treatment controversial?

7.   What are policy implications if antipsychotic drugs could be refused by most patients?

8.   How might the Mental Health Systems Act Bill of Rights best be implemented?

9.   What is the duty to warn of dangerousness suggested by *Tarasoff, McIntosh,* and *Hedlund?*

10.   What is the possible conflict of interest in commitment of mentally retarded children by their parents? Are *Parham* safeguards sufficient?

11.   Why have many elderly persons been committed to mental institutions in the past? What is the problem illustrated by *Lake?*

12.   What is the primary purpose of incompetency statutes? What reforms are needed?

13.   When did states begin to enact sex offense statutes? What is the definitional problem?

14.   What is the argument for treating sex offenders as criminals?

15.   Should alcoholics be treated as criminals or as patients? What is one difficulty implicit in a treatment approach?

16.   Is drug addiction a crime? What problems have been encountered in involuntary commitment of addicts?

17.   Who is incompetent to stand trial? What are potential consequences of incompetency?

18.   Are most persons held for the purpose of pretrial evaluation judged incompetent? Summarize *Jackson.*

19.   What three points must be considered in evaluating insanity as a defense? What are consequences of proposed reforms?

Questions for Debate and Discussion

1.   The medical model of mental illness has recently been criticized. What legal problems does it produce?

2.   Has the use of nursing homes rather than mental hospitals for older persons resulted in a higher regard for individual rights?

3.   What policies would you like to see advanced by the Supreme Court concerning rights to obtain treatment, to refuse treatment, and to refuse medication?

4.   Evaluate the civil rights provisions in the mental health statutes in your own state.

Selected Readings   Herr, Stanley S. *Legal Rights and Mental Health Care.* Lexington, Mass.: Lexington Books, 1983.

Lacoursiere, Roy B. "A Footnote to Parham: Was J.L. a Casualty of the Mental Health Bar?" *American Academy of Psychiatry and Law Bulletin* 11 (1983): 279–285.

Legal Rights of Mentally Disabled Persons. New York: Practising Law Institute, 1979.

Mabbutt, Fred R. "Juveniles, Mental Hospital Commitment, and Civil Rights: The Case of Parham v. J.R." *Journal of Family Law* 19 (1980): 27–64.

Merton, Vanessa. "Confidentiality and the Dangerous Patient: Implications of Tarasoff for Psychiatrists and Lawyers." *Emory Law Journal* 31 (1982): 477–531.

Morris, Grant H. "Dr. Szasz or Dr. Seuss: Whose Right to Refuse Mental Treatment?" *Journal of Psychology and Law* (1981): 283–303.

Ray, Joyce M., and F. G. Gosling. "Historical Perspective on the Treatment of Mental Illness in the United States." *Journal of Psychology and Law* 10 (1982): 135–161.

Rubin, Jeffrey. "A Survey of Mental Health Policy Options." *Journal of Health Politics Policy and Law* 5 (1980): 234–249.

Stone, Alan A. *Law, Psychiatry, and Morality: Essays for the 80s*. New York: American Psychiatric Association, 1984.

Wexler, David B. *Mental Health Laws: Major Issues*. New York: Plenum Press, 1981.

Yohalem, J. B., and J. Manes. "The Rights of the Mentally Disabled: Progress in the Face of New Realities." *Trial* 19 (1983): 8, 68.

Zlotnick, David. "First Do No Harm: Least Restrictive Environment Analysis and the Rights of Mental Patients to Refuse Treatment." *West Virginia Law Review* 83 (1980–81): 375–448.

Legal and Social Services

CHAPTER

25

Legal Services

LEGAL ASSISTANCE DEFINED

Legal assistance, also known as legal aid, provides the services of a lawyer to people who cannot afford to hire one. Legal-aid attorneys are generally employed full time by a specialized organization supported by private contributions or government grants. The services are means-tested. Users must provide data on their incomes and assets to demonstrate that they are "legally indigent." Such means tests ensure that legal-aid programs do not compete with private attorneys.

Current eligibility guidelines for federally sponsored legal aid authorized in the Legal Services Corporation Act of 1974 (42 U.S.C. 2996 Sec. 100a.2) concern not only financial inability to afford legal assistance but disqualify an applicant when "such individual's lack of income results from refusal or unwillingness, without good cause, to seek or accept an employment situation." The stated goal is to give preference to the persons least able to afford such assistance, since the demand for legal services exceeds the supply.

Two kinds of cases are excluded by legal services programs: criminal cases in which the defendant is provided legal services by the court and personal injury cases in which the lawyer's fee is based on a proportion of damages awarded, i.e., a contingency fee.

THE NEED FOR LEGAL ASSISTANCE

How great is the need for legal assistance? A Denver study projected that there are about 10 million legal problems among persons whose incomes are below the poverty line. In San Francisco, where legal services have been relatively adequate, thirty cases per 1,000 population were handled in one year. Projected for the nation, the total is 6 million cases. About 1 million cases are now handled each year. To meet the need, 12,000 to 15,000 lawyers might be required, but we have about 25% of that number.

There are probably more unmet needs for legal services than for medical services. The poor are unpromising clients for the private attorney. They are frequently unaware of the need for service until an emergency makes legal advice absolutely necessary. The need for prompt action then precludes thorough legal work.

SCOPE OF LEGAL AID

While legal aid is often thought of in terms of litigation, in many legal-aid offices less then 5 percent of legal-aid matters actually come to trial. The problems involved in legal aid require advice-giving, negotiation, and education.

Four types of matters constitute roughly 80 percent of legal assistance activities: domestic relations, housing, consumer law, and welfare law.

Domestic Relations The greatest need for legal assistance is for divorce. Many of the so-called single-parent families maintain a tenuous relationship with a spouse, whom they would divorce if legal services were readily available. Child dependency and neglect, child abuse, and problems with the legal status of an institutionalized family member constitute other typical domestic relations problems. A social worker may be as helpful in resolving these problems as a lawyer, and social workers are increasingly included on the legal-aid team.

Housing Landlord-tenant relations for the poor are frustrating because owners are rarely interested in investing money to improve property in deteriorating neighborhoods, whether or not the condition of a building would justify such an investment. Legal-assistance lawyers have been successful in helping tenants of such buildings obtain the right to withhold rent legally with cause in an effort to force landlords to make necessary repairs and upgrade dwellings in accordance with the law. As Chapter 21 shows, many problems are simply the result of poor enforcement of existing housing codes.

Consumer Law Consumer law involves the issues of price and quality of merchandise, sales techniques, and the use of credit. These issues were included in the consumer cases in Chapter 20. Legal assistance is particularly important in cases of consumer fraud because of the long-term obligations created by signing conditional sales contracts.

Governmental Services Welfare and other governmental services give rise to many legal problems. Eligibility laws and regulations frequently restrict the rights of the poor. In addition, agencies may employ extralegal means to discourage the poor from applying for welfare or to terminate their eligibility. The emphasis on detection of welfare fraud may impose restrictions on the personal freedom of applicants and recipients alike.

Over and above the legal issues of the welfare system, provision of basic universal governmental services may also be inadequate. Irregular garbage collection, substandard schools, and dangerous parks are conditions with which the average citizen must frequently cope. Legal action may bring about improvement.

SERVING MINORITIES Members of minority groups are especially vulnerable in dealing with legal problems including, but not limited to, the four types discussed above. They are often confused by the legal process required to deal with their difficulties. For some, a lack of proficiency in written and spoken English creates a special problem. Yet even English-speaking people find the legal system difficult to negotiate. For example, one study reported that blacks prefer teachers and social workers from their own race, but they prefer white lawyers, on the assumption that whites are better able to negotiate the judicial system (Brieland, 1969:171).

While minorities have a great need for legal protection, they have the least information about the law and little access to legal services. They are potential recipients of legal action, but seldom use it to assert their rights or to redress grievances.

HISTORY OF LEGAL ASSISTANCE Legal assistance has gone through four stages of development: (1) the era of private support (1900–1965); (2) public support through the Anti-Poverty Program of Lyndon Johnson; (3) establishment of the Legal Services Corporation; and (4) attempts of the Reagan administration to eliminate federal funding of legal services.

The Era of Private Support (1900–1965)

Until the 1960s, legal assistance was offered through a limited number of voluntary agencies and was often financed in part from contributions of lawyers through local bar associations. Otherwise legal services had to be obtained by *pro bono* services—lawyers donating their efforts.

In 1963, less than $4 million was spent on such services—only two-tenths of 1 percent of legal expenditures to serve almost 50 million Americans. The proportion of persons served per 1,000 population was about the same as it had been in 1916 (Johnson, 1974:9).

Some of the early private legal-aid services were supported by predecessor organizations of the United Way. In the beginning, the primary function of legal-aid lawyers was to attend to cases and little else. Sometimes the service of the legal-aid staff was supplemented by lawyers who volunteered to work an occasional evening or Saturday. With such limited service, only dire emergencies were likely to receive attention to the exclusion of routine divorces, consumer fraud, and issues involving small claims. The narrow focus of the traditional legal-aid program and its inadequate manpower stand in contrast to the legal services following the advent of the War on Poverty.

Legal Assistance Through the Office of Economic Opportunity

The early 1960s saw demands for more adequate legal services. By the time the Economic Opportunity Act was passed, objectives for legal services included:

■ Asserting legal rights which, although recognized in law, remain unimplemented. Housing and welfare law are two common examples. The enforcement of housing codes and the use of fair hearings for welfare clients left much to be desired.

■ Facilitating the development of legal rights in areas where the laws are vague or biased. Competent legal representation tends to bring about reassessment and change. Due process has been one of the major emphases.

■ Bringing pressure to increase the fairness and reasonableness of adjudicative procedures and to ensure more positive and sympathetic implementation of legal policies. In short, advocacy can serve the poor and increase the responsiveness of agencies.

■ Assisting in the creation of contractual relations and legal associations to maximize the opportunities and benefits the law provides. Lawyers need to provide a voice for their clients in the decision-making process. This involves negotiation more than litigation.

Legal assistance was first offered as part of the Community Action Program of the Office of Economic Opportunity (OEO) in 1965. The Legal Services Program was given separate identity by Congress in 1969, so it survived after the Poverty Program had been abandoned. Legal assistance expanded rapidly in this period. In fiscal year 1966, $20 million was appropriated, rising to $61 million by 1972. Legal-assistance programs of the late 1960s and the 1970s stressed education of clients and the general public. For the first time, there was enough personnel to provide such public education. A need for consumer law reflected a comparable need to educate clients about credit options and product warranties—means to arm people against questionable sales practices and unconscionable contracts. Since the problems of the poor are principally related to low incomes, some legal-assistance attorneys offered fiscal management programs to individuals and groups. Their activities are not unlike those of the social worker who tries to help public assistance recipients live on a standard budget. Attorneys in legal-service programs also fulfilled an important role in educating the general public on the needs of the poor.

In such educational efforts, the attorney became an advocate with influential members of the community, whose support is essential to improve the lot of low-income citizens. Modern legal assistance, then, is a combination of litigation, advocacy, negotiation, and education of both the poor and the general public.

Rapid growth during the OEO period made legal services politically controversial because poverty attorneys frequently opposed landlords, police, social service agencies, and members of state legislatures. Government funds were sometimes used to sue other government agencies. Members of Congress responded by trying unsuccessfully to forbid such suits. Vice President Spiro T. Agnew (1970: 329) commented that the legal services program was "manned by ideological vigilantes who owe their allegiance . . . only to a system of social reform."

The Legal Services Corporation (1974–1981)

Advocates of legal aid felt that the program had attained permanent funding and increased status when the Legal Services Corporation was authorized in 1974. Its board included leading lawyers and legal educators and its budget continued to expand to provide much more adequate coverage. The activities were similar to those developed under OEO. The budget increased from $205 million in 1978 to over $321 million in 1981. It employed 3,850 attorneys in 1978 and 6,337 in 1981.

The Reagan Era (1981 to the Present)

The opposition to legal services was stated unequivocally by President Ronald Reagan. The administration tried to eliminate the entire appropriation for legal services, including appropriations for legal services to the elderly under provisions of the Older Americans Act. Failing in this, the President nominated conservatives to the board of the Legal Services Corporation and was successful in reducing appropriations by $80 million in 1982 and 1983 and cutting staff attorney positions to 4,800. Current staff members complain that newer rules inhibit their activities and reduce their effectiveness.

LEGAL AID AND LAW REFORM

Some of the achievements of law reform efforts during the OEO phase of legal aid are interesting because they involve cases with which you are already familiar from previous chapters. Earl C. Johnson, Jr., national director of the Legal Service Program at that time, estimates that such decisions as *Shapiro v. Thompson* on residency and *King v. Smith* in the "substitute father" issue resulted in an annual increase of $300 million to $400 million in public assistance income (Johnson, 1974: 204). Had challenges to maximum and flat grants been successful, further gains would have been achieved.

Poverty lawyers also obtained increased benefits for education by successfully challenging the property tax as a fair way to finance schools, in Serrano v. Priest, 487 P.2d 1241 (Cal. 1971), a decision that held variable property valuations to be an inequitable means of school financing (see Chapter 22).

Johnson provides examples of how challenging the actions of public and private institutions has resulted in greater personal freedom for clients.

> Goods, services, and even opportunities, generally are provided to the poor through government and quasi-governmental agencies, welfare departments, public housing authorities, the Social Security Administration, unemployment compensation boards, and scores of other local, state, and Federal agencies which administer the transfer payments that supply half of the goods and services enjoyed by the bottom fifth of the population. Poor people not only have a stake in the amount of goods and services

distributed, a decision generally beyond the control of these agencies, they are also interested in the manner of distribution.

■ Are the eligibility standards well advertised and applied uniformly?

■ Is there undue interference with the privacy or life-style of the recipients?

■ Do the administrators apply all rules and policies without discrimination?

■ Are the poor given adequate notice and a fair hearing before termination of their transfer payments?

■ Do agency personnel treat the recipients with the respect due fellow human beings?

All of these questions involve matters within the control of the agencies charged with the responsibility of redistribution. A complex body of law, consisting of regulations, rules, and policies, has been formulated to deal with these questions by the agencies themselves. This special legal system has tolerated and sometimes promoted abusive, unfair, discriminatory procedures and practices. Some examples:

■ "Midnight raids" on recipients by investigators seeking to unearth violations of welfare rules.

■ Denial of aid to applicants who fail to measure up to some arbitrary moral standard, that is, no member of family was ever arrested, no illegitimate children.

■ A quantity of detailed rules and regulations so onerous as to unduly constrict the daily lives of recipients.

■ Termination of welfare assistance or public housing tenancy for any reason before the recipient has an opportunity to refute the allegations at a hearing (Johnson, 1974: 217).

All these issues have been subjects of litigation.

Private agencies also exercise great power over the lives of the poor. As Johnson indicates:

■ Unless an industry is unionized, an employer usually can still take away a worker's job for any cause, or none, without even telling the employee why he is being fired.

■ In most states, a landlord can take away the tenant's shelter for any reason, or none, and in some states without any kind of hearing.

■ Until recently, an alleged creditor could take away most of the debtor's income, through garnishment, without even proving a debt is owed.

■ Creditors also can harass a debtor unmercifully: contacting him at inconvenient hours, bothering his children, embarrassing him with his employer, and so on.

■ Employers, landlords, and creditors have been known to disregard even the few protections that exist when dealing with people who lack legal counsel or an understanding of their rights (Johnson, 1974: 219).

JUDICARE   An alternative to legal-aid offices, Judicare involves the use of attorneys in private practice to serve the poor. Although such lawyers serve as volunteers, they are usually paid according to an established fee schedule. A special credit card system has been used to make it possible for the potential client to complete eligibility requirements in advance of the need for legal services.

Judicare provides clients with the services of attorneys who have been in practice longer but whose knowledge of problems typically experienced by the poor may be less than that of the regular legal assistance staff. Although Judicare offers greater freedom in choice of lawyers, this freedom is of relatively little importance to low-income clients who are not sufficiently informed to know whom to choose. In regular legal-aid programs, a client may request transfer to another attorney if the first relationship proves unsatisfactory.

Cost studies indicate that Judicare runs higher than legal-assistance services. A Judicare divorce costs three to seven times as much as a divorce delivered by full-time legal-assistance attorneys (Johnson, 1974: 40). The main value of Judicare is that it gives more attorneys firsthand experience in dealing with problems of the poor.

USE OF PRIVATE ATTORNEYS

Although the Reagan administration did not succeed in eliminating the Legal Services Corporation, the corporation was required to make available 10 percent of its funds in 1983 and 12.5 percent in 1984 to promote involvement of private attorneys in delivery of legal services to the poor. In some instances this simply involved the development of Judicare arrangements, but other approaches have also been used, including contract attorneys, lawyer referral services, co-counseling arrangements with private lawyers, and volunteer lawyers working inside legal services offices (Smith, 1983: 187–189).

Smith summarizes potential positive aspects of the private attorney involvement program:

> Motivation for private attorney involvement as an integral part of all programs' delivery systems.
>
> Use of federal funds to obtain increased client services by (1) tapping the "voluntarism" of the legal profession to obtain *pro bono* and reduced fee services, (2) improving the quality and range of services available through the special expertise of private attorneys, and (3) increasing the pool of attorneys who are experienced with the legal needs of the poor.
>
> Means to translate the Code of Professional Responsibility into actions that serve the poor.
>
> Use [of] the resources of the private bar to develop new local funding sources.
>
> Expansion of positive working relationships between legal services programs and private attorneys, breaking down barriers and overcoming stereotypes by introducing legal services programs to possibilities for participation of private attorneys and introducing the bar to the legal problems of the poor.
>
> Incentives for continued exploration of innovative methods for delivering legal services to the poor.

PREPAID LEGAL SERVICES

Prepaid legal services are often called legal insurance. Cost sharing through membership plans for middle-class people have shown gradual growth. The American Bar Association began a pilot program in Shreveport, Louisiana, fifteen years ago, which has been copied elsewhere. It involves an "open-panel" plan in which anyone who pays the membership fee may join and choose from a wide range of lawyers when service is needed.

In a closed-panel system, a group or organization contracts with one or more law firms providing legal services for its members. Labor unions often enter into such plans. In both the open and the closed panel, legal matters included under the agreement are carefully specified and limited.

RECENT DEVELOPMENTS IN LEGAL AID

Some innovations in the use of legal services have already been mentioned. Further developments include the growth of clinical programs sponsored by law schools and staffed by their students. These programs have induced graduates to seek employment in legal aid offices. In states that allow law school seniors to appear in court, students gain useful experience by providing legal assistance.

Some bar associations supplement legal-aid services by providing clients an initial interview with a private lawyer free or for a nominal fee, perhaps $10 for a half-hour. This facilitates preliminary analysis of the problem, with subsequent referral to a private attorney or legal assistance as appropriate.

DIFFERENTIAL STAFFING AND SOCIAL WORK ROLES

Further innovations have been implemented in the staffing of legal service. While there is no general national shortage of lawyers, staff shortages because of limited budgets have encouraged innovations in the use of personnel. The range of cases handled by legal-aid offices forms a repetitive pattern where the same types of situations arise. Often clients have a greater need for advice and education than for litigation. In such a setting, paraprofessionals can make a valuable contribution to resolution of problems and free lawyers to do work for which only they are qualified. Paralegal training is available both through college programs and commercial sponsorship. While there is still resistance to the use of such personnel, their efforts have generally been successful. Many legal-assistance operations and procedures have been effectively routinized to save time and costly personnel.

With the high volume of domestic problems handled by legal aid, social work personnel are especially useful. Their knowledge of community resources often supplements that of the attorney. Social workers are ideal for working on behalf of persons with medical and mental health problems, child welfare problems, and difficulties with public assistance.

Just as the law student obtains useful clinical experience in a legal-assistance office, the student social worker finds that the legal-aid program can provide a varied and stimulating field placement with opportunities for both service and advocacy. Interdisciplinary teams in legal assistance will develop as the volume of cases increases and specialization is seen to be efficient.

Questions for Review

1. How widespread is the need for legal aid?

2. How are the typical legal-aid activities classified?

3. What was the basic purpose of traditional legal aid? How was it financed?

4. What were the major objectives of the Legal Services Program under the OEO?

5. Give an example of the educational role of legal services.

6. What court decisions on welfare cases resulted in the provision of more money to the poor?

7. Summarize the major criticisms of legal services advanced by the Reagan administration and the policy of the administration toward legal service.

8. What are some functions of paralegal personnel? Of social workers in legal services offices?

9. Explain Judicare.

10. In prepaid legal insurance, what is the difference between a closed plan and an open plan?

Questions for Debate and Discussion

1. What are the most important issues in legal services for the elderly?

2. What is the difference between legal services and Judicare? Which do you prefer?

3. Should legal services place less emphasis on law reform and more on such services as divorce?

4. How can the issue of social workers practicing law be avoided in using them as staff members in a legal-aid office?

Selected Readings

Garth, Bryant. *Neighborhood Law Firms for the Poor*. Rockville, Md.: Sijthoff & Noordhoff, 1980.

Katz, Jack. *Poor People's Lawyers in Transition*. New Brunswick, N.J.: Rutgers University Press, 1982.

Starkey, Debra L. "A Partnership of Professionals: Need for Social Workers in Public Defender Offices." *National Legal Aid and Defender Association Briefcase 38* (1981): 58–68.

Zander, Michael. *Legal Services for the Community*. New York: International Publications Service, 1978.

CHAPTER
26

Legal Issues in Social Work Practice

The law can bar social agencies or individuals from offering child care or nursing home services unless they are licensed to do so. The law can require anyone calling himself or herself a social worker to qualify for a license to practice. In the case of malpractice, the law also may authorize revocation of a license and subject the social worker to possible suits for damages.

LICENSING OF FACILITIES

State statutes regulate the way children or adults are placed and cared for outside their homes. Licensing of social agencies and of individuals performing social welfare functions is an important element of regulation. Hospitals are licensed by the state Department of Health, and their social service activities receive sanction by this means. Voluntary and proprietary agencies offering residential or day-care services for children are generally licensed by the state Department of Social Services. Licensing is ordinarily not required for agencies that provide only outpatient programs. Public agencies are also not usually subject to license, although their programs are expected to meet licensing standards.

The reason for licensing is simple. In care given outside a child's home, for example, the state provides supervision on behalf of the welfare of the child. A license tells the public that minimum standards have been met. State v. Hay, 131 N.W.2d 452 (Iowa 1964) establishes the principle of minimum standards as the basis of licensing.

Licenses are usually available without charge. State licensing specialists visit and evaluate facilities. Initial approval is particularly important in licensing, for in licensing-renewal studies numbers of staff are sometimes inadequate for in-depth study.

Children's agencies that provide adoption, foster family care, institutional services, and group day-care must be licensed. Individuals or families providing day care are generally required to have a license. This requirement is often ignored by care-givers because of the informality of arrangements and the difficulty of enforcing the law. Only homes that advertise are likely to be known to licensing authorities.

In administrative law, which includes licensing, the statutes tend to provide definitions and a general framework. A regulatory agency has the authority to draft detailed standards based on the statutes. Licenses related to the provision of social services are similar to those that authorize the conduct of a business or the practice of any profession. Licensing statutes specify behaviors, demand conformity, and impose sanctions. Standards should be based on research and sound knowledge and be interpreted carefully to the community. Without a license, a person or organization may not engage in the activities covered by the particular statute. An applicant who is denied a license has recourse through the courts.

Six criteria are important in evaluating a licensing law:

1. Statement of purpose
2. What activity is prohibited
3. Constitutionality
4. Means for implementation
5. Rights and responsibilities of licensee
6. Provision for citizen participation

Several controversial questions remain: (1) Should a state agency that operates programs of its own also have the authority to license others? (2) To what extent should goals beyond minimum standards be a part of the licensing program? (3) Do licensing standards deal with personality factors and management techniques or only objective data such as square footage per occupant, play equipment, fire prevention, and formal educational credentials of the staff?

LEGAL REGULATION OF SOCIAL WORKERS

Legal regulation of a profession is provided as a part of administrative law primarily for the protection of the public. Licensing is most important as a means of quality control. When a physician displays a license, the public is assured that state educational requirements to practice medicine have been met and that the physician has been examined by peers for evidence of competence. The implications of social work regulation are similar.

Many of the problems implicit in regulation of the profession arise from the diverse roles of social workers. The term **social worker** has been applied to many subprofessionals—most notably personnel in public assistance who determine client eligibility, a task generally performed by people with limited education and status. Inadequacies of the public assistance system have generated hostility toward the whole field of social work. The public understands direct service social work roles better than the roles of advocate or social planner, but it does not understand distinctions between professionals and nonprofessionals.

By the beginning of 1985, thirty-five states and the Virgin Islands and Puerto Rico provided some form of legal regulation of social work. The status and the type of regulation in each are identified in Figure 26.1. The National Association of Social Workers (NASW) has been the major advocate of legal regulation. The NASW has been joined in its interest in legal regulation of the profession by various societies for clinical social work (which emphasize the practice of psychotherapy at an advanced level) and by the National Association of Black Social Workers. As we shall see, the three groups take quite different positions on regulation.

The psychotherapeutic market in social work is linked with the medical profession through psychiatry, with education through the counselor role, and with psychology through its clinical specialty. At one extreme, some people contend that psychotherapy should be performed only under close medical supervision. At the other extreme, some support therapeutic help by lay self-help group members.

FIGURE 26.1
STATES WITH ACTS REGULATING SOCIAL WORK

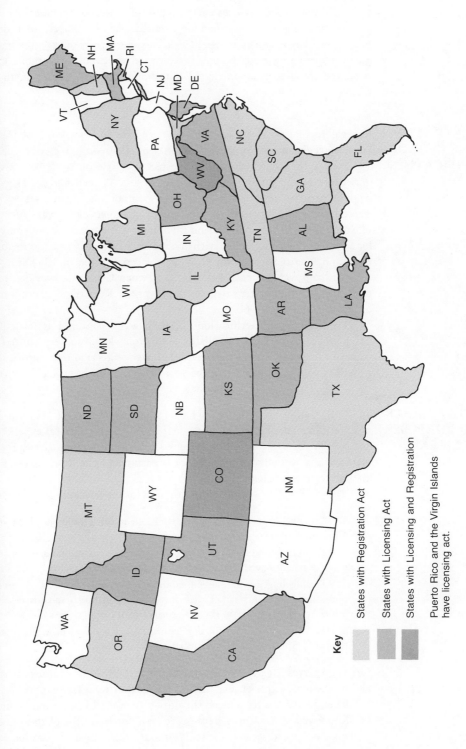

Key

States with Registration Act

States with Licensing Act

States with Licensing and Registration

Puerto Rico and the Virgin Islands
have licensing act.

Such diverse approaches result in ambiguity about professional boundaries and areas of expertise and ultimately hinder passage of legislation.

Legal regulation involves enacting a state statute to provide for peer review of persons wishing to be certified or licensed. At the outset, in order to assure professional involvement to establish a membership base, a "grandfather clause" grants experienced practitioners certification or licensure without examination. After the specified start-up period, all applicants must take a qualifying examination.

REGISTRATION OR CERTIFICATION

In legal regulation of social work practice, an understanding of the differences between **registration** (or **certification**) and **licensing** is essential. Certification acts bestow the exclusive right to the use of a title on those who possess certain qualifications and are registered. A typical title is "certified social worker." Any helping persons without such credentials cannot call themselves social workers. These laws characteristically lack teeth. Practitioners can always substitute a title like "counselor." Since registration is voluntary, there may be no strong motivation for social workers to comply with the requirements and pay the membership fee. Although Puerto Rico approved an act for certification in 1934, the first law on the mainland was not passed until 1945, when California provided for voluntary registration of the master's degree social worker. Registration laws were advocated until the end of the 1960s.

The registration/certification approach was recognized as inadequate for the development of necessary standards, and professional concern shifted toward advocacy of licensure. Licensing provides greater protection than certification because it defines who can practice and because a license can be revoked for cause.

RATIONALE AND PURPOSES OF LICENSING

In 1968, California passed an act licensing the practice of "clinical social work" with requirements for the master's degree and specific clinical experience. In 1969 the NASW Delegate Assembly adopted a position favoring licensure. Two model state statutes were developed, one for licensure and one for registration. Now only the former is advocated.

The NASW (1975) stated four purposes for the licensure of social work practice:

1.   Establishing a public, legal definition of the profession which recognizes the differential levels of social work practice
2.   Protecting consumer and clientele rights and raising standards of service competence of practitioners in both agency and independent practice
3.   Establishing a public accountability in the delivery of social services based on professional standards rather than inconsistent, private standards of performance to protect the practitioner in the performance of social work tasks
4.   Providing a basis for the development and advancement of the profession within the context of other social institutions and professions

Licensure serves a gatekeeping function by establishing educational qualifications and professional experience as the professional criteria for practice.

The NASW has recognized the difficulty of establishing public understanding of professional social work. Because at least three-fourths of the persons engaged in delivery of social services are still without professional preparation and may have limited awareness of professional and ethical standards that should govern their activity, the public's failure to consider licensure as an indication of professional quality is hardly surprising. In addition, state legislators may perceive "social work" as activity carried out within the state's public welfare program, where mounting costs are a source of constant irritation; they do not always view social workers as skilled and disciplined service-providers.

However, many state legislators and a sizable portion of the public are concerned about the quality of services provided. They may come to recognize that effective help is cheaper and more humanitarian than bureaucratic processing of people by untrained social workers. The task is to build public support for the social work profession that will result in more appropriate use of trained personnel.

REQUIREMENTS FOR LICENSING OF SOCIAL WORKERS

A licensing statute should require:

1. Minimal educational credentials. With the exception of the initial grandfather period, there are to be no alternatives to traditional academic degrees.

2. Professional experience for each level of professional practice as set forth in the act.

3. An examination procedure to ensure competence.

4. Sanctions against persons guilty of malpractice or those who are otherwise unfit, to be accomplished through an initial refusal to grant a license or through provisions for suspension or revocation of licenses.

Traditionally the qualifications and ability of license applicants has been assessed through both written and oral examinations. Because these means may be discriminatory against people who lack traditional educational requirements, the need for innovative approaches to the problem of qualification criteria is great. While the NASW model statute refers to the use of written examinations, a recent policy statement proposes that NASW units study and attempt to develop less rigid approaches to the assessment of applicants. Since the profession's basic concern should be with the quality of service provided and the breadth of practitioners' competence, new examination models are often used as substitutes for the usual pen-and-paper procedures. In addition, the NASW insists that licensing cover all levels of social work practice.

A MODEL STATUTE FOR LICENSING OF SOCIAL WORKERS

The key sections of the model statute developed by the NASW follow.

EXCERPTS FROM NASW MODEL STATUTE FOR LICENSING OF SOCIAL WORKERS

1. Purpose

Since the profession of social work profoundly affects the lives of the people of this state, it is the purpose of this act to protect the public by setting standards of qualification, education, training, and experience for those who seek to engage in the practice of social work and by promoting high standards of professional performance for those engaged in the profession of social work.

2. Definitions

"State regulatory agency" means the (name of the existing professional regulatory body to be charged with the responsibilty of this act).

"Board" means the Board of Social Work Examiners established under this act.

3. Practice of social work

a. After (date), no person may engage in the practice of social work unless he/she is licensed under this act as a certified social worker or social worker, and no social work associate may practice except under the supervision of a certified social worker or social worker.

b. For the purposes of this act, "social work practice" is defined as service and action to effect changes in human behavior, a person's or persons' emotional responses, and the social conditions of individuals, families, groups, organizations, and communities, which are influenced by the interaction of social, cultural, political, and economic systems. The practice of social work is guided by special knowledge of social resources, social systems, human capabilities, and the part conscious and unconscious motivation play in determining behavior. The disciplined application of social work values, principles, and methods in a variety of ways includes but is not restricted to the following: (1) counseling and the use of applied psychotherapy with individuals, families, and groups and other measures to help people modify behavior or personal and family adjustment, (2) providing general assistance, information, and referral services and other supportive services, (3) explaining and interpreting the psychosocial aspects of a situation to individuals, families, or groups, (4) helping organizations and communities analyze social problems and human needs and provide human services, (5) helping organizations and communities organize for general neighborhood improvement or community development, (6) improving social conditions through the application of social planning and social policy formulations, (7) meeting basic human needs, (8) assisting in problem-solving activities, (9) resolving or managing conflict, and/or (10) bringing about changes in the system.

Nothing in this act shall be construed to prevent licensed physicians, surgeons, psychologists, psychotherapists, attorneys, court employees, marriage counselors, family counselors, child counselors, or members of the clergy from doing work within the standards and ethics of their respective professions and callings, provided they do not hold themselves out to the public by title or description of service as being engaged in the practice of social work. Any profession licensed under state law shall be exempt from the purposes of this act. Students enrolled in recognized programs of study leading to social work degrees may practice only under the direct supervision of a certified social worker or a social worker licensed under this act.

Violation of the foregoing shall be a misdemeanor punishable by fine of not less than $(amount) nor more than $(amount), by imprisonment for not less than (period of time), or by both fine and imprisonment.

4. Representation to the public

After (date), no person may represent himself as a social worker by using the titles "certified social worker," "social worker," "registered social worker," "social work associate," or any other title that includes such words unless licensed under this act.

After (date), no person may represent himself as a certified social worker, social worker, registered social worker, or social work associate by adding the letters CSW, SW, RSW, or SWA unless licensed under this act.

Violation of the foregoing shall be misdemeanors punishable by a fine of not less than $(amount) nor more than $(amount), by imprisonment for not less than (time period) nor more than (time period), or by both such fine and imprisonment.

5. Titles and qualifications for licenses

The state regulatory agency shall issue a license as a certified social worker, a social worker, or a social work associate.

a. The state regulatory agency shall issue a license as a "certified social worker" to an applicant who

1. Has a doctorate or master's degree from a school of social work approved by the state regulatory agency.
2. Has passed an examination prepared by the board for this purpose.
3. Has satisfied the board that he is a person of good moral character.

b. The state regulatory agency shall issue a license as a "social worker" to an applicant who

1. Has a baccalaureate degree in a social work or social welfare program approved by the state regulatory agency from a college or university approved by the state regulatory agency or a baccalaureate degree in another field, two years' experience in a social work capacity, and completion of courses equivalent to a social work or social welfare program approved by the state regulatory agency from a college or university approved by the state regulatory agency.
2. Has passed an examination prepared by the board for this purpose.

3. Has satisfied the board that he is a person of good moral character.

c. The state regulatory agency shall issue a license as a "social work associate" to an applicant who

1. Has a baccalaureate degree in a non-social-work field or discipline or an associate of arts degree in the human services in a program approved by the state regulatory agency from a junior college, college, or university approved by the state regulatory agency or equivalent as determined by the board.
2. Has passed an examination prepared by the board for this purpose.
3. Has satisfied the board that he is a person of good moral character.

6. Private, independent practice of social work

a. After (date), no person may engage in the private, independent practice of social work unless he

1. Is licensed under this act as a certified social worker.
2. Has had two years of experience under appropriate supervision in the field of specialization in which the applicant will practice (e.g., psychotherapy, community organization, or planning).
3. Has passed the examination prepared by the board for this purpose.

b. Violation of the foregoing shall be a misdemeanor punishable by a fine of not less than $(amount) nor more than $(amount), by imprisonment for not less than (time period) nor more than (time period), or by both such fine and imprisonment.

7. Exemption from requirements (grandfather provisions)

a. From the effective date of this act to (cutoff date), an applicant shall be exempted from the requirement for any examination provided for herein if he satisfies the board that he is and actually has been engaged, for at least two years, in the practice for which the examination would otherwise be required.

An applicant shall be exempted from the requirement for any examination provided herein if

1. He satisfies the board that he is licensed or registered under the laws of a state or territory of the United States that imposes substantially the same requirement as this act.
2. Pursuant to the laws of such state or territory, he has taken and passed an examination similar to that for which exemption is sought.

b. From the effective date of this act to (cutoff date), an applicant shall be exempted from any academic qualifications required herein if he satisfies the board that he is and has been actually engaged, for at least two years, in the practice for which the academic qualifications would otherwise be required or if he has a post baccalaureate degree in a social work program approved by the state regulatory agency from a college or university approved by the state regulatory agency.

8. Grounds for disciplinary proceedings

a. The state regulatory agency may refuse to renew, may suspend, or may revoke any license issued under this act on proof after a hearing that the person

1. Is guilty of conduct defined as a misdemeanor in this act.
2. Has been convicted of a misdemeanor under this act.
3. Has been convicted in this or any other state of any crime that is a felony in this state.
4. Has been convicted of a felony in a federal court.
5. Is unable to perform the functions of his license by reason of (a) mental illness, (b) physical illness, or (c) addiction or intoxication.
6. Has been grossly negligent in the practice of social work.
7. Has violated one or more of the rules and regulations of the state regulatory agency.

b. These grounds for disciplinary proceedings may be waived by the state regulatory agency on the advice and counsel of the State Board of Examiners. (This item may be inserted *only* if state law governing professional licensing permits it.)

9. Privileged communications

No licensed certified social worker, social worker, or social work associate or his employee may disclose any information he may have acquired from persons consulting him in his professional capacity that was necessary to enable him to render services in his professional capacity to those persons except

a. With the written consent of the person or persons or, in the case of death or disability, of his own personal representative, other person authorized to sue, or the beneficiary of an insurance policy on his life, health, or physical condition.

b. That a licensed certified social worker, licensed social worker, or licensed social work associate shall not be required to treat as confidential a communication that reveals the contemplation of a crime or a harmful act.

c. When the person is a minor under the laws of this state and the information acquired by the licensed certified social worker, licensed social worker, or licensed social work associate indicates that the minor was the victim or subject of a crime, the licensed social worker, the social worker, or the social work associate may be required to testify fully in any examination, trial, or other proceeding in which the commission of such a crime is the subject of inquiry.

d. When the person waives the privilege by bringing charges against the licensed certified social worker, the social worker, or the social work associate.

For violations of acts regulating social work, existing laws provide fines of up to $500 in some jurisdictions and sentences of up to one year.

SOCIAL ACTION FOR LEGAL REGULATION

Public understanding of professional social work, uniformity of proposals in the various states, unity within the profession, and complementary strategies and tactics among related professions are major issues in facilitating the passage of licensing legislation in the remaining states. In this section, we shall draw on the NASW analysis.

The NASW believes that the basis of licensing legislation is the need of the public to understand the professional nature of social work and the appropriate use of professionally trained personnel in providing social services. This need is a fundamental issue confronting the profession, because legal regulation is essentially a public mandate. It implies that, in the interest of the public and of society, one should be required by law to meet certain standards in order to practice social work. If there is no *public* purpose, there is no basis for public, legal sanction.

The public must be educated to recognize that professional training makes a difference, that persons served by unqualified and untrained practitioners are deprived of adequate service and risk having their problems exacerbated as a result of incompetent but well-meaning efforts. Lack of agreement among such groups as the NASW, Clinical Social Workers, and the National Association of Black Social Workers may be fatal to the passage of regulatory legislation. Although the present movement toward licensure of social work is conducted mainly by NASW units, other organizations of social workers are also active. Advancement of the profession and successful passage of legislation depend largely on achievement of common legislative objectives within all factions of the social work community. Separate legislation for each level of professional practice has been opposed by some state clinical social work groups who oppose a multilevel approach.

On the other hand, the National Association of Black Social Workers has questioned state licensure as a threat to the profession's potential for social change in that it may restrict entry into the field by minorities. Objections are also raised to inequitable, discriminatory "examination barriers" that favor academic achievement over effectiveness in practice and fulfillment of client expectations. As is true with any legislation affecting a specific group of people, state legislators are loath to pass a bill that is still a matter of dispute and disagreement within a profession. In recent years this situation has blocked passage of social work licensure bills in several states.

The development of model statutes helps assure uniformity among state laws and paves the way for closer cooperation in the administration of licensing among the several states. In order to minimize incompatible and inconsistent state acts, the movement to secure licensure of social work practice should be unified and strengthened. Variations in legal requirements diminish public understanding and improved quality in services.

State licensing or examination boards now communicate and work together. Further efforts at stimulating communication among states would reveal a potentially rich source of data and information on the practice of social work from state to state.

Related helping professions, including psychiatry and psychology, have led the opposition to licensure of social workers. Opposition generally stems from the relationship between licensing and third-party payments for mental health services. Reimbursements from insurance companies are much easier to obtain if the social work therapist is licensed. Various other helping professions, such as marriage and family counselors, personnel and guidance counselors, pastoral counselors, and alcohol and drug abuse counselors, are also actively seeking legal recognition. In spite of paragraph 3 of section 3 of the proposed model act, which disclaims any attempt to regulate these non-social-work activities, practitioners in the other counseling fields may not look favorably on licensing bills. Disagreements within social work and opposition from other professions can only serve to confuse and irritate legislators and to defeat bills to license social workers.

There are three major hazards to the rapid extension of licensing laws: public confusion about social work in general, differences of opinion within social work itself, and pressures from related professions in health and other fields.

Many of the suggestions for lobbying discussed in Chapter 3 of this book are useful in promoting passage of a licensing act.

MALPRACTICE IN SOCIAL WORK

Malpractice is an issue in social work as well as in medicine. Professional people operate on their own judgment based on educational background and other professional credentials. They are expected to be competent and to act in a proper manner, according to the code of ethics of the profession. A social worker becomes liable for damages if injury or harm is inflicted on a client, if the client is treated improperly, or if the social worker neglects to do something that should have been done, which constitues negligence. The need for social workers to carry liability insurance is demonstrated by the following cases:

■ The California Supreme Court ruled that a psychotherapist treating a patient who committed murder was liable for damages to the parents of the murder victim. The therapist failed to warn third parties of the patient's announced intentions to do bodily harm. This decision is indicative of the tendency of courts to place increasing responsibility on the therapist, not only for the choice of treatment method, but also for treatment outcome.

■ A suit charging child abuse was brought against a children's home in which a six-year-old's shoulders were broken. The child's parents sued the agency, including the supervisor of the social worker charged with the act. The agency, the supervisor, and the worker can all be sued.

■ While on a picnic supervised by a social worker, a child drowned. Unnoticed, the child and a companion left the group to go swimming, disregarding the social worker's explicit instructions. The child ventured into deep water and went under. Later the parents sued the social worker for negligence.

■   A woman had had twelve years of mental health problems and received in-patient and out-patient treatment. She brought suit against the social work therapist for repeated acts of sexual intercourse. While it was her word against the worker's, the suit was settled out of court. Even if the worker had successfully defended himself, his career would probably have been ruined.

Sexual intercourse used as a therapeutic technique is especially likely to be an issue in malpractice. Roy V. Hartogs, 381 N.Y.S. 2d 587 (1976), involving a psychiatrist, is illustrative.

ROY v. HARTOGS

Supreme Court,
Appellate Term, First
Department,
381 N.Y.S.2d 587
(1976).

PER CURIAM:

A complaint should not be dismissed on the opening statement of counsel unless, accepting as true all facts stated in the opening and resolving in plaintiff's favor all material facts in issue, plaintiff nevertheless is precluded from recovery as a matter of law. . . . Counsel asserted in the opening statement that the defendant, a psychiatrist, had treated the plaintiff, as his patient, during the period March, 1969 through September, 1970. It was further averred that, during the last thirteen months of her treatment, plaintiff was induced to have sexual intercourse with the defendant as part of her prescribed therapy. As a result of this improper treatment, counsel alleged that the plaintiff was so emotionally and mentally injured that she was required to seek hospitalization on two occasions during 1971.

The right of action to recover a sum of money for seduction has been abolished by Article 8 of the Civil Rights Law and the predecessor legislation found in Article 2-A of the Civil Practice Act. These statutes were passed, as a matter of public policy, so that marriages should not be entered into because of the threat or danger of an action to recover money damages and the embarrassment and humiliation growing out of such action. . . . However, this legislation did not abolish all causes of action wherein the act of sexual intercourse was either an "incident of" or "contributed to" the ultimate harm or wrong. . . . In this proceeding, the injury to the plaintiff was not merely caused by the consummation of acts of sexual intercourse with the defendant. Harm was also caused by the defendant's failure to treat the plaintiff with professionally acceptable procedures (cf. Zipkin v. Freeman, 436 S.W.2d 753, 761, 762 [Mo. 1969]; cf. Anclote Manor Foundation v. Wilkinson, 263 So.2d 256, 257 [Fla.App.1972]). By alleging that his client's mental and emotional status was adversely affected by this deceptive and damaging treatment, plaintiff's counsel asserted a viable cause of action for malpractice in his opening statement. . . .

Generally, evidence of other acts or transactions, even of a similar nature, are not admissible where such acts can only be deemed relevant through the inference that the party would follow the same course in the transaction in issue. . . . However, the physical condition of the defendant in this appeal became relevant when he stated that he did not have sexual intercourse after 1965 because of a hydrocele. . . . At that juncture, the testimony of witness Stern was correctly received in rebuttal on defendant's physical condition in 1969 and 1970 when he was treating the plaintiff. Because witnesses Cuttler and Sherwood were unaware of the defendant's physical capability during the period in issue, their testimony was properly stricken by the court below. In the context of this protracted trial, the jurors were not so unduly influenced by this stricken testimony as to warrant a reversal on this ground. . . .

Since the brief and unsolicited meeting between juror Smith and Witness Sherwood occurred after the rendition of the verdict on liability, the defendant cannot meritoriously contend that the resolution of the liability issue was tainted by juror misconduct. The propriety of the transfer from Supreme Court to Civil Court . . . was not raised below and will not be considered, for the first time, upon appeal.

The award of $50,000 in compensatory damages for defendant's aggravation of plaintiff's pre-existing mental disorders, is, however, in our opinion excessive. Plaintiff's condition was of long standing, and began years before she became defendant's patient. There is no evidence to support a permanent worsening of the condition by defendant's acts; nor is there proof demonstrating a permanent impairment of her ability to work in a position comparable to that she had before or during the period she was defendant's patient. Given the fact that she may recover only for the aggravation of her condition by defendant (Schneider v. New York Telephone Co., 249 App.Div. 400, 292 N.Y.S. 399), we conclude that an award of more than $25,000 would be excessive.

The jury's finding, implicit in its award of punitive damages, that the defendant was actuated by evil or malicious intentions when the parties had sexual intercourse was against the predominating weight of the credible evidence. Viewing all the facts and circumstances incident to the occurrences most favorably to the plaintiff as disclosed in this record (Sanders v. Rolnick, 188 Misc. 627, 67 N.Y.S.2d 652, affd. 272 App.Div. 803, 71 N.Y.S.2d 896), the weight of the evidence did not justify the jury's finding that defendant's conduct, while inexcusable, was so wanton or reckless as to permit an award for punitive damages. . . . The other points of error raised in defendant's brief are clearly without merit and need not be explored in this decision.

Judgment, entered July 29, 1975 (Myers, J. and jury), reversed and new trial ordered limited to the issue of compensatory damages, with $30 costs to appellant to abide the event that plaintiff recovers less than $25,000 in compensatory damages, unless respondent within ten days after service of a copy of the order entered hereon with notice of entry, stipulates to reduce the recovery to $25,000, in which event judgment modified accordingly and as modified, affirmed without costs.

MARKOWITZ, Presiding Justice (concurring):

I concur in the Per Curiam but would like to add the following observations.

The subject matter of this case was highly sensational forcing the participants to operate in a charged atmosphere rather than the calm almost cloistered climate of the routine civil courtroom. However, since this State has not closed the door on all actions merely because sexual relations are part of the core facts, and does permit civil prosecutions where the wrong alleged is grounded on conventional tort (Tuck v. Tuck, 14 N.Y.2d 341, 251 N.Y.S.2d 653, 200 N.E.2d 554) there is no question that the facts adduced in this record were properly presented to the jury as a possible basis for malpractice which had a causal connection to plaintiff's subsequent psychotic episodes.

While cultists expound theories of the beneficial effects of sexual psychotherapy, the fact remains that all eminent experts in the psychiatric field including the American Psychiatric Association abjure sexual contact between patient and therapist as harmful to the patient and deviant from accepted standards of treatment of the mentally disturbed.

Dr. Ernest Jones, in his encyclopedic treatment of "The Life and Work of Sigmund Freud" (New York, Basic Books, Inc. 1953) sets forth (Vol. 3, p. 163) a letter written by Freud to a colleague which is relevant to the discussion here.

It reads in pertinent part as follows:

"13. XII. 1931

"Lieber Freund:

". . . You have not made a secret of the fact that you kiss your patients and let them kiss you; . . .

"Now I am assuredly not one of those who from prudishness or from consideration of bourgeois convention would condemn little erotic gratifications of this kind. . . . but that does not alter the facts . . . that with us a kiss signifies a certain erotic intimacy. We have hitherto in our technique held to the conclusion that patients are to be refused erotic gratifications. You know too that where more extensive gratifications are not to be had milder caresses very easily take over their role, in love affairs, on the stage, etc.

"Now picture what will be the result of publishing your technique. There is no revolutionary who is not driven out of the field by a still more radical one. A number of independent thinkers in matters of technique will say to themselves: why stop at a kiss? Certainly one gets further when one adopts 'pawing' as well, which after all doesn't make a baby. And then bolder ones will come along who will go further to peeping and showing—and soon we shall have accepted in the technique of analysis the whole repertoire of demiviergerie and petting parties, resulting in an enormous increase of interest in psychoanalysis among both analysts and patients. The new adherent, however, will easily claim too much of this interest for himself, the younger of our colleagues will find it had to stop at the point they originally intended, and God the Father Ferenczi gazing at the lively scene he has created will perhaps say to himself: may be after all I should have halted in my technique of motherly affection *before* the kiss.

"Sentences like 'about the dangers of neocatharsis' don't get very far. One should obviously not let oneself get into the danger. I have purposely not mentioned the increase of calumnious resistances against analysis the kissing technique would bring, although it seems to me a wanton act to provoke them. . . .

With cordial greetings
Your
Freud"

Thus from the font of psychiatric knowledge to the modern practitioner we have common agreement of the harmful effects of sensual intimacies between patient and therapist.

Of interesting note is an annotation entitled Civil Liability of Doctor or Psychologist for Having Sexual Relationship With Patient (33 A.L.R.3d 1393), in which the notewriters state: "Apart from Nicholson v. Han [12 Mich.App.

35, 162 N.W.2d 313, 33 A.L.R.3d 1386, a case whose facts are not applicable here] research has failed to disclose any case in which the courts have discussed or passed upon the civil liability of a doctor or a psychologist, as such, who while the doctor-patient relationship substituted, had established a sexual relationship with a patient." However, where the sexual contacts are themselves the prescribed course of treatment and where such treatment is outside of accepted professional standards, what remains is a simple malpractice action as to which research would be merely cumulative.

On the question of punitive damages, such recovery is allowed in cases where the wrong complained of is morally culpable, or is actuated by evil and reprehensible motives, not only to punish the defendant but to deter him as well as others, from indulging in similar conduct in the future. (Walker v. Sheldon, 10 N.Y.2d 401, 404, 223 N.Y.S.2d 488, 490, 179 N.E.2d 497, 498.)

In the instant case all that has been established is professional incompetence. It was established that plaintiff was influenced to participate on a theory that it would solve her problems.

Sex under cloak of treatment is an acceptable and established ground for disciplinary measures taken against physicians either by licensing authorities or professional organizations (see 15 A.L.R.3d 1179). Whether defendant acted in such manner as to seriously affect his performance as a practitioner in the psychiatric field should be left to these more competent fora, rather than seeking deterrence by way of punitive damages. The only thing that the record herein supports is that his prescribed treatment was in negligent disregard of the consequences. For that, and that alone, he must be held liable.

RICCOBONO, Justice (dissenting):

The plaintiff pursued her action for malpractice by alleging that over a period of some 13 months the defendant made sexual advances towards her with a lewd and lascivious motive and that he did in fact engage in sexual intercourse and other acts of carnal knowledge with her, in a purported furtherance of psychiatric treatment. Plaintiff further asserts that instead of assisting and curing her, the defendant's therapeutic methods caused her permanent mental and emotional harm. This harm, it is alleged, was caused by the defendant's failure to treat the plaintiff by acceptable medical procedures.

The right of action to recover a sum of money for seduction was abolished by virtue of former Article 2-A of the Civil Practice Act, now Civil Rights Law, section 80-a et seq. Article 8 of the Civil Rights Law must be liberally construed to effectuate this purpose (Civil Rights Law, § 84). This legislation was passed as a matter of public policy because of the threat or danger of an action to recover money damages and the embarrassment and humiliation emanating from such scandalous causes of action.

In the case at bar, although the plaintiff was suffering from a number of emotional problems her competency was never placed in issue. Is it not fair to infer, therefore, that she was capable of giving a knowing and meaningful consent? For almost one and a half years while this "meaningful" relationship continued, the plaintiff was not heard to complain. Upon the defendant terminating the relation, this lawsuit evolves.

The defendant obviously did not help his cause by denying what the jury found to be the fact, viz., that the defendant did have sexual relations with the plaintiff. Nevertheless, however ill-advised or ill-conceived was the choice of his defense, in my view this did not constitute malpractice. The plaintiff was still obliged to prove her case by the preponderance of the credible evidence, regardless of the defendant's defense.

I neither condone the defendant's reprehensible conduct, nor maintain that it was not violative of his professional ethics and Hippocratic oath. If, however, the defendant has committed a crime, let him be brought before the criminal halls of justice. For violation of his Hippocratic oath, if there be any, let him suffer the sanctions of the Medical Ethics Board or other appropriate medical authority. But let him not be convicted of his acts of misfeasance and malfeasance by virtue of an action in malpractice. I might parenthetically add, that if the plaintiff is to succeed I am in total agreement with my colleagues that the plaintiff is not entitled to punitive damages and am likewise in full accord that her recovery should not exceed $25,000.

The relief sought by this plaintiff constitutes the closest approach to a conventional action for seduction, and hence must be treated as such. This is barred by section 80-a of the Civil Rights Law (Fernandez v. Lazar, N.Y.L.J., September 15, 1971, p. 19, col. 6, N.Y.Supreme Ct., Leff. J.; Nicholson v. Han, 12 Mich.App. 35, 162 N.W.2d 313 [1968]). As so inextricably intertwined, I would reverse and dismiss the complaint.

Other common bases for malpractice actions involve breaches of confidentiality, malicious prosecution in cases of child protection, custody suits involving "child snatching," and the prescription and/or supplying of medicine—a role restricted entirely to the physician.

Professional social workers are expected to know the statutes related to malpractice and to practice within their framework. The best protections against malpractice are caution in one's practice, following the code of ethics and carefully recording and documenting transactions with clients and family members. Such records can be admitted as evidence in many states. Finally, great care should be taken to disguise records used for teaching purposes to preserve confidentiality. In no way should a client be recognizable, especially if the details are to be published.

Although malpractice actions against social workers are relatively uncommon compared with those against physicians, malpractice insurance for social workers is desirable. It is available at relatively low cost for professional social workers and for agencies. Because a suit is likely to be brought against the agency as a corporation and against staff as private individuals, protection is needed for both. Because of the doctrine of sovereign immunity, which may prohibit suing a state, it may be difficult to collect damages from a public agency, so people press suits against staff members.

MANDATORY CONTINUING EDUCATION

Licensing requirements are beginning to include continuing education as a condition for renewal of a license. Several states have adopted such a provision. State requirements are very general. Credentialing for continuing education has become a function of the colleges and universities, with workshops and short courses generating formal academic credits. The professional is generally enthusiastic about educational standards because they provide a means to encourage agencies to support continuing development of knowledge and skill.

Questions for Review

1. Why is legal regulation of practice in the professions necessary?

2. What kind of helping service is offered by the three professions—social workers, psychologists, and psychiatrists?

3. Why are there "grandfather clauses" in most statutes on legal regulation of professions?

4. How does certification differ from licensing?

5. Explain and evaluate the definition of "social work practice" offered in the model bill.

6. How does the section of the model bill on representation to the public restrict the use of professional titles?

7. What are the major concerns of clinical social workers relating to licensing? What are their objections to typical licensing laws? How can they be dealt with?

8. What competing efforts from other professions affect licensing of social workers?

9. Why does the social worker need to give increasing attention to malpractice?

10. Concerning malpractice, how does the position of the social worker in private practice differ from that of the agency employee? Does the public agency employee need to carry malpractice insurance?

Questions for Debate and Discussion

1. What does the term *social worker* mean to the general public? Why does the public image of the title make legal regulation difficult? Can this image be clarified?

2. What are some of the criticisms of educational qualifications as requirements for licensing of social workers?

3. Should there be provision for substituting professional experience for academic degree requirements? Why or why not?

4. What are the major objections of black and Hispanic social workers' groups to traditional licensing requirements? How can the objections be met?

5. Why do malpractice insurance policies tend to exclude coverage for a therapist's use of sexual intercourse in treatment of a social work client? Do the same restrictions apply for medically sponsored sex therapy programs?

Selected Readings

Bross, Donald C. "Professional Agency Liability for Negligence in Child Protection." *Law Medicine and Health Care* 11 (1983): 71–75.

Jankovic, Joanne, and Ronald Green. "Teaching Legal Principles to Social Workers." *Journal of Education for Social Work* 17 (1981): 28–35.

Sharwell, George R. "Avoiding Legal Liability in the Practice of School Social Work." *Social Work in Education* 5 (1982): 17–25.

"Social Workers and Liability: Who Should Pay When Negligence Occurs?" *Legal Rights Journal* 4 (1983): 6–7.

Spear, John Barlow. "Computers in the Private Sector: Right to Informational Privacy for the Consumer." *Washburn Law Journal* 22 (1983): 469–490.

Bibliography

Aaron, Henry. *Shelter and Subsidies—Who Benefits from Federal Housing Policies.* Washington, D.C.: Brookings Institution, 1972.

Abrams, Harvey A., and Sheldon Goldstein. "A State Chapter's Comprehensive Political Program." In *Practical Politics,* edited by Maryann Mahaffey and John W. Hanks, pp. 241–260. Washington, D.C.: National Association of Social Workers, 1982.

Agnew, Spiro T. "What's Wrong with the Legal Services Program." *American Bar Association Journal* 56 (1972): 930–932.

Andrews, Lori. "Removing the Stigma of Surrogate Motherhood." *Family Advocate* 4 (1981): 220–25, 44.

Annas, George, and Sherman Elias. "In Vitro Fertilization and Embryo Transfer: Medicolegal Aspects of a New Techinque to Create a Family." *Family Law Quarterly* 17 (1983): 199–223.

Avner, Judith I., and Kim E. Greene. "State ERA Impact on Family Law." *Family Law Reporter* 8 (1982): 4023–4035.

Babbitt, Bruce. "The New Federalism Debate." *Public Welfare* 41 (1983): 9–15.

Bean, Philip. *Rehabilitation and Deviance.* London: Routledge and Kegan Paul, 1976.

Beis, Edward B. *Mental Health and the Law.* Rockville, Md.: Aspen Systems Corp., 1984.

Bell, Derrick. *Race, Racism, and American Law.* Boston: Little, Brown, 1973.

Bell, Cynthia, and Wallace S. Mlyniec. "Preparing for a Neglect Proceeding." *Public Welfare* 32 (1974): 26–37.

Berger, Curtis, J. "Housing." In *Law and Poverty: Cases and Materials,* 2nd ed., edited by George Cooper et al., pp. 619–838. St. Paul: West Publishing Co., 1973.

"Berkeley, California Okays ECT Ban." *Behavior Today* 13 (1982): 1.

Bernstein, Barton E. "The Social Worker as Courtroom Witness." *Social Casework* 56 (1975): 521–525.

———. "The Social Worker as Expert Witness." *Social Casework* 58 (1977): 412–417.

Besharov, Douglas, J. "Protecting Abused and Neglected Children: Can Law Help Social Work?" *Family Law Reporter* 9 (1983): 4029–4037.

———. *Defending and Prosecuting Juveniles—Practice in a Unique Court.* New York: The Practising Law Institute, 1974.

———. *Criminal and Civil Liability in Child Welfare Now, the Growing Trend.* Washington, D.C.: National Legal Resource Center for Child Advocacy and Protection, 1983.

Bittner, Egon. "Policing Juveniles: The Social Context of Common Practice." In *Pursuing Justice for the Child,* edited by Margaret Rosenheim, pp. 69–93. Chicago: University of Chicago Press , 1976.

Black's Law Dictionary, 5th ed. St. Paul: West Publishing Co., 1983.

Boland, Barbara, and Bryan Forst. *Prevalence of Guilty Pleas.* Washington, D.C.: U.S. Department of Justice, Bureau of Justice Statistics, 1984.

Brennan, William C., and Shanti K. Khinduka. "Role Expectations of Social Workers and Lawyers in the Juvenile Court." *Crime and Delinquency* 17 (1971): 191–201.

Brieland, Donald. "Black Identity and the Helping Person." *Children* 16 (1969): 171–176.

Brieland, Donald, Lela Costin, and Charles Atherton. *Contemporary Social Work,* 3rd ed. New York: McGraw-Hill, 1975.

Butler, Robert N. *Why Survive?* New York: Harper and Row, 1975.

Caplovitz, David. *Consumers in Trouble: A Study of Debtors in Default.* New York: Free Press, 1974.

———. *The Poor Pay More: Consumer Practices of Low Income Families.* New York: Free Press, 1963.

Cardwell, George L. "Destroying the Presumption that Homosexual Parents Are Unfit: The New Burden of Proof." *University of Richmond Law Review,* 16 (1982): 851–866.

Cates, Willard, Jr. "Legal Abortion: Public Health Record." *Science* 215 (1982): 1586–1590.

Chandler, Joann, and Sterling Ross. "Zoning Restrictions and the Right to Live in the Community." In *The Mentally Retarded Citizen and the Law,* ed. by Michael Kindred et al., pp. 305–342. New York: Free Press, 1976.

Chicano Ad Hoc Committee. *Chicanos: A Student Reform of Social Work Education.* New York: Council on Social Work Education, 1971.

Christoffel, Tom. *Health and the Law.* New York: Free Press, 1982.

Clancy, Tom. "The Attack on the Poor." *NASW California News* 11 (May–June, 1984): 1.

Clark, Homer. *Domestic Relations,* 3rd. ed. St. Paul: West Publishing Co., 1980.

———. *Law of Domestic Relations.* St. Paul: West Publishing Co., 1968.

Coles, Robert. *The South Goes North.* Boston: Little, Brown, 1971.

Costin, Lela. "Education." In *Contemporary Social Work,* edited by Donald Brieland, Lela Costin, and Charles Atherton, pp. 141–157. New York: McGraw-Hill, 1975.

Costin, Lela B., and Charles Rapp. *Child Welfare Policies and Practices.* New York: McGraw-Hill, 1984.

Dallek, Geraldine, and Lucien Wulsin, Jr. "Limits on Medicaid's Patients' Rights to Choose Own Doctors and Hospitals." *Clearinghouse Review* 17 (1983): 280–289.

Davis, James F. *Society and the Law.* New York: Free Press, 1962.

Davis, Karen, and Cathy Schoen. *Health and the War on Poverty: A Ten-Year Appraisal.* Washington D.C.: Brookings Institution, 1978.

Delgado, Richard. "Euthanasia Reconsidered—the Choice of Death as an Aspect of the Right of Privacy." *Arizona Law Review* 17 (1975): 474–494.

Deutch, John. "Reactions to Zoning Restrictions and the Right to Live in the Community." In *The Mentally Retarded Citizen and the Law,* edited by Michael Kindred et al., pp. 343–348. New York: Free Press, 1976.

Dickson, Donald. "Law in Social Work: Impact of Due Process." *Social Work* 21 (1976): 274–278.

Emling, Diana. "The Reagan Scheme as Welfare Reform." *Public Welfare* 41 (1983): 22–26.

Evans, Marie W. "Child and Parent: *MJP* v. *GP*: An Analysis of the Relevance of Parental Homosexuality in Child Custody." *Oklahoma Law Review* 35 (1982): 633–658.

Fanshel, David. *Far from the Reservation: The Transsocial Adoption of American Indian Children.* Metuchen, N.J.: Scarecrow Press, 1972.

———. "Parental Visiting of Children in Foster Care: Key to Discharge." *Social Service Review* 49 (1975): 493–514.

Federal Bureau of Investigation. *Uniform Crime Reporting Handbook.* Washington, D.C. Government Printing Office, 1980.

Fiss, Owen M. "The Charlotte–Mecklenburg Case" *University of Chicago Law Review* 38 (1971): 697–703.

Fogelson. F. B. "How Social Workers Perceive Lawyers." *Social Casework* 51 (1970): 95–101.

Foster, Henry H. "Marriage and Divorce in the Twilight Zone." *Arizona Law Review* 17 (1975): 465–473.

Fox, Sanford J. *Law of Juvenile Courts in a Nutshell.* St. Paul: West Publishing Co., 1984.

Funston, Richard. "Educational Malpractice: A Cause of Action in Search of a Theory." *San Diego Law Review* 5 (1981): 743–812.

Gallant, Claire. *Mediation in Special Education Disputes.* Silver Spring, Md.: National Association of Social Workers, 1982.

Gifford, James, and Frank Macchiarola. "Legal, Technical, Financial, and Political Implications of School Finance Reform in New York State." *Tulane Law Review* 3 (1981): 716–734.

Gitlin, Joseph H. "Attempts to Resolve the Conflict." *Family Advocate* 4 (1981): 18–19.

Goldberg, Harriet. "Social Work and the Law." *Children* 7 (1960): 167–171.

Goldberg, Nancy. "Pretrial Diversion: Bilk or Bargain." *NLADA Briefcase* 31 (1973): 490–493, 500–501.

Goldstein, Joseph, Anna Freud, and Albert J. Solnit. *Beyond the Best Interests of the Child,* New York: Free Press, 1973.

Goodman, Gail S., ed. "The Child Witness." *Journal of Social Issues* 40 (1984): 1–192.

Hagen, Jan L. "Justice for the Welfare Recipient: Another Look at Welfare Fair Hearings." *Social Service Review* 57 (1983): 177–195.

Hazard, Geoffrey. "The Jurisprudence of Juvenile Deviance." In *Pursuing Justice for the Child,* edited by Margaret Rosenheim, pp. 1–19. Chicago: University of Chicago Press, 1976.

Henderson, Charles, and Bok-Lim Kim. "Racism." In *Contemporary Social Work,* edited by Donald Brieland, Lela Costin, and Charles Atherton, pp. 176–196. New York: McGraw-Hill, 1975.

Herr, Stanley. *Rights and Advocacy for Retarded People.* Lexington, Mass.: Lexington Books, 1983.

Herr, Stanley, Stephen Arons, and Richard Wallace, Jr. *Legal Rights and Mental Health Care.* Lexington, Mass.: Lexington Books, 1983.

Howe, Ruth-Arlene. "Adoption Practice, Issues, and Laws 1953–1983. " *Family Law Quarterly* 17 (1983): 173–197.

Huntington, Jane F. "Powerless and Vulnerable: The Social Experiences of Imprisoned Girls." *Juvenile and Family Courts Journal* 33 (1982): 33–34.

Johnson, Earl. *Justice and Reform—The Formative Years of the OEO Legal Services Program.* New York: Russell Sage Foundation, 1974.

Joint Commission on Mental Health of Children. *Crisis in Child Mental Health.* New York: Harper and Row, 1969.

Jonas, Stevens. *Health Care Delivery in the United States,* 2nd ed. New York: Springer, 1981.

Kadushin, Alfred. *Child Welfare Services*. New York: Macmillan, 1980.

———. *Adopting Older Children*. New York: Columbia University Press, 1970.

Kahn, Alfred, and Sheila Kamerman. "Income Maintenance, Wages, and Family Income." *Public Welfare* 41 (Fall 1983): 23–30.

Kahn, Alfred, Sheila Kamerman, and Brenda McGowan. *Advocacy: Report of a National Baseline Study*. Washington, D.C.: Office of Child Development, 1973.

Katz, Sanford N. The Lawyer and Caseworker: Some Observations. *Social Casework* 42 (1961): 10–15.

———. "Rewriting the Adoption Story." *Family Advocate* 5 (Summer 1982): 8–10.

Kelly, R. and S. Ramsey. "Do Attorneys for Children in Protection Proceedings Make a Difference? —A Study of the Impact of Representation Under Conditions of High Judicial Intervention." *Journal of Family Law* 21 (1983): 393–455.

Kerper, Hazel B. *Introduction to the Criminal Justice System*. St. Paul: West Publishing Co., 1972.

Kirp, David L. "Student Classification: Public Policy and the Courts." *Harvard Educational Review* 44 (1974): 7–52.

Knitzer, Jane E. "Child Advocacy: A Perspective." *American Journal of Orthopsychiatry* 46 (1976): 200–216.

Larson, John Farr. "Model Statute on Juvenile and Family Court Records." *Juvenile and Family Courts Journal* 32 (1981): 8–15.

Lehr, Richard I. "Legal Issues." *EAP Digest* 4 (May/June 1983): 12.

———. "Legal Issues." *EAP Digest* 3 (January/February 1983): 15, 17.

Levi, Edward H. *An Introduction to Legal Reasoning*. Chicago: University of Chicago Press, 1963.

Litwak, William. *North of Slavery*. Chicago: University of Chicago Press, 1961.

Lopata, Helen, and Kathleen Fordham. "Changing Commitments of American Women to Work and Family Roles." *Social Security Bulletin* 43 (June 1980): 3–14.

MacDougall, Priscilla R. "Women's, Men's, and Children's Names: An Outline and Bibliography." *Family Law Reporter* 7 (1981): 4013–4018.

Model Penal Code. Philadelphia: American Law Institute, 1962.

Morris, Norval, and Gordon Hawkins. *The Honest Politician's Guide to Crime Control*. Chicago: University of Chicago Press, 1970.

Murase, Kenji, Jane Egawa, and Nathaniel Tashima. *Alternative Service Delivery Models in Pacific/Asian American Communities*. San Francisco: Pacific Asian Mental Health Research Project, 1981.

Nakao, Annie. "The Best and the Worst the Bay Area Schools Have to Offer." *San Francisco Examiner* (April 11, 1984): A4.

Nathanson, Paul S. "Legal Services for the Nation's Elderly." *Arizona Law Review* 17 (1975): 275–292.

National Association of Social Workers. "Delegate Assembly Position Statement on Legal Regulation of Social Work Practice." *NASW News* 20 (1975): 15.

———. "Bill of Rights for Children and Youth. *NASW News* 20 (1975): 27–28.

"National Association of Social Workers Policy Statement on Abortion—1975." In *Compilation of Public Social Policy Statements*, p. 1. Washington, D.C.: National Association of Social Workers, 1983.

National Conference of Lawyers and Social Workers. *Law and Social Work*. Washington, D.C.: National Association of Social Workers, 1973.

Nejelski, Paul. "Diversion: Unleashing the Hound of Heaven." In *Pursuing Justice for the Child*, edited by Margaret Rosenheim, pp. 94–118. Chicago: University of Chicago Press, 1976.

"1974 Developments in Welfare Law—The Supplemental Security Program." *Cornell Law Review* 605 (1975): 825–826.

Olson, Jay, and George H. Shepard. *Intake Screening Guides: Integrating Justice for Juveniles.* Publication No. 77–504, pp. 18, 21. Washington, D.C.: Department of Health, Education, and Welfare, 1975.

Pabon, Edward. "The Case for Alternatives to Detention." *Juvenile and Family Courts Journal* 34 (1983): 37–45.

Paulsen, Monrad, and Charles Whitebread. *Juvenile Law and Procedure.* Reno, Nev.: National Council of Juvenile Court Judges, 1974.

Pierce, President Franklin. "Veto Message—An Act Making a Grant of Public Lands to the Several States for the Benefit of Indigent Insane Persons." Quoted in June Axinn and Herman Levin, *Social Welfare: A History of the American Response to Need,* 2nd ed., p. 50. New York: Longman, 1982.

Pierce, William L. "Survey of State Laws and Legislation on Access to Adoption Records—1983." *Family Law Reporter* 10 (1984): 3035–3041.

Platt, Anthony M. *The Child Savers.* Chicago: University of Chicago Press, 1969.

"Policy Statement." *Family Law Quarterly* 3 (1968): 107.

"Product Warranties: Congress Lends a Helping Hand." *Consumer Reports* 40 (1975): 164–165.

Rodham, Hillary. "Children under the Law." *Harvard Educational Review* 43 (1973): 487–514.

Rothstein, Laura F. *Rights of the Physically Handicapped.* Colorado Springs: Shepard, 1984.

Ryder, Charles F., and Norman B. Westoff. *The Contraceptive Revolution.* Princeton, N.J.: Princeton University Press, 1977.

Sarri, Rosemary C. "Gender Issues in Juvenile Court Justice." *Crime and Delinquency* 29 (1983): 381–397.

Schottland, Charles. "Social Work and the Law: Some Curriculum Approaches." *Buffalo Law Review* 17 (1968): 719–731.

Schrag, Peter. *Consumer Protection.* St. Paul: West Publishing Co., 1973.

Senna, Joseph J. "Changes in Due Process of Law." *Social Work* (1974): 319–325.

Shanker, Albert. "What If We Need the Public Schools?" *The New York Times* (February 19, 1984): E7.

Shapiro, Stephen, and Wade Henderson. "Justice for Aliens." In *Our Endangered Rights,* edited by Norman Dorsen, pp. 160–178. New York: Pantheon, 1984.

Sheehan, David. "Who Gets the Child?" *Family Advocate* 4 (Fall 1981): 2–6.

Sheridan, William, and H. W. Beaser. *Model Acts for Family Courts and State and Local Children's Programs.* Publication No. 75–26041, pp. 9–41. Washington, D.C.: Department of Health, Education, and Welfare, 1975.

Shoeshy, Norman, and Marya Mannes. "A Radical Guide to Wedlock." *Saturday Review* 55 no. 31 (1972): 33–38.

Siegel, Larry, and Joseph Senna. *Juvenile Delinquency—Theory, Practice and Law.* St. Paul: West Publishing Co., 1981.

Silberman, Linda J. "Professional Responsibility Problems of Divorce Mediation." *The Family Law Reporter* 7, no. 15 (1981): 4001–4012.

Sloane, Homer. "Relationship of Law and Social Work." *Social Work* 12 (January 1967): 89–91.

Smith, Audrey. "The Social Worker in the Legal Aid Setting: A Study of Interprofessional Relationships." *Social Service Review* 44 (1970): 155.

Smith, Ken. "The 1982 Private Attorney Involvement Effort: A Status Report." *Clearinghouse Review* 17 (1983): 183–189.

Sobelson, Roy. "Termination of Indigent Parents' Rights after *Lassiter*." *University of Richmond Law Review* 16 (1982): 731–771.

Sparer, Edward. "Social Welfare Law Testing." *The Practical Lawyer* 12 (1966): 14.

Sperling, Gilbert. "Poverty Law." *1980 Annual Survey of American Law* (1980): 461–481.

Stone, Alan. *Mental Health and Law: A System in Transition.* Rockville, Md.: National Institutes of Mental Health, 1975.

Tamilia, Patrick R. "Neglect Proceedings and the Conflict between Law and Social Work." *Duquesne Law Review* 9 (1971): 579–589.

Tancredi, Laurence, Julian Lief, and Andrew Slaby. *Legal Issues in Psychiatric Care.* New York: Harper and Row, 1975.

Tapp, June. "Psychology and the Law: An Overture." *Annual Review of Psychology* (1978): 359–404.

"Texas Involuntary Commitment Statute Held Unconstitutional." *Clearinghouse Review* 17 (1983): 1047.

Thorsell, Bernard A. and Lloyd W. Klemke. "The Labeling Process: Reinforcement and Delinquency." *Law and Society Review* 6 (1972): 393–413.

Thurman, David S. *Right of Access to Information from Government.* Dobbs Ferry, N.Y.: Oceana Publications, 1973.

Tierney, John G. *How to Be a Witness.* Dobbs Ferry, N. Y.: Oceana Publications, 1971.

Tottenberg, Nina. "Behind the Marble, Beneath the Robes." *The New York Times Magazine* (March 16, 1975): 15, 58, 60, 63–67.

Twentieth Century Fund. *Task Force on Criminal Sentencing Fair and Certain Punishment.* New York: Twentieth Century Fund, 1976.

Uniform Adoption Act, Revised 1971. Chicago: National Conference of Commissioners on Uniform State Laws, 1971.

United Nations. "Official Records of the General Assembly." *Fourteenth Session Supplement No. 16,* 1960.

Vargus, Ione. "The Minority Practitioner." In *Contemporary Social Work,* edited by Donald Brieland, Lela Costin, and Charles Atherton, pp. 417–427. New York: McGraw-Hill, 1975.

Wald, Michael S. "Child Custody Disputes: Are We Abandoning the Child's Best Interests?" *Stanford Law Review* 16 (1981): 16–19.

Wald, Patricia. "Pretrial Detention for Juveniles." In *Pursuing Justice for the Child,* edited by Margaret Rosenheim, pp. 119–135. Chicago: University of Chicago Press, 1976.

Warner, S. B. "The Uniform Arrest Act." *Virginia Law Review* 28 (1942): 315–417.

Weidell, R. C. "Unsealing Sealed Birth Certificates in Minnesota." *Child Welfare* 59 (1980): 113–119.

Weil, Marie. "Research on Issues in Collaboration between Social Workers and Lawyers." *Social Service Review* 56 (1982): 393–404.

Weil, Marie, and Ernest Sanchez. "The Impact of the Tarasoff Decision on Clinical Social Work Practice." *Social Service Review* 57 (1983): 112–124.

Weitzman, Lenore J. *The Marriage Contract: Spouses, Lovers, and the Law.* New York: Free Press, 1981.

Weyrauch, Walter O., and Sanford N. Katz. *American Family Law in Transition.* Washington, D. C.: The Bureau of National Affairs, Inc., 1983.

Wilkins, Lawrence P. "Children's Rights: Removing the Parental Consent—Barrier to Medical Treatment of Minors." *Arizona State Law Journal* 1975 (1975): 31–92.

Winslade, William J., and Judith Wilson Ross. *The Insanity Plea: The Uses and Abuses of the Insanity Defense.* New York: Scribner's, 1983.

"Working Definition of Social Work Practice." Quoted in Harriet M. Bartlett, "Toward Clarification and Improvement of Social Work Practice." *Social Work* 3 (April 1958): 5–9.

"Working Statement on the Purpose of Social Work." *Social Work* 26 (1981): 6.

Name Index

Subject Index

618   SUBJECT INDEX

Patronage, 69
Rule-making powers, 70

PURE FOOD AND DRUG ACT OF
1906, 494

RACISM
Generally, 381–402
Access to private facilities, 390–391
Access to public facilities, 388–390
Affirmative action, 395
Alien land laws, 383
American Indians, 382–383, 399
Asians and Pacific Islanders, 381–384
Blacks, 387
Bracero Program, 384
Chicanos and Hispanics, 384–387
Chinese Exclusion Act, 383
Civil Rights Acts, 387–388
Definition, 381
Emancipation Proclamation, 381
Fifteenth Amendment, 381
Fourteenth Amendment, 381
Hispanics, 384–387
Illegal aliens, 384–387
Indian Citizenship Act of 1924, 382
Indian Child Welfare Act, 399–400
Japanese Internment, 382
Marriage, interracial, 396–398
Native Americans, *See* American Indians
Origins, 381–382
Persons of color, 381
Remedies, 382
Resident aliens, 386
Scott, Dred, Decision, 381–382
Simpson-Mazzoli Bill, 386
Social workers' roles, 398–400
Thirteenth Amendment, 381
Treaty of Guadalupe Hidalgo, 384
Voting rights, 391–395

RACIAL MINORITIES
Generally, 18

RAPE, 78
In marriage, 238

REAGAN ADMINISTRATION
Welfare Policies, 65–66

REAL EVIDENCE
See Evidence, types

RECONCILIATION IN MARRIAGE
Means to encourage, 321, 327

REGULATION
Federal, example of, 39–42

REGULATION OF SOCIAL
WORKERS
State coverage, 577

RELIGION
As adoption requirement, 306–312

RENT WITHHOLDING, 463–464

REPLEVIN
See Repossession

REPOSSESSION
Default on conditional sales contract,
448

RES JUDICATA
Defined, 326
In divorce, 326
Remarriage followed by annulment,
242–244

RESIDENCE REQUIREMENTS
In divorce, 322, 325
In public assistance, 424

RETALIATORY EVICTION, 464

RETARDED CHILDREN
Community opposition to facilities for,
467–468

RIGHT TO DIE, 375–376

RIGHT TO LIBERTY
Mental patients, 523–527

RIGHT TO TREATMENT
In mental health, 516–519, 523–528

RIGHTS OF CHILDREN AND
YOUTH
Generally, 347–366
Advocacy, 351, 364–365
Age of majority, 347, 353–357
Bills of Rights, 348–351
Consent to medical treatment, 362–363
Contracts, 353–357
Emancipation, 358
Enforceability of contracts, 353–357
Legal assumptions, 347–348